D0441734

"COOL!"
— Tim Barkow, WIRED Magazine

"An unquestionably masterful work. Somehow the folks at Goofy Foot manage to strike a perfect balance between the informative and the entertaining, the serious and the silly."
–BUZZ, The Weekly Newspaper from Penn State University

"The hottest thing to hit sex since... AA batteries!"
— Colorado Daily, University of Colorado

"Fantastically funny and enticing. Throw it on your coffee table, it's one heck of a conversation starter. "
–Daily O'Collegian, Oklahoma State University

"It's playful without being corny, sensitive without being sappy and informative without being condescending. Definitely the best sex you can buy for $19.95."
–Rob Hill, Bikini Magazine

"The most appealing sex manual I've encountered."
–Robert Lavett Smith, SEXlife Magazine

"Able to do what a large collection of battery operated devices and blow-up dolls could not... put fun back into sex!!"
–Jeff Katz, WRKO, Boston

"Absolutely the best sex book out there!"
–Vanessa Wilde, WRZX, Indianapolis

"Makes learning about sex almost as much fun as doing it!"
–Pam Winter, Alternative Lifestyles Directory

"It's got all the kinds of things in it that even if you know them, you've never thought about them quite that way before."
–K.C. Rourke, Spectator Magazine

"Witty, irreverent, yet completely straightforward, intelligent and downright USEFUL. Honestly if you only pick one book on sex in all its wonderful practicalities, this should be it."

–AK Press Catalog
(For Book Stores)

Sex Therapists Speak!

"Must reading for anyone who counsels couples."

–Sandi Khani, M.S., L.M.F.T.

"I think it is the best book on this subject I have ever seen. It is factual, interesting to read, and has a wonderful approach to the subject. I love the humor. It can be read cover-to-cover or used as a reference."

–Steven Wales, M.C., C.P.C. Phoenix Interfaith Counseling

"Excellent! Covers the details others don't or won't discuss and in a language and style that is down to earth and respectful. As non-biased as any book I have found on sex."

–Virginia A. Shannon, M. Ed.

"Down to Earth, clear, simple, language. Valuable. Well worth recommending. I could truthfully say much more, I believe everyone should read it."

–Daniel H. Cannon, M. D.

"I love it! I use it as a reference for my human sexuality class!"

–Katy H. Steinkamp, M. Ed.

"I've rarely read a book of this sort with such open-minded yet sound medical comments expressed both humorously and respectfully."

–Adam Moore, M.D.

SELECTION! PSYCHOTHERAPY BOOK CLUB

Sex Educators Speak!

"Loved the *Guide To Getting It On!* so much that I am ordering it as a required text for my Human Sexuality class at Santa Barbara City College. The faculty that have seen it so far have flipped! Thanks for the funny, sane & sexy approach."

–Janice Hamilton, M.F.C.C., Santa Barbara City College, CA

"As an instructor, the Guide helps me to promote an open discussion of sexuality. There is no air of embarrassment. I highly recommend the Guide for adoption to others teaching human sexuality courses."

–Debra Hanson, College of the Sequoias, Visalia, CA

"My students like the Guide as the book talks to them rather than at them. Most appealing to me is that the Guide is sensible and down to earth."

–Robert Pollack, Ph. D., University of Georgia at Athens

Students Speak !

"The up-front and shameless approach helped me to explain myself clearly to my boyfriend when he asked what pleased me. It also helped me find out what really felt good for him. He and I were quite amazed."

"All in all it was a great book. You know it is when your parents are asking to borrow it."

"The book made me look at sexuality with a smile."

"I stayed up late at night not being able to put the book down. It is the first required textbook I've enjoyed reading."

"The *Guide To Getting It On!* made it really easy for me to talk about sex with my partner. Things that have totally embarrassed me in the past were brought up in ways that I could understand and identify with."

The Guide To Getting It On!

America's Coolest & Most Informative
Book About Sex

For Adults Of All Ages

The Guide To Getting It On!
2nd edition

Publisher's Cataloging-In-Publication
Joannides, Paul N.
Guide to getting it on! / Paul Joannides, author;
Daerick Gross, illustrator.-- 2nd ed.
p. cm.
Includes bibliographical references and index.
LCCN: 98-86365   ISBN: 1-885535-00-7
1. Sex instruction. 2. Sex. 3. Man-woman
relationships. 1. Gross,Daerick. 11. Title.

HQ31.J63 1999   613.9'6   QBI98-878

The Goofy Foot Press
fax: (310) 652-2995
P.O Box 69365
West Hollywood, CA 90069-0365

Printed in the heartland of America
Arkansas City, Kansas

Written & Created by Paul Joannides
with ideas by many
Illustrated by Dærick Gröss, Sr.
Goofy Foot logo by Brent Myers

Fair Use
Feel free to copy up to 250 words of this book, except for quotations and song lyrics, as long as the title and publisher are cited. That's called fair use. Reproducing more than 250 words by any means (electronic, internet, mechanical, photocopying, recording or otherwise) without written permission from the publisher is theft. It is illegal. The only exception is if you are writing a legitimate book review. Copy the illustrations from this book without written permission, and we will send Guido to break your kneecaps.

Bed of Contents

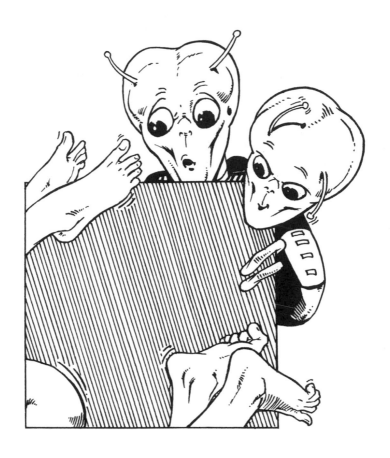

Distribution & Foreign Rights

Distributed in the U.S. & Canada by
Publisher's Group West
(800) 788-3123

Distributed in the UK by
Airlift
(+44) 181 804-0400

Italian Edition
Il Pratiche
Milan, Italy

German Edition
Goldmann (Bertelsmann)
Munich, Germany

Czech Edition
Alpress
Prague, Czech Republic

Elsewhere in the Federation
Goofy Foot Press
(310) 659-8430

Warning—Disclaimer

Hard as we tried, this guide isn't perfect, nor was it intended as a final authority on sex. There will be times when it is better to consult your beautician, bartender, or best friend. You might also speak to a physician or licensed sex therapist. Ultimately, it is your body and your sexuality — venture beyond the bounds of common sense at your own peril. Also, this book talks about sex acts which are illegal in some states, particularly North Carolina. Know your state's laws about sex and break them at your own risk.

No one involved with the writing or publishing of this book is a physician or licensed sex therapist, although members of these professions have been consulted on thorny issues. The people who have contributed ideas to this book are mostly psychologists, psychoanalysts, social workers, lawyers, teachers, writers, a couple of surfers, and even a prostitute and a priest. The actual writing was done by a mental health professional. Just because some of these people have college degrees doesn't mean they know any more about sex or sexual relationships than you do. They all struggle at times. Still, their perspective might be helpful and even refreshing.

While the techniques mentioned in this book work well for some people, they might not be good for you. Check with a physician or licensed sex therapist before attempting any sexual act that you are unfamiliar with, or do so at your own risk and with the understanding that bad things might happen. Consult with a physician if you have any condition which precludes strenuous or sexually exciting activity.

All readers, except those who are trying to get pregnant, are encouraged to use birth control and to adopt a medically sound strategy for avoiding sexually transmitted diseases. However, no form of birth control is foolproof, and diseases have been known to break through (or climb around) even the finest of barriers. These are normal consequences of having sex and are not the fault of this book.

This book was written to help expand the consciousness of its readers. Neither the Goofy Foot Press nor any of its minions shall be liable or responsible to any person or entity for any loss, damage, injury or ailment caused, or alleged to be caused, directly or indirectly, by the information or lack of information contained in this book.

If you do not wish to be bound by the above, you may return the book to the publisher for a refund.

Goofy Foot: When a surfer leads with the right foot instead of the left (regular foot). Results in a different orientation towards the wave.

This book is dedicated to Sisyphus.

Chapter 1
The Alpha Chapter

Sometimes I think, life is just a rodeo,
The trick is to ride, and make it to the bell
But there is a place,
Sweet as you will ever know
In music and love
And things you never tell

"Rock and Roll Girls" by J.C. Fogerty, Wenaha Music Company

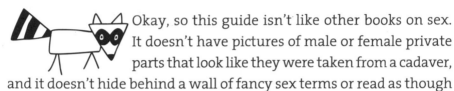 Okay, so this guide isn't like other books on sex. It doesn't have pictures of male or female private parts that look like they were taken from a cadaver, and it doesn't hide behind a wall of fancy sex terms or read as though it were written by Mr. Rogers.

This guide encourages you to explore dimensions of sexuality that people in our country usually aren't told about—from the emotional part of getting naked together to why a guy who takes his penis too seriously might have trouble pleasing his sweetheart. It covers subjects like hand jobs and heart throbs, kisses above and below the waist, vibrators, friendship and even sex on the interstate.

But most important of all is the Goofy Foot Philosophy which says that it doesn't matter what you've got in your pants if there's nothing in your brain to connect it to.

Do With It What You Want

Since this is a book about sex, it might be a good idea to include a definition of what sex is. But trying to define sex is a lot like trying to insert a diaphragm. Just when you think you've got it in, the thing turns ninja on you. For instance, here are only four of several issues that need to be answered if you are trying to define the term sex:

People think of intercourse as the ultimate sex act, the real thing—*ipsum fuctum*. If intercourse is the ultimate act, then how come making out or holding hands is sometimes sweeter and more meaningful?

🐄 Almost all sex acts can be painful, obnoxious, or boring unless you do them with someone who turns you on. Does this mean that the mental part of sex is more important than the physical part?

🐄 Why does one couple find a particular sex act to be highly erotic while another couple finds the same act to be downright disgusting?

🐄 How can a song, car, or piece of clothing be sexy?

Needless to say, we have given up on trying to pin a tail of definition on the big donkey of sex. It seems that any definition of sex needs to fit who you are as an individual as well as your particular situation. Instead of pretending to know what that might be, consider the following:

Learning about sex and intimacy is a lifelong task. Even with years of experience, we still blow it on occasion. The best we can do in the pages that follow is to tell you what we wish we had known about sex twenty years ago. Do with it what you want.

Morality and What's In Your Pants

In much of America we still try to equate morality with whether or not you keep your pants on. We also associate morality with religion. But the truth is, there are Christians, atheists and Jews who are moral people; and Christians, atheists and Jews who are immoral people. The same is true for people who are sexually active and those who aren't. Morality, from this guide's perspective, is your ability to respect and care for your fellow human beings. It has little to do with the way you enjoy your sexuality, unless what you do breaks a special trust or violates the rights of others.

Birth Control & Gnarly Sex Germs

This book's chapter on birth control and sex germs talks about everything from scruffy sex rodents to things you can do to make a rubber feel right. Hopefully, its perspective on sexuality will help you avoid things like unwanted pregnancies and an early funeral. In the meantime, it might be helpful to remember that just about anything in this world that's worth doing will kill you if you're stupid about it. Having sex can be far less risky than driving on the freeway or even driving across town. It just depends on how smart you are about sex and how badly you drive.

How It Fits In...

There are many different reasons why people have sex, some having to do with love, others not. For instance, many of us have sex because it can be a great deal of fun, especially with someone who you care deeply about. It's also an activity that couples do when they have a primal urge to get physical or need to relieve erotic tension (aka horniness). Some individuals offer sex to please or placate a partner, and some use it as a way of gaining security or status. In addition, people have sex when they want to have a baby. That kind of sex has an added dimension which can bring partners incredibly close.

An important aspect of sex is how it can mean different things at different times in your life. For instance, you might find yourself in one relationship where the sex helps to enhance and deepen your love for each other. In another relationship the sex leaves you feeling anxious and empty. Early in a long term relationship, the sex might excite you and rev you up, at another point it might provide you with comfort and calmness. In most long term relationships, there will be stretches where the sex begins to bore you. That's when you need to work on making it better.

For those of you who are younger, people sometimes refer to matters of the younger heart as puppy love and treat it with disrespect. That's silly. The most powerful feelings in life are often puppy love. Cherish them. As for having sex with your puppy love, far be it from this guide to say yes or no. It might be wonderful, but then again, maybe not. Just be aware that there's usually more to a good carnal experience than the simple hydraulics of sticking hard into wet. For some people, what separates the good sexual memories from the bad are intangibles like fun, friendship, love, and caring.

It might also be helpful to remember that as you get older, your expectations about sex may change. For instance, if you just turned seventeen, getting laid in-and-of-itself can be a huge thing. But by the time you turn thirty-four, you'll have more experience under your belt. By then, you might want your sex life to take you someplace different than when you were younger. Perhaps you will be searching for different qualities in a partner than you did when you were seventeen. Hopefully, you will want sex to be special no matter what your age.

A Red Flag—Matters Of The Heart

On an emotional level, sex can be as powerful as you want to make it. But good luck if you are trying to have sex without it becoming emotional.

The emotions that accompany sexual relationships can be magical, enchanting and wonderful. Then again, they can be really awful. Hopefully your love life will bring you bundles of joy, but occasionally it won't. For instance, a cherished relationship can crash and burn, leaving you with so much heartache that you might wish you were dead. Sometimes the tears pour from a place so deep inside of you that you wonder if they'll ever stop. On the other hand, lovemaking can become a sacred ground for working through all sorts of fears and crises, as well as a place for growth and forgiveness.

No Assumptions Here

Most of us make assumptions about the sex lives of other people. Consider for instance Mark, who is a quiet, college-aged computer geek, and Jake, who is a well-liked, twenty-seven-year-old shortstop on his company's baseball team. Mark is biceps-challenged while Jake looks like he just stepped out of the pages of Men's Health. Mark has a wonderfully creative and fulfilling sexlife with his girlfriend Elvira, while Jake lives in fear that someone will find out that the closest he has come to having sex with a real live woman is when he masturbates to X-rated videos.

This book is just as much for Mark and Elvira as it is for Jake and Rosie. It doesn't matter if you've been around the block more times than even a supercomputer can count, or if you haven't yet hit the ball out of the infield; this guide makes no assumptions about you except that you're curious about sex and might want to enjoy it even more.

The other thing to keep in mind is that no matter how old you are, there is still time left for you to have a rewarding sex life. Even if you're darned near senile, get yourself a magnifying glass and give the Guide a gander.

Charts, Graphs & Sex Surveys

This book has no charts or graphs. If you are the type who's bamboozled by such things, consider the following: how do you graph the value of a loving glance or heartfelt hug? Yet try to enjoy sex in a long-term relationship without such things. Rather than assuming which graph is best for you, this guide tries to accommodate a full range of sexual tastes and beliefs, be they conservative, eclectic, or kinky. (Are any of us just one or the other?)

In addition to charts and graphs are sex surveys. These are published every couple of years with each claiming to be the ultimate sex census. But think about it for a moment; big as it is, the federal government has trouble doing an accurate census of its own citizens, and the only two questions it needs to ask is if a person's heart is still beating and what their address is. Imagine a team of five or ten researchers trying to document the sexuality of 250 million people! Even if all you ever do is masturbate, your sexuality is probably too complex to be summarized by charts, graphs or surveys.

A Second Edition First—Reader's Comments

Over the past year, we have sent out more than seven hundred questionnaires to men and women who ordered copies of the first edition of the Guide.

We received far more completed questionnaires from women than men. The women's responses were a hoot to read. The men's responses were, for the most part, boring and uncreative. (Are these the same guys who brag about their sexual prowess?) Even the women in the office who helped read and tabulate the responses snored through most of the men's answers, while thoroughly enjoying the sexual creativity of their own gender.

Since there was nothing scientific about the design or distribution of our questionnaires, it is impossible to jump or even crawl to conclusions. But in case you ask "Why did you include so many more women's responses?" it's because they were far more interesting, instructive and downright sexy.

Final Alpha Note

Most people would probably agree that sex is best when it's honest, caring, and fun. The same should be true for books on sex. Hopefully, you'll never find a more honest assessment of love and sex than in the pages that follow, or a publication that has more respect for its readers than this one does for you.

For the fun part, please keep reading.

Chapter 2
A Brief History of Sex

This chapter describes a brief history of sex in modern America from the 1950s to the time of the millennium. Don't worry, it's nothing like George Washington crossing the icy Potomac, although people have been known to do things every bit as drastic when they haven't had sex in a really long time.

Some writers give the impression that there was no sex in the 1950s, and that sex wasn't even invented until the 1960s when humanity supposedly started making love instead of war. This is not true. People who were young adults in the 1950s claim that there was plenty of sex. It's just that couples often waited until they were married, or at least until they were 18 or 21 before having intercourse. Also, couples usually dated for a longer time before getting sexual. Since a woman's virginity was more of a commodity then, it's possible that unmarried couples shared more hand jobs and oral sex than intercourse.

Sexual expression was sometimes a challenge for single women in the 1950s, since they were often expected to put-out enough to keep a man interested, but not so much as to gain a bad reputation. (Have things changed all that much?) Some women used this double standard to their advantage, while others found it oppressive. For readers interested in learning about the 1950s, David Halberstam's book "The Fifties" might be a fine place to start. Talking to people who were sexually active during the 1950s could also prove interesting.

The Rolling Stone Orgasm, Circa 1966-1977

For young people in the late 1960s and 1970s, there were at least three different types of sexual experience.

The first type of sexual experience was getting yourself off by hand. This provided a really intense jolt of sensation that left you feeling relaxed and settled. It required little social skill or effort. (Some

Sex In The 1950s

of us who went to religious school would try giving up masturbation for Lent, which is how Palm Sunday got its name.)

The second kind of experience was better. Much better. The second kind of sexual experience was what happened when you were lucky enough to have a sweetheart. It happened when your eyes met, when you held hands, when your lips touched, and when you talked on the phone. The second kind of sexual experience sent a herd of butterflies somersaulting through your stomach and made you feel happy just to be alive. It tugged at the edges of your heart and nearly tossed you off your still clumsy feet.

The third type of sexual experience is what happened when the second type of experience started to include intercourse. It's what happened when you went "all the way."

Did the third type of sexual experience rate as being the best of times? Not always. For instance, your author can still recall what going "all the way" was like for him. Getting a hard-on usually wasn't a problem, but he had to keep it that way at the same time he was trying to get his sweetheart wet enough for intercourse. Then he spent the rest of the time thinking about baseball so he wouldn't embarrass himself by coming too soon.

Pathetic. Really pathetic. And awkward.

For him, the best of times were taking long walks, playing football in the mud, breaking various laws and ordinances, and summer nights with his head in a special friend's lap, gazing at her moonlit face outlined by a billion stars from the sky above. The best of times were also listening to rock'n'roll, music having been the heart and soul of everything.

Fortunately, there were plenty of other people who had no hesitation whatsoever when it came to enjoying intercourse. And the introduction of the birth control pill during the 1960s helped give an even greater sense of sexual freedom. Other factors that helped change the sexual climate in America during the 1960s included the invasion of rock'n'roll bands from Britain, the use of LSD and other psychedelic drugs, the media, marijuana, the mini-skirt, the women's movement and the anti-war movement.

The Clitoris, 1966 A.D.

Aside from landing an astronaut on the moon during the 1960s, science also introduced men and women to the word "clitoris." While the clitoris was by no means an invention of the 1960s, few people had ever known what to call it and many men as well as some women were ignorant of its function.

An unfortunate aspect of this new discovery is that people started to describe the clitoris as a mini-penis. As a result, men who were earnestly trying to please their partners began rubbing the clitoris with the kind of intensity that they wished women would use when rubbing their not-so-mini male penises. Of course, rubbing a clitoris in this way can result in extreme discomfort for a woman. (Who knew?)

In spite of the great clitoris stampede that continues to this day, one should be wary of excessive clitoral fawning. Far more important is the ability to make a lover feel wanted, safe and silly.

If men had learned only one lesson during the 1960s, it should have been to ask a lover what feels best. Instead, we often thought to ourselves "I gotta find her clitoris" and went for it like militant Moslems on a mission for Allah. Still, with the discovery of the clitoris there was simply no turning back, or so we thought

Sex In the 1980s & 1990s — Love Takes A Backseat To Cash Flow

Much can be learned about sex during the 1980s and 1990s by considering the plight of a conservative and popular United States president who held office during that time. During the 1980s, this president spent millions of taxpayer's dollars to establish an executive office of celibacy, a governmental agency whose job it was to sell the American people on virginity. However, during the 1990s, this same president's flesh and blood daughter could be found posing buck naked, legs spread, in a popular men's jerk-off magazine. Go figure.

Not to be outdone, a more recent U.S. president who was trying to boost his own moral image fired the surgeon general for expressing an opinion about masturbation. This same president signed into law bills that allocated millions of dollars for abstinence-only sex educa-tion–but who should know better than he, since one of the bigger legacies of his second term was to introduce the words "oral sex" into the vocabulary of nearly every first-grade child throughout the land.

And that's how sex has been here in America during the past decade or two–a kind of Siamese twin with one head being puritanical and the other hedonistic. Or maybe that's how sex has always been, but TV and the media are now highlighting it in a way that is harder to ignore. Whatever the case, it is now a sad truth that people in the 1990s who hear the word "sex" are just as likely to think of disease as fun or healing, and the 1960s notion of sexual freedom has given way to warnings about sexual abuse and harassment. And while younger teenagers who haven't even started to grow pubic hair are now having intercourse, college students on some campuses in the Midwest are proving to be more conservative than their grandparents were in the 1950s. Who knows how to summarize what's going on in this country sexually, except to say that there are many different people with many different points of view.

If ever there was a time when we needed to be tolerant of each other's sexual tendencies, whether they involve total celibacy or the occasional weekend threesome, now seems to be it.

Learning From The Past

Learning from history is often important, but it seldom happens when the subject is sex. For instance, can you imagine a grandmother telling her sixteen-year-old granddaughter or grandson: "You know, I didn't start having multiple orgasms until I was forty-five, after your grandfather brought home that vibrating Swedish scalp massager..." or "If you masturbate right before a date, it might help take the edge off the evening," or "It wasn't particularly easy being pregnant at seventeen; I wouldn't recommend it."

If this guide were limited to one page of advice about sex, it wouldn't be concerned with how much, what way, or even when. It would, however, try to express the following, with the first part being directed to a typical young adult, and the rest applying to us all:

There isn't a feeling in the entire universe that you and your sweetheart don't have stored somewhere in your bodies, feelings that are waiting to be touched, shared and released. Yet the extent of your current lovemaking is to stick your tongues down each other's throats, tweak each other's nipples a perfunctory number of times, lick each other's genitals because that's what the sex books say you should do, and then thrust away until one of you goes 'Ooo-ahh, Ooo-ahh', and the other goes squirt, squirt, squirt. For you, sex is still an extension of grabbing for the cookie jar, which is fine as long as your expectations aren't very high.

Fortunately, there are a lot of wonderful dimensions to sex besides just huffing and puffing while the bedsprings squeak. Sharing sex with a partner allows you to discover where the different emotions are stored in each other's bodies, where the hopes and dreams are hidden, where the laughter and pain reside, and what it takes to free the fun, passion and hidden kink. To achieve that level of sharing you have to take the time to know someone, to feel what they are feeling, to see the world through their eyes, and to let a partner discover who you are in ways that might leave you feeling vulnerable. This can be scary.

Granted, there will be plenty of times when all you want from sex is a quick jolt of sensation, but if that's all you ever expect from sex, then you might be coming up a bit short.

The Next Chapters

One of the problems with adult sexuality is that few of us started with a philosophy or overview. The next couple of chapters attempt to remedy that. Please be aware that the Goofy Foot Press has about as much passion for philosophy as for rattlesnakes and flat cola. As a result, we worked hard to create chapters that are fun, interesting, and hopefully relevant.

Chapter 3
To Draw Or Not To Draw

What? A sexbook without drawings of couples doing the wild thing in positions that would cripple even a Dallas Cowboy cheerleader? (The illustration on page 385 doesn't count. It's a parody.)

While producing this book, the Goofy Foot Press did several flip-flops on whether to include illustrations. The following might help you understand why we almost decided to go without any illustrations at all, which is significant since it's the illustrations, rather than the intelligence, that sell most books on sex.

Confucius Says...

Many years ago, a fortune cookie maker by the name of Confucius made the observation "One picture is worth a thousand words." But in those days pictures were often works of art done by master craftsmen. Today, pictures flood our senses in the form of television, movies, billboards and magazines. While some of these pictures are rich in meaning, others distort the truth.

For instance, consider one picture showing fingertips on skin and another picture showing a penis entering a vagina. The penis/vagina shot is by far the more powerful visual image, yet running your fingertips up and down a lover's back is a sexual act that can create wave after wave of delicious pleasure. Fingertips on skin can be just as meaningful and important as intercourse, but you seldom get that feeling from looking at pictures. As a result, we had hoped that you might create your own glossies in the theater of your mind. That way you wouldn't be burdened by someone else's notion of what should or shouldn't turn you on. On the other hand, a book on sex without any pictures would be, well, boring.

The Illustration Nightmare

Sexuality has all sorts of dimensions—from the feel of your lover's hair and skin to the sound of his or her voice and way that he or she makes you laugh. Imagine trying to capture all of those nuances

in illustrations where the only tools the artist has to work with are black lines on white paper.

Another limitation of sexbook art was highlighted by this book's illustrator when he said "What you want me to show in these illustrations takes several seconds or minutes to unfold when done between a man and a woman. To capture all of it in a single frame is impossible. To capture the erotic parts of a sexual act, we might need to leave out a smile that shows appreciation and love. Art is a compromise. "Bah humbug."

And then came the wishes of the reader. While most of the young adults who previewed these illustrations kept saying to make them more explicit, others, especially those over thirty-five, felt uneasy. What follows is a verbatim interchange with one female reviewer in her mid-forties:

Reviewer: When I first looked through the illustrations, I was sure they were too explicit. I hid them until nighttime, when my husband and I could look at them in bed after the kids were asleep. Contrary to my initial reaction, I want to thank you. We ended up having the best sex that we've had in years!

Needless to say, it took a full year to illustrate the 1st edition of this book, and another year to do the new illustrations that were added to this, the second edition. The time was spent designing and re-designing each and every element, trying to get a look that felt right in spite of the inherent limitations of dirty pictures.

In Praise Of Anatomical Incorrectness

A fully grown woman was recently recalling her childhood Ken doll, of the petrochemical icon family Barbie & Ken. She stated that her Ken doll had not only been anatomically correct, but extremely well - endowed. When informed that Ken has always been a neuter, this woman was taken aback. Could those amazing genitals have been a product of her childhood imagination? Absolutely. This is why some child development experts feel that dolls are best left without genitals. The power of a child's imagination is so great that they wouldn't want to limit it by sticking pre-formed genitals on dolls. Perhaps it's not totally different with adults. Maybe this is why we sometimes find it more titillating to be visually teased; a scantily clad image allows our imagination to run wild in different ways than one that is in your face. With this in mind, we have made some of the illustrations in this guide merely provocative, while others are fully explicit.

"Too Explicit"— Cosmo

As you may have noticed, the "Guide To Getting It On!" comes fully illustrated. This has led to some interesting situations. For instance, Judy's Book Store in Porterville, California called to say that they were removing the book from display for a few days because one of the local preachers was coming into the store to pick up a religious book that he had ordered. And while the lovely little book store in Newport, Oregon was deciding whether to carry the book, the doctors and nurses at the local hospital in Newport ordered seventeen copies direct from the publisher. (They not only decided to order it, but gave it a generous review in their monthly newsletter. However, they do keep it behind the counter, so if you are on the coast of Oregon, you will need to ask for the "Guide" in order to see it.)

Equally intriguing was a letter from Cosmopolitan Magazine explaining that they wouldn't print excerpts from the 1st edition of this book because it was "too explicit and goofy." Mind you, one of the more prestigious book clubs in the country chose the "Guide To Getting It On!" four times as a selection for their 50,000 psychotherapist members, while the September 1996 issue of Cosmopolitan Magazine was banned from WalMart stores because its cover was—you've got it—too explicit.

End Of Chapter Notes: While some child development experts might not want dolls to be anatomically correct, they fully encourage parents to teach their young children the proper names of male and female body parts.

Since the subject of Ken and Barbie came up in this chapter, we couldn't help but include the ultimate treatise on Barbie and Ken by the parents of a young girl who has a new Barbie doll. It's from an essay by

Margaret Atwood titled "The Female Body" in the *Michigan Quarterly Review*, edited by Laurence Goldstein, Vol. XXIX, No. 4, Fall 1990:

He said, I won't have one of those things in the house. It gives a young girl a false notion of beauty, not to mention anatomy. If a real woman was built like that she'd fall flat on her face.

She said, If we don't let her have one like all the other girls she'll feel singled out. It'll become an issue. She'll long for one and she'll long to turn into one. Repression breeds sublimation. You know that.

He said, It's not just the pointy plastic tits, it's the wardrobes. The wardrobes and that stupid male doll, what's his name, the one with the underwear glued on.

She said, Better to get it over with when she's young. He said, all right but don't let me see it.

She came whizzing down the stairs, thrown like a dart. She was stark naked. Her hair had been chopped off, her head was turned back to front, she was missing some toes and she'd been tattooed all over her body with purple ink, in a scrollwork design. She hit the potted azalea, trembled there for a moment like a botched angel and fell.

He said, I guess we're safe.

Chapter 4
The Dirty Word Chapter

You might be wondering why a chapter on dirty words would be stuck so close to the front of an otherwise fine and upstanding book like this. Perhaps there is more to this chapter than just dirty words.

Whether you agree with this guide's observations about dirty words is not the point. This chapter, like all of the others in this book, was written to encourage you to think.

Hans, Sven & Yellow Snow

We at the Goofy Foot Press probably use the word fuck more times each day than the pope says amen. The sad thing is, we mainly use our fucks to express anger or frustration. Seldom do we use them in the fun way. This is often the case with sexual slang here in America, where swear words and sex words are often one in the same.

In Sweden, a culture that is more sex-friendly than our own, sexual slang is not usually used to express anger or frustration. If Sven or Hans are really annoyed, they are more likely to yell something about yellow snow than sex. Even our own Pueblo Indians had no history of using sexual slang for hurling insults. If a Pueblo Indian was really bent-out-of-shape, he or she might have inferred that the offending party was a lousy farmer or kept a sloppy wigwam. But then again, the Pueblos had a less repressive attitude about sex than our Pilgrim forefathers.

Calling People By The Female Genitals

Back when he was a kid, the worst thing your author knew to call another person was a "cunt." He never could bring himself to use the word, but then again, he had yet to work with anyone in the entertainment industry.

Another slang word that kids often use is "pussy." While pussy is a term that refers to the female genitals, it is also an expression that boys use to taunt other boys who are being wimps or cowards.

Why does our culture associate cowardice with being a woman or having a women's genitals? And why would we want to discredit the very female genitals that so many of us craved (and still crave) to touch and know more about? What kind of number was our culture doing on us, anyway?

Mother Fucking, Titty Sucking, Blue-Balled What?

There is a researcher by the name of Warren Johnson who studied how normal eight-year-old boys and girls use slang. According to Johnson, the children's favorite expression when out of parental earshot was "mother fucking, titty sucking, blue-balled bitch." Johnson hadn't expected to find America's eight-year-old children capable of out-swearing his former marine troop.

Of particular interest is Johnson's observation of an eight-year-old girl yelling "Suck my dick!" to another child who was annoying her. As long as she needed to use sexual slang for swearing, why didn't the little girl yell the more anatomically correct "Eat my pussy!" instead of "Suck my dick!?" Perhaps even an eight-year-old child knows that the way to insult someone in our society is by telling them to take the woman's place when she is having sex, with terms such as "You cocksucker!" "Screw you!" and "Get fucked!" being a crude way of saying "You're the woman in sex, you scoundrel!"[1]

It is difficult to understand how something as sweet and delicious as sex could be linked to anger or frustration. It is equally difficult to understand why being the woman in sex is a put-down. Yet these are the premises about sex that we Norte del Americanos grow up with.

When Eight Turns Eighteen

What's going to happen when the little girl who was just mentioned wants to share sex with a boy? How is she supposed to enjoy performing the very insults that our society has taught her to hurl at others? Is she going to require the young man to swear

---

[1]It could be argued that the implied insult behind terms like "fuck you" or "suck my dick" is that the receiver of the insult is homosexual. But wouldn't that be

undying love and adoration before she "sucks his dick"? Will she extract a measure of revenge by making him deliver on various goods or promises? Will she use sex as a commodity, weapon or way of achieving security? Will she learn to hide her sexuality, or perhaps become numb to it? Will she turn men into sex objects? Equally disconcerting is what this attitude does to boys. The message is that you either screw or get screwed, the former being associated with winning, the latter with losing. This turns sex into some sort of competition.

Sluts, Whores, Virginity & Sewers

Western religions have never done too well with the notion of women and sexuality. For instance, early Christians taught that a virgin daughter occupied a higher place in heaven than her mother, since the mother must have had sex for the daughter to have been born. And around 400 A.D., Christianity's Saint Jerome wrote "Though God can do all things, He cannot raise a virgin after she has fallen" (Epistles 22). Pretty dirty stuff, losing your virginity, if you are a woman anyway. It's never been a problem for us men, but then again, we're the ones who wrote the scriptures. (You don't have to be religious to know that when a boy in our society has intercourse for the first time he becomes a man. Yet a girl who has intercourse loses her virginity and is no longer pure as the driven snow, assuming she was in the first place.)

Rigid as St. Jerome may have been about women's virginity, he was quite the feminist when compared to some of his Christian and Jewish predecessors. For instance, one early church father described woman as "a temple built over a sewer," with sewer referring to her genitals. (Men who made statements like these were later declared saints.) This kind of negative imagery requires women to deny their own sexual desires lest they end up singing the afterlife blues.

---

just as true for the hurler of the insult, who seems to be inviting the act? Besides, if someone wants to imply that the offending party is gay, there are plenty of expressions that do just that and few people hesitate to use them.

Perhaps it's no coincidence that many adult women who are unable to have orgasms were raised in households where the temple/sewer notion still holds sway.

To this day people still equate a woman's personal reputation with her appetite for sex: if her sex drive is too low, she is cold or frigid; too high and the sewer floods the temple, in which case she is called a slut, whore, 'ho, nympho or easy. In Britain, the term is slag. While young men are free to strut their sexuality, young women learn to carefully regulate theirs. Otherwise, they risk being called dirty words.

Note: Contrary to what makes sense, women are often the first to accuse other women of being sluts or whores. Men may have been the Bozos who wrote the anti-woman theology, but women are sometimes its cruelest enforcers. Also, it is well known that Jesus of Nazareth was loving and respectful towards women. Why did the church fathers who followed him have so many problems in this area? And if the human body was made in the image and likeness of God, as church scripture says, why were church leaders so rejecting of women's genitals and sexuality? Had God been drinking the day He crafted the clitoris and vagina?

Dicks, Pricks & Morons

Why do we refer to a person who is being a total jerk as a "dick" or "prick"? A dick should be someone who brings pleasure, but that's not what our culture teaches us.

For instance, adults will praise a young boy for showing his latest drawing or for making it to the toilet on time, but if he proudly displays his pint-sized boner, throats get cleared. Boys in our society are encouraged to spend eons learning how to make a baseline jump shot or to hit an A-minor flat nine on a guitar, yet they are taught to ignore their own sexuality in hopes that it will simply go away until they get older. Maybe that's why many of us grow up having more sensitivity for what happens in music, art or sports than for what happens in bed.

Power-Booting & Name-Calling At Dartmouth

While our culture encourages its straight men to strut their sexuality, this doesn't mean we always do. For instance, the following story tells of how the term faggot is used by straight guys to deride other straight guys for preferring women to beer. It is from Regina Barreca's fine book "They Used To Call Me Snow White But Then I Drifted" published by Viking/Penguin, New York, 1991:

"When I started my first year as a student at Dartmouth College, there were four men for every woman. I thought I had it made. Dartmouth had only recently admitted women, and the administration thought it best to get the alumni accustomed to the idea by sneaking us in a few at a time. With such terrific odds in my favor socially, how could I lose? I'd dated in high school and although I wasn't exactly Miss Budweiser, I figured I'd have no problem getting a date every Saturday night. But I noticed an unnerving pattern. I'd meet a cute guy at a party and talk for a while. We would then be interrupted by some buddy of his who would drag him off to another room to watch a friend of theirs 'power-boot' (the local vernacular for 'projectile vomiting'), and I realized that the social situation was not what I had expected."

"Then somebody explained to me that on the Dartmouth campus "They think you're a faggot if you like women more than beer." This statement indicated by its very vocabulary the advanced nature of the sentiment behind it. If a guy said he wanted to spend the weekend with his girlfriend, for example, he'd be taunted by his pals, who would yell in beery bass voices 'Whatsa matter with you, Skip? We're gonna get plowed, absolutely blind this weekend, then we're all gonna power-boot. And you wanna see that broad again? Whaddayou, a faggot or something?'"

While many boys who end up at colleges like Dartmouth have intercourse by the age of sixteen, a fair number remain crude in their ability to value friendship with sexual partners. While they may be coordinated enough to guide a penis into a vagina, on an emotional level some still belong in the arms of their drinking buddies. Equally as puzzling are the young women who agree to have sex with these emotional giants.

Sexuality here in America remains a confusing entity. A "just say no" mentality thrives in a culture that uses sex to advertise and sell everything from soap to beer. As a result, there are times when we flaunt our sexuality, and other times when we deny it completely.

Origin Of The Bimbo & Stud

Bimbo and stud aren't dirty words per se. But they achieve dirty word status when you consider the following observation made by a female friend who was sitting on the beach:

> A father was standing a few feet into the surf with a young boy on his right side and a young girl on the left. The children were the same size. Whenever a wave came in the father would keep his right arm rigid. This helped the boy brave the oncoming splash. At the same time, the father would lift his left arm, pulling the girl into the air so she could avoid the splash altogether. The little boy was being taught how to face the wave, the little girl was being taught to expect a man to rescue her.

Bimbo training starts early in our country. All too often, the first step is getting little girls to believe that they are more fragile than boys. And ads in women's magazines spawn the belief that there is something unsexy about the female body unless it's plugged with a scented tampon and accessorized with perfume and high heels.

Seldom does our society encourage boys and girls to value and respect each other. More often, boys are taught to protect girls because the latter are supposed to be weak and dainty, and many girls are still taught that their self-value is determined by the desirability of the boys they date.

Blow Jobs & Bounced Checks

Consider the following statement by a modern American wife of five years:

"My husband's going to be furious when he finds out about the check I bounced, so I better give him a really good blow job tonight."

As you will discover in the chapters that follow, this book has no problem with really good blow jobs, but not when they are motivated by fear, lack of power, or crass manipulation. Yuck. This sort of thing gives blow jobs a bad name.

Counterpoint: Female readers might claim that trading blow jobs for money is one of the few ways that women have had throughout the ages to even the score economically, and who are we to get on our high horses by condemning such a practice? They might argue that trading sex for money brings far more joy into the world and is less destructive than the ways that many men earn their paychecks. They might also take this guide to task for ignoring the possibility that the above-mentioned housewife finds the situation to be a sexual turn-on and might totally enjoy doing the payback blow job!

Re-arranging The Bed Sheets On The Titanic With The New Word "Foreplay"

The term "foreplay" was invented by people who write books on sex. Foreplay is what you are supposed to do to get a woman wet enough so the two of you can have intercourse. It may seem strange that this book considers foreplay to be a dirty word, since caring guys are usually encouraged to embrace the concept. Yet there is nothing caring about the underlying premise of foreplay: that women are somehow a little retarded and need to be warmed-up before they want to become sexual. Shoot, you have to warm up the old Ford on cold days, so why not the woman you love?

Most sex books forget to mention that a woman who is masturbating can get herself off just as fast or slow as a man. Perhaps the problem isn't that women have a slower warm up time, as the notion of foreplay seems to imply. Perhaps the real problem is our culture's concept of sexuality, where being a woman (e.g. getting fucked) is a common insult, where "scoring" makes a boy feel like a man, and where respect, friendship and caring are not necessary conditions for sex.

Unfortunately, the concept of foreplay implies that tenderness is little more than a tollbooth on the big highway to intercourse. Nonsense. Tender kisses and caresses do not need to be trailed by intercourse to justify their importance or necessity. They are just as important as intercourse, if not more so.

If you can't get past the notion of foreplay, try to think of it as everything that's happened between you and your partner since the last time you had sex. How you treat each other with your clothes on has far more impact on what happens in bed than carefully planted kisses right before intercourse. This is just as true for the way that women treat men as for how men treat women.

Why Even Care?

Studs, bimbos, bounced checks — why even care? How can you not care? These are the myths about each other that we take to bed with us. It's what gets in the way. 🐟 🐟 🐟

End of Chapter Notes: Regarding the wigwam comment at the start of the chapter, just seeing if you were on your feet. Pueblo Indians either live in adobe/stone pueblos or caves. Unfortunately, life on the reservation has not been good to the sexual habits of the Pueblo, and incidences of rape are now being reported. 🐟 In unnatural settings like prisons and expensive private boys schools, heterosexual males sometimes coerce other males into having sex as a sign of power or superiority. Once returned to the mainstream of society, the object of desire becomes women and the sex is referred to as "making love." 🐟 It's sometimes strange to hear modern women use various fuck-this/fuck-that expressions, since the implied insult is to be the receiver of intercourse. Women might reply "And who would know better?" ◄ Did the little girl mentioned earlier in this chapter actually understand the premise of the slang phrase suck my dick or was she simply mimicking the correct social usage? Does it matter? Is there any difference in the long run? ◄ Expressions like "Fuckin' great" are examples of how sexual slang is used in a positive sense. They tend to be role neutral and refer to the act of intercourse itself. ◄ The creation of foreplay was actually an improvement over what had come before, or so it is said..

Special thanks to the writings of Ira Reiss, Paul Evdokimov, David Schnarch, Regina Barreca, Carol Tavris, the late Bob Stoller, and many others for inspiring concepts used in this chapter. Thanks also to Paul Kroskrity, Anthro Professor at UCLA, for the information about the Pueblos. And finally, thanks to the famous sex researchers who originally suggested that people think of foreplay as everything that happened since the last time you had sex.

Chapter 5
Romance

Dear Dr. Goofy,

This romance thing is making me crazy. I'm dating a wonderful girl named Valerie and last night I took her to a romantic night out at an expensive restaurant. I spent more than $100 for the two of us. She seemed to be having a good time. I figured that before the night was over my Little Willy would be seeing some serious action. But when I took her home all I got was a thirty second good night kiss. At this rate, I figure I'll have to spend at least $2000 on a weekend in Acapulco just to get a hand job. Do you have any suggestions?

Dude,

You might be confusing romance with prostitution. This is a bad mistake, unless the woman you are romancing also enjoys turning tricks on the side. If what you are looking for is sex, you shouldn't have any trouble finding a woman who will give you a lot more than a hand job for $100. If what you are looking for is romance, then sex should not be the goal. That's because romance is a special way of connecting with someone that has its own unique universe that resides somewhere between Platonic love and carnal lust. Sure, romance can evolve into sex, but it's just as possible to have a perfectly romantic evening and still end up in bed alone, with you lathering up Little Willy with his favorite brand of hand lotion and romancing him that way.

In case you find this answer confusing, please keep reading. You'll probably get the concept by the end of the chapter.

How Pulp Novels and The Free Market Have Given Romance A Bad Name

Dear Dr. Goofy,

Romance is that mushy stuff that fills Harlequin Novels. It is an entirely feminine construct. Men only become romantic when sheer raw sex is assured. Every time I see those pathetic diamond commercials, I nearly throw up on my television. What I want to know is if any guy has ever been romantic without the possibility of sex hanging in the balance? male age 24

Dude,

Owwie ouch! We hate to think what else your parents taught you about relationships... Do you realize that there is not a single solitary woman in the entire universe who would date you if she knew you submitted this question? Were you abused as a child? We're taking bets that your own penis cringes with fear whenever it sees your cynical hand approaching!

In your defense, you make the same mistake that many men and women do: you associate romance with capital outlay–the proffering of diamonds and stuff. Although you probably consider yourself to be a free thinker and quite the amazing philosopher, when it comes to romance you appear to be a witless puppet of the mass media.

TV and Magazine ads constantly distort the notion of romance, given how we hardly see it portrayed without some credit card being hyped in the process. The fact is, none of the huge corporations (or small ones for that matter) make a single dime when you do something simple but thoughtful for your partner. They don't want you to know that the possibility even exists.

Contrary to what your television is telling you, romance does not need to cost a thing. Romance has a lot more to do with thoughtfulness, kindness and fun than capital outlay. It has to do with special gestures, like taking the time to help your partner do taxes, or scouring the tile in her skanky-looking shower, or getting him a bottle of his favorite imported beer, or taking a whole day to help her organize a troublesome closet or garage. Maybe it's washing her car

Romance In Action
Dating At The Goofy Foot Press

and getting its oil changed, or just leaving a note on the refrigerator or car seat saying "I love you." Maybe it's telling him how much you appreciate how hard he works.

Of course, there's no reason to trust the Goofy Foot Press. Consider instead what some of our guy readers have to say about the subject of romance:

> "Romance is being kind, gentle and thoughtful. Sometimes intense as when making love, sometimes only on pilot light, but never off." *male age 70*

> "Romance is when we go rollerblading together at the beach." *male age 32*

> "Romance is kissing at every red light while on a date, or feeling tingly when you see each other again after being apart for hours or days." *male age 38*

> "Romance is when she and I can absolutely forget that the rest of the world exists. Just today we both had a million things to do to prepare for the coming work week but I turned on the

**Romance In Action
Commuting To Work At The Goofy Foot Press**

CD player and played a great Spanish song about a bull that falls in love with the moon. Soon we had dropped our work and were spinning each other around the living room like two people who had no idea how to dance Flamenco..." *male age 25*

"Romance is being naked in the sun." *male age 42*

There's not a single thing these guys mention that will require the folks at MasterCard to increase your credit limit. Of course, maybe they are deluding themselves, thinking they can be romantic without seriously increasing the national debt. So let's check with what our women readers have to say.

Women Readers On Romance

"What is romance? Stroking my hair, holding my hand, helping me with the housework, cooking, talking, sharing the day with me." *female age 43*

Romance In Action
Lunch At The Goofy Foot Press

"Romance is waking up in my partner's arms and being told that he loves me." *female age 27*

"Romance is sitting on a hammock together reading our books." *female age 26*

"Romance is talking to each other when we are frustrated or upset and then making love." *female age 27*

"It's bringing home a single rose or a little something to say I was thinking of you today." *female age 34*

"Doing things that shows he values me as a life partner and not just a bed partner." *female age 45*

"Being a friend AND a lover!" *female age 37*

"For romance, I enjoy a great bubble bath together with candles and wine, lots of great smelling scents whether it's perfume, incense or just the smell of my man." *female age 36*

Romance In Action
Dinner At The Goofy Foot Press

"If he brings you flowers or jewelry and he's not there in any other way, it's not romance." *female age 45*

Romance In Long Term Relationships— Getting The Mix Right

When it comes to long term relationships, all the romantic gestures in the world are meaningless if you aren't trustworthy and don't help maintain the mutual nest. Cooking a special dinner or sending an unexpected card won't get you far if you didn't do any of the chores that your partner was counting on you to do.

For romance to work in a long term relationship, it needs to be based on a foundation of reliability and trustworthiness. Then, the kind and thoughtful gestures that we are calling romance have a footing on which to stand. They help take your relationship beyond the functional and into the sublime.

On the other hand, when you hear people who have been together for a long time say that the sparkle is gone in their

Romance In Action
Weekends At The Goofy Foot Press

relationship, they have sometimes worked so hard on being reliable that they have forgotten about the little gestures that help to make a relationship fun.

Dear Dr. Goofy,

My husband of fifteen years is the most trustworthy and hard-working man on the face of the earth. He's a great father to our kids and I love him dearly, but the romance in our relationship is gone. I can't remember the last time I received flowers from him that weren't for Mother's Day. The big trouble is, I've been noticing the pool man a lot more than I should. He compliments me on what I am wearing, asks me about the projects I am working on, and makes me laugh. By the time he leaves every Wednesday, I find myself wetter than the pool deck! It's not that he's some sort of physical ten or that we've had sexual contact, it's just his wonderful attitude and the way he takes the time to notice me. How do I get my husband to do the same?

Dude(ette),

We'll be hand-delivering this reply next Wednesday afternoon, just as Mr. Chlorine pulls out of your driveway... Here are some things to consider: It's quite possible that in your husband's mind, his way of being romantic is by working his rear off for you and the kids. Worse things have happened. Be sure that at least a couple of times a week you tell him how much you appreciate how hard he works. Do this from now until the end of time. Next, think back over the past fifteen years and come up with a couple of things that both you and he have enjoyed doing together—without the kids. Hopefully, it will have nothing to do with his work or yours. Maybe it's river rafting, maybe it's shopping for antiques or going to a carnival. Whatever it is, plan it for just you and he. Don't expect much from the first five or ten excursions, rusty wheels take a long time to loosen. At the end of each of your special outings, give him the best blow job he's ever had (pretend you're doing the pool guy). When you're done, tell him something like "When you work so hard for us, that makes me love you deeply. And when you spend time with me like you did today, it makes me want you to fuck me. I'd really love to do this again next week." Come up with your own variation of this theme, but do something that will help thaw the glacier that your relationship has become. Of course, if you and he are locked into some kind of sick transference where you are acting out stuff from your respective childhoods, best to get marital or individual counseling.

Some of you might say that in this example, sex is being used to get romance. Perhaps, but what better reinforcement for making emotional connection once again.

FOR GUYS EVERYWHERE
HIGHLY RECOMMENDED!!

It's a book called "How To Romance The Woman You Love." This book will do more for you and your relationships (present and future) than a thousand books on sexual technique. It has hundreds of suggestions, but maybe you will only find two or three that turn your lights on... That could be all you need to separate you from the rest of the pack. The author is Lucy Sanna, and the publisher is Prima Press. If you can't find it at your local bookstore, call the publisher at (916)632-4400.

FOR COUPLES

Laura Corn's books can be a lot of fun for couples. Consider trying her "101 Nights of Great Romance" (800-547-2665). Also, there are certain board games designed to enhance romance. If the notion of playing a romantic board game doesn't cause you to throw up on the spot, you might check out "Enchanted Evening" (800) 776-7662.

FOR WOMEN

Daphne Rose Kingma has written about a zillion books on romance. She's a very thoughtful and caring person. One of her publishers is Conari Press, whose catalogue oozes with of the type of romance stuff that no self-respecting male would be caught dead reading, but a lot of women seem to enjoy. (800)685-9595. For men and women: When romance fails, you might try reading Ms. Kingma's "Coming Apart: Why Relationships End and How To Live Through The Ending Of Yours."

Chapter 6
Kissing—Lip-Smacking Good

This chapter is about kissing on the upper body as opposed to kissing on the genitals, although one often follows the other, and a lot of couples mix the two together—a little peck, a little suck, a little peck, a little suck...

Sometimes kissing is used as a starter, to help stir-up various body fluids. Sometimes kissing is all there is. Whatever the case, it doesn't matter if the only person you've ever kissed was your grandmother, or if your lips could dock space shuttles for NASA, you might find some helpful reminders in the pages that follow.

The Power Of Talking In Tongues

It's funny how kissing a partner on the lips usually makes more of an emotional statement than kissing him or her on the genitals, even if the latter sometimes feels better. For instance, one woman who makes her living by having sex with different men reports that she won't let anyone other than her husband kiss her on the lips. And when a relationship starts to go sour, couples usually stop kissing on the lips long before they stop having intercourse.

There are reasons why kissing on the lips has such emotional power. From the moment we were born, most of us were kissed constantly by moms, dads, aunts, uncles, grandparents, and anyone else whose approaching lips we couldn't successfully dodge. At the same time, our genitals remained virtually unkissed or unsucked, in most families anyway, until we could get old enough to talk a friend or partner into doing it.

Another reason for the added emotionality of kissing is because four of the five senses have major outlets on the human face: sight, sound, smell and taste. Also, the human face is a welcome receptor of the fifth sense which is the ability to feel touch. (Ever hear the term "in your face?")

Interestingly, the ability to have an orgasm is not considered one of the basic senses, although it totally overwhelms the other senses when it actually happens.

When Kissing Is The Main Course

Kissing is often a prelude to other things, but there are plenty of times when kissing is all you get. Like when you are sixteen and necking all night long. Or when you are older but want to feel like you're sixteen. But don't for a moment think that extended kissing sessions are kid's stuff. Some people experience make-out sessions as hotter than a lot of the intercourse they have had.

NOTE: If all you plan on doing is making out, be sure to put your gum in a safe place where you can find it afterwards. It will help take the edge off until you can go home and masturbate.

Reader's Smooch Advice: The Basics

"Please don't eat my mouth. A good kiss can make me wet with desire, with only the softest touch." *female age 23*

"Kissing is not just a preliminary to fucking. Gently explore with your tongue, lightly suck on her lips and tongue. If she is into it as much as you, kiss with good suction, not lazily." *female age 45*

"When you're kissing be gentle, don't swallow the women's entire face into your mouth or dig your teeth into her cheeks."
female age 36

"Start really light. Barely brush your lips against hers. Be very aware of her response. Increase the pressure ever-so-slightly when she begins to meet your lips. Eventually, touch the tip of your tongue to her lips. If she opens her mouth, you can let your tongue enter just the smallest bit, but try not to force her mouth open." *male age 25*

French Kissing

French kissing is not a tongue-to-tonsils regatta. Try swallowing first and don't go shoving your tongue down your partner's throat.

Pretend your tongue is Barishnakov instead of Rambo and you will do just fine. There is always time for tonsil sucking later.

When you are French kissing, keep in mind that mouths, like numerous other body parts, enjoy variety. Don't treat your partner's mouth like a New York City parking space. Bring your tongue out for air and change the pace with a little lip-to-lip or lip-to-neck action before re-probing the deep.

"Take it slow and easy, but not too easy." *female age 26*

"Don't jam your tongue down someone's throat until she invites you in." *female age 38*

"Getting deep throated for fifteen minutes at a whack is no fun." *female age 48*

El Nino You Are Not

People who are new at kissing sometimes ask what to do with their noses when they smooch, and whether they should kiss with their eyes open or closed. We don't know. As for the issue of water-works, e.g. serious salivary action, take these comments to heart:

"Turn off the water works! There is nothing worse than a big slobbery wet kiss." *female age 27*

"Try not to slobber!" *female age 25*

"An overly wet mouth is a turn-off." *female age 32*

"Girls love slobber. At least that's what they tell me. Maybe that's 'cause I slobber, though. Hey, wait a second!" *male age 22*

Lip Sucking Good

Keep in mind that eyelids, ears, noses, cheeks and foreheads are sometimes excellent areas to kiss. And for heaven's sake, don't forget the neck. We're not talking vampire action, but something this side of raising a hickey might help create a welcome reception in body parts further to the south.

What About Hickeys?

Hickeys are what happen when a lover sucks on your neck or other body parts with enough force to cause internal bleeding. The hickey is the resulting bruise. Some people are proud of their hickeys and display them like bikers do tattoos. Other people feel mortified when they discover a brownish or bluish blotch that wasn't there the day before. They even wear turtlenecks in the middle of summer to cover the things up.

Most drug stores and larger supermarkets have cosmetic sections with different shades of make-up that can help hide hickeys. If you buy one of these concoctions, make sure that it matches your natural skin tone. Otherwise it will look like a big smudge.

Keep in mind that people with certain skin types hickey-up worse than others. As for hickeys between the legs, who much cares unless you are going to the beach or having an extra-marital affair?

(One woman who called a local radio talk show said that her boyfriend had given her a hickey in the middle of her forehead. How do you explain that one at work?)

Great Kissing Advice:

"The best thing you can do during a good kissing session is to ask your partner to kiss you the way he or she likes to be kissed. It really works. Just sit back and let him or her take over, you'll learn all kinds of things." *male age 26*

Flossing, Brushing & Garlic

It is raunchy to kiss with pieces of food stuck in your teeth. Flossing and brushing can make you far more attractive to a partner than wearing expensive cologne or sucking on a fistful of breath mints. (If you are concerned about bad breath, check with your dentist, and ask if it would help if you scraped the back of your tongue once or twice each day with the flat edge of a spoon.)

If you are eating food with garlic or onions, make sure that the person you plan to smooch shares a couple of large bites. Flossing and brushing won't put a dent in breath that's laced with garlic. Your only defense is to share the offense.

If You're Wearing Braces...

For people who have braces with rubber bands, consider taking the rubber bands out ahead of time. One reader barely escaped mid-smooch tragedy when a rubber band on his sweetheart's braces came unhooked and nearly shot him in the uvula. A direct hit would have triggered the same reflex that causes projectile vomiting.

Also, be aware that a tongue entering from the opposite direction as your own might get scratched or caught on metal edges that don't pose a problem for you. You might even tell your partner that you are concerned about this, and would feel much better if he or she slowly and thoroughly explored the inside of your mouth with his or her tongue... WOW!

Kissing On The Edge Of Town...

In nearly every community where people have lips, there tend to be special places where the locals go to make out.

In the town where your author grew up there were two favorite places where people went to kiss and grope—well, three if you count the local drive-in, but that was more like an extra bedroom. One of the favorite places was at the river east of town. Another was in the local orange groves. Each had its own hazard, which merely added to its allure. The road to the river twisted along a steep mountainside, which sometimes posed a problem if you were either low on gas or high on beer. As for the orange groves, a busted ditch or recent watering could result in hidden mud traps. Tires could spin aimlessly until your best friend's father arrived to tow you out...

Eskimo Pies & Eskimos Kisses: Kissing In Other Cultures

You may have heard that Eskimos don't kiss like we do. Instead of kissing on the lips they allegedly rub noses. What's closer to the truth is that Eskimos put their noses in close proximity to inhale the breath of a loved one. Perhaps they do this to keep their lips from freezing together. (They may want to avoid oral-genital contact for the same reason...)

Eskimos find that inhaling the breath of a lover is erotic; those of us from more temperate climates prefer exchanging wads of saliva. People raised in different cultures don't always agree on what's erotic.

The Real Estate Between Your Neck & Knees

This guide places way too much emphasis on the standard Blue Chip kissing zones — lips, nipples and genitals. Lovers who really enjoy each other sexually will often go from head to toe, discovering and rediscovering where a partner loves to be kissed and touched the most. Here are a few areas to consider when kissing your partner:

🐇 Skin Folds. The places on the body where the skin folds or creases tend to be very sensitive and love to be kissed. These include the backs of knees, the fronts of elbows, the nape of the neck, under breasts, on eyelids, armpits, crotches, between fingers and toes, and behind ears.

🐇 Bellies & Navels. Think of the navel as a little vulva rather than a mere collecting point for lint. Some people love to have their navels licked and caressed. Plenty of people enjoy having the area between their navel and genitals kissed. The same is true for the skin that's over the hip bones.

🐇 Long Licks. Don't hesitate to get your tongue really wet and take a long lick up your partner's body, from hip to armpit or tailbone to neck.

🐇 Lower Back & Buns. The lower back and rear end can be an exquisite area to lavish kisses.

🐇 Human Serving Tray. Fruits, desert foods, and certain liquors can be served on various parts of the body with pleasing results.

🐇 Love Bites. Teeth on skin can feel really nice or really ugly. If this is what you would like to try, lube your lover's skin with oil or saliva so your teeth glide along the surface. Then raise your lips up like Dracula and gently run your teeth back and forth. You might try a little biting action on large muscle groups such as the shoulders or rear end, especially during intercourse. Be sure to get lots of feedback from the bitee, and for heaven's sake, stop short of violating federal statutes.

Be Sure To Ask

Kissing is such a powerful thing, yet we seldom take the time to ask a partner how he or she likes to be kissed. Maybe he or she is turned-on more by delicate little butterfly kisses than by some overly-dramatic lip lock that you saw at the movies. You'll never really know unless you ask, and it really is a shame not to ask.

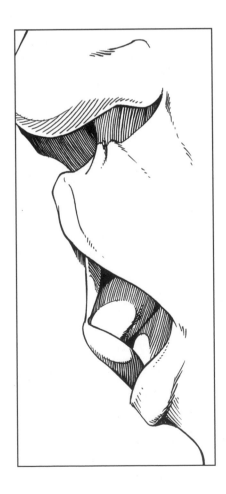

Chapter 7
The Importance Of Getting Naked

In human relationships, there are different kinds of nakedness. For instance, in one-night stands or short term relationships, getting naked mainly means exposing skin. Lots of skin. While this kind of sex can be exciting, a steady diet of it may leave you feeling a bit trashy and wanting for a partnership with more depth. That's when you might start seeking a lover with whom you can get emotionally naked as well as physically naked, or maybe that has been your goal from the start. Whatever the case, this chapter talks about taking your clothes off, and suggests a kind of nakedness that has emotional as well as physical grit.

Getting Naked — An Overview

For some people, getting naked in front of a lover is as easy and natural as drinking a glass of water, but for others, getting naked can cause distress or embarrassment. There are even people who engineer things so they can get it on without taking their clothes off in front of the other person. Perhaps this gives you an idea of how powerful getting naked can be, and how vulnerable we feel about our bodies here in America.

As a culture, we are so upset about nakedness that we don't have street corner fountains with fat marble cherubs peeing into large pools of water or public paintings of naked Botticelli babes. The mere mention of a Norman Rockwell frontal nude is enough to make most people squirm, and a bare crotch on network television is about as common as a snow storm in Siam. At the same time, we are clearly interested in nakedness, given how so many ads and images in our society drip with prurient fury. Perhaps we have learned to cope with our society's mixed messages about sexuality by becoming more aroused at near-naked images instead of actual nakedness. If you doubt this, look at the drawing on the next page. With its suggestion of impending nakedness, the picture has more intrigue than if the couple were shown buck naked.

Getting Naked — Hidden Possibilities

If you and your sweetheart are in the process of becoming more physical, you might consider some of the hidden possibilities that getting naked has to offer. A lot of honesty and trust can be generated when you are naked together, something that rarely develops if the sole purpose of taking your clothes off is for having intercourse. It's how you can learn to relate physically with more than just your crotches. It's how a guy can learn to have his penis resting on a woman's soft warm skin without feeling like he has to perform with it. It's how you can be holding each other without a stitch of clothes on and it's way more than just a milestone on the way to getting laid.

Naked Logistics

If it feels like your relationship is ready, you might consider planning a time and place where the two of you can work on getting naked. Some couples enjoy undressing each other, while others make a game out of taking their clothes off—from playing strip poker to light-hearted wrestling. Sometimes getting naked just happens naturally if you go skinny-dipping or hot-tubbing, and some couples enjoy undressing each other while dancing, slow or fast. (If you try this, be sure to have birth control handy in case you get swept away by the moment and suddenly start doing the polka.) There are also occasions where one partner blindfolds the other before undressing him or her.

Occasionally, people find it helpful to tell each other some of the things that they do and don't like about their bodies. Some women worry that their butts are too big or their breasts are too small or big. Some guys worry that they aren't hung well enough, or that they might be hung too well. Just getting your fears out in the open will usually help you feel more comfortable. If it doesn't, then maybe the relationship you are in isn't such a good one.

For couples who are particularly self-conscious, writer Jay Wiseman suggests getting naked in total darkness. Each partner then takes turns examining the body of the other with a small flashlight — one of those little penlight things that excites just enough photons to light up an area the size of your thumbnail. This can be a fun game that taps into all sorts of fantasies as well as helping to decrease the anxiety of being seen naked all at once.

Guys Worry: Wood Good, Wood Bad?

When it comes to getting naked, men sometimes worry about whether they should or shouldn't have a hard-on. It doesn't matter. It's fine if you have one, it's fine if you don't. The whole point, if there needs to be one, is learning to associate nakedness with something other than just sex and taking a shower. With a little work, you might discover that being naked helps create the kind of space where you and your partner can talk about important things. **Naked Note:** Some people don't have the slightest hesitation to get naked for having sex, but good luck if you suggest getting naked with the sole purpose of talking or holding each other. They sometimes become fidgety and fire off a rapidly dismissive "Sure, we'll have to try that sometime..."

Naked & Getting Off

While getting naked together doesn't need to include orgasms, some couples find it uplifting to have one or two somewhere along the way. So plan your naked time to include lots of holding and touching, an attempt at an orgasm or two, and then even more holding and touching afterwards.

Coming is usually the last thing that couples do when they are having sex. Yet it might be nice to spend extra time holding and touching each other after you have orgasms, rather than simply rolling over and falling asleep or running off to work. That's because coming clears the senses in a way that allows many of us to share a special kind of warmth and tenderness.

Sex Tips With A Cranky Marxist Edge

Sometimes a half-peeled banana is more exciting than one with no peel at all, or so we've been led to believe. This type of philosophy has helped fuel the multi-million dollar lingerie business, which for years has made a handsome profit selling flimsy wisps of underwear to women under the name of lingerie. And now, manufacturers are gouging men with similar intent. They embroider the name of some fancy clothes designer or tennis shoe manufacturer into the spandex band of men's briefs and suddenly charge $10.00 to $20.00 for a pair that you could otherwise buy at Kmart for $2.50.

Anyway, if you find underwear to be erotic, here are a couple of possibilities:

🐮 Women who wear nylons and garters might consider putting their panties on over the garter belt instead of under, so their panties can come off while leaving the stockings and garters intact. *Fine tips such as these can be found in Cynthia Heimel's wonderful book, "Sex Tips For Girls." Her lingerie chapter offers insight about women's underwear that no male writer short of a transvestite would ever get right.*

🐮 A common garter faux pas, according to the owners of Los Angeles' Trashy Lingerie store, is when the woman wears the rear garter all the way back instead of to the side. On the right leg, the front garter should be worn at dead center (12:00) and the rear garter should attach to the nylon at 3:30-4:00 as opposed to 6:00. On the left leg the front garter attaches at 12:00 and the rear garter at 7:30 or 8:00. This helps keep the seams straight. The "Western Woman" pictured on page 346 almost has it right, although her rear garter is closer to 5:00 than 3:30-4:00.

Another Trashy Lingerie tip: if you are wearing a push-up bra, put it on and then reach across your chest with your right hand. Grab your left breast from under your armpit, lifting it up and dropping it into the bra cup. Do the same thing with your left hand and right breast. Another bra misdemeanor: incorrectly adjusting the straps so the bra rides up too high or droops down too low.

When out on a date, a woman should never hesitate to let a man know that she is not wearing any underwear, or reach into her purse and pull out a pair of panties while saying "Oops, guess I forgot to put these on!" As for men doing the same thing — not around here, but maybe in your neighborhood.

When sitting down to lunch or even for a long plane flight, some women briefly hike up their dress and intentionally adjust a garter in view of a man whose salivary glands they hope to make flow. The art of doing this, of course, is in the ability to disguise the purposefulness of the act.

One oral sex variation is to go down on your partner while she or he is still wearing underwear. You can reach under the material with your tongue, push it to one side for proper access, or pull it off with your teeth. You'll probably need a fingertip assist, but the gesture is what counts!

If you're having a quickie, you might not fully get out of your underwear before the action begins. Darn! Also, some couples enjoy having oral sex and intercourse while one or both partners is wearing crotchless underwear. (It used to be that crotchless underwear were just for women, but then that equality thing happened.)

Dry humping with only your underwear on can be fun, as well as taking a shower or bath while still wearing your underwear. The same is true while wearing swimsuits, assuming you aren't sporting a nasty sunburn and your trunks and bikini aren't harboring a billion grains of sand.

🐮 Women shouldn't hesitate to take their lovers with them when shopping for lingerie. Shopping for a new bra or skivvies might seem mundane to a woman, but it could be a fun treat for a man. It will also help give him ideas for when he wants to get you a special gift. If it's possible, ask him to accompany you into the dressing room, but don't try on every bra in the store. His tolerance for that sort of thing might not be as great as yours.

🐮 For guys, the next time you are in a big department store with your sweetheart, nudge her into the men's underwear department and ask her what style and colors she thinks might look best on you. This can make for added pleasure the next time she reaches down and pops the buttons on your blue jeans.

Crotchless Pantyhose

Dear Dr. Goofy: I get seriously turned on when my girlfriend is wearing pantyhose. There's something about the feel of them on her legs that makes Mr. Winky pop straight in the air. Any advice about this?

Dude,

Given how most of our mother's wore nylons or pantyhose, and considering how often our toddler selves stood next to them with arms wrapped around their legs, it's a wonder why more guys aren't stirred into action by the feel of a woman wearing pantyhose.

Assuming your girlfriend is understanding and willing, ask her to cut out the cotton crotch on a pair of pantyhose. She can then let you go wild while she is wearing nothing but. Thanks to the new ventilation system, you'll be able to go down on her as well as have intercourse while she is wearing her customized pair of pantyhose. Make sure she cuts out the crotch on the inside of the seam so they won't unravel. Also, be sure to bring her off orally first, because it isn't likely that you'll be lasting for long once the intercourse begins. If she isn't handy with scissors, she can purchase crotchless panty hose in some stores, but probably not Mervyns or Target.

P.S. You're going to love the illustration on page 396!!!

Men's Underwear

Men have a choice of wearing briefs, boxers, nothing, or even women's underwear if they're of that ilk. Most of us end up wearing whatever it was that our mothers bought for us as kids, usually briefs or boxers. Each provides its own separate kind of feeling that a man gets used to, thus casting him for life as either a briefs guy or a boxer guy, although there are probably some men who are switch-hitters. While a briefs guy might experiment with boxers for a couple of months or even years, there's probably a tendency to go back to what he started with. Same with a boxer guy. A woman shouldn't push the issue one way or the other, unless the man doesn't care or is the type who tells her when to wear a bra.

Cramped Penis Alert

A guy's penis usually hangs downward when it's soft, but as it stiffens it needs extra head room to accommodate the expansion. Yet if a man is wearing briefs under his jeans, the expanding penis either gets trapped in a downward position (ouch!) it gets stuck in a horizontal pickle. So if you are fooling around for an extended period of time with your clothes on, the penis will usually need a quick assist to rise above the resistance that's provided by the blue jeans and briefs. While it might be a bit presumptuous for a woman to lend a helping hand the first time you have an extended grope, this can be a really nice gesture in a longer term relationship. When the bulge starts to grow, just reach inside his pants and pull the penis up so its head is pointing toward the man's chest!

Jocks & Cups

Some men like to wear athletic supporters for erotic purposes. Perhaps one reason is because the athletic supporter, by the nature of its design, emphasizes a man's rear end by keeping it naked while highlighting his genitals by keeping them covered. While this might be more prominent in the gay community, we know of straight women who get turned-on by seeing a lover in an athletic supporter, as long as he isn't wringing wet from playing rugby for six hours.

NOTE: They're beginning to find that some guys who are sterile as adults got that way because they were playing sports without a cup and took a significant knock in the nuts. Any guy who is involved in a contact sport should wear a cup, whether he's an adult or kid. Ditto for if he's playing catcher in baseball. Fortunately, they have soft cups these days which are a lot better than nothing for a game of grab-ass whatever, and they'll make you look like you're really well hung to boot. *See "cup" in the Goofy Glossary at the end of this book for tips on wearing a cup.*

Special Lingerie Supplement — Learning From Lady Lawyers

During the 1970s and 1980s, there suddenly arose a large number of lady lawyers in this country who began to penetrate the traditional male lair of the law. Being confused about how to be taken seriously, most of these women started wearing boring wool suits with blouses that had floppy bows (the lady lawyer uniform). The intent was to look as nonsexual and unalluring as humanly possible, as femininity was considered to be some sort of liability when arguing matters of law. Short of wearing a body bag to court, most of the women succeeded handily. Interestingly, some of these lady lawyers made it a point to wear steamy lingerie under their boring suits. It was a way of saying to themselves "At least some part of me is still feminine."

In our society, wearing lingerie has been an important way for women to feel feminine. In fact, some women feel sexier wearing lingerie than they do being naked. (Some women feel better masturbating while wearing lingerie or underpants.)

As for guys feeling more masculine while wearing boxers, briefs, or jock straps, nobody around here felt overwhelmed by the idea — although men sometimes feel sexy in their underwear. What feels best of all is when a lover pulls off a man's briefs or boxers.

Thanks to the writings of Barbara Keesling, Linda Levine,
Lonnie Barbach, Cynthia Heimel, and Jay Wiseman for naked inspiration.
Ditto to the folks at Los Angeles' Trashy Lingerie.

At Work

At Home

Chapter 8
On The Penis~
The Penis And The Man Behind It

This chapter was specifically written for women readers, although the men who have seen it claim to be amused. The topic is boys and their toys. Hopefully the following pages provide some insight into the love (and sometimes hate) relationship between a man and his weenie.

Toys, Pain & Pleasure

As a woman, the first thing you will find out about penises (and testicles) is that most guys take them way too seriously. There are reasons for this:

◄ The penis is the only childhood toy that a guy gets to keep and play with throughout his entire life. It is the only toy he will ever own that feels good when he tugs on it, it constantly changes size and shape, and it is activated by the realm of the senses. Try to find that at Toys'R'Us.

◄ One of the first things a man does when he wakes up in the morning and the last thing he does at night is to touch his penis and testicles. It is a male ritual of self-affirmation that has little to do with sexual stimulation. A daytime extension of this practice is known as pocket pool.

◄ The average male pees between five and seven times a day. Each time he pees he has a specific ritual, from the way he pulls his penis out and holds it, to the way he wags it when he is done. When he is peeing alone a guy will often invent imaginary targets in the toilet to gun for. An especially fine time is had when a cigarette butt has been left in the commode. Floating cigarette butts are the male urinary equivalent of the clay pigeon. While this may be a difficult concept for a woman to fully grasp, it does make for a certain amount of familiarity, friendship, and even self-bonding between a man and his penis.

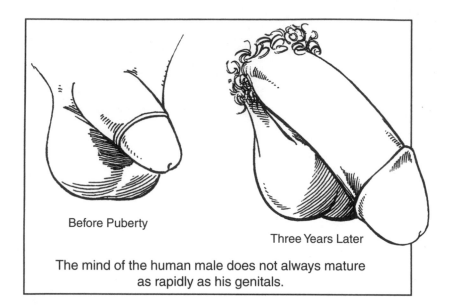

Before Puberty

Three Years Later

The mind of the human male does not always mature
as rapidly as his genitals.

◄ You wouldn't believe how often the human male experiences a jolt of pain in his testicles. It is a discomfort that gives a guy the kind of extra personal relationship with his reproductive equipment that menstruating women have with theirs. The source of agony can be anything from an elbow during a game of basketball to simply bending over and having your pants crimp the very life force out of you. One of the great culprits in male testicular angst is the horizontal bar on the bicycle frame. Why is it that girls' bicycle frames are V-shaped when it is guys who need the V? Not only did this confusion among bicycle makers result in our younger selves not getting to look up girls' dresses when they were mounting their bikes, but many of us still have the words Schwinn® engraved on the underside of our testicles from each time a foot slipped off the pedal.

◄ This may be difficult to fully appreciate, but there is the matter of the unwanted hard-on. The unwanted hard-on usually strikes with predictable ferociousness first thing in the morning. Not only does it interfere with the ability to relieve a full bladder, but it provides logistical problems for a guy who has to traverse shared hallways to get to the bathroom. The unwanted hard-on can be partic-ularly excruciating and even painful for its most frequent victim, the adolescent male. The unwanted hard-on is much less of a problem after a man turns 30, and by the time he's 40 it is an event accompa-nied by a sigh of relief and a moment of thanks.

◅ When guys are naked together we sometimes glance down to check each other out. (Do women make similar comparisons regarding their breasts?) Since we males do it amongst ourselves, we figure that women check us out in the same way. This can make us extra conscious about what we've got between our legs.

◅ When life is full of despair, the one thing that a guy can usually count on for a good feeling is his penis, unless matters are totally out of hand, in which case he needs to consider something stronger like tequila or prayer.

◅ Our society teaches us that sexual pleasure between a man and a woman depends on the man's ability to get hard and stay hard. (What a demented view of sex.) This puts a lot of pressure on guys to be consummate cocksmen. It makes us more dick-oriented than necessary, at the expense of everyone.

These items aside, the most important thing for a woman to know about a penis is how it figures into a man's concept of his own manli-ness. Ridiculous, but important.

Manliness — A Goofy Definition

Masculinity and femininity are inventions of culture that have little foundation in science or nature, yet they remain powerful forces in the way we view ourselves and each other. In our society, everyone has an idea of what a real man is, but few people know how to define it. This guide suggests that there are at least two influences which help a boy become a real man:

A parent-figure who provides physical and emotional tender-ness without being too controlling, and someone with a solid sense of values and work ethics whom the boy can look up to and believe in.

OK, so these are the same ingredients that are essential to raising a real woman. They lead to the following definition:

> A real man in American culture is a fairly responsible person who can stand alone when the occasion demands, but who can also be warm, comforting and kind; a person who doesn't need to prove his masculinity by trying to scare or intimidate others.

Of course, there are plenty of males who have none of these qualities, but appear to be total studs nonetheless. These are the guys who usually take their penises way too seriously. That's because the only way they can convince themselves that they are real men is by performing manly activities, drinking a lot of beer or doing drugs, and having a vagina close by that they can stick themselves into.

While most of us resort to these behaviors on occasion, some guys make a lifestyle out of it.

Penis As Camouflage: Why It's Difficult To Be Satisfied By A Guy Who Takes His Penis Too Seriously

A hard penis is sometimes used to camouflage what's missing inside a man, as well as what's missing in a relationship between a man and a woman. Consider the following analogy from the world of surfing:

> A skilled surfer mounts his surfboard in a way that permits the ocean to cradle him with its fury and passion. If the surfer is all hung up about his equipment, then the synergy between man and ocean is seriously compromised.

If a guy is all hung up about his penis being a symbol of his manliness or demands that it have a disproportionate amount of attention, then it gets in the way of his being at one with a woman. The same is true for a guy who needs to always play a manly role. He sometimes feels more warmth for his car or computer than for his wife.

Unfortunately, a lot of women grew up thinking that a distant, self-involved, dick-centered type of guy is what manhood is all about. As a result, they end up being attracted to guys who they can never really get close to, and spend the rest of their lives belly-aching about what duds we men are.

Narcisso' Gasms

Biologically, most women can have a couple of orgasms (or extended wavelike pleasure runs) to the average man's one. This is just fine with most men, since most of us would like to see our partners have as much pleasure as their hearts and loins desire. But for a man who takes his penis too seriously, orgasm giving sometimes becomes too important. His partner's orgasms become reassurance that he is a total guy. (We all do this to some extent, but for those men it's a matter of narcissistic life and death.)

If your man is like this, you may discover that your main function in life is to look good and have lots of orgasms. Or maybe it's just to look good. Consider yourself an offering to the great Dick God.

The Penile Pumping Regatta

Some men lose emotional connection with a woman once intercourse begins. The woman starts to feel like a commodity, as though she has become the guy's masturbation machine. Sex becomes a virtual pumping regatta, with the man using intercourse to prove dick-worthiness. This can be really boring for both partners.

To give you an idea of how much insecurity is involved in all this, consider the words of a twenty-nine-year-old man who is starting to question why he takes his penis so seriously:

> "It's like, I attack sex. I'm afraid of slowing it down. If I'm gonna be fucking, I'll fuck like crazy, gotta have a huge dick and fuck like crazy to avoid dealing with whatever's making me anxious. Women have always said to me, 'God, you can't get enough.' But I think the reason I can't get enough is that if I slow down, the fears start to crowd in on me: Does this woman really want to be with me? Is she going to leave? Is my cock good enough? It's hard for me not to use sex as a seal of approval." (In Harry Maurer's "Sex: An Oral History" Viking Press, New York, 1994)

Of course, there are plenty of women who have their own insecurities. For instance, is getting breast implants all that different from this guy's need to have a big penis?

The Diagnosis and Cure

How do you distinguish a man who takes his penis too seriously from one who doesn't?

The man who doesn't take his penis too seriously is able to be kind, caring, and doesn't beg out when it comes to doing the dishes, shopping or changing diapers. He may have various passions in life, often sports, music, business or trying to fix things (sometimes successfully), but these help to center rather than isolate him, except at critical times like during playoff games or the week of a big presentation. Sex with him is a natural extension of your friendship that makes all the sense in the world.

As for "curing" the kind of man who does take his penis too seriously, you can't. Hard as you might try, no human being has ever changed just because someone else wanted him or her to. It's something that has to come from within. Friends and lovers can sometimes help if they are willing to call the guy on his own nonsense, but they can't make the changes for him.

Sexual Awareness: Hood Ornaments Vs. Wet Triangles

When it comes to sexual awareness, the penis is positioned like the hood ornament on a car. It's difficult to ignore what your hood ornament is telling you when it is sticking straight in the air. Sometimes we guys aren't even aware that we are sexually aroused until we feel ourselves starting to get hard.

Women are not conditioned from early childhood to associate sexual arousal with specific body cues in the way that men are. While their genitals often swell and lubricate, no flags get waved. Most of the changes happen on the inside and can be more easily ignored than a hard-on. Besides, "nice" girls are often taught to ignore their body's sexual cues.

While the penis can be a reliable indicator of sexual excitement, it does have its share of false positives and negatives.

Unwanted Wood

"For some reason, out of nowhere, your penis starts to get hard and it is extremely difficult to stop." male age 25

"It's totally embarrassing. You just want to get up and go, but you can't. So you start pulling on your shirt or sweater to try to cover up the bulge. You become very self conscious, you think everyone is looking at your crotch." male age 43

"It's like being in an elevator with an umbrella that will not go down." male age 42

"It can physically hurt, when your penis is trapped in your jeans pointing downward and it suddenly gets hard for no reason whatsoever." male age 26

"Most of my memories of unwanted erections were at school. Generaly during class, and I was terrified that someone would notice." male age 24

"I travel a lot for business and sometimes wake up after a flight, erect. It is just terribly embarrassing. If I can't think the damn thing down, then I have to go through the tricky maneuver of flipping it up, trapping it under my waistband (without being noticed) and then keeping my briefcase in front me when I stand." male age 25

Women usually assume that the presence of a hard-on means that a man is sexually aroused, and that no rise in his pants means he isn't. Were it that simple. Consider the occurrence of the unwanted hard-on. The average teenage male is capable of getting a totally unwanted hard-on in the middle of an algebra test for absolutely no reason, unless he is a member of that rare breed who finds polynomial equations sexually arousing. When you are a young man, hard-ons just happen; nobody is more befuddled than the possessor of the penis. To say that all hard-ons are a sign of sexual arousal badly overstates the case. One reader took a bad grade in an early morning high school class because he couldn't go to the board due to his unwanted erections. (Unwanted erections aren't helped by sitting,

THE GOOFY DICK GAME
REAL PENISES OF REAL GUYS

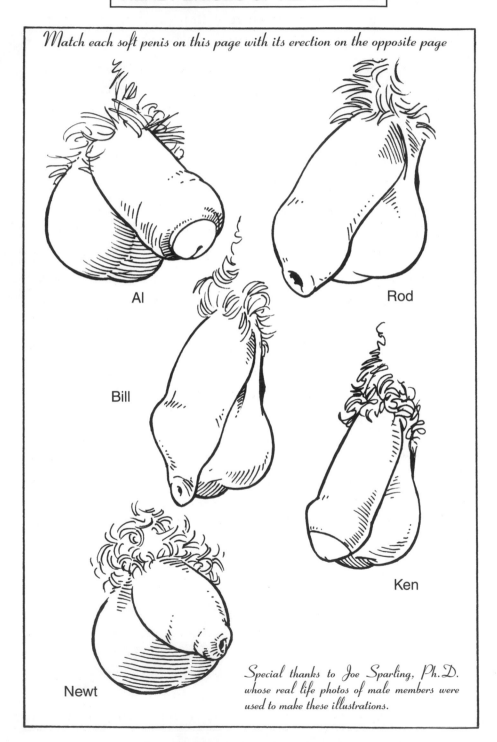

Match each soft penis on this page with its erection on the opposite page

Al

Rod

Bill

Ken

Newt

Special thanks to Joe Sparling, Ph.D. whose real life photos of male members were used to make these illustrations.

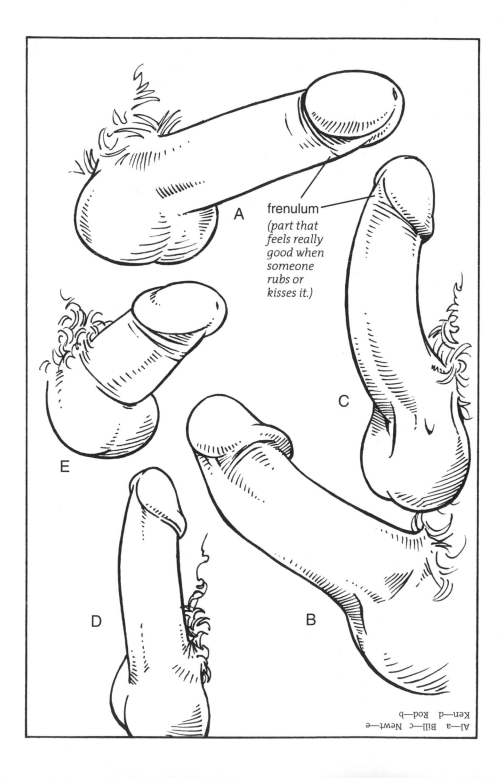

frenulum

(part that feels really good when someone rubs or kisses it.)

A

B

C

D

E

Al—a Bill—c Newt—e
Ken—d Rod—b

since sitting can cause the veins that carry blood out of the penis to be partially or fully closed.)

In addition to getting unwanted hard-ons[1], there are times when a man can feel highly aroused, yet either fail to get hard or have it go limp when he needs it the most (floppus erectus).

False Negatives: When Gravity Dings The Dong

Confucius say: If limp dick is worst thing that happens to your relationship, you live charmed life.

Hopefully your lovemaking isn't solely dependent on the man's ability to get hard. If it is, your sexual relationship might be somewhat limited. It's also disconcerting to think that your entire sex life might be centered around the whims of the average penis, hard or soft.

Regarding the biology of erections, it is perfectly normal for a hard penis to partly deflate every fifteen minutes or so. Regarding the psychology of erections, be aware that hard-ons have been known to fly South for varying periods of time, from a single day to who knows how long.

The most unhelpful thing a woman can do when a guy can't get it up is to become defensive. Women often assume that erection failures mean the man doesn't find them attractive, or that he might be gay. These are possibilities. But there are about a billion and ten other reasons for not being able to get an erection, from fearing that you won't be good in bed to what just happened on Wall Street. Given the stress of living in the modern world, it's a wonder we men are able

---

[1]Fear of an unwanted hard-on might be one reason why teenage guys instinctively wear their shirts untucked. As for the issue of being aroused by polynomial equations, one woman recently recalled that her first orgasm as a teenager occurred spontaneously during a high school algebra test. She thinks it had more to do with the way she was sitting than the subject matter. She was so astonished and overwhelmed by the flood of sensations that she left the entire test blank, although she was an A-student and well-prepared. She suspects her female teacher understood what was happening, since nothing was ever said and she wasn't marked down. With more experience and self-awareness, this woman's earlier sense of being overwhelmed by her orgasms evolved into feelings of delight and amazement.

to get it up as often as we do. And given the lack of tenderness or excitement in some relationships, an unerect penis might be a signal that the man and woman need to get closer emotionally before anything more can happen sexually.

While most of us have been raised to think of a limp penis as a sign of failure, perhaps it might be more productive to view it as an opportunity to bring a man and woman closer. For more on this, please see Chapter 45, which discusses the penile nose-dive and other forms of male hydraulic failure. In long term erection failures, one should first rule out physical causes which can range from the side-effects of prescription drugs to failing arteries in the penis due to cigarette smoking or diseases that impact the circulatory system.

Betty On Dick

The following passage is from Betty Dodson's neat little book "Sex For One" (Harmony Books). In addressing the issue of misbehaving penises, Ms. Dodson speaks with welcome concern:

> "Although I ran only a dozen men's groups, the experience helped me to let go of my old conviction that men got a better deal when it came to sex... I thought they could always have easy orgasms even with casual sex, and I envied their never having to worry about the biological realities of periods or pregnancies. But the truth is that not all men are able to be assertive studs who make out all the time... The most consistent sex problem for many men in the workshops was owning a penis that seemed to have a will of its own. An unpredictable sex organ that got hard when no one was around and then refused to erect when a man was holding the woman of his dreams in his arms..."

If this situation sounds familiar, tell your man that there probably isn't a woman alive who wouldn't be happy to receive a long, lingering back rub and oral sex in the place of intercourse. In other words, if his woody won't work, let him know in no uncertain terms that there are plenty of other ways to please you sexually. This guide's philosophy: *Never ever let a recalcitrant penis ruin your time or his!*

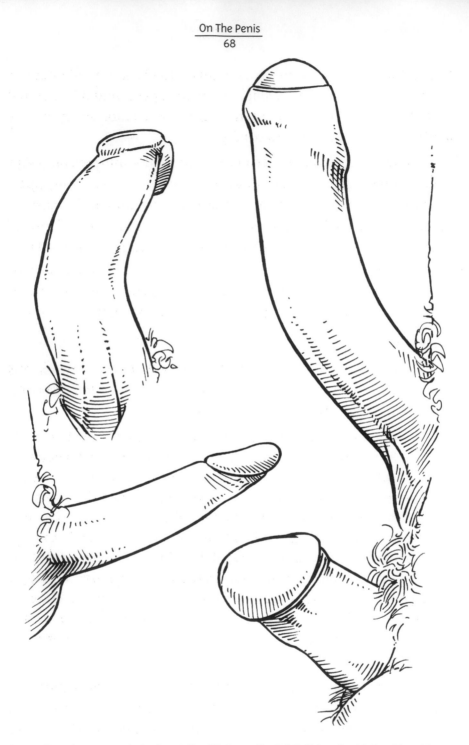

According to a recent study at the University Of California At San Francisco, the average length of a flaccid penis is 3.4", while the average length of an erect penis is 5". Most guys are within 2" of these figures.

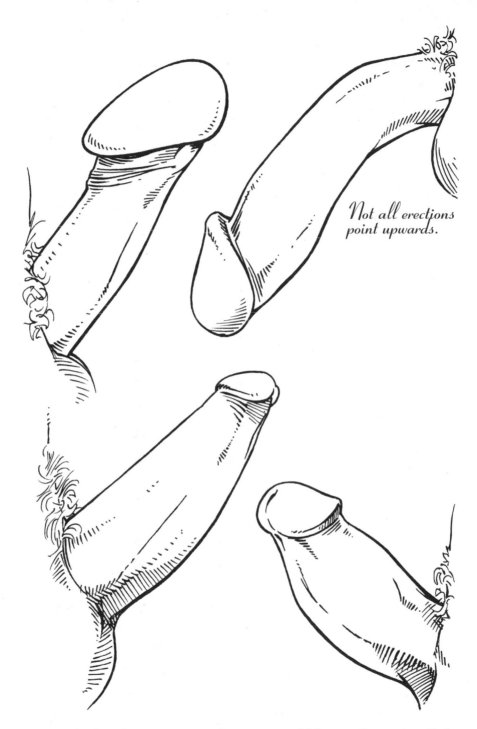

Not all erections point upwards.

When you look at the erections on these pages, which were drawn exactly to scale from real photos, you begin to see how terms like "6 inches" and "normal" are somewhat meaningless. All of these penises are "normal," yet are very different from each other. *Thanks to Joe Sparling, Ph.D. for most of these penis photos. They are from an upcoming book he is doing on erections.*

Dick At Dawn

Guys often wake in the morning with erections. There may be three different causes, none having to do with horniness unless the man also had dreams that left him aroused upon waking:

1.) Dream sleep usually leaves a man with an erection regardless of what he's dreaming about, be it tractors, football, being chased, or even having sex. Since the amount of dream sleep increases significantly towards the morning hours, it's likely that your man's early morning erection was simply the body's ante for letting him dream. (Dream sleep also causes a woman's sexual organs to go into arousal mode, but a congested vagina is more easily ignored than an erect penis.)

2.) Some people believe that the hard-on helps keep a man from peeing during his sleep, especially towards dawn when his bladder is more likely to be full. The reason why it is so difficult to pee with a hard-on is because the erection closes off the passage to the bladder so the man's ejaculate won't backfire during orgasm. However, men who wake with empty bladders still get morning hard-ons, and men who wake with a full bladder but no erection don't necessarily wet the bed.

3.) It's been suggested that the level of testosterone is elevated in the AM. However, elevated testosterone does not necessarily cause an erection.

Contrary to what you might think, a man's first feelings upon waking with an erection usually aren't sexual. They are more along the lines of "I wish this stupid hard-on would go down so I could pee," or "Damn, I hate having to wake up this early." While some men enjoy having sex first thing in the morning, not all men associate early morning erections with horniness. In fact, a man who wakes up in a grumpy mood might feel seriously annoyed if a woman assumes that his early morning wood is for sex. She may need to coax him into having sex, although his penis is rock hard.

A Wet Warning — Ain't Love Grand!

Every once-in-a-while a girlfriend will ask a guy if she can stand behind him and hold his penis while he pees. This is a completely normal request born of completely normal curiosity. But be forewarned that you are sometimes giggling so hard that the entire bathroom becomes a target. On the other hand, women sometimes do a better job of aiming the darned thing than we men. As for penile calligraphy skills, one female friend of this guide loves grabbing her husband's penis and writing their names in the snow with its amber stream.

Men Checking Out Other Men

Guys often have a powerful curiosity to check each other out. You might assume that this curiosity is greatest when they are kids and decreases as they get to be adults, but not according to a recent study by a group of Ph.D. students. These students hung out in restrooms at a San Diego Padres game and secretly studied a hundred different men who were peeing. They found that nearly every guy made an attempt to check out the equipment of whomever was peeing next to him. Furthermore, guys who were well-endowed went out of their way to show their meat to the other men who were peeing. Of course, these tendencies might be more true of Padres fans than say, White Sox fans, who are usually too busy weeping in the men's room to check out anyone else's wood.

As for generalizations, if you are a guy who has ever glanced down at another guy's penis when you are peeing, you can take comfort in knowing that you're probably normal.

First Ejaculation

Before starting puberty, a guy can stroke his little pecker until it nearly falls off and his orgasms will mostly be dry except for maybe a few drops of clear, slick, slightly viscous fluid. Sometime during puberty, this changes. He starts to produce an adult-sized wad when he has an orgasm. Instead of being clear and thin, it's white and thick, and instead of being a drop or two, it shoots or oozes all over the place.

This process can be quite wonderful if you know what to expect and know that it's normal. It can be quite disturbing if a guy doesn't have a clue about masturbation except for knowing how to do it. It can be particularly disturbing if he has no clue about ejaculation and masturbates for the first time after entering puberty, since by then he's fully loaded and ready to shoot.

> "I didn't really know what I was doing. I was about eleven and discovered this new feeling when I rubbed this silky part of my blanket over my penis, so I kept doing it. Eventually, I got this intense feeling in my groin and then there was this goop everywhere. I was completely freaked and grossed out. I thought that I broke myself, but was too afraid to tell my parents." *male age 24*

> "I was sure anything that felt THAT good had to be sinful, and that my ejaculate was evidence that I was damaging my insides. Each time I'd masturbate (almost daily) I would feel horrible guilt afterwards and swear to God that I would never do it again." *male age 44*

> "I had heard about masturbation while sitting in the back of the school bus. When I tried it just the way the kid told me, it was almost like pain. For weeks I would stop short of actual orgasm for fear that I would do some sort of internal damage to myself. Finally, one day I kept rubbing through my fear and found that I enjoyed the hurting tremendously." *male age 25*

The Couch Potato Penis

As they get older, many things start to petrify or harden. This is true for logs, fossils, and the human brain. Unfortunately, it is not true for the human penis. In fact, as a penis approaches its fifth decade, it tends to petrify less fully than it did earlier in life. It also squirts less fluid during ejaculation. Some women will cling to this information as a ray of distant hope, while others will be a bit disappointed. Whatever your situation, it shouldn't make much difference. That's because as the bearer of the penis gets older, he becomes wiser in the ways of love. By then, he can hopefully compensate with wisdom and skill for whatever he loses in hardness or volume.

NOTE: Older men seldom make an effort to stay in good aerobic shape. It's being out of shape, rather than increasing age, that often causes the couch-potato penis and decline in libido. However, age alone seems responsible for changes in ejaculation, with the middle-aged man sometimes feeling nostalgic for his teenage genitals which sometimes propelled ejaculate a foot or more.

Bebop & Squirt — Men and Multiples

Most males experience orgasm as an overlapping two-part process—sensation and ejaculation. Some guys have learned to separate the two events, experiencing a series of orgasm-like sensations before they finally ejaculate.

While this ability may come easily for some men, it usually requires a great deal of practice, more than some of us care to expend. Nonetheless, it can be worked on during hand jobs and oral sex. The woman brings the man close to ejaculation, but slows the stimulation before the squirting begins. Eventually she lets him ejaculate, but not until he has had a good workout. You will find more on this in various Taoist, Tantric or Zen-like books on sex, as well as in other chapters of this guide. (If you absolutely insist on exploring this route, you might check out the work of Jack Johnston (800)349-9886.)

On Men's Hormones

Research indicates that men have mood shifts every bit as strong (if not more so) than women's, making total nonsense of the myth that men are more emotionally stable than women. Researchers are also finding that sex hormones affect the moods of different men in different ways. Some men become irritable or depressed when their testosterone level is elevated. How men respond to the increased level in sex hormone is an individual matter which probably has more to do with social conditioning than biology.

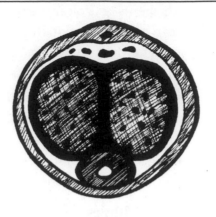

head of a large insect
or
cross-section of a human penis

As for hormones and sexual desire, a certain level of male hormone is necessary for sexual arousal, but it isn't very high. Increasing the amount of male hormone above this level doesn't make men any hornier. The only time when added hormone increases a man's horniness is when his testosterone level is below the minimum level to begin with. *Do not take things like testosterone and DHEA without first having your blood levels tested, and then under the direction of a skilled physician if lab results show a deficiency.*

Guys & Horniness

It is sometimes assumed that the average male wants to have sex each and every hour of the day as long as the opportunity presents itself. There are some guys for whom this axiom simply doesn't apply, at least around these parts. Maybe it's a problem with our masculinity, maybe we're latent homosexuals, or maybe we have nervous systems that are sensitive enough to be impacted by some of the really disturbing things that happen in the world around us. Or maybe we are really tired and simply need a good night's sleep. Whatever the case, it is sometimes difficult to drop everything and have sex. As often as not, it's nicer to cuddle up close to a sweetheart and simply enjoy falling asleep in each other's arms.

The Vicissitudes Of Mercy Sex — Making A Man Come Sooner

Let's say you are getting your man off as an act of kindness and aren't particularly into it, or really need a good night's sleep but won't be able to get one until you've made his woody sneeze. Here are a few things you can do to help make a man come sooner:

◅ **Tighten The Foreskin.** Pulling the foreskin taut around the base of the penis can cause a man to feel more sensation when his penis is stimulated. This might help speed up your lover's ejaculation during oral sex and hand jobs, as well as during intercourse. *See page 199 for specifics.*

◅ **Focus On The Frenulum.** The frenulum is the most sensitive part of the penis. It's just below the head of the penis, on the side where the seam runs up the shaft. During oral sex, you might focus on this area. If doing him by hand, make sure that your fingers run over this area with a fair amount of pressure during each stroke. (Pumping too quickly may numb out the penis and be counterproductive. Also, using a well-lubricated hand rather than masturbating him dry will speed up most men's ejaculation if that is your intent.)

◅ **Adding A Squeeze Or Twist**. Try giving a well-lubricated hand job where your entire hand wraps around the penis and twists up and down it as though it were following the red stripe on a barber's pole. Try a similar twisting motion with your head during oral sex (just a slight turn of the neck is all that's needed, nothing to give you whiplash). At the same time, work the area between his testicles with one of your hands.

◅ **Visuals.** If the man is turned-on by your naked body, for heaven's sake, crank up the lights and park the parts he enjoys most in full view.

◅ **Play With Yourself.** Never hesitate to play with your nipples or vulva. Some men will be so turned-on by watching you play with yourself that they will begin to masturbate and finish themselves off with their own hand.

◅ **Pleasure Toggles.** Some men have a spot along the part of the penis that is buried beneath their testicles or all the way back to the rim of their anus which deepens the degree of sensation when pressed upon. Knowing your man's sexual anatomy and keeping a finger on this spot may help move up launch time. (Women who give superb blow jobs often work these areas with one hand while tending to the end of the penis with their tongue and lips.)

◄ **Nipples.** Some guys nipples are quite sensitive, other's aren't. If your man's are, tweaking them with your fingertips or caressing them with your lips and tongue can speed up arrival time.

◄ **On Or Up His Rear.** A wet finger on or up a guy's rear end can speed up some men considerably.

◄ **Etc.** If he gets turned-on by talking dirty to him, do it if you're in the mood. If he likes X-Rated movies, load his favorite in the VCR. If you're having intercourse, try slowing down the thrusting rather than speeding up, or somehow change his pace. If he's thrusting shallow, have him thrust deep.

If His Weenie Goes Pop...

OK, so let's say you are riding your cowboy in a sexual way and you suddenly fall off, or you are trying one of those ridiculous inter-course positions that's suggested in the fancy sexbooks and one of you slips. Or perhaps you've had a wicked week at work and the kids have the flu and the last thing in the world you want sticking inside of you is your partner's penis, but he has the nerve to insist nonetheless. Whatever the cause of the calamity, should your man's erection suddenly bend in a direction that God didn't intend and makes a cracking sound or goes POP, get it to a hospital right away. Although rare, the pop might be from the snapping of a ligament in the penis that acts a bit like the suspension cables on the Golden Gate Bridge. If it breaks, internal bleeding can result which might permanently damage the penis. Urologists can usually save the wounded soldier within the first few hours post pop, but wait more than a day and your guy could end up going to the grave with a penis that's shaped like a deflated circus balloon, or worse yet, an Allen wrench.

While the above-described popping action is fairly uncommon, an erect penis can still be damaged if it is repeatedly bent mid-shaft. This sometimes happens during sloppy intercourse and might eventually lead to Peyronie's disease. Peyronie's disease can cause painful and/or bent erections. Some physicians believe that Peyronie's disease results from patches of calcium that collect on the penis at points where it has been torqued. The calcium or plaque decreases the elasticity of the expanding penis, which is like pinching together the side of a balloon when you are blowing it up. This condition can be improved with vitamin E in approximately 30% of cases. Some urologists feel that vacuum pumping can also help to straighten out a bent penis.

Warning: The intercourse position that can cause the most potential damage to the penis is when the woman is on top. Be sure to use lots of lube and understand that sloppy intercourse in this position can damage your pecker. Any kind of genital pain that lasts more than ten minutes, whether it's caused by torquing your pecker or a pop in the balls, needs to be attended by a physician. Long term damage can often be averted if you get medical help right a way. ◄◄◄

"Why are guys always touching and grabbing at their genitals?" female age 19

When the skin on the balls sticks to the thighs, and the skin on the penis sticks to the balls, you get a claustrophobic feeling. It's like if you had to keep your arms pressed against your sides all of the time. (Try it for just five minutes without lifting them.) You just gotta dig to lift and separate. Body powder can help. Underwear that doesn't fit right can make matters worse.

What's Inside A Girl ?

Whoa... there's some things baby I just can't swallow
Mama told me that girls are hollow
Uh-uh... What's inside a girl?
Somethin's tellin' me there's a whole nuther world

Ya gotta pointy bra... ten inch waist
Long black stockin 's all over the place
Boots... buckles... belts outside
Watcha got in there yer tryin' a-hide?
Hmmmm?... What's inside a girl?
Ain't no hotter question in the so-called civilized world

Can't see it by satellite, baby that's cheatin'
The President's callin'an emergency meetin'
The King of Siam sent a telegram
sayin' "Wop bop a loop a lop a lop boom bam!"
Wooeee... What's inside a girl?
Somethin's telling me there's a whole nuther world

(chorus)
Whatcha got... watcha got...
Watcha got in the pot?
Whatcha got... whatcha got...
Whatcha got in the pot?
In the bottom of your bottomless bodypit
You got somethin' and I gotta get it
Come onnn... What's inside a girl?

Like da itty bitty baby takes apart his toys
I'm gonna find what's rilin' up the boys
Sugar and spice is just a bluff
You can tell me baby... what is that stuff?
Come on... What's inside a girl?
That wavy gravy got my head in a whirl

Chapter 9
What's Inside A Girl?

 Most books on sex present female genitals as though they were a static entity that is easy to comprehend. They give you a few carefully illustrated diagrams and proceed to speak of women's genitals as one would a carburetor. This is a big mistake.

Of course, some people might say this puts women down since it implies their genitals are more complex or more mysterious than men's. Nonsense. Our goofy little brains aren't so totally fried that we don't value "complex" every bit as much as "simple." We are simply acknowledging that if a man approaches a woman's genitals in the same way that he does his own, he and his partner might be missing out on a lot of fun.

This chapter approaches women's genitals differently than most books on sex. It begins with a boy's quest to discover what's between a woman's legs. It then discusses some of the realities and myths about women's sexuality, although it is nearly impossible to separate the two in our society. Then it talks about specific body parts, like vulvas and vaginas, and ends with a look at phenomena such as G-spots, female ejaculation and multiple orgasms.

Instant Pussy

What follows is an experience that the author of this book had with women's genitals back when he was eleven-years-old and very, very curious.

He had been sent to the big city to visit relatives and it was now time to return home. Since the northbound bus didn't leave until noon, he got to spend the morning in the downtown area next to the Greyhound depot. That's when he found himself taking a leak in a big city men's room which was a far cry different from the one-seater he had grown up with. For instance, right next to the towel dispensers sat three different vending machines.

One of the machines had men's colognes in it; you could spritz yourself with Old Spice or Brut for a quarter. Next to that was a machine that contained a product which was totally baffling. And next to the mystery machine was a dispenser that said *Instant Pussy—2 Quarters*. To put this into proper perspective, back then candy bars weren't much more than a nickel, and two quarters amounted to a near fortune. But then again, the front of the machine promised a facsimile so exact that you couldn't tell instant pussy from the real thing.

For the next hour or so, the young boy pondered the ultimate existential question: ten candy bars or instant pussy, ten candy bars or instant pussy, ten candy bars or instant pussy. A rush of guy hormones apparently kicked in at this very moment and he returned to the porcelain rain forest with two shiny quarters in hand.

The rest of the day was spent in quiet anticipation, with thoughts of instant pussy overwhelming whatever interesting sights and sounds the big city had to offer. Finally, after he had arrived home, fed the dog and did his other chores, the anxious boy opened the small box and read the instructions. "Place capsule in a large glass of warm water." He spent the next half-hour trying to decide just how warm the water should be. He even took out the thermometer and tried to make it a perfect body-heated 98.6. Then came the big moment. He crossed himself and rewed up his courage. With an Enola Gay-like swoop, his trembling fingers dropped the capsule into the glass. Then he waited. And waited. And waited.

To make a long story short, forty minutes went by before the gelatin capsule finally melted. The instant pussy was nothing more than a thin piece of sponge cut out in the shape of a cat.

What's Inside A Woman?

A fine way to learn about what's inside a woman is to hold her. For hours. Your skin against hers, the weight of her body and emotions pressing against yours. And if you really want to learn about a woman, consider having babies and raising them together. Hopefully you will like what you discover, although there are no guarantees for either of you. As for understanding a woman's sexuality, some women will let you deep inside of them, others will only have sex with you. It's no different than with men. Just because it's sex doesn't mean it has emotional depth, even if you are married and having intercourse the prescribed 2.3 times a week.

Myth #1—Men Are Hornier Than Women, And Men Peek Sexually In Their Late Teens While Women Peek In Their Late Thirties

There is a silly notion in our society that young men are hornier than young women, and that the cause is biological (hormones, chromosomes or the will of God). It is also said that women don't reach their sexual peak until they are in their late 30s.

It is interesting how these myths don't exist in cultures that are more accepting of women's sexuality than our own. Perhaps it's not until American women get into their late thirties that they start to realize what a crock of sanctimonious nonsense they have been swallowing all their lives about themselves and their sexuality. That's when they start to let go of their silly illusions about men being hornier, and begin seeking their fair share of pleasure. Unfortunately, by that time a lot of their male contemporaries have gotten fat or are simply out of shape, which makes them less receptive to anything that requires physical effort and stamina.

Myth#2—Tampon-Related Insanity: Rosie The Riveter Has PMS?

The next biological myth, one that is more prevalent now that doctors and pharmaceutical companies can make a lot of money off of it, is that women become incompetent or emotionally unstable during "that time of the month." You know, PMS. To this day, PMS remains such a loosely defined concept that most men qualify as having it. Perhaps the concept of PMS has become so bloated that it no longer resembles reality.

During World War II, when the bulk of American males went to war, millions of American women manned the nation's industrial war machine. Our female dominated workforce turned out an armada of planes, tanks and guns that was unprecedented in history. It wasn't until the men returned from war and needed their old jobs back that the myth of women's so-called hormonal instability began to rear its head once again. It's a myth that fit well with our society's need to get women out of the workplace and back into the home.

One reason why PMS is such a negative concept is because it helps fuel the notion that women as a group are flakier than men. (Just as flaky, yes; flakier, no.) While menstruation may not feel wonderful, it doesn't make a woman emotionally unstable unless she's fairly depressed or fragile to begin with, which most aren't. (Around 3% of women are emotionally unstable, the same number as men.) While most men don't menstruate, not officially anyway, we do have just as many mood swings each month as women.

The following quote by Harriet Goldhor Lerner helps put the hormone matter in proper perspective. This quote was found in Carol Tavris' most excellent book, "The Mismeasure of Woman:"

> "Let's face it. Do you stay off the streets at night because you fear attack from uncontrolled, irrational women in the throes of their Premenstrual Syndrome? Probably not. We stay home at night because we fear the behavior of men."

Myth #3 — Wrestling With The Concept Of "Womanhood"

People make all kinds of assumptions about "womanhood," yet not many of these assumptions hold up to scrutiny. For instance, a conservative female's definition of "womanhood" might not have much in common with that of a radical lesbian feminist, which might not have much in common with that of a heterosexual feminist. And that's just the opinions of women; most of us men gave up trying to define womanhood sometime around 1970. Still, it might be instructive to consider some of the following contradictions about womanhood:

Intuition is said to be a defining element of womanhood. Yet there is not a single respectable study on intuition that has ever shown women, as a group, to be any more or less intuitive than men. Besides, you don't have to know too many women who date and marry total jerks to have serious doubts about the assumption that women are the more intuitive gender.

In the past, motherhood was thought to be an essential element of womanhood. Yet we all know plenty of women without children who are far from deficient in the area of womanhood, whatever womanhood might be.

It is often assumed that women are the less aggressive gender, and that men's aggression makes them more bullying or controlling than women. Yet what about those women who rule the domestic roost with an iron fist that redefines the word controlling, or the self-sacrificing matriarch who manipulates everyone around her by being the consummate martyr, or those women who nag, whine, or criticize with an intensity that's the psychic equivalent of domestic violence?[1] While women don't always do it with bullets and knives, there are just as many aggressive, controlling and unpleasant females as males. And there are just as many aggressive female drivers, when you factor in the number of miles each year that men and women drive. Aggression, or the lack of it, is not a defining element of womanhood.

One female professor-type recently penned a best seller that claims there are significant style differences in the way that men and women express themselves. Perhaps this is a defining element of womanhood. Yet when an interviewer noted that this woman's own style was more like the men she describes in her book, she fully agreed and added that her husband's style is more like a woman's. It's a good thing she didn't include herself and her husband in her studies.

There are women who still equate womanhood with a sense of approval that's reflected in a man's eyes. So what do men think about womanhood? One totally normal heterosexual male said he wondered what it would be like to have women's breasts with sensitive nipples, apparently subscribing to the myth that all women's

---

[1]Statistics indicate that women initiate as many incidences of domestic violence as men.

nipples are like detonators of nuclear bombs. Another straight man said he wondered what it would be like to have women's genitals, to have a penis inside of you during intercourse. A third man whose wife had recently given birth wondered what pregnancy would feel like, and what it is like to nurse a baby who had grown inside you from the time it was a single cell.

Why do these men equate womanhood with having a woman's body, leaving out the various social and political features that a professor of woman's studies might include? Perhaps they are being insensitive clods, or maybe they have known and dated enough women to appreciate the huge range of personalities, capabilities and perspectives that different women offer. Perhaps the only unifying attribute they can ascribe to "womanhood" is having a female body.

Perhaps some of today's women feel equally challenged in trying to define womanhood for themselves. Hopefully you and your sexual partners will feel safe enough to be whatever you need to be, whether it is society's stereotypes of manly, womanly, boy-like, girl-like, passive, active, or bits and pieces of each.

Women's Sexual Anatomy — The Nerve Of It All

In the late 1950s, a scientist named Kermit Krantz explored how women's genitals are wired. It is difficult to find a single research report on the topic of women's sexuality that is of more value than what Kermit Krantz discovered. What Dr. Krantz did is painstakingly dissect the genital regions of eight dead women. (Sorry, there's no other way of putting it.) Krantz found a great deal of variation in the way the nerve endings were distributed throughout the different women's genitals. While there tended to be a higher concentration of nerve endings in the clitoris, the amount varied significantly with each woman, e.g. some had more nerve endings in the labia minora (inner lips) than in the clitoris, and some women's nerve endings were highly concentrated in one area while other women had nerve endings that were spread out over a larger area. To quote Kermit Krantz:

"The extent of innervation in different females
varies greatly"

What this suggests is that no two women get off sexually in the exact same way. Each woman needs to explore her own unique sexual universe, from where to touch to the kind of fantasies that get her off. No matter how experienced her partner might be with other women, he won't know exactly what she likes until she tells him. It's not the sort of awareness he is going to assimilate during a one night stand. A female reader comments: "Talking about this is as much her responsibility as his." A male reader comments about her comment: "Sex is a hundred times better when a woman can actually show or tell you what she wants."

Note: For a man, prior experience can be as much of a hindrance as a help. For instance, stimulating his current partner's vulva in the exact same way that used to drive a former lover wild could be about as effective as calling her the name of the former lover.

Show & Tell

Most guys know what other guys' penises look like. That's because male genitals stick out. You can't help but notice them when you have showered together or peed together. On the other hand, women have no subtle way of looking at other women's genitals, even if they are buck naked. In addition, women have traditionally been discouraged from looking between each other's legs. It's not ladylike. One female reader comments: *"While women speak to each other in graphic terms about things like menstruation, blow jobs and the ratio of penis size to male ego, we usually don't talk to each other about what our crotches look like, not that we'd necessarily want to."*

Still, some women have found it reassuring to see what other women's vulvas look like. They are often surprised to find that there is a lot of variation. If you are a woman who would like to know what other women's vulvas look like, plenty of graphic displays can be found in men's jerk off magazines. There are also a few photo books on vulvas which have been published by some feminists.

Interestingly, the muff shots in some of the politically correct beaver books have a clinically sterile edge that's not particularly arousing. In fact, these mug shots of women's crotches are every bit as unerotic as mug shots of men's crotches. Makes you wonder if it isn't the rest of the picture or the sexual situation, rather than just our genitals, that makes us sexy.

Perhaps the missing element in some of the feminist beaver books is an attitude that says, "What we have between our legs is a good thing. It's fun, it's sexy, we like it." Maybe that's the difference between a picture that's clinical and one that's erotic. Of course, some women will claim that men should value sour pusses every bit as much as happy ones. But some of us enjoy knowing that women find their own genitals to be sexy. Perhaps that's why a lot of us nearly ejaculate on the spot if a partner enjoys masturbating and lets us hold her or watch while she's doing it.

Note: In our culture the vulva is usually wrapped with anything from silk to spandex and leather to lace. This wrapping is known as lingerie. Lingerie is thought to give a sense of allure, like the wrapping that covers a precious gift. Or perhaps the allure is in knowing that the woman finds her genitals sexy enough to cover them in an erotic way.

Vulvas, Vaginas, Beavers & Bear

While many of us can correctly label the male genitals, we usually don't know stem from stern about the female organs of sex. For instance, people refer to everything between a woman's legs as her vagina. Yet this is far from true. What sits between a naked woman's legs is her vulva.

You might ask "What difference does it make if you call it a vulva or vagina?" One female educator answered this question by asking another: "What if parents taught their children that they had no eyes, ears, nose or mouth, but instead gave them one word for their entire face and called it 'tongue'?"

This would be confusing and limiting. It might even suggest that parents are afraid of faces and all the wonderful things they can do.

For the record, a vulva is composed of:

🐦 The outer lips.

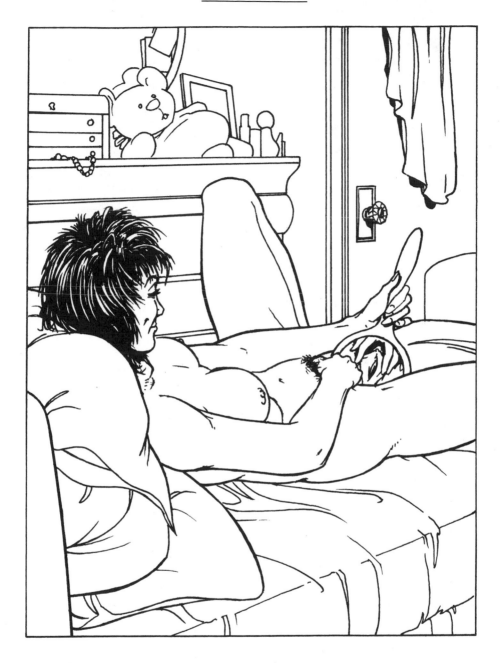

The inner lips and the clitoral hood.

The tip or glans of the clitoris, if it's the kind that peeks through the clitoral hood.

The urethral opening (peehole). Good luck finding it!

The opening of the vagina. (You might need to open the lips to see it.)

The mons pubis, a fleshy little mound that sits on top of the pubic bone and is usually covered by pubic hair, unless the woman has been trying to wear a string bikini with grace or simply likes to have her pubic area trimmed, close-cropped, or cleanly shaven. The mons pubis is a wonderful love-making ally that men often ignore.

Lips, Lips, Lips

Wouldn't you know it, even the ancient Romans got it wrong. They named the outer lips "Labia Majora" (big lips) and the inner lips "Labia Minora" (small lips). But in a lot of women, the outer lips aren't particularly prominent, while the inner lips fan out in all kinds of ways and shapes.

The outer lips often have hair on them, while the inner lips are bald as can be. For most women, the inner lips are more sensitive than the outer. In fact, a lot of women play with the inner lips or gently stroke them when they are masturbating. The lips are so grateful for the attention that they often swell and open when sexually aroused. Their color tends to deepen as they swell, which is nature's way of saying "I'm ready for all the attention you can possibly muster."

The inner lips are often bigger players during intercourse than the clitoris. It's the inner lips that are pushed and pulled with each stroke of the penis. They are the medium that transmits the message to the clitoris.

Clitoris — Point Guard For Women's Genitals

If you don't know a clitoris from a bunion, ask your sweetheart to show you. If you don't have a sweetheart, ask a female friend and then duck. Here's the definition of clitoris from the Goofy Glossary:

clitoris — Latin for "darned thing was here just a second ago." The only organ in either the male or female body whose sole purpose is pleasure, which from a biological perspective might indicate that the female genitals are more highly evolved than

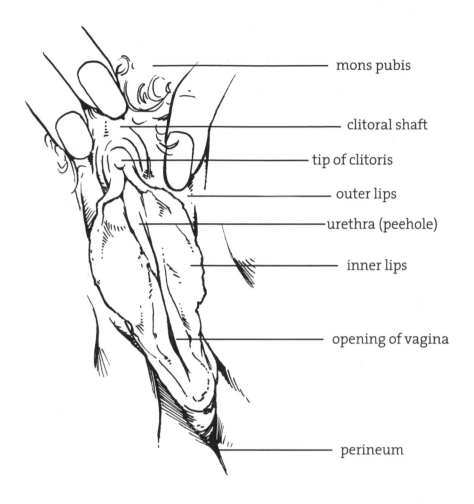

mons pubis

clitoral shaft

tip of clitoris

outer lips

urethra (peehole)

inner lips

opening of vagina

perineum

the male's. 2. Sometimes regarded as the Emerald City of women's orgasmic response. 3. Not to be approached in haste. 4. Sometimes wants to be caressed with vigor, other times can hardly tolerate being breathed upon.

Some clitorises nearly pop out at you and shake your hand, others can hardly be seen. Some clitorises are extremely sensitive, others aren't. Some change sensitivity with the time of the month. Not to worry, the sensitivity of the clitoris has nothing to do with its size, which can range from 2 to 20 millimeters in diameter.

As a woman becomes aroused, the tip or glans of her clitoris often swells. The clitoris also has a foreskin or hood. Manipulating the hood of the clitoris is an art form that is discussed in Chapter 12: The Zen of Finger Fucking. **Note:** Newer theories describe the clitoris as being much larger than was previously thought. Some people now envision the clitoris as being a wishbone-like structure, with the legs of the wishbone running beneath each of the labia.

As The Clitoris Retracts...

As a woman approaches orgasm, her clitoris often disappears or seems to retract. This can be confusing for the man who is trying to stimulate the clitoris by hand or mouth. The confusion is in knowing whether to play Hercule Poirot and give chase, or to simply wait until the clitoris returns...

One researcher, Beverly Whipple questions whether the clitoris actually retracts, or if it simply gets lost in the swelling tissues that surround it. Also, as a woman becomes more aroused, she may want her partner to stimulate her in a different way or on a different spot. Discussing this with your lover makes a great deal of sense.

Incoming

The clitoris is seldom positioned to rub noses with an incoming penis. This is why a number of women enjoy the added stimulation of a finger or vibrator during intercourse, or they sometimes push the clitoris against the shaft of a sweetheart's thrusting penis, or grind it against his pubic bone while his penis is all the way inside. Other women do just fine with thrusting alone. It all depends on how the man's anatomy interfaces with the woman's, where the particular nerve endings are located, how long the man is able to last, and the woman's level of arousal.

A Final Note On The Clitoris — How Do You Pronounce It?

One day the author of this book found that he had to address a classroom of students and might need to say "clitoris." There he was, with almost twelve years of college under his belt, not knowing how to pronounce the word clitoris. To prepare, he wrote "clitoris" on one card and "penis" on another. He then asked friends of both sexes to say the two words out loud.

No one had any hesitation in pronouncing penis, but almost everyone approached the word clitoris with a perplexed look and said "Well, here's how I've always pronounced it..." Some said cli-TOR-is, others said CLIT-or-is. As he was exploring his own usage of the word, he realized that the only time he had referred to it was in bed with a woman, and then he called it "it." (The dictionary says that either pronunciation is correct, although it lists CLIT-or-is first.)

Papa Freud & The Viennese Vagina

Not too long ago, Freudian psychiatrists proclaimed that women had defective egos if their orgasms didn't originate from deep inside the vagina. Sex researchers in the 1960s did society a huge service in showing that the majority of women's orgasms involve the clitoris rather than vagina. However, they may have gone too far in discounting the vagina as a source of pleasure. In fact, some women feel that having something in the vagina (penis, dildo, fingers) during orgasm changes the character of their orgasm and makes it more of a full-body experience. It's not necessarily better, just different from an orgasm that's all clitoris.

Busy Little Beavers

People often view the vagina as passive or inactive. Not so. Consider the following:

🐾 The human body is made up of many different tubes. The favorite tube of many straight males is the vagina, a hollow canal with walls that contain nerves and blood vessels. When not aroused, the walls of the vagina lie flat against each other like a firehose without water. When aroused, a vagina often straightens out and puffs up even more than an erect penis, often doubling in length or depth.

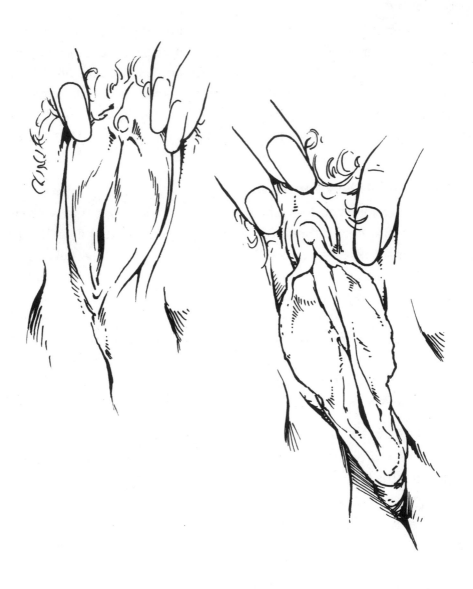

Different Women...

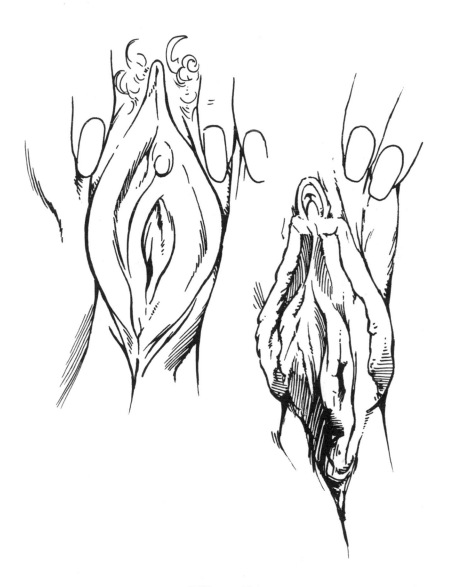

...Different Vulvas

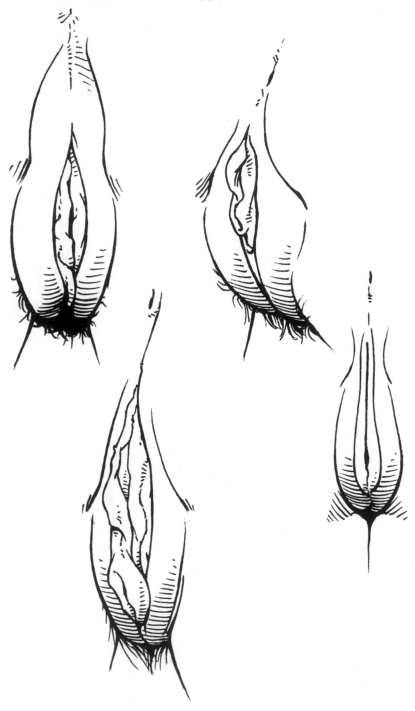

View From Behind.
(What? No Anuses?)

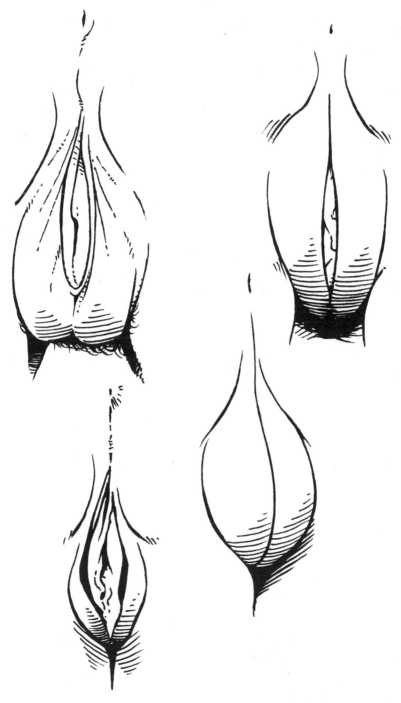

One way to find out how your vulva looks is to sit on a large Xerox machine, and press the copy button! The cover is glass, so sit very gently, and be sure you have the permission of the machine's owner!

☙ When sexually aroused, the first third of the vagina becomes narrower while the back part expands and sometimes balloons open, a little like the bottom half of an hour glass.

☙ The first third of the vagina is often sensitive to touch, while the back two-thirds is more sensitive to pressure. The walls of the first-third tend to have more tiny folds, while the back two-thirds tend to be smoother.

☙ For some women, the back part of the vagina expands before orgasm and then contracts. This might cause a longing to have something inside the vagina which the rear walls can grasp during orgasm. This also causes women to utter various which often contain the Lord's name.

☙ We could try to map out a vagina for you, but why not make your own vaginal love maps? What nicer way to spend an afternoon than exploring the tender shoals of a lover's warm moist vagina... (More on this in Chapter 12: The Zen of Finger Fucking.)

Variations In Preference

Some women like coffee first thing in the morning, others don't. Some like tomatoes, others find them slimy and odd. The same is true with intercourse; some women can't get enough of it, others prefer their crotches just as they are without a penis begging to get inside. This has little to do with a woman's sexual orientation, but rather with her sexual perspective which is determined by a combination of physiology, temperament and prior life experiences, or experiences from prior lives if you are into that sort of thing.

As for variations, one woman might prefer oral sex to intercourse. Another might prefer masturbating while her partner either holds her or masturbates along with her. A third woman might not feel satisfied unless sex includes intercourse. And a fourth woman might prefer oral sex with John, but intercourse with Bill.

Variations In Wetness

When sexually aroused, some vaginas get so wet that the woman needs to wring out her underwear. Other women can be every bit as aroused, but their vaginas remain dry. Also, some women become wetter during certain phases of their menstrual cycle. Men shouldn't be so silly as to gauge a woman's level of sexual arousal upon vaginal wetness alone.

Women who remain dry even when highly aroused are smart to keep a bottle of water-based sex lube handy. Some women insert a glycerin suppository or similar product into the vagina to make it wet and sensually sloppy. Others find that glycerin-containing lubricants bring on infections. And no matter how wet the woman gets naturally, she should consider using lubrication when her partner is wearing a condom or is inserting a dildo or sex toy.

Aliphatic Acid Trip

Researchers have discovered that about one-in-three women have vaginal secretions that contain certain types of scent-producing aliphatic acid chains (organic chemical compounds). The scent of these women's vaginas varies with the phase of their menstrual cycle. For the other 66% of women there is no such vaginal scent, and the perfume of the vagina (or lack of it) remains the same no matter what day of the month a lover's face might find itself between their thighs. Unfortunately, the researchers did not say if the added scent is encouraging or discouraging to the male of the species.

Four Scores & Seven Vaginas Ago

If you have had the good fortune to experience sex with a number of women and were of a clear mind when doing so, you may have noticed that not all vaginas are created equal. (Not all penises are created equal either, as you may have noticed.)

While most vaginas feel quite nice, some feel even better. And once or twice in a lifetime a man might encounter a vagina that feels so amazingly wonderful that the mere memory of it redefines his personal concept of heaven. Interestingly, one never knows how a particular vagina is going to feel based upon the appearance of the female to whose body it belongs. For instance, steam might be billowing out of your ears at the mere sight of a certain woman, but after having intercourse with her your penis complains that jerking off in the shower feels better. At the same time, a woman who seems quite plain on the surface may be the one whose vagina you remember most throughout life.

Also, you might find that some women's genitals lend themselves more to one type of sexual activity than another, e.g. you may love going down on Mary Jane, but intercourse with her is only so-so; the exact opposite might be true with Dixie May.

Vaginal Farts

"My boyfriend was performing oral sex on me and fingering my vagina. When I sat up, all of the air in my vagina came rushing out and made a huge fart-like noise. I was totally embarrassed; it was completely unexpected. I looked at my boyfriend with shock on my face, and then we both started laughing."

female age 25

Occasionally, air gets trapped inside the vagina, and makes a fart-like noise when it comes it. This happens all of the time and is nothing to be embarrassed about, given how both of you created the situation and hopefully had a fine time doing so.

The Cervix

The cervix is a fleshy little dome on the top rear part of the vagina. Nature put it there as a sort of valve or gatekeeper that joins the uterus and vagina. The cervix can be as small as a cherry in a woman who has not delivered a baby through her vagina, or it can be much bigger. It has a little dimple in the center through which female fluids come down and male fluids go up. It sometimes feels softer when a woman is ovulating. During that time, mucus passes through the opening in the cervix and bathes the vagina. This keeps it clean and more acidic, conditions which encourage conception. At the point when conception is most likely to occur, the mucus becomes clear and slippery. (Danger! Danger!)

The cervix has a space around it that is called the fornix. This is a delightful area to explore with a finger. It is also a good space to know about when the woman's vagina isn't particularly deep or her lover has a long penis. Such couples will want to find intercourse positions that encourage the penis to slither under the cervix and into the rear fornix. This will add an extra inch or two of runway space, so to speak.

Birth Control Note: Diaphragms are little latex hub caps that cover the cervix and attempt to block male ejaculate from sneaking through the little dimple in the center.

Gynecology 101 — The Wonders Of Nature

There are two ways we know of to see a cervix. The first is the traditional way of using a speculum. This is a metal or plastic device that physicians insert into a woman's vagina to help push the walls apart. This allows the physician to see parts of a woman that most boyfriends and husbands never do. If you have a healthy sense of curiosity, get a speculum from your physician or medical supply store. Lubricate it with KY or contraceptive jelly, gently insert it into the vagina, and add the krypton beam of your favorite flashlight as well as the reflection of a hand held mirror. This will give both of you a bird's eye view of the cervix.

Another way of seeing inside a vagina is to get an acrylic dildo with a view port that is optically designed to give you 5X magnification. The Xandria people sell one that's called "The Observer." It's not cheap ($75!) but might be neat to try. To order, call (800) 242-2823. Once you insert it, the cervix should be in there somewhere.

A statement of disbelief that is often made upon seeing the slit in the middle of the cervix is "A baby is supposed to fit through that?"

Ovaries — Gynecology 102

A man's testicles tend to announce themselves wherever he goes. Not so with a woman's ovaries. In fact, it's possible to have a long term relationship with a woman and not even know her ovaries are there, except through events like pregnancy or menstruation.

Assuming you want to, the best way to feel a woman's ovaries is when she is lying on her back and is in an "It's OK if you feel my ovaries" kind of mood. Otherwise, don't even try. Rest one hand over her lower abdomen below her belly button. Place a lubricated finger or two from your other hand deep into her vagina. When you encounter the rear wall of her vagina, veer to the left or right and push up gently while pushing down with the hand that's on her abdomen. You will need to rely on her instructions from there. (If a woman doesn't know where her ovaries are, she might ask her gynecologist to show her during her next exam.)

While some women enjoy having their ovaries explored, others experience such attempts in the same way that a man does a pop in the balls. It might also depend on where she is in her menstrual cycle. Ask, and the truth shall set you free.

Menstrual Note: Highly astute males know that some women prefer different types of sexual stimulation during different phases of the menstrual cycle. This can be particularly true for nipple and breast stimulation. Learning about these variations can take months or even years, but is definitely worth the effort.

Charms? Quarks? G-Spots? Super-Orgasms?

Some people swear by the G-Spot, others aren't so sure. One theory about the G-Spot that helps clear up the matter has been advanced by Drs. John Perry and Beverly Whipple. They feel that women's orgasms are transmitted to the brain through two neural pathways instead of just one. This makes a great deal of sense when you consider the findings of Dr. Whipple's research with women who are paralyzed due to spinal cord injuries. She found that a large percentage of these women are still able to have genital orgasms, which indicates that a secondary pathway to the brain exists for orgasms besides the one that runs up the spinal column.

Of the two neural pathways to the brain, the clitoris is connected to the pudendal nerve, and the G-Spot is connected to the pelvic nerve. As a result, a clitoral orgasm travels to the brain by a different pathway than a G-Spot orgasm. Perhaps this is why women who have G-Spot orgasms describe them as being "deeper" in the body. It might also be why stimulation of the G-Spot area makes a lot of women feel like they have to pee, since the same nerve that transmits G-Spot sensations to the brain also transmits bladder sensations. (Can a woman have G-Spot and clitoral orgasms at the same time? Heavens!)

Theoretically, the G-Spot is made up of tissue that surrounds the urethra. This places it on the roof of the vagina about a third- to three-quarters of a finger deep. Some people say the G-Spot is close to a small patch of vaginal tissue which might feel rough. The roughness is from several small folds in the tissue. Others refuse to get specific and seldom mention landmarks. Some people say the G-Spot is small when unaroused (about the size of a pea), but that it grows bigger when fully aroused (about the size of a quarter). That's inflation for you.

Some women feel a slight discomfort or bladder fullness with G-spot stimulation. G-spot afficionados suggest that women let go of their concern about bladder fullness and allow their muscles to relax in order to enjoy the benefits. (Why not put a towel down just in case? That might help her feel more relaxed.) Also, it's best to wait until the woman is fairly aroused before exploring for G.

One way of stimulating the G-Spot is by inserting a finger or two into a wet and awake vagina and making a "come here" motion. A woman who is exploring on her own might find it easier while squatting. In addition, there is an interesting vibrator attachment which is especially designed for G-spot stimulation. It can be ordered from Good Vibrations.

One intercourse position that you might try when exploring G-Spot potential is as follows: the woman kneels on the floor next to the bed and leans on the mattress. She is leaning on her elbows and her upper body is diagonal to the mattress. Her partner enters her from behind. Experiment with various types of thrusting, shallow to deep. If it's more comfortable, she should try this standing, with her elbows resting on a table or dresser.

As for the feelings that accompany G-spot stimulation, some women enjoy them tremendously while others couldn't care less and some even find them to be obnoxious. Also keep in mind that sexual satisfaction is part of a much larger process. How you treat each other when you aren't having sex will probably impact your level of satisfaction far more than simply romancing a woman's G-Spot.

If you are looking for more on the G-Spot, consider reading "The Good Vibrations Guide To The G-Spot" by Cathy Winks, from Down There Press, San Francisco, 1998. While we laud the cheap $7.00 price, it is hard to understand why the publisher printed the book with type so small that your eyes ache from trying to read it.

Female Ejaculation Vs. Bum Bladders

For years, physicians have known that some women ejaculate following orgasm. Rather than trying to find out more about this, the doctors assumed that the fluid was urine from a leaky bladder. There are now people who dispute the leaky bladder theory. They claim that the fluid is similar to male prostate fluid which provides the lion's share of male ejaculate. (Two different studies have been done where samples were collected from a number of female ejaculators. One study found the fluid to be chemically similar to male ejaculate, while the other study found it to be primarily urine.)

There are now a number of X-rated videos that show female ejaculation. Some of the women in these videos expel fluid with the force of a busted fire hydrant. These female ejaculators claim that the pints of fluid they are shooting across the room were from tiny prostate-like ducts. Nonsense. Other women in the tapes spouted smaller amounts of fluid that may have realistically had a source other than the bladder.

Whatever the case, women who do squirt as part of the orgasm process should feel relieved to know that there's nothing unusual about it. On the other hand, some of the tapes on female ejaculation got awfully evangelical about the subject, with some of the women who did squirt trying to make women who don't feel inadequate. That's ridiculous.

Women ~ Multiple Orgasms

"Usually I am too sensitive following an orgasm for any stimulation. But occasionally, when I've had a real shake-the-walls, body-mind-soul climax, I'm still in a state of high arousal and if my husband stimulates me again a few seconds later I go off with a bang. Sometimes this can happen two or three times in a row. It feels like a firecracker exploding without any prior warning, and we often start laughing at the surprise and delight of it." *female age 47*

"It feels like having a baby, except all the pain is replaced with pleasure." *female age 34*

"It was very intense, almost too intense, like my body was out of my control." *female age 45*

While some women are able to have multiple orgasms, most are quite pleased with a single orgasm and some work hard to get even that.

Unfortunately, giving a concise definition of multiple orgasm is a problem. One hitch is that people usually associate "orgasm" with the ejaculation type of orgasm that men often have. Adjectives like multiple have to be added to make it fit the kind of experience that some women have, although multiples don't necessarily feel like a series of singles. Another problem in defining multiple orgasm is that the experience varies from woman to woman. Whatever the definition, here are a couple of reasons why some women are capable of having multiple orgasms:

ANATOMY: Despite the extreme sensitivity following her first orgasm, a woman's genitals often stay primed and ready for more. This gives some women the potential to have an extended wave-like orgasm or separate orgasms but with little time in between.

EMOTIONS: Gynecologist David Cheeks did a series of hypnotic regressions on a number of his women patients. One group of these women routinely enjoyed multiple orgasms, while another group had difficulty reaching orgasm at all. ("Hypnotic regression" means to explore early childhood memories while under hypnosis. Whether such memories describe what really happened or are simply metaphors for early emotional experience is a subject of much debate these days.)

The women who were able to have multiple orgasms could recall feeling wonderful sensations in their genitals that were not only present during events like baths or diaper changing, but also during moments of happiness and joy, especially when parents expressed love or acceptance for the child. These women had no memories of being scolded for playing with their genitals. This contrasted sharply with memories of the non-orgasmic women who recalled few early associations between happiness or joy and sexual sensation. Under hypnosis these women could often recall being scolded for playing with their genitals.

It doesn't take a genius to figure out what this suggests. On the other hand, there are plenty of women with rather hideous childhood sexual experiences who now love sex and get a tremendous amount of comfort and joy from it. Tragic early experience needn't shackle one for life.

Possible Parallels Between Girl'Gasms & Giving Birth

Some people claim that a woman's sexual experience occasionally transports her into another dimension, one that incorporates aspects of Disneyland, the Taj Majal, and maybe an orbit or two around the moons of Jupiter. Perhaps some of the parallels between a woman's ability to bear children and her sexual response might give the latter extra kick. For instance, consider the following associations which were culled from the writings of an early feminist by the name of Niles Newton:

🐑 During early sexual arousal and the first parts of labor, a woman's breathing often becomes deep and slow. Then, at the point of orgasm and the second stage of labor, her cervix opens up and her breathing pattern becomes interrupted. Her face often tenses and strains, and she experiences uterine contractions. (Uterine contractions, whether part of orgasm or child-birth, are thought to be triggered by the release of similar hormones.)

A woman's clitoris is usually engorged (swollen) with orgasm and immediately following birth, moments when most women experience a sense of joy and well-being. Some women have orgasm-like experiences after giving birth.

During both sex and childbirth, a woman's behaviors and expressions become less inhibited. She is less aware of her immediate environment. If the sex is good, anyway.

Uterine contractions and nipple erection often occur during orgasm and while nursing a baby. There are accompanying changes in the skin temperature of the breast during both orgasm and nursing, and it's not unusual for a woman to experience sexual pleasure while nursing. It's likely that some of the same hormones mediate both milk release and uterine contraction. (Some babies respond to sucking on the breast with rhythmic movements and penile erection. Many of us grown up guys do the same.)

Here is one that Ms. Newton may have missed: Some women who have really powerful orgasms push down as they are coming, perhaps a little like a woman who is pushing out a baby.

Perhaps these parallels allow a woman access to sexual feelings that might be different from a man's. Then again, the sexual journey could be an individual matter that has little to do with whether you are male or female.

Beware Of Womb — Ovary Exorcism

If a woman in our society has her reproductive organs removed no one takes much notice. It is an everyday surgical event. But if a man has his testicles removed, we tend to gasp in shared pain. We are sensitive to the man's loss, but not to the woman's. It seems that American medicine has an inborn prejudice about women's reproductive organs. The prejudice is that women are better off without them — although unnecessary surgeries on the male prostate are on the rise, too.

In America, approximately 665,000 hysterectomies are performed each year. The average age of women having the surgery is 42.5 years. In her book "The Mismeasure of Woman," psychologist Carol Tavris notes that many hysterectomies are unnecessary. Tavris quotes a university professor who is a second opinion expert for Blue Cross as saying "The patients who had the recommendations for the hysterectomies either had no pathology whatsoever or had pathology that was so minimal it was inexplicable to me how anybody could have recommended surgery." If a woman is told that she needs to have a hysterectomy, she should be sure to get a second opinion from a gynecologist who doesn't do surgery, especially if the reason for the hysterectomy is a pre-cancerous pap smear. (Perhaps a positive effect of managed health care will be a decrease in unnecessary hysterectomies and C-sections, since the profit margin won't be so high.)

Reader's Comments

What does it feel like in your genitals when you are sexually aroused?

"Tingling starts in my clitoris and spreads to my labia. My whole vulva starts to throb, literally. The throbbing is extremely pleasurable. Then my vulva gets swollen and almost hot. Once it is swollen every slight touch sends lightning bolts of pleasure all around my whole body."   *female age 23*

"Sometimes it's an ache not unlike having a full bladder. Other times, a sensation of heat and congestion in my labia, clitoris and vagina. If I'm highly aroused, or if my clothing is tight, I'll be able to feel my pulse between my legs. Sometimes I'll feel my tendons and muscles twitching as well. "   *female age 36*

"My labia feel swollen and tight, my clitoris becomes hard. Sometimes my clitoris feels like it's huge, and it sort of throbs. If I am extremely aroused, my whole vulva feels as though it's pounding, with my clitoris as the center."   *female age 26*

"You know the feeling you get right before your leg or arm falls asleep? I mean, before it's annoying or hurts. It's a really intense tingling feeling. It makes my whole body feel warm and excited. There are moments however, right before my partner enters me when my vagina actually aches." *age 27*

When did you first make the connection between being sexually aroused and being wet?

"When I was around ten or eleven, while watching a sex scene in a film. My panties got wet, and I realized that was why. If I'm really turned-on, I'll drip down to my ankles."

female age 25

"I first connected being wet with sexual arousal when I was 13. I was watching a silent, vintage erotic film with a friend. When I went to the bathroom, I was soaked!" *female age 26*

"The first time I connected wetness with sex was when I was 9 or so and got all wet and throbby when I was watching a couple kissing at the beach. But I don't always get wet when I feel aroused, it isn't an indicator for me." *female age 38*

"When I first masturbated, I only touched myself on my clitoris, so I was very surprised when I eventually felt my vagina and it was dripping fluid." *female age 23*

Comments about being wet...

"Being wet is hard to explain, I don't know if I can offer insight because it just happens. The most annoying thing is that if you don't wear panties and get wet, it tends to be very messy, but arousing!" *female age 36*

"For me, the degree of my wetness varies greatly from time to time and seems to be largely affected by how mentally 'into' having sex I am at that given time." *female age 34*

"If my boyfriend just starts kissing me and wants to have sex, I am not automatically wet. I need to be turned-on. This could be by way of slowing down and paying attention to my body, or it could be by talking sexy, reading, looking at or listening to erotica." *female age 26*

"It does not work when my partner concentrates solely on doing mechanical things to get me wet. Yet a simple very tender kiss can do it, especially when the whole day is relaxed." *female age 48*

"I enjoy sex a great deal, but seldom get wet." *female age 32*

End Of Chapter Notes: While this chapter might not pay the usual homage to sex researchers of the 1950s, 1960s and 1970s, it was the work of those researchers that paved the way for books like this. Also, it is difficult to truly appreciate the prejudice and resistance that the early sex researchers must have faced. It is a resistance that continues to this day. Kermit Krantz' work arrived via a book titled "The Classic Clitoris." Carol Tavris' excellent book "The Mismeasure Of Woman" was very helpful throughout this chapter. Thanks to Philosophy Professor Michael Russell from Cal State University at Fullerton for his work on Sartre and sex.

Chapter 10
Sunsets, Orgasms & Hand Grenades

"Define orgasm? It's somewhere between a hand grenade and a sunset."

Mr. Billy Rumpanos, lifetime surfer
& early supporter of the Goofy Foot Press.

One of the many neat things about sharing sex is having orgasms, also known as coming. This chapter describes what an orgasm is and where it might come from. It talks about the sometimes fine line between pleasure and pain, styles of coming, faking orgasms, and how some people use orgasms for control rather than pleasure (orgasm dementia).

Perhaps it might be helpful to begin with a few comments from Dr. Frieda Tingle, the world's leading expert on sex:

Q. *Dr. Tingle, what do you think of "Sex in America"?*

A. I think it would be a good idea.

Q. *Do you think Americans are too concerned about orgasms?*

A. Whose? Their own or their neighbor's?

Q. *We mean in general.*

A. Orgasm is very important for many Americans because it tells them when the sexual encounter is over. Most of these people enjoy competitive sports, where some official is forever blowing a whistle or waving a little flag to let them know the event has ended. Without orgasm, they would be fumbling around, never knowing when it was time to suggest a game of Scrabble or a corned-beef sandwich.

Q. *What kinds of things affect a person's ability to have an orgasm?*

A. One important factor is diet. Many times I have been told that it is impossible to have an orgasm after eating an entire pizza. I assume this has something to do with the Italian religious taboo against sexual abandon. Another factor is the weather. Many patients have told me that if the window is open and they are being rained on, it is particularly difficult to have the orgasmic experience... (Dr. Frieda Tingle is the alter ego of Carol Tavris and Leonore Tiefer.)

Orgasm Defined

The best way to define orgasm is to put your hand in your pants and give yourself one. A more cumbersome way is to read the following definition:

Orgasms are extra special sensations that people sometimes experience while being sexual, either alone or with a partner. They occur after a certain threshold of excitement has been crossed, and can last from seconds to minutes or longer. A sense of well-being and relief often follows, perhaps because orgasms are thought to release pain inhibitors in the body. (Studies have shown that people with arthritis sometimes get pain relief for three to four hours following orgasm.)

Orgasms often feel as if they are being broadcasted from the genitals or pelvic floor, although there is no reason why they can't originate from other parts of the body.

Some people experience orgasm as a single, tidal wave-like surge of sensation with a couple of brief aftershocks; others experience orgasm as a series of waves, genital sneezes, or bursts of light, color, warmth and energy. Some describe orgasm as creeping up on them, slowly flooding their senses; some refer to it as a change in consciousness, and some experience it as a brief but potent explosion. (People occasionally use the term "congestion" to describe the feelings in their genitals just before orgasm; this should not be confused with nasal congestion, unless it's the kind that makes you sneeze.)

Some orgasms make you feel great, others can be wimpy and disappointing. Some orgasms are strictly physical, others are physical and emotional. Some reach into the body, others reach into the soul. Some are intense and obvious, others are diffuse and subtle.

The way an orgasm feels can vary with different types of sexual activity; for instance, oral sex orgasms might feel different from intercourse orgasms. Masturbation orgasms are often the most intense. One reason might be that there's very little anxiety or tension when a person masturbates. (No worries about performance or if your

In our dreams...

partner finds you attractive.) And it's unlikely that a partner will be able to find the exact grip, pressure, finger movement and speed that you know because you are getting instant feedback from your own body.

Orgasms with the same partner are likely to run the gamut from totally spectacular to downright disappointing. It depends on the particular day, and whether your worlds are colliding or are in sync.

Some people have orgasms when a lover kisses them on the back of the neck, others need a stick or two of dynamite between the legs. The amount of stimulation needed to generate an orgasm has nothing to do with how much a person enjoys sex. (Orgasms which require more effort are sometimes more intense.)

When shared with someone you love, orgasms and the feelings that follow often make it possible to experience a special kind of intimacy.

⌂ Some people feel pleasantly amped or energized following orgasm, while others feel mellow and might want to sleep. For some people, one orgasm begs for another or at least calls for more hugging and tenderness.

⌂ Genitals can become extremely sensitive after having an orgasm. Stimulation that may have felt wonderful moments before orgasm often feels painful or abrasive immediately after. This is why a woman might suddenly pull your hand away from her genitals after she seems to have been enjoying whatever it was doing. It never hurts to ask your partner about this, since it's true for some but not all.

⌂ Some people are easily derailed on the road to orgasm. For others, the phone can ring, the earth can shake and a dam can break, they come no matter what.

⌂ An interesting and highly philosophical property of orgasm is that it may cause partners to become momentarily estranged. That's because when we are highly aroused, we often enter our own private orbit which might cause us to lose awareness of a sexual partner except as a generator of physical sensation. Many couples make up for this temporary separation by feeling extra close right after orgasm.

⌂ It is not necessary or even desirable for partners to come at the same time. For instance, it can be wonderful to feel or watch your partner have an orgasm, which is difficult to do if you are coming simultaneously. On the other hand, it might be nice to occasionally blast off together. Just be aware that not many partners actually come at the same time.

⌂ Some people have orgasms with their legs squeezed together, while others come with their legs wide apart (innies vs. outies). People who prefer coming one way sometimes find it difficult to come with their legs the other way. Do you have a preference?

Your Partner's Orgasms

We often assume that a partner who has an orgasm is fully satisfied, while one who doesn't is somehow disappointed. Yet for many people there is more to lovemaking than just having orgasms. For instance, most of us can usually get really intense orgasms from masturbating, but not many of us can get profound feelings of closeness, friendship, and love when we do ourselves solo. For some people, these latter feelings are the most important part of lovemaking. So try to be sensitive, but not too paranoid, about your partner's orgasms.

Note: If wanting orgasms were the sole reason for doing a particular sex act, not that many women would bother with intercourse. Only about 30% of women have orgasms from intercourse alone. Plenty of women who have orgasms during intercourse need extra clitoral stimulation in addition to thrusting, or they need the guy to ride high so his pubic bone rubs against their mons and clitoris. Lots of women prefer having an orgasm before intercourse. They say that the intercourse feels better after they've come.

Things that increase the chance of orgasm: Being seriously into your partner, exercise and a healthy diet (these increase levels of hormones that enhance the sex drive), reading and seeing erotic images, and whatever else happens to turn you on.

Things that decrease the chance of orgasm: Being annoyed or angry with your partner, smoking (chemicals in tobacco constrict blood flow to the genitals and may lower the level of testosterone in both men and women), stress (notice how you tend to have more sex while on vacation), not sleeping enough, and being Catholic (nearly 60% of Protestant women report they nearly always have an orgasm during sex, while 26% of Catholic women do; perhaps one problem for the Catholic women is the Catholic church's strident prohibition against touching yourself, which is how a lot of women learn to have orgasms, especially during intercourse).

Expressions, Decibels & The Way People Come In The Movies

People sometimes worry about how they behave when having orgasms. Some are self-conscious because they lose control, others because they don't. The answers? There are none. There is no correct way to come. Sexuality is an altered state of mind; what you do with it is strictly a matter of personal choice.

For instance, some people fear that they will look weird if they allow themselves to be overwhelmed by an orgasm. They fear that their partner will laugh or find them ugly. Quite to the contrary, it is far more likely that a partner will think something like the following:

"WOW! Her face got all twisted and contorted when she came. She looked like Whistler's mother on a really bad acid trip. She must have had a major orgasm. Maybe I'm not so bad in bed after all..."

Of course, there are plenty of people who have sensational orgasms but hardly show it at all. Their orgasms are an internal phenomena that remain hidden to the outside world. Unfortunately, many of us labor under the notion that women are supposed to make a lot of noise when they are coming. Quite to the contrary, there is little correlation between decibels and delight. Some women sound like freight trains when they come, others become rather quiet except for an occasional twitch and sigh. The same is true for men. If your partner comes in a quiet way and you would like to know more about it, why not ask?

Keep in mind that many of us learned to come quietly at a very young age. That's because there might not have been much privacy where we masturbated; letting out a large bellow would have informed the entire household. This was particularly true if you shared a room with siblings, and even worse if you had the top mattress in a bunk bed. The same difficulties are faced by people living in dorms, sororities, fraternities and military barracks, where roommates often sleep only a few feet away. In these situations, we pretend to be asleep when masturbating — a funny notion when you consider that our roommates are probably doing the same thing.

The great sex noise dilemma is also faced by moms and dads while making love (or trying to) when there's a household full of kids.

Is It Possible To Have Too Many Orgasms?

Some of the various Tantric Yoga/Zen types nearly hemorrhage at the notion of a man ejaculating more than once or twice every ten years. They feel that the male body is seriously depleted when it ejaculates. As a result, they hoard the white sticky stuff like generals do with weapons-grade plutonium. Some even teach themselves to have dry orgasms.

Is there any reality to this seed spilling fear? It has been written that the Nazis pondered this same question. To test it out they forced a prisoner of war to masturbate every three hours, day and night, for the duration of World War II. Thanks to the allied invasion, the prisoner finally got to stop jerking off. He apparently went on to father several children and lived to a ripe old age, certainly as old as most seed-retaining monks if they didn't fib about being 128 when they are really only 55-years-old. As for other living examples, one male friend of the Goofy Foot Press is now in his .arly 70s, but his mind is incredibly sharp and he doesn't look a day over fifty. He currently has at least five ejaculations per week, down from the ten or so he has been having since he was a teenager. According to Tantric Yoga semen retention theories, he should either be dead or a zombie.

Regarding women and orgasm: nobody in his or her right mind has ever worried about a woman having too many orgasms, except for the people who live next door or in the apartment below.

Where Does Coming Come From?

The following quote is from a woman who had a spontaneous orgasm while riding public transit — a rather scary thought if you have ever taken the bus in places like Los Angeles or Detroit:

> "I've perfected this wonderful ability to orgasm without touching myself. It started one day on the BART train when I was ovulating, and I felt myself throbbing. I started running a fantasy in my mind and discovered I could bring myself to orgasm. The only trouble with a public place is you have to control your breathing..." (Words of a former high school homecoming queen who grew up in the Midwest, as found in Julia Hutton's helpful book "Good Sex" Cleis Press, 1992.)

Not only is it possible for some people to have an orgasm without genital stimulation, but it can even happen spontaneously without sexual thoughts. For instance, some women have spontaneous orgasms during highly charged debates or intellectual discussions that have nothing whatsoever to do with sex. One female reader had her first orgasm as a teenager while her hair was being brushed, and as a 40-year-old she still has orgasms when her hair is brushed.

While not many of us are able to have orgasms without genital stimulation, the notion of a hands-free orgasm does suggest that there is more to orgasm than genital contact. For instance, there are plenty of people who have suffered nerve injuries and can no longer feel sensation in their genitals, yet they learn to have orgasm feelings in other parts of their bodies, such as their faces, arms, necks, lips, chests, and backs. They often find that these feelings are as satisfying as their former genital orgasms. This indicates that the power to experience an orgasm resides somewhere in the senses and not simply in the groin. (One woman whose clitoris and vagina were removed due to cancer surgery was able to experience the same kind of intense multiple orgasms after the surgery as before.)

People who have lost one of their senses do not suddenly grow new ones to compensate. Rather, they are forced to better use the senses that remain. This suggests that many of us could achieve greater sexual pleasure from other parts of our bodies if we learned to allow it. One way of doing this is mentioned later in this guide, where the woman stimulates her partner's penis with one hand while using her other hand or lips to caress another part of his body not normally associated with sexual feelings.

Pain Next To Pleasure

Receptors for pain and pleasure are located next to each other throughout the body. These receptors often fire at the same time. It is the brain's job to decide whether the overall experience is one of pain or pleasure.

Fortunately, each of our brains makes its own unique decision about what is pleasurable or painful. While one person might enjoy masturbating to the fantasy of seeing Johnny or Amber naked, the mere hint of Johnny or Amber's presence might make another person feel sick to the stomach. Or one person might find spanking to be painful and a turn off, while another might find spanking to be painful and erotic. The stimulus is the same, but how we feel about it depends on how our brain interprets it.

Most people who enjoy an occasional slap on the rear during sex usually don't like the pain unless it is done when they are in a state of sexual arousal. Being sexually aroused causes the brain to throw normal caution to the wind, perhaps converting feelings that are usually painful into feelings of pleasure.

One By Land, Two By Sea

There seem to be at least two different neural pathways that transmit signals from the groin to the brain. Researchers John Perry and Beverly Whipple suggest that G-Spot stimulation might be conveyed to the brain through one set of nerves, and clitoral stimulation through another. Perhaps the same is true in males for penis stimulation vs. prostate stimulation. This could explain why one type of orgasm might feel more intense in the area of the clitoris or penis, while another not as well-defined but resonating deeper in the body.

Possible Assist For Women's & Men's Orgasms

When women are about to come they often pull in or tighten their pelvic muscles. Yet doing just the opposite, pushing out, might make their orgasms more intense. Some women will hesitate to do this from fear that it might cause them to pass gas, but what the heck, you'll both live if she does. And if you consider the gas-passing habits of men and women over the lifetime of the average relationship, chances are she owes him a few.

Whether you are male or female, you might occasionally experiment with relaxing the muscle tone in your pelvis and rear end when you come. For instance, some men find that they can prolong the feelings of orgasm if they relax their crotch and rear end as orgasm is about to come. Other men find this to be uncomfortable. Also, contracting the muscles in the rear end during intercourse might contribute to premature ejaculation, as is mentioned in the chapter: Dyslexia Of The Penis — Improving Your Sexual Hang Time.

What Was It Like?

Lovers sometimes ask each other if they came, but not what coming feels like. Granted, sexual experiences are hard to put into words, since they often exist on the cusp between physical and emotional sensation. But asking a partner to describe what it feels like when he or she comes might lead to some interesting insights and discussions.

Faking Orgasm

People lie a great deal in our culture. Lying is often the basis for marketing and advertising. In fact, just using a credit card is often a form of lying where we spend money that we don't even have, telling ourselves that it is really OK. With so much lying and deception around us, perhaps it would be nice for people to make their sexual relationships a fortress of truth and honesty. Yet that's not how we always do it. In fact, some of us have even — gulp — faked orgasm.

Some people fake orgasm in an attempt to reassure their partner. This takes the pressure off to come, which then allows them to enjoy sex more or to roll over and fall asleep if that should be their goal.

Assuming that you have at least some social skills and are able to proceed with kindness, what's so horrible about saying to your partner "I didn't come" instead of faking orgasm? Then you might discuss what you do and don't like about sex. Maybe you will want to say "I like having sex with you even when I don't have an orgasm..." or "I enjoy intercourse, but it's not the way I have orgasms; here's how I usually come..." or "If I reached down and rubbed myself when we did that I might have an orgasm..." or "I'd really love it if you got me off by hand, or held me while I masturbate..." or "Your need for me to have an orgasm is annoying and actually puts me off..." or "It's not easy for me when you ejaculate so quickly after the start of intercourse; let's read Chapter 44 of this book together..." or "It's hard for me to get really excited when you are so: passive about sex... preoccupied... into yourself... insecure... distant... angry... out of shape... thin.. fat... rude... drunk... stoned..." or "When I reach a certain level of sexual excitement, my mind sort of goes blank and my body starts to feel numb."

If Your Partner Fakes Orgasms

One of the worst things you can do when a partner fakes an orgasm is to try to help him or her to have one. This usually makes matters worse. (There is sometimes a fine line between helpful concern and obnoxious fretting, especially if the reason why you need your partner to have an orgasm is for your own reassurance that you are a good lover.)

Rather than trying to help your partner have an orgasm, why not try to discover the things that give him or her physical comfort? Contrary to what you think, this might simply be holding each other for an extended time, taking long baths together, or not grabbing for your lover's crotch the minute you feel horny. If your partner has suggestions about technique, all the better, but this might not be where the problem lies. The trouble might be within the greater context of your relationship, or maybe you are great friends but not a good sexual match, or perhaps your partner has always had trouble having orgasms.

Orgasm Dementia

Sometimes it's fun to count orgasms and go for it like pigs to mud. But for some people, orgasm production and/or procurement has a suspicious edge. Here are a few reasons why:

⛭ Some people get a sense of smug superiority by claiming how many orgasms they either had or "gave" a partner. They confuse sex with pinball.

⛭ Some people use pleasure-giving as a way of controlling a partner. They might hardly come at all while making sure that a partner comes several times. While this might not sound like such a bad problem to have, keep in mind that partners who won't surrender the reins sexually are sometimes very controlling in other aspects of life as well.

⛺ There are people who expect their partners to supply them with numerous orgasms. This can breed resentment over time.

⛺ Some people need to have sex or masturbate several times a day to help numb a chronic state of anxiety or ease feelings of deadness. Having a constant stream of orgasms can be their way of keeping an emotional funk at arm's length.

Reinventing The Sexual Wheel — Marketing & Orgasm

In order to sell books and tapes on sex, publishers want us to feel sexually inept if we don't buy whatever kind of sexual experience they are currently hocking. For instance, during the last couple of years we were supposed to buy books and tapes on G-Spot orgasms, female ejaculation, extended orgasms, one-hour orgasms, Tantric sex orgasms, extraordinary orgasms from boring people, and now, books on multiple male orgasms. It's only a matter of time before publishers start to sell "Better Orgasms For Your Dog and Cat," and try to make the public feel like pet sadists if we don't plunk down $29.95 for the videotape.

Many of us would enjoy having bigger and better orgasms if we could. But sometimes the consumer simply has to say "enough is enough." On the other hand, sex can be a fun topic to learn more about. Since we are the physicians of our own sexuality, it wouldn't hurt to at least stay current. This book does what it can to steer you in that direction.

Reader's Comments

For Men: What does an orgasm feel like?

"My knees get weak and I tingle everywhere. It feels like I am numb all over." *male age 21*

"Like an energy emanating in the soles of my feet, up the back of my legs, in and through my rear end, to my belly button, and out through my balls and penis. Awesome, warm, exhausting." *male age 26*

"When I'm getting close, it feels like every ounce of fluid in my body has been forced into my penis. My whole body is in anticipation of the moment when my penis can no longer take the incredible pressure and bursts. Flames envelope the entire thing and the shock reverberates throughout my entire body." *male age 25*

"Orgasm make me feel very connected to my lover, like I'm becoming a part of her." *male age 39*

"It feels like all your vital matter collects in your penis and then shoots out of you!" *male age 22*

For Women: What does an orgasm feel like?

"Every orgasm I have is different! Sometimes I feel like I'm just melting, floating away. Sometimes I feel like I'm running or pushing into the orgasm. Sometimes an orgasm will sneak up on me, other times I will be able to control its arrival and duration." *female age 45*

"All my orgasms seem to be the same beast, but with varying levels of intensity from 'Gosh, was that it?' to an ache so sharp it's almost hard to bear. My most intense orgasms tend to come from using a vibrator but, oddly enough, they're not always the most satisfying." *female age 36*

"Orgasms range for me from a simple response in my genitals, without much sensation and even some numbness, to a mind-blowing, explosive force of nature that permeates my whole body, mind, and emotions, encircles my partner, and fills the room around us. Sometimes it's the physical sensations that are the most intense part of orgasm, other times it's the emotional quality and being with my partner that take top billing. Even when the physical sensation isn't very intense, I generally feel much more whole and integrated after an orgasm." *female age 47*

Your first orgasm...

"With a vibrator at age 38, Finally!!!" *female age 49*

"It didn't happen until seven months after my first sexual experience. I had no idea what was happening. We were through having sex. When I began to put my clothes back on, I started to tingle and fluids started flowing out. It felt great, but I was actually kind of scared and embarrassed." *female 21*

"I had an electric shaver that had an attachment which was a massager. After about an hour of moving it around on my clit (and praying that the pillow between my legs was muffling the sounds so my parents didn't hear) I had an orgasm. I'd already had sex many times with my boyfriend, but I felt like I was really sinning now!" *female age 25~raised Catholic*

"I didn't really know what I was doing. I was about ten or eleven and discovered this new feeling when I rubbed this silky part of my blanket over my penis, so I kept doing it. Eventually I got this intense feeling in my groin and then there was this goop everywhere. I was completely freaked and grossed out. I thought that I broke myself, but was too afraid to tell my parents." *male age 24*

"My first orgasm took place at age eighteen, when my fiance introduced me, despite my initial reaction of revulsion and disbelief, to the delights of cunnilingus. I thought he was depraved. I was sure I was going straight to hell. I couldn't wait for it to happen again!" *female age 55*

"I had my first orgasm during one of my first menstrual periods. The feeling of a clean pad against my genitals made me feel a warmth I had never experienced before. I rubbed against it to see if I could prolong the sensation, although I had no idea what the sensation was. I just knew it felt good!"
female age 45

"I didn't know what was going on. My body felt like it was convulsing. I tried not to let the guy know this was happening. I didn't know at the time I was supposed to let myself go and enjoy it." *female age 26*

"The first one I had was clitoral—it tickled (I was probably ten). The second type of orgasm I had was when I was twenty. I felt it more in my vagina. It was overwhelmingly emotional and I came in a flood, and I do mean flood. I thought I had peed all over my partner. Now I have both kinds of orgasms. I get to pick, let's see, lobster or steak?" *female age age 26*

"My first orgasm was when I was making out in the back seat of a car. I was on top of my boyfriend and there was a lot of bumping and grinding going on and I just climaxed, with my clothes on." *female age 49*

"I was surprised by how sensitive my clit was, but I wasn't sure the actual orgasm was an orgasm because it didn't seem nearly as explosive as what happened in the bodice rippers I'd been reading. I couldn't believe I'd gone through all this work for that. Happily, many years of practice improved the results!" *female age 36*

"Age twenty. One morning before arising I was idly rubbing my clit and fantasizing, and from out of nowhere excitement began building more intensely than it ever had before. I rubbed myself quite vigorously and for a very long time, until suddenly there was a mind-blowing explosion. I was certain that everyone in the house figured out what I was doing. I was very embarrassed. However, I repeated the experience every night—it took over an hour of heavy-duty stimulation at first." *female age 51*

"My first orgasm was by a male friend (not a lover). I told him that sex was not that great. He used his fingers to teach me what it could feel like. I remember thinking 'Oh God, this is an orgasm!'"   *female age 48*

Chapter 11
Sex Fluids

In order to enjoy sex, you need to feel OK about getting wet and slobbery. That's because no matter how you sort it out, sex here on the mainland is a wet adventure, an erotic monsoon of sorts. Various body fluids get sloshed around during sexual encounters, from saliva and sweat to male ejaculate and female lubrication (and sometimes female ejaculation). Some of these fluids, like ejaculate, arrive abruptly while others, like saliva, sweat and lubrication are more constant in flow. Also, menstrual fluids can double as sex fluids, but there's an entire chapter on lovemaking during periods later in this book.

Fluid Understanding

Sex fluids mean different things to different people. For instance, one woman might find it wonderful when her lover ejaculates. It leaves her feeling valued and powerful being the one who makes his fluids flow. Another woman might find her boyfriend's ejaculate to be a sticky mess that she would rather not have to deal with.

Men usually welcome women's sexual wetness, although there are exceptions. For instance, your author can remember a conversation from his freshman year of high school with a fellow member of the track team who had just felt up a woman for the first time. The young man described "it" as being wet, sticky and yuckie, and indicated that "her thing" accommodated nearly half his arm. Considering this was a farm town, your author has since wondered if the woman in question might not have been a cow.

Most grown men feel good about their own sexual fluids, although some young men who ejaculate for the first couple of times worry they might have broken something inside. Proper education about masturbation can help alleviate most of these fears. Single moms who want to explain ejaculation to their sons might find it helpful to know that prior to puberty, male ejaculate is clear and there is not much of it, perhaps a drop or two. After puberty it becomes white and there is more, about a teaspoonful. Whatever his age, it might be nice if a young man were taught to respect his own ejaculate as the catalyst for new life as well as a sign of his own sexual maturity and pleasure — all three being good things that should bring pride as well as new levels of responsibility.

As for women's feelings about their own sexual wetness, most seem to enjoy it. However, young women who don't understand or fear their body's sexual response may feel uncomfortable if they suddenly find themselves getting wet while having sensual thoughts.

Other Sex Fluids

Two other body fluids that switch-hit as sex fluids are saliva and sweat. These flow in steady and sometimes subtle ways, unless propelled by a sneeze or when making love when it's hot or humid and you are sweating like swine. Another body fluid that some people think of as a sex fluid is urine. (See "Golden Showers" in the glossary.) People who view urine as a sex fluid are said to be into kink, although a curiosity about seeing others pee is perfectly normal.

Urine Note #1 Believe it or not, urine from most physically healthy humans is more sterile than saliva. In fact, urine is considered to be a mild antiseptic, although you might not want to replace the bottle of Bactine with it. If for some reason you find yourself seriously cut, can't get medical attention for a long time and have no first aid handy, consider peeing on the cut with your own urine. It might stop or slow the onset of infection. Also, consider doing the same following any unpleasant run-ins with sea urchins. Urine is said to help dissolve sea urchin spines that are embedded in human flesh, although it is best to check with a physician about such matters. (For cuts caused by sea coral, a plaster made of the food additive MSG and water is said to help draw out the toxin and hopefully lessen the agony, but again, check with a physician first.)

Urine Note #2: We didn't know where else to put this, but some people, more than you might think, have trouble peeing in a public restroom. For instance, some men aren't able to use a urinal if other men are either going next to them or waiting in line. While some of these men are able to go in a closed stall, others can't even go then. The same is true for some women. Needless to say, this can be a source of great frustration for the people with the problem. It can also make them feel socially inept, as well as isolated if their pee-shyness keeps them from attending certain day-long events. At the very least, the person avoids having Cokes or beers while at football or baseball games; at its worst, the problem can result in kidney damage. The underlying causes can be many, from feeling performance anxiety to shame about being heard or seen urinating. The occasional psychologist might say that the problem is hiding an unconscious desire to pee on everyone! Whatever the underlying cause(s), most people with this problem would welcome even a 50% improvement. Unfortunately, there is no single therapy that has a consistently high batting average in curing this condition. While some people might find a lessening of symptoms with desensitization therapy or hypnotherapy, others might find help with psychodynamic therapy. Others continue to struggle with the problem no matter what they try, and for some, the situation improves with age, especially when the bladder can no longer hold fluids with the tenacity that it did in its younger years.

Urine Note #3: Guys & The Bowl — *"When guys are peeing, why can't they aim it right? Would it kill them to get all of it in the bowl?"*

The problem is not with the aim, but with the unpredictable nature of the stream It tends to break up about as often as the signal on a cellular or digital phone. Sometimes a rebel tributary will suddenly appear and shoot off to the side, sometimes a healthy stream will suddenly turn into a spray, and sometimes it goes just where you aim it, but the toilet water splashes up and makes a mess on the rim.

Of course, this is no reason why a guy shouldn't grab a wad of toilet paper and clean up after himself (bowl, floor, walls, shoes, etc.).

The How-To Part Of This BooK

There's one way that dogs do it, one way that sheep do it, and one way that each kind of bug does it. This is also true for elephants, lemurs, and wildebeests. Unicorns need to be extra careful when it comes to oral sex, and the female praying mantis eats her male sex partners—to death. So does the black widow.

The animal with the greatest potential for a varied sex life seems to be the human. Human brains are a bit beefier, which means that our minds and emotions, rather than our hormones, guide us in our sexual choices. We are also the only animals who do our sex indoors and in private, which makes getting it on somewhat of a mystery, in this culture anyway.

The upcoming chapters attempt to shed light on the mystery of sex. They describe various tips and techniques for giving your partner monster amounts of sexual pleasure. Hopefully you will find these techniques useful. But first, it might be a good idea to mention a few things about give and take, shame, and the Guide's policy on when to call it quits.

Give And Take

Author Julia Hutton interviewed eighty different people about sex. She asked each person how he or she defined Good Sex. Needless to say, she got eighty different answers. According to Ms. Hutton, "The interviews suggest that sexual savvy depends less upon *how-tos* than on self-knowledge, which evolves slowly, awkwardly and through many different routes."

Please keep Julia Hutton's words in mind as you read the how-to part of this book. Also, people usually assume that if both partners are sexually amped then all they need to do is get naked and good sex will follow. Were it that easy... Even when the sex is great, it often takes time to feel comfortable with a partner. For example, consider the following quote from a 29-year-old kindergarten teacher whose comments appear in Julia Hutton's excellent book "Good Sex":

> "With Chris [her husband] I like having him in me, that warm good feeling. I've discovered I can ask for what I like, that there's nothing wrong with wanting your nipples pulled taut. I've learned that keeping a vibrator by the bed is not a crime. I've learned that Chris can come, and then I can come, and we can both enjoy watching each other come—as opposed to having this simultaneous orgasm that's supposed to move the world. If we have intercourse that's fine, if we don't that's fine. Sometimes we come home weary from work and it's: what do you want? Do you want to masturbate? Do you think you can focus enough for intercourse? It's negotiation, which I never thought it would be. I always thought it would be this mystic experience, but it's become a verbal experience." (From Julia Hutton's "Good Sex" by Cleis Press, 1992.)

Again, while some couples have good sex from the start, other couples take months and sometimes years to find a satisfying groove. In addition, most couples report that their sexual desire for each other waxes and wanes, although sometimes it just wanes.

Shame Between The Sheets

> *"Because Ford never learned to say his original name, his father eventually died of shame, which is still a terminal disease in some parts of the Galaxy."*
>
> From Douglas Adams' "Hitchhiker's Guide To The Galaxy"

Entire civilizations have been built upon the notion of guilt and shame. However, since modern psychology has become a new form of religion, the old standbys of guilt and shame have gotten a bum rap. No one is supposed to feel guilt or shame anymore, and everybody is supposed to have good self-esteem, whatever that might mean. Yet there is plenty in this world to feel guilt and shame about, and it's stupid to think that people should feel good about themselves when they haven't done anything worth feeling good about.

Still, some of us might do better in bed if we felt a little less guilt and shame about what turns us on sexually, assuming it does no harm to others. This is especially true for people who are too bashful to tell a partner what does and doesn't feel good.

When It's OK To Go For It

Since this book is being used in educational settings, we thought it important to include a few words about relationship hygiene, or when it's OK to go for it and when it's not. As a result, we created the following:

The Guide To Getting It On's Policy On When To Call It Quits

If a potential partner doesn't want sex every bit as much as you do, go home and masturbate. At least you will still have your self-respect. If the relationship is worth it, phone the next day and talk it over.

If you don't have that much self-control or the ability to know when another person doesn't want to have sex with you, nothing this book says is going to help. Still, here are a few answers to questions from inquiring minds: *To Mindy at University of Wisconsin:* OK, so you can feel him getting hard but it's no enchilada when you reach down and rub his crotch. (He pushes your hand away.) Just because a guy is hard doesn't mean that he automatically wants to have sex with you. Believe it or not, there are rare but important times when a man actually pleads with his penis to stay soft, but the thing goes BOING just to spite him. Mindy, there are reasons why we refer to genitals as "private parts." Maybe he has his reasons for not wanting your hands all over his. Why not ask? *To Mark At University of Georgia:* Dude, when it comes to sex, we've all been misled (or led on) at one time or another. Some of us have even misled others. The fact is, we live in a society that is so weird about sex that it's not unusual for a person to appear incredibly seductive, but become confused or angry if you actually go for it. You end up feeling like some sort of pervert, when from all appearances, it seemed like they wanted sex as much as you.

In the future, why not make sure that it's your date who makes the first move—she kisses you first, she takes off your shirt before you reach under hers, and she unbuttons or unzips your pants before you touch hers... *To LouAnne at Santa Barbara City College:* You say that you and he had been "slamming down Kamikazies in his bedroom and he was wearing blue jeans three sizes too small in all the right places and had on one of those little half-length tee shirts that was exposing each and every one of his washboard abs..." LouAnne, it wouldn't matter if he were buck naked and had a red tassel on the end of his penis, when he said "No more" you should have respected his wishes. None of us has a right to ignore another person's protests no matter how hot, horny, hard, wet, willing, stoned, drunk, or sexually amped we might be. And even if a person has their tongue half way down your throat for the better part of an hour, if they suddenly pull it out and wag it in a way that says "stop," then you better be ready to stop. The same is true even if the two of you have been married for ten or twenty years.

Chapter 12
The Zen Of Finger Fucking

"Rubbing lightly is what I do when I masturbate, so I like it even more when my boyfriend does it. I love it when he runs his fingers along my inner lips, up and down. I also love my genitals to be rubbed and tickled when I wear jeans or corduroy. I can come from that kind of stimulation."

female age 23

Some men, especially younger ones, take the term "finger fucking" quite literally. They think that a woman's idea of a good time is having a man cram his fingers up her vagina. Other men attack a woman's clitoris as if it were a hydraulic pump, believing that the more they rub it the closer she gets to the big "O." (The only "O" she sometimes experiences is "OUCH!" rather than orgasm.) The truth is, finger fucking is not something a man does to a woman, but something he does with a woman. It's all of him; his smile, kiss, laughter, strength, and tenderness focused in the ends of his fingers.

What follows is a great deal of information about pleasing a woman with your fingertips. Hopefully you will find some of this to be helpful, especially if you are able to leave your bulldozer behind and are willing to feel things with your fingers that maybe you've never felt before.

A Note On Terms Of Art

In the pages that follow, this guide occasionally does minor violence to the English language by using words such as "masturbate" incorrectly. For instance, while masturbation is something you do to yourself, expressions such as "masturbating a partner" or "masturbating yourself" are sometimes used. This kind of usage helps certain sentences to be more easily understood, even though "masturbating a partner" is a contradiction in terms, and "masturbating yourself" is as redundant as saying white cow's milk.

Coaching, Patience & Practice

"I had to learn how to touch her clit... I can remember being clumsy about it early on. She'd have to stop me — I was going too fast, going too hard. I can remember her saying, 'You're in the wrong place.' Well, show me where. I mean physically, show me... Rub so I can see it. Okay, now I understand. Over time, I've learned where the places are. I can find them in the dark now. But early on I couldn't. I'd say 'Okay, show me. Are you sure?' Other times she would take my hand, or my finger, and she would put it right exactly where it was supposed to be, and she'd move it the way she wanted me to move it, and she would apply pressure to the back of my fingers, the amount of pressure she wanted, until I got the hang of it, and then she would take her hand away. If I got out of sync or something, she'd put her hand back and show me until I got it right. A few weeks later I might need some re-education, so she'd show me again." (From Harry Maurer's "Sex: An Oral History" Viking, 1994)

A truly civilized way of learning how to get a woman off by hand is to make an agreement with her that she will provide lots of coaching and patience.

That's because hands that are used to throwing a baseball, holding a shovel, or torquing down engine bolts tend to get a little frustrated when it comes to finessing a woman's genitals; and that's only part of it. There's the additional matter of knowing when to speed up, slow down, push harder or stay your course. For instance, some women might prefer that guys stimulate them with a constant speed and rhythm as they are approaching orgasm. This might not make sense to a man, since when we masturbate we sometimes speed up as we get close to coming. Other women cherish variety. They will want your fingers to go slow, fast, soft, hard, and have more speeds than a Kenworth big rig (or Ferrari if you grew up on the rich side of town).

Differences In Attitude

"I've seen a couple of guys masturbate. I can't believe how rough they are with themselves!" *female age 26*

Take this woman's comment to heart. The reason she can't believe how "rough" we guys are with ourselves is because she would never dream of finessing her genitals in the way we do ours. ˙

The best thing you can do when it comes to giving a woman pleasure by hand is to forget everything you know about giving yourself pleasure by hand. Do not even think for a moment about stimulating her clitoris in the same way you do your penis.

With a penis, you can slap it, yank it, and nearly choke it to death, all it does is get hard or harder. In fact, think of how you squeeze or wag it when you are finished peeing. Try approaching a clitoris with than kind of careless abandon, and you're likely to be a dead man.

When it comes to touching a woman's clit, assume that softer is better. Always err on the side of tenderness. Push just hard enough to move the skin back and forth over the shaft of the clitoris, assuming you can find the shaft of the clitoris.

In time, your lover may want you to be more vigorous. For instance, some women enjoy it if you put your fingers on the outside of the big lips and push all the way down so you can roll the entire vulva between your fingers. This is more like a deep tissue massage of the entire crotch, but there can be a time and place for it if you know the woman well and her feedback is reliable and forthcoming.

Showing Instead Of Telling

> "When women moan or gasp, it encourages me to press harder
> or faster on the clit... Always with poor results." *male age 41*

Be aware that a woman's understanding of her own sexuality is sometimes on a body level and may have few words. Our society wants it that way and often teaches women from day one that they aren't supposed to tell men about their sexual needs. Getting all frustrated and yelling "just tell me" does absolutely no good. She probably would if she could, but it's a little like asking someone to tell you the meaning of life. She may simply have to show you by putting her own hands over yours and guiding your fingers as they go. Or maybe she might say "Please keep trying different ways – I'll let you know when it feels right" or "Maybe if you didn't press quite so hard..." or "Try it here." One reason why feedback is so important is because a woman might say "harder" when she actually means faster, or visa versa. And most guys make the mistake of thinking that if a little pressure feels good, a lot of pressure will send her through the ceiling. This is true, minus the metaphor. Guys also reason that if slow feels good, fast will feel even better. This kind of thinking is seriously flawed. If faster is what she wants, work together on establishing some kind of signal that will let you know.

Mix-ups will happen. You can get all frustrated, or you can view this as part of the fun of exploration. After all, it's not like anybody's going to die or lose their job because you confused harder with faster!

Another suggestion is for a woman to use her partner's fingers or penis to masturbate with. That way he'll get a good feel for the

different kinds of speed and intensity that she likes, and the way she likes the process to unfold.

Intrigue Along The Inseam

> "I like to wait until I can't stand it and beg him to put his fingers inside of me." *female age 25*

Men make a big mistake when they forget to give their fingers a sense of humor. Fingertips that tease and dance will find an especially warm welcome between a woman's legs. For instance, gently running your fingertips up and down a woman 's inner thigh is about a zillion times more enticing than shoving your middle finger up her crotch. When she's ready to have your fingers inside of her she will let you know in no uncertain terms, and even then it's sometimes wise to hold back and tease and play some more.

Finger fucking is definitely more effective if your fingertips are playful and melodic rather than serious or hyper.

Zen Boot Camp — Learning Her Style

"It's not a dish of salted peanuts down there, don't just grab and hope for the best. It's very sensitive. Even the slightest movement can produce a reaction, good or bad." *female age 45*

The latter part of this chapter is dedicated to special types of fingerplay that a woman probably doesn't use on herself when she masturbates. But first, it helps if you can learn how to stimulate her in the exact same way that she stimulates herself. (What if she doesn't masturbate? Then both of you can learn together!) With time, you will add your own special twists, but it's a big mistake to get fancy before you learn the basics — her basics. Give yourself at least a month or three in Zen boot camp with your sweetheart as master and you as grasshopper. Assuming you currently have a partner, you might also ask her to put a small red heart in parts of this chapter where she thinks you could use a little brushing up, in the way that some restaurants flag menu items that aren't supposed to kill you nearly as fast as the others. Here are a few suggestions that might be helpful:

Cut Your Fingernails. Make sure there are no rough edges.

Contradiction In Terms. Sony, but finger fucking does not necessarily mean pushing your finger in and out of your partner's vagina. Much of the action occurs on the the outer part of a woman's genitals.

Hand & Arm Placement: When a woman masturbates, she often rests her wrist on her lower abdomen just above the pubic bone. If this is what your partner does, try to do the same, since it will definitely influence the way that your fingers feel on her vulva.

MAJOR HINT: Try lying parallel to your partner and reaching your arm over her body until your fingers touch her crotch. This allows your fingers to approach her vulva in the same way that her own fingers do when she masturbates. Another position that allows for a similar approach is for the two of you to be in a sitting position with her in front and you behind. And some men like it when a woman lies on top of them, with her backside on his frontside. The pressure of the woman's body on top of you can be nice, as well as allowing the option of rear entry intercourse at the same time that you are caressing her vulva with your fingers. The worst way to masturbate a woman is while sitting between her legs, facing her vulva. This can be a fine position to use for genital massage, which is discussed later, but it's an ineffective approach if you are trying to imitate the way she touches herself.

The Proper Invite. Let The Vulva Come To You, Grasshopper. Guys who are more experienced at lovemaking often begin with a light, gentle, caress that barely touches the inner thighs and pubic hair. They don't go much further until a woman's legs spread open and/or her pelvis begins to arch upwards. They tease and caress until the lips of her vulva invite their fingers inside.

Forget Ground Zero. Too often, the main focus of a guy's fingers is to get them on a woman's clitoris and keep them there, or to go mining up her vagina, searching for that darned g-spot. Never hesitate to interrupt a bout of clit-play by running your fingertips up and down her inner thigh, or by massaging her mons, pulling gently on her pubic hair or reaching down a little lower and giving her inner lips a gentle massage or tug. Predictability is hobgoblin of finger fucking.

Fingers On The Hood. Given how the clitoral area is often more sensitive than any single part of the penis, you don't want the rough skin of your fingers rubbing across it. This is why some men gently push and pull on the clitoral hood and labia (lips) when first touching a woman's genitals. Using the lips as leverage can provide pleasing stimulation without painful friction.

Lubrication: Does your partner use lubrication when she masturbates, e.g. saliva, baby oil, etc.? Do the same when masturbating her. Never be shy about using extra lubrication, especially if you'll be at it/or long periods of time.

Wrist Motion. When men try to masturbate women, they often use just one finger. However, when a woman does herself she might incorporate a bit of wrist into the motion, even if only one finger is actually touching her vulva. This can be a subtle but important detail, and may require practice.

〰〰 **Focus.** A good reason for watching your partner masturbate is that it will help you to learn where she likes to place her fingertips. Does she like to dip her fingers inside her vagina? If so, this might not happen until she gets more aroused.

〰〰 **Favorite Side?** Find out if your sweetheart has a favorite side of her clitoris or labia that she likes to stimulate. Be sure to follow her lead. (This is a lousy time to be dyslexic, but we all feel that way at times.)

〰〰 **Don't Lose Sight Of The Bigger Picture.** Some books on sex are guilty of excessive clitoris worship, as though the female of the species were little more than a pair of arms and legs attached to a clitoris. While this may be true at certain moments for certain women, your lovemaking technique is going to be awfully raw if all you do is woo & lasso your lady's clitoris (or genitals).

〰〰 **Pubic Bone.** You wouldn't be worth a darn as a basketball player if you didn't know how to use a backboard. The same can be said for a lover who doesn't know how to utilize his lady's pubic bone — inside as well as out. It's a fine perch for a tired hand, and offers all sorts of leverage when caressing a woman's genitals. The added bonus is that a woman's pubic bone is usually much easier to find than her clitoris!

〰〰 **Mons Pubis.** The mons is the little fleshy mound at the top of the vulva just above where the lips begin to open. It usually has hair on it. Men often ignore the mons pubis and head straight for the clitoris, yet women often use the mons when masturbating. For instance, some women masturbate by putting moderate fingertip pressure on the mons and making a circular or back-and-forth motion with it. If your partner is highly aroused, she might want you to do this while the fingers of your other hand are rubbing her clit or filling up her vagina. Some women enjoy it when a partner kneads the mons (illustrated on page 150) or taps on it with his fingertips.

〰〰 **Amplification.** When a woman is giving a guy a handjob with lubrication, she can increase his sensation if she pushes the foreskin down towards the testicles with one hand, and twists her lubricated hand up and down the shaft of his taut-skinned penis. Pulling the skin taut on the penis has an amplification effect. For some women, there is an amplification effect if you pull up on the mons with the fingers of one hand while tending to the clitoris with the fingers of the other.

Imitations. An excellent way to learn more about pleasing your partner is to rest your fingers over hers while she is masturbating herself. Then do the reverse, with her fingers acting as guides for your own. Note: A woman should never hesitate to take a man's fingers and put them exactly on those parts of her body where she likes to be touched. Most men will appreciate the assist!

Feeling Her Arousal. *Body Cues For Changing Gears.* Another advantage of having your arm resting across your partner's body is that it allows you to feel when she is tensing up, when her hips start to arch, and if her body begins to writhe or twitch as it sometimes does when highly aroused. These are important signals, because as a woman becomes more aroused she may need you to stimulate her in a slightly different way. This is the lovemaking equivalent of learning how to type without looking at the keyboard.

Range Of Motion. When they masturbate, some women direct the stimulation to just one spot. Others might stimulate themselves in a more global way, tugging and pulling on the surface of the entire vulva. Plenty of women use a circular motion when rubbing their genitals, while others move a finger side-to-side or up and down like plucking at a guitar string or turning on and off a light switch. Some even tap lightly with a finger, and many have a preferred side of the vulva which they stimulate.

Tempo & Rhythm. Most women appreciate it if your fingers achieve a certain tempo and rhythm as they traverse her vulva. This can change as she becomes more aroused. How to proceed can be confusing until you learn your partner's responses. Helpful indicators include the little sounds she makes, changes in her breathing, the way her body moves—especially her hips and legs, the changes in her vulva, and if her clitoris starts to retract. While one woman might want you to maintain the exact same rhythm and hand motion from start to stop, another might need an array of tempos because she quickly habituates to the same finger motion and it loses its effect. Finding the right rhythm and tempo often feels awkward (and even hopeless) for the first few weeks or months, but with time, you will learn when to mix it up and when to stay your course.

Fill'er Up? Does your partner like to have something inside of her when she comes? Your fingers, a dildo, etc.? Ask. Also, some women have sensitive spots inside their vaginas which they might love you to stimulate with the fingers of one hand while doing their clitoris with the other. You may want to do the clitoris with whichever hand you use for writing, since stimulating a clitoris tends to require more fine motor skill than massaging a vagina. Simple pressure often works well in the vagina once you learn where to touch.

One Joint At A Time. You never want to bogart a woman's vagina by shoving an entire finger into it. A more satisfying approach is to ease your finger in one joint at a time. For instance, once you get the signal that she wants your finger inside of her, slide it in as far as the joint that's between your fingernail and first knuckle. Use it to make sensuous circles inside her vagina, gently tugging the tissue this way and that. After a while, she'll give you a cue to up the ante. Then gently glide your finger in a little further until you reach the first knuckle. Stop and play some more. At that point, she might want it to go all the way in, or maybe she'll prefer the added fullness of a second finger. She might want you to do an in-out motion with your fingers, or maybe she'll want you to stimulate the roof of her vagina. Perhaps she'll want you to jiggle your hand or pull upwards with it as your finger make an "L", with the fingertip part inside her vagina and knuckle part pushing against the shaft of her clitoris. There are many different options; it's best to experiment with her telling you what feels best.

Nipple Ripple. Some women love having their nipples caressed, sucked-on, or pulled while being masturbated. The added nipple pleasure makes it easier for them to come. Other women find this annoying. Be sure to inquire.

⌇⌇ **Lips:** The outer lips often have hair on them, the inner lips don't. The outer lips are usually more prominent, although sometimes the inner lips are. Some women like it if the man clasps each lip between his thumb and forefinger and tugs on them. Some women like this to be done very gently, others with more force than you might think. If you try this, do it very gently at first, increasing the amount of tension to where your lover finds it most pleasing.

⌇⌇ **Finger Variations:** While lying next to your partner, rest your arm across her body with your fingers on her vulva. Separate her labia with your first and third fingers, and stroke between her inner lips with your middle finger, bringing lubrication up from inside her vagina. (If she isn't already wet, lubricate your finger with saliva or store-bought lube. And try to be gentle since the belly of the clitoris is sometimes extremely sensitive.) Some women like to have their vulvas tapped with fingers, and some even like to be lightly slapped on the genitals — but only a moron would try something like this unless his partner requested it.

〰️ **Further Variations.** When lying parallel to your lover, try reaching across her body and resting the heel of your hand above her pubic bone. Then put your index finger on one of her labia and your middle finger on the other. Move one finger in an upward direction and the other downwards so that her labia are gently rubbing against each other.

〰️ **Sunnyside Down.** There are women who enjoy being touched from behind, either when they are lying on their stomach, on all fours (as in the illustration on page 143), or while leaning over something. You simply reach between their legs from behind. This changes the angle that your hand makes with their genitals and can be a delightful change of pace. It's also a neat way to massage the roof of the vagina with your thumb!

〰️ **Ovaries.** Ask your partner to help you locate her ovaries, assuming she knows where they are. They can usually be felt in the deepest part of the vagina and to the far left or right. Some women will like you to massage this area, others will find it painful. Sensitivity will also vary with her menstrual status.

〰️ **Wet Humping.** There's no reason why a woman shouldn't lube up a favorite part of her lover's body and rub up against it with her vulva. Some women like to do this on a man's back or thigh. (There are women who feel that the penis would be far more useful if it had been mounted on the front of man's thigh instead of between his legs. There is even a special dildo harness that mounts a dildo on the thigh, achieving this very feat in an amusing way.)

〰️ **Using Your Head.** Some women enjoy using the head of a sweetheart's penis for masturbating. This can be an invigorating experience for both partners. Keep in mind that even if the male doesn't ejaculate, unwanted sex germs can be passed on or the woman can get pregnant from such activity. You can greatly diminish these risks if the man is wearing a rubber that is well-lubricated with something like contraceptive gel or KY.

᭄ᜡ **Natural Lube.** If pregnancy or sex germs aren't a considera-tion, some women like to use a man's ejaculate as a lubricant to masturbate with. This might be fun to do when he comes first. She might add some saliva or her own lube, otherwise it's likely to dry up fairly fast.

᭄ᜡ **Robot Alert.** Some men follow the exact same protocol each and every time they have sex. This makes them very boring lovers. It never hurts to experiment with new ways to touch your partner, both with your fingers and your heart.

᭄ᜡ **A Special Note For Women.** It maybe difficult for a man to know when you are feeling pleasure as opposed to pain. Sometimes the noises for each sound identical, even if your experience of the two might be very, very different. It's up to you to help your man learn the difference.

More Than A Peace Sign

In reviewing porn movies done by lesbian producers, author Jay Wiseman noticed that when lesbian performers feel each other up they almost always use two fingers—not one or three. Wiseman asked a number of women about this, and most replied that two fingers simply feel better. Some of this guide's women readers said they enjoy one finger, three fingers, an entire fist or even a big toe, but most agreed that two fingers is a fine number. The number of fingers a woman wants inside of her will also depend upon her level of arousal and sometimes upon her body's menstrual status.

You might consider wearing latex gloves when spending long periods of time with your fingers inside a woman's vagina. The smooth latex surface sometimes feels nice for the woman and helps to keep your fingers from stinging when they marinate in vaginal fluids, which are fairly acidic. (Try putting a dab or two of water-based lube inside each fingertip of the glove. You might prefer the way it feels when your fingers are inside of your partner's vagina.)

Female Reader's Advice On Fingers In Their Vagina

"I like it if he inserts one finger until the opening relaxes, then adds a second finger. When I begin to breathe faster, he should start flexing his fingers. The motion is similar to when you are signaling a person to 'come here.' " *female age 32*

"When I am sufficiently wet, I enjoy two fingers. I like it when he puts them in gradually and 'fucks' me with them gently. But no fingernails and no rushing!" *female age 35*

"Start with one finger, then go up from there. To find the G-spot. put your thumb over my clitoris, then insert your first finger into my vagina and feel for the rough spot on the upper wall. Rub this spot!!!" *female age 26*

"I like a finger in there, but please, don't dig for China."

female age 48

"I don't necessarily care for fingers in my vagina. I'd rather have a penis in there." *female age 43*

"I like him to rub the entrance of my vagina in a circular fashion, but don't particularly like a finger all of the way inside."

female age 30.

Playing The Over In Your Sweetheart's Under

There's a time to bunt and a time to hit straight away; a time to bring the infield in and a time to respect the hitter's power. It's no different with women's genitals: with a little skill and strategy, you're on your way. The next couple of pages offer techniques for knowing a woman's genitals in a way that's profound. Most women will love the kind of detailed and caring attention that's involved.

Learning To Massage A Woman's Genitals

Giving a woman a genital massage differs from giving her traditional handplay in a couple of significant ways:

First: You almost always use some kind of massage oil or lubricant.

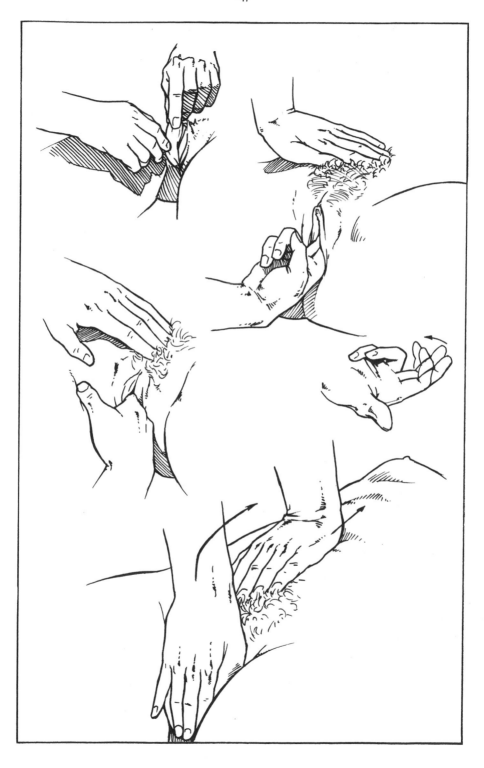

Second: You sit facing her, either between her legs or to one side. The drawing on page 137 is a good example.

Third: You are not trying to imitate the way she masturbates herself.

Fourth: What you learn about a woman's vagina from massaging her genitals can be used to increase her pleasure during intercourse. The sensitive spots or areas that you find in her vagina can sometimes be massaged with the head of your penis.

Fifth: Clocks. Think clocks. In female genital massage, clocks are everything. So are lips.

Big Ben Gets A Woody

Sit facing your partner's crotch, either between her legs or on the side of her body that allows you to easily touch her genitals with whatever hand you might use for making obscene gestures.

Now, close your eyes and think of clocks—the old fashioned type of clock that has a big hand, little hand, a second hand, and a Cuckoo bird if you must. There are six or seven clocks (or pelvic time zones) to consider when massaging a woman's genitals. An effective way to explore a woman's vulva and vagina is to image each part as having a clockface over it.

For instance, place an imaginary clockface around your partner's clitoris. Then put your fingertip at twelve o'clock, press lightly, and stimulate as long as she likes. Do this at each hour of the clockface. Hopefully your sweetheart will let you know when you hit a really good spot by saying something profound such as "There!" You can then say "2:00?" and she might reply "try 1:45." Go back and forth until you have it just right. Instead of having to say something out loud, she might prefer to hold your penis, ankle or big toe in the same way that kids use joy sticks. She can then squeeze this particular body part to indicate a direct hit.

TECHNIQUE TIP #1. When massaging different parts of a woman's genitals, apply just enough pressure to move the skin back and forth over the tissue that's under it. Press harder if she asks.

TECHNIQUE TIP #2. Genital massage requires massage oil. One loving way of applying this oil is by first putting your hand over your lover's genitals. Then slowly drip the oil on your fingers so it seeps through them and onto her vulva. Nuke the stuff for a few seconds beforehand if it is cold, or rub it between your hands to warm it. More is mentioned about lubricants at the end of the next chapter.

Clitoral clock: Imagine that there is a clockface surrounding your partner's clitoris. Start with a single finger at twelve o'clock and lightly jiggle or massage that spot for a minute or two. Then move your finger into the one o'clock position, and jiggle or massage it there. Repeat this at each one-hour interval until you have circled her entire clitoris. Of course, if for some reason or another you have your finger at one o'clock and she suddenly starts moaning and her whole body contorts and writhes in pleasure, consider keeping it there. There is no point in being a slave to protocol. If you don't get to two o'clock for another week or two, who cares? Also keep in mind that points which bring subtle pleasure can be just as important as those which set off fireworks.

Clitoral Suburbs: When they masturbate, some women focus finger pressure on the smaller labia or on the inner part of the larger labia rather than upon the clitoris proper. Be sure to explore the parts that are clitoris adjacent.

Urinary Meatus Clock: Finding a man's peehole is not a particularly taxing exercise; finding a woman's can take a bit of work. Why would you want to? Because the little dome of tissue that surrounds a woman's urinary opening has sometimes been compared to the head of the penis. Some women might enjoy it if you stimulate this area, others won't.

Note: The urinary tube runs along the ceiling of the vagina from the outside of a woman's body into her bladder. It's a bit like an air conditioning duct that is above a suspended ceiling. The urinary tube is surrounded by a special type of tissue that occasionally contains a multitude of nerve endings. Some women refer to this area on the

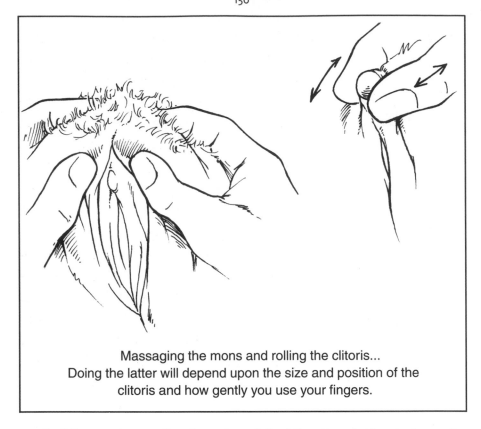

Massaging the mons and rolling the clitoris...
Doing the latter will depend upon the size and position of the
clitoris and how gently you use your fingers.

roof of the vagina as the G-spot and find its stimulation to be quite pleasurable. One way of stimulating it is by making a "come here" motion with a finger that's put inside the vagina.

Outer Vagina Clock: Think of the vagina as a tube that's about four inches long. Start at the rim (opening) of the vagina. Put pressure on each part of the tissue as your finger eventually makes a complete circle. Then move the imaginary clockface deeper inside, and do the same thing all over again. Keep repeating this until you have done the whole thing. It helps to be extra thorough about clocking the first third of the vagina, because that is where it is most sensitive to touch. Pay special attention to the roof of her vagina between 9:00 and 3:00. A number of women report pleasurable responses in this part of the vagina.

Inner vagina clock: Some women feel a certain dull but enjoyable sensitivity around the base or deepest part of the vagina, a full finger deep. This part of the vagina is more sensitive to pressure than touch.

TECHNIQUE TIP: Lay your free hand over the lower part of your lover's abdomen. Experiment by applying different kinds of pressure with the tophand while fingers from your other hand are inside her vagina.

Cervix clock: A woman's cervix can usually be found in the upper rear part of her vagina. It is easily felt if she is on all fours or brings her legs to her chest. The cervix feels like a little dome of tissue that's fun to run your fingers around. It may also have a small cleft in the middle, like your chin. Carefully stimulate the area surrounding the cervix. Some women may enjoy this and want you to do it more often; others won't. Cervical sensitivity can vary with a woman's menstrual cycle; massaging it may release some blood if she is close to her period.

Perineum clock: This is the area between a woman's vulva and rear end. It really isn't a clock at all, but more like a mini football field with the end zones being her vagina and anus. Explore this entire area thoroughly, but try not to leave any divots.

Anal Clock: The ring of the anus contains a multitude of nerve endings. Women and men who don't have aesthetic problems with anal stimulation might enjoy a clocking of their rectal areas. You may find that one part of it is more sensitive and putting a finger on it generates pleasure. But be careful about going from a woman's rectum to her vulva without washing your hands.

The Lip Part Of Erotic Massage

Most women's genitals have two sets of lips—the labia majora which form the outer folds of the vulva and the thinner labia minora which are the inner lips. The inner lips are particularly significant since they also form the hood of the clitoris. In erotic massage, much time is spent stimulating these various lips.

Tracing: After applying lubrication, it might be nice to begin with one of the larger outer lips. Place the lucky lip between your thumb and forefinger, clasping it at the base where it attaches to the main part of your partner's body. Then run your fingers (or fingertip) from the lower to upper part of the lip, as though you were tracing one side

The Hand Held Shower Head

While pleny of women might welcome a few more showers such as this, one reader offers the following counterpoint: "This illustration shows more of the same old thing: Man acts upon woman's genitals, woman passively swoons in man's arms..." Another reader says, "I'm a feminist too, but if given the opportunity, I'd happily swoon."

of a parenthesis. Repeat this as long as your partner's feedback is positive. You can also make an upside down horseshoe pattern with a fingertip by starting at the lower inside part of one lip and finishing at the lower inside part of the other. It could be fun to do this with both inner and outer lips.

Off The Edge: Another form of genital massage can be done by holding a lubricated lip between your thumb and forefinger. While squeezing just a little, pull your fingers straight away from the woman's body. Your fingers will end up in the air an inch or two above her body, as though you had pulled them off the edge of a table top or sheet of paper. If she likes this, repeat it many times.

Clock Madness — What Did You Discover?

"My clitoris gets more sensitive so when he hits just the right spot, I want him to stay there with his touch."   *female age 34*

Sometimes it will take months to fully clock a woman's genitals. Maybe you will find one special place, or maybe you will find ten. Whatever the case, after you know the various locations you can throw away your mental clocks.

You can also try to stimulate these spots while having intercourse or oral sex. Experiment with different positions that might allow you to caress them with the head of your penis. Also, much fun can be derived from stimulating one spot with the fingers of one hand while doing another spot with your other hand or tongue.

Obsession Alert

Hopefully you will approach genital massage in a spirit of playfulness and fun rather than as some sort of mission or quest. And while the sensations won't necessarily pack the kick of a mule, the overall effect can be quite pleasing when done for extended periods of time.

Palms Between Her Legs

Here is a form of genital massage with no clocks attached. It is illustrated on the bottom of page 147. Sit above or next to your partner's abdomen while facing her feet. Place a well-lubricated hand between her legs with your fingertips resting just below her vulva but not touching her anus. Pull the hand all the way up to her belly, with your fingertips gently separating her labia with each stroke. Immediately do the same thing with your other hand, alternating strokes like a dog does when he's digging a hole in your garden, but not nearly as fast. (Sorry about the canine imagery.)

Hydropower—Aquatic Version Of Finger Fucking

Many couples find it sensual to hold and grope each other in the shower, hot tub or bath. Trouble is, the H_2O tends to wash away any kind of natural lubricant. A good solution is to keep a plastic squeeze bottle with oil in it next to the tub. Stand and lube the outside of your dry genitals with vegetable oil, then ease your way into the water. This will keep your genitals slick and slippery, and should greatly enhance aquatic hand play.

Two recent advancements in hydrotechnology have been a great boon to women's sexual pleasure:

Hand-held shower head: If you don't have one of these gadgets, consider running to your local hardware store to get one. It shouldn't take more than fifteen minutes to install, unless your plumbing is really old and rusty. Hop in the shower with your sweetheart as she tries out the various settings on the shower head. Some women like their partner to hold them from behind while focusing the spray between their legs. This can be combined with rear entry intercourse. Also, keep in mind that when you hold the shower head point blank against the skin it causes the water to bubble somewhat like the jet on a hottub. This might feel good. Don't point the jet of water into a woman's vagina as it might force air inside of her body. This could be dangerous.

(Some men enjoy the feeling of the spray against the side of the scrotum. Depending on how you hold the showerhead, it's a sensation that can be on the cusp between pleasure and pain. This might have something in common with the kind of sexual experiences that some women report, where the line between pleasure and pain is a fine but pleasant one.)

Note: Different brands of hand held shower heads create different kinds of spray. Some people might prefer one brand over another. Also, the sensation will vary with the water pressure in your area. You can often find some units for under $40. Hardware chains generally put them on sale every month or so.

Power jets in the hottub: The possibilities for genital stimulation nearly cripple the imagination. Check with your hottub repair person about fitting an extension hose on one of the massage jets so you can direct the flow where you want. Cut the air to the jets so none of it will get into the vagina.

Note: They are actually starting to make waterproof vibrators. These are tiny things which only have one conceivable purpose, yet the box shows a woman in a tub using the point of the vibrator against the side of her neck!

Final Perspective: A Man's Fingers On A Woman's Body

"The first time I felt a woman's vagina was with my first love. We were taking things very slowly and when I would ask if I could go down her pants, the answer was "no." I respected her wishes and we always did something else, usually making out. One day she finally told me I could proceed below the waistline. It was warm and wet and very soft. The wetness of her vagina was the most exciting feeling I'd ever had." *male age 25*

For some men, putting their fingers between a woman's legs is a moment that has its own wonder or magic. They love feeling the woman's warmth and the start of her wetness, and how her body sometimes tenses, squirms and writhes. The arc that jumps back and forth from fingers to thighs is sometimes quite intense. Other times there isn't as much chemistry or energy, but this doesn't mean that the partners don't love each other dearly It just means that sex is different for different couples.

Also, there might be other parts of a woman's body where touch produces intense sensation. For instance, one reader reports that his lover has a small area on the lower part of her back that is so erotically sensitive that her knees nearly buckle whenever he strokes or caresses it. He once nearly caused her to have an orgasm in the middle of a busy hardware store by caressing the small of her back. Another woman reader is so sensitive to having her fingers touched that she has actually had orgasms while getting a manicure.

For better or worse, the focus of this chapter has been on touching a woman between the legs. Hopefully, you will explore your partner's entire body, searching for the places where she loves to be touched the most.

Final Words About Caressing A Woman's Genitals

As kids we used to hold sea shells up to our ears to hear the ocean. It was magic, of course. As adults, some men find themselves pressing an ear against a partner's chest while pirouetting a hand and fingers over the sweet spot between her legs, listening to her heart beat as she starts to enter a state of sexual bliss. It might not tell you the meaning of life, but it's a start.

Chapter 13
Hand Jobs: Different Strokes For Different Blokes

The hand job is like the Swiss Army Knife — a fine, multi-purpose tool that is useful in many different situations. This chapter is about hand jobs that women give to men, as opposed to the kind that men give themselves when no one else is around. This chapter is divided into two parts: giving your man a traditional (classic) hand job and doing genital massage.

The Classic Hand Job: In giving a classic hand job, the goal is to bring the man to orgasm — rub rub, squirt squirt. This is usually most effective when you are able to do him in the same way that he does himself. He will think you are brilliant.

Erotic Genital Massage: Erotic massage uses techniques that men don't always perform on themselves. The goal is to make every stroke an experience in and of itself, turning a man's entire body into one giant sex receptor. Rather than racing towards orgasm, the intent is to delay ejaculation while building erotic tension in the man's body. In erotic massage, there is no need for the man to have a full erection, with half to three-quarters of an erection sometimes being optimal.

How Men Masturbate

Before offering different techniques to use on your partner, it might help to explain how men masturbate. This might seem too elemental to male readers, but female readers have found it helpful.

While each man might have his own unique spin or variation, there are two basic ways that men masturbate. The first is by doing it dry, the second is with lubrication. Believe it or not, these are as different as wearing briefs or boxers.

Dry: The man wraps one or two fingers around the shaft of the penis at a strategically placed point. He then moves the entire foreskin up and down with each stroke. Although the fingers are firmly clasped around the shaft, the elastic nature of the foreskin allows the fingers to glide smoothly over the tissue below. The bulk of sensation occurs as the fingers move over a highly sensitive part of the penis which is called the frenulum.

Lubricated: Using lubrication allows for a handjob that feels more like intercourse. When giving himself a lubricated handjob, the man often wraps his whole hand around the penis. The lubrication allows the hand to glide over the surface of the foreskin. This makes it possible to stimulate the head and shaft without moving the foreskin up and down. Some men keep the foreskin stationary by pulling it taut around the base of the penis with their free hand. Details on how to do this are given later in the chapter.

Dry Vs. Lubricated: The lubricated handjob tends to be a more sensuous experience than doing yourself dry. However, plenty of guys prefer doing it dry, and there are many times when masturbating dry is more practical. It's less of a production, and you are able to come into a tissue or a sock instead of all over your hand, which often happens when you do it with lubrication. On the other hand, if a man has the time and is so inclined, masturbating with lubrication can be a delightful treat.

What Does A Penis Feel Like?

When a penis is soft, it feels a bit like human lips. The skin has a silky smooth, almost translucent texture that slides over the tissue beneath it. A soft penis is extremely flexible. It can be warm or cold to the touch, and feels more like a squid than a hot dog.

To know what a hard penis feels like, find a fairly buff guy who lifts weights and ask him to flex his arms. A hard bicep feels similar to a hard penis, although a hard penis won't be nearly as big around except in some guy's dreams. Poking a finger into a man's unflexed pecs will give you an approximate idea of what a semi-erect penis feels like.

Here are some women's recollections about the first time they touched a penis:

"It was sort of like 'Oh my God, What do you do with it?' I knew if you did something to it in the right way, that was good. I felt very, very careful, not sure what I was dealing with at all. It was like an alien creature that you were supposed to automatically know how to please... As I listen to myself describing it, I am aware that I must have considered it as separate from the individual who it belonged to!"

"It was not a pleasant experience then, but it sure is now."

"I had intercourse a number of times but never touched it. I didn't get into that until much later."

"I didn't like the way it felt when flaccid. A couple of years later I finally got around to making friends with it, and it became exciting... When you make friends with a person, you make friends with his penis."

"It took me awhile to figure out that you could really handle it, that it wasn't fragile."

Intent & Intensity

"I could never move my fist that fast for so long. He really man-handles that sucker and it doesn't seem to hurt!" *female age 55*

Some people say that the difference between giving a great hand job and a mediocre one is a matter of intent; if a woman isn't turned on by the situation, she can pump a penis 'till Tinkerbell commits a felony, nothing special is likely to happen. Other people say that giving great hand jobs is a matter of skill and endurance. Whatever the case, few women realize that they have the potential to control nearly every cell in a man's body with each stroke of their hand. Instead, they often just jerk away until things get sticky. One female reader comments, "Not true. Plenty of women are aware of the potential control they have, but choose not to pursue it."

Traditional Hand Jobs (THJ)

Taking The Jerk Out Of Jerking Off

This section is about giving a guy a handjob without using lubrication. Ways of doing it wet are described in the second half of this chapter.

Some women give hand jobs that are jerky. This is understandable, since it might appear that when guys masturbate we use a single 'up' stroke followed by a single 'down' stroke, all in rapid succession. But that's not how we do it. We usually have a more fluid motion, so to speak. The hand doesn't stop or even slow down as it changes direction from up to down. As a result, the motion is smooth rather than jerky — which means the term "jerking off" is a misnomer.

Another potential problem occurs when a woman slows down or stops pumping as the man begins to ejaculate. While some guys may want you to stop right away, others will greatly appreciate it if you keep stroking for a few minutes after they ejaculate ("stroking through"). Some might even want you to proceed as though the penis were an udder, with you milking out each drop.

As the hand motion becomes more familiar, you might want to caress your man's testicles with one hand as you are jerking him off with the other. Your lover might also enjoy being kissed while you are giving him a hand job. And some people claim that sex can be greatly enhanced if you stare into each other's eyes as you are coming. Others think that this is a silly thing to do.

To find the optimal hand position, lay parallel to your man and reach across his body like he does when he is masturbating. Ask him to form your fingers around his penis in the same way that he does when he's alone and thinking about you. The way he holds the penis and where he puts his hand on the shaft are more significant factors than you might think. Try to imitate the exact place where he grips himself. There are reasons for this. One of the most sensitive areas of the penis is just below the head on the side that's away from the man's belly when he has an erection. It shows good form to rub a finger over this spot when masturbating a man. Rub the middle part of your finger over the frenulum, not your fingertips.

Another reason to position your hand exactly where he does is because the foreskin is only so elastic, if he is circumcised, anyway. If your grip is too high or low, the foreskin will be pulled beyond its stretching point. Again, much confusion can be avoided if you simply ask him to place your hand and fingers where he likes them. Then have him guide your hand up and down so you will get a sense of how high and low to stroke.

Variation: Consider doing your man when he is standing or kneeling as opposed to simply lying prone. This could be nice for both of you.

Pressure. Chances are, your partner might want you to clasp or squeeze the penis more tightly than you feel would be comfortable for him. (How do you think we guys develop such firm handshakes?) It never hurts to ask if he would like you to squeeze tighter.

Ball Trick: When masturbating, some guys push a finger from the stroking hand against the lower part of the penis near where the testicles attach. (Usually a little finger, or combination of little finger and ring finger.) This causes the testicles to jiggle or vibrate with each stroke, which can feel really nice. But it's always best to seek your man's input when first trying to do this, since your finger might inadvertently poke him in the nuts.

Ultimately, there is no way that you are going to get your sweetheart's hand motion exactly right unless you have him show you. That's because each guy varies in terms of grip, stroke, and rhythm — not to mention anatomy. Don't be surprised if it takes a number of tutorials before you get it right, especially if your hand is considerably smaller than his. If your own man is too uptight to teach you, it's likely that any number of his friends will be more than willing to let you learn the basics on them, or maybe one of your girlfriends can demonstrate on her own boyfriend... Then again, she might use a banana.

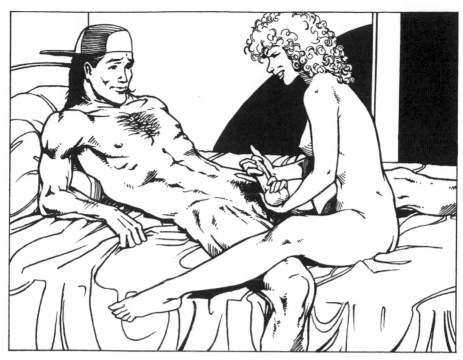

This position is fine for doing erotic massage, but not so good for giving a traditional hand job.

It can be both fun and helpful talking to your friends about their own special techniques for getting guys off, although you shouldn't assume that they know better than you when it comes to your own man.

In his wonderful books "Tricks: 125 Sex Tips To Make Good Sex Better" author Jay Wiseman lists several tips to make a traditional hand job more fun. For instance, he suggests caressing the penis for ten seconds with your fingertips, followed by one quick up-and-down hand stroke. Then caress the penis for ten more seconds, followed by two quick up-and-down hand strokes. After every ten second period of caressing, increase the stroke total by one. *For information about ordering Jay Wiseman's books, see page 607.*

There are plenty of other techniques for making traditional hand jobs more fun. One is when the woman makes a vagina with her warm lubricated hands and the man thrusts his penis in and out.

Some couples enjoy it when a woman lubricates her breasts and holds them together while the man thrusts between them. And more than one man has nearly exploded on the spot when a woman runs her hair or nipples along his torso and over his genitals.

Also, some women like it when their partners ejaculate on them; other women don't find this to be such a wonderful idea.

Male Genital (Erotic) Massage

We now up the ante and offer techniques for doing male genital massage. What follows may seem a bit mechanical or complicated. Not to worry; keep it fun and use these suggestions in any way you like. While genital massage tends to be different from the traditional hand job, there is no reason why you can't mix and match various strokes and strategies (layering?).

Lubricating your hands and his genitals is essential for doing male erotic massage. As is mentioned in greater detail at the end of this chapter, any number of oils will work rather nicely, as long as you're thinking peanut oil instead of Penzoil, and canola or coconut oil instead of Castrol. (It's a penis you are massaging, not a piston.) Also, hand moisturizers absorb into the skin too quickly to be of much use.

The Point Of No Return

The ante for doing male genital massage is learning to keep your man highly aroused for long periods of time without letting him ejaculate. (No, we haven't lost our minds, it is possible. An entire chapter of this book, Dyslexia Of The Penis—Improving Your Sexual Hang Time is dedicated to this very subject.) Let's say your partner ejaculates at 9.5 on an imaginary pleasure scale of 10. In doing genital massage, you will want to keep him between 7 and 8 on the same scale for as long as possible before finally letting him squirt, an event that might be rather powerful when it finally occurs.

One way to keep your man at such a high level of excitement is to learn his body language for when he is about to ejaculate. For instance, the veins in his penis may start to bulge or his penis might give a sudden throb, the color of the head may darken, his testicles may suck up into his groin, his muscles may suddenly tighten, his hips may thrust, and he might start to groan like a dying bull or invoke the names of various saints. Change the stroke or decrease the intensity when this happens.

Some women find it very helpful if the man is able to report his levels of excitement by saying something like "6", "7","8" or "9". Even the cues "more" or "less" are often enough. This will help you learn when to up the pace and when to back off. After a while you will become so familiar with his body language that you won't need him to actually tell you.

Ready, Set, Relax

When attempting genital massage, the first thing to do is to get your man completely naked. This is usually not a difficult task.

Next, find those parts of his body where tension gathers. For instance, do what you can to massage the tension out of your man's upper body before touching his genitals. (Who knows why, but the shoulders and back often become the body's collecting points for tension. There is no point in doing good work on a man's genitals when the weight of the world is parked between his shoulder blades. This is also true for women's bodies.)

Some men believe that the only important part of sex is when a penis is being rubbed, sucked or fucked. They might not even care about the tension in their shoulders, and will sometimes direct your hands straight to their crotch. If that's the case, go ahead and fondle your man's testicles with one hand. At the same time, repeat your request that he close his eyes and relax, and inform him straight away that you will do to his body what you like, when you like, and how you like. If he still objects, slap him upside the head and remind him what you are holding in your other hand!

Finally, lube him up. The most civilized way of greasing a man's groin is to cup one hand over his genitals and drip massage oil over it. Gravity will pull the oil through your fingers and onto his genitals unless you are in outer space. Make sure that your man's testicles and penis are thoroughly basted with oil. Also consider smearing some massage oil over his inner thighs from knees to groin and over his lower belly. Putting a plastic sheet or a thick towel or two under him might be a good way to catch the excess oil. Large plastic garbage can bags work really well. If clean-up is going to pose serious problems, use less oil.

Different Massage Strokes

What follows are a few of the different strokes that make up male genital massage. These strokes appear in videotapes on erotic massage by sex experts like Joe Kramer, Ray Stubbs, Michael Perry, and the NSS organization. **Massage Note:** It is not necessary for a man to have an erection for genital massage to feel great. In fact, many guys remain semi-erect when receiving genital massage.

Fists Going Up: Be sure all skin surfaces are well lubricated. Wrap one hand around the base of the penis, squeeze lightly, and pull it up along the shaft, over the head, and into the air. As this hand is making its upward stroke, grab the base of the penis with your free hand, squeeze and do the same thing. Create a fluid motion with one hand constantly following the other. Be sure to slow the pace if the man shows signs of impending orgasm, lest he create fluid of his own. This technique is shown at the top of the next page. The folks who did the NSS video suggest giving a little extra squeeze or snap on the upward stroke just as your hand reaches the head of the penis.

Fists Going Down: Same technique as above, only in the reverse direction with your hands going from the tip of the penis to the base. Downward strokes such as these usually require an erection. Otherwise, the thing just flops there in your hand. Also, use a more open grip so you don't shove the penis into the body.

Thumbs Up: While facing your man's crotch, clasp your fingers together as you might do when praying that the check you just wrote doesn't bounce. The only difference here is that your hands are

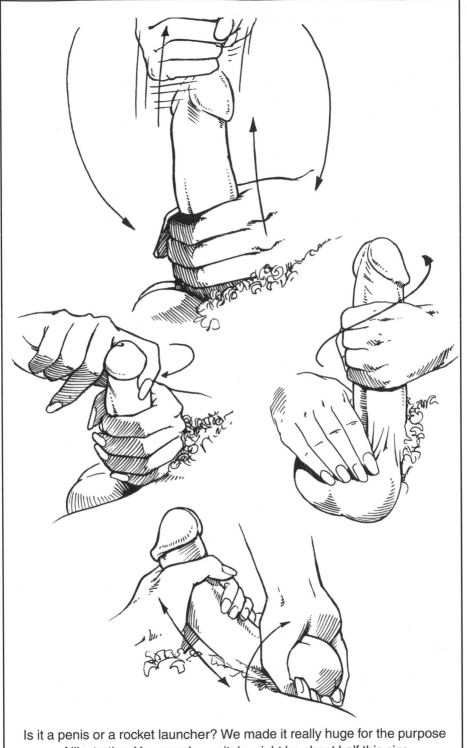

Is it a penis or a rocket launcher? We made it really huge for the purpose of illustration. Your man's genitals might be about half this size.

clasped around your man's penis. Use the pads of your thumbs to massage the front part of the penis where nature left the seam showing. Spend extra time rubbing the area where the head attaches to the shaft, or just below it, as this is usually the most sensitive part of the penis. (Some people compare the sensitivity of this area to that of the clitoris, although they are probably over-stating the case.)

⟿ **Open Palm Rubbing Head Of Penis:** Some guys might like this, others won't... Hold the shaft of the penis in one hand so it is sticking straight out from the man's body (perpendickular). Open your other hand flat and rub it in a circular pattern over the head of the penis, as though you were buffing it. Make sure that the palm of your hand is well-lubed.

⟿ **Twisting The Cap Off A Bottle Of Beer Stroke:** Hold the shaft of the penis near to the base. With your other hand, grasp the head of the penis as though it were the cap on a bottle of beer. Twist it as if you were opening a beer bottle, with your thumb and forefinger running along the groove under the ridge where the head attaches to the shaft.

⟿ **Wringing A Towel Dry Stroke:** Grasp the lower part of the penis with one hand, and the upper part of the shaft with the other. There should be no gap between your hands unless mother nature mistakenly endowed your man with an elephant trunk instead of a penis. Twist your hands back and forth in opposite directions.

Strokes Where The Skin On The Penis Is Pulled Taut

The penis can usually be made more sensitive by stretching the foreskin. As mentioned earlier, guys who masturbate with lubrication sometimes use one hand to pull the foreskin taut while stroking the shaft with the other.

This also helps to keep the baggy skin on the scrotum from rising up onto the shaft of the penis. There are a couple of ways to achieve this:

⟿ **Palm On The Side:** Clamp your thumb and forefinger or middle finger around the shaft of the penis just above where it joins the testicles (scrotum). Pull the skin down a bit, and then wrap your other fingers and palm around the testicles. This will make the foreskin taut. If the man is uncircumcised, reach higher up on the shaft to pull the extra skin down.

⇰ **Taut Variation:** To keep his foreskin taut, it is possible that your partner hooks his thumb around the shaft of his penis and uses the other four fingers to cup, squeeze, or caress his testicles. Then again, if he's the outdoor type with a history of running power equipment, he may need to improvise depending upon how many fingers he still has left. Some guys might even make a sideways or downward pointing peace sign, with the peace sign fingers straddling the lower part of the penis, pushing the foreskin down into the scrotum. The ring and pinky fingers then lay over the top of the testicles.

Tightening the skin over the penis might enhance the feeling of some of the following hand strokes, as long as the hand that's doing the stroking is well- lubricated:

⇰ **Penis/Belly Rub:** The penis should be lubricated and resting flat against the man's belly. Pull the skin taut at the base of the penis as mentioned above. Open your other hand and lay it flat on top of the penis. Then drag the hand up towards the man's chest, as if you were trying to push the good feelings out of his penis and onto the skin of his belly. Repeat. As with any of these strokes, feel free to vary the angles, pressures and grips to form your own unique style. And don't hesitate to do a series of one stroke followed by an entirely different type of stroke.

⇰ **The Corkscrew Stroke — Or— Following The Stripe On The Barber's Pole:** Pull the skin taut at the base of your partner's penis. Wrap your other hand around the base of his lubricated penis. Squeeze lightly, and twist it upwards as though you were following a corkscrew or the stripe on a barber's pole. If his penis is hard enough, do a reverse downstroke which should return your hand to the same position where it started. If there isn't enough erection to make the downward stroke work, just do a series of upward strokes.

Note: When it comes to giving either lubricated hand jobs or oral sex, never hesitate to use a twisting motion up and down the shaft of the penis, especially on the ridge that's beneath the head.

➤ **Thumbs Up — Thumbs Down:** This may sound complicated, but it isn't. There are two ways to grasp a penis that is lubricated. One is with your hand facing up, so the little finger is towards the base of the penis and the thumb is towards the head. The other is with your hand facing down, so the thumb is around the base and your little finger is around the head end of the penis. It can be quite impressive when a woman alternates hand orientation while doing the corkscrew stroke that's listed above.

➤ **Octopuss(y) Fingers:** Lay the palm of your hand over the head of the penis and drop your fingers down along the sides of the shaft. (Your hand will look like an open parachute or an octopus when it swims.) Your fingers will stimulate the sides of the penis as you move your hand up and down. You can also twist your hand sideways, or do a corkscrew stroke that combines both motions.

Cross-Modal Stimulation

There's never any harm in running a hand up and down a man's inner thighs or across his chest and stomach at the same time that you are stimulating his penis. For instance, you might make a complete "U" by going up one thigh, around his crotch and down the other thigh. The same is true for rubbing his chest and stomach with one hand while stimulating his penis with the other. And there aren't too many men who would mind receiving tender kisses while your hand is stroking or massaging their genitals. If your partner is the type who enjoys nipple stimulation, consider kissing or caressing his nipples at the same time that you are massaging his genitals.

Massaging Under The Testicles

If the skin over the testicles is tight, heat the room and put a warm washcloth over them. Let the scrotum warm up for a couple of minutes until the testicles hang freely. Press into the middle of the scrotum with your fingertips. They should be touching the part of the penis that is covered by the testicles. Massage this area all the way back to where the man's rear end begins. There is often a single spot on this part of the penis where a number of ligaments, muscle fibers, and nerve endings seem to converge. Putting fingertip pressure on this spot while massaging the "regular" part of the penis with your other hand can make the entire shaft—from the base of the pelvis to the head of the penis—experience a subtle, warm feeling that some men will find enjoyable. You might also try massaging this area when giving a blow job.

This part of the penis is smaller than a dime and is either tucked under the testicles or it might be located more towards the man's rear end. Also, it might be on one side of the shaft rather than in the middle. As for testicles that get in the way, do what we guys do: push your fingertips into the space that is between them or just behind them, or push them to the side.

Note: A man's testicles will nearly cripple him with pain if they get hit, knocked or flicked, but not when a partner caresses and massages them. Being massaged in this area can feel like getting a really nice backrub, only it's between the legs. Still, be gentle at the start, and keep in mind that while some men find the sensation to be delightful, others don't like to be touched there.

Massage That Includes The Testicles

Here are a few techniques to try on the testicles, as well as some strokes that include the testicles and penis. None of these strokes should cause any pain or discomfort. If they do, stop.

⟿ **Simple Testicle Massage:** Explore with your fingertips the space between the testicles. Be gentle at first, and seek plenty of feedback. Once you find a form of massage that pleases the man, do it often. For some men, the sensation feels like it's part backrub and part orgasm. They might even prefer that you do this to stroking their penis. Once you get it just right, try not to vary the pressure or finger position, since the margin between delight and no pleasure is small.

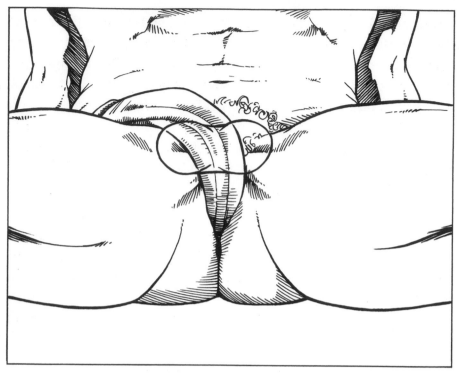

The Man With Invisible Balls

Women often assume that the penis is somehow glued or stapled to the front of a man's pelvic bone. In reality, it runs beneath his testicles and anchors inside his pelvis. Some men enjoy having the "invisible" part of the penis massaged. Push into the space between the testicles with your fingertips and gently rub, or try massaging the flat space between his balls and anus.

⇜ **Penis Up, Balls Down:** Be sure that your hands are well-lubricated. Grasp the lower part of the penis with one hand. Clamp the thumb and forefinger of your other hand around the base of the scrotum where it attaches to the groin. This should cause the testicles to pop out a bit and the skin covering them should become taut. Squeeze both hands lightly, and then do an upwards stroke with the penis hand while the testicle hand pulls gently in the opposite direction. Find a tempo that works for both of you and keep repeating these strokes.

⇜ **Ball Rub:** With the thumb and forefinger of one hand, make a ring around the part of your man's scrotum where it attaches to his groin. Squeeze gently until his testicles are popping out a bit, but not enough to cause any pain. Run the fingertips of your other hand up and down the sides of the scrotum with a light tickling touch.

⤙ **Flat Handed Doggy Dig:** Straddle your partner's chest while facing his feet. Lay his penis flat against his belly with the head pointing up toward his navel. Place one of your well-lubricated hands between his legs with your fingertips resting below his testicles. Pull the hand all the way up to his belly, dragging your fingers over his testicles and penis. Repeat with your other hand, rhythmically alternating strokes as a dog might when digging in the dirt. This same stroke is illustrated in the chapter "The Zen Of Finger Fucking" but it is being done on a woman.

Spreading The Excitement — Pavlov Between The Legs

Genital massage can be used to help a man link the sensations in his crotch with other parts of his body. For instance, Zen/Buddhist types might have you stimulate the man's genitals with one hand while caressing various chakras (e.g. upper abdomen, heart, third eye) with your other hand. It might help if he inhaled deeply, as though he were sucking the warm glow from his genitals into the upper part of his body.

Western psychology types might suggest kissing or caressing your partner's neck, shoulders or chest while massaging his genitals. At various intervals, stop stroking the man's genitals but continue to kiss or caress the other designated body parts. If he were a dog and his name was Pavlov, he might eventually learn to have genital sensations any time you caress these other body parts. Likewise, he might learn to have pleasant sensations in other parts of his body whenever his penis is stimulated. The ultimate goal is to help a man experience greater sensation over his entire body.

"FOR GUYS"

Helping A Partner Learn How To Please You

A man can help both himself and his partner if he will turn the lights up, get naked, and let her do an introductory physics lab on his genitals. The purpose is for her to tickle, squeeze, tug and poke each part of the man's sexual anatomy so she can become more confident in handling his genitals. Hopefully she will begin very gently, increasing the pressure until the man says something earthshaking such as "Ouch!" At that point, the woman eases up until he says "Ah, that's perfect!" Here are a few specifics:

> **PENIS:** Have her tug it, gently yank it, and squeeze it until she's able to distinguish your Ouch! zone from your Perfect! zone. Then show her how to grasp your penis to give you a hand job. Indicate how far up and down you like the strokes to go, as well as how fast to do them and how long you wish she would keep stroking after you come.

> **TESTICLES:** First, if the room is cold and your cujones are in frost bite mode, turn up the heat and put something warm over them until you have managed to coax them back down. Once they are hanging freely, let her tickle, caress and play with them, telling her what feels good and what what doesn't. Then have her slowly squeeze each testicle until you say "Ouch!" Also, have her put a finger or two in the space between your testicles and push in until she is massaging the shaft.

> **PROSTATE:** For couples who are either curious about or into anal stimulation, consult Chapter 21 "Up Your Bum — Anal Sex" which explains prostate massage.

Lube Specs — For Both Male & Female Genital Massage

Most hand creams and moisturizers are designed to absorb into the skin so people won't feel like greased pigs after they use them. This means that the macro-molecules that make up moisturizers are designed to go flat fast. As a result, most hand moisturizers aren't adequate for doing massage.

When it comes to male genital massage, the best kind of lubricant is a super slick potion that will leave your man's woody wet and slippery for as long as possible. This will require one of the new water-based lubes with silicone, or an oil-based lubricant. Possibilities range from canola or coconut oils to vegetable oil, mineral oil, almond oil, baby oil, various massage oils, and heaven only knows what. A popular and nearly legendary jerk-off lubricant is a facial cleanser called Albolene. Anything that's good for jerking off is also good for male genital massage.

The outside of most women's genitals do well with oil-based lubricants, but that's not necessarily true for inside their vaginas. Consider keeping a water-based lubricant handy for putting fingers inside the vagina. Most water-based lubricants mix nicely with a woman's own natural lubrication, and a few drops of water or saliva can be added if they start to dry out. Never, use Vaseline (petroleum jelly) inside a vagina, as it blocks the ability of the vagina to cleanse itself and may result in infections. Scented lotions should be avoided because they can cause irritation, and some women get infections from water-based lubes that contain glycerin.

For the latest on lubes, check out the web site for Condomania, which is listed in the resources section. The better mail order catalogs will also provide you with a good summary. The raunchier male order catalogs will try to sell you anything.

Reader's Comments

What did you think the first time you saw a guy ejaculate?

"I did it right! Good job! I was proud of me. Then I thought, 'Geez, I hope my mom doesn't come home early.'"
female age 22

"I remember being disgusted and oddly fascinated at the same time, and I couldn't believe how far that stuff could shoot out!" *female age 32*

"It just kind of oozed out. For some reason I thought there was supposed to be more of a stream." *female age 37*

"I was jealous he could actually project it from his body and I couldn't."   *female age 23*

"I was kinda grossed out by the whole thing."   *female age 45*

"I was proud that I made him ejaculate, but I couldn't believe that people actually would let that go in their mouths. I was a senior in High School."   *female age 25*

"I was a little shocked. I was young, 15, and I don't think I understood exactly what was going on. It's also when I realized that tissues weren't just for noses anymore."
female age 27

"I wondered what it felt like. I wondered what it tasted like. Also, I wondered what it would feel like to have that happen inside of me."   *female age 25*

"I vaguely remember thinking, it's amazing how their bodily process is. Also, there is what is needed to help form a human being."   *female age 36*

End Of Chapter Notes: In case there are any physics major readers who also jerk off, Sir Isaac Newton might have said that while the motion of the hand alternates in opposing directions (up and down) its velocity remains constant and its acceleration is zero, except for the first and last few strokes. In other words, there's not much jerkiness to a good hand job... Thanks to the writings of Brooks Peters for suggesting that "jerking off" is a misnomer.

Chapter 14
Balls, Balls, Balls

Testicles may seem like a mystery, because guys tend to be fixated on the penis as the source of all pleasure. In fact, you may need to teach your lover about the delights of caressing his testicles. That's because a lot of guys aren't used to experiencing how wonderful it can feel when a woman uses her fingertips on the testicles and inner thighs. As one reader comments, "When my wife gently massages my testicles and runs her hands up and down my inner thighs, it's one part excitement, two parts relaxation, and six parts total bliss. I didn't appreciate this a few years ago, but now I enjoy it every bit as much oral sex. The sensation is entirely different, but it's every bit as satisfying."

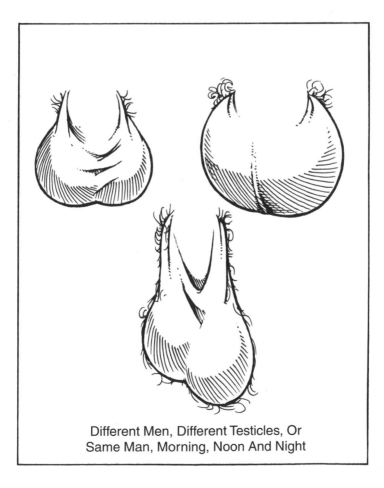

Different Men, Different Testicles, Or
Same Man, Morning, Noon And Night

Ball Rules

Testicles are far more rugged than you might think and can usually be handled with impunity, but pop them with a simple flick of a finger and you might have to peel their owner off the ceiling. Heaven only knows why. Testicles should feel a little like hard boiled eggs without the shell, but they won't be quite that big unless your lover is related to the racehorse Secretariat.

As a man becomes aroused, his testicles tend to swell or become bigger. When he is highly aroused or just about to come, his scrotum and testicles will rotate and hug the shaft of the penis, like bungee jumpers on the upswing. Another thing to know about testicles is that they can easily go from feeling soft to feeling hard. It depends on the temperature and on the man's level of sexual excitement.

Testicle Embryology

In the womb, males and females start off with the same genitals. These are female. If the fetus is bathed with masculinizing hormones, the female genitals will turn into male genitals. If not, the fetus is born with female genitals.

Embryologically speaking, if your man hadn't morphed into a male while in his mother's womb, the skin that made up his scrotum would have remained the outer lips of his vulva. If you look carefully, you'll notice a seam along the center of his scrotum. That's where his fetal labia fused together to make a scrotum. This is a long-winded way of saying that a man's scrotum has about the same sensitivity as the outer lips of your vulva. And his inner thighs are just as sensitive as yours, a fact he might not have noticed because he's been so busy all these years stroking his penis.

Ball Tending

The preceding chapter "Hand Jobs, Different Strokes For Different Blokes" has an entire section on testicle massage. For now, there's no need to try anything fancy, just experiment and see what he likes. You might start out by placing your fingertips on the sides of his scrotum and caressing as lightly as you can. Let his verbal feedback guide you from there.

You might also try resting the palm of your hand over his penis with your fingertips pointing down. Experiment with lightly massaging the back part of the scrotum, where it attaches to his groin. Every minute or so, push your palm down against the penis. This should give his penis a pleasant, isolated jolt of pleasure, which might mix nicely with the more subtle sensations that your fingertips are providing his balls.

Some guys will also find it pleasurable if you caress their testicles while they are face down. Reach between their spread legs, like in the illustration on page 178.

Intercourse Extra

You can tend to your man's testicles during intercourse if you are in a position which allows it. The most direct way is if you are on top facing his feet. Different rear entry positions may also allow you to reach between your legs and caress his testicles. Experiment and see what you and he like best.

Liking His Licking

Some guys enjoy it if you lick and suck on their balls when they are on all fours and you are on your back beneath them. The added benefit for you is that you get to rest your head on a pillow!

The Exquisite Brush Off

Get yourself a make-up brush or a Japanese bamboo artist's brush, have your cowboy spread his legs, and gently brush his inner thighs, testicles, penis and abdomen. Doing repeated circles around the outside of his balls can feel especially nice. The sensation is subtle, somewhere between a feather and a fingertip. It can feel relaxing and titillating at the same time. If you enjoy a bit of bondage, tie him up first. After about thirty minutes of this, a guy might actually come from the brush strokes alone.

When brushing a guy off, don't limit your strokes to just his genitals. Try his face, back, feet and hands. If you're lucky, he'll grab the brush and return the favor.

Perineum

There is a patch of anatomical real estate between the testicles and rectum which is often ignored but has the potential for much sensation. It is called the perineum. (Women have one, too.) Buddhist types get all excited about this particular area and regard it with the same kind of awe that we Westerners sometimes do the reset button on the garbage disposal. Place your fingertips on this area with just enough pressure so the skin moves over the tissue beneath it. Experiment and see what feels good.

Another Kind Of Tenderness

If you are so inclined, don't hesitate to reach between your man's legs and cup or cradle his genitals at nonsexual times, like when watching TV or while falling asleep. Some men will find this to be extremely thoughtful and caring. Others will find it too arousing, and some like this kind of tenderness.

Chapter 15

Doing Yourself In Your Partner's Presence

A lot of women have never seen a man masturbate, nor have many men seen a woman masturbate. Yet plenty of us, male or female, would find it interesting if not highly erotic to watch a partner masturbate. That's what this brief chapter is about, masturbating together or in your partner's presence.

In Front Of A Partner

For straight people, masturbating in front of a partner can sometimes take a lot of trust. That's because masturbation tends to be more self-disclosing than other types of sex. It can also leave you feeling vulnerable if your partner finds you doing it. ("Oh, hi honey, I was just sitting here jerking off.") Still, most of us continue to masturbate even when we are in a relationship, and being open about it usually helps to expand sexual enjoyment for both partners. Here are eight reasons why:

There is often something erotic and even forbidden about seeing your partner masturbate. This is just as true for women watching men as for men watching women.

If your partner can see how you please yourself, it might help him or her understand more about pleasing you.

Orgasms from masturbation are often the most intense kind of orgasm. It might increase the level of intimacy in your relationship if you can ask your partner to hold you while you bring yourself to orgasm.

Masturbating together is an excellent way to share intense sexual feelings without the risk of unwanted pregnancy.

People often have unreal expectations that a partner can satisfy all of their sexual urges. There will be plenty of times when one of you is in the mood and the other isn't. There may also be times when your partner is so pleasantly drained by what you have just

done (oral sex, genital massage, etc.) that he or she curls up and falls asleep on the spot. If the two of you are comfortable about masturbation, then the spent one can simply offer to hold the horny one while he or she masturbates, or you can masturbate while your partner conks out.

◄ There are times when people feel like doing it solo. If this is an accepted part of your relationship, you won't have to hide or feel like some sort of weirdo when you want to control your own orgasmic destiny.

◄ Sometimes your partner may want to lie down beside you and masturbate too!

◄ Summers in the East, South, and Midwest are sometimes so miserably hot and muggy that the last thing you'll want to do is hug an equally hot and sweaty partner. Masturbating together is one way you can share sexual pleasure without full body contact.

When you do masturbate in each other's presence, don't forget that a partner's pleasure might be greatly enhanced with a special assist on your part. For instance, a man might enjoy it tremendously if his partner caresses or massages his testicles while he masturbates, and a woman might find it delightful if her partner licks her nipples or whispers sweet but nasty things into her ears while she masturbates. The possibilities abound.

CAUTION: If you are a woman and have your partner's ejaculate on your fingers, be sure to wash your hands before touching your vulva. One woman actually became pregnant from masturbating right after giving her high school sweetheart a hand job.

Reader's Comments

"I wish he would do it in front of me more often... I've even named his penis Squeegy Loueegy." *female age 37*

"I never realized it was possible for a guy to be turned-on by seeing a woman touching herself. Needless to say, once I figured this out about him, I put on a good show." *female age 45*

"It took awhile for us to get comfortable with it, but I like to watch my husband stroke his penis. He enjoys watching me, too. I often masturbate as part of our loveplay because I like stimulation in more places at once than two hands are capable of doing."

female age 47

"During intercourse one of us always has to touch me so I can have an orgasm, so in that respect, he's seen me do it. And we both chat about how we masturbate when we are alone sometimes." *female age 30*

"It's very intimate, sort of like sharing your most personal thoughts! And it's very arousing." *female age 26*

"I masturbate in front of my husband, mostly with a vibrator. I still find it a bit embarrassing." *female age 35*

"We never masturbated together until my wife bought your Guide To Getting It On! After reading it, we now talk freely about masturbation. We've both had some wonderful orgasms this way!" *male age 38*

"I have watched her masturbate and even helped her, and she has done the same with me. It is fun and important for both of us."

male age 70

Chapter 16
Nipples, Nipples, Nipples

This chapter talks about ways of using your fingers and mouth to tweak your partner's titties. Plenty of men and women have mega-nerve endings in their nipples, providing the potential for sensations that can be both pleasant and annoying.

For instance, one woman might find it heavenly when a lover barely breathes on her nipples, but convulses in pain if he is the slightest bit rough. So the guy learns to traverse her tender nipples like a butterfly and becomes a master at the art of subtle stimulation. Another woman might want her man to handle her nipples with authority and doesn't find it erotic until his lips latch on like an industrial vacuum cleaner. (It's amazing how hard some women want you to squeeze and suck on their nipples, while others don't like having their nipples touched at all.) Also, some women's breasts become more sensitive during certain stages of their menstrual cycle, especially if they are taking birth control pills. Know your lover's body, and be sensitive to this.

In our society it is assumed that men are the ones who stimulate women's nipples instead of it being a mutual experience. Too bad. Guys probably have the same variation in nipple sensitivity as women. One man might get an erection when his nipples are caressed, another might find it annoying.

No matter what the sex of your lover, here are a few things to consider when kissing and caressing nipples and chests. Keep in mind that you may feel clumsy the first umpteen times.

Size Vs. Performance. As with a clitoris or penis, the sensitivity of a breast has nothing to do with its size. Small ones can be like lightning rods, while big ones might not be sensitive at all.

Five-Finger Nipple Grab. This works best if the breast and your hand are lubricated with massage oil. Rest the palm of your hand over the breast with your finger tips around its circumference. As you lift your hand let your fingertips caress their way up the sides of the

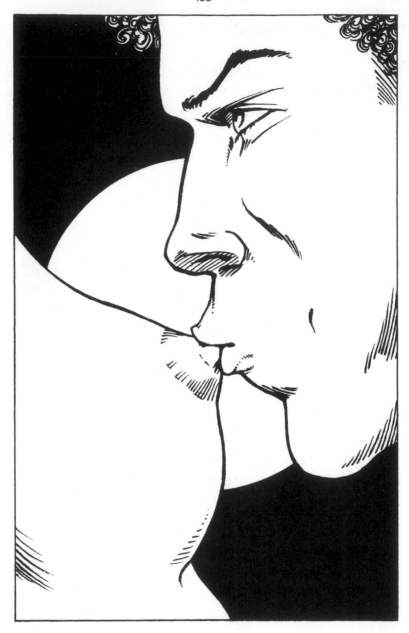

breasts, until they are clasping the tip of the nipple. Pull on the nipple just a little or a lot, depending on what your partner likes and her level of arousal.

Nipple Between Your Index & Middle Fingers. The ability to do this will depend upon the size and shape of the nipple. Cup your hand over the breast in such a way that the tip of the nipple rests in the space between your middle finger and index (or other) fingers. Squeeze the fingers together so that when you lift your hand the nipple follows, pulling the rest of the breast up with it.

In And Out. Pucker up your lips and use them to make a gasket around the nipple. Then suck in and out without breaking the seal — so the nipple feels alternating currents of vacuum and pressure. This method is described in more detail in Ray Stubbs' book "The Clitoral Kiss," and also works well on ear lobes and the clitoris. However, if you are sucking ear lobes in this way, be sure that earrings are removed first. As for jewelry in the nipples or clitoris, what's a boy to say?

Making The Nipple Taut. Place your fingers on each side of the nipple, not quite touching the nipple but around the perimeter of it. Push down lightly and pull or slide your fingers apart. This will make the nipple taut. Begin licking or sucking on it.

Nipple & Penis. Some women find it highly arousing when a man caresses their nipples with the head of his penis. If he pulls apart the opening of his penis, he can sometimes stick the tip of an erect nipple into it. This is particularly true if he is uncircumcised.

The Whole Enchilada. Women who like having their breasts and nipples caressed sometimes complain that men don't spend enough time doing this. It's hard to lavish too much attention upon your partner's breasts if she enjoys it. Also, consider licking and sucking the entire breast and not just the nipple, and remember to alternate breasts every once in a while.

Hand And Mouth. Chances are, your partner has two breasts and you only have one mouth. Perhaps she might like it if your fingers are caressing one breast while your lips are tending to the other. Or maybe she'll find this distracting, or perhaps she would prefer your hand to be caressing some other part of her body. The best way to find out is to ask.

Variations In Sensitivity. Sometimes, one breast or nipple is more sensitive than the other. Find out if your partner prefers you to spend more time on the sensitive side.

Different Temperatures. An ice cube in the mouth can be a rousing way to greet a partner's nipples. Or for nipples that are already cold, drinking something warm just before licking or sucking them can feel quite exquisite.

🐄 **Fruit Salad,** All kinds of fruits, dessert foods, and certain liquors can be served on nipples, chests, abdomens, backs and other body parts with extremely pleasing results. (Do what you can to keep sugars out of the vagina. Also, you might check out the definition of "body shots" in the glossary at the back of the book.)

🐄 **Getting To Watch.** Some people find it highly erotic to watch while a partner plays with her (or his) own nipples and breasts. So if you enjoy playing with your own nipples, there's no point in keeping it a secret.

Hard Nipple Alert

Let's say you are playing with your partner's nipples and they get hard, is this a good sign? Sometimes yes, sometimes no. Until you learn more about your partner's body, don't assume that hard nipples mean happy nipples. Nipples can get hard from unpleasant stimuli as well as pleasant, e.g. roughness, abrasion, cold—so be sure to ask your partner if he or she likes what you are doing. Also be aware that what a person wants in terms of nipple play can vary with their state of sexual arousal.

Reader's Comments

"Kissing my breast depends upon my mood. Sometimes I like being touched gently with fingertips and then gentle circles of a tongue followed by a very light sucking on the nipples."

female age 27

"Most of the sensitivity is in the nipple, but there are good feelings from having the whole breast caressed and sucked. Swirling your tongue around the nipple is good. Sucking the nipple is great! Biting the nipple is a MAJOR no-no." *fem. age 34*

"Depending on how aroused I am I like to be sucked hard and even gently bitten on the nipple." *female age 45*

"There doesn't seem to be any logical pattern or reason behind it, but sometimes even touching the breast area can hurt. Other times, pretty much of anything is O.K." *female age 32*

🐄 🐄 🐄

Chapter 17
Oral Sex: Popsicles & Penises

 Some women truly enjoy giving oral sex to a man. It provides them with feelings of intimacy and closeness that can be both soothing and erotic. It also gives some women a feeling of power and control. Other women don't find anything special about doing oral sex, but will go down on a guy if he enjoys it. And some women would rather suck on a rusty old pipe than let their lips stray south of a man's beltline.

Whatever your preference, this chapter offers tips and techniques about giving oral sex to the male of the species. It starts with a candid discussion about male ejaculate, and then offers various techniques for giving splendid blow jobs. It also includes a series of suggestions for the man who is receiving oral sex — things he can do to help make it a neat experience for both partners.

When Gay Guys Blow

Straight women often get the feeling that they need to swallow a guy's ejaculate in order to give a truly fine blow job. If this were true, you'd think it would apply just as much in the gay community where the giver of the blow job knows exactly what it feels like to receive a blow job. But that's not true. Gay guys usually don't swallow when giving blow jobs. As one gay male reader says, "No way am I going to do all that work getting a partner to come and not watch him ejaculate. Besides, I don't exactly love the taste."

Of course, you might love swallowing whatever your man can pump. But do it only because you want to and not because there's some Emily Post of Blow Jobs who says it has to be.

To Swallow Or Not To Swallow—Taste & Texture

Considering what happens if you suck on a penis for long enough, a woman who gives a man oral sex eventually has to decide if she wants to swallow his ejaculate. While some women don't mind swallowing, others find it weird. For many women the salient factors

are how they feel about the guy and how they feel within the relationship. For others, it's a matter of taste and texture.

Different guys come in different flavors. They also have different textures and volumes. For instance, one man's ejaculate might be viscous while another's is thin. One man might taste good while another tastes bitter or salty, or as a female reader states: "My current lover tastes great, I like swallowing his ejaculate. But when my former boyfriend came, it felt like battery acid in the back of my mouth." Another reader comments that she has no problem with the taste or texture of male ejaculate, but that it sometimes upsets her stomach. A British sex expert with a Margaret Thatcher-like voice says that male ejaculate is an acquired taste, like swallowing raw oysters. She says it's nothing to get worked-up over. We're not so sure, given how nobody around here likes swallowing raw oysters. As for the smell of male ejaculate, it's like a weak solution of Clorox—original scent rather than Lemon Fresh or Spring Rain.

Who knows what to advise about swallowing male ejaculate, except to say that a man shouldn't push the issue one way or another unless he is willing to swallow a mouthful of his own, although the actual amount is closer to a teaspoonful. *Suggestions for how to give a really good blow job without swallowing are listed later in this chapter, so are tips for improving the taste of male ejaculate.*

To Swallow Or Not To Swallow, Hormonal Considerations

Women sometimes wonder if they are going to get a dose of male hormones when they swallow male ejaculate. Not to worry. While the testicles produce the lion's share of male hormone, these hormones are not released into a man's ejaculate. Instead, they are dumped directly into the blood stream where they can have an impact on the rest of his body. A woman is not going to sprout a beard or grow a big Adam's apple from swallowing her partner's cum. She will get more male hormone from giving him a hickey. As for the question of calories, the only way you will gain weight from male ejaculate is if it makes you pregnant, and it is biologically impossible to get pregnant from oral sex alone.

Regarding the issue of health, ejaculate from a healthy guy has far fewer germs than saliva. It seldom causes an allergic reaction. The main health concern about male sex fluids is if the man has a sexually transmitted disease, which is somewhat common these days. More on STDs in Chapter 39: Birth Control & Gnarly Sex Germs.

Suggestions For Giving A Really Good Blow Job

Going down on a man isn't as much a mystery as going down on a woman, given how the penis is pretty much in your face from start to finish. The childhood experience of sucking on popsicles will give you an idea of how to begin. However, popsicle sucking does not make for an excellent blow job unless your man keeps his penis in the freezer.

There are many different kinds of blow jobs. Some women like to give blow jobs that include lots of kissing and licking, others mainly suck on the thing and do fine at that. Using your hands while giving oral sex also adds an extra dimension.

It never hurts to ask your partner what he likes, but these discussions are usually more productive after you've been down on him a time or two. The shared experience provides both of you with a point of reference, e.g., he can say, "I really liked it when you..."

Dozens of tips are listed in the pages that follow—just about anything you'd ever want to know about giving a really good blow job. But if the doorbell is ringing and you need a quick primer in ten lines or less, you might start by tossing the lucky guy on his back. Lick his penis to get it wet with your saliva. This provides pleasure and lubrication. Then, make a ring around the penis with your lips. This will create a gasket. Slide your head up and down, but only as far as you feel comfortable. There is no need to suck. Each time you pull your head up, suction will build naturally in your mouth. *But please, don't take our word for it.* Try it first on one of your fingers. Notice how good this makes your finger feel!

Of course, there are about a hundred other factors to consider, from what to do with your saliva to keeping yourself from gagging.

Gag Prevention

Some women complain that they gag when giving blow jobs. When asked if they ever bothered to tell their partners about this, the gagging girls usually reply "no." Perhaps their male partners were inconsiderate oafs, or maybe these men had trouble reading the women's minds. Whatever the case, many men would do back flips to please a partner if only they were told what she does or doesn't like. The last thing most men want is to hurt or displease a woman sexually.

What follows are four suggestions to help keep yourself from being gagged while giving a blow job, but the most important and intelligent suggestion is clearly the first:

TELL HIM! If he thrusts and it gags you, let him know. Tell him that the two of you need to work on it, because you enjoy giving him blow jobs except for that part. Be specific! If a little thrusting is OK, help him recognize the difference between good and painful thrusting.

FIST ON SHAFT. Make a fist around the shaft of your lover's penis, with your little finger resting on his pubic bone. This will give you four knuckles' worth of washer or buffer. If your man has an average-sized penis, there should be less than three remaining inches to go into your mouth. If your man is luckier than most, use two hands instead of one, like you would if swinging a baseball bat or even a golf club. As an added benefit, keeping your fingers around the shaft can be nice for him if you use them to pump the foreskin or pull it taut. More on the pleasure aspects later.

ON HIS BACK. Some guys thrust involuntarily when they come. To deal with this, keep your bronco on his back and position your body between his legs. When he is close to coming keep both of your hands around the base of his penis and your forearms flat against his pelvis. The weight of your body distributed against his pelvic region will help discourage any unwanted thrusting, and if he does thrust it will pull you up with him.

BALLS. Clamp your thumb and forefinger together around the upper part of the man's scrotum where it attaches to his groin. This will place the testicles in the palm of your hand. Some men find this pleasurable, especially if the woman gently pulls downward. Then, if he thrusts more than you want, increase the downward pull, as though you were pulling back on a horse's reins.

Positions For Penis Sucking

A highly effective position for doing oral sex is to place yourself between your partner's legs, facing his body. This gives your tongue direct access to the most sensitive parts of his penis and scrotum, and the angle minimizes the tendency for the head of the penis to bang against your molars. It's a comfortable position for most women, and it lets a man watch you giving him head, which some men find to be reassuring, loving and a turn-on. Another variation is to sit, kneel, or crouch in front of your partner while he is standing or sitting.

Some couples like the woman to straddle the guy's chest. In this position, she faces southward like she would if the couple were doing 69. This can be particularly nice for the guy if staring at his sweetheart's crotch and rear end provide an extra turn-on. But it places her mouth in a lousy position to give his penis maximum stimulation, as it puts her tongue in contact with the backside of the penis which isn't as sensitive as the front.

In the positions mentioned so far, the guy lies still and the woman provides the up and down motion. Another way of doing a blow job is where the woman keeps her head still and the guy moves his penis in and out of her mouth. The fancy term for this that nobody but the pope ever uses is *irrumation*, which is Latin for "altar boy, hold still!"

The position the woman usually takes in irrumation or "face-fucking" is on her back with her head propped up on a pillow. The man sits astride her upper body and gently thrusts his penis in her mouth. The woman lets the guy do some of the work and she has good access to his testicles and rear end, or she can easily masturbate while he's receiving the blow job. The couple can also alternate penis thrusting with French kissing. On the other hand, some women become bored or feel claustrophobic giving a blow job with the guy on top, or they fear that the man might be rough or thrust too deep. Putting your hand around the shaft of his penis while he thrusts will greatly decrease any chance that he might thrust too deep.

A final position that some couples enjoy is where they lay side-by-side, with the woman's mouth in front of the man's genitals. She can lay her head on a pillow and do the up-and-down motion by moving her neck or he can thrust with his hips. On the other hand, one of her arms may be out of commission because she's lying on her side, and her head motions are limited.

Deep Throat Myth—Where To Suck And Where Not To

You wouldn't stick an entire popsicle down your throat, so why try it with a guy's dick? Truly great blow jobs have nothing to do with deep-throating a man. Deep-throating is more of a novelty than something that makes a penis feel great. If your man insists that you deep throat him, go to the market and buy a vegetable that's the same size as his erect penis, hand it to him and say, "OK, let's see you shove this thing down your throat!"

Also, don't confuse a penis with a clitoris and think that every square centimeter is packed with thousands of nerve endings. As was said in the porn film *How To Perform Fellatio:* "The most sensitive part of the penis is the top part, so stop wasting your time on the bottom," and the male actor who uttered this profound statement had a penis with a great deal of bottom part to suck if he had so wanted.

The average pe.iis has certain parts that are sensitive, and other parts that are mostly for show. For some guys, especially those who are uncircumsized, the head might be really sensitive. Work out with your man if and how he likes you to suck or lick the head. Also, there is a sensitive nickel-sized area just below the head on the side of the penis that's away from his body when he has an erection. It's called the frenulum, and some guys can be brought to orgasm from stimulating this area alone. (See the illustration on page 65.) The seam of the penis that runs from the scrotum to the head usually responds to tender kisses, as does the entire scrotum.

Note: If you still insist on deep-throating your man, two resources to consider are the videotape "How To Perform Fellatio" with tonsil aerobics host Karen Summer, and the book "Ultimate Kiss" by Steve & Jacqueline Franklin. Do not get the video by the same name, as it has nothing to do with the book and is truly dreadful. It might also help if you position your body so you are either on top of the man in a 69-type position or are lying on your back with your head over the edge of the bed. These positions will help to straighten the pathway down your throat. They are better for deep-throating but not nearly as good for regular blow jobs.

Blow Job Basics

Several tips and techniques are listed in this section for giving a really good blow job. Enjoy!

Slobber: People who are neat freaks often try to swallow all of their own drool when giving blow jobs. Such people have been known to nearly drown. Smart women let gravity carry their saliva down a lover's penis. They can also use it as a lubricant for pumping the bottom part of the penis with one hand while doing the upper part by mouth. Don't hesitate to toss a towel under the man's rear or to wedge one beneath his testicles; that way there won't be a big wet spot or stain on the mattress or couch.

If It's Still Soft: Some women enjoy sucking on a soft penis and feeling it grow inside their mouth. Just because it's soft, don't think for a moment that each kiss, lick and suck doesn't feel exquisite. One of the few times when a man can be totally passive and feel no need to perform sexually is while he is receiving a blow job. Don't assume it's a negative sign if it takes a while to get hard or if it doesn't get hard at all. A guy can still have a really enjoyable orgasm with a soft dick.

Lubrication For Licking: When you first lick a man's genitals coat your lips and tongue with extra saliva. This will make it feel better. Honest. If you suffer from the dreaded pre-blow-job-dry mouth, try sucking on a mint beforehand to help kickstart your salivary glands.

Teeth: Some women wrap their lips over their teeth when giving a blow job, given how the mere hint of teeth on the penis scares the tar out of some men. However, a set of sexy choppers can sometimes feel erotic, assuming you're not in a pit bull kind of mood. Ask, experiment, and see what you come up with.

Little Kisses & Flickering Tongues: Never hesitate to lavish your man's genitals or any other part of his body with neat little flicks of the tongue or sweet little lip locks. The kisses not only feel nice, but they allow you to rest your jaw without totally stopping the action. It usually works better if the area you are flicking your tongue over is already lubricated with saliva or massage oil, so get it good and wet.

Twisting Your Head: Twisting your head when going up and down the penis (in a corkscrew pattern) provides a higher level of stimulation, especially when focused on the upper half of the penis. Try it on your finger.

Further Twisting/Corkscrew Action (for the experienced): While on the upstroke, wait until you are half way up the shaft and put the tip of your tongue under the ridge of the penis head. Not only does your tongue press against the sensitive frenulum while your head is twisting, but the tip of your tongue adds extra stimulation to the sensitive ridge.

The Shirley Temple: You can lick the penis with the pointed end of your tongue, or you can soften your tongue and give it a long flat lick that covers more real estate. The latter is called a "Shirley Temple" because it's similar to the way a person licks a big lollipop.

Uncut: For Men Who Aren't Circumcised: Without retracting his foreskin, stick the tip of your tongue inside his foreskin and run it in a circle around the head of his penis. You can pull the foreskin down with your fingertips. NOTE: Guys who are uncut usually have a more sensitive penis head than guys who are circumcised.

The Long Lick: Mother nature left a seam on the penis that runs from just below the head to half-way down the scrotum. Never hesitate to take a long, wet lick from beneath your partner's testicles all the way to the tip of his penis, along the length of the seam.

Using Your Hand As A Buffer: Just about anyone who writes about oral sex recommends that women who are new to it or who are giving a blow job to a new partner wrap one hand around the shaft of the penis while sucking the upper part. This protects you from accidental gagging, and is especially recommended if you don't yet know how to read the man's body reactions or they are unpredictable. Protecting yourself in this way can also add to his pleasure, by using your hand to pull his foreskin taut or by pumping the shaft with it.

Making The Foreskin Taut: Using your hand to pull the skin taut over the shaft of the penis can sometimes enhance the pleasure of a blow job. It might also encourage the man to come sooner if that's what you want. The way you do it is by wrapping your thumb and forefinger, or your entire fist, around the shaft of the penis an inch or so above the base. Then pull it down to the base. This makes the skin tighter on the penis and usually increases the sensitivity in the upper part of the penis.

Pumping The Shaft: While your lips are focusing on the upper part of the penis, there's no reason why you can't be pumping the bottom part of the shaft with your hand or fingers. Let your saliva flow down the shaft, lubricating both it and your hand, and start pumping.

🐟 **Pumping The Shaft, Part II:** Some women synchronize the shaft pumping with their head bobbing, so their hand follows just beneath their lips at all times.

🐟 **The Vacuum Factor (Hoover Fellatis):** Some men will like it if you draw a light vacuum with your mouth. One way to draw a vacuum is to take as much of the penis in your mouth as feels comfortable, make a seal around the shaft with your lips, and suck some of the air out of your mouth. Then, as you pull your head back, a vacuum is created.

🐟 **Na-Na-Na-Nipples.** Some guys have nipples that are highly sensitive. Caressing them with your finger while doing oral sex might add to the man's overall pleasure. Other men won't like this at all. The best way to find out is to experiment and seek feedback.

🐟 **Inner Thighs And Other Places.** The inner thighs of both men and women can be extremely sensitive. There's no reason why you can't lick and suck on your man's inner thighs, or caress them with a free hand while giving him a blow job.

🐟 **Fingers In His Mouth.** When you are blowing him, you might try sticking your fingers in his mouth. Some guys will find this added touch to be very erotic.

🐟 **Perineum (Between The Testicles And Rear End):** There is an area behind the testicles called the perineum that is often overlooked but has the potential for wonderful feelings. Licking this area can light some guys up. A gentle finger massage down here can also add an extra dimension to oral sex.

🐟 **The Blow Hole:** This is the little slit in the head of the penis where the ejaculate comes out. It might be fun to explore it with the tip of your tongue.

🐟 **Rear End:** Some men find that a finger on or up the rear when receiving a blow job can feel wonderful. Some men claim that the most intense orgasms they have ever had is when a woman was giving them oral sex while massaging their prostate. Other men hate this sort of thing. Also, a small vibrator up the rear might catch some men's attention, and some couples enjoy rimming (oral-anal contact).

For more on playing with his bum while giving him oral sex, see Chapter 21.

Visual Glee. There are plenty of men who enjoy watching a woman give them head. Some women might be offended by the notion, thinking that this has something to do with submission. If the truth be known, the chances are that the man is way too appreciative to be thinking anything other than adoring thoughts. **Note:** In her video on how to give blow jobs, porn star Nina Hartley comments "It took me a long time to be able to do a blow job in the light and not get embarrassed." (She apparently got over it.) Ms. Hartley also says "Some people get scared of erections; I used to be terrified of them before I understood that they're just a guy's way of saying 'Hi.'" (Nina's epiphany?)

Oral Intermission: If your mouth gets tired, do your man by hand for a while, or run your hair over his genitals. You might also masturbate for a bit, giving him the treat of watching you do that. Some women say that they give their best blow jobs when they are just as turned-on as their partners. Don't be afraid to let him know about it if you are!

Tap & Hum: It might enhance the feeling of a blow job if you occasionally hum or tap the shaft of the penis when the head and frenulum are in your mouth.

Hot, Cold, Etc.: Never hesitate to suck on ice cubes to make your mouth cold, or drink hot liquids to make it extra warm before and during oral sex. The same applies to licking nipples.

Going Down After Intercourse: Some women enjoy giving blow jobs after intercourse. They find it highly erotic to suck on a penis after it has been inside of them. Other women don't like this at all.

Size: Oral sex may be problematic if your man's salami is on the enormous side. While it may be difficult to suck, you can still lick and kiss it into submission. Also use your hands to pump the shaft while focusing your efforts on the frenulum and head. Chapter 35: Techno 'Breasts & Weenie Angst lists a number of tips for having sex

An Effective Way To Get Him Off Orally Without Swallowing

This feels so good that a lot of guys won't be able to tell that you aren't swallowing unless they are actually looking. The trick is to focus your lip action on the sensitive frenulum area while cradling the penis with your hand. This area is just beneath the head of the penis. Use lots of saliva and put plenty of tongue into it—almost like you are French kissing this part of his penis. Occasionally fill your hand with your hot steamy breath. This also works well if your lover's penis is a little on the huge side and you'd more easily fit a zeppelin in a one-car garage than get it in your mouth.

---

with the extra-well endowed, and the illustration above might give you a few ideas.

🐟 **A Little Help From Your Friends:** If you have a friend who is more experienced at giving blow jobs, consider asking her (or him) for pointers, but keep in mind that you will soon be evolving your own personal style. What you do will also vary depending on the guy who you are doing it with.

Cujones

What you do with your hands sometimes separates the good blow jobs from the great. Better blow jobs often include lots of finger and hand work. For instance, at the same time that your mouth is on his penis, consider caressing your partner's testicles. Also, there might be places along the lower shaft of the penis — the part that is covered by the testicles — that respond nicely to fingertip massage. Massaging this area with your free hand when giving a blow job can substantially increase the sensation. Make handplay an active part of the blow job, and he's not as likely to notice when your lips need a rest.

Two Balls, One Tongue

> "I love my boyfriend's testicles. I like taking them into my mouth one at a time and sucking on them. The skin on the sack is really soft and feels great in my mouth."   *female age 23*

Some men will feel highly appreciative if you take one or both of their testicles in your mouth. Don't fear doing this. Just go slowly the first couple of times until you get the hang of it. The skin around the testicles (scrotum) also loves being licked and kissed The sensitivity of the scrotum has been compared to the outer lips of women's genitals.

If he doesn't have an erection, you might be able to fit his testicles in your mouth as well as his penis.

Sage Blow Job Advice

In the video "How To Perform Fellatio" porn starlet/host Karen Summer encourages women to listen to the man's body. Ms. Summer says that if the man moves, move with him, but once he starts to moan or grunt, keep doing exactly what you were just doing, because it's working extremely well.

Right Before He Comes

There might be certain things that you can do just before a man starts to come that will increase his pleasure. Some women wrap a hand around the bottom part of the penis so the entire shaft feels like it's inside a vagina. Others place their fingertips along the seam on the front side of the penis and apply a bit of pressure. They might be able to feel the ejaculate surge through the penis when they do this. Some men might appreciate it if you increased the vacuum in your mouth as they are about to come. Others enjoy it if you hold or caress their testicles, or massage the part of the shaft that's beneath them. Since this is a highly individual matter, issue a warning that you would like to experiment with a couple of new things and seek his feedback.

Note: An extremely intelligent and highly experienced prostitute who consulted on this chapter said she finds that many men like to have their nipples pinched as they are about to come.

Learn When He's Coming

If you know the right signs to look for, you can often learn when your man is about to come. This will give you options if you don't want to swallow.

While it's not like Mt. St. Helens, there are definite signs. Until you learn his body's signs, ask him to tell you when he's about to come. But after a while, you'll hopefully notice that his little willy starts to swell and contort just before it spurts. You can feel this in your mouth. Also, a hand over his testicles may also be a good source of information, as they tend to draw close to his body when he is about to squirt. In addition, his body might tighten up or his hips might give a small thrust when coming is inevitable.

If You Don't Like The Way He Tastes

If you know you're not going to swallow, keep a hand around the base of his penis while you are sucking on the upper half. As the signs of ejaculation present themselves, free your mouth from the line of fire, slide your hand up the shaft, to just below the head, and start pumping for Old Glory. Be sure your grip is firm and pump fast and furious. This is no time for a gentle touch.

Another way of bringing him off without swallowing is shown in the illustration on page 202. Also, you might read the part at the

end of this chapter titled "Improving The Way Your Ejaculate Tastes."
Here are some other suggestions that you might find helpful:

◄ **Tartar Control...** Sticking a bit of toothpaste in your mouth
before inserting a penis can improve the taste greatly. The same is
true for sucking on a mint beforehand. The flavor of blowjobs can also
be enhanced by sipping on your favorite sherry or liquor, or by glazing
your man's yam with things like honey, jam, or whipped cream.
Champagne blow jobs can also be fun. (While you might enjoy experimenting with minty liquors such as Creme de Menthe, be sure to do
a small test patch on the side of the penis beforehand. While a little
menthol on the skin can feel great, especially when you blow on it, too
much can burn. It takes a few minutes for the full intensity of the burn
to peak, so wait awhile before declaring your test a success.)

◄ **The Condom Factor.** A competent prostitute can slip a condom
over a man's penis with her mouth alone and he will never know it is
there. This suggests that the problems some guys have with wearing
condoms might be psychological. (So what else is new?) Here are two
highly acceptable approaches to consider if you want your man to use
a condom while blowing him but he balks. 1.) In a loud and clear voice,
say "Forget it, Charlie! If you think it tastes THAT great, suck on it
yourself." [Actually, he probably would if he could, and maybe even
tried a couple of times when he was a kid.] 2.) Try making the whole
process of oral sex more fun and pleasurable for both of you. If he
knows that the blow job is going to be lots of fun, putting a condom on
won't be such a big deal. **Condom Tip:** You might try sticking a drop of
water-based lube or contraceptive jelly on the head of a man's penis
right before bagging it with a condom. Once you have rolled the
condom over his penis, squish the lube around the entire head. Some
guys say that sloshing around in a rubber that's been lubricated on the
inside feels better. If you don't have any lube handy, hock a small wad
of loogie on the head of his penis before putting the condom on.
Non-lubricated: If you use a condom for oral sex, try finding ones that
aren't lubricated. Condoms with lubrication often taste bitter. There
are also varieties of condoms made of flavored latex. At the time

of this book's printing, a condom that many people favored for blow jobs was the unlubricated Gold Circle. **Saran Wrap:** If you're in a jam or don't exactly cherish the taste of latex, you might experiment with Saran Wrap. It's neat because you can see through it, and you'll probably like the feel of it better than latex. You can lay it over the penis if you're using the technique that's shown on page 202, or if you decide to tent the penis with it, put the gathers on the side of the penis that's away from the frenulum and faces his stomach when he's got an erection.

🐟 **To The Rear.** If you are going to swallow but want to decrease the taste, place his penis as far back in your mouth as you can while still being comfortable. Then start swallowing fast. Unless he comes in buckets, it should decrease the amount of ejaculate that hits your taste buds.

🐟 **Sublingual Ejaculation.** The following tip is mentioned in the excellent book "Tricks — 125 Ways To Make Good Sex Better" by Jay Wiseman: When it feels like your man is close to coming, put your tongue over the head of his penis so the ejaculate does not squirt directly on the taste-bud side of your tongue.

🐟 **Let Him Help.** Some guys won't mind finishing themselves off with their own hand if you have taken the time and energy to give them a really good blow job. It might be a special treat if you kiss or suck on their testicles while they pump themselves to orgasm.

After He Comes

The head of the penis can become extremely sensitive immediately after orgasm. If you keep his penis in your mouth while he is coming, be sure to find out what he wants you to do while he is coming as well as after. Some guys might want you to keep it in your mouth, but to slow the action way down. Others will want you to stop completely at some point, and some might want you to keep going full force. Another option is to stop the sucking action, but to keep pumping the shaft with your hand.

The trick is to know when to stop or switch gears. The only way to learn this is from experience and plenty of helpful feedback on his part.

What If He Doesn't Come?

This is a situation where one woman's blessing is another woman's curse... A lot of guys don't come from oral stimulation alone. This doesn't mean that they didn't love every minute of your blow job. It doesn't mean that you haven't given a great blow job. It just means that they don't come from lip action alone.

Beginner Jitters

Some people who are new at sucking on penises, as well as some seasoned veterans, experience a brief paralysis or mini-dread right before the thing ejaculates. There are two things that might be helpful: reread the preceding section "If You Don't Like The Way He Tastes," and try to talk to your partner about it. Maybe he can give you plenty of warning so you can stop sucking and start pumping by hand long before the sticky stuff starts to ooze. With time and experience, it's likely any dread will go away.

Hands On Your Head

Men will often put their hands on a woman's head when she is giving oral sex. For most guys, this is a very loving gesture which can also be used to let a partner know what feels good and what doesn't. However, some men will put their hands on a woman's head and attempt to forcibly push it down onto the penis. Not only is this rude, but it is a form of assault. **Counterpoint:** One woman says, "This can be particularly exciting, when a man pushes my head down on his penis. But then again, I would never have sex with a man who I didn't love going down on. Also, you make a joke out of it when a woman grabs a man's head and pulls it into her crotch (page 237, *Feeling Like A Crash Test Dummie*), but call it assault when a man does this to a woman. You present a double standard that says we women are either more fragile than men, or are more easily offended when it comes to sex."

Research Findings

One of the more interesting research findings of all time is an article about the hazards of oral sex. It was written by a group of dentists and published in a medical journal called Military Medicine (145:787 1980 by Bellizi, Krakow and Plack—honest, his name is really Plack and he's a dentist). The article is titled "Soft Palate Trauma Associated With Fellatio."

The article tells about the daughter of an officer who was taken to the base hospital because she discovered a black and blue blotch in the back of her mouth. Several dentists eventually converged on the mystery blotch, trying to discover its origin. After eliminating all other possibilities, the dentists finally asked the officer dad to leave the room and then popped the big question: "Gotta boyfriend?"

In the back of the mouth near where the tonsils hang is a highly vascularized mass of tissue (highly vascularized means lots of small blood vessels). An erect penis hitting against this rather sensitive tissue can cause a bruise.

This isn't a common injury. It goes away like any other bruise, but it is a reminder that the woman, and not the man, should control the level of movement during a blow job. For instance, it's fine if she wants a lover to thrust in and out of her mouth, but the choice needs to be hers.

Ejaculate-Related Sinus Infections

When some women give blow jobs, they like to create a slight to moderate vacuum around their lover's penis. Men who enjoy this this kind of sensation find it to be heavenly. However, one problem with this kind of blow job can occur when a man comes with the head of his penis in the back part of the woman's vacuum pulling mouth. Apparently, the vacuum can sometimes draw ejaculate up into the woman's sinus cavities, creating what might be a cum-related sinus infection. If this is the case, the woman and her partner need to work on keeping the head of his penis in the middle part of her mouth when he is coming. Another solution, of course, is for him to wear galoshes (a condom).

Lasting Shorter (As Opposed To Lasting Longer)

"Why is it when you are giving men head, they take forever to come, but are so much faster when having intercourse?"

During vaginal intercourse, most guys make an effort to last as long as their partners want, sometimes successfully. While this might be a noble gesture during intercourse, it is not appreciated nearly as much during oral sex. That's because oral sex, whether done on a man or woman, tends to tucker out the mouth of the giver. So if the purpose of the blow job is to get the man off, he shouldn't necessarily try to hold back his climax just to show what a stud he is. As always, the best course of action is to discuss this matter with each other. If the male is one of those lucky guys who can pretty much come at will, he and his partner might devise a signal for when she'd like him to come. For the rest of us, the woman can ease up if we are approaching orgasm faster than she would like, or she can try some of the measures listed on page 75 to speed us up if her jaw is starting to feel as though it's about to drop off.

Do Men Blow Men Better Than Women Blow Men?

In researching different sexual techniques, we have reviewed many videos on sex. Video tapes made by women, many of whom are bisexual or lesbian, are often (although not always) a good source of information. The absolute worse source of information on any kind of sexual technique is traditional straight pornography.

It wasn't until this book was nearly finished that we took stock of the fact that no gay male videos had been reviewed—except those on male genital massage which were very informative. With this in mind, the following question about oral sex was posed:

*Is it possible that gay men give better
blow jobs than straight women?*

Armed with several gay videos, this question was examined by a small group of straight men and women, with the men being somewhat uncomfortable and the women being highly curious. Of course, the videos themselves caused a few unanticipated comments.

Most of the actors in the gay videos were exceptionally good looking and appeared totally straight. At the very least, these men were far more buff, attractive, and likable than many of the actors in traditional straight porn movies. Upon making these discoveries, one female reviewer exclaimed "It's a straight woman's nightmare, five naked men who are physical gods and I couldn't get one of them to look at me if his life depended on it!" Another woman viewer stated: "It's one of the few times in my life when I wish I had a penis. I'd let that cute blonde guy with the dimples and shoulders suck on it all night long."

As for conclusions, it seemed that these men handled each other's bodies with a kind of skill and effectiveness that some straight women might do well to imitate. However, the actual difference in doing oral sex wasn't so much from technique but rather from intensity, although the gay men did seem to use their hands more than most women do when giving blow jobs. It's difficult to put into words, but viewers had the feeling that the gay males (or gay male actors, anyway) had the ability to form an intense relationship with the penis itself. No matter how much they might enjoy doing oral sex, few women make an emotional connection with a man's genitals in quite the same way as these gay men appeared to.

Granted, few people who have ever worked with actors consider them to be representative of average people, or not the kind you would necessarily want as a close friend. And this guide's methodology is clearly lacking in scientific rigor, but the conclusion is, yes, it's quite possible that gay men blow men better than women blow men; at least in porn movies.

In turning the question around, it can be asked if women do a better job of giving oral sex to women. The answer? Who knows, although one female reader who is bisexual was kind enough to offer the following comment:

"Having received oral sex from many men and women, I believe womens' superiority at this activity is mostly myth."

An Oral Sex Postscript Over At The Beta House

Let's say a very straight, homophobic, college fraternity man who prides himself on his conquests with women has just volunteered to take part in an experiment on sexual response. The researchers put EKG leads on his chest, blindfold him, restrain his hands, and inform him that he is going to receive a blow job from "a very sexy blond." After receiving the blow job, he responds that she seemed to know more about how to please him orally than any sorority girl he's ever dated, and pleads for "her" phone number. We then inform him that the sexy blond is a male who starred in one of the previously mentioned gay videos, and show him a tape of the sexy blond doing him. Suddenly, our fraternity brother's enthusiasm isn't quite the same and he's not sure if the blow job was all that exceptional. More importantly, if this subject had been told the true identity of the sexy blond ringer before receiving the blow job, it is quite possible that he wouldn't have been able to get an erection or ejaculate.

In this hypothetical experiment, our subject's pleasure was determined as much by his fantasy of who was giving the blow job as the reality of it, assuming the blow job was competently done. MORAL: Never underestimate the role of the human mind in determining what does and doesn't work sexually.

Things A Guy Can Do To Help A Woman Who Is Trying To Give Him Oral Sex

Carefully read the preceding pages about bruising, gagging and lasting shorter. Also try reading this chapter with your partner. The keys to a really good blow job are being willing to explore and giving each other feedback.

Clean: Keep in mind most women won't go down on guys who smell rank. Whether you are going out on a first date or have been married for twenty years, here are a few things to keep in mind: **Clean #1:** Shower at least once a day, unless you are seriously into grunge or are a holdover from the court of Louis XIII, in which case bathing is irrelevant. **Clean #2:** Don't wear the same socks or underwear for more than one day without washing them. If everyone including the dog and cat run out of the room when you take your shoes off, use foot powder or spray. **Clean #3.** While not particularly popular with the organic crowd, deodorant can be a wonderful thing. **Clean #4:** Brush and floss your teeth often. **Clean #5:** Cut your fingernails and toenails often. **Clean #6.** If you wear cologne, ask your partner or a woman friend how she likes the smell of it, as well as how much you should use. Maybe she will prefer you without cologne. Some guys smell great from just bathing alone. On the other hand, she might like you marinated with a bit of citrus or spice.

Pube Tug: Tug on your pubic hair ahead of time so you'll pull out the strays that might end up in her mouth.

Attitude Issues: #1: Arrogance: Don't assume that a woman automatically wants to suck on your penis just because you like the way it feels. (How would you like to suck on some guy's dick?) Never take blow jobs for granted, and be thankful whenever you get one, even if your partner loves doing it. Tell her how good it feels. Also, it never hurts to ask yourself, "What have I done lately to deserve a blow job?" Did you give your partner a long lingering body massage? Did you help her with a project she's been struggling with? Did you do more than your share of the housework? Did you respond kindly in a situation where most men would have been jerks? Are you a loving partner and good friend?[1]

Attitude Issues: #2: Downfield Coverage: Think of what a catastrophe it would have been if Joe Montana or Steve Young had never discussed patterns and coverage with Jerry Rice. Oral sex requires a doer who is willing to accept helpful feedback, and a receiver who is willing to give it.

---

[1]Of course, there are those situations when you might be a total prince among men, but your partner doesn't like to give blow jobs, doesn't like sex at all, or likes sex but not with you.

🐟 **Attitude Issues: #3: Mutuality:** Never, ever cop an attitude such as "My last girlfriend blew me really well. Why can't you?" There are reasons why you aren't with your last girlfriend. Giving and receiving great blow jobs is a shared responsibility. With enough mutual caring, love and experimentation, the chances are excellent that you will soon be getting fine oral sex, but don't expect it to happen magically without your help.

🐟 **Attitude Issues: #4: The Deep Throat Fantasy:** Ever since the "Deep Throat" movie, some men have been all hyped up over the notion of having a woman do a sword swallowing act with their penis. Get over it. A throat is not a vagina, and any extra thrills you might get from this are mostly psychological. Besides, why would you encourage your partner to do something that might trigger a natural gagging reflex? And if she gags on your penis, do you really think she's going to be excited about putting it in her mouth again?

🐟 **Attitude Issues: #5: He Who Gives, Gets:** A fine way to get great oral sex is to give great oral sex. This assumes that the rest of your relationship is in good shape. Some guys are great in bed, but total jerks otherwise. Do not expect that being great in bed will make up for being a selfish person. Some women will overlook bad manners and social lunacy for a good lay, but they tend to have their own emotional problems and will make your life a living hell in other ways.

🐟 **Asking Vs. Not Asking:** Every once in a while you might have a really horrible day or week and are totally frazzled and in desperate need of a blow job lest you decompensate even further and have to be hauled off to the loony bin. If you don't abuse the privilege and have a loving partner who hasn't had an equally bad day or week, she will usually do the mercy blow job even if she's not particularly into it. For this type of situation, it is fine to ask (OK, beg) for a blow job. However, in the course of normal lovemaking, it might not be such a good idea to routinely ask for oral sex. That's because some women don't take well to being pestered for blow jobs. Granted, they might love blowing you and will do so often, but only if it's from their own initiative. Of course, there are other women who are just fine with being asked.

🐟 **Improving The Way Your Ejaculate Tastes:** Some people claim that vegetarians, both male and female, taste better than their carnivore brethren, or maybe this is just propaganda from cows and chickens. At the very least, red meat is said to make some men taste strongly. Dairy products are said to make ejaculate taste bad, but not nearly as bad as asparagus. Also, smoking and/or drinking coffee might cause a guy's ejaculate to taste strong or bitter. (Perhaps Starbucks can formulate a new blend of beans and call it "Ejaculate Lite." Also, the combination of smoking and coffee drinking make for hideous smelling breath.) A guy might also try holding off on the garlic and pasta sauce to see if it improves the way he tastes. One common suggestion for improving the taste of male ejaculate is to eat fruit or celery each day. Especially pineapple and apples. The sugar in the fruit is supposed to give a guy's ejaculate a bit of a sweet edge. Perhaps this is just useless folklore. However, if this is what a partner wanted before doing more blow jobs, most of us guys would happily go to work each morning munching on a few stalks of celery and finishing our lunches with slices of fruit. Whatever the case, if your partner is willing to be the taster, experiment with different combinations of food. Does ingesting a little cinnamon make any difference in the way you taste? What happens if you drink less coffee or eat less broccoli?

Bitter taste due to infections: If your partner says that your ejaculate is really bitter, consider seeing a urologist to screen out the possibility of an infection in your prostate or urethral glands. Although you might not be feeling any pain, it's still possible to have an infection. Unfortunately, in this day and age of HMOs, you will probably need to see a family physician or internist first, and might be a bit embarrassed saying "Heather says my cum tastes bitter." (Urologists see genitals all day long, and it's usually easier to say something like that to them.) In either case, rather than telling the receptionist or nurse the exact reason for the appointment, you might just say that you suspect having a urinary tract infection. Then tell the physician the real reason once you see him or her in private.

Reader's Comments

"I am certain that women would give more blow jobs if they didn't feel like they had to swallow!" *female age 43*

"Cum is not a gourmet treat, but not unpleasant either. I'd rather be eating mocha chip ice cream, but getting there isn't half as much fun. My partner's orgasm is often a total turn-on for me, and occasionally just a relief that the blow-job is now over with." *female age 47*

"I don't find oral sex repulsive in the least if he is conscious of good hygiene. If he smells bad down there it's a turn-off for me." *female age 34*

"I swear by pineapple, it helps take the bitter taste away." *female age 24*

"It feels funny when he squirts in my mouth. His cum often gives me an upset stomach so I usually spit it out." *female age 23*

"If I'm in the mood it's really sensual. If I'm not it's like a job." *female age 43*

"It is a major power trip for me if he comes in my mouth. I like knowing I have the ability to take this big strong man and turn him into a sack of jello." *female age 37*

"It is great! I like running my tongue around the head and sliding it in and out of my mouth. I like to take his penis in my mouth as far as possible and rub my tongue on the underside of it, pushing the head into the roof of my mouth. It seems to drive him crazy!" *female age 37*

"When it comes to blow jobs, let the lucky son of a bitch treat you like a queen, honey, because you are." *female age 48*

"More than anything it feels so good because I am in control."

female age 23

"I have to open my mouth wider than normal and it gets tired pretty fast. I don't really like it much, but he loves having it so it makes me feel really good and loved to be giving him oral sex."

female age 32

"I never was very good at blow jobs until I had a lover who had a small penis. Then I felt comfortable with him in my mouth."

female age 45

"I like to give head, so I don't need much persuasion. I get really wet from giving someone that kind of pleasure, and I always feel so powerful when I do it." *female age 23*

"It feels very sensual if he lets me take it at my own pace. I think the penis has the most wonderful velvety skin." *female age 38*

"I only like it if I can keep the hair out of my mouth. I enjoy it only because I know he enjoys it so much." *female age 35*

"I like it. I especially like the little leaks before he comes, it gets me excited to know he is so excited. I think cum has an interesting taste, sort of fizzy." *female age 38*

"I have discovered that we both find it erotic to have him come on my face or on my breasts when I give him head. I don't care for the taste of his semen." *female age 22*

"I find it helpful to open my mouth a bit when he's coming, then swallow quickly." *female age 26*

"I really don't like it when he comes in my mouth. I kind of gag on it." *female age 26*

"I used to tell my partner that I was semen-intolerant." *fem. age 26*

"It's O.K. as long as I can spit it out. I don't like to swallow it." *female age 43*

"One thing that's really neat about sucking on a guy's cock is watching it change shape, color, and get harder as it gets more aroused. You're right up there in the front row! You don't get that with intercourse." *female age 42*

"It's fun to take a limp penis, put it in your mouth, and suck on it until it hardens." *female age 37*

"I've observed that not all guys come as much: some have very little, and other lots and lots!" *female age 27*

"Never forget to caress and tickle the balls." *female age 44*

"Usually it's very erotic and sexy, especially if I'm particularly in the mood to suck him. Sometimes (rarely) it feels too much, invasive." *female age 48*

"My lover likes to hold my head and slowly slide in and out of my mouth. I trust him to do that without going too deep or choking me." *female age 37*

"My mouth and hand work as a team. As I pull away with my mouth, I twist my hand almost like a cork screw." *female age 26*

From Female Readers For Men Who Are Receiving Blow Jobs:

"Be very clean. Feel free to moan when you feel pleasure. Speak up if there is something I am missing." *female age 30*

"Keep your genital area clean and pleasant smelling." *fem. age 34*

"Tell me what you like. If you want to grip the shaft or caress your testicles while I am sucking, go ahead and do so." *fem. age 37*

"I love to give head, but I hate to feel pressured into doing it. Also, remember what goes around comes around. If I'm the only one going down, I'll be less likely to do so again." *female age 26*

From Male Readers For Women Who Are Giving Blow Jobs:

"Please don't do it like they do in the porno flicks, where the girl just about bobs her head off. Not a turn-on." *male age 46*

"Don't be fooled by the name. Blowing has nothing to do with it."
male age 26

Chapter 18
Oral Sex: Vulvas & Honey Pots

Sometimes, having powerful feelings for a woman can leave a man with an insatiable need to kiss and lick her genitals. It's hard to explain why, but it's a primal need that can be triggered by a mere wink of her eye. Other men are happy to give a woman oral sex because it pleases her sexually, but aren't fully into it. And some men would rather eat a cat.

Whatever your preference or level of desire, this chapter is loaded with tips and techniques for giving a woman all of the oral pleasure her heart and thighs could possibly want.

Talking To Elvis From Between Your Sweetheart's Thighs

It's a funny thing about oral sex, at least when you are a guy on the giving end. The woman who you are giving oral sex to, a person whom you know and often love, sometimes just disappears. All that's left is a strange, twitching, moaning protoplasm which only partially resembles the person who was there just minutes ago. You are left virtually alone, with your tongue feeling like it's running the Boston Marathon. You might as well be talking to Elvis. After it's over, you might want to ask "Hey, where did you go?" but you learn not to because she'll usually just give you a big smile and want to curl up in your arms.

Comment: One female reader offers a possible explanation. She says that when she is receiving oral sex, she isn't as aware of her partner's presence, so it's easier to let her fantasies run wild. She wouldn't necessarily want to tell him "where she went," since her fantasy might have been with someone else! Little does she know, guys who are sexually secure might get off on hearing about her fantasy escapades, even if they're with someone else.

The Way Women Taste

The previous chapter on blow jobs begins with a discussion of how guys taste. This chapter turns the tables and talks about the way women taste.

Most guys who enjoy going down on women know that some vulvas taste great, while others don't exactly leave fond memories. Beyond that, men are fairly useless when it comes to discussing genital taste. Lesbian and bisexual women, however, will talk your ear off about the subject of how women taste. What follows are some of their comments. But, first is a brief discussion about female genital chemistry.

While most of the skin on the human body has a pH between 6.0-7.0, the optimal pH of the vulva and vagina is between 4.0-5.5. (Vaginal secretions contain lactic acid which helps to maintain the lower pH.) A lower pH helps eliminate unfriendly bacteria which can cause anything from a rank odor to vaginal infections. Unfortunately for women's genitals, most body soap has a pH of between 6.0 and 14. This can raise the pH of the vulva and may challenge nature's own system for eliminating unfriendly bacteria. It might be why women who bathe more than once a day tend to get more vaginal infections.

Fortunately, there are now low pH soaps with lactic acid that are made especially for women's genitals. They contain no artificial deodorants or fancy scents. One woman who has been using the soap for almost a year says that it allows her genitals to stay fresh for a full twenty-four hours. Another says she no longer hesitates to let her husband go down on her twelve hours after her last shower. Physicians especially recommend this soap for women who have frequent infections.

The bad news is that as of press time, few of these soaps were available to American women.[1] They are mainly being sold in France, Italy, Switzerland, and Ireland. Interestingly, gynecologists in those countries can't agree on exactly which pH is optimal, so the soap is made with a slightly different pH in each country.

---

[1] Perhaps the big pharmaceutical giants make more money from the treatment of vaginal infections than from their prevention, which could be why they don't make the soap available to American women.

The good news is, one American company does produce a low-pH soap that some women use on their genitals. The name is Nature's Plus Natural Beauty Cleansing Bar. It has a pH of 4.5. Unfortunately, it does not have a lactic acid base and was not formulated with women's genitals in mind, but some readers say it is far kinder to their genitals than regular soap. To find where it is sold, call (800) 937-0500.

Soaps aside, here are a few comments that bisexual women and lesbians had to say about the taste of their female lovers:

🐦 "One woman who I loved going down on suddenly began tasting different—not nearly as good. As it turned out, she had started taking vitamin pills. It was never a problem if she took herbs, but vitamin pills would ruin the way she tasted."

🐦 "A former girlfriend was a tennis pro. Sometimes she would play tennis for a few hours and I could go down on her without her taking a shower and she would still taste sweet. There are other women whom I have gone down on right after we showered, and they still didn't taste good. In making my own inquiries, I found that the sweeter tasting women didn't eat red meat."

🕊 "Some women spend more time filing their toenails than they do taking care of their pussies... When I'm in the shower, I always separate the lips of my vulva and use a wash cloth to clean between them. I'm also careful about little bad-tasting pieces of gunk that might collect under my clitoral hood. These are what uncircumcised males get under their foreskin if they don't pull it back and clean it." **Note:** A Q-tip dipped in mineral oil works well to get rid of any "little pieces of gunk" or smegma that stick under the clitoral hood.

~Talking With Tongues~
Suggestions For Pleasing A Woman With Your Mouth

According to some women, a smart and loving tongue between their legs can offer feelings of pleasure that fingers or a penis simply can't. Yet many a male merely pushes his face into a woman's crotch, sticks his tongue out like when the doctor asks you to say "ahhh," and wags the thing mindlessly.

This is about as smart as pitching out when nobody's on base. What follows are suggestions to help cure a nagging case of tongue wagging.

On The Tip Of Your Tongue

The human tongue, like the penis, can be made hard or soft. To understand the difference between a soft and hard tongue, spend the next couple of minutes licking the palm of your hand. This may not be as much fun as when Lulu Belle sits on your face, but a moment's practice on the palm of your hand can be a good way to learn about subtle variations in oral sex technique.

For starters, if you have just been installing a new head gasket or fertilizing the lawn, it might be a good idea to wash your hands. Then, pretend your palm is a woman's vulva and give it a good licking.

The first thing you might notice is how quickly the end of your tongue goes dry. This creates drag or friction. The same thing can happen when you first start licking a woman's vulva. Men tend to assume that a tongue and vulva are naturally wet. But they aren't, which is why you'll need to coat your tongue with saliva before licking a woman's private parts. Not so much that you drool, but enough to blow a good-sized bubble. After a few minutes, saliva from your mouth will automatically run down your tongue and keep everything well-lubricated, but not necessarily at the start.

Next, you will probably find that your tongue is somewhat taut with the tip hard and pointed. Try to let it go soft, in a way that would cause you to slur your words if you were attempting to speak. You may need to push your hand closer to your face, since a soft tongue is not as long as a hard tongue. Some women will prefer a more rounded tongue when you are licking the naked underbelly of the clitoris, given how it isn't insulated by the clitoral hood.

This may all sound like French if you have yet to go down on a woman. Not to worry; no matter how experienced you might be, she will still need to teach you where and how she wants you to lick. This can take months or years. Also, it's normal to feel clumsy when you are with a new lover or if you haven't done oral sex in a while.

The Initial Approach — Getting There

"Gentle teasing brings me to an orgasm. I like him to start off gently, with light licks and kisses all over my vulva. I can't take too much pressure on my clitoris though, and sometimes that ruins it for me." *female age 23*

When you are shooting a freethrow, you don't want to hit the rim. When you are landing a plane, you don't want to brush the treetops. When you are going down on a woman, it's an entirely different story. The best approach to a woman's genitals is anything but direct.

Once you've been with a woman for awhile, you'll discover what body parts she likes to have licked. For instance, one woman might love it when you kiss her inner thighs or rear end, but hate it if you kiss her abdomen. Another woman might want just the opposite. Find the body parts close to her vulva that she likes having kissed, and spend plenty of time on them. Plant occasional kisses on her vulva, but only as a preview of what's to come.

Kissing and caressing in this way help assure a warm welcome when your tongue finally drops into your lover's saddle.

Your Goal: Orgasm Or Pleasure?

Some guys feel they haven't pleased a woman unless they have given her an orgasm. That would be fine if sex were football and orgasms were touchdowns, but this kind of philosophy can spoil your lovelife. Instead of trying to delight your lover's senses, you'll always be playing to her clitoris. This can get tedious.

Of course, there are times when it's important to be single-minded about a woman's orgasm, but not as a rule. You'll do a lot better if you let yourself have fun, be close and want her dearly. If your lips convey this when they are between her thighs, you'll have a leg up on most guys.

Beard Burn

When it comes to receiving oral sex, one thing that women often complain about is men's beards. Their advice: grow a full beard or keep your face clean shaven. Grunge does not feel good on a woman's thighs.

If you're the kind of guy who grows a five o'clock shadow ten minutes after you shave, find a favorite set of towels and drape one over each of her legs, like mechanics sometimes do on the fenders of cars when they are working on the engine.

Warning To The Wise

Three oral sex caveats:

🐦 Until shown otherwise, do not assume there are any similarities between the way you like your penis sucked and the way your partner likes having her genitals licked.

🐦 If your main exposure to oral lovemaking has been through watching porn videos, forget all you have ever seen. Rather than showing the back of a man's head buried between a woman's thighs, the porn industry has invented its own version of oral sex. In porn-oral sex, a woman sits with her legs about six miles apart while some guy tries to lick her vulva without blocking the camera shot. While this is good for the cameraman, it's not necessarily going to please a woman.

🐦 A mediocre lover always knows what a partner wants without having to ask. An accomplished lover is a wise grasshopper who implores a partner to give him copious amounts of advice.

Body Positions

There are some oral sex positions that might look great, but don't work as well as others. What follows is a description of four oral sex positions where your heads are both pointing in the same direction. These provide the best face-to-crotch alignment, which means that when you lick, your tongue has clear access to the tip and shaft of the clitoris.

🐤 Your sweetheart is on her back and you sit, kneel, or lie between her legs. In this position, you will be staring up at her navel, rib cage, and perhaps her face.

🐤 She can sit in a chair or on a bar stool, with you sitting or kneeling between her legs. To allow proper access, she'll need to slouch so you don't get a mouthful of chair cushion, oak or leatherette.

🐤 The two of you can lay on your sides, with your head between her thighs and the rest of your body behind hers, e.g. if you were standing in a swimming pool and she was sitting on your shoulders, but facing the other way so you couldn't see where you were going. It's like that, only you're laying on your sides.

🐤 Another oral sex position is when she is "sitting on your face." Go back to the swimming pool with her sitting on your shoulders. Again, she's facing the other way so you can't see a thing and you are getting a mouthful of bathing suit crotch material. Imagine if the two of you fell all the way back so you're on your back and she's above you on all fours. Get rid of the swim suits and trade the pool bottom for a bed, and there you have it.

There are other oral sex positions, like the ones you would use if you were doing 69. In these positions, your head is pointing in the opposite direction from hers and the face-to-crotch alignment is not optimal. When you open your eyes in these positions you usually get a close-up view of your sweetheart's butt cheeks, and your nose is nearly knocking on her rectum door.

Ground Zero

Perhaps you are a total pro at giving oral sex, or maybe you know more about the dark side of the moon than licking a woman's genitals. Regardless of your experience, what follows is a blueprint for giving really good oral sex—as long as you get reliable feedback from the woman you are trying it on.

🐦 **Saliva:** The tongue can be an abrasive little organ unless it is lubricated. Coat your lips and tongue with extra saliva as you approach your lover's vulva.

🐦 **Saliva & A Towel To Catch It:** Doing oral sex tends to make your salivary glands sing. Instead of swallowing or letting all that saliva pool in your mouth, try allowing your slobber flow wherever gravity wants to take it. That way, you're less likely to drown and you won't have to worry as much about pubic hair wrapping themselves around your tonsils each time you try to swallow. Putting a towel under your sweetheart's rear end will help to keep the mattress from turning into a giant sponge. Some women will appreciate it if you push an edge of the towel against the area that's just below their vulva so the saliva doesn't trickle down their butt crack.

🐦 **Leg Flexing:** When a woman flexes her legs, her pelvis arches forward. This will provide the access that a guy needs to give her good oral sex. A lot of women will do this themselves by putting their legs over your shoulders, or by planting one or both feet on your shoulders. Some pull their legs up to their chest. The guy can also wrap his arms around the back of the woman's thighs and push them forward.

🐦 **Changing Legs:** As a woman becomes more aroused, she might want to change her leg position or flex her thighs in ways that help to get her off. This might limit your access to her vulva, but if it's what does the trick, so be it.

🐦 **Under Her Rear:** As with any kind of sexual activity, a strategically placed pillow under your partner's rear end can provide better access to her genitals. And never hesitate putting a pillow under your head if it makes you more comfortable.

✿ **Parting Her Lips:** Some women provide all the oral access a man needs by simply spreading their legs. On the other hand, you may want to separate the outer labia with your fingers. This gives your mouth better access to the inner lips, and can sometimes feel like the difference between kissing a woman whose mouth is open as opposed to closed. Some women will offer a helping hand by separating the lips themselves. This can be highly erotic.

✿ **Between The Inner And Outer Lips:** Lavish the outer lips with licks and kisses. Then try running the tip of your tongue up and down the furrows between the outer and inner lips of your lover's vulva.

✿ **Pushing Or Pulling Up The Mons.** The mons pubis is the little mound of flesh that sits directly above the labia. It is where the bulk of the pubic hair grows. Some women enjoy it if you rub the mons in a circular pattern. Also, pushing or pulling up the mons while doing oral sex can heighten the intensity for some women.

✿ **Brushing The Bush.** Some women will enjoy it if your run your fingertips through their pubic hair, and some will particularly enjoy it if you tug lightly on it or nibble gently on the mons beneath it.

✿ **Tugging On The Inner Lips.** The inner lips of women's genitals tend to be longer around the vaginal opening. Some are prominent enough to clasp between your fingers and tug upon gently. When a woman is highly aroused, she may enjoy this tremendously. As with everything else, be sure to ask!

Her Clitoris

"Don't immediately dive into the clitoris and stay there. Warm up by licking all of the vaginal area. Suck on the labia. Then turn your attention to the clitoris. I like my clitoris to be licked, flicked and sucked. Sometimes I get off faster if my partner licks lower on the clitoris, rather than at the top of the hood. It makes for a different kind of orgasm." *female age 25*

No matter how small your penis is, nobody's going to have trouble finding it. No matter how large her clitoris is, nature designed it to play a mean game of hide'n'seek. In addition, you may need to find it in order to avoid it!

After kissing and caressing the other parts of the vulva, most women will appreciate it if you focus your oral efforts in the vicinity of the clitoris. You may need to take this quite literally, as some will want you only in the vicinity, while others will want you right on the clitoris. In this section, we try to discuss the various landmarks so you will at least have an idea of which is which.

🐦 **Getting The Shaft:** The parts of the clitoris you will be most interested in are the shaft and the tip. The shaft is in the upper part of the vulva. It might be anywhere from less than a half-inch long to more

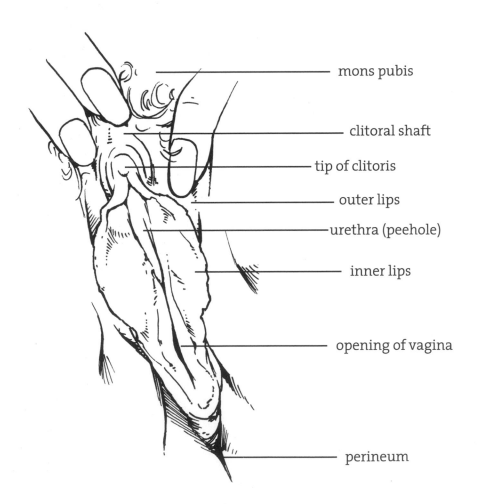

mons pubis

clitoral shaft

tip of clitoris

outer lips

urethra (peehole)

inner lips

opening of vagina

perineum

than an inch. Pushing the labia apart and upwards with your finger-tips will help to expose it.

🐦 **The Hood:** The shaft of the clitoris is covered by a thin little wet-suit which is called the clitoral hood. This hood is similar to the foreskin on a guy who is not circumcised. It protects the shaft from the rigors of crotch life. Oral sex pros manipulate it to great advantage. With practice, the clitoral hood will be your friend, too.

🐦 **The Tip:** The glans or tip of the clitoris is somewhere near the juncture where the clitoral hood splits into two. The tip of the clitoris can be the size of a pen tip or a small finger, depending on the woman. It's sensitivity has nothing to do with its length or diameter. The tip is usually more sensitive to your tongue's caress than the shaft because it's easier to expose than the shaft which is covered by the clitoral hood. This is why some women prefer it if you use a softer more rounded tongue against the clitoral tip. Others will want you to lick with authority.

🐦 **Exposing The Tip:** Sometimes all it takes to expose the tip is a single finger to pull the hood up. Sometimes it takes both hands and a litany of prayer.

🐦 **Finding The Tip With Your Tongue:** Separate the outer lips with your fingers. Make sure your tongue has plenty of saliva on it for lubrication. Take a long slow lick from the vagina to the top of the vulva where the big lips meet. Somewhere along the way you will most likely feel a small knob or slight protuberance. Find out from your partner if this is the tip of her clitoris, and have her explain to you exactly how she likes to have it licked.

🐦 **As The Clitoris Swells:** As your sweetheart becomes more aroused, it is likely that the tip of her clitoris will swell. Some swell predictably, others don't. This process can be a bit challenging until you become more familiar with the way her clitoris changes, and changes, and changes. In fact, with some women, you learn to lick on a specific spot rather than relying on finding her clitoris with your tongue. You simply have faith that after awhile, it will appear.

🐦 **Working The Steps:** You might think that the surest way to arouse a woman would be to start at the tip of the clitoris, since that's where so much of the action seems to be. But this is not the way it usually works. For most women, you don't even approach the clitoris until you have planted plenty of kisses in the surrounding area. Then, you might focus on the clitoral shaft, working the hood with your tongue and avoiding the tip until she is more highly aroused. With some women, you don't touch the tip at all. **Note:** These are just suggestions. If your lover wants you to start by throwing a lip lock on the tip of her clitoris, far be it from this guide to suggest anything different.

🐦 **Mouth Motion:** Some women enjoy it if you kiss their vulva in the same way that you do their mouth. Some crave a gentle nursing action on the clitoris. Some like it if you flick the tip of your tongue over the clitoris in a sideways direction, others prefer an up and down motion as though you were rapidly turning a light switch on and off with your tongue, and some enjoy a circular motion. These different motions may seem awkward at first, but you will eventually learn to flick your tongue back and forth (or is it hither and yon) with enough grace to humiliate the average humming bird. Also keep in mind that some women will want you to speed up or change locations as their arousal grows, while others prefer a constant and steady mouth motion. Interestingly, once some women reach a certain threshold of arousal, they can't tell which direction your tongue is moving in. All they know is if it feels good or not.

NOTE: Be sure to pay close attention to your partner's body language as your tongue touches her exposed clitoris. If her body suddenly convulses or jolts, you have probably hit the right area but too early or with too much force. It never hurts to retreat and find a safe spot along the clitoral shaft that's protected by plenty of hood. She will usually let you know when she wants more tongue. Ways she might do this include telling you, pulling your head into her body with her hands, or grinding her crotch into your face. Hopefully she won't grab you by the ears, although men's ears make fine rudders for oral sex.

🐦 **Taking Sides.** Your partner might have a favorite side of her clitoris where she prefers you to lick. To help improve access to the favored side, she might try flexing one leg while the other lays flat and a bit to the side.

🐦 **When The Clitoris Disappears:** The clitoris sometimes disappears right before orgasm. This can be a bit discouraging, because you might have spent the last twenty minutes finding the thing. Once it retracts or simply gets lost in the swelling labia that surround it, you will need to make an educated guess, and let The Force guide you from there. With helpful input from your partner you will eventually learn how to respond, but it may take a long time to get it right. Patience is your ally, assuming she doesn't divorce you first. **Note:** When a clitoris disappears on you, you might try giving a little suck to pull it back out.

🐦 **More On The Clitoris:** After learning more about your partner's responses, you might experiment by puckering your lips around her clitoris and making a light vacuum. You can then push the clitoris in and out of your mouth either with your tongue or by reversing the suction every couple of seconds. (Tricks like this can be found in Ray Stubb's book "The Clitoral Kiss," published by Secret Garden Press.)

🐦 **If Her Pussy Starts Starts Pulsing:** After you get to know a woman's responses really well, you might find that her clitoris or the area around it begins to pulse once she is approaching orgasm. This is a clear indication that whatever you are doing you should keep doing without the slightest variation in speed, tempo or rhythm. (You might reason that if she's pulsing at this speed, you'll double the tempo or do it harder and she'll pulse even more. WRONG!) These pulses seem to happen every second or so, and are in direct response to the stimulus of your tongue. If you speed up any faster you quickly loose them. **Note:** The contractions of orgasm are said to happen every seven-tenths of a second. Some men say that the best way to simulate a woman's clitoris either by mouth or by hand is to use strokes that last seven-tenths of a second. Some women don't agree.

🐦 **Hormonal Considerations:** Some women prefer different kinds of stimulation depending on the time of the month. For instance, at one point in her menstrual cycle you avoid the tip or glans, but two weeks later you know to lick the tip silly. It's nothing you're going to learn in a one-night stand, and simply doesn't apply for a lot of women.

Her Vagina And Beyond

🐦 **The Space Between Her Clitoris And Vagina:** Using terms like "urinary meatus" or "the area around her peehole" can cause an aesthetic flat tire. However, the part of a woman's vulva between her clitoris and vagina which contains the urinary meatus is definitely worth exploring with the tip of your tongue. For some women its stimulation might be the difference between good oral sex and great oral sex. (If you have aesthetic problems with this notion, think about what your lover dips the tip of her tongue into when she is caressing the head of your penis. Also keep in mind that urine and the urinary passageway is more sterile than the human mouth, and that kissing her down here is far more sterile than kissing her on the mouth.)

🐦 **Vagina:** The opening of the vagina can be found in the lower half of the woman's vulva. A man might occasionally be swept away by an urge to stick his tongue far into his lover's vagina. This, of course, is ridiculous unless he shares the same gene pool as Lassie. Still, it's a nice thing to do, or want to do. Realistically, your tongue will be able to stimulate the outer edges of your partner's vagina and maybe an inch or two inside of it. Reaching too far inside a woman's vagina can cause your tongue to get a nasty cramp.

🐦 **Fingers Inside Her Vagina:** Some women will treasure a finger or two inside the vagina when you are doing oral sex, but usually not until you have been at it for a while. As for what to do with your fingers once they are inside, you will need to ask. Some women like them to stay perfectly still, while others will enjoy it if you twist, jiggle or thrust your fingers in and out. Also, there might be special spots in her vagina that your partner enjoys having stimulated.

🐦 **Dildos:** The inner part of a woman's vagina often balloons open when she is sexually aroused. A number of women enjoy having this filled up. While a man's fingers will usually do the job, some women find that a silicone dildo works better. (For some couples, inserting a dildo during oral sex can be quite a turn-on, others would find this to be strange.) Also, a woman might fantasize about having one man's penis inside her vagina at the same time that another man is licking her clitoris. Using a dildo while receiving oral sex can help satisfy this fantasy unless you are actually into threesomes. *For more about dildos, see Chapter 23* You might keep the dildo in a bowl of warm water until it is ready for use. Believe it or not, there are special oral sex dildos that strap onto a guy's chin!

🐦 **Anal Assist.** One highly athletic advisor to this guide so loved doing oral sex on his women friends in high school and college that he was considered an important resource off the court as well as on. His secret? When a woman was about to have an orgasm, he would gently insert a fingertip into her rectum. He says this would invariably launch a cascade of pleasure. If you want to try this, there is no need to stick your finger in very far; just putting pressure on the rim around   a lover's anus might light up thousands of happy little nerve endings. (Don't put it in her vagina afterwards.) Another variation is to insert   a small, well-lubricated vibrator in the woman's rear while doing oral sex. Other couples like to use their tongues for anal stimulation. This is called rimming. *See Chapter 21 for more information about putting fingers and anything else you can think of up your partner's rear.*

🐦 **Triple Play.** Lips on her clitoris, one finger in her vagina and one up her rear.

🐦 **Approaching Orgasm:** Some women push a man's head away from their vulva after they begin to come. Other women pull it in tighter. (Don't fret if she pushes it away. This will give your tongue a well-earned rest.) Some women are extremely sensitive after orgasm, when barely breathing on their genitals can feel overwhelming.

If She Starts Bucking

It's not unusual for some women who are receiving oral sex to start bucking their hips with pleasure. This kind of motion can knock a guy off the mound.

While it is important to discuss this with your partner, a response that some women seem to appreciate is as follows: Wrap your arms around her thighs from behind, as in the illustration on page 221. Put your hands firmly on her hip bones. The female hip bones provide a perfect handle and were clearly put there by Mother Nature for this very purpose. Flex your arms so that she has to lift the weight of your upper body in order to buck. This shouldn't hurt her at all, and will keep her pelvis still enough so you can give her more of what's causing her to buck in the first place.

Fun At The Y — Random Tips & Techniques

⚘ **Hands, Tits & Toes.** Find out if your sweetheart likes you to reach up and play with her breasts or other body parts while you are going down on her. One reader loves her partner to squeeze her toes when she's receiving oral sex—it can be the difference for her between coming or not.

⚘ **Oral Exams.** One female reader suggests writing each letter of the alphabet with your tongue on your partner's vulva. Before long, she might start requesting specific letters or even whole syllables!

⚘ **Helping Her Into Hyperspace.** Here is a game suggested in the helpful book "Ultimate Kiss" by Jacqueline & Steven Franklin. Bring your lover to the edge of orgasm with oral sex and then pull your mouth away for a count of 50. Then bring her to the edge of orgasm again, and pull your mouth away for 25 seconds. Then bring her to the edge of orgasm, and pull your mouth away for 10 seconds. Do this once more, pausing for just a few seconds. Be sure to explain this game beforehand so your partner doesn't become seriously annoyed when you stop for the first 50 second pause. Also, one female reader suggests that this kind of game can work equally as well when masturbating a woman.

🕊 **Lingerie One.** Sometimes it is fun to give a woman oral sex when she is still wearing her panties or bikini bottom. Start with your lips on her inner thighs, work them up to her crotch, and then sneak your tongue under the material and into her vulva. Eventually, you might want to push the material to one side with your tongue, teeth, or fingers. This will provide more working room.

🕊 **Lingerie Two.** Some women might like it if you blow warm moist air through the front panel of their underwear, others won't. But never blow air directly into a woman's vagina.

🕊 **Lingerie Three.** Consider pulling your lover's panties off with your teeth. But be careful not to leave any holes or rip the material, given how fancy little underthings often cost an arm and a leg; it's best that she not remember you as the one who destroyed her favorite undies.

🕊 **She Stands As You Deliver.** It is next to impossible to do oral sex on a woman who is standing. The access is just too limited. Think nothing of crawling under her dress when she is standing to plant tender kisses in places where other guys only dream of touching, but she'll need to sit or lay down to receive your oral finest.

🕊 **Vibrating Tongues.** After the women is highly aroused, place the tip of your tongue on the side or bottom of her clitoris. Then push the tip of a small vibrator on the other side of your tongue.

🕊 **The Sixty-Second Lick.** Separate the outer lips with your fingers and lay your tongue flat against her vaginal opening at the lowest part of her vulva. Take a slow, long, wet lick that lasts for about sixty seconds. This way, her clit gets a long slow protracted licking as your tongue creeps its way up her vulva like a red hot glacier.

🕊 **Pillows Regular.** Placing a pillow or two under your partner's rear can greatly enhance access to her genitals.

🕊 **Pillows Plus.** Some women like so many pillows under their rear ends that their entire body is on an incline with their crotches angled up in the air. This provides wonderful access as well as an intriguing view. It may also cause lots of blood to rush into the woman's head.

🕊 **Humming.** A more subtle way of making your tongue vibrate is to hum while placing it on your partner's clitoris. A well-hummed aria can push some women into orgasmic orbit. Others will start laughing hysterically.

🕊 **'Hot'n'Cold.** On a hot muggy day, ice cubes can always spice up any kind of sex play. Some women enjoy an occasional ice cube in the vagina. If you try this, use small cubes that won't cause frost burn. During the cold of winter, sipping a warm drink before kissing a woman's vulva can leave her with warm and sensual feelings.

🕊 **When Pooh Has Oral Sex.** Some couples enjoy placing a piece of fruit like a banana, slice of mango or papaya inside a woman's vagina for the man to retrieve with his tongue. (Honey and syrup should be used with caution. While they are fine on nipples and other parts of the body, residual sugar in the vagina might inspire its resident yeast cells to procreate with painful delight. This may not be a problem for most women, but is worth noting.)

🕊 **Love Swings — Going Up On Her.** There are special swings that are great for doing oral sex. They can be hung from a door jam or ceiling rafter. The swing is a bit like a harness that automatically spreads the woman's legs and places her at the perfect height for a man to give her oral sex while he is sitting upright. By far and away the best and most reasonably priced swings that we have seen are made by a man in Southern California. Check out the resources section on page 613.

🕊 **Toasting At The Y.** Some couples occasionally pour champagne into a woman's vagina when her legs are elevated. (Vamosa?) Her partner then licks out the champagne, although this is not recommended for men in twelve step programs or for women whose vaginal tissue might become irritated. (An extremely dry champagne with low residual sugar might be preferable; avoid putting cold duck in a woman's crotch and be sure that she checks with her gynecologist first.)

🕊 **Kissing Above After Kissing Below.** Some women have a problem with being kissed on the face after being kissed on the crotch. If that's the case in your household, consider keeping a wet washcloth handy. Run it across your face while on route from her lower lips to her upper lips.

🕊 **Air Stream.** Blowing air on the genitals can feel refreshing, but never blow air into a woman's vagina.

Safety Note: It can be very sexy to blow warm moist air over your lover's vulva, but very dangerous to blow air into her vagina. Never lock your lips on your partner's vulva and blow air into it, unless your partner is made of plastic and gets inflated that way.

Female Ejaculation

Some women who are highly aroused occasionally ejaculate fluid around the same time that they have an orgasm. One female reader who ejaculates says that her male partners find it exciting. Other guys who aren't quite as thrilled with the notion should discuss it with their partners and figure out ways of ducking when the drenching is about to begin.

If your partner ejaculates and you have a problem with it, take solace in knowing that you've done something incredibly right to get her to that point.

Feeling Like A Crash Test Dummy

Some women are not particularly subtle when it comes to signaling their oral sex wants and desires. In fact, it is not unheard of for a woman in the heat of oral passion to suddenly grab a man's skull and yank it one way or another with enough force to cause whiplash.

If she grinds your face into her crotch with a nose-flattening swoosh, she probably wants you to up the tempo a bit. But don't be silly and let your tongue go full throttle, because this might cause her to whip your head in the opposite direction. Learning to shift tongue-gears gradually can add years to the life of your neck and spinal column.

Neck Pain, Lock Jaw & Tongue Cramping

Tongue cramping and jaw paralysis are common side-effects of giving oral sex. These usually occur just moments before the woman blurts out "There, that's perfect, don't stop!" Being able to continue when every ligament and muscle fiber from your neck up are screaming for mercy is what separates the oral sex men from the oral sex boys.

With experience, you will discover which positions land you in traction and which don't. Do not suffer in silence. Discuss this with your partner, so you can find oral sex positions which are mutually pleasing. That way you'll be able to give her more of what she likes.

Also, if your jaw is jamming, don't hesitate to give it a breather by gently replacing the tip of your tongue with the tip of your finger.

Damn Those Dental Dams & The New Latex Beaver Tarps

About ten years ago, when the AIDS concern reached full steam, some bozo decided that a way to safely go down on a woman was to spread a dental dam over a woman's crotch and lick away. While dental dams work great for dentists, we challenge any loving couple to enjoy oral sex through a dental dam. Why not just use neoprene or naugahyde?

Lately, they've come up with an alternative that's supposedly thinner and more lick friendly. Hogwash. It may be made for vulvas and not molars, but we challenge anyone to give good oral sex through latex. First of all, you have no clue as to what you're licking. It might as well be the President's face, for all you can tell. And then there's the texture problem. Try whipping your tongue back and forth over a surface of latex. No matter how much slobber you throw into the mix, your tongue drags and your RPMs go straight to hell. Giving a woman oral sex through even the thinnest of latex barriers makes you appreciate how much subtlety is involved when it comes to making her little lips sing.

A far more satisfactory barrier was a simple piece of Saran Wrap. You can see through it, it doesn't slow your tongue action, and you can always use it for other purposes, like to cover the Peach Melba or Apple Brown Betty.

When A Woman Doesn't Like Her Own Body

"I have a lot of hang ups about oral sex because I think the guy wants to get out of there as soon as possible. So I need to be reassured you really enjoy it. The orgasm I have with oral sex is the most wonderful, but it often takes a long time and would try the patience of anyone." *female age 38*

Some women don't like their bodies and are uncomfortable when a man has a close-up view. If this is the case in your relationship, it might help ease your partner's mind by doing oral sex with the lights out. On the other hand, if your partner is looking for an excuse to feel bad about herself, she will assume that you turned the lights out because you find her body ugly. Either way, it never hurts to talk about this.

One possible solution is to start doing oral sex on her when the two of you are in the shower. She might feel more comfortable with this, hopefully believing that she is clean enough for you to enjoy.

Maintaining A Hard-On While Giving Oral Sex

If a guy is giving his sweetheart oral sex, it might be nice if he kept doing it long enough to at least get her off. But once he feels his hard-on starting to go, a man will sometimes surface from between a woman's legs and try to have intercourse before it's "too late." Otherwise he feels unmanly about going soft.

So why does a man sometimes lose his erection while going down on a woman? First of all, doing oral sex requires the kind of concentration that isn't always conducive to maintaining an erection. It's a little like playing catch or strumming a guitar, things that are immensely enjoyable but don't necessarily make a guy hard. Also, for some men, doing oral sex on a woman can bring up all sorts of primal feelings that aren't necessarily in sync with getting a hard-on. These can be pleasant and even deeply moving feelings, but they might not be the stuff that erections are made of. For other guys, it's instant wood the second tongue touches thigh.

There is also the matter of mouth fatigue. It's not easy to keep a hard-on when your tongue and jaw start cramping. On the other hand, it's kind of fun to see how far you can lick a lover into an altered state of sexual consciousness even if you can't talk too well afterwards.

Whatever the cause, it's not unusual for a man to lose his erection when he is going down on a woman, but not because he is unhappy or a wimp. (Women might consider what a drag it would be if they had to stay hard while doing oral sex. Nobody ever gets on their case for losing an erection.)

Things A Woman Can Do To Help A Partner Who Is Going Down On Her

Here are a few suggestions for the woman who likes to receive oral sex:

🐦 **Tugging On Your Bush.** Stray pubic hairs in the mouth can sometimes put a damper on wanting to lick a woman's genitals. Take a moment to tug on your bush before your man goes down. You'll pull out the lose hairs that would otherwise end up sticking to the back of his throat.

🐦 **Trimming Your Triangle.** Getting a mouthful of pubic hair can sometimes put a damper on wanting to lick a woman's genitals. While some women feel that trimming the triangle defiles the natural appearance of the female body, others take pride in showing off more of their genitals. A woman so inclined should never hesitate to put her lover in charge of muff maintenance ~ coiffure. Many men find this to be a joyful duty and take the responsibility quite seriously.

🐦 **Labia Laundering.** Separating the labia and washing between them once a day will help to keep your genitals clean and tasty. Douching usually isn't necessary or advisable.

🐦 **Helpful.** Some men find it to be an extra turn-on if a woman reaches down and separates her labia with her own fingers when he is going down on her. And no man has ever complained about a woman playing with her breasts if that is what she wants to do when receiving oral sex.

🐦 **Not Helpful.** Women who think that their own genitals are dirty or not likable seldom do themselves any favors when it comes to oral sex. For instance, a guy might be having a wonderful time kissing and caressing his partner's genitals when she suddenly pulls him up because she's decided that he surely can't be enjoying something "as gross as that." If a woman fears that her genitals don't taste good, she should ask her partner. And if she feels there is something bad about her genitals, she should tell her partner lest he become seriously annoyed by her rejecting behavior. Perhaps his reassurance will be helpful. (What if he brought her roses and she said "Yuck" or made him return them? It's no different when she thinks her genitals are not worthy of his kisses, assuming he enjoys kissing them.)

🐦 **Information.** As long as it's done with sensitivity, most men will appreciate any input or suggestions that a woman has about giving her oral pleasure. If you feel shy, hand your lover a copy of this chapter and ask if he'll read it with you. And if your man's ego is so fragile that he can't handle your input, perhaps he would do better with a mindless partner who has no input to give. If you aren't equal partners in sex, you aren't equal partners period. Is that what you want?

🐦 **Masturbating.** Don't hesitate to reach down and masturbate while your partner is doing oral sex. Of course, this may be more easily said than done, so be sure to let him know that you want him to keep licking while you masturbate. While this can be fun, it may require some interesting tongue-finger logistics.

🐦 **Elective Stroking.** One of the best parts about receiving oral sex is not having to do anything but enjoy the sensations that are coming from your partner's mouth. Still, some women enjoy holding or stroking a partner's penis while he is going down on them.

🐦 **Attitude Issues.** There is a section at the end of the preceding chapter on blow jobs that is similar to this, only it is addressed to men. You might look over attitude issues , on pages 212-213. If the shoe fits...

🐦 **Humor:** Next to bathing, humor is the most important sex aid there is. Try not to forget this.

Oral Sex During Menstruation

Some couples are fine with oral sex while the woman is menstruating, others wait a few days until the menstrual flow has stopped. Here are three possibilities if you don't want the mess but don't want to wait:

🐦 Instead. It's the name brand of a new tampon alternative that fits over your cervix in the same way as a diaphragm. Pop one in before oral sex and it will catch most if not all of the bloody flow. You can get them at your grocery store. **NOTE:** These are not for birth control.

🐦 A woman who is menstruating can douche and insert a couple of tampons before a man goes down on her. The tampons will usually catch most of the flow, assuming that you don't attempt to tickle the woman's cervix with the tip of your tongue. If you douche, which might do more harm than good, consider using a solution that has a lower pH.

🐦 Some women get a diaphragm for the sole purpose of having sex during their periods. The diaphragm becomes a barrier that traps the menstrual flow. Some couples use the diaphragm for oral sex but not for intercourse, since menstrual secretions can help make intercourse feel extra nice. If you do this, be sure to use an alternative method of birth control.

🐦 A simple way of dodging menstrual flow is by putting plastic wrap over the woman's vulva before going down on her.

NOTE: For couples who are concerned about AIDS transmission: Whether AIDS can be transmitted through oral contact is still not known, but why take the chance? Use a latex barrier until more is learned about the transmission of AIDS. Also, you should never do unprotected oral sex on a partner if you have a chancre sore or active oral herpes in your mouth, or if your partner has a herpes outbreak on his or her genitals. Germ-proof that beaver with a latex tarp and have at it.

69

69 is when a man does oral sex on a woman at the same time that she does oral sex on him.

There are plenty of couples who enjoy oral sex but don't necessarily like doing 69. That's because when a person is on the receiving end of oral sex, he or she might want to kick back and not have to worry about getting the other person off. 69 should also be avoided if the female partner involuntarily clenches her jaw during orgasm...

On the other hand, there might be times when 69 is great fun. Some couples enjoy it as their favorite way of having sex. They love the feeling of simultaneously sucking and being sucked. 69 might also be good for people who can't tolerate receiving pleasure without giving it at the same time, or visa versa.

There are three standard positions for doing oral sex— with the man on top, with the woman on top, or with the couple on its side. Some women prefer being on their sides or on top because in these positions it is easier for them to control the depth that the penis goes into the mouth.

Reader's Comments

Advice On Giving Oral Sex

"Lick around the area of the clitoris, not directly on it, until I am more aroused and then only part of the time." *female age 35*

"Get a good rhythm going, don't suck or lick too hard on the head of the clit. Also, be either smooth-shaved or have a beard, but no in-between. Razor burn really kills down there!"
female age 45

"Stubble on the face is not welcome in tender areas down below." *female age 48*

"Please quit when I say so, it gets really tender and ticklish after I come." *female age 43*

"Start out slowly working around the outer area with your tongue. Don't just push in. Do a lot of gentle rubbing and caressing on the insides of the leg. Gradually probe the vulva with your tongue. Develop a rhythm and keep going until I come." *female age 32*

"If my partner's tongue gets tired, he uses his finger and sometimes it feels the same." *female age 25*

"I like a man to first shave me smooth, then gently kiss and finger me." *female age 34*

"It's great when he puts a finger into my rear while giving me oral sex. It makes for quite the explosion!" *female age 38*

The Xandria Catalogue has a chin device called "The Accommodator." It's like a penis that fits on a guy's chin. He can insert it in his lover's vagina while licking the area around her clit, or if he is attending a meeting of the Fraternal Order of the Big Dildo, he can strap it on upside down and have a latex penis sticking out of his forehead, like a rhinoceros horn.

🐓 🐓 🐓

Chapter 19
Massage, Body Rubs, Back Rubs
The Ultimate Tenderness

In doing research for this book, almost every way that human adults get each other off was considered. Attempts were made to view sex through the eyes of mate-swappers, Buddhist sex masters, gays, lesbians, conservative born-again Christians, bondage enthusiasts and even those whose sex lives are really boring. Having left no sexual stone unturned, one and only one universal truth about human sexuality emerged:

No matter what your sexual beliefs, fantasies, kink or persuasion nothing beats a good backrub.

Nobody, absolutely nobody, had a single bad thing to say about a good back rub. Ditto for foot massage.

Hard Vs. Soft? Male Vs. Female?

Just about every book ever written on sex loves to state that men touch women too hard, and that women touch men too soft. Baloney, says a straw poll taken by the Goofy Foot Press. Here are two types of touch that both men and women like a great deal:

Feather Light To Light: This is where the fingertips lightly dance across the surface of the skin, resulting in a delightful tingling sensation that may or may not raise goosebumps. It can also be done with the flat of the hand doing light, long, gentle strokes. Optimal feather light touch time: from five to fifty minutes. Some people who were held down as kids and mercilessly tickled might not like this kind of touch.

Deep & Hard: This is when muscles are kneaded with a strength and authority that chases away stress and tension. The men commented that they often fear they are doing this too hard, but their female partners almost always say it's just right or to do it harder. Optimal deep & hard massage time: from half an hour to how ever long the giver wants to keep doing it.

Fortunately, numerous books on touch and massage have been published in the last twenty years. There are also several nicely done videos on the subject of massage. An hour spent reading one of these books or watching a tape will probably do more for your relationship than a lifetime of looking at Playboy or Penthouse. Pay special attention to the chapters on foot rubs, hand rubs, scalp and facial massages. These body parts are often ignored because they aren't considered blue chip erogenous zones.

Spectators Vs. Participants

Some people struggle to get fully into their bodies. Some are perpetually stuck in "prepare to defend" mode, and have trouble relaxing enough to enjoy what is being shared with them sexually. For whatever reason, they need to be hyper-vigilant about what is going on around them. Another problem results when the person always needs to perform, and has difficulty becoming passive enough to allow sexual things to happen to his or her body.

Learning to massage and be massaged is one way that might help you to temper your body's armor. This might be anxiety producing at the start, if sexual trust is an issue for you. As you work through these issues with your partner, your ability to enjoy physical pleasure should increase substantially.

Combining Sex & Massage

One reader comments: "My husband often massages my shoulders while I'm giving him head. It feels wonderful and serves to relax me so I can become more easily aroused." Another reader ties her naked partner's hands together above his head, lets him watch as she slowly removes her satin panties, and then caresses his entire body with them. A third reader drags her long hair across her lover's naked body and eventually wraps it around his genitals. One man reports that the best way to drive his partner into total ecstasy is for him to brush her hair or massage her scalp with his fingertips. Another lights candles in the bathroom. Both he and his partner then take long showers together, shampooing each other's hair and soaping each other's body.

Perhaps you have your own favorite ways of combining massage with sexplay. Whatever your inclination, if there is only one thing you take from this book, take the resolve to make massage and body rubs an integral part of your sexual relationships. Touch and massage might be the most important aspects of human sexuality, outside of the occasional need to replenish the species.

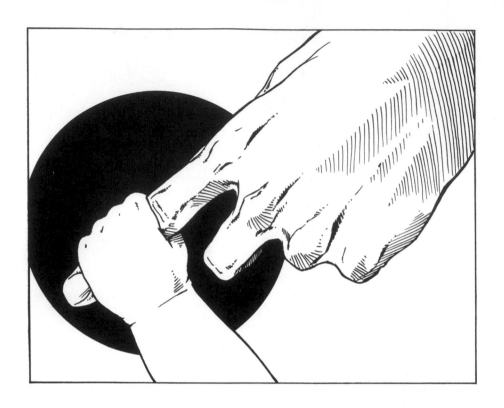

Intercourse Alert

There are a number of fun, exciting and highly satisfying ways of sharing sexual pleasure besides vaginal intercourse.

If you are not fully prepared to become pregnant, to support ($$$) and parent a child for the next eighteen years, to give your baby up for adoption, or to have an abortion, then you shouldn't be having vaginal intercourse.

Even the best birth control methods fail. Intercourse is also the most common means of passing on sexual diseases.

Chapter 20
Horizontal Jogging (Intercourse)

Intercourse can mean different things to different people. As presented in this chapter, it's an intensely private act. You can use it to honor and expand your relationship at the same time that you're doing really nice things with your body. It's also what couples do when they want to create new life. We don't take it lightly, and try to present it with a level of feeling and intelligence not normally found in popular books on sex.

Dick, Laura & Craig

To learn more about the role of intercourse in sexuality, this book has invaded the privacy of three young adults, Dick, Craig and Laura. Laura used to go out with Dick, and now she's involved with Craig. Here are their goofy stories:

DICK

Dick is a very nice-looking guy who won his fraternity's "Mr. All-America" title two years in a row. Dick has a nice social manner, drives a nice sports car, wears nice clothes, has nice biceps, triceps, and pecs, and goes out with nice women. Since this is a book about sex, you might as well know that Dick has a tree-trunk of a penis that stays rock hard from dusk to dawn. A former girlfriend referred to it as "the sentry."

CRAIG

Craig is the same age as Dick. Craig's a sportswriter. Craig is no longer eligible for your average "Mr. All-America" contest. During a football game a few years ago, Craig went airborne to catch an overthrown pass. On the way down he got sandwiched between two spearing linebackers. Craig's spinal cord snapped and he hasn't been able to walk or have an erection since.

LAURA

Laura is a fine young woman who just left a big corporation to form her own company that makes sporting gear. Laura's had sex with both Dick and Craig. Let's see what Laura has to say about these two different men.

"Dick's the kind of guy that many American women have been raised to worship. Parading him around your friends or taking him home to your parents would win you the female equivalent of the Breeder's Cup... I've always really enjoyed sex, and until recently I could never understand why a woman would want to fake an orgasm. But it didn't take too many nights with Dick before I started faking orgasms. There was Dick, Mr. Right Stuff, making all that picture perfect love. I didn't want him to think there was something wrong with me since I couldn't get into it like he was, so I started faking orgasms."

"Craig is nowhere near as perfect as Dick, but he has a great sense of humor and he is genuine. Craig is able to laugh at himself, which Dick never could. Craig has taken the time to learn exactly how to kiss, touch, and caress me, and the sex I have with him is great. When I'm with Craig I don't need to fake a thing."

"This may not seem relevant to your question about sex, but I work in a totally male-dominated business. I have to think like a guy from morning to night. Sometimes it leaves me feeling alien from my femininity. With Craig it's easy to find it back again... Craig never wakes me up at 3:00 a.m. with a hard-on poking in my back, but he feels just as masculine as Dick. With a lot of guys there's a huge difference between how they treat you in bed and how they treat you the rest of time; with Craig that's not the case. Maybe that's another reason why sex is so nice with him, even if it's not intercourse."

OK, so here we have Dick, more functional than a Sidewinder Missile. He fulfills everybody's definition of what a true sexual athlete should be. Then we have Craig who redefines the term 'sexually dysfunctional.' If Craig had the same erection failure but no spinal cord injury, a bunch of psychologists and sex therapists would collect a small fortune trying to make him 'normal.' At the very least, they would have him munching down Viagra pills like they were M&Ms. And probably Prozac, too.

CLOSED CAPTION

And finally, there's Laura, a woman who enjoys sex a great deal. She's saying that the guy who can't get it up is a more satisfying lover than Mr. Erectus Perfectus.

In telling you about Laura, Dick and Craig, the intent was not to dump on intercourse. Intercourse, when it's good, can be one of the sweetest things there is. What this book is dumping on is the assumption that intercourse is good just because it's intercourse, and that a man is a man because he can get hard and fuck, or that a woman is a woman because she can get wet and fuck him back.

When Ms. Dworkin Has Intercourse

If it weren't bad enough that we started our intercourse chapter with a story about a gimp sportswriter who can't get it up, now we're quoting from a radical feminist who can't get it down. What follows is Andrea Dworkin raging about intercourse, or as she calls it, "violation."

"The vagina itself is muscled and the muscles have to be pushed apart. The thrusting is persistent invasion. She is opened up, split down the center. She is occupied physically, internally, in her privacy... Violation is a synonym for intercourse." (Andrea Dworkin, "Intercourse" Simon & Schuster, New York, NY 1987)

In case you think Ms. Dworkin is talking about rape, she isn't. It seems that she doesn't see much of a difference between intercourse that a woman desires and rape. In order to find out if Andrea was just having a bad day, or if she was genuinely speaking for all women, we asked our women readers the following question, " What does it feel like when you have intercourse?" Mind you, these women are clearly describing intercourse with partners who they care very deeply about.

What Does It Feel Like When You Have Intercourse?

"Oh God – It's like describing the universe. It feels like I might explode and can't wait to but at same time want it to last forever. Breathless, hot, turned-on in the extreme. I want to engulf and squeeze his penis, get it in me as much as possible. I love the connection of it."

female age 48

"When his penis first enters me I want to feel every inch of it because it is exquisite. I feel like I need it inside me and I don't know if I can describe that. The actual sensations of his penis sliding in and out of me are sometimes overpowered by the pleasure I feel all over my body, so I don't necessarily concentrate on the intercourse."

female age 23

"As he enters me I feel myself spreading open to accomodate him. Emotionally it feels right that he is inside of me. I have a feeling of fullness when he is inside me. I can feel the head of the penis as it slides in and out and can feel my vagina collapse or expand around him. If he plunges deep I can feel the head of the penis bump my cervix, a not altogether unpleasant feeling. From rear entry I can feel the penis more acutely rubbing the top of my vagina." *female age 37*

"It feels different everytime. Sometimes it is very satisfying. Some-times it hurts inside my vagina if I'm not lubricated enough. And sometimes when his penis hits my g-spot it takes my breath away!"

female age 34

"At first I feel the light pressure of my partner's penis against my unopened vagina. It is often deeply pleasurable to feel the head penetrate, and then a slow, smooth slide all the way in, and a jolt of excitement when my lover's penis is completely inside me. The most sensation is around the outer part of the vagina, but there is also a pleasurable feeling of fullness when he is fully inside me. My hips want to move and match his strokes, or create my own rhythm for him to match. Different types of strokes and rhythms create different sensations." *female age 47*

"The first thrust is the most vivid for me. I like to slowly slide down his cock and feel it go up me. I love it when he is trying to hold back from coming, I can feel him get more swollen and hard and I get very excited when I feel that. It actually is the time when my vagina gets the most pleasure from intercourse." *female age 23*

"It depends on how sexually excited I am and whether I'm in the mood or if I'm just doing it because he wants to. If I'm into it, it's like ecstacy!" *female age 43*

"I enjoy the pumping and grinding a great deal. I love it when we are rubbing our pelvic bones together and when the penis is in deep."

female age 21

"My favorite part of intercourse is when he comes, his entire body stiffens." *female age 55*

"I'm strictly a clit person. I love having sex with men, but I don't like intercourse." *female age 36*

At The Start—New Relationship Or New To Intercourse

For a lot of couples it takes time and familiarity for intercourse to get that kind of sloppy-intimate-erotic edge that makes it so much fun. This means that intercourse won't necessarily knock your socks off at the start. It may not even feel as good as masturbation.

Also, each partner brings his or her own hopes and expectations, as well as physical anatomy and body rhythms. Patience can be a virtue. For instance, some couples who are having dynamite intercourse during the fifth year of their relationship had lousy intercourse during the first year. And even if the sex is great at the start, chances are there will be periods in any relationship when sexual desire falls flat. Hopefully you will continue to grow as a couple during those times.

Your First Intercourse

In a recent, well-designed study on first intercourse that included 659 college students, researchers Schwartz, Sprecher, Barbee and Orbuch found the following:

🐜 While 79% of the men reported that they had an orgasm during their first intercourse, only 7% of the women reported having an orgasm.

🐜 Males had far more overall pleasure than females.

🐜 The mean age for first intercourse was 16.5 years, although those who waited until they were 17 years or older reported having a better experience than those who were younger. Not that anything gets better with age automatically, but sometimes a year or two of added life experience can go a long way when you are only sixteen.

🐜 Women experienced more guilt than men. (Society teaches men that having their first intercourse is a good thing, a passage of sorts, but for women, losing their virginity is still problematic.)

🐜 Males reported having more anxiety than females, probably having to do with performance concerns, but the increased anxiety did not keep them from experiencing greater pleasure than their partners. Perhaps some anxiety is a good thing.

🛏 The report states: "Both males and females reported more pleasure if they had intercourse for the first time in a more serious or long-term relationship than in a casual or brief one." This suggests that sex is more pleasurable when there is love or commitment.

🛏 Individuals in long term relationships reported having less guilt during their first intercourse than those in more casual relationships, although they did experience more anxiety, perhaps from having more at stake or a greater desire to please their partner.

🛏 Individuals who used contraception reported more pleasure than those who didn't.

🛏 People who used alcohol during their first intercourse (about 30% of the total) reported significantly less pleasure and more guilt than those who did it sober.

BIRTH CONTROL NOTE FOR POTENTIAL FIRST TIMERS: It's easy to get pregnant the first time you have intercourse. You can also become pregnant from having intercourse during your period.

The Approach

Sometimes you're both so horny that you hardly get your shoes and socks off before the hungry vagina has lapped up the hard penis. But a lot of the time, one of you is ready for intercourse before the other. Now if it's the man who isn't ready, it's a no-brainer who needs to get turned-on a bit more, unless it's one of those times when the man is all turned-on but his erection detonator is all turned-off. As we said in a prior chapter, when that happens, it's time for him to pull out his trusty tongue and dive. Muff dive, that is.

If he's the one who's ready first, it wouldn't hurt him a bit to tease his partner until she's more or less pleading to be entered. You can always get a little extra mileage before taking the big plunge by letting the head of your penis caress the lips of her vulva. She'll know it's there, but she won't know when it's going in.

One problem with this is if the big dude is worried that his little dude won't stay hard. For some guys, it might help to know just how hot you're making her by playing the tease. For others, the anxiety of losing it is just too great to delay.

Some women are able to enjoy intercourse a lot more if they have an orgasm before the penis ever goes in. If that's where a guy has put his pre-thrust efforts, then he deserves to put it in without delay.

One In The Hand... Who Sticks It In

"I generally prefer to put it in, otherwise we seem to miss a lot."
female age 32

"I always want him to put it in," *female age 25*

"I like to put his penis in me because it seems no matter how many times we have had sex, he still misses a little bit when aiming. Also, I find it exciting to hold him while he thrusts into my vagina." *female age 23*

"It's really whoever grabs ahold first." *female age 36*

"He prefers to put it in, because if I do, he thinks I think he doesn't know where in the heck that hole is." *female age 38*

"She always does. No matter how many years we've been doing this, I still manage to miss!" *male age 43*

This may seem like a dumb thing to talk about, but the issue of who sticks the penis into the vagina can sometimes be significant. A rule of thumb, so to speak, is that the woman should be the one who sticks it in—at least for the first few times until both partners have their signals in sync. That's because only a woman knows when she is ready to have a penis inside, and all those years of inserting tampons has taught her exactly where the head of little Tonto needs to go. Of course, some women might be shy about grabbing a guy's penis and guiding it in for a landing. This kind of reticence is silly, but understandable.

If it becomes the man's job to put the penis in, he should wait until getting some sort of go-ahead signal. At the very least, he should check out the readiness of his partner's vagina with a finger. If it's not

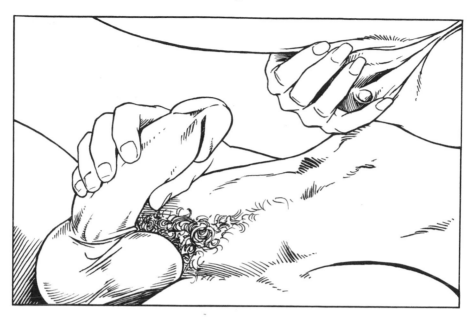

particularly wet but the woman still wants him inside of her, he should lube himself up with a water-based lubricant such as KY, contraceptive jelly, or one of the newer generation of store-bought sex lubes. Also, a wad of saliva slapped on the head of the penis is a time-honored antidote for a willing but arid vagina.

Lube Note: If you are using a water-based lube and it dries out with extended thrusting, add a few drops of water or saliva rather than more lube. A drop or two of water will give it new life, while more lube will just gum things up. The women at Good Vibrations suggest keeping a water pistol handy for just this purpose, although women without humor will find this to be offensive, and wives of NRA members should be careful to not grab the Uzi by mistake.

The First Thrust

As we were reading the survey results of our women readers, an amazing thing began to happen. A large number of women said that the part of intercourse they liked best was the first stroke. For a lot women, it seems like the first stoke is a nearly religious happening, assuming they're primed and eager for the thrusting to begin.

While we offer a number of tips later in this chapter, asking your sweetheart about how she likes you to do your first stroke might be one of the most significant. Does she like you to tease with a bunch of short little strokes first, going in only an inch or two? Or does she like one big straightforward glide for the gold?

Legs Bent Or Straight, Open Or Closed

The Physics Of Intercourse Pt. I: The biggest single variable in the physics of intercourse is often the position of the woman's legs—whether they are straight or bent, open or closed, over your shoulders or in your face. For instance, when the woman's legs are straight, penetration is not as deep, but the clitoris tends to receive more stimulation. (The penis rides higher in the saddle, so the clitoral hood gets pulled and pushed a bit more.) When a woman bends her legs and brings her knees closer to her chest, the penetration is deeper. This can be nice if she likes more pressure in the back part of her vagina, although this sometimes pulls the clitoris away from the penis. It also changes the angle of the penis in the vagina, causing a different feel for both the man and woman.

If the woman's legs are together, the penis is hugged more snugly. This might offer better clitoral stimulation, because the added snugness may push the inner labia more tightly against the shaft of the penis as it goes in and out. When she opens her legs, there is greater skin-to-skin contact between her vulva and the man's genitals. This can also result in more bouncing-testicle action if the man is on top.

Some couples enjoy intercourse with one leg straight and the other flexed. And some women compensate for decreased clitoral contact by reaching between their legs and pushing the clitoris against the penis with their fingers. Got all of that?

Note: Keeping their legs straight and together while flexing their thighs is a trick that some women use to help push them over the top.

Legs Bent Or Straight, Anatomical Consideration

A woman's decision to keep her legs straight or bent might also vary with the length and thickness of the man's penis. A woman whose partner has a really long penis may find that she gets poked in the cervix if she opens and bends her legs during intercourse, while a woman whose man has a short penis might prefer the feeling of deeper penetration that bent knees allow.

Porn star Nina Hartley has a shallow vagina and can't take guys who are really long. Mind you, "shallow" and "long" are defined differently in the world of pornography than in the average bedroom. Ms. Hartley suggests that women can add another inch or two of thrusting room by using positions that allow the penis to move into the space behind the cervix that is called the fornix. (You will need to experiment on your own, as she doesn't say what these space enhancing positions might be.)

Note: Sex books these days don't use the term "short penis." Instead, they say a penis that isn't overly long. The latter phrasing is meant to protect the allegedly fragile male ego, yet this guide hates to think that today's male is so fragile that he can't say "I've got a short one" without experiencing a crisis of character. As for the sentiment expressed by the recent 20 Fingers hit song "(Don't Want No) Short Dick Man," Chapter 35 discusses penis size.

Thrusting — Shallow Vs. Deep

The Physics Of Intercourse Pt. 2: The walls of a woman's vagina change shape with each thrust of intercourse. This means that with each stroke, thousands of nerve endings are being pulled and tugged, which, neurologically speaking, can feel extremely nice. (This doesn't feel half bad for guys, either.) The most sensitive part of the vagina is usually at the opening, up to an inch or two deep. This also becomes the snuggest part of the vagina when it is aroused. Shallow thrusting allows the ridge around the head of the penis to stimulate this sensitive part of the vagina. (An exception might be if the man's penis has a small head and is thicker around the middle part of the shaft, in which case the woman might prefer the thicker part to be in the vaginal opening.) Shallow thrusting also encourages the snuggest part of the vagina to wrap around the most sensitive part of his penis, just below the head.

Deeper thrusting offers its own advantages. Unless the man's penis is really long or the woman's vagina is shallow, deep thrusting can help to position his pubic bone in direct contact with her clitoral area. Rubbing against a man's pubic bone helps some women to have orgasms during intercourse. Deeper thrusting may also allow the penis to pull on the labia minora (inner lips) for a longer period of time providing more simulation to the clitoral area. In addition, the deeper part of the vagina is often sensitive to pressure. As some women approach orgasm, they find it pleasurable if there is a penis or penis-like object in the back part of the vagina which it can contract around.

The Zen Police Talk Thrust

The various Tantric sex masters usually caution about deep thrusting during intercourse. They feel that the vagina does best with a ratio of five-to-one or nine-to-one shallow-to-deep thrusts. This is an interesting observation on their part, given how they don't allow women to be monks and masters, but they sure do sell a lot of books and tapes these days. Anyway, the nine shallow for every one deep thrust is a pattern that pretty much wins you the Tantric intercourse exacta. Then, as your partner becomes more aroused, increase the ratio to two deep for every four shallow, or what the heck, live dangerously and go for a little one shallow to one deep.

This is definitely something to experiment with, but if your partner starts threatening you with serious grief if you don't knock off the shallow stuff and start thrusting deep, you can safely assume she wasn't an Asian princess in a past life.

Battering Ram Or Pleasure Wand? Mosh Pit Or Symphony?

Some men use a penis as a kind of battering ram, believing that women enjoy being slammed during intercourse. Other men, perhaps a bit more sensitive or experienced, realize that there are different thrusting rhythms that can help make intercourse feel more symphonic than metallic. A lot of it also depends on what style or styles of thrusting the woman enjoys.

An excellent way to find out what works best during intercourse is when the woman is on top. That way the man can feel what she does with his penis, how she moves up and down on it, and what parts of her vagina she focuses the head on to. For instance, does she thrust rapidly with it, or does she keep the penis deep inside of her and rub her clitoris on the man's pubic bone? Does she like to massage her clitoris or breasts while a penis is inside of her, or would this be an unwelcome distraction? Where does she like to look, and what does she do with her mouth?

Eager For Beaver—Intercourse As Two Separate Acts

If you are feeling terminally reflective and have nothing else to do, it might be helpful to think of intercourse as two separate acts— the thrusting or rocking part, and the orgasm part. If the sole purpose of the former is to achieve the latter, then the intercourse might not have much emotional depth to it. That's because it is during the thrusting part of intercourse (before orgasm) when feelings of love, friendship and gratitude are often shared. Most couples have a variety of thrusting modes; e.g. hot and furious, fun and playful, giggly, tearful, passionate, powerful, passive and maybe even angry at times. This becomes part of the private language that lovers share.

Using Your Head

Keep in mind that the first inch or so of a woman's vagina is sensitive to touch. That's why a bit of gentle finger or penis head action around the rim can be a nice way to begin. The art, of course, is in making those shallow little thrusts without pulling out too far and having your dick fall out. If it falls out enough times, she'll start thinking your middle name is "Goober."

Beyond the first inch or so, you need to start thinking pressure. That's because the back part of the vagina feels stretching and pressure more than it does light little touches. This is when it's wise to learn which parts of her vagina respond best to pressure, i.e. the kind that happens when the head of your penis pushes against it. If you pay close enough attention, you'll find that you can combine certain positions with certain angles to pressure almost any part of her vagina that she likes.

A good way to learn about a woman's genitals is with your fingers as well as with your penis. This will give you a better under-standing of what needs to be done with your penis. (As one female reader says, "It wouldn't hurt for women to know this about themselves.")

Popping Out

During some orgasms, the vagina contracts so much that it can expel a penis. When asked about this, most women say "Push It Back!!!" With this kind of contraction, it feels good to have a penis deep inside a vagina, even if it might take quite a thrust to keep it in or get it back in.

Thrustless In Seattle

Some couples don't thrust at all during intercourse, but move their entire bodies in sync or the man might do a circular motion with his penis or pelvic bone pushing against the woman's clitoris. And some couples occasionally stay really still during intercourse and simply try to coordinate their breathing. For instance, one partner breathes in at the exact moment that the other breathes out.

You don't have to be a Zen master to achieve wonderful experi-ences with breathing instead of thrusting. You don't even need to meditate six hours a day or stand on your head while chanting some mysterious incantation. All you need to do is be in sync with each other.

Another interesting way of enjoying intercourse without thrusting is to play "squeezing genitals." It is based upon the anatomical fact that when the male squeezes or contracts his erect penis it momentarily changes diameter, and when the woman squeezes her vagina it hugs the penis—sometimes rather snugly and with memorable results. To play "squeezing genitals," partners alternate squeezing their genitals. This can be extremely satisfying if your pelvic muscles are in really good shape, and it doesn't require a particularly high I.Q. Exercises for males to beef up their pelvic muscles are listed in Chapter 44: Dyslexia Of The Penis — Improving Your Sexual Hang Time. Women can do something similar by sticking a finger or finger-like object in the vagina and then squeezing down on it. Repeating this ten times in a row a couple of times a day will help tone the muscles that surround the vagina. Some women feel that this also helps them to achieve a stronger orgasm.

Riding High — Tom Landry Remembered

Each year a new book comes out that promises to reinvent the wheel sexually. For instance, a recent entry talks about a radical "new" way of having intercourse. The couple starts by assuming the traditional missionary position with the man climbing on top. Right before the thrusting begins, the man makes a quick shift towards the head of   the bed, like the Dallas Cowboys used to do at the line of scrimmage before the set call, back when they were America's team and Tom Landry was coach.

During this quick shift, the male pushes his entire body a couple of inches forward over the head of the woman. Not only does this tempt a man to obnoxiously rest his chin on his partner's third eye, but it puts him in the position of being able to say "Honey, your roots are showing something awful, time for a new bleach job." This new intercourse position is supposed to bring the man's penis in more direct contact with the woman's clitoris, assuming his poor weenie doesn't snap off between the down and set call.

There is no in-out thrusting motion to this new form of inter- course. The couple simply moves their hips back and forth in synchronized form, like those women swimmers do at the Summer Olympics. Fortunately, the founder of this new position says nothing about wearing ugly swim caps, or Dallas Cowboy football helmets for that matter.

This intercourse position does attempt to maximize clitoral stimulation by making the man "ride high." Guys who are sensitive lovers figured this one out long ago, although an occasional man may have had the knowledge forced upon him by a rambunctious lover who rode so low that she made him wonder if his penis would survive the night. Her low riding is the equivalent of his riding high. Again, a good way for a man to learn what angles his partner prefers is to pay close attention when she's on top. Or ask.

Nasty Reflections

Watching your genitals at work or play during intercourse can be an amusing and fun way to pass time. ("Sexy and hot" adds a woman reader.) There are several positions which allow one or both partners to watch the vagina swallowing up the penis and then spitting it out again — oops, passionately enveloping it. A good-sized hand mirror can offer a nice view of genital play until one of you accidentally kicks it over. Also, try using the magnifying side of the mirror. It will make you look huge! A woman reader comments: "That's a frightening thought."

Some couples also like to pull out the Camcorder and tape themselves when having intercourse. Entire books have been written on this subject. Precautions for making home movies are mentioned in the fantasy chapter, such as putting a big X on the cassette and keeping it in a separate place from the movies that go back to Blockbuster. There are also special video locks that can be put on tapes of mom and dad having sex so the kids don't accidentally watch and suddenly have the ammo to blackmail you out of every last dollar in your retirement fund.

Kissing When Thrusting — Size Vs. Intent

Sometimes there's nothing nicer in the world than kissing passionately when your genitals are locked in a loving embrace, but this simply isn't possible for some couples. For instance, if a woman is 5'1" and her partner is 6'4", there is no way her tongue is going to comfortably play inside his mouth at the same time they are having intercourse unless she has a really deep navel or a foot-long tongue.

One reason why it's impossible to make recommendations regarding intercourse positions is because different couples come in different sizes. For instance, some positions will feel better for certain couples who are relatively the same height and weight, while those same positions might be a total disaster for a union between Twiggy and the Jolly Green Giant. Likewise, certain positions will feel better or worse depending on the size and angle of your respective genitals. And some positions that feel best during the first part of a woman's menstrual cycle might give way to other positions during the later part of her cycle. And that's just physical differences. It really gets complicated when you factor in each partner's emotional desires and needs.

Ends & Odds

Here are some observations on intercourse that you might find helpful:

Some couples enjoy it greatly when the woman uses a vibrator during intercourse. The sensations can be very pleasing for both partners. You can do this in any number of positions that actually feel comfortable, or you can get all artsy fartsy and try doing it like the couple on page 322.

A woman who is on top and facing her man's feet can easily watch his penis as it bebops in and out of her vagina. She can also reach forward and play with his little piggies, or reach down and play with his big piggy and testicles.

Rear entry positions allow the head of the penis to focus on the upper front wall of the vagina, a place that some women find extra sensitive. It also provides extra padding, which can be very welcome if one or both of you is really bony.

Rather than thrusting, some couples find that rocking back and forth with a penis inside can feel quite pleasant.

Some couples enjoy taking an intercourse break in order to have oral sex (oral intermission); other couples like to have oral sex after intercourse, and some women have their orgasms by receiving oral sex before or after intercourse.

In Veronica Monet's video of women masturbating, some of the women used dildos. However, they used the dildos differently

Studies show that the guy who helps out around the house gets laid more often than guys who don't, causing speculation that Windex and 409 are better aphrodisiacs than oysters, expensive cars and a medicine chest full of Viagra.

than men use their penises during intercourse. For instance, it was not unusual for the woman to run the dildo between her labia rather than plunging it into her vagina. Some women enjoy a well-lubricated penis moving between their labia in this way, like a hot dog going back and forth through a hot dog bun, although you might skip the relish and mustard. The ridge around the head of the penis can feel especially nice as it glides back and forth over the clitoris. The woman can increase the pressure by pulling the penis tighter against her vulva with her fingertips. This is also called femoral intercourse. *For more information about Veronica, see page 600.*

🐏 In the highly recommended books "Tricks — More Than 125 Ways To Make Good Sex Better," author Jay Wiseman suggests having the man lie on his back and the woman places a pair of her panties over his penis. The penis sticks through a leg-hole, with the panties draping down over his testicles and between his legs. The couple then has intercourse with the woman on top. If the panties are silky or rayon-like, the material will stimulate him each time she moves up and down. *To order Jay's books, see page 607.*

🐏 Some couples find a well-trimmed and freshly bathed big toe to be a fun penis substitute. Also, the pad of the big toe or heel can be used rather nicely to stimulate a woman's genitals.

🐏 There are couples who like to gently bite each other's shoulders or run their teeth along each other's skin while having intercourse. This works best when the skin is well-lubricated and the lovers let each other know when it starts to hurt.

🐏 Some men and women particularly enjoy the feeling of intercourse after a woman has had an orgasm.

🐏 If for some reason a vagina doesn't get as wet as a couple might want, be sure to keep some water-based lube handy, or pick up glycerin suppositories from the drug store that can be put into the vagina ahead of time. As the former baby boom generation hot flashes its way into the next century, a plethora of pricey new "personal moisturizers" will flood the market, many of which contain glycerin. If vaginal infections are a problem, you might experiment with water-based lubricants that have no glycerin.

🐜 Women might not lubricate very well for the first couple of months following pregnancy. Extra lubrication can also help if the woman is taking certain drugs such as antihistamines, alcohol, pot, and if the man is wearing a condom or the couple is playing with sex toys.

🐜 Why not try feeding each other while having intercourse? That's what nature created papaya for...

🐜 Some couples enjoy putting a finger, thumb, small vibrator, gerbil, or butt plug on or in each other's anus during intercourse.

🐜 Most sex stores sell little plastic thingies that fit over a man's penis and provide extra stimulation to the woman's clitoris when she rubs up against his pubic bone. There is also a plastic device called a vibrating cock ring that some couples enjoy using, and a special vibrator in a harness can be strapped in place over the clitoris for use during intercourse.

🐜 Some vaginas make fart-like noises during intercourse. This is due to air that has been pushed into the back of the vagina. If you get embarrassed about these sounds, it might be helpful to remember that it wasn't just one of you who "farted," but that the noise was the result of the two of you doing wonderful things to each other.

🐜 There is one position where the man sits on a chair and the women sits in his lap, wrapping her legs around his waist. While this doesn't work for heavy-duty thrusting, the penetration can be really deep. Sitting up also allows more blood to pool in the pelvic region, which can help some men get better erections. You might try a similar position where the man sits in the chair and the woman sits on his lap but facing away from him (sitting spoons position?).

Signaling

Sex seldom works well when one partner is too passive or inhibited to let the other know what feels good and what doesn't. Fortunately, signaling during intercourse doesn't need to include words, because hands on a partner's hips or rear end can be great rudders—as long as the partner with the hips is hip to the hands.

To Come Or Not To Come...

People have this silly notion that women are supposed to come during intercourse and by thrusting alone. The fact is, way fewer than fifty percent of women have orgasms during intercourse. One reason is because the clitoris does not usually receive direct stimulation from the penis during intercourse. It gets its stimulation from the pushing and pulling of the inner lips while the penis does its thrusting.

As you will see from the comments below, many women who do come during intercourse need a little help from either their own or their partner's fingers.

> "I very rarely have orgasms with intercourse, unless I'm playing with myself at the time. The best way for me is oral sex or using a vibrator." *female age 36*

> "I don't usually have orgasms during intercourse. In a very open relationship, I can have an orgasm after intercourse by manually stimulating my clitoris, or by rubbing myself on his flaccid penis." *female age 26*

> "I usually have them with intercourse if my husband is rubbing my clitoris or using a vibrator while he is thrusting. Sometimes when I am really excited, I can have one just with thrusting." *female age 35*

> "I come faster sometimes when he's inside me, but I always have to rub my clit to climax." *female age 25*

In case you think these women don't like intercourse, think again. A woman can love the feelings she gets from intercourse, but still not have orgasms from it.

When Is Intercourse A Success?

Most books imply that intercourse is a success if you give each other orgasms and a failure if you don't. Hardly. This guide takes the position that intercourse needs to convey certain feelings between partners that are too primal for words alone. These feelings rest on the boundary between body and soul, and are transmitted from one person to another in many different ways. If orgasm is part of that process, fine, but simply having an orgasm is no guarantee that anything special has taken place. At the same time, it's possible to have intercourse with no orgasm at all, and experience it as being wonderful or enchanting.

When is intercourse a success? Intercourse seems successful when it leaves you feeling a little more solid, less grumpy, more able to face the day, and less afraid of the world when it's an overwhelming place. Intercourse is successful when it allows you to both give and get something from your partner that makes you feel a bit more whole   or wholesome and secure.

When is intercourse a failure? This book's criteria for failure is waking up at three or four in the morning, looking at the person who's sleeping next to you, and thinking "I wish I were home in my own bed, ALONE." This can be a particularly nasty dilemma if you are married or living together. Also, intercourse that conveys less pleasure than when someone leaves you a free hour on a parking meter is not necessarily worth having.

Pillows On Parade

Never underestimate the power of a pillow to help enhance intercourse. For instance, consider trying a pillow under the rear of whomever is on the bottom. For some couples, the change in angle increases sensation. (Depending on who's doing what, optimal pillow placement might be higher above the tailbone, or further down under your rear. Experiment to find what placement, if any, is good for you.)

If you like intercourse from the rear, keep a lookout for the right big pillow that might provide support and raise the woman's rear end to an angle that is both comfortable and inviting. The more humongous the pillow, the more fun. Experiment with bolsters and oddly shaped pillows.

Environment

If intercourse is seeming a bit stale, it might help to start doing it in a new location. Of course, it never hurts if that new location happens to be a four star hotel somewhere in Europe, but if you haven't saved up quite that many frequent flyer miles, here are a few other possibilities:

☞ **The Kitchen,** Always a fine place for intercourse until you have kids. But once the kids reach school age, the kitchen is usually free for an occasional nooner.

☞ **In Front Of The Fireplace.** There's nothing quite like doing it in front of the fireplace, until the woodsman delivers wet pine instead of seasoned oak and a slew of hissing, burning embers shower your naked back and rear end.

☞ **The Yard.** It's a shame to spend all that time and money making the grass grow and never fuck on it. Go ahead, give the gophers a show.

☞ **In Water.** Hot tubs, bath tubs, pools and other large bodies of water can be great places for people to do all sorts of nasty things to each other. But intercourse in water provides its own unique hazard because water washes away natural lubrication. The best solution is a silicon based lubricant. *Check out pages 174-175 for more info on this type of lube.* Another solution is to slip the penis inside of the vagina while both sets of organs are outside of the water. Then slither your way under the surface, penis-in-vagina. Aqua fucking is now do-able if you limit yourselves to a muted kind of thrusting. Oil-based lubricants can also help, but these sometimes mess with the vagina's ability to clean itself. If this isn't a problem for you, rub your genitals with a little massage oil before going under. Also, to help facilitate underwater handplay and other forms of sexual groping, coat your genitals with something oily while they are still dry-docked.

☞ **Sex At The Office.** Sex at the office often has the right elements of risk and mischievous fun. One reader is a commercial real estate agent who has keys to some of the finest offices in all of Los Angeles. When he and his girlfriend want a dramatic change of scenery, they check out the upper floors.

☞ **Candlelight.** An old standby for erotic ambiance is candlelight. Make sure that the candle wax doesn't drip on your carpet, because it will cost you a fortune to have it commercially removed. Also, one reader cautions that some types of candle holders get hot enough to scorch furniture.

After Intercourse — The Drip Factor

Unless a guy is wearing a rubber or pulls out and squirts to the side, he usually leaves ejaculate inside a woman's vagina following intercourse. OK, so where does the ejaculate go?

"Runs down your leg" says one female respondent. "It usually drips out" replies another. "Like water in a cup that's turned upside down" says a third. This might not be a problem if you are going to sleep, except for the wet spot on the mattress, but what if you had intercourse in the morning or at lunchtime? "You can usually get it out in the shower" was one response, while another woman says "Not true. It tends to drain out at its own pace, and all the showering in the world isn't going to hasten it along." Either way, what if you already took a shower or don't want to take one just then? "Sometimes I'll wear a panty liner" said one woman, "but it's not worth a tampon." All of the women who were asked said they know of other women who douche right after intercourse even when they have it at bedtime. Most thought this was silly and unnecessary. As one woman said, "It's not dirty; I put the stuff in my mouth!" Another woman said "I don't have sex with a man unless I really care about him... While this might sound a little weird, I find the occasional dripping to be a sweet and sometimes exciting reminder that he's been here."

Top Dog

It has been said that people who always need to be on top during intercourse are basically insecure, while people who have it more together are happy to switch off. If this is true, then intercourse is no different from life in general.

Also, feminists claim that intercourse usually follows a prostitute model of sex— once the male comes the sex is over. Maybe this book is terribly out of step, but it seems like a shame to end that way. It's also rude. Perhaps the two of you can talk about ways to help the woman get her share of pleasure if the man comes before she's ready to stop.

On Not Pulling Out

Staying inside your sweetheart after the thrusting is done can sometimes feel magical. Since most men lose their erections after coming, the two of you need to be somewhat clever, keeping the fading member in while getting comfortable enough to stay in each other's arms. Some couples like to fall asleep this way.

The desire to stay inside your sweetheart after ejaculation is one of the downsides of using a rubber. A man who is wearing a rubber needs to pull out soon after he's come. Otherwise he might leave the rubber inside his partner.

Too Early, Too Late

Men who have trouble coming tend to pump faster during intercourse, hoping this will provide extra stimulation to help them ejaculate. This is a bad idea. The rapid thrusting desensitizes the penis even more, and it's possible the female partner won't be able to walk right for a few days afterwards. This is discussed further in Chapter 45: When Your System Crashes.

While some women wish they had a partner who had trouble coming, it's a problem that is often more difficult to deal with than premature ejaculation, which is the topic of Chapter 44: Dyslexia Of The Penis—Improving Your Sexual Hang Time.

Passive Intercourse Vs. Masturbation

This section was included with an awareness that only some couples might be interested. Other couples will find that it has no place in their relationship or that it might even seem perverse.

Let's say a woman wakes up at 5:00 a.m., horny as can be, and would like to have something approximating intercourse. Her partner, on the other hand, is not a morning person and is pretty much comatose until noon. Assuming he's not the type who is an early morning grouch, he allows her to stimulate his penis to a point of erection, or maybe he's already got an early morning (REM state) hard-on. They then have intercourse in a position where he can be passive while she is active, or she massages her clitoris while his penis is inside of her. In a sense, she is using his penis as a dildo.

Or, let's say it's nearly midnight and this woman's partner is feeling sexually amped, but she is pretty much dead to the world. She doesn't mind him using her vagina for intercourse, but doesn't want to have to be into it either. So she rolls on her side, and allows him to have rear entry intercourse. (Women have been doing this sort of thing for years, but the difference here is the lack of false pretenses. She doesn't need to pretend that he is giving her an earth-shaking orgasm. It also helps if the form of birth control is the pill, implant or IUD, rather than something she has to make an effort to prepare or insert.)

Ah, you might say, why didn't the horny partner simply mastur-bate instead of bothering the one who is zoned-out? Sometimes a partner honestly doesn't mind being "used" for sex as long as he or she isn't expected to get all turned on. He or she might even enjoy the partner's pleasure. However, it is essential that the passive partner feels comfortable saying "Naw, not now," and the horny partner should be willing to masturbate if that is the case. And it requires a sex life that is fairly rich at other times, given how an entire diet of passive sex might leave the active partner feeling unvalued or the passive partner feeling used.

What's The Frequency, Dan?

When it comes to frequency of intercourse, people who ask "what's normal" usually aren't asking the right question. For instance, if you are in a relationship, good questions to be asking are "Do we have intercourse as often as each of us likes?" "Do we have inter-course more often than one or both of us likes?" The reason why these questions are far more important than "what's normal" is because the only thing that matters about sex is what feels best for you—whether it's three times a day or three times a decade.

Betty On Intercourse

What better way to wind down a chapter on intercourse than with a few passages from feminist writer Betty Dodson's book "Sex For One"? These quotes refer to things that transpired during Ms. Dodson's sex groups for women. Part 1 is a summary of women's experience with orgasm, part 2 describes a role-playing exercise where Betty Ann had the women take the man's role in intercourse, and part 3 includes general comments on intercourse.

1. On Orgasms

Some women had good orgasms with oral sex but not with intercourse. Others could come with intercourse but couldn't get off alone. Still others were having orgasms with themselves but not with a partner. All of the orgasmic women agreed on one thing: Their experiences of orgasm varied greatly from one orgasm to the next...

2. On Pretending You're A Guy During Intercourse

One amusing and informative exercise was called 'Running a Sexual Encounter.' It involved reversing sex roles with the women on top. We made believe that our clitorises were penetrating imaginary lovers, and we had to do all the thrusting. I would set the egg timer for three minutes, a little longer than the Kinsey national average. As the fucking began, I would participate and at the same time comment on everyone's technique. 'Keep your arms straight; don't crush your lover. You're too high up; your clitoris just fell out. Don't stop moving, you'll lose your erection. Don't move so fast; you'll come too soon. And don't forget to whisper sweet things in your lover's ear between all those passionate kisses.'

Watching the egg timer, I coordinated my theatrical orgasm with the ding of the bell, frantically thrusting for the last ten seconds. Then, falling flat on my imaginary lover, I muttered, 'Was it good for you?' and promptly began snoring loudly. It was always hysterically funny. Panting and exhausted, [the women] all exclaimed, 'How do men do it?' Complaints included tired arms, lower-back pain, and stiff hip joints. Most of the women had fallen out long before the bell went off. After that, there was always more empathy for men, and the women showed an increased interest in other positions for lovemaking...

3. Odds & Ends

Some of the women talked about experiencing pain with deep thrusting intercourse, while others claimed to want a hard fuck. In my youth, I'd confused hard pounding intercourse with passion, and experienced internal soreness afterward. I explained that I felt a sensitive lover would never thrust with violence. While I enjoyed a strong fuck when we were two equal energies in sync, I also loved the slow intense fuck.

Another problem the women complained of was lack of lubrication and the pain of dry intercourse. Some women felt inadequate if they weren't wet with passion. My experience varied; sometimes I lubricated when I wasn't even thinking about sex. Other times I could be dry even though I felt sexually aroused... (From Betty Dodson's book "Sex For One," Harmony Books, New York.)

Reader's Comments

Some of your favorite positions?

"My favorite position is doggy style, with me on my hands and knees, and him behind me. I like this best for two reasons: my vagina is tighter this way, and I can easily rub my clitoris and have an orgasm. I also love to sit on a guy while he is sitting up. This just feels wonderful. Our bodies are so close." *female age 26*

"Good old missionary, with me on the bottom and him on top!" *fem. 32*

"One of my favorite positions is sitting in his lap in a chair. He can kiss my neck or armpits, which drives me nuts, and I can move freely. If we are on the bed, I can also lie back and touch my clit if I want."
female age 38

"My favorite position is sitting on top of him. That way I can stroke my clitoris or I can watch him do it." *female age 43*

"I enjoy having him on top but recently discovered that if we lie on our sides with me in front and I throw my upper leg over his, he can enter me from behind and it's very exciting." *female age 45*

"I like it best when we're doing it doggy style and I hold the vibrator and rub my clit with it. The sensation is wonderful!"
female age 25

"I like to bend over a table and have my partner insert his penis from behind. We get great penetration this way, and he is also able to hit something in there that makes me feel really good!"
female age 34

"I like to be on my back with my legs up while he is on his knees entering me and rubbing my clitoris. We started using this position when I was pregnant and I still like it best." *female age 35*

What do you like the most about intercourse and what do you like the least?

"Worst part—the big wet spot. Best part—making the big wet spot." *female age 27*

"It is wonderful when we first start having intercourse and I love the cuddling after. I don't like how, if you don't clean up afterwards, the ejaculate runs out of you (sometimes cold) and drips down your butt onto the sheets." *female age 30*

"I like it when he first inserts his penis into my vagina the best. The thing I like least about sex is having to really work for a long time to get him to orgasm when he's had too much to drink."
female age 34

"I like the beginning the most and orgasm, of course. If somebody takes too long, the middle gets dull." *female age 25*

"The first moments of penetration are the best. The wet spot on the bed, the worst." *female age 44*

"The part I like best is when my man spends a long time getting me hot until I want him so badly I can't wait and he finally sinks his penis into me, it's such a relief to finally be joined together. I like it least when he enters too soon and comes too fast and says "I'm sorry" when I had my hopes up for more." *female age 38*

"I love feeling him on top of me, kissing and caressing, and I love the feeling of his penis inside me. The part I don't like is the mess." *female age 35*

Considering only 7% of women have orgasms during their first intercourse, we asked our women readers to offer their suggestions about having intercourse for the first time.

"Make him read the 'Guide To Getting It On' first!" *female age 30*

"Use protection!!!" *female age 26*

"Be choosy. Take your time. Touch and explore everything, maybe tie him up and you take total control, it's amazing the feeling you get by doing that." *female age 36*

"Make sure you really want it and it's not about being pressured. Masturbate together first. Be comfortable together. My first time was painful and humiliating, there's got to be a better way."

female age 38

"It was very hard to do, but I waited until I was 18 to have intercourse. It was with a guy who I know cared deeply about me, which made my first experience very fun and comfortable."

female age 36

"Relax and don't expect it to be like the romance novels."

female age 32

"Make him go slowly and be sure that you are aroused sufficiently before you let him enter you because it will probably be a little uncomfortable the first time. If he rushes, it will hurt and you won't enjoy it at all." *female age 35*

WARNING: Certain kinds of intercourse injuries can cause your penis to forever bend in strange ways. The damage is often permanent and might not start showing up until years after your penis hits the wall, so to speak. The intercourse position where most of the injuries occur is when the woman is on top. Urologists strongly suggest that when using this position, you make sure the woman is very well-lubricated, and that she restricts her up-and-down motion. This can help decrease those instances where she sits down on your penis, but at a funny angle, or when it comes out on the upstroke and gets crunched on the downstroke instead of sliding in easily the way it's supposed to.   A good way to compensate for the decreased thrusting is to put a pillow under the man's rear end. This can help make his pelvic bone more accessible, and his partner might delight more in pushing down against it (grinding) than in moving up and down. That way she's got the penis deep inside, and gets her clitoral area worked too. She might also try squeezing, like if she's peeing and trying to stop the flow.

El Goof!

In typesetting this book, we goofed and ended up with two blank pages at the end of this chapter. Use them as you like, perhaps to doodle, or maybe to write your sweetheart a nasty note, or maybe to write us a nasty note. Your input is always appreciated, and may even end up in a future edition of the Guide, with your permission.

Chapter 21
Up Your Bum ~Anal Sex

The following recollections are of a seventy-one-year-old woman: "I grew up in the country... We had neighbors, Amos Wheatley and his wife. One night while washing dishes, Mrs. Wheatley told my mother that she let Amos 'use the other hole.' Then they had a baby girl, and I heard my father comment that Amos must have got it right at least once! Sometime later, Amos, who was uneasy about the expense of having a new baby, told my father he'd rather have had a team of horses. My father said, 'Isn't that expecting rather a lot of Mrs. Wheatley?'"

-As told to Julia Hutton in her book "Good Sex"
Real Stories From Real People" (Cleis Press 1992)

Anal Sex—Statistical Lowdown

Some couples would rather drink goat sweat than try anal sex; others enjoy an occasional rear end soiree. The reasons for doing it, as explained later, have more to do with stimulating certain nerve pathways than just for the perverse thrill of it all. This is why a number of heterosexual women and men, as well as some gay guys, like having their rear ends plowed.

Anal sex—*Penis Into Recutus*—is often associated with homosexuality. However, 30% to 40% of all heterosexual couples in this country have tried anal intercourse, with up to half of these continuing to do it on an occasional basis. While two- to five-million straight American couples are said to practice anal intercourse with regularity, only about 50% of gay males are into backdoor sex. Of course, straight or gay, these statistics refer only to anal intercourse. Here are some reader comments that indicate there are other ways to tickle your hemorrhoids than with a penis:

> "My boyfriend likes me to rub a finger on his anus while I give him oral sex. Gentle pressure and a rotating finger add a lot to his pleasure." *female age 23*

"I hate admitting this, but I like it when Dave wets one of his fingers and slides it into my anus. It is a huge turn-on, and there are times when it makes me orgasm. The only problem is pulling out. It always hurts coming out and usually throws off my bowel movements for the next few hours. It feels like I have to go..." [Editor's note: You didn't think we'd leave out the last part, did you?] *female age 26*

Whether you are straight, gay, or somewhere in-between, the chances are good that at some point in your life you might try anal sex. That is why the topic is covered in this book, although it may catch severe grief from the self-righteous and anally oppressed. Please be aware that this guide couldn't care less whether you do or don't practice anal sex, but it does have a few suggestions in case curiosity nips you in the rear.

Big Mama Nature ~ The Human Backside

When Big Mama Nature designed the female body she gave it a vagina that's rough, tough and durable. She made the walls of the vagina so they would stretch, swell, lubricate, and straighten out at times of sexual excitement. This allows objects of desire to slide in and out with a fair amount of ease and enjoyment.

Mother Nature was working from a different set of blueprints when she built the human rectum. That's because the rectum's main purpose is for elimination rather than romance. As a result, the walls of the rectum don't stretch and lubricate like those of the vagina, although they comfortably fit objects that are even larger than a penis on a nearly daily basis. (Think about it.) Reports that anal sex will damage your rectum are not backed up by medical fact as long as you use lots of lubrication and leave your crowbar in the tool shed.

Another difference between the rectum and vagina is that nature included a pair of pugnacious sphincter muscles to guard the gates of your anus. These muscular rings were designed to facilitate outgoing rather than incoming objects, although they can be taught to yield in either direction. The anal sphincters are two of the most important muscles in the human body as long as you plan on living and working in the vicinity of other human beings.

A Brief Historical Summary Of The Structure & Function Of The Human Rectum From The Time Of Cro-Magnon Man Until The Founding of Ancient Greece

If you consider the history of the human rectum, say from the time of Cro-Magnon Man up until the founding of Ancient Greece, its sole purpose was to hold things in. It wasn't until the Ancient Greeks invented sodomy that our rear ends became multipurpose. (In giving credit where credit is due, the Old Testament may have had an interest in the subject of anal sex that possibly predated the Ancient Greeks. At the very least, one of the early Biblical plagues visited upon the Egyptians apparently included hemorrhoids.)

Down & Dirty At The Acropolis

Thanks to the inventiveness of the Ancient Greeks, we now have things in our lives like politicians, lawyers, doctors and anal sex. The only one of these that should never cause you any pain is anal sex. If it does, you are doing it wrong, says psychologist Jack Morin who has written an entire book on the subject called "Anal Pleasure And Health." It is doubtful whether you will find this title at your local B. Dalton.

The key to pleasurable anal sex is training the anal sphincter muscles to open for incoming objects. One set of these muscles is under conscious control. It's what people use to maintain their dignity when waiting to use the bathroom. The second set of sphincter muscles is a total free agent that automatically closes whenever something pushes against it. In order to have comfortable anal sex, the second set of sphincters must be taught how to relax when you ask.

Rectal Aerobics —'a One and 'a Two and 'a...

> "When a guy stimulates my anus with his fingers or a dildo before entering it with his penis, it's much easier to take him that way. It's a very intense feeling, and can be very pleasurable, but it has to be slow & gentle, otherwise it's too painful."
>
> *female age 26*

This section has been written as if the male is doing the inserting and the female is receiving. Far be it from this guide to say how it is in your own relationship. Make sure that your fingernails are trimmed and your hands are washed. Wearing a latex glove and/or condom is recommended. Also, some people prefer to give themselves a quick enema ("short shot") with a bulb syringe or a pre-prepared store-bought solution before having anal sex. Others might equate this with removing the patina from the Statue Of Liberty.

Psychologist Morin suggests the following technique for teaching your rectum to relax: Each night for a week or so the male partner lubes up a clean finger and gently inserts it into the female's rear, pushing very softly and slowly.

Rectal expert Erik Mainard— known as Avatar of Ass—encourages a gentle massage of the anus and suggests angling the finger slightly upwards towards the tailbone, since that's how the rectum curves. He says to push in quite slowly and only as the resistance eases. This kind of digital exploration should feel very good for the receiver, otherwise the person who is inserting the finger is either rushing it or being a brute.

One way to help relax the anal area is for the receiver to push down as though she were trying to move her bowels. In addition to relaxing the sphincters, this adds a bit of suspense to the exercise. However, anal purists say that with the help of a patient, caring partner, one needn't trick the sphincters into relaxing.

The receiver should feel comfortable with finger penetration before attempting any further unnatural acts. It is also suggested that the receiver try inserting her own finger, i.e. when she is in the shower, so she can get a better sense of how her second sphincter works (digital-rectal bonding...). It is not until the second sphincter learns to relax that anal sex will feel comfortable, and if it doesn't feel comfortable, you shouldn't be doing it. If there is any discomfort other than a feeling of fullness which shouldn't be painful, spend an extra week doing the finger exercises or give up the concept of anal intercourse entirely.

Butt...

"I like to have my anus stimulated when I'm receiving oral sex. I like to have one finger inserted, but it doesn't have to be very far—just past the sphincter muscle will do. And rather than sliding all the way in and out, it is better if there is just a slight tugging movement. It adds one more sensation to the myriad of sensations involved in oral sex." *female age 37*

If you want anal stimulation, you need to ponder the profound question of exactly how you want it. Do you want it thin like a finger, or wider like a penis or dildo? Do you want it to move in and out, or do you want it to go inside and stay there, for the purpose of filling you up? (When it comes to purchasing sex toys, the former would call for a dildo-like object, the latter might best be served by a butt plug.) Anyway, when it comes to anal sex, you've got more choices to make than at a Bloomingdale's After Christmas Sale, and you need to think carefully about your choices because your anus is probably one of the more sensitive parts of your anatomy.

Rear end connoisseur Erik Mainard claims that people tend to stick fingers or a penis into a partner's rear end ("rosebud") when they would be better off spending more time massaging and caressing the external butt and anal parts. Until watching Mr. Mainard's "Rosebud Massage" tapes, we'd always assumed that a man either left his sweetheart's rectum alone, which seemed like a fine idea, or tried to stick   a penis up it, assuming that's what she wanted. But Mr. Mainard teaches several different ways of massaging a partner's rear end which seem pretty interesting if the two of you are into backdoor stimulation. To get Mr. Mainard's videos, call (510) 428-9063.

Romancing The Rear

Any kind of anal play, be it using a butt plug or a real-life penis plug, goes best with relaxation. Make sure the receiver receives a long, lingering massage, a candle-lit bath or whatever it is the two of you do to get really relaxed. That's because one of the places in our body where we tend to carry a lot of tension is between our butt cheeks. If you are going to do anal sex, you want that area to be as relaxed as possible before anything goes in. That could well be the difference between an experience that is pleasing and one that is painful.

Anal Sex Tips From Lucas, May He Rest In Peace

The rectum isn't encased with muscle except at the very end. This means that it can't hug a penis as a vagina might. Aside from possible pain and aesthetics, this is may be one reason why some couples only try anal intercourse once.

One suggestion for having a good time rectally is if the receiver occasionally contracts her upper thigh muscles. This helps to massage the penis, and the woman might enjoy the added sensations too. This may make it unnecessary for the man to thrust in and out. Also, it is recommended that the receiver be the one who backs into (or lowers herself onto) the penis or penis substitute, at the start anyway. And always apply massive amounts of lubrication.

When Playin' The Back Nine, Bag It First

Straight or gay, single or married, monogamous or slut from cyber-hell, it's always wise to use a condom when having anal sex. There are really good reasons for this that extend way beyond concern about AIDS.

Fluids deposited in the rectum are absorbed more easily into the body than fluids deposited into the vagina. In other words, deposit a wad of male ejaculate up a partner's rear, and chances are her hungry little colon is going to slurp it right up. Heaven only knows how her immune system is going to respond, but there is some speculation that it's not a healthy process. Again, this has nothing to do with AIDS. If you bag the penis before it goes up her bum, you've eliminated a very legitimate source of concern.

Also, some males get urinary tract infections from having anal sex without wearing a condom. In addition, no matter how hard you wash your penis after a rectal rendezvous, little pieces of poop still remain inside your peehole. This is not good for either of you, and at the very least can give her an infection if you follow with vaginal intercourse.

When it comes to condom use, there are two new possibilities:

REALITY: This is the new female condom, designed to be used in a woman's vagina, but what the heck. Some women like to use it for anal intercourse. This might give a girl greater feeling of control, and her old man doesn't need to wear a condom on his penis before plowing her rear end with it. Of course, sticking that bottom ring of the Reality Condom up your own rectum might be a bit of a challenge, but it is an option that you might consider. **Note:** As of press time, the FDA had not approved Reality Condoms for the purpose of buttfucking. However, an inside source tells us that tests are being conducted daily in the very halls of congress.

AVANTI: The new polyurethane condom, currently marketed under the name "Avanti," should be a butt pirate's dream. These are made thinner than traditional latex condoms and can be used with oil-based lubricants. On the other hand, they may have a higher rate of breakage than the old latex war horses.

Do not used ribbed or studded condoms for anal sex. And it's always a good idea to put a new condom on any sex toys that go into the rectum, and to wash the toy afterwards.

Beware The Butt Fuck Video

If you like the thought of doing anal intercourse, chances are good you like to watch anal sex videos. In her book, "The Ultimate Guide To Anal Sex For Women," Tristan Taormino warns that anal intercourse requires lots of patience and a slow, relaxing approach. This is the part that the anal sex videos leave out. Even in X-rated movies, they don't just go plowing some porn starlet's rear end without lots of preparation and anal foreplay—none of which the viewer actually sees in the video. So while it's fine to enjoy the hot action shown in *Anal Invaders Number Six Million And Thirty-Two*, don't for a moment try to replicate it in real life with a real life partner, unless she's inflatable and has a polyurethane rectum.

In Slow—Out Slow

No matter what you are putting inside a rectum, it needs to go in very slowly and come out very slowly.

Most people have no difficulty grasping the former, but they don't realize that anything being pulled out of a rectum, whether it's a finger, penis or butt plug, needs to be pulled out slowly. Otherwise, extreme discomfort and even physical damage can result.

Anal Intercourse Alternatives

One of the most sensitive parts of the human body is the skin that surrounds the outer rim of your anus. It's easy to stimulate this area with a thumb, finger, tongue or butt plug as opposed to sticking a penis all the way up it. For instance, some women who are receiving vaginal stimulation enjoy it when a partner puts pressure on their anus with a thumb or finger. Just be sure to avoid putting something that's been up an anus into a vagina.

Why Do People Do It?

Why do people have anal sex? Some women offer anal sex as a way of keeping their virginity. Some men offer anal sex as a way of getting work in the entertainment industry. Some couples like anal sex because it's forbidden. But the most obvious reason why people do anal sex is because they enjoy the way it feels.

"Anal sex helps me feel a whole different part of my vagina and vulva. The fact that it is so tight and kind of nasty is a turn-on to me too." *female age 23*

"My wife asks for anal intercourse on occasion, usually late at night when she is very aroused and her inhibitions are down." *male age 41*

"When Hillary is all worked up, she sometimes really likes me to massage her anus. When I slip a lubricated finger inside her, it is often the thing that puts her over the edge. If I have a finger inside her vagina and one in her anus, she reacts very well to the sandwiching of the wall when I press the two together. Other times, she really hates it when I touch her there. I can never quite guess when it's going to be a green light." *male age 25*

"Both of us like it. I will sometimes put a finger in her anus while we are having intercourse. It's very exciting for her, and I can feel my penis through the wall which I find to be very erotic." *male age 39*

A lot of people have the notion that the only reason women do anal sex is to please a male partner. Not a single woman in our survey who does anal sex mentioned anything about pleasing a partner.

Each one said she did it because she liked the way it feels. Aside from the obvious reason, which is that the anus is filled with lots of nerve receptors, it seems that the wall between the vagina and rectum may swell when the woman is sexually aroused. This wall might tug on the same nerve that transmits G-Spot orgasms to the brain. As a result, some women experience extra pleasant sensations on the wall between the rectum and vagina during anal intercourse that they don't get otherwise. Some women report getting an extra intense orgasm when they stimulate their clitoris at the same time that they are having anal sex. This makes sense, since the extra anal stimulation would intensify the orgasm signal that is going to the brain, as well as providing extra stimulation to the pelvic nerve.

As for men's pleasure, some enjoy having their anus massaged or penetrated, and some report having their finest orgasms when their prostate gland is being massaged. This could be, in large part, because the nerve pathway from the penis to the brain runs through the rectum. One large nerve bundle is located beneath the prostate. Another reason for why a prostate driven orgasm might feel "deeper" than a penis orgasm is because the nerve that transmits sensations from the bladder to the brain might also be getting extra stimulation.

A final reason why some couples do anal sex is for birth control. Anal sex is widely practiced as birth control in countries like Brazil that take seriously the Catholic Church's opposition to contraception. Perhaps this isn't what the Vatican had in mind. Or maybe anal sex is simply a hot concept down in the southern hemisphere. Is anal sex an effective means of preventing pregnancy, or can ejaculate run out of the anus and into the vagina? Pregnancies from anal sex are common enough that the term "Splash Conception" is used to describe them. Perhaps this is how people with anal compulsive personalities are conceived.

All Things Considered: Zucchini Revenge

It's only fair that if a guy wants to stick his penis up a partner's rear end, she should be able to stick something of comparable size up his. If vegetables are used, don't forget to check with your grocer or family doctor as to which are safest and most suitable. You don't want a vegetable breaking off and taking up permanent residence inside your man's rectum, do you? Couples who are less organically inclined might use a silicone penis substitute known as a dildo or butt plug.

Butt Plugs Galore

Butt plugs are dildo-like objects made specifically for the rear end. They have flared bases to keep them from getting lost on the hershey highway. Butt plugs come in many different sizes, and some even vibrate. People use butt plugs to give their rear ends a feeling of fullness. They are much better suited for this purpose than a dildo, which is made for thrusting.

Dildo Deluxe

OK, so you thought you finally had this sex toy thing under control when suddenly your old man informs you he wants you to fuck him up the rear. What's a girl to do? Pull out her real-life soft rubber version of Jeff Stryker's monster dong? Or does she use her silicone Rocketeer, or what about her Billy the Kid with the vibrating head?

When it comes to violating a loved-one's rear end, wisdom has it that a dildo which curves upwards is the way to go. That's because our rear ends tend to curve. The nice thing about using a dildo instead of a real life penis is that you can turn the dildo upwards or downwards to hit the right spot. The other nice thing about using a dildo is that you can call the women at Good Vibrations and get their catalog, which shows you which dildos are best for anal penetration. They'll also be able to tell you dildo will fit into your new Malibu Two Strap harness. (Your Jeff Stryker dildo won't—it's too big!)

Note: If you plan to use a dildo for both vaginal and anal recreation, it is a very good idea to get a separate one for each hole. Having dedicated dildos helps decrease the chance that fecal matter will get into the vagina.

When A Partner Straps One On

"My boyfriend of five years actually made the suggestion that
I penetrate him anally. I lubricated the finger with the shortest
nail on it and slowly slid it into his anus. He enjoyed it so much
that he asked for two fingers and then three. While doing this,
I also alternated sucking and manually pumping his cock with
my other hand. He had a mind-blowing orgasm. He tells me it's
the kind you feel deep down to your toes... I'm now looking for
a strap-on that stimulates me as well as him!"   *female age 40*

Some women hold a dildo with their fingers, others put it in
a dildo harness and propel it with their hips. A dildo harness looks
somewhat like a jock strap and holds the dildo in the same position as
a man's erect penis. This allows the woman to thrust-in-and-out,
more or less. Learning how to use a dildo in a harness is an acquired
art that takes time and patience. Also, keep in mind that a man's anal
sphincters need just as much rectal foreplay as a woman's.

Consider trying a harness that straps to your thigh. It might
be easier to control than the crotch model.

Toy Precautions

🐂 Contrary to what you might think, rectums are hungry little
orifices. Make sure that anything going up them is firmly anchored
on the outside of the body so it can't get sucked up inside. Dildos or
butt plugs with flared bases are best for anal play, as it is unlikely you
will need the assistance of an emergency room crew to get them out.

🐂 Be sure that anything inserted into the rectum is smooth
with no points or ridges.

🐂 Anal beads consist of five large beads on a string. They
resemble worry beads, but each bead is held in place on the string so
it doesn't slide. While anal beads can certainly be used to count your
worries on, people usually stick them up their rear end. They are
slowly pulled out, often at the point of coming, which is said to make

for a kick ass orgasm. Anal beads can be as small as mothballs or as big as tennis balls (OK, golf balls). If the beads are plastic and have sharp blow-mold edges, be sure to file them down first. Also, people sometimes encase them in a condom before inserting.

Prostate Stimulation

A number of straight men experience pleasant sensations from rectal stimulation, especially in the area of the prostate. Yet the only time most straight men get anal stimulation is during a physical exam. Then and at tax time.

If prostate stimulation is what you would like to try, consider the following, some of which was suggested by Kenneth Stubbs in his excellent book "Romantic Interludes" but translated into this guide's own homespun style:

For hygiene and comfort, wear a latex exam glove. With your cowboy naked and on his back, sit to one side or between his legs. Spend some quality time massaging his penis. Then work your hand down to the perineum area which is between his testicles and anus. Using the pads of your fingertips, press and rub in a circular way so that the skin moves over the tissue that's beneath the perineum. This is the equivalent of rectal foreplay. Eventually, slip a well-lubricated finger with a non-lethal fingernail over his anus. Massage it in a circular pattern, a bit like the Indians did when circling a wagon train. Gradually ease the finger inside, with the same gentleness and tenderness that you wish men would use when sticking fingers inside of you. Once your finger is fully inserted, make a "come here" motion. This should put your fingertip in the immediate vicinity of the prostate. The prostate of a young man feels like a walnut-shaped mini-mound of gristle, but in older guys it can grow to the size of a baseball. Let your finger gently explore and massage the prostate gland and area around it. With patience and feedback you should be able to generate some very pleasant sensations. You can also give your man a blow job or masturbate him with your other hand while stimulating his prostate. This can result in a very intense orgasm which gay men refer to as "a gusher." If you are really adventurous and have nothing better to do, you might try intercourse at the same time that you are tickling his prostate, mounting him while facing his knees so you can reach between his legs without dislocating your finger. Be sure to stop if there is any pain or discomfort, and don't even think about doing any of this if your lover has a pair of big old hangin' hemorrhoids... If you have any questions at all, be sure to ask your family doctor or nurse practitioner, and don't forget to tell them that the Goofy Foot Press sent you.

Men who are curious about feeling their own prostate can do so by reaching between their legs and sticking a well-lubricated finger up their own wazoo. Pressing on the prostate will probably cause a dull, subtle sensation in the penis. Some men find that physical contortions necessary to reach their own prostate can result in unanticipated trips to the chiropractor. A better approach might be to call Good Vibrations and order their catalog. Tell them you are interested in prostate stimulation. They will be able to help you with several specially curved sextoys that will help you stimulate your prostate comfortably.

Rimming

Rimming is a slang word for kissing ass, literally. It means sticking your tongue up or around your partner's deep space nine. Keep in mind that it's probably not a good idea to rim just anyone, unless he or she is your boss or the chair of your dissertation committee. One reason to avoid indiscriminate rimming is because it can be an effective way of getting hepatitis. It's the sort of thing to save for long term relationships, if you are so inclined. Good hygiene is a plus.

Note: One Gastroenterologist has said that by the time a couple has been together for a couple of years, they pretty much share the same anal flora. This means you wouldn't get anything more from licking your partner's asshole than you would get from licking your own. On the other hand, if you are in anything even remotely resembling a casual relationship, use a barrier before licking ass. Otherwise, you can get things like hepatitis. For the latest information on the medical advisability of rimming, call your local Gay & Lesbian health center or call one of the sex information hotlines listed in the resources section of this book.

Anal Fisting

Yes, Martha, there is such a thing. It can be very dangerous if done by the inexperienced. If you absolutely must have someone else's fist up your ass, the best book on the subject is said to be Bert Herrman's "Trust: The Hand Book — A Guide To The Sensual and Spiritual Art Of Handballing" from Alamo Square Press, San Francisco, 1991. Be sure to check with a physician first, perhaps one from your local Gay and Lesbian health center first. Even if you're not gay, they're more likely to know about the practice than a regular family practitioner.

Rules Of The Rear — A Pocket Guide

Here's a following list of precautions for anal sex:

1.) Straight or gay, married or whatever— if you're doing anal intercourse, use a condom.

2.) Make sure that anything about to go up your rectum is both clean and well-lubricated. Reapply the lubrication often.

3.) The human rectum curves in a funny way and your partner won't know which angle feels best unless you specify. This means that you'll need to discuss which positions and angles feel best. Positions are similar to those used with vaginal intercourse.

4.) Except for anal beads, remove anything you have placed in the rectum very slowly. This includes a penis.

5.) Don't stick a finger, penis, or other object directly into a vagina when it's just been up a rear end. Wash it first with soap and water. Make sure that your nails are well-trimmed.

6.) People who have anal intercourse should occasionally get a rectal swab done to check for VD, yet few individuals want to own up to doing anal sex so they don't tell their doctors. It might be easier if doctors simply asked "Have you ever tried anal sex?" but it seems unlikely that the answers given would exactly become a barometer of truth.

7.) Never, ever have anal sex unless your rectum is in 100% good health. Do not do anal sex if it is painful. Unless you are sure of what you are doing, check with a physician or qualified sex expert first.

Note: The senior author of this book went to a university with a top reputation in the sciences. Many of his classmates became medical doctors. A number of these did not seem emotionally equipped to deal with questions about sex, anal or otherwise. If you have medical questions about any kind of sex, it is possible that you won't be comfortable asking your private physician. An alternative is to call your local free clinic or national sex hot line. And while you may not be homosexual, a good place to call with questions about anal sex might be the nearest Gay & Lesbian health center.

End Of Chapter Notes: If anal sex puts people at higher risk for AIDS, why do a chapter on it? Driving a car puts most straight couples at greater risk for death than having anal sex. This guide would be more reckless asking most of you to start your car than in writing on anal sex. Thanks to the late Dr. Bruce Voeller, Mariposa Foundation, for help.

RECOMMENDED: If you are into anal recreation, consider reading the following two books:

"The Ultimate Guide To Anal Sex For Women" by Tristan Taormino, Cleis Press, San Francisco, 1998. In spite of its title, it's just as informative for men.

"Anal Pleasure And Health" by Jack Morin, Ph.D, from Yes/Down There Press, San Francisco, 1998. A competent source, covering all aspects of anal sexplay.

Chapter 22
Playing With Yourself

Before the 1960s, people who wrote books on sex stated with an almost religious fervor that playing with yourself (masturbation) was a very bad thing to do. Today, people who write books on sex speak with the same kind of religious fervor, only now they are saying that playing with yourself is a very good thing to do.

It doesn't seem as though anything has changed. That's because none of the so-called experts are asking you what you want to do. When it comes to the question of whether you should or shouldn't be masturbating, this book doesn't have any answers. It's your hand and your pants, if you want to stick one into the other, that's totally up to you.

What we can tell you is that as teenagers we felt certain that masturbation was an adolescent thing, something we would grow out of when we become adults. Silly us. There have been times when we've done it a lot, and times when we have hardly done it at all; times when it's felt great, and times when it's been a letdown. Whatever the reason for doing it, masturbation can usually be counted on to help take off some of the edge. It's also a wonderful nighttime aid that helps ease the transition between wakefulness and sleep, and contrary to what you might think, it can have an important role in relationships even when the sex between partners is totally satisfying.

> "If I have a test to study for and am getting burned out, sometimes I'll masturbate just to take a break from it. After I'm done, I'll be relaxed and ready to work again. I'll masturbate as a way to get to sleep. I'll masturbate when I'm having a bad day or am bored. And of course, I'll masturbate when I'm feeling sexually aroused." *male age 20*

Playing With This Chapter

Playing with yourself can be a way to explore and pamper your body, as well as exploring the sexual feelings that you might be having about someone else.

Some people find that their bodies simply work better if they have an orgasm every day or two, with masturbation being a natural way to help this happen. Do you ever get into a certain state of mind where you need to masturbate just to relax enough so you can get the rest of your work done?

Whatever your motivation, if you are going to get yourself off by hand, why not try to get the most out of the experience? That is the focus of this chapter.

Vital Statistics

The following was told to Harry Maurer by a young woman for his book titled "Sex: An Oral History" (Viking Press, 1994):

> "My mother has a vibrator that my father gave her one year. When I used to come home from college, I knew where she kept the vibrator, and I knew they never used it, so I would put it into my room and use it for the vacation. One summer I came home and it wasn't there. I was going crazy, I'm really a vibrator addict. Finally I was just so horny I said 'OK, Mom, sit down. Where's the vibrator?' She's like, 'What!' I said 'Look, here's the deal. I've been stealing your vibrator for three years, and I need it now.' She was blown away, but she goes into her room, comes back with the vibrator, and says 'By the way, have you ever used the jet in the hot tub?'"

According to just about everyone who has ever researched the subject, somewhere between 80% and 95% of guys eventually masturbate. Depending on whose statistics you look at, between 50% and 80% of women do the same.

Contrary to what you might think, people don't masturbate any less as they get older. In fact, many people who are married or deeply involved in a sexual relationship still get themselves off by hand.

Masturbation doesn't decrease a person's desire for shared sex. For some people, it increases it.

How often do people masturbate? It varies from a couple of times a day to sometimes never. As for the number of orgasms per effort, researcher Thore Langfeldt interviewed children in Norway from kindergarten through high school about sex. Langfeldt found that the younger boys and girls could give themselves multiple orgasms when they masturbated. But as they got older, the boys started reporting fewer orgasms per attempt, while the girls reported more. This is a trend that continued with increased age and experience.

What The Sandman Knows About Masturbation

"In my younger years, it usually took an hour or so before I had an orgasm. Now, if I'm especially hot, five minutes with a vibrator can do it, or about fifteen to twenty minutes by hand. Sometimes I like to keep things slow, I prolong it by starting and stopping. Other times, I just want to get off as fast as I can. Sometimes I masturbate, but not to orgasm. It feels good and relaxes me without wanting to come." *female age 47*

According to the sandman, the most common time when people masturbate is at night before they go to sleep, or before taking a nap. He says it makes his job much easier. People get themselves off at other times, too. For instance, it sometimes feels good to masturbate after a workout, since workouts can be sexually arousing. Plenty of people masturbate as a study break or when they have to spend long hours doing a paper or a project. It helps them refocus and return to the work at hand. Some people masturbate before a date so they will be more intellectually present. Women sometimes masturbate during their periods to help relieve cramping, or before intercourse to help it feel better. Some people wake up feeling really horny. They sometimes masturbate early in the morning, when the cock crows, before having their Wheaties®.

Note: We should have said Corn Flakes instead of Wheaties, since Kellogg's Corn Flakes were created to give children more stamina so they wouldn't want to do horrible things like masturbate. John Harvey Kellogg MD, founder of the flake, thought masturbation to be so evil that he encouraged parents to lift their sleeping children's nightshirts to make sure that no little fingers strayed into private places. To keep Dr. Kellogg spinning in his grave, this book encourages its readers to occasionally masturbate while eating a bowl of Kellogg's Corn Flakes. For more about modern religious prohibitions against sex and masturbation, see Chapter 29: Sex & Sects.

How Guys Learn

"When I was ten, an older friend showed me how to masturbate. He had a full ejaculation; nothing came out of my penis except for a few drops of clear sticky fluid. This was back in the 1960s, when astronauts first orbited the earth, and I believed that technology could fix anything. So I pulled out my erector set and decided to create a jack off machine. Planning and building it kept me busy for days. Unfortunately, it didn't make anything more come out of my penis than my hand did. Time, rather than technology, was the answer to that problem..."   *male age 45*

A lot of guys learn to masturbate from other guys, often a big brother or friends. One shows the other how he does it, or the experienced whacker might put his hand on the novice guy's penis and jerk it off for him. Guys who don't learn about jerking off from other guys eventually learn on their own. That's because a teenager has to be pretty numb to himself to miss the obvious connection between soaping the thing up in the shower and the nice feelings that result. Also, when laying face down on a mattress with a hard-on, most guys are eventually compelled to hump. Males eventually learn to masturbate because of all human organs, the penis is the only one that pleads to be yanked, stroked, lubed and squeezed.

Note: If they haven't been taught about ejaculation, some guys will experience anything from concern to terror the first time they ejaculate, e.g. "Oh no, I broke something," to "Please God, I'll never ever do it again! I promise, just make it OK." *For more on this, see page 71-72.*

The Group Thing

"I can understand all sorts of things about guys' sexuality, except for why they jerk off together. It seems so gay. Why do they do it?"

Good question. Maybe it has to do with the maturation process. Most young guys need little encouragement to take their pants off and explore. Getting naked can be so exciting for some boys that they get hard-ons from that alone. It's also natural for boys to share experiences, whether it's checking out an abandoned house or cave, or showing each other the things you do with your dick. After all, you'd want to show your best friend the model you just built or take turns doing the latest skateboard trick, so why wouldn't you want to jerk off together and see what happens when you get hard or come?

> "When we became teens, some of us boys would get together for a masturbation meeting in the tree house, but it was more the thrill of something exciting and forbidden than anything else." *male age 26*

Of course, plenty of guys will shake their heads and say "No way. You'd never catch me jerking off with another guy when I was a kid." Perhaps they represent the majority. Other guys will say "Sure, that's how I learned" or "That's how we did it." And some might even say, "It was neat back then; simpler and a lot of fun."

As far as masturbatory etiquette goes, some males have guy-like tea parties called circle jerks where everybody stands around and masturbates. There might be games connected with this, like who shoots the farthest or who comes the fastest (it's interesting how priorities change as you get older!) It's even been said that some young men feel terribly excluded until they have been allowed to beat off with members of the local gang. The urge to beat off together seems to peak before high school age, and drops off significantly after that. However, there seem to be plenty of adult males who, while identifying as heterosexual, enjoy beating off together.

The following answers to a survey in "Sex & Health" helps summarize some of what's involved:

"While partying with fraternity brothers, someone suggested a contest to see who could ejaculate the farthest. Each of the five of us took our turn in a tiled shower room. Surprisingly, the least endowed among us won!"

"Sometimes when I'm camping with a couple of my buddies and our girlfriends are otherwise occupied, we get to joking about sex. We soon get so aroused that when one of us whips it out to pee, we start joking and the others whip theirs out, too. Then we just start stroking ourselves and talking about our favorite techniques. We don't touch each other, but we do comment on each other's members and may cheer one another on to climax. We're all good friends and have become much closer sharing our sexuality this way."

Sex & Health has a large straight male readership. It's a newsletter we recommend highly. Here's a summary from their recent survey:

"95% of the men who responded to our survey characterized themselves as strictly heterosexual. Most (89%) were married and many had children. 84% of the survey respondents reported fantasizing about masturbating with or in the presence of other men, e.g. 'Although I'm happily married with two children, I do sometimes fantasize about masturbating with friends. I've thought about asking one friend in particular, but I haven't had the nerve.'"

Before you start saying "That guy's a closet case," consider why the most significant part of straight male porn flicks is the "money shot," where the guy pulls his monster schlong out of whatever female orifice it's been parked in, and then strokes himself to ejaculation—with a full camera close-up. Perhaps it's acceptable to be curious about another guy's ejaculation if he's just had his penis in a woman's body, but not acceptable if it's just two guys together.

How Girls Learn

"When I was young, climbing a flagpole always brought on such intense tingling feelings that I was only able to hold on tight and my legs would clamp around the pole. When the feelings subsided enough, I would resume climbing."

female age 37

"It was my freshman year of high school. I was kissing this guy and was getting really turned-on. He put his hand on my inner thigh and I was going crazy! This was my first heavy petting session. I didn't quite know what to make of it. When I got home, I went to the bathroom. My underwear was very wet. I went to touch myself and BAM! —instant orgasm! My very first. I've never had it that easy since." *female age 27*

"When I had my first orgasm I kept saying "Oh my God!" over and over. I was really shocked because I didn't know I could do that to myself!" *female age 25*

Girls don't do the "show and tell" game nearly as often as boys. They tend to learn about masturbation on their own or by reading about it. Sometimes women learn how to masturbate from the sensation they experience while cleaning or wiping their genitals, from climbing trees, poles or ropes, while on swings or when riding bicycles. Sometimes they learn by putting a pillow between their legs or by leaning up against something such as the washing machine when it's on the spin cycle. It might also happen when they have a sex dream and wake up before it's over—the sensation is still alive in their genitals and all they need to do is reach down and rub. One woman reported learning to masturbate by pushing a sanitary napkin against her vulva. Another by stroking the shaft of her clitoris with a pencil. The possibilities for discovering how to masturbate are way too many to name here.

Tools Of The Trade — Girl Variations

"I did it in front of a mirror with a condom-wrapped candlestick, and another time with the end of a comb." *female age 21*

"Bathtub, vibrator, boyfriend's fingers (my own don't work). Electric toothbrush handle, my ex-husband's hammer (the handle), even celery once." *female age 26*

"I get the most intense orgasm by leaning on a hard surface like a counter and wiggling around 'till I come. I also use a dildo, and I use my fingers to massage my labia and clit, occasionally fingering my vagina." *female age 37*

"I use a finger, then fingers." *female age 49*

"Occasionally I use my hands, but usually I use a running faucet before I take my bath." *female age 19*

"I rub my clit in a circular motion with my fingers, or use a trusty old Prelude 3 (vibrator). I've tried putting things inside my vagina, but so far that's been a very neutral experience — I need my lover's hand or torso to be attached to what's going inside. Sometimes I gently rub my chest as I masturbate, or run a soft piece of cloth over my nipples." *female age 47*

"I do it while reading a book or having a fantasy. Usually I stimulate my clit directly with one or more fingers. Only rarely do I put anything inside my vagina, although I do like the feel of a tampon. I also like anal stimulation. That will make an orgasm more intense and more diffused." *female age 36*

It is virtually impossible to list all of the different ways that women masturbate. A lot of women use their fingers while lying on their backs or sitting in chairs. Some do it on their sides, or while laying face down so nobody can see what they're doing. Some women may even occasionally prefer to squat.

Men sometimes have the fantasy that a woman who is masturbating sticks her fingers inside of her vagina. Some women do, but many don't. Instead, some women like to squeeze together the lips of their vulva or push against their vulva in ways that create pressure rather than penetration.

Plenty of women use lubrication when they masturbate, either their own (vaginal or saliva) or store bought. Lots of women like to use vibrators for masturbating, and some use dildos. *Chapter 23 is all about vibrators and dildos.*

Some women like to masturbate by using the faucet in the bathtub. After you get the water temperature just right, lay down in the tub and push your rear end up against the wall of the tub where the faucet comes out. It might help if you have an inflatable pillow to put under your rear to get the angle just right. Some women say it works better if they spread their labia open with their fingers so the water cascades onto their awaiting clitoris. **WATER SAFETY:** When masturbating with a water jet in a whirlpool or Jacuzzi, sit back at a distance and aim the jet towards your genitals. The current might be stronger than you think, so approach slowly. Some women like to pull their labia apart, others don't. Do not get extremely close to the jet and aim it up your vagina or rectum.

A woman who has extremely responsive nipples may make nipple stimulation an enjoyable part of her masturbation.

Thigh High

Some women are able to masturbate by squeezing their thighs together. The woman writer who contributes to the female part of www.JackinWorld suggests that some women can teach themselves to come by squeezing their thighs together. She suggests that you start by masturbating in the normal way, but press your thighs together when you start to have an orgasm. After a few weeks of doing this, masturbate yourself to the point where you almost have an orgasm, but pull your fingers (or whatever) away at the last minute and try to finesse yourself into orgasm by squeezing your thighs together. Once you are able to do this successfully, start with the thigh squeezing action a little earlier each time. Some women might prefer doing this with tight jeans on so they get an assist from the seam   in the crotch.

Additional Ways

One of us knew a woman who could have an orgasm by doing thirty-seven stomach crunches (mini sit-ups). What an incredible incentive for keeping your abs in shape!

Other women get off by humping pillows, water bottles, swinging on swings, tugging on underwear, rubbing up against things, with peeled cucumbers, and on bicycle seats when riding down bumpy roads. Some like to stimulate their rear ends, either by putting pressure on the anus or by sticking a finger or butt plug inside of it. Some like to look in mirrors, some get turned on by wearing their boyfriend-or girlfriend's, shirt or underwear, heck — fill in your own blanks.

Rubbing The Nub? Beating The Bush?
Giving Girl-Masturbation A Name

There are numerous slang terms for male masturbation. This   is not the case with female masturbation (Diddle? Jill Off? These are not exactly universal terms). Since women don't usually masturbate together, they haven't needed to establish slang terms to convey what they are doing. In fact, it has only been during the last thirty years that our society has even acknowledged the existence of women's masturbation. Maybe it's time that women adopt a universal slang term for masturbation, perhaps one of the women's magazine's could have a contest, or maybe the first lady could announce what she calls it.

Women Rock'n'Rollers Touch Themselves

While there are several rock'n'roll references to male masturbation, there seems to be only one song that mentions women's masturbation (on a major record label, anyway). This is a 1980s song by the Divinyls about a woman who touches herself when she thinks about her lover. Blessed with a great melody and steamy vocals, the touching herself song became an instant mega-hit. According to the lyrics of this song, the woman is so into her man that she doesn't seem to have much of an identity without him. This amplifies an age-old double standard: guys can masturbate because it feels good, but women need to frame their sexuality with love for a man.

Goofy Music Note: In a Rolling Stone interview, Christina from the Divinyls says that the song doesn't refer to masturbation. Perhaps she hasn't seen her own video. A reader disagrees: "First, I think the song is speaking of how thoughts of her man make her horny. Second, I fail to see how the song implies that she doesn't have her own identity without him. Do you think you might have read too much into the lyrics?" Editor's note: We stand by our guns. Unfortunately, the song is owned by four different publishers, one of which wanted an obnoxious amount of money for print rights. So if you are interested, you will need to listen to the "Touch Myself" song on your own.

Women, Masturbation & Intercourse

Some women give themselves orgasms during intercourse by pushing against a partner's pubic bone or by reaching down with their fingers and playing with themselves while the penis is inside of them. Is this masturbation, intercourse, or both? It clearly doesn't matter, except to mention that it is so normal maybe even Tipper Gore does it.

Also, it's not unusual for a woman to masturbate before intercourse to help her genitals be more into it, or after intercourse because she needs more stimulation or simply enjoys the feeling. It is unfortunate that women often hide this, or that their partners might not want to know about it. We consider it a sign of a good relationship when a woman feels free to finish what we couldn't, or when we help her get started and she takes it from there.

It's also nice when a partner feels free to masturbate on his or her own. Far from being a sign of deficit, this might be an indication there is a great deal of love and understanding in the relationship. See Chapter 15 for more about this.

As a cultural aside, the Eastern religions of Taoism, Buddhism, and Vishnu seem to encourage female masturbation. From their perspective, a woman's energy, like her orgasm, is considered to be infinite and life-affirming. The whole world is thought to be a better place when she masturbates.

Girls, Their Horses, & The Fifty Minute Hour

> "My first orgasm? I was riding my horse and I felt a strange sort of pleasure between my legs. I felt like I wanted it to stop so I could concentrate on my riding, but it felt so good..."
>
> *female age 18*

> "I was standing in the barn with my horse when I had a spontaneous orgasm. I gushed and everyone laughed at me for peeing in my pants. I was fourteen or so. I didn't discover masturbation until I was twenty, and then I thought orgasm was so incredible, I wanted one every day."   *female age 37*

Having grown up in a farm town, your author knew from a young age that it was unwise for any man to come between a woman and her horse. But can you imagine his amazement years later when an occasional female patient would describe the euphoria she gleaned from the back of her favorite gelding? It's information that's usually relayed in hushed tones of revelry and delight — warm, pleasing, primal sensations with one of nature's most magnificent creatures between her legs. Women rarely speak about their husbands or boyfriends with the kind of knowing sensitivity that is reserved for their favorite horse.

From Trigger To Vishnu...

After having an orgasm, women's genitals often stay primed longer than men's. Since their genitals stay pumped-up, some women experience waves of orgasm that can be finessed for the better part of an hour. Other women find a single orgasm to be very satisfying.

Because of the different possibilities, one woman might masturbate on and off for an entire evening, reaching between her legs every page or two while reading a book. Another woman might masturbate with the sole purpose of reaching a single, discrete orgasm, going from beginning to end without pause.

Of course, there are plenty of women who don't like to masturbate. Some never feel the urge. For others, touching themselves implies an uncomfortable investment in their own sexuality. While it may be perfectly fine to enjoy sex with a man, masturbation might feel dirty. This might be true even if their body badly needs an orgasm to help it unwind. There are also women who like to masturbate but don't like to touch their genitals. They might use a vibrator or masturbate with their fingers on the outside of their underwear.

The Limitations Of One Grip-One Rhythm (For Both Sexes)

If you always use the exact same touch and rhythm when you masturbate, you might be teaching your body to expect that and only that. Given how it's difficult for someone else to do you in the exact same way that you do yourself, you might consider occasionally mixing it up. For instance, if you usually get yourself off dry, you might try it with lotion. If you use your right hand, experiment with your left. Women might try it with a vibrator one time and another time in the bathtub, but not with a vibrator in the bathtub unless your vibrator is waterproof.

On Sucking Air (For Both Sexes)

Learning to breathe right is an essential part of being an athlete, unless maybe your sport is billiards. It's no different with sex.

When you are in the process of having sex, be it solo or with a partner, you might occasionally pay attention to your breathing. The Zen types encourage taking long, slow deep breaths where you imagine pulling the air all the way into your groin. This helps some people to have a more intense experience. From this book's more geriatric perspective, the extra O_2 helps keep us from having a coronary.

Guy Tricks — "First, Nuke A Jar Of Miracle Whip, Then..."

"I made a false pussy out of bicycle tire inner tubes, and it worked quite well. I have also used banana peels, watermelons, and a hole in a piece of wood." *male age 42*

A lot of guys use their hands to jerk off with. Some do it dry and some add lubrication which includes saliva, soap, hair conditioner, vaseline, vegetable oil, coconut oil, baby oil and anything else under the face of the sun that can make your pecker slick. Guys do better using an oil-based lubricant, and some even use a special type of facial cleanser called Albolene which is greatly admired for its jerk off properties. The trouble with standard moisturizers is that they dry up quickly, as do water-based lubes when exposed to air. If you use a water-based lube, try adding a few drops of water or saliva as it dries instead of adding more lube. Otherwise, you might end up with two sticky messes instead of one. See page 271-272 for information on different lubes. See page 167 for a more detailed description of how guys use their fingers to masturbate.

A lot of guys masturbate in the shower using soap as a lubricant, but that's kind of iffy because the soap can get up your peehole and irritate the living daylights out of you. A fine substitute is hair conditioner, or you might start each stroke by grabbing your penis around the base and pulling outward only. As soon as one hand reaches the head, grab the bottom of your penis with the other to keep an uninterrupted rhythm going. The hand motion is the opposite   to what you would be doing if you were pulling in a rope.

Another way that guys sometimes masturbate is by lubricating the inside of a condom with a water-based lube like KY Jelly or Astroglide. They slide the condom on an erect penis, wrap their fingers around it and pump away. A variation of this is to lube up the inside of a Baggie or plastic bag and put it between your pillows or

This young buck is taking his time.

mattress and box springs. You then get on your knees and hump the bag, being careful not to get your mattress pregnant.

Note: If you make an artificial vagina and heat it in a microwave, be cautious. It could feel nice and warm around the outside, but sizzle your little pecker when you stick it in the center.

Rushin' Roulette (For Men)

Guys tend to rush themselves when they are masturbating. There are a couple of reasons for this. First, a man who is jerking off often wants to get to the heavy duty pleasure part as soon as possible. Second is the matter of privacy, or lack of it, when you are growing up. The last thing most guys want is for someone to walk in on them when they are stroking themselves, so they teach themselves to come quickly and quietly. Also, if they are doing it in the shower, the extra speed helps them finish before the hot water runs out.

In employing the basic theorem of jack off relativity, $M=Q^2$ (masturbation= quick x quiet — Betty Dodson), the body becomes numb to anything but the rush of coming. This might desensitize a man to some of the more subtle sensations that can feel so wonderful when he is sharing sex with a partner.

Learning To Live In The Zone Of Subtle Sensation

Taking extra time when masturbating might help a man learn about subtle sensations that he won't notice if he's red-lining it. For instance, if he slows down as ejaculation approaches, he might discover a rush of feelings in his stomach, bladder, or from inside his rear end. Instead of going for the big squirt, he might try to back off a bit, teaching himself how to live in the zone of subtle sensation. If allowed to emerge slowly, pre-squirt feelings can be quite intense and last for long periods of time without becoming an actual ejaculation. Learning to stay with these feelings might help a man experience deeper levels of intimacy when he is with a partner.

Also, instead of reaching for his crotch each time he masturbates, a man might start by touching or massaging other parts of his body: scalp, face, neck, shoulders, chest, hands, feet, etc. This can be a way of reminding himself that sex is a full-body activity rather than something that just happens between his legs. (One female reader suggested that this section should have been written for women as well as men.) For new ways of stroking yourself that you might not have thought about before, check out page 167.

Socks Or Tissue?

In case you were wondering, Sex & Health reports that younger men tend to use socks to jerk off into, while older men prefer tissue.

Warnings

URETHRA SAFETY: Some people, both men and women, are tempted to stick things up their urethra (peehole) when they play with themselves. This can be a dangerous thing to do, and end up requiring an embarrassing visit to a hospital emergency room and maybe even surgery if the object gets lost in your bladder. If you absolutely must do this, find a physician or nurse who can show you how to correctly use a catheter and get sterile ones from a medical supply house or one of the mail order houses that include fetish and kink. Even then, you might end up getting infections.

BUTTHOLE SAFETY: Some people, both men and women, enjoy sticking things up their buttholes when they play with themselves. The advantage of using a finger is that it's not likely to get lost up where the sun don't shine. Just be sure it is well-washed ahead of time and that your fingernails don't look like Elvira's. A good alternative is to use a butt plug. See Chapter 21 for the skinny on butt plugs.

REALLY TWISTED STUFF: Over the years, we have heard of some seriously dangerous and life threatening ways of jerking off. If you are into that sort of thing, there are two ways to go. Maybe you need to act out some various scenes or kinds of kink that are best done in the company of people who know how to do that sort of thing as safely as possible. If that's the case, please read Chapter 31 which talks about kink. The other way is to get yourself some therapy, because some form of anger, confusion, self-hatred or fear is trying to express itself in the way you touch yourself. It is likely that your life in general, in addition to your sex life, will start to be more satisfying if you can begin to deal with these emotional issues.

End of Chapter Notes: Dr. Tom Szasz made a presentation which was similar in content to this chapter's introduction. This similarity was discovered after this book was already written and is strictly by coincidence.

Reader's Comments

Have you ever needed to masturbate while away from home?

Guess which answers are men's and which are women's!

a. "I have done so occasionally in the car, while driving. Tricky, but do-able." *age 37*

b "I would pretty much masturbate anywhere if I could. I know it sounds silly, but when I am on the beach or catching a killer wave I get kind of horny." *age 23*

c. "Yes. Although never at my current job, I have masturbated at work." *age 26*

d. "Yes. I've masturbated driving in my car, down the road, the urge was just too great and had to deal with it right then." *age 36*

e. "It has happened. I feel pressure like I'll go nuts if I don't get relief, and I'll sneak off." *age 38*

f "Except for when I was on a long vacation, I've always been able to wait until I got home." *age 26*

g. "One time I was driving and I had a terrible urge so I brought myself to orgasm. I've also done it at work once." *age 43*

h "I was once on a long distance bus trip and a teenage boy was next to me. I don't remember why, but I got very aroused so I put my coat over me and masturbated while he slept." *age 45*

i. "While my partner lived in a different city, I used to all the time. I would lock myself in the bathroom and put my feet on the wall while sitting on the toilet, with my legs bent and above my head. It was most satisfying this way." *age 37*

j. "I was using the computer at my brother's house when no one was home. While on the net, I was talking to someone who was so hot that I had to masturbate to release enough tension so I could keep talking online." *age 27*

a. female b. female c. female d. female e. female f. male g. female h. female i. female j. female Darned stereotypes....

Chapter 23
Oscillator, Generator, Vibrator, Dildo

Some people claim that the light bulb was the most important electrical invention of the last 150 years, others say it's the vibrator. This chapter is about vibrators and dildos. Its emphasis is on the use of sex toys by couples as opposed to individuals, although many people use these toys for solo sex. Please keep in mind that there are lots of people who don't like to use sex toys. They should be spared the sometimes evangelical prodding of sex toy enthusiasts.

Confusing Vibrators With Dildos

People often confuse the vibrator with the dildo, which is like confusing a rhino with a giraffe. Both are native to the bush, but that's where the similarities end.

Vibrators are valued for their buzzing properties and are usually rested on the outside of the genitals rather than placed inside of them. Dildos are penis-shaped and are used as such. They don't vibrate like a vibrator, but are made to be kept inside the vagina to give a feeling of fullness or to be thrust in and out. They can also slide up and down between the lips of the vulva.

Note: The common, battery operated, plastic vibrator is sometimes thought of as a dildo. While some women use them as such, the vibrating part of these little devices is usually located on the tip, which means a woman can't insert it deeply inside of her vagina and expect it to keep her clitoris happy. These are also made of hard plastic and they don't pack much of a wallop compared to the more adequately appointed AC models. While fine for business trips or weekend camping, these devices aren't in the same league as a well-made dildo or vibrator, although some highly devoted users would clearly disagree. One of these is illustrated on the next page. It is to the right of the dildo.

Vibrators, Dildos & Couples

Most guys have no problem with a partner who uses sex toys; many find the situation a total turn-on. However, some males worry that their sweetheart will start preferring the vibrator or dildo to them.

On the surface, this is not an irrational fear. First of all, the vibrator keeps running long after most men have delivered the mail, and nobody's ever heard of a dildo that couldn't get it up. Also, women can put the vibrator or dildo anywhere they want and totally control the proceedings. But strangely enough, if you are a considerate, caring, real flesh and blood guy, most women will still want you regardless of how often they fire up the old Magic Wand. In fact, it's hard to have a meaningful conversation with a vibrator, and no dildo has ever played catch with the kids or gotten up in the middle of the night to feed the baby. Also, sex toys aren't the sort of thing that you can cuddle up next to and feel safe with — not that you can with all men, either.

In purchasing a new vibrator or dildo, a woman who is in a relationship should consider making her partner a part of the selection process. This way, her partner won't feel left in the dust, resentful or inadequate. Perhaps it might not hurt to show him this chapter which encourages men to take pride in a woman's sex toys. It might also help to let him know that women who buy vibrators and dildos are often extremely happy with their male sex partners.

Making Friends With Your Lover's Toys

Rather than feeling at odds with your lover's vibrator or dildo, ask her to show you how she uses it. Hold her tight while she's getting herself off with it. If she has a vibrator, let her use it on you. And for heaven's sake, be sure to have her use it during intercourse. Some couples find the sensations to be sensational. It's even possible to combine vibrator play with oral sex. The man pushes a small battery operated vibrator against the bottom of his tongue while the tip of his tongue is touching his partner's clitoris. Or the man can gently push a dildo in and out of her vagina while planting warm wet kisses on her clit.

Vibrator Bits & Pieces

Here are a few vibrating facts that might be helpful if you have never used a vibrator before. (People with medical conditions such as phlebitis should check with a physician before using a vibrator.)

Coil Vs. Wand. There are two different types of vibrator design: wand-like vibrators with longer bodies and large heads, and coil vibrators with compact heads. Each type delivers a different sensation. For instance, coil vibrators are smaller and nearly silent. The sensations they produce tend to be more localized. The more popular wand vibrators are bigger and make a distinct humming noise. Newer models are rechargeable and will hum for up to an hour per charge. Some come with two heads which can be used for a variety of purposes, including on your genitals and rear end at the same time, or for up and down your spinal column.

🐛 **Be A Brand Name Snob.** While some people swear by the little battery operated cylinder vibrators, plenty of other people swear at them. The beefier AC powered vibrators, such as those crafted by Hitachi, Oster, Wahl, and Panasonic, deliver much more bang for the buck and won't let you down at critical moments. They are also well made and have warranties. Many of these units are now rechargeable and do a great job. Note: If you are new to vibrators, be sure to use it on the lowest possible speed at first while you learn to navigate the head around your pubic bone. Some new users have actually bruised their pubic bones by plopping the head of a vibrator on a bony pelvis.

🐛 **Geography.** Some women move a vibrator around the entire vulva rather than parking it in one particular place, others find a favorite spot and leave it there as though it were welded.

🐛 **Speeds & Mufflers.** Some users like the sensations of a vibrator full blast, others like to muffle the vibrator with a towel or even a pillow, and some hold the vibrator in a way that allows their fingers to transfer the vibrations. Some of the wand vibrators have variable speed controls, and many vibrators have a low and hi option.

🐛 **Hands.** Some vibrators strap on the back of your hand. Your fingers deliver the vibrations. These can be great fun to use, but they do tend to numb out the fingers (only temporarily).

🐛 **No Hands.** Some women rest a vibrator between their legs so they can use their hands for other things such as for holding a book, playing with their nipples, touching a partner's body, or channel surfing. There are also special harnesses which hold the head of a vibrator snugly between a woman's legs. There are even small vibrators with built-in straps that are sometimes called a Joni's Butterfly. They can be worn during intercourse, in public, at work, on a date, or wherever a woman might want to get her own private buzz in a public place. However, this type of vibrator can sometimes be heard in super quiet places like elevators or libraries, so plan accordingly. (One woman says that when she gets really bored she sometimes tucks a vibrating pager in her underwear and phones herself repeatedly...)

Good Vibrations is an excellent source for esoteric vibrators and vibrator accessories (800)289-8423.

〰️ **Positions.** Unlike most men, vibrators are meant to be abused. Be sure to try different positions with it on top of you, you on top of it, and on your side with it between your legs.

〰️ **Vibrator Vacations.** People sometimes worry that a woman will become used to the vibrator and want only that. This seldom happens, but if you are worried about it, consider taking vibrator vacations for one week every month, or alternate with different ways of getting yourself off.

〰️ **Attachments.** There are a number of vibrator attachments such as the G-Spotter and the Clitickler that can deliver a 'finger' of vibration to any specific location a man or woman wants.

〰️ **Vibrators And Boys.** Women aren't the only ones who appreciate an occasional mechanical assist. For instance, some boys learn to wrap a towel around their dad's hand-held vibrating sander and hold it against their genitals for a quick and easy orgasm. In fact, just about anything around the house that vibrates will eventually find a young man leaning against it to see how it feels. Likewise, a number of girls first learn about good vibrations by leaning against the washing machine when it's on the spin cycle. Leaning against the handles of some vacuum cleaners can also be enlightening.

〰️ **Vibrators And Men.** Given how many times the average male masturbates during his lifetime, it makes a certain amount of sense to try out a couple of gadgets and special sleeves that are made for that purpose. Some are interesting, most are disappointing, and few are anywhere near as convenient as simply using your hand. For instance, there is a special attachment for certain types of vibrators called a come cup which fits over the head of the penis. (Be sure to lube up the cup first.) Some men push the head of a vibrator against their hand as it is holding their penis. And some wrap a vibrator with a towel and lean into it. The towel helps to muffle the sensation, since vibrators numb some men out (temporarily). There are even special

vibrating sleeves that a penis can fit into. If the establishment that you buy from is reputable, the sales person should be able to tell you which of these works best.

Battery Operated Personal Massagers. There are many different vibrators crafted in every possible she known to woman or man, from cute little lady bugs to vibrating silver bullets and even vinyl hummingbirds. While some of these are made by reputable companies, few deliver the same kind of sensation as those that plug into the wall.

Ⲷⲷⲷ **Flying High?** When viewed through X-ray, some vibrators resemble detonating devices on bombs. As a result, security people might make you open up purses, briefcases and suitcases that have vibrators in them. Resist informing them about what your vibrator does and doesn't detonate.

Dildo Logic

Vibrators have become so socially acceptable that most department and drug stores prominently display them. Of course, few stores or manufacturers mention the real reason why people buy the vibrators, although most of the boxes show scantily clad women using them on their calves. With dildos, there are fewer options for subterfuge and denial. Big stores would be hard-pressed to advertise that dildos help relax tense muscles, although they clearly do. And if people hear a woman say the word "dildo" in a public place, they are more likely to think that she is referring to a male member of Generation X than something that gives her pleasure.

The next couples of pages offer enough information about dildos so you won't be in the dark if you decide to order up and join the Age Of The Dildo.

Dildo Vs. Penis

It is a known biological fact that the human penis when fully anchored to the human crotch imposes certain limitations upon a woman's sexual pleasure that the silicone dildo does not. For instance, a real penis can't be radically flipped upside down without necessitating a trip to the hospital for the man whose body it is (or was) attached to. There is also the matter of hardness: the male penis isn't always hard when a woman wants it hard, nor for as long as she might desire. And finally, a penis is not like a car that you can trade in every couple of years. Even if her spouse's penis might not be the best size and shape to fit her psyche or anatomy, a married woman is pretty well glued to it 'til death or divorce does them apart. Fortunately a woman needn't ditch the man she loves just because she prefers a Chevy-type penis when nature gave him a Ford or, gulp, Yugo. She can purchase a dildo instead.

In Search Of The Perfect Dildo

Dildos are made from a large variety of materials, including jade, acrylic, alabaster, latex, leather, glass, brass and wood. However, the most highly regarded dildo material is usually silicone. Silicone has a soft but firm texture with a smooth surface that is durable and easy to clean, although it doesn't stand up to cuts too well. The silicone material also warms up rather nicely, which is an added plus unless you like cold things in your vagina.

Since there is a fair amount of craftsmanship involved in producing a high quality dildo, be sure to purchase dildos from places that carry only proven products and take pride in pleasing their customers. One such place is Good Vibrations in San Francisco, where all of the products are approved by a member of the staff before going on the shelf. As for dildo particulars, here are a few to consider:

Price. Expect to pay from $35 to $75 for a good quality silicone dildo. Vinyl or rubber dildos are much cheaper, but each has its own set of drawbacks. For instance, rubber dildos have little divots in the surface which make them next to impossible to keep clean. You should always use a condom over rubber dildos.

Size. The most important consideration in sizing a dildo is width. One strategy for determining which width is best for you is suggested by the women at Good Vibrations. They say to buy a couple of different sized zucchinis, carrots or cucumbers that have an inviting width. Steam or nuke them for just a few seconds so they won't be cold, wash them and put condoms over them. Add lubricant and then try them in your vagina. Don't hesitate to use a vegetable peeler to fine tune the width. When you find one that feels just right, cut it in two and measure the diameter, which will most likely be somewhere between one and two inches. If you are the one who will be inserting the dildo, order one that's sized just right. However, if a friend will be doing the inserting, consider getting a dildo with a slightly smaller diameter. As for length, a four to five inch long dildo should be just right if you plan to keep it stationary inside your vagina, while a six to eight inch length might be easier to handle if you like thrusting.

Shape. When it comes to dildos, there are plenty of variations within a basic theme: Some dildos are made to look like penises, complete with veins and testicles, some look like dolphins or bears, and some have ridges. Dildos also have different sized heads. With a small amount of effort, you are likely to find the dildo of your dreams.

Lubrication. No matter how wet you might be, it's best to lubricate both the dildo and yourself before inserting, but don't lose track of where you put the bottle of lubrication. You may need to add more as you go.

Whadda'You Do With It? Contrary to what most people believe, women don't necessarily use dildos for thrusting in and out. For instance, she might like a dildo to be stationary inside of her vagina while she uses her fingers, a vibrator, or while a partner provides her with oral or anal attention. Or she might enjoy running the dildo up and down between her labia.

Numbers. Some women have one favorite dildo; others have a different size and shaped dildo for every day of the week.

Clean. Dildos should be washed and dried after each use, or used with a condom over them. If not properly cleaned, the porous surface of some dildos will grow microorganisms that are best not introduced (or reintroduced) into you body. If you are sharing sex toys, sterilize your dildo with hydrogen peroxide, rubbing alcohol, or a light bleach solution (nine parts water to one part bleach).

Anal Play. If you use the dildo in your own or your partner's rear end, be sure to wash it with soap and water before putting it into a vagina. Better yet, slap a condom on it before it goes up anyone's rear. Also, it is wise to limit your anal play to dildos with a flanged end or use a butt plug which won't get lost up your rear end. (People who enjoy both anal and vaginal penetration are wise to have dedicated dildos for each orifice.)

🌀 **Dildo Harnesses For Outer Wear.** Dildos with a flared base can be worn in harnesses which make them appear somewhat like erect penises. With a moderate amount of skill and effort, the person wearing the harness can use the dildo to penetrate a partner. This can be disappointing, though, because the dildo isn't connected to the wearer's nervous system like a real flesh and blood penis and she can't feel what the dildo is feeling. (Talk about an existential crisis!) Nonetheless, there are plenty of couples, both straight and lesbian, who enjoy using a dildo in a harness. The best harnesses are made of leather or nylon webbing. The actual geometry of harness construction and fastener application can be tricky; the catalog of Good Vibrations is full of advice about the do's and don'ts of dildo harness buying and wearing. Also, there are other kinds of dildo harnesses such as those that fit on the thigh. Users of these marvel at the versatility of such an arrangement and claim that the human penis should have been attached to the thigh of the male rather than between his legs. There is even a dildo mounted on a beach ball that a person can bounce up and down on. (Author Dorthoy Allison has written an interesting essay on her experiences with dildos and dildo harnesses. This can be found in her 1994 book titled "Skin.")

🌀 **Dildo Harnesses For Inner Wear.** So let's say you've got to go shopping at the supermarket or have a hot date and want to spice things up a bit. No matter where you go or what the purpose, you can now do it with your favorite dildo sticking inside of your vagina and no one will ever know. That's because they now make dildo harnesses that hold the dildo inside a vagina so it won't pop out when you are at the supermarket or making that special presentation before the chairman of the board.

🌀 **Techno'Dildo.** Some dildos are motorized and move in circles, as well as having a vibrating appendage that can be parked over the clitoris.

🐛 **Beware Of Gumby-Like Dildos.** Some dildos are embedded with wire rods to help keep whatever shape the person bends them into. Be aware that if the wire separates from the dildo material it will become embedded in the wall of your vagina or rectum.

🐛 **Menopause.** Masturbating with a dildo fully inserted might help some menopausal women without partners to keep their vaginas in good shape.

🐛 **Full Court Press.** Some women like to be penetrated in both the rear end and vagina at the same time. In lieu of doing a three-some, the dildo can stand guard at one gate while her partner fills the other.

🐛 **Suction Cups.** There are even dildos with suction cups on the bottom so the woman can stick them on a wall or the floor while she moves her entire body up and down or forwards and back while the dildo remains stationary. These can also be planted on the wall above your boss or supervisor's desk.

Sex Toy Layering — Dildos & Vibrators

Some women who have never enjoyed masturbating with their fingers or a vibrator go to town once they get the right dildo. The dildo provides an internal fullness that makes it much more satisfying when they stimulate the vulva with their fingers or a vibrator. Other women consider this to be sex toy overkill, and do just fine with their fingers or vibrator acappela.

Backdoor Men & Women

Good Vibrations reports that about half of the dildo harnesses they sell are to heterosexual couples, where the woman wears the dildo to do her man in the rear. So much for the notion that only gay men like an occasional rod up the rear. 🐛🐛🐛

End Of chapter Notes: Is David Bowie's "TVC-15" about a vibrator? .Special thanks to the "Good vibrations" catalog for technical help, to the "The Good vibrations Guide To Sex" by Cathy Winks and Anne Semans, and to those movers and shakers who shared their own personal tips.

Highly Recommended: Get yourself some of the catalogs from sextoy Mail Order houses like Good Vibrations, Xandria, Blowfish, Adam & Eve, etc. Each has it's own style (one is a bit raunchier than the others), but they are all fun to open, especially when the only other things in your mailbox are bills and supermarket ads. See the resources section at the end of the book for numbers to call for these catalogs.

Consumer Report: A very expensive ($90+) vibrator called the Euroscillator is now available. It recently made the rounds around the Goofy Foot Press, and we are happy to offer the following report: It's a bit like an electric toothbrush on amphetamines. The sensation is similar to a coil vibrator, but different enough to be interesting. It doesn't feel very well made and seems like it should be half the price. On the other hand, if you aren't satisfied with a wand or coil type of vibrator and don't mind forking out the bucks, don't hesitate to give it a try. You might find the sensations to be pleasantly pleasing.

Chapter 24
Basic Brain Weirdness & The Mind-Body Interface

This chapter is about mental events that can get in the way of having a good sex life, or just having a good life period. Some people would call these mental glitches, others might say that they are a normal part of the human condition.

Shyness

Shyness is a funny thing. Sometimes it sits like a shroud over everything you do. Other times it is highly selective, making only certain parts of your life sheer hell. Shyness can take many different forms and can be a great deal more mysterious than people give it credit. For instance, shyness can make you babble like a fool and say really stupid things or it can make you seem cold and aloof when you're really not.

To illustrate what happens when shyness gets the better of you, consider the following true life story a former high school student whom we will call Andrew.

It was a beautiful spring day about a month or two before the beginning of a somewhat magical time that later became known as the Summer of Love. This was the same year when nearly half a million young people gathered at a now famous farm in upstate New York for three days of rock'n'roll that became known as Woodstock. It was also a time when other people gathered on other farms throughout the country to do more mundane things like milk cows and tend crops. Regrettably, Andrew was more than three thousand miles away from that very special farm in New York. As for the summer of love, he had never even put his hand up a woman's shirt.

None of this stopped him from having an overpowering crush on a very popular young woman who was older than he. (Back then, younger guys rarely dated older women.) This female heartthrob just happened to be the local homecoming queen, or first runner up, or Future Farmer's Princess, or whatever it was that a young woman became in a small town when everybody claimed to like her. She was so special that he was too embarrassed to tell even his best friend about his lick-the-mud-off-her-shoes-if-that's-what-she-wants crush. Instead, he focused his energies on trying to act cool whenever she passed by.

To make matters worse, the young goddess was constantly surrounded by senior guys who had their own cars, lettered in football and baseball, and got drunk and never even threw up. He, on the other hand, saw himself as just another underclassman who had less than a snowball's chance in hell of attracting this woman's interest.

One day about an hour after school, some strange and peculiar force caused this special young woman to toss her books and pompoms into the back of her car and aim it for the very address where this young man lived. When the doorbell rang he figured it was probably the paperboy or a Jehovah's Witness selling the Watchtower. When he walked outside and saw who it was his lower jaw dropped so radically that a big wad of drool nearly fell out of his mouth. All things considered, he did well to maintain bladder control.

He stood staring at this babe like a deer in front of headlights. He felt so paralyzed that he couldn't even mobilize the words to invite her inside. When he did start talking it was in an almost glib way that didn't allow the slightest bit of closeness. He was clearly blowing it. After about ten awkward minutes of trying to deal with the situation, the young goddess blew the baffled boy a puzzled kiss and drove away never to return.

Many years have passed since this fellow botched the summer of love. He still feels just as clumsy and awkward when he meets a woman who he is really attracted to.

One-Night-Stands & Back Seat Bangers

You will simply have to find out about things like one-night stands on your own, and even then you may disagree with this book's stand. But working up a good fantasy and getting yourself off by hand tends to be less of a headache and is often just as satisfying as most one-night stands. The fantasy of a one-night stand is usually better than the reality of it.

Counterpoint: One reader from London clearly disagrees: "A one-night stand can be an immensely exciting and rewarding experience which you may remember your whole life."

On Being A Sex Object

People usually associate "being a sex object" with being a woman. However, this is about a guy named Steve whom women treated as a sex object. Steve was tall, blonde, blue-eyed and had a perfect body. In addition to being a fine surfer, he was a male model who was actually straight.

Everyone was thrown into total shock one night at Steve's tearful lament that he wished women would stop wanting him just for sex. (It's a problem none of us could relate to.) Steve was in a total funk because women were constantly diving for his crotch.

It's difficult to imagine that physical attractiveness can get in the way of leading a happy life, but people who are physical 10s are sometimes rather lonely. Friends of the same sex are often envious and sometimes feel threatened by the attention that the 10 seems to get. Members of the other sex tend to stare or else act bizarrely. People who are extremely attractive sometimes marry simply for protection.

What's Wrong With This Picture?

The opposite problem of being a physical 10 is being less than beautiful, and having someone who is drop dead gorgeous show a romantic interest in you. Instead of responding romantically, you might be saying to yourself "Naw, can't be true. Big mistake here."

While the physical 10 may be begging for romance, the less-than-10 is turning a great opportunity into a self-fulfilling prophecy of doom.

People Who Claim "The Opposite Sex Is Worthless"

Some people choose sexual partners who can't supply any of their emotional needs. It's as if they would be horribly overwhelmed to find someone who could be both a friend and lover, and therefore not quite so "opposite." Perpetual victims such as these claim that they are more mature and able to love more than their moron partners.

The fact is, people who have a healthy self-regard do not suffer the presence of fools and jerks, let alone sleep with them. The perpetual victim is just as immature and has as many problems with intimacy as does the jerk whom he or she dates or marries. Neither has much to brag about.

Giving Friendship A Chance

The only male-female relationships that we usually teach our children to value are those with romantic potential. As a result, men and women tend to approach each other as potential sex partners rather than as potential friends.

Platonic male-female friendships are a wonderful thing, but they sometimes become endangered if one person starts to feel sexual and the other doesn't. A lot of male-female friendships never happen because people are unable to work it out when one of them wants sex or romance and the other just wants friendship. Knowing that a friend wants romance when you don't can be uncomfortable. However, if he or she were given the time and understanding to cool his or her jets, the nonsexual friendship might be able to flourish for years to come. As for the person who feels smitten and then bitten, keep in mind that a platonic friendship often lasts for years, while that is not always the case with romantic affairs. You might be losing out on something special if you aren't able to accept the person as a friend instead of as a lover. (Another factor that often destroys male and female friendships are jealous spouses.)

Counterpoint: One reader comments, "This is a cursory and shallow discussion of this issue." We apparently struck a nerve. She's right; the matter is often far more complex than presented here. Sometimes it is filled with all kinds of hopeful expectations and excruciatingly painful disappointments, when one person feels romantic love and the other feels "only" friendship.

Initiating Sex When Holding Is What You Need

Some people find it hard to acknowledge that they simply need to be held, since asking to be held might make them feel weak, wimpy, vulnerable or frightened. Instead, they sometimes initiate sex when what they really may have wanted was physical tenderness and comfort. Fortunately, the desire for sex and tenderness often overlap, which allows us to receive both at the same time. But sometimes we need more of one than the other. Hopefully you can evolve a set of clear signals that will help your partner know what it is that you need, assuming you know yourself.

In Love But Out Of Sync

It's the saddest thing in the world when people have powerful feelings for each other but can't make their relationship work. For instance, one of you might become more settled and grounded earlier in life than the other. You may feel like putting down roots or becoming established while the other is still an emotional tumble-weed who needs to experience the outside world and soak in whatever it has to teach. The lack of synchrony forces a break-up. While you may not have any desire to get back together, there might always remain a place in your heart for the other person.

Breaking Up

Breaking up is the sort of thing that you either write a whole book about, or not much at all. Otherwise, you risk being trite about a phenomena that can leave even the strongest of hearts and minds crippled for months if not years.

The one thing we will mention is that breaking up doesn't always happen with a big fight or hellstorm of hostility. In fact, sometimes you spend your last hours together holding each other tightly, with tears flowing and a kind of desperate, profound sadness in both your hearts. And even if you are the one who is doing the leaving, the final steps toward the door can sometimes feel awfully lonely or empty.

Forgiving Yourself

Every once in a while we say or do something so stupid that even friends talk about having us committed. This can be particularly devastating when it results in the loss of friendship or love.

The best thing you can do in these situations is to figure out how and why you messed up. Then do what you can to mourn the loss and get on with your life. While there is much to be gained from intro-spection, there is little to be gained from beating yourself up. On the other hand, if you suffer from a perpetual case of foot-in-mouth disease, it is possible that there is some kind of chronic confusion or anger in the depths of your soul that prevents you from using good sense. In that case, the input of a respected friend, teacher, colleague, relative or even therapist might be an important thing to seek.

Stupid Mistakes — Young Vs. Old

If anyone ever tells you that making stupid mistakes is a part of being young and will pass as you get older, don't make the really stupid mistake of believing them.

True, you usually don't make as many mistakes as you get older, but that's only because your brain doesn't work nearly as fast. As your brain slows down you simply don't have the opportunity to make mistakes with the same lightning speed that you once did.

The Fantasy Of Love & Commitment

When you feel particularly empty inside it's easy to labor under the illusion that things will be better if you can just find someone to love.

Love is a special way of sharing friendship that can bring tremen-dous joy. It allows you to think and worry about someone other than yourself, which can be a much needed relief. It also lets you know that there is someone who believes in you when you don't particularly believe in yourself. But in spite of all its pluses, it's unlikely that love will take away your personal fears and insecurities, organize your chaos, cure your bad habits, help you lose weight, stop smoking, get in shape, or turn you into a better human being, not in the long run anyway. These are personal demons that we need to conquer on our own.

The Dark Side — Nights Of Quiet Despair

Sometimes you get hit by a certain mood, one that's a quiet mix of frustration, hopelessness and despair. It's when something deep inside you isn't working right, something incredibly human, but you can't put a finger on it.

Being in a relationship does not always help the bad feelings to go away.

Sometimes it becomes a contest between you, the despair, the beer, pills, sleep, food, sex or whatever it is that helps make you feel better. President's wives tell you to just say no, the disc jockey on the all night radio station never plays the song you need, and a river of pain cuts your heart in two.

Nights of quiet despair sometimes go away by morning.

Reader's Comments

One-Night Stands Vs. Long Term Relationships

"Not to sound like a dick but, a 'one-night-stand' is all about me. I am there to get and to be fucked. Sex in a relationship is about both of us. Adding in love and respect make sex in a long term relationship better." *male age 25*

"In 'one-night stands', the expectations far exceed the experience. I'm not in tune to what turns my partner on sexually as I would be in a long term relationship." *male age 39*

"'One-night-stand" sex can be exciting because you just don't know what you're gonna get." *female age 25*

"Sex in a 'one-night-stand' has it's own excitements. But, most of those are related to the 'naughtiness' of the situation and having to live with the thoughts and fears of possible exposure to STD's, as well as guilt concerning 'what type of person do I want to be.'"

female age 37

"I am a very horny person and I was surprised that I could not get wet when I was with a 'one-night-stand.' It was almost like a business deal. I felt no release and passion that I do in my relationship with Chris." *female age 23*

"My 'one-night-stands' have varied, some guys pass out drunk, or they plain just can't get it up no matter what you do. I really haven't had much luck with the one night stands." *female age 36*

How Does Sex Impact Your Long Term Relationship?

"I find that if we go without sex for a few days it throws my boyfriend and I off and we lose our common wavelength. After sex we are right back in tune with each other and there's nothing like that." *female 23*

"Sex enhances just about everything in my life. It relieves my stress and anger, and it increases our love and romance. It leaves me happy and with a certain glow. It's as though I can conquer anything!" *female age 36*

Chapter 25
Men's & Women's Experience Of Sex

Men's and women's genitals are generally found in the same location: behind the buttons of a person's blue jeans. But what about the way we experience sex? Do men and women experience sex differently? That's what this chapter is about. But first...

Forget Everything Else!

Forget penises, vulvas, and chromosomes. The biggest difference between male and female sexuality throughout the ages has been the fact that men don't get pregnant and women do. Forget the "behavioral influences" of estrogen and testosterone — instead, consider how differently we might approach sex if men were the ones who got knocked up and had to carry a baby inside themselves for nearly ten months, and if men were expected to be the child's primary caregiver for the next eighteen years.

Of course, there are other factors that influence men's and women's experience of sex. While most of these factors have to do with cultural roles and expectations, some reflect differences in biology. For instance, there are subtle differences in brain anatomy which may influence behavior. Consider how the female brain responds to the smell and taste of chocolate. Think of how different life would be if the female brain responded to the penis with half as much craving as it often does for chocolate.

There are also claims about differences in the behaviors of male and female newborns. The author of this guide spent a number of years in graduate school holding and studying babies, from 2 lb. premies to drug-addicted newborns of crack-smoking moms. He can assure you that the only difference between boy and girl babies that means a single thing is how the babies pee. Boy babies have the capacity to wipe out your favorite shirt, tie, glasses and notepad, while girl babies tend to be more forgiving. Working with boy babies requires a quickness of hand which some women report is just as necessary when working with the babies' adult fathers.

Perhaps a more relevant finding of infant research is that girl babies are every bit as strong and healthy as boys at birth, if not more so. Yet we often treat girl babies as though they were more fragile. For instance, researchers have dressed the same baby as a boy and then as a girl. When caregivers thought that the baby was a girl, they said things like "Aren't you pretty and dainty." When they thought it was a boy, they said "Aren't you a big one, look at how strong you are." Furthermore, if you want to know the sex of a baby from ten yards away, just observe how its daddy plays with it; girl babies get a plethora of hugs and kisses while boy babies get the rough'n'-tumble. With such profound differences in the way we raise our children, it's hard to imagine how subtle variations in neurology or genetics   even matter.

Typical Male Porn Vs. The New Female Porn

What happens to these babies twenty years later when they are having sex and maybe even thinking about making babies of their own? Do the women's experiences fall into the "pretty and dainty" category? Are the men's "big and strong?" Perhaps not, but our culture does have specific insults which it hurls at women whose sexuality appears to be "big and strong" and at men whose sexuality is "pretty and dainty.

To help illustrate possible differences in men's and women's experience of sex, we have included a few samples of pornographic writing. The following is a typical letter to a male magazine that is commonly used for masturbation. It has a monthly audience of around 5 million people:

It wasn't long before a wet area began to appear in the front part of DeAnne's bikini panties. I slowly started to pull them down, at first revealing a neatly trimmed patch of silken blonde down, then the glistening tip of DeAnne's swollen clit, and finally the rest of her hidden steamy treasure. The mere sight made me so hot I nearly exploded.

DeAnne must have sensed my excitement. Without saying a word, she ripped open my bulging blue jeans and started ravaging my nine inch cock with her pleading lips. Within seconds I was filling her hungry mouth with load after load of white hot cum. DeAnne kept sucking and slurping on my throbbing rod until she milked my big balls dry.

OK, so getting your rocks off is the name of the game in traditional male porn, with the focus being on the particular body parts that get you there the fastest.

Typical male porn holds the premise that within every woman sits a raging nymphomaniac begging to wrap her lips and legs around the teeming bulge of the nearest available guy. There is little concern that a woman's idea of fun might not include deep throating her teacher's 9" penis, that she might need a plumber for something other than a hard pounding fuck, or that she might find it less than pleasing when an out-of-shape salesman with muttonchop sideburns starts coming all over her face and chest.

The next two passages are from "Erotic Interludes," a collection of women's pornography — ah, erotica — edited by Lonnie Barbach (Harper & Row, 1986):

...J.B. tenderly caressed my breasts until I could feel the space between my legs grow warm and wet. His kisses were different than ever before, long and slow at first, then his tongue licked mine like fire dancing in the dark. His long, slender legs gradually, rhythmically inched mine apart. The tip of his cock played on my belly, and I couldn't resist rising up to meet him, opening my legs as far as the backseat would allow. A soft flash of red filled my vision when he entered me, his kisses wild on my face. I remember only the sense of infinite motion that followed. (Written by Sharon S. Mayes.)

Amy groaned with pleasure as his large hand cupped her gently and his third finger came to rest on the one sweet spot he knew so well. As he touched it she felt an electric current flow from his hand into her. His energy swirled inside her till the whole universe seemed to start spinning around... The spinning sensation rose up and flooded her whole body, pushing at the boundaries of who she thought she was... Finally, unable to hold the energy back any longer, she let it explode through every cell in her body, cleansing her with light and pulsating out into the room. (By Udana Power.)

Blinding light? Infinite motion? Spinning senses that rise up to flood her whole body, pushing at the boundaries of who she thinks she is? This has a different edge than "Within seconds I was filling her hungry mouth with load after load of white hot cum."

On the other hand, one female reader protests that the samples of women's porn "left me bored," while she found the male passage to be "erotic for me until he wastes his cock in her mouth." Several female readers have echoed this same sentiment, but with phrasing that is somewhat more delicate. At the same time, a male reader says that he finds the women's passages to be more erotic. Perhaps it's not so easy to generalize about the preferences of men and women, although the samples could easily be tagged as typical male or typical female.

Is It Really Different?

Are men's and women's experiences really different, or do they just use different words to describe them?

Researchers asked men and women to write a paragraph describing their experience of orgasm. A panel of judges could not tell the women's descriptions of orgasm from the men's. (So much for those charts on orgasm that make men and women look like they come from different planets.) Nonetheless, studies have shown that there are some sex-related differences in the attitudes of men and women, but mostly when they are with members of the same sex.

These differences decrease greatly when men and women are in mixed company.

But this isn't what Madison Avenue wants us to think. Advertisers work hard to make us believe that men and women are very, very different. That's because manufacturers can often charge more for products that are targeted to a specific sex, e.g. cigarettes, deodorants, and even hemorrhoid ointments which are for one sex only. It's a little surprising that we haven't seen toilet paper that's made just for a man's or woman's "special needs" — although one manufacturer, Kleenex, did try to sell man-sized facial tissues, which by the way, really were better for jerking off into than normal-sized tissue.

How Men And Women Experience Visual Pornography

It is often said that women aren't as turned on as men by X-rated movies, and that women aren't as sexually aroused by what they see. However, research is showing that rather than being turned-off by visual pornography, women are mainly turned-off by the premise of most male pornography which portrays females as submissive bimbos. When shown X-rated movies which are smart, fun, and where the sexuality conveys affection, both male and female viewers prove to be highly aroused. (If men were the ones who risked pregnancy during sex, perhaps traditional male porn might have a more caring premise!)

Note: In research on pornography, college students were hooked up to devices that measure blood flow in the genitals. They were then shown X-rated movies. Although these devices indicated that many of the female students were as sexually aroused as the males, several of the women were not consciously aware of their arousal. This may have been due to an experimental glitch. On the other hand, it might reflect how women are often raised to ignore their body's sexual cues. Also, it is possible that males wouldn't be nearly as conscious of their own sexual arousal if they didn't have a penis that's difficult to ignore when it gets hard. Whatever the case, women do rent about 40% of X-rated videos, the absolute numbers of which are staggering.

Role Reversal — Fingers Up Men's Rear Ends

Getting a finger up the rear during a routine physical exam makes many guys feel like they've been raped, yet they don't think twice about sticking their own fingers up a woman's vagina. It's possible that a woman's experience of sex might feel more private than a man's since her body is the one that is usually being penetrated. One woman reader comments:

"Even if he's wearing a condom, it still feels like a man leaves something inside of me during intercourse. He's got to have something I really want inside of me, or I won't do it."

One of the few times when a woman gets to stick something of hers inside a man is during French kissing. Some men love the feeling of a woman's tongue inside their mouths, while other men are only comfortable with French kissing if it imitates intercourse. Also, some couples are into certain kinds of anal sex where the woman penetrates the man's rear with her fingers or various kinds of sex toys.

Intimacy — Men Vs. Women

In our society, we often assume that women are better at intimacy than men. Is this true?

The answer depends upon how you define intimacy. While women are often better at some levels of intimacy (sharing feelings, talking about how the day went, etc.), neither sex fares particularly well when it comes to getting extremely close. Psychologist David Schnarch speaks to this issue in his book "Constructing The Sexual Crucible" (Norton, 1992):

"Popular wisdom suggests that women are more interested in intimacy than men... However, sharing feelings is not the same as open self-confrontation in the presence of the partner. When the focus is intense intimacy, there is no consistent gender difference in intimacy tolerance: almost no one wants it... When intimacy is distinguished from dependency and fusion, many women don't want it either."

A Final Perspective

Some evolutionary experts believe that nature has programmed men to ejaculate into each and every available vagina (the victory plunge), while women are programmed to couple with males who will offer the best chance to successfully raise a family (relationship material). The people who take these theories most seriously are the evolutionists themselves, but there is little in this chapter that contradicts such a position.

On the other hand, a man who is highly masculine and heterosexual might experience sex in the way that we would typically expect of a woman—sensitive, monogamous, intimacy seeking, while a very feminine, heterosexual woman might enjoy sex with numerous men, value it for the rush of sensation that it offers, and be turned-on by visual pornography. In other words, it's dangerous to generalize about how any of us, male or female, experiences sex.

The most important thing to be aware of about sexual differences is that your partner might experience sex differently than you do. Instead of pretending to know what that might be or making silly assumptions based upon even sillier generalizations, why not ask, explore, and find out for yourselves?

Also, as we get older, life presents us with opportunities for growth and change. Hopefully, you will be able to use these opportunities to increase the intimacy and satisfaction in your relationships, even if it means being more "male" or "female" in bed than your gender's stereotype currently allows.

End of chapter Notes: Our society uses the term "opposite sex" when comparing men and women. Are men and women really opposites? Few psychological test batteries are able to distinguish male from female test takers.

Chapter 26
What's Feminine, Masculine & Erotic

Guys, Girls & Gorillas: When a human male walks into a class-room of human females he can't tell which ones are ovulating (able to get pregnant). Few of the women even know themselves. However, when a male gorilla walks into a room full of female gorillas he automatically knows which ones are ovulating. That's because the rumps of female gorillas turn red and they put off an irresistible sex perfume that make male gorillas weak in their big hairy knees.

Most animals are highly influenced by the reproductive cycle of the female, except for humans. One reason is because we have bigger forebrains. Our souped-up forebrains allow us the choice of having sex when we want, how we want, and with whom we want. We also rely upon cultural cues in deciding what is masculine, feminine, and erotic.

Does having bigger forebrains mean we have it better than the other animals? Not really. While gorillas may not have as much choice about sex, they don't sit around reading books about it either. Nor do they seem to experience as much sadness and anguish as we humans.

What Society Finds Erotic

Each culture has its own definition of what's erotic and what isn't. Here are some examples of how these definitions differ from culture to culture year to year:

In Japan, it's a common practice for people to strip naked and bathe together. Nobody finds this kind of public nudity to be erotic or shameful, but Lord help two Japanese who kiss in public. In our society, it's nearly the opposite, with kissing being fine but public nudity being a legal offense.

Who Is The "Sexual Prisoner"?
a. The Moslem Woman
b. The Western Woman
c. Neither
d. Both

🐦 Women in Muslim cultures cover themselves from head to toe when appearing in public. Women in Hollywood appear in public wearing a few molecules of black spandex, designed more to tease than to cover. The women in Hollywood claim that their Muslim counterparts are sexual prisoners. The Muslim women feel that the real prisoners are the females in Hollywood. A neutral observer might call it a toss up. One female reader says that neither women are sexual prisoners, since they both use sex to control the people around them!

🐦 During the Summer Olympics, male gymnasts from the Russian team often celebrated good performances by kissing other male team members on the lips. Our U.S. male gymnasts wouldn't be caught dead doing that, not in public anyway.

🐦 In America, many straight women now wear their hair short, and straight men wear their hair long. Forty years ago this meant that you were homosexual. And think of the public outcry if a 1950s professional baseball player appeared in billboard ads wearing a pair of red bikini briefs; or if his 1950s beehive-coiffed girlfriend went to the grocery store wearing Doc Martins and a pair of male boxers. Or what if a straight American male tried wearing a pierced earring before the 1980s?

🐦 In America, there is nothing unusual about an unmarried 18-year-old woman having sex; but on the West Bank of Palestine or the Gaza Strip such a woman risks being brutally murdered by her own relatives for harming the honor of her family. This type of murder, which is called "honor killing," is supported by the girl's family as well as the rest of the village. Even the girl's mother and sisters support the murder because it protects the family name. The murderer, who might be the girl's father or brother, is usually exempt from criminal prosecution. In one village, they favor throwing the accused girl off the minaret of the local mosque, in other areas the father or a close blood relative murders her with an axe, knife, strangles her, or burns or buries her alive. All of this for having sex while unmarried, which millions of American women do by the age of sixteen or seventeen.

🐦 In Africa, nearly 80 million adult women had their clitorises and inner labia crudely cut out of their bodies as children. This type of "surgery" is considered an important passage to womanhood which many African mothers have done to their young daughters. In the Western world, a mother who did such a thing to her daughters would be put into jail. Of course, African women might claim that the clitoridectomy is just as cosmetic and feminine as our Western penchant for mutilating female bodies with breast implants. Mohammed only knows what an African woman might say about liposuction.

🐦 In the Hispanic culture of East Los Angeles some males don't feel masculine until they have gotten a woman pregnant ("given her a child"). Likewise, some Hispanic females don't feel good about themselves until they have borne children. Twenty miles to the west, in Pacific Palisades and Malibu, the last thing a teenage couple wants to do is get pregnant. They often seek an abortion if it happens. Furthermore, a Malibu woman who is pregnant often worries about losing her hard-earned, occasionally anorexic shape, while the pregnant Hispanic woman might relish the feeling of fullness that pregnancy offers.

🐦 Kim Edwards is a woman who taught English in a rigid Islamic country for two years and then moved to Japan. In the Islamic country, an exposed female body is considered to be the tool of the devil, and women cover it from head to toe to save the souls of men. After a few years in a rigid Islamic country, Ms. Edwards literally started hating her own body. When she finally moved to Japan, she was shocked to find herself treated as a normal person no matter what she wore. She could even bathe naked in public bath houses, while she would have been stoned to death for doing this in an Islamic country. (Kim Edwards' story is from her work "In Rooms Of Women" published in Laurence Goldstein's "The Female Body, Figures, Styles, Speculations" University of Michigan Press.)

🐓 Until the last couple of decades it was considered unfeminine for women in our society to enjoy sex as much as men. Valuing sex was a masculine trait, and some women even believed that it was unladylike to have orgasms. Yet there are plenty of other cultures which take it for granted that the sex drives of men and women are equally intense. In some cultures, parents even teach their children about enhancing sexual pleasure.

Masculinity and Femininity

Masculinity and femininity are concepts that make all the sense in the world as long as you don't try to define them.

For example, people in this country think of masculine as being rough-and-tumble, and feminine as being dainty and nurturing. Yet this isn't nearly as true in preschools that require little girls to wear the same kind of clothes as little boys. Once freed from wearing dainty outfits, little girls get rough-and-tumble too. Likewise, if little boys had to wear precious outfits that needed to be kept clean, they would probably act more daintily.

Equally as puzzling are all those rough-and-tumble men who become extremely nurturing and maternal when it's time to feed the baby. Do their aggressive male hormones suddenly dry up at dinner time? Do their brains change shape? And if you assume that women are less aggressive or the more nurturing sex, try talking to a random group of female lawyers, advertising execs, or women in entertainment.

While hormones may have some impact in determining male and female behaviors, what we learn from culture about our respective sex roles is clearly the larger force in shaping the way we behave. That's why it is hard to talk about the definitions of masculine and feminine unless we also know the particular country, culture, and year.

Ethics Vs. The Law

There is sometimes a big difference between laws and ethics. For instance, there are groups of professional people who have drawn up codes of conduct which they sometimes refer to as "ethics." As a result, it is unethical for certain professionals to have sex with the people they serve. It is important that these ethics be upheld in order to maintain the fabric of society. On the other hand, many states have laws telling married couples what they can or can't do in bed. Laws like these are silly.

Hypothetical: State Trooper pulls over a speeding motorist. Motorist says "Betcha' never had a blow job on this stretch of highway before." Officer lies, says "No, I haven't. Maybe we should do something about that." Which person, cop or motorist, is being unethical? Hint: The last time you took a driver's test, did you have to pledge that you would never offer sex to get out of a speeding ticket? Sometimes it's not unethical to offer, while it is unethical to accept. Also, while not unethical, it might be against the law in some states to offer a blow job to get out of a ticket (attempting to bribe an officer of the law).

Upcoming Chapters

From this guide's perspective, any culture's definition of masculine, feminine and erotic is arbitrary, transient, and often artificial. Nonetheless, people take these definitions seriously and get really bent out of shape if you ignore their local customs. In some of the chapters that follow, we consider society's sacred cow rules and traditions, as well as the perspective of people who don't abide by them.

Counterpoint: One reader from France writes "You have done a great job in this chapter explaining cultural differences, yet you blow it with the first sentence of your final paragraph. In my mind, it's a culture's rules and definitions that make it unique. It would be a very boring planet if we were all the same, and especially if we were all like Americans." 🐔 🐔 🐔

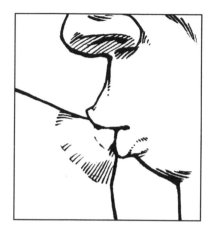

Thirsty?

Chapter 27
Goofy & Gay

Let's face it, ours is a culture based on the great hetero-sexual dream — marriage, kids, house in the 'burbs, and a rock-solid pension plan. Straight or gay, people who don't fully subscribe to the great heterosexual dream tend to feel left out. This is particularly true for teenagers who are gay, many of whom are desperately trying to fit in and behave like future breeders.

This chapter is about people who are turned on by members of the same sex, people who often feel left out in a big way. But first, the following is from the very funny book "Who Cares If It's A Choice? Snappy Answers To 101 Nosy, Intrusive, And Highly Personal Questions About Lesbians And Gay Men" by Ellen Orleans, 1994, Laugh Lines Press:

At What Age Do You Know You're Homosexual?

As you might imagine, this varies greatly. Guys seem to be aware of their sexuality early on. A single erection while watching Batman free Robin from the clutches of the Riddler provided many young men with their first clue. One gay friend told me that his childhood role models were Bert and Ernie. For others, it was Skipper and Gilligan.

Women seem to discover their sexual orientation more from personal experiences. Although I didn't realize it at the time, my first clue was when I zipped up Bobby Wolinsky's fly for him in the second grade. My teacher said this was not proper— that that was a boy's private area. At the time, I didn't see what the big deal was. Guess I still don't.

One man in Frontier's Magazine said he knew he was gay when it became clear that he preferred masturbating to the men's under-wear part of the Sear's catalogue instead of Playboy.

Gay, Straight Or In-between?

What's straight and what's gay?

Straights are turned-on by people who have genitals that are shaped differently from their own. *Gays* are turned-on by those whose sex organs are cut from the same cloth. *Bisexuals* are people who don't fit neatly into either category.

As for statistics, it is estimated that at least 60% of the population is straight, that 15% to 30% or more might be bisexual, ranging from barely bi to full blown bi, and that 2% to 7% of the population is gay. The numbers derived from different sex surveys vary hugely, depending upon how the questions are worded and how each category is defined. For instance, how do you categorize someone who occasionally fantasizes about having sex with a member of the same gender, but would never want to actually do it?

Of the various sexual orientations, which is best? We have no clue. There are times when life and relationships totally suck no matter what your sexual orientation; being straight is no guarantee of happiness. Nonetheless, it's what the majority of people are, and it is usually easier to be part of the majority no matter what the subject. Easier, but not necessarily more satisfying.[1]

When Your Minister And His Wife Have Anal Sex

While it's one thing to feel uncomfortable about another person's sexual orientation, it's quite another to make fun of them, occasionally beat them up, and pass laws that discriminate against them. Yet that's what a number of straight people have done to gays.

Consider the following: Straight or gay, most men enjoy having their penises sucked. If your partner is a woman, you have a woman sucking your dick. If your partner is a man, you have a man sucking your dick. Did some prophet come down from the mount and announce that a woman's mouth is better suited to suck a penis than a man's? Are her molars somehow penis friendly while a man's aren't? And believe it or not, just as many heterosexual couples in this country had anal sex last night as did gay couples. Maybe even your minister and his wife enjoy anal sex, not to mention some of our country's ultra-conservative senators and congressmen. Are they bad people because they enjoy an occasional butt fuck?

---

[1]Most studies measuring the satisfaction of straight, gay male, and lesbian couples find few differences, although the data often suggests that lesbian couples are likely to be more satisfied than their heterosexual or gay male counterparts.

Human beings have a long history of being uncomfortable with perspectives that differ from their own. As Americans, we have a history of being squeamish about sex. Add these two together, and it makes sense why so many straight people feel uncomfortable about gay sex. Still, if you are secure about your own sexuality, why should someone else's sexual preference cause a hostile or fearful reaction?

Gay Bashers & Reaction Formation

The University of Georgia is a truly fine institution of higher learning, and not simply because they use the Guide To Getting It On! as required reading in one of their classes, although it does speak well of them. The University of Georgia did a fascinating study on homophobia.

Psychologists gave a questionnaire about homosexuality to a group of sixty-four men. Based upon their responses, the men were divided into two sub-groups: those who were homophobic, and those who were not. The testers placed sensors on the guys' penises to determine if they were having erections. They then showed the subjects hardcore X-Rated videos of men having sex with women, and men having sex with men.

While only 34% of the non-homophobic men had erections while watching the homosexual tapes, 80% of the homophobic men did. 80% of the homophobic men got wood while watching men having sex with men. Get the picture?

Naturally, almost all of the homophobic men denied feeling aroused while watching gay guys having sex.

Heather & Cher's Place

While this guide doesn't care what your sexual orientation is, it does care that you respect your sexuality. This puts it at odds with what has been happening in some of the more visible parts of the gay male community.

For instance, several years ago the author of this book moved to Los Angeles to begin graduate school. That's when he joined one of the glitzy health spa chains whose spokespersons were celebrities like

Cher and Heather-someone. Being a person who loved taking a steam bath after a workout, it's also when he discovered that the men's steamroom at Heather and Cher's place is where some of the local actor wannabe types congregated to jerk off.

Call it provincial, call it petty, but there's something really annoying about taking a steam bath and having to worry about sitting in a puddle of actor-wannabe cum. This was before people knew much about AIDS, so the complaint was strictly aesthetic.

Livestock sexuality can be a lonely thing. This is just as true for straight people as for gays cruising locker rooms with pumped-up dicks hoping to attract the hand or mouth of a nameless faceless stranger. (Actually, if you consider the history of homosexuality here in America, being able to troll inside of Heather & Cher's locker room is quite an achievement. That's because before the 1960s, being a homosexual in America was a greater crime than being a robber or rapist. Having gay sex in the privacy of your own home could land you in jail and leave you branded as a sex offender for life. Even today it's illegal to perform a homosexual act in more than twenty states, in spite of the fact that approximately one-out-of-five Americans will take part in a homosexual act at some point in their lives.)

Given this rather frightening history of oppression, it's easy to see why gays may have viewed the freedom to jerk off in Heather and Cher's locker room as a tremendous victory. But there comes a time to stop measuring the present strictly against the past. Instead of encouraging its members to respect their sexuality, the gay community in the '70s and '80s went out of its way to sanction the practice of livestock sex. The implied message became "love me because I'm gay," which is about as dumb as saying "love me because I'm straight."

Of course, one doesn't criticize this sort of activity without being called homophobic or anti-gay. But maybe it's possible that this section was included out of love and concern, and an awareness that whether you are gay or straight, life is even more difficult without a sense of dignity and self-respect.

Some people might argue that this perspective is ten years out of date, and that anonymous trolling in the gay community is a thing of the past. If that's true, is the reason due to increased self-respect, or simple fear of the plague? If AIDS were to disappear tomorrow, how long would it be before 70s style cruising would return?

Postscript — That's Entertainment

Recently, the author walked past a group of young women who were swooning in front of the poster of a good-looking actor who has made it big in the last couple of years. This actor has had quite an impact on the American public—women want to sleep with him, their boyfriends wish they could be him.

Your author couldn't help but chuckle because he rarely forgets a face, even if it was through the fog in the steamroom of Heather and Cher's gym more than ten years ago.

Straight Male Friends Can Be Important

Contrary to what some heterosexuals fear, the last thing most gay men want is to have sex with a straight guy. While there are exceptions, most gay men would be bored by the concept. And if you are a straight guy who gets hit up for gay sex, it's quite easy to say "Sorry, but I'm one of those boring breeder-types."

Straight men should also be aware that within the gay community, conversations sometimes boil down to one of three topics: sex, AIDS, or gay politics. This is one reason why some gay men value their friendships with straight men. With straight men they are only friends and not potential sex partners, and they can have conversations about things like baseball scores and new car tires without the added postscript of who just died. Furthermore, their straight male friends aren't invested in the sometimes vicious politics of the local gay scene. Likewise, there are plenty of straight men who can use help with fashion, design, or advice about women from their gay male friends.

Straight or gay, most men prefer to be known for what they are rather than who they fuck. Yet there are large portions of both the gay and straight community where this is not possible.

A Sad Note About Teenage Runaways And Suicides

Statistics show that more than 50% of runaway teenagers living on the streets of New York City are gay or bisexual. A disproportionate number of teenagers who commit suicide are also gay, and that's only counting the ones who had come out before they killed themselves. Is there something about being gay that predisposes these kids to being depressed or not welcome in their own homes, or are these statistics an indicator of just how alienating it is to be gay in a society that is so uneasy with homosexuality?

Going Both Ways~Bisexual Considerations

At one time or another many people have a homosexual feeling or ten. It's no big deal unless you are also homophobic, which can necessitate all sorts of mental gymnastics. For instance, Queer bashers are allegedly straight men who enjoy beating up homosexuals. In beating up gays, are these men trying to punish or eradicate the queer part of themselves? And what if you admire the bodies of people who are the same sex as you. Does this mean that you have bisexual tendencies? Does anyone know, does anyone care? Also, plenty of straight people occasionally have dreams or fantasies of a homosexual nature. Does this mean that they have bisexual elements to their personality?

People who give full rein to both hetero- and homo- desires are called switch-hitters and are said to go both ways. While the ability to switch-hit might win a baseball player an added bonus, this is not the case when it comes to human sexuality. Both the gay and straight communities regard switch-hitters with suspicion. This is especially true in parts of the lesbian community where a *good lesbian* isn't supposed to even think about having sex with a man, and where you would probably get a black eye if you referred to a dildo as a *penis substitute*. As a result, the switch-hitter sometimes feels alien in both the straight and gay communities.

While bisexual women might by shunned by ardent lesbians, they fare much better overall than do bisexual men. For instance, a former hit song by a female singer named Jill Sobule is all about how she kissed a girl. Do you think that a song like this would have even been cut, let alone become popular in the straight community, if it had been titled "I Kissed A Guy" and had been performed by a male singer? Perhaps one reason for the discrepancy is because a large number of

straight males get off on the notion of two women making love, with a common fantasy being to watch their wives or girlfriends make it with another woman. On the other hand, not many women fantasize about their husbands making it with another man. Whatever the case, the following words of a bisexual woman might be helpful in explaining how a bisexual experiences his or her sexual feelings:

"It's funny to talk about the difference between male and female partners, because we did a lot of the same things. What I'm realizing now is that if I've got the emotional, intellectual connections, then the physical stuff can be about the same... There's a chemistry that happens, and I don't know if it's going to be with a man or a woman."

From Julia Hutton's "Good Sex," Cleis Press.

Life As A Lesbian, As If We Had A Clue...

People often think of gay men and women as being similar just because they are both homosexual. Silly them. To give you an idea of how dissimilar gay men and women can be, consider these statistics: while the majority of gay males in this country will have sex with at least a hundred different partners in a lifetime, the average gay woman has sex with a lifetime total of two to five partners. And while less than 20% of gay males have had sex with a woman, more than 80% of gay women have had sex with a man.

Setting a stereotype for gay women is not possible, says sex researcher Ira Reiss. While common personality traits and pathways to homosexuality have been found among some groups of gay males, Reiss has found few among gay women.

Lipstick Lesbians

People sometimes think that all lesbians are bull dykes or motorcycle mamas. That's ridiculous. This guide is willing to bet its left foot that there were as many lesbians entered in last year's Miss America Pageant as were on the women's professional golf tour. Lesbians are just as feminine (or unfeminine) as straight women. A number of very hot looking actresses and models are lesbians.

Equally off base is the notion that gay women make love in a delicate or particularly poetic way. The fact is, gay women get it on with as much passion (or lack of it) as straight women.

Beyond Brown & Yale

In the past, women who preferred women still dated and married men. And women who had lousy experiences with their fathers often replaced them with equally difficult boyfriends or husbands. In fact, it was usually expected that women should remain in heterosexual relationships even if they preferred being with women. There are at least five reasons why this is not necessarily the case anymore:

1.) Mothers used to teach their daughters that it was hugely important to marry a man and have his children. This is not as true as it used to be; 2.) Appealing lesbian role models used to be few and far between. There now exists a group of very appealing, successful, high profile lesbian role models in sports, business, rock'n'roll, and entertainment; 3.) It is now acceptable for lesbian couples to have children by artificial insemination, spawning a whole new market for turkey basters; 4.) It is now the height of academic chic for angst-filled coeds to have lesbian affairs at schools other than just Brown and Yale; and 5.) Straight women get no respect at the Dinah Shore Golf Classic.

Mistaken identity?

Women in our society can hug, hold hands or dance together and it is not considered a sign of homosexuality. As a result, they can have homosexual feelings without acknowledging them as that. The following statements by two lesbians help describe how this lack of labeling can impact female homosexual thought (from "Women's Sexual Development" edited by Martha Kirpactrick, published by International Universities Press):

> "I never thought of homosexual as relating to women, only to men..."

> "Our sexual relationship we kept to ourselves, and I was more excited about it than anything else. I thought it was just a delicious secret. And at the same time I had a mad crush on a guy."

Avoiding a label of straight or gay seems like a refreshing idea in this current age when one's sexuality is considered part of the community agenda. On the other hand, there are times when it is important for people who are gay to band together en masse, especially when their civil rights are endangered.

Lambs & The Biology Of Sexual Orientation

Much has been written in the past few years about how sexual orientation might result from biological factors. For instance, researchers have injected sheep with hormones that cause male-type behaviors. The female offspring of these sheep turned out to be stud muffin lambs who displayed so many stereotypical male behaviors that the other sheep treated them like males. These lady lambs even mounted other females, giving rise to speculation that lesbian lambs had been created by the injection of male-type hormones.

Other researchers are claiming that there are differences in certain structures human brains which they believe cause homosexuality. Stories like these tend to make headlines, yet there are plenty of researchers who say that we still have a long way to go before anyone will be able to demonstrate that homosexuality in humans has a strictly biological origin.

The sad thing about these studies is the way that some people use them as an excuse for being gay, e.g. "My son had no choice about being gay." Does one need an excuse for his or her sexual orientation? Whose business is it, anyway?

When it comes to needing excuses, the vast majority of serious crimes in this country—from violent attacks and child molestation to bank fraud and illegal drug importation—are committed by hetero-sexual males. If anyone needs excuses, it's the straight males who commit these crimes and the parents who raised them. ⚣ ⚣ ⚣

End of Chapter Notes: Are you a straight woman in love with a gay male? The best ever written on this subject can be found in Cynthia Heimel's wonderful book "Sex Tips for Girls." Two other books on this subject are listed in the resources chapter, e.g. when your husband comes out of the closet. We know of no books for husbands whose wives come out of the closet.

Chapter 28
I Knew The Bride —
Long Term Relationships

This chapter is about marriage and long term relationships. It doesn't even pretend to be comprehensive, but it does speak about weddings, tradition, sex in marriage, fights, kids, and divorce.

I Knew The Bride

> I can see her now in her tight blue jeans
> Pumping all her money in the record machine
> Spinning like a top, you should have seen her go
> I knew the bride when she used to rock 'n 'roll

"I Knew The Bride" performed by Dave Edmunds,
Written by Nick Lowe, Anglo Rock, Inc./USA,
RockMusic Co. LTD/The World

One of the fun things about weddings is watching the white-laced bride taking her vows of marital bliss and wondering if she has ever handcuffed the groom and done some of the outrageously nasty things to him that she once did to you. The memory puts a smile on your face and maybe even makes you blush. But it's not the kind of question you ask as you are working your way through the reception line — not with everyone's parents standing there presenting an array of cold clammy hands sticking out of pastel gowns and rented tuxedos.

Weddings — What's Love Got To Do With Them?

You don't have to go much farther than the average magazine rack to realize that weddings are big business. Plump, glossy 'zines with names like "Modern Bride" nearly bite your arm off as you walk by. The ads in these magazines reflect the many segments of our society that thrive on marriage-related businesses — bridal wear shops, tuxedo rental centers, wedding gift registries, boutiques, kitchen appliance stores, caterers, florists, bakers, diet plans, ministers, priests, rabbis, justices of the peace, churches, synagogues, reception halls, hotels, resorts, etc.

In our society, traditions like marriage (and Christmas) have become an economic spectacle rather than a symbol of love and commitment. Today's marriages are so choreographed that you seldom get a feeling that two people are making a promise to be there for each other no matter what, to be inseparable partners on the great rock climb of life. Instead, what you often get is the all too familiar bride-to-be psychosis, where the future bride and her mother become so savagely obsessed about things like table centerpieces and bridal gowns that any sense of love and devotion is pretty much out the window.

What if couples put as much effort into improving the level of intimacy and fun in their relationship as they do into selecting wedding invitations? And what about those bizarre, adolescent feeding frenzies known as bachelor parties? If guys need to see high-priced women getting naked or want to lick whipping cream off silicone-filled breasts, why not just do it? Why use weddings as the excuse?

Marriage is a big step, an important step. Hopefully you won't get too caught up in our culture's market economy view of marriage as a generator of crippling debt, and will instead work to make your relationship a safe haven in a world that is sometimes anything but.

Also, marriages might do better if people worked to maintain them instead of assuming that they are going to last forever. Maybe relationships would be kinder and gentler if each partner knew that the other could get up and leave if subjected to continual bitchiness or jerk-like behavior—the words "I do" being no guarantee of emotional or physical servitude. And what if couples took the money that they spent on weddings and set it aside for one long weekend each and every month, just to be with each other and have fun?

Sex After Marriage

Studies show that within a year of saying "I do," most couples start saying "I don't want to." A recent study by Call, Sprecher & Schwartz investigated factors that influence levels of sexual activity in marriage. Contrary to what they expected to find, the authors state:

Couples who want to make time for sex do, even with the obstacles of schedules, fatigue, and work related emotional complications. The DINS dilemma (double income, no sex) may be a myth.

The authors of this well-designed study about sex in marriage suggest that one reason why sex declines within a year after the wedding is because marriage makes sex legitimate. This might cause it to lose some of its erotic edge. It also seems that once the wedding ring is welded to the finger, people are less inclined to use sex to help make things better. According to this study, the following factors significantly influence the rate of sexual activity in marriage:

BUMMER 🐛 FACTORS

Factors that contribute to less sex in a relationship
are as follows:

🐛 **BEING OLDER.** Couples in their 20s had sex an average of three times a week, while those in their 30s averaged twice a week. Frequency tended to decrease with age for most, but not all couples.

🐛 **AN UNHAPPY MARRIAGE.** Who wants to make love when they are angry all the time?

🐛 **MUCH SCHOOLING & LITTLE SCHOOLING.** People with moderate levels of education tend to have more sex than people with a little or a lot. None of the researchers had a clue as to why. A reader comments, "You mean if I hadn't gone to law school I'd have more sex?"

🐛 **POOR HEALTH.** Who wants to have sex when they feel lousy?

🐛 **BABY OR CHILD UNDER AGE 5 IN THE HOUSEHOLD,** Parents of young children won't argue with this one.

🐛 **BEING CATHOLIC.** No kidding, being Catholic contributes to having less sex. No other religion had a negative impact on sexual activity.

🐛 **WIFE PREGNANT.** Plenty of couples love having sex when pregnant, but others don't.

HAPPY FACTORS

The following factors contributed to an increase
in sexual activity:

 FIRST YEAR OF MARRIAGE. This is a fine time for sex. While the
second year of marriage might not be as sexually active, it still
has a positive effect.

⌇ **MARRIED MORE THAN ONCE,** People seem to get it right the second time around.

⌇ **BEING STERILE:** Disabling reproductive hardware adds to sexual activity. Everybody is able to relax and enjoy it more when there's no danger of pregnancy.

⌇ **LIVING TOGETHER BEFORE MARRIAGE.** People who live together before tying the knot might be more sexually liberal to begin with, but this is a factor that leads to greater sexual frequency over the   long haul.

⌇ **A CHILD AGE 5-18 IN THE HOUSEHOLD.** Cherish your child's fifth birthday, since at age five and beyond he or she stops being a bummer factor and becomes good luck for getting laid.

Styles Of Problem Solving

Besides feeling love and friendship for each other, important ingredients in keeping a relationship happy is a couple's ability to solve conflicts. Couples with a knack for problem solving tend to have much happier marriages. (Da...)

Such couples approach conflicts with a willingness to talk things over and work them out. We are sure that such couples exist. Somewhere. The rest of us who don't do so well at conflict solving sometimes resort to sarcasm, name-calling, stubbornness, making threats, automatically giving in, taking blame needlessly, becoming silent, or pretending that there is no conflict when all hell is about to break loose. (Thanks to researchers Michael Metz et. al for specifics on conflict resolution.)

Single Vs. Hitched

Being single makes it easier to maintain the illusion that you are a perfect human being. Long term relationships force you to confront parts of yourself that many of us would rather not. For instance, in a long term relationship, your husband or wife will probably get fed up with your worst faults and remind you of them at least six times a day. If you are the rigid type who is incapable of change and compromise, then you might not be well-suited for marriage. On the other hand, a reader from San Francisco comments, "It could be just what you need."

Birds Of A Feather Get Bored With Each Other

Long term relationships can sometimes be a challenge to keep fresh and vital unless both partners make a constant effort to enjoy each other.

For instance, think about all the extra things you did to impress each other when you first met; you probably even cut your toenails or trimmed your bikini line. Why would there be any less need for romance and wooing after you've known each other for a number of years? If anything, mature relationships require more rather than less effort at romance and improvement—from cards, flowers and special dates to extra attempts at tenderness and even reading books like this.

Your Partner's Bad Moods

Like colds and flu, occasional bad moods are part of the human condition. In better functioning relationships, the partner who is in the good mood is sometimes able to maintain a healthy perspective when confronted with a partner's bad mood. He or she might even take steps that will help the other's bad mood to go away. But in difficult relationships, all bets are off.

In a difficult relationship, the partner who is in a good mood tends to experience the other's bad mood as a personal attack, even if it has nothing to do with him or her. Attempts to help are often filled with so much anxiety that they only make matters worse, and the partner in the bad mood might lash out at his or her spouse just for the heck of it. Such couples usually do better if one spouse has a job that keeps him or her on the road for long periods of time.

Waiting Until Cooler Heads Prevail

Contrary to what you may have heard about the value of releasing anger, trying to resolve a conflict when you are still fuming at each other is not always productive. Sometimes it is best to wait until cooler heads prevail. Of course, some people will use this as an excuse to avoid confronting a partner altogether. Then nothing ever gets worked out.

The Good, Bad, & Ugly

When you enter into a marriage or long term relationship, the chances are good that you will discover hidden but wonderful aspects to your partner's character. Cherish, respect and admire these. To deal with the less perfect parts of your sweetheart's character, consider the following:

1. Learn how to fight constructively. This means that no matter how nasty or unpleasant your fights might be, try to keep them issue-oriented so they can work their way towards a solution or compromise. This is quite different from fights that revert to name-calling or rehashing past hurts. These accomplish little, except to degrade whatever dignity you may have once had.

2. Fighting is preferable to indifference, unless you are getting violent.

3. Every once in a while, when you feel like wringing your partner's neck, do something really nice for him or her. This could end up being far more satisfying than fighting, and it might even get you laid.

4. Instead of blaming your partner for things that are going wrong or wishing that he or she would somehow change, try to find ways that you might be setting your partner up to be the bad guy. Also try to make changes that will help you to be a better or more effective person. This doesn't mean that you should stay in a relationship that's no longer working, it just means that the things you control most in a relationship are those that you put into it. If your efforts to change yourself don't inspire changes in your partner, then there's not much more you can do.

Sex After A Fight

Fights leave most couples worn out or sad. However, some couples enjoy sex after a good fight, given how their neurotransmitters are already fired up and ready for action. (On a biological level, the body might confuse a fight with sexual excitement, thus eliminating the need for tender preliminaries.) Hopefully, the reasons for the fight have been resolved and the sex isn't simply being used as a cover-up.

Sex After The Baby Arrives

Our society doesn't provide many role models for caring parents who are also sexual beings. We sometimes separate the two roles entirely, as though being a good mom or dad precludes you from giving great head or loving the feel of your partner's naked body next to your own. Just identifying as a parent may make you feel less sexual than you really are. Hopefully you will take take the time to talk this over with your partner before having children, as well as after. There is no reason why you can't be great parents and have

We sometimes forget about the potential of sex to create new life,
sustain love, and offer hope.

The illustration on the left is from the first edition of this book. However, some people got all worked up over the notion that the couple might be having intercourse while holding junior. We liked the original illustration, and still do, but for those of you who are uncomfortable with it, we bring you the above revision.

great sex — although the latter might not be as spontaneous as it was before the children arrived. *A married reader comments: "We had lots of sex during nap time and Sesame Street."*

Also, never discount the extent to which exhaustion might erode the desire to have sex, and don't expect to have sex if you aren't doing your fair share of the childcare and housework. While you've probably never considered vacuuming and taking the garbage out to be romantic acts, good luck getting laid without doing these sort of things once the new baby arrives. One reader who is a prostitute adds, "And for heaven's sake, buy a diaper service before you spend the money on a prostitute."

Divorce & Your Children

If your marriage has fallen upon rough times, don't assume that kids automatically do better if their parents stay together. While some children feel a terrible sadness when their parents get divorced, others feel relief. It usually depends on how bad the marriage was, how bad the divorce is, and if the kid gets to live with his or her favorite parent, if there is one. The absolute worst arrangement for most children is spending half of their week or a month at one parent's house, and half at the other. This is the psychological equivalent of cutting the baby   in two.

What often destroys kids more than the actual divorce is the parental lunacy for years before and years after. In an emotional sense, children of divorce often end up having no parents at all because their parents are sad, joyless, hateful or frightening to be with. If you are getting a divorce, do what you can to reach through your own pain, remembering that children need to see at least some form of hope reflected in their parent's eyes. And remember that your child's psychological health will in large part be determined by how amicably you and your former spouse are able to co-parent when divorced. We cannot emphasize this point enough.

End Of Chapter Notes: Special thanks to the Rosewoman, Daphne Kingma, for thoughts on divorce. Ms. Kingma has written many books on all aspects of relationships, from the rise to the fall.

Chapter 29
Sex & Sects

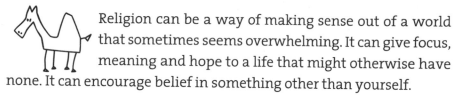 Religion can be a way of making sense out of a world that sometimes seems overwhelming. It can give focus, meaning and hope to a life that might otherwise have none. It can encourage belief in something other than yourself.

Religion can also be used as a force of oppression. Perhaps that's why so many people refer to their personal beliefs as spiritual rather than religious. This allows them to believe in something greater than themselves without endorsing the capriciousness and greed that has characterized so many organized religions throughout history.

Sex

It's interesting how some religious leaders obsess more about sex than even people who run adult book stores.

It is sometimes helpful to remember that what these religious leaders call "the word of God" is actually the word of man. For instance, in the Koran it states that women need to dress modestly in public. But it is a human religious leader who decided that "modestly" means covered from head to toe.

As it turns out, interpreting religious scripture is a lot like interpreting the Constitution of the United States. It is generally done by a small group of males who have won positions of power and title. They often claim that God is speaking through them.

Guns, Dollars & Faith

It doesn't matter if you are a Christian, atheist, Moslem or Jew, we live in a country that was founded with a Bible in one hand and a firearm in the other. As a result, many of our society's values are rooted in a rather strange trining of gunpowder and holy scripture. Faith is important, but it never hurts to have a Smith & Wesson handy...

The Party

Painting by Masaccio, 1425 AD. Wouldn't he just croak if he knew his work was in the Guide To Getting It On!

The Morning After

If you believe that religion has no influence over your daily life, grab your purse, wallet or conk your piggy bank over the head. Pull out any form of U.S. currency from a penny to a hundred dollar bill. Each piece of money bears two four-word phrases. One is "United States Of America." Check out the other.

The Bible

There is no question that the Bible has much wisdom to offer. Take for instance the passage from Luke that reminds us how easy it is to love those who love us, but how important to love those who don't. And what about the story of the poor fellow who was mugged and left for dead. A priest passes by and does not help, nor does a man from a blue-blood religious family. (They were probably on their way to church.) Finally, a traveler from a much-maligned country stops to offer aid. And that's how we got the story of The Good Samaritan. The Bible abounds with many thought provoking passages, including Matthew 18:23-35, which presents much wisdom about fairness and debt.

In addition to the many good things that it offers, the Bible is often blatantly unfair to women. Why did the Bible has such awful things to say about women and sex?

Virgins & Prostitutes

In the reference classic called "Butler's Lives Of The Saints," the name of each saint is written in bold black ink. Next to the names of the women saints is the additional inscription of "virgin or widow." The sexual status of the male saints is not listed. It is fortunate for men like St. Paul and St. Augustine that women saints were the only ones who had to account for their personal sexual histories.

It is also interesting that the majority of women mentioned in the New Testament are either virgins or prostitutes. There was little room for virtuous women who enjoyed sex, nor was there room for women to become priests, preachers or popes.

It seems that the Bible as we know it had many different sources. Some had more to do with war, politics and Real Estate than religious salvation. For instance, The Old Testament is filled with anti-woman sentiment, because some of the outlaying tribes of Israel worshiped a female god. The other Israeli tribes worshiped a more aggressive male god, and so they provided us with anti-female scripture such as the Bible's account of the creation, which denies women's role in birth and portrays Eve as a total bimbo. Not only does Eve cavort with the wily snake, but she leads Adam into sin via the fruit tree fiasco, thereby blowing the gig in the garden.

Sex & The New Testament

The New Testament shows Jesus of Nazareth accepting women and speaking to them in a way that shocked some of his contemporaries. Yet if Jesus did show a loving acceptance towards women, some of his followers failed to notice. Even Mary, mother of Jesus, wasn't considered a major player in church dogma until the 11th to 14th centuries, when a romantic wave of sentimentality toward women forced the church fathers to significantly upgrade her role. And during the early years of Christianity, the church forbid husbands and wives from enjoying sexual pleasure. For instance, St. Augustine proclaimed that husbands and wives were no different from pigs and geese unless they abstained from sex. Also, the church administered more punishment for oral sex than for premeditated murder, and a virgin daughter was accorded a higher place in heaven than her mother because the mother had to have intercourse for conception to take place.

Fortunately, some modern religions, both Christian and Jewish, are moving away from their early anti-woman and anti-sex biases. However...

Women Are Subservient To Men, & Masturbation Is Really, Really Bad

You think certain thresholds have been crossed, and then the Southern Baptists let us know that this modernization thing is out of hand. They've just announced that men are the head of the household, and that is that. Now word has it that they are taking their message into Utah, trying to convert Mormons, who are having their own little fuss over the legalization of Polygamy.

But that's nothing compared to the most recent Catholic Catechism Book for Junior High students. Published within the last two years, it states in no uncertain terms that masturbation is bad. Really, really bad. Religiously speaking, the Catholics have placed jerking off somewhere between grand theft and shooting heroin.

Bad Acts & Queer Angels

Religious leaders have often ranted and railed against certain sexual practices, from masturbation and oral sex to homosexuality, as though these acts were the handiwork of the devil. But what if God feels more honored when a person joyfully masturbates as opposed to saying a speedy rosary or spending an obligatory hour in church? After all, God created orgasm, while prayers and churches are the creations of men. What if God receives more joy when an unmarried couple lovingly shares oral sex than when a church-going husband and wife have passionless, missionary position intercourse? And who is to say that God hasn't created a group of homosexual angels to guard the gates of heaven? Maybe God has a sense of humor and brings out the queer angels whenever a redneck preacher or one of his intolerant parishioners has just died and is awaiting judgment.

Kindness & Warmth

The most important thing that this guide has to say about religion is something remembered from childhood:

There is sometimes a priest, minister or rabbi whom the children feel safe with and to whom they will tell the truth. To the other clerics they withhold or lie. Perhaps children are aware of something that we adults forget—that what's needed from spiritual leaders is warmth, kindness and understanding rather than the propensity to judge, preach and chastise.

As adults, we often forget how contagious kindness and warmth can be. In so doing, we forget the essence of God.

End Of Chapter Notes: There are interesting similarities between the Bible's Eve and Greek mythology's Pandora. ⚕ The Mormons have a different take on the apple biting incident in The Garden. They believe that Eve did us all a big favor by pursuing knowledge. Of course, this is not to imply that the Mormon church is the Rome of feminist thinking. ⚕ Carl Jung's "Answer To Job" provides a captivating exploration of the Yahweh of old. ⚕ The so-called pagans who worshiped a male and female god also practiced human sacrifice. While not such an inviting practice from a public relations point of view, it is hard to believe that the number of human lives lost in this way was even a fraction of those lost in the religious wars that have dominated the globe since the Yahwehs seized power. ⚕ There may have been a translation error between the early Greek, Latin and Aramaic languages; the expression for "young woman" may have been confused with the term "virgin," perhaps explaining some of the Bible's jones for virgins. Also, the notion of the Assumption didn't exist until a church council in the mid-1800s decided to invent it. ⚕ Readers who are interested would do well to consult Bishop Spong's books on the bible. They are very readable, thought provoking, and are published by Harper/San Francisco. ⚕ Thanks to Elizabeth Berlese for spurring memories about warmth and kindness, to Presbytera Donna Pappas for mentioning how people often refer to themselves as spiritual rather than religious, to Carol Tavris for the Muslim "head to toe" example, to Robert VanSweden on the Mormons & Eve, and to the writings of David Schnarch, Bishop Spong, and Paul Evdokimov. Evdokimov's writings were suggested by Father Andrew Barakos. Because these people are being thanked does not mean that they necessarily agree with the perspective of this chapter.

Chapter 30
Do Buddhists Shave Their Pubic Hair?

It is not unusual for some women (and men) in our society to trim or shave their pubic hair. People who are Buddhists would probably think us crazy for even considering such a thing. Buddhists often have a different take on sex than we Westerners, at least on the surface anyway. They refer to male sex organs as jade stocks and worry about unclogging special centers in their bodies called chakras.

This chapter discusses a few of the Buddhist and other Eastern Religion attitudes regarding sex. Some of these attitudes are admirable, others less so.

How Buddhists View Sex

Buddhists and members of other Eastern cultures make sexuality a part of their religion. They view sex as an important blending of energies that helps with one's spiritual transformation. Many of their most sacred shrines and altars show pictures of people having sex, and they sometimes speak of finding god through getting it on. Here in the West, sex is also an important part of religion. Everything that's bad is at one time or another blamed on sex. You get the feeling that sex was invented by the devil himself.

Our Western slang for female genitals include cunt, crack, pussy, beaver, snatch, bearded clam, and muff. Buddhists refer to women's genitals as honey pot, pleasure grotto, valley of joy, golden crevice, grotto of the white tiger, and shady valley. (Grotto of the white tiger?) Buddhists claim to honor the female genitals as the gateway to life. Early Christian doctrine called women's genitals a sewer.

Buddhist men believe that female sex secretions are both energizing and harmonizing, which is why oral sex is viewed as a spiritual fueling rather than a manly duty or foreplay. Even the saliva (sweet spring) of a sexually excited woman is thought to strengthen and revitalize the man who absorbs it. Orgasm is also viewed a little differently. Partners are encouraged to synchronize the sensations (energies?) that lead to orgasm. This allows the sensations to build and circulate rather than spilling out all at once.

To give you a better idea of how some Eastern Religions view sex, consider the following passages from a book called "Taoist Secrets Of Love" by Master Mantak Chia, Aurora Press 1984:

> "Enter slowly because woman grows aroused more slowly than man. Untaught man is quick to begin and quick to finish... With reverence, light the sacred candles in her thighs. If she is taken too abruptly, the flush of pleasure has insufficient time

to spread over her entire nervous system. Sensation remains fixed in the genitals... The essence of this thrusting technique is to go nine shallow and one deep. The one deep thrust, besides varying sensory stimulation, forces the air out of the vagina. This allows you to create a vacuum inside your partner with the nine shallow thrusts which follow. You never withdraw completely: this would break the vacuum seal. Rather, you hover at those outermost inches of the vagina which are covered with a dense net of nerves. The nine shallow, one deep rhythm delights your partner. The vacuum has tremendous effect: she feels empty then full, empty then full. This pleases because you constantly refresh her senses with change..."

This is fun to try. But what about the notion of a man "taking" a woman? Sounds a little like the Old West. And as mentioned in an earlier chapter, this guide takes exception to the idea that women arouse more slowly than men. Women who are masturbating can reach orgasm just as quickly as men.

Reservations About The Wheel Of Karma

Zen Buddhists have gotten some pretty favorable press when it comes to matters of the body and soul. Much of it is deserved. Yet it seems that Buddhists have their own share of hang ups, just like the rest of us. For instance, Buddhists give the appearance of having a much better attitude toward women than we Occidentals. However, if you read the big Buddhist death manual (Book of the Dead) you will find signs of deeply ingrained sexism at the very heart of reincarnation.

A Buddhist male who has led a good life and freed himself from the wheel of karma won't have to come back again. However, a Buddhist female who has led a good life gets to come back as a man. The fact that she was even born a woman is because of bad karma in a past life. It seems that we men are the only ones who are allowed a chance at the Big Spin! Ever quick to sense a public relations glitch, some Buddhist monks now claim that women, too, can go for the Big

Spin, they simply need to resonate with a male energy to do so. How white of them.

Eastern religions or spiritual paths such as Hinduism and Vishnu claim to have a more enlightened attitude toward sexuality than we Westerners. That might be true if you ignore what goes on in the society as a whole. For instance, we Westerners may have problems with various aspects of women's sexuality, but it has never been a common practice here in the West to murder female babies because they are considered to be a liability, nor have we ever made it a point to throw the wives of dead men on the funeral pyre. Can this be said of the countries where the "more enlightened" Eastern religions hail?

Learning Vs. Conversion

Some Americans adopt Eastern thought with a kind of rigid, controlling, fanaticism. They become evangelical about Buddhism, and sometimes feel superior after obsessively meditating several hours a day. Is this what Eastern thought teaches?

There is much that we Americans can learn from Eastern religion and culture, especially about sexuality. But there is a difference between benefiting from another culture's perspective and adopting it lock, stock, and incense. Keep in mind that other cultures sometimes appear more ideal from a distance. 卖卖卖

NOTE: One reader from Japan said she'd heard of Zen, and heard of Buddhism, but never Zen-Buddhism! Sorry about the inaccuracy. We have apparently invented a new religion! A reader from Southern California said we were on the money about all religions but Buddhism, which she feels we have maligned unfairly. We enjoyed her comments, but stick by our guns.

Chapter 31
On Culture & Kink

On the surface, men in our society seem more into kink than women. But maybe that's because we define kink differently for men than for women. For instance, a woman who wears her boyfriend's boxers or briefs is at the height of fashion, but if he wears her underwear we consider him to be weird. Our society relishes her kink, but gets very uncomfortable with his.

In our society women touch each other at will. However, if men were to touch each other with half the frequency that women do, they would be called queer. Once again, our culture labels men as being strange for something that women do all of the time. Most male-to-male touching in our society is limited to handshakes and contact sports — which may be a reason why men feel such an affinity for football. For a guy to experience much physical contact with another guy, he needs to be a jock, a homosexual, or both.

There are plenty of other things that are considered kinky when only men do them. For instance, a woman who routinely undresses in front of an open window is thought to be a neighborhood resource. Double that for a woman who plays with herself and/or makes love with the window shades up. But a guy who does these things is considered to be a pervert and may even be locked up. There is also the biological fact that some women can masturbate without even being noticed. Guys can't masturbate with that kind of subtlety. The occasional male who gets himself off in a public place is at much greater risk of being caught and labeled as a pervert than the occasional female who does the same thing. One reader comments, "Not only is he labeled a pervert, but if convicted he would be forced to register as a sex offender."

Bondage Lite

The United States was originally settled by a group of religious outcasts, malcontents, criminals, and slaves — the fact that we're not all into some form of bondage is a little amazing.

Bondage is the application of restraint, pain or humiliation in a way that some people find erotic or satisfying. One form of bondage ("light bondage") includes having your arms or feet tied together while being kissed, tickled, caressed or otherwise made love to. In parts of California, New York, and Chicago this type of activity isn't considered bondage, but merely good bedroom technique.

Those who are into light bondage often enjoy it because they are rendered passive and have no choice but to totally enjoy what a partner is doing to them. They don't have to worry about being a "good" sex partner who provides pleasure in return. Performance anxiety is virtually eliminated.

If you are into light bondage, be aware that scarves and ties tend to form tight knots that are hard to undo; wrists and ankles can be permanently damaged. Bondage enthusiast William Henkin says that professionally made cuffs may seem expensive to couples who simply like to tickle and spank, but they are much safer than the restraints that people improvise at home. In the event that professionally made cuffs aren't available on your TV's Home Shopping Network, check with places like Good Vibrations or The Pleasure Chest.

Painful Contradictions

You don't have to be into bondage or SM to appreciate the following social ridiculousness: here in America parents can spank a child and it is not called bondage or sadism. Yet fully consenting adults who spank each other are ostracized and even considered morally corrupt.

Spanking is a form of sexual kink that can be considered either light or heavy bondage, depending upon how it's done. For instance, some participants like their spanking hard and with a hostile edge, while others enjoy a little spank here and there when highly aroused.

Why do some adults enjoy spanking or being spanked? One theory states that people sometimes sexualize their childhood shame or humiliation. Turning it into erotic sensation helps it to become more bearable. They might even secretly identify with the person who is spanking them, feeling a sense of power even though in reality they are the ones who are powerless.

Another reason why some people enjoy an occasional swat on the rear is because they find that it feels good, as long as they are sexually aroused and it is their own personal choice to be in the situation.

Bondage By Choice — A Feminist Contradiction?

People who are feminists or socially progressive (whatever that might mean) sometimes feel that they are deserting their own cause if they enjoy submission or S/M fantasies. For instance, consider a feminist lawyer whose favorite fantasy is being tied up and sexually violated. She occasionally acts out this fantasy with her male lover. Does this contradict her political beliefs? Not really, since the relevant issue is the freedom to choose rather than what's being chosen.

The lady lawyer believes that each person should be able to choose what to do with his or her own sexuality. In acting out her bondage fantasy with her lover, this woman chooses to give up her position of equality, as well as choosing the man whom she wants to give it up to. In the criminal rape cases that she handles in court, the rape victim had no choice. The act was forced upon her, rather than being part of a shared fantasy between two consenting adults.

Note: The term feminist no longer has the meaning that it once did and is currently rife with contradiction. For instance, some feminists are opposed to pornography and feel it demeans women, while other feminists believe that women should be proud of their bodies and free to display them sexually if that's what they want to do. Some feminists hate men, others don't; some embrace lesbianism, others are alienated by feminist groups who are more concerned with lesbian issues than those of straight working mothers. Some feminists feel that intercourse is a form of oppression that women have been brainwashed to have by the patriarchy (straight white guys). Other feminists view intercourse as a satisfying activity where a vagina is as active and powerful as a penis. Some feminists consider motherhood to be a form of slavery for women, while others welcome motherhood. In fact, most women in this day and age describe themselves as being feminists, regardless of their political, social, or religious views.

Heavy Bondage — A Little Like Life?

Heavy bondage, (B&D or S&M) can get fairly brutal. It can be a world of whips and chains and devices that might even put a chill up the spine of the average PE teacher. When it comes to heavy bondage, the only comment this guide knows that even comes close is, "Toto, I have a feeling we're not in Kansas anymore."

In heavy bondage, having an orgasm isn't nearly as important as the bondage scene itself, with its undercurrent of domination, submission and sometimes humiliation. People into heavy bondage seem to process pain differently than people who aren't. Bondage lovers find serious doses of sexual pain to be invigorating and intimate. They speak about sexual pain with the same kind of clarity and relish as religious pilgrims who are describing a visit to a holy shrine or the Dalai Lama.

People into heavy bondage tend to be very serious about their kink. In fact, there are even well-established bondage clubs like the Portland Power and Trust, Chicago Hellfire Club, Bound and Determined in Massachusetts, Society of Janus in San Francisco, and Leather and Lace in our very own City of The Angels.

There are mainstream bondage publications like Domination-Submission, Dungeon Master (which probably takes the prize for being the Boy's Life of kink), and Prometheus, the Quarterly of the Eulenspiegel Society. There are numerous magazines on latex fashion. There are also bondage reference guides like "The Leatherman's Handbook," "The Lesbian S/M Safety Manual" — cross their hearts and hope to be humiliated.

If you have an irrepressible need to get into heavy bondage, please consider the following advice: don't pick up a stranger who enjoys beating the crap out of people and confuse that with bondage, even if you are a woman who loves too much. In heavy bondage there are established rules and etiquette that keep the participants from getting seriously hurt. Mind you, the definition of *seriously hurt* is a personal matter. If heavy bondage is what turns you on, learn the rules and make sure that your partner knows and respects them. (See "alternative lifestyles" in the resource part of this book.)

Even if you aren't into bondage, don't get roped into thinking that mild-mannered people prefer being bottoms (slave role) and that aggressive types prefer being tops (master/dominator/dominatrix). There are plenty of business executives, lawyers, doctors, politicians, policeman, and even East Coast publishing types who prefer being on the bottom when it comes to sexual kink. In fact, it's a known dilemma around the bondage community that a good top is hard to find. It's also true that a number of people into S-M enjoy alternating roles between top and bottom. They are called "switches."

Readers who are copy editors might be chomping at the bit because of our inconsistency in writing "SM." As it turns out, SM writers use any of the following forms: SM, S/M, S-M, and S&M. In an attempt to discriminate fairly, each form has been used at least once.

Lite Or Heavy Bondage — Safety Considerations

No matter if you only use bondage once a year, or are a full-fledged bondage brute, the SM book by author Jay Wiseman titled "SM-101" (Greenery Press) makes the following suggestions:

🐑 Any time a body part that is tied up feels numb or goes to sleep, untie it immediately. And never tie anything around a partner's neck.

🐑 In anticipation of catastrophes like fires, earthquakes or an unexpected visit from your mom and dad, be sure that you have a flashlight and pair of heavy scissors handy. "SM-101" recommends paramedic scissors which can be found at medical supply stores. They cut through almost anything except handcuffs. Keep the scissors and flashlights in a place that you can readily find in the dark. Ditto for the handcuff key if that's what you are using.

🐑 Never leave the person for long, and check them often. If any injuries were to occur, you would be legally and morally responsible.

🐑 Always establish a safeword which means to stop. Some people use "red" for stop and "yellow" for easing up a little. No one who is seriously into dominance & submission uses "stop," "don't," or "no more" for safewords, since any good bottom says them often but doesn't mean them one little bit.

Fetishes, An Overview

Several years ago, a singer named Randy Newman wrote a song whose lyrics entreat his lover to take off all of her clothes, except for her hat. If Mr. Newman couldn't enjoy sex unless the woman had a hat on, then we might say he had a hat fetish. The Glossary at the end of this book offers the following definition of fetish:

FETISH—1. Reliance on a particular prop, body part or scenario in order to get off sexually. 2. The prop can either be fantasized or exist in actuality. 3. One philosopher has described "fetish" as a hungry person sitting down at a dinner table and feeling full from simply fondling the napkin.

If both people in a relationship enjoy a particular fetish, then acting out the fetish will be a welcome event. But if only one partner is into the fetish, the other partner might feel that she or he is not nearly as important as the fetish itself. For instance, if the woman in the above-mentioned song loves wearing her hat while otherwise naked, then she has found the perfect man. Otherwise, she may start to feel like a human hat rack.

Fetishes, Specifics

Festishes come in many different forms. What follows are two examples where dirty words and cross-dressing might be considered fetishes:

Talk Dirty To Me. Some couples enjoy saying dirty things while having sex. But what if one partner can't perform sexually without hearing the dirty words? This takes it beyond simple sexplay and hints of a fetish, especially if the other partner feels stupid screeching things like "Fuck me harder, fuck me harder you big stud, Mama wants it all," or degrading things like "You miserable, worthless, little turd." Particularly troublesome are situations where the partner with the fetish needs to say degrading things to you, unless of course, you find something endearing about being called a smelly old cow, fat whore, or pencil-dicked imbecile.

What A Drag… Some women occasionally dress up like men, to the point of wearing a fake penis (a form of accessorizing known as "packing"). And some men feel a powerful need to dress like women ("transvestism"). Psychologically, a man who cross-dresses might do so to help ease the pain of early humiliations at the hands of a domineering mother or sister figures. Dressing as a woman helps him to feel like one of the power elite, and therefore not so vulnerable. This might be just fine with his wife or girlfriend, in which case all is well. However, problems might arise if he keeps stealing her favorite bra and panties to wear under his suit whenever his law firm assigns him to handle a high-profile case.

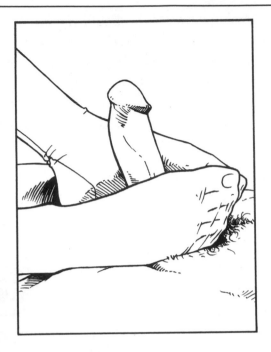

Is this activity:

a. fun
b. a fetish
c. both
d. who cares?

This wouldn't be considered a fetish or kink if it's something you enjoy doing but can also do without. Psychologists would call it a fetish if the man couldn't become aroused without seeing or touching the woman's feet, or if her pantyhose were so important to him that he needed them rather than her to become sexually excited. How do psychologists know? Because they're as twisted as everyone else.

People with fetishes usually love them immensely and resist giving them up. Therapy is seldom effective in loosening the love for a fetish. As long as the partner is fine with the fetish and it causes no ha:m to others, there seems to be little reason for abandoning it.

It is interesting how in our culture, men with certain conflicts might deal with them one way while women sometimes give them a different spin. For instance, more men probably have foot fetishes than women, yet more women obsess about shoes (and spend far more hours shopping for them) than men. An obvious and time-honored solution, of course, is for men with foot fetishes to work in women's shoe stores!

Piercing & Tattoos — On Pins & Needles

Is getting tattooed a sexual thing? Who knows. It sure is popular these days, especially among women who are sporting little butterflies, flowers and the like in highly private places.

Piercing, like tattooing, has been around for a long, long time. Women have traditionally had their ears pierced, as have various pirates and sailors who have sailed the seven seas. Nowadays everybody seems to be getting into the act, although the recent male ear piercing craze appears to be slowing.

In a highly sexualized version of piercing, body parts like noses, navels, nipples and genitals are potential sites. People who are seriously into piercing will stick earrings or gold posts through just about anything. Some do it for sport, others experience it to be on the sacred side with body as altar. If you are into this kind of thing, be sure to have it done at a well known establishment with a solid reputation. Not enough can be said for sterile technique and skill on the part of the piercer, as infections and botched insertions tend to be common. There is also a fair amount of wisdom involved in selecting the proper ring or post for specific body parts, given how those that are too thin eventually pull out.

Some people say that getting nipples pierced hurts more than having genitals done, others disagree. One woman who sports gold rings along the sides of her labia says that the jewelry dresses up her genitals and makes her like them even more. Another woman who has had her clitoris pierced loves the new sensations and claims that just sitting down can sometimes give her an orgasm, although less than one-in-three women has a clitoris that's plump enough for a bull's eye insertion. As for male genitals, the head of the penis can be skewered in several different ways, and earrings can be placed anywhere from the bottom of the testicles to the tip of the foreskin.

Ah, life in the big city.

Vaginal Fisting (Handballing)

Vaginal fisting is finger fucking and then some. This guide first became aware of the concept when reviewing lesbian tapes produced by and for women. It seems that some women enjoy having a partner's fist inside their vagina. In fact, most women who enjoy fisting share the experience with near religious awe — an awe that seems to be felt as much by the fister as the fistee.

The trouble is, the kind of vaginal fisting these women are talking about is usually being done by a woman to a woman. This is an important distinction, since most women usually have significantly smaller fists than men. A fist the size of a man's could take a potentially pleasurable experience and turn it into something akin to childbirth. On the other hand, some women claim to like a bigger fist. Either way, it needs to be a mutual decision and not something one partner pushes on the other.

The reason this guide decided to include information about vaginal fisting is because friends in the lesbian community as well as some straight sex therapists believe it is being done, and people who are doing it need access to information. Please do not think that we encourage fisting. It's not anything that anyone around here has ever done. Also be aware that any kind of fisting is a potentially dangerous activity, especially if done quickly and without the fistee controlling each part of the action. For instance, some women experience a slight amount of bleeding following fisting. Fisting enthusiasts say this is normal but gynecologists might not agree. Interestingly, an exercise called "perineal massage" which is sometimes taught in childbirth classes is similar to vaginal fisting.

Please check with a gynecologist before attempting any kind of fisting, and in no instance should you proceed if you experience anything but the slightest amount of pain. Perhaps you can find the name of a physician or nurse practitioner who is familiar with fisting through a gay & lesbian health center, since your local HMO night not be particularly well-versed in the practice, or not willing admit it anyway. Also, you should never attempt fisting if either of you have been drinking or doing drugs.

If vaginal fisting is an experience a woman genuinely wants to try and is certain she can handle it physically, here are a few things to consider as mentioned in a 1992 article on the subject by Carol Queen which was published in the woman's magazine "On Our Backs!"

1. Always wear a well-lubricated latex glove, as much for the woman's comfort as for germ prevention. (Even a jagged cuticle can cause discomfort, which is why you need the glove.) There should be no rings or untrimmed nails, and the woman should pee first.

2. Ms. Queen: "Don't try this on a dry, sleepy pussy. Wake her up! Make her want it! And please, allow sufficient time." Be sure to add lots of lubrication.

3. The fistee starts by inserting one finger into the vagina, moves up to two, then three. The way to introduce the fourth is to bring the fingers together into a point, but while still extending them. This should be a familiar gesture for people who grew up dipping fingers into holy water each morning. (The things you learn from a religious education...) For others, the hand will look like a caricature of a bird's head when viewed from the side. Be sure to turn it upside down before inserting.

4. Knuckles down, palm up. It's the bottom part of the vagina that stretches, not the top. This means that your knuckles (the back of your hand) should be facing the bottom part of the vagina, or as Ms. Queen so eloquently states "...Stretch assward instead of clitward. When she is sufficiently relaxed, your hand will likely slide right in, the fingers naturally curling up into a fist." Be sure to let the woman control the action, and stop if there is resistance.

5. Some women will only want three or four fingers inside rather than the whole fist. Respect this and never think of it as a failure. The goal should be mutual pleasure rather than getting a whole fist inside.

Never hesitate to call it a day and move on to some other form of sexual activity that doesn't stretch the bounds of comfort.

6. Only with a great deal of feedback will you know whether the woman wants you to twist your hand or keep it stationary, or to move your fingers.

7. Some women will want to orgasm with the fist inside, others will want to wait until it is out. To quote Ms. Queen: "I find that when my partner is fisting me I love to play with my clit and keep myself on the edge of orgasm... But when the hand comes out, I come like crazy... With smaller-handed partners I like getting fist-fucked and coming, squeezing down on their wrists. As a fister, feeling those contractions in my partner is my favorite moment — that and when my hand first slips inside."

8. When you finally pull your hand out, do it very, very slowly and straighten your fingers as you go. The slowness can help minimize discomfort and increase sensation. Also, if a woman has had an orgasm her vagina may tighten up around your fist. It might help if she pushes down at the same time that you are slowly pulling your hand out.

9. Afterwards. Plan to spend plenty of time holding each other after you are done, as fisting tends to be a powerful experience that needs protracted coming down time. Also, don't hesitate to follow it up with oral sex or anything else that gives the two of you pleasure, although having a penis inside of a woman's vagina immediately after a fist might be somewhat of a letdown for a woman.

If you are thinking of getting into vaginal fisting, Greenery Press has recently released a book titled "A Hand In The Bush: The Fine Art Of Vaginal Fisting," by Deborah Addington, Greenery Press, San Francisco, CA. (415)831-2220.

Anal Fisting

Some couples, straight as well as gay, are into anal fisting. Technically, this act is possible without causing irreparable damage, since surgeons occasionally stick an entire hand up a person's rear end while doing surgery, and how many of us haven't had a boss who didn't try to do nearly the same thing, at least metaphorically? On the other hand, receiving an entire fist up the rear end requires the kind of relaxation that is well beyond the capacity of the average asshole.

Couples into anal fisting often recommend a book on the subject by Burt Hermann titled "Trust — The Hand Book." At the very least, consult with your family physician before attempting anal fisting. "Hello, Dr. Welby... You have? Really? Lots of lube?"

RESOURCE NOTE: *The Black Book*; An annual web/phone media/consumer directory for kink & fetish. Provides you with all the resources you'll ever need, from the National Foot Network and Northeast Erotic Spanking Society to suppliers of quality enema equipment and other insertable devices. P. O. Box 31155 -GF, San Francisco, CA 94131-0155, (415) 431-0171.

FOR MORE RESOURCES ON KINK OR ALTERNATIVE EXPRESSION: See the resources part of this book, pages 621-624.

End Of Chapter Notes: Thanks to the writings of Chris Gosselin and Glenn Wilson for some of the ideas used in the introduction to this chapter, and to the works of Carol Queen, Cathy Winks, Anne Seamans, Bert Hermann and Jay Wiseman.

Chapter 32
Talking To Your Partner About Sex

While most of us will see angels before we'll see our teenage years again, it never hurts to look at the truly unfortunate advice that Teen Magazine offers its 4.4 million American girl readers about sexual matters. Many of us, both male and female, still abide by the Teen philosophy long after we've reached the legal age of reason:

> "When you're French kissing, it helps to let the guy take the lead. Part your lips gently, and let him explore your mouth with his tongue..." (from a 1992 Teen Magazine piece titled "Kissing Anxiety? Lip-To-Lip Lowdown").

Teen's smooch advice gives the impression that we guys come out of the womb knowing how to French kiss. Don't the editors of Teen realize that the average American male's preparation for sex is jerking off to the centerfold of whatever dirty magazine he can successfully hide from his mother's grasp? This is supposed to teach us how to French kiss, or anything else for that matter?

And why are guys always supposed to know what to do? Why aren't men and women encouraged to explore sex together, teaching each other what feels good along the way? And why are magazines like Teen still trying to push the tired old notion that sex is something a man does to a woman—unless she needs something from him or wants a big favor? One way to avoid being a Teen Magazine type of lover is by learning to talk to your partner about sex, about what feels good and what doesn't, and by exploring beyond what's familiar. Unfortunately, that's not as easily done as said. That's why we've included this chapter. It starts by exploring different parts of the problem, and finishes with a concrete plan of action.

Naked And Tongue Tied

Consider the following conversation between two people who are about to have intercourse for the first time:

"Ah, should I...?"

"Yes."

"OK, I'll put one on."

That's it. The intercourse begins. Less than ten words, all single syllables. Grunting cavemen were probably more expressive. And then, there's the prolific verbal exchange at the end of the event:

"That was really good."

"Me too."

While most of us aren't too ashamed to have sex, plenty of us approach critical mass when it comes to talking about it. One problem has to do with a lack of a comfortable, shared vocabulary about sex. We often feel limited to one of two extremes, e.g. "When I was giving you cunnilingus..." or "When I was eating your pussy..." No confusing these for Kodak Moments. In order to talk about sex with a partner, it helps to find a comfortable middle ground between stiff Latin terminology and sexual slang that is more commonly used for swearing.

After Marriage — Grow Or Die

Partners often start talking less about sex after they've been married for awhile. Things like the interest rate on a credit card or replacing the kitchen cabinets garner more excitement than finding new things that turn each other on. Sexual interests and desires start getting hidden, and we sometimes feel embarrassed or shy about things that would have kept us up all night a few years earlier.

Maybe when a relationship is new, having sex becomes a way of exploring each other's emotions as well as each other's crotches. After awhile, finding new things that turn each other on either takes too much effort or becomes scary, and sex has no room to grow. "I don't want him/her to know that about me" becomes more powerful than "It might be exciting if she/he knew this about me." Perhaps we have too much to loose if a partner disapproves, or maybe we give our partners the kind of power that our parents once had to make us feel ashamed.

Knowing Vs. Asking

Imagine going to a restaurant where the chef served you whatever he or she felt like fixing instead of giving you a choice. Imagine a gardener who never asked "How do you like your bushes trimmed?" Imagine a laundry who didn't say, "Light Starch, Heavy Starch, No Starch, Hangers or Folded?" Yet when it comes to sex, many of us assume that we know what our partner wants, or we clam up instead of giving feedback.

After So Many Years...

Let's say after ten years of being a sexual mute, you suddenly decide to raise the issue. Perhaps your partner will be happy that you finally spoke your mind. Or maybe he or she will be annoyed, "You mean it's been bothering you for ten years and you never said a word?" Or you might receive a suspicious reply, "How did you learn all of that new stuff all of a sudden?" We often become fragile beings when it comes to hearing an honest critique of our sexual technique. One solution is to make talking about sex part of the fabric of your relationship from the very start. This can be tricky, though, because a lot of couples are so satisfied by the newness of their sexual relationship that they don't find it a priority to learn how to talk to each other about it.

Learning To Speak

Props. There are certain props that will make it easier for you to exchange information about sex when you have your clothes on instead of off. That way, there won't be this huge pressure when there's something specific you want to talk to your partner about. By discussing sex on a regular basis, if only every month or two, your partner will feel much less criticized when you suggest that he or she try something new.

To help provide such a prop, we were considering starting a monthly newsletter on sex that would bring you interesting updates and findings about sex, in a way that men and women would feel comfortable discussing together. But then we found "Sex & Health," a monthly newsletter that is so informative, helpful and up-to-date that we decided to scuttle our own plans and recommend it instead. "Sex & Health" (800) 666-2106 is about twelve pages long. It has no nasty pictures or X-rated sex columns, but will provide any couple with an easy, comfortable and informative forum for bringing up the subject of sex on a monthly basis. Other magazines you might consider are Sexlife (650)968-7851 and Libido (800)495-1988. Sexlife is a new magazine for younger couples, while "Libido" has explicit pictures and stories that are aimed to help warm the crotches of any couple. There are other new magazines on sex that we haven't included simply because we haven't seen them yet. (While magazines like Playboy and Penthouse offer excellent advice about sex, they are designed for men rather than couples. There are also magazines for women that have interesting articles about sex, but not in a way that appeals to men.)

Another great way to you discuss sex is to say to your partner "Let's get at least one new book or magazine on sex every month or two." We're not suggesting glossy jerk off tombs with the human

crotch splayed wide, unless you're both into that sort of thing. But do consider picking up books like Susan Bakos' "Sexational" (St. Martin's Press), Kathy Winks "G-Spot Book" (Down There Press) or even "The Ultimate Guide To Anal Sex For Women" by Tristan Taormino (Cleis Press). Believe it or not, the latter is a fairly cool book by a female author and it's an interesting read for both men and women. Or maybe you'll want to get Laura Corn's "101 Nights Of Great Sex" (Park Avenue Press) which is more action-oriented and good at giving permission if that is what you need.

You can always highlight parts of this book that you find meaningful and would like your partner to know about. Or you can read parts of it to your partner, as a lot of couples seem to do. It's amazing how a bit of humor helps any discussion that might otherwise be filled with a bit of anxiety.

There are some really good sex videos that are both informative and erotic. For instance, Pacific Media's "The Complete Guide To Oral Lovemaking" and their video on using sex toys were fun to review

(800)262-7367. When searching for erotic videos, you'll find some winners and plenty of yawners. But the search is half the fun.

Why not get yourself on the mailing list of the big sex-related catalogues such as "Good Vibrations," "Adam & Eve," "Xandria," "Blowfish," "Sexuality Library"? Their phone numbers are in the resources part of this book. We at the Goofy Foot Press have great fun receiving these catalogs. Perhaps you will too.

Some couples find it fun to play board games that promote discussion about sex or physical exploration. The nice thing about these games is that there are no losers. One game to consider is "Enchanted Evening" (800) 776-7662.

Prevention

You'd think your sex life would be just as important as gardening, sports, business, travel and entertainment. Couples don't hesitate to get magazines or books on subjects like those. In fact, they often value and appreciate them, and discuss with their partners the things they have just read.

Of course, you might say "Our sex life is just fine right now. We don't need anything like that." Hopefully, your luck will hold, but therapists often see couples who had great sex lives two, five or ten years earlier. Things break down when we take them for granted, and the process of getting them right is not always pretty or fun.

Dear Dr. Goofy,

I just wanted to comment on my sexual pleasure now as opposed to twenty years ago. In the past, I was way too concerned with my body image, with being too verbal or aggressive, and striving for the Big "O." But the biggest obstacle to experiencing sexual pleasure was the passive role I assumed. I expected great sex to just happen. I finally realized, after frequently saying to myself, "Is that it?" that I had to take an active role in the process in order to make sure that my needs were met. Now they are. I'm no longer afraid to talk about sex, and the results are wonderful!

female age 42

Chapter 33
Sex Fantasies

 Given how sex fantasies are nearly universal, it's a little surprising that we tend to be embarrassed about them. On the other hand, why bother fantasizing about something that everyone else approves of?

Some people have a single reliable sex fantasy that they go back to time and again. Others have a virtual rolodex of scenes and images that help to get them off.

Some people know they're horny because of the sexual fantasies they've been having. For others, horniness is something they feel in their bodies, with very little mental imagery.

The content of sex fantasies varies; some are sweet, kind and silly, others are weird, kinky, and bizarre; some are action packed and exciting, others are really boring. Some sex fantasies are populated with current or past lovers, rock'n'roll singers, people in uniforms, movie stars, teachers, priests, family members, total strangers, and even furry friends from another species. Here's just a partial list of the scenarios that people sometimes fantasize about:

Being held or cuddled; doing all kinds of sex acts; sex with more than one partner; having anonymous sex with a highly attractive partner or partners; being forced to have sex; watching or being watched doing heaven only knows what; being adored, desired, spanked, tortured or humiliated; being the one who dominates; watching a partner have sex with someone else; having gay sex when you otherwise feel straight (a related fantasy is to have sex with a male/female couple, which can camouflage homosexual interest and make the fantasy easier to swallow if that sort of thing bothers you).

Fantasies Of Rape

It is not unusual for people to have fantasies in which sex is forced, nor is it unusual to fantasize about sex with policemen, priests

Lucky's Home

or others in uniform. Consider the following passage from Betty Dodson's fine book "Sex For One" published by Harmony Books:

"A friend who considered herself a radical feminist got concerned that her sexual imagery wasn't politically correct because it wasn't 'feminist oriented.' I assured her that all fantasies were okay. Lots of people imagine scenes they never want to experience. I also pointed out that we can become addicted to a fantasy like anything else, and suggested she experiment with new ones. One of her new assertive fantasies is about moving her clitoris in and out of her lover's soft wet mouth while he's tied down. Whenever she gets stuck or is in a hurry, she brings out her old fantasy of being raped by five Irish cops and always reaches orgasm quickly."

Just because someone has a fantasy of being raped doesn't mean that he or she wants it to happen in reality. Sometimes being raped in fantasy is a way for the person to enjoy sexual pleasure that would otherwise cause guilt. Sex that is out of your control keeps you from having to feel responsible for wanting it, and in a typical rape fantasy the rapist is usually someone whom the victim finds appealing and would like to have sex with anyway. It is also a way to feel sexually desired and valued, since the perpetrator would do anything to have you. For more about wanting sex that is forced, see page 391 "Bondage By Choice—A Feminist Contradiction?"

Men's Vs. Women's Sex Fantasies

Young girls in our society are raised on fashion magazines that highlight gorgeous female models, gorgeous if you don't take into account how many meals these women barf up to stay slim and how much silicone they have surgically packed into their chests. As they look through these magazines, American girls often grow up thinking about other women's bodies, particularly the ideal woman whom they hope to someday become. Boys, on the other hand, often grow up fantasizing about doing things, for instance, being firemen, sports heroes, musicians, stuntmen (here in Los Angeles, anyway), and

eventually stud lovers. In other words, our society wants its girls to be admired for how they look, and its boys for how they perform.

Psychologist Karen Shanor believes that when women see an erect penis in their fantasies they often relish it as a sign that the man finds them irresistible, and not as an object of worship as we men tend to think. In fact, Shanor speculates that many young women learn to include men in their fantasies as an afterthought, with the fantasized male being little more than a woman retrofitted with a penis. Perhaps this is one reason why teenage girls so often fawn over totally androgynous male rock'n'roll singers.

If you doubt Shanor's formulation, keep in mind that when a woman walks into a formal affair like a dance or prom, the first thing she often notices is how the other women look, and how she feels in comparison. The first thing a man notices is often the same thing: how the other women look. Men usually aren't concerned with how the other men look, unless they are actors or gay.

Interesting as it is, this theory does have its limitations. For instance, it doesn't explain why some women clearly prefer the sexual touch and feel of a man's body which can be quite different from their own.

Your Lover's Sex Fantasies

Every once in a while, one partner will tell the other about his or her private sex fantasy. (Stranger things have happened.) But don't expect to see the fantasy plastered on a billboard surrounded by neon lights. Most of us are a little embarrassed by our sexual fantasies, sometimes with good reason. As a result, we tend not to reveal our sex fantasies in a way that's particularly direct.

You Only Get One Chance

Let's say you are a guy, and your sweetheart casually or jokingly makes an off-the-cuff statement that she likes seeing guys in jocks.

Boom, ball's in your court.

Now, if you have half a brain, and not many of us do, you won't laugh and tell her how much better you feel in boxers than wearing some old athletic supporter. Instead, you will consider buying about a dozen or so new jocks, maybe in colors, maybe one with a cup, what the heck. So there you are later that night, your sweetheart's warm familiar fingers are slowly popping the buttons on your blue jeans, and bingo — she discovers that you are wearing a jock underneath! Before you know it, she's in sexual orbit and you are the happiest guy on your block! On the other hand, she might discover that her fantasy was best when it was only imagined, and that it feels silly or loses its erotic edge when acted out in reality.

Beat The Rut

As with life in general, sex can be really boring if you never vary the routine. Mind you, this hasn't stopped many couples from doing the exact same thing in bed week after week, month after month, year after year.

Adding variety to a boring sex life is a favorite topic of the magazines that people read in check-out lines at the grocery store, especially when the person in front of you pulls out an entire shoe box full of coupons and you suddenly find yourself with an extra half-hour on your hands.

Odds & Ends: Compromises, Big Xs & The Truth

While it's great that you and your partner might be open to hearing each other's fantasies, this doesn't mean that you need to act them out. For instance, when one partner has a Jones to do something that the other finds loathful, you might try working out a compromise, e.g. It's likely that there are plenty of videos depicting whichever fantasies are currently oozing from the darkest recesses of your sexual mind. Why not rent one and use it as a masturbation aid? At other times acting out your sex fantasies can be great fun.

People occasionally have sexual fantasies about someone other than their partner. Sometimes it's prudent not to share these fantasies (e.g. "The reason I got so hot is because I pretended you were Mike"). Other times your partner might find these fantasies very arousing.

If you are going to make your own adult videos at home, keep in mind the fate of the poor sheriff from the Midwest who accidentally returned a custom-made X-rated video of he and his wife to the local video store. Be sure to mark an unmistakable X on both sides in brightly colored nail polish or maybe even Liquid Paper, and keep it in a separate location from where you put the rental tapes.

There are special locks available that fit into the sprocket hole of video cassettes. By using these, you are safe even if your five-year-old accidentally grabs your homemade orgasmo-tape instead of "Fantasia" or "Bambi." ("Mommy, Mommy, you'll never guess what we saw Amber's mom and dad doing on videotape!")

Responsibility

Knowledge of your partner's fantasies is a trust that remains with you for life. This trust holds true even if you break up and otherwise find yourselves hating each other. (No one forced you to be in a relationship with the person, so don't go blabbing personal stuff just to be hurtful. In the long run, it reflects badly upon you.)

To put it another way, people who gossip about a current or former partner's sexuality are both shallow and deceitful. The laws of karma will some day haunt them, assuming there are laws of karma.

Reader's Comments

"At work I daydream a lot about sex and what it would be like with certain people that I am especially attracted to. Since I am about to get married, I sometimes feel bad thinking of others, but as long as you don't act on it, you're pretty much O.K."

female age 30

"My sexual fantasies always involve my current real life lover. We're making romantic love somewhere that is new to us, a beach, forest, remote island, in front of a fire in a cabin."

female age 34

"I probably have similar fantasies to anyone who watches the Sci Fi channel too much." *male age 30*

"My fantasies don't play a huge part in my life, except that I get confused why I have fantasies about other girls when I love penises and my boyfriend very much." *female age 23*

"I had always fantasized about my girlfriend being totally naked with her legs spread apart when I came into the room. One day she actually did this! It was awesome!" *male age 21*

"I don't have any clearly defined fantasy. They are more fleeting feelings and don't effect my life much." *female age 38*

"As a working mother, I get sex and orgasms, but I rarely get romance, so that is what I fantasize about." *female age 36*

"My husband and I have been married for ten years and still love to act out our sexual fantasies. Last month he was a customs agent and I was trying to sneak something across the border. After he completely searched me, I had to bribe him with sexual favors until he let me go. Later, I was a physician and he the reluctant patient. Acting out your fantasies can be great fun, and it keeps your sex life young!" *female age 33*

"I'd love to see my girlfriend get it on with another woman and I know it would be a turn-on to see her get it on with another guy, but I don't know if I could keep from getting jealous."

male age 39

Have you ever had homosexual fantasies?

"I used to fantasize about women all of the time. Finally, I decided to give it a try and had sex with one of my best female friends, who is mostly heterosexual. It was fun and every now and then we play with one another. I have never developed an emotional attachment to her or any other woman, and I no longer fantasize about women." *female age 26*

"I fantasize about being with another woman often, but I also fantasize about my boyfriend and Brad Pitt!" *female age 25*

"I am aroused by images of women with women; also by stories of multiple partners. On occasion, I use these fantasies to help me reach orgasm." *female age 32*

"I've had no fantasies or gay experiences, although I wonder sometimes if I could get turned-on by another guy." *male age 30*

"Gay fantasies? I've never even considered being gay. I'm not gay. I swear it." *male age 22*

Chapter 34
Love Dreams, Sex Dreams & Sweet Dreams

Some people have dreams of misty-eyed romance, the kind of dreams that leave you floating in the clouds until noon the next day. Some people have dreams that include sex. These are the dreams that this chapter is about. And some people have dreams that combine sex and romance. These are the dreams that we dream about dreaming — the rocket fuel variety of dream that fills the soul and tugs at the edges of who we are.

Sex Dream Statistics

Less than 10% of American parents inform their children about sex dreams, yet the majority of young adults at one time or another have them. More than 50% of women have sex dreams, yet many women don't start having them until they are in their twenties. With the male of the species it is different. Males often experience sex dreams as teenagers, with the frequency tending to decrease as they get older.

Sex Dream History

In the mid-1800s, it was assumed that sex dreams were caused by immoral thoughts. Bizarre operations were proposed for the penises of men who had wet dreams, and all sorts of devices were patented that a man was to wear on his penis at night to prevent him from having erections and the dreaded sex dreams that were thought to follow. One device was designed to wake him up by pulling on his pubic hair when he got an erection. Another machine poured cold water on him whenever he became erect during his sleep.

Dreamtime Sex Cinema

During an average night of sleep, human genitals get hard or wet several times. This usually happens whenever you are dreaming regardless of the dream's content, even if the dream is about your grandmother or someplace you once visited. A "wet dream" happens when you are actually dreaming about sex and have an orgasm.

Note: Almost half of the "wet dream" orgasms that men have are actually dry and don't include ejaculation, which makes the term wet dream   a bit of a misnomer when it is used to describe men's sex dreams. However, it is an accurate description of what happens during women's sex dreams.

While having an orgasm in your sleep isn't much of a problem for a woman, it sometimes leaves a guy with a sticky mess. In a more understanding world, a male wouldn't have to feel embarrassed about wet dream stains. But wet dreams often leave a splotch on the sheets or in your underwear and what's a boy to say? Since there is no way of predicting when you will have a sex dream, packing your shorts with Kleenex at bedtime isn't going to help.

Sex Dreams Vs. Masturbation

Talk about difficult bedtime decisions... When the author of this book was a teenager he assumed that he would be more likely to have a wet dream if he didn't masturbate. Not so. Sometimes a person can have a wet dream the same night that he or she masturbates or has sex. On the other hand, not masturbating won't increase your chances of having sex dreams.

There is simply no way to will yourself a wet dream, unless you are good at lucid dream enhancement, or whatever the people at Stanford are calling it these days. Books on the subject of lucid dreaming are published by Ballentine and authored by Stephen LeBerge.

Sex Dream Complications

Not only are sex dreams a sign that you are growing up, but they are a great way of having sex when it is not readily available. Some people even have their first orgasms while asleep and dreaming. Still, some people feel upset by their sex dreams. For instance, you might have a sex dream that includes someone you know, maybe a friend, boss or teacher. This might make you feel a bit sheepish when you see that person in real life. Not to worry, you have done nothing wrong. This book's suggestion is to scope out the person from head to toe.

Check everything from subtle mannerisms to what kind of clothes he or she is wearing. Then ask yourself: "Is he or she as good (or bad) in real life as he or she was in my dream?"

There can also be wet dream downers. For instance, wet dreams can leave you feeling frustrated when the love of your dreams doesn't want much to do with you in waking life. This can be particularly bittersweet when the person is a former lover and is now with someone else or is no longer living. Also, it is not unusual for hetero-sexuals to dream about having sex with members of the same sex. There are many ways of interpreting this sort of thing, e.g. the sex in these dreams might represent accepting part of yourself.

Whatever the content, it would be nice if your sex dreams could be a safe and welcome place to explore a full array of sexual activity that you wouldn't ordinarily do when awake.

The Family That Dreams Together...

People sometimes have sex dreams that include members of the family. This doesn't necessarily indicate a problem. Again, actions that transpire in dreams are often symbols for something very different than meets the eye, so you can't assume that the sexual partners or the sexual activity in a dream truly reflects the deeper meaning of the dream. If, however, this happens on a regular basis and you are disturbed by it, consider seeking the help of a trained mental health professional.

Another reason to get outside help is if you usually end up frustrated, hurt, frightened or angry in your dreams. You don't have to be Sigmund Freud to realize that repeated dreams of a disturbing nature reflect an inner struggle of major proportion. The exception is with children, since bad dreams are quite common during the younger years. It is not uncommon for children who are happy and whose emotional development is normal to have bad dreams two to four times a week. If, on the other hand, the child is also struggling during the waking hours, it might be prudent to seek a professional assist. 🐑🐑🐑

Chapter 35
Techno'Breasts & Weenie Angst

People who feel sexually inadequate sometimes focus their angst on body parts. For women, the focus is often on breast size or body shape; for men it is on the penis and sometimes height. Of course, it is silly to obsess about something that you had no say in getting, yet that is what many of us do.

When it comes to generating a physical balance sheet, it might be helpful to remember that even Man-O-War had his weaknesses. It might also help to remind yourself that sexual attractiveness is not like a steel chain, where one weak link makes the whole thing useless. All of us have weak links sexually, as part of our bodies and minds.

Of course, this will offer little solace to people who feel convinced that certain of their essential body parts are deficient. They will keep telling themselves "Everything would be better if I just had a bigger this or a smaller that..." To address such fears, this chapter offers a lengthy discourse on men's genitals, then ruminates on breast implants, and ends with a few suggestions about alternative strategies.

Body Concerns: Guys & How They're Hung

While most books on sex say that penis size doesn't matter, there are two groups of people to whom it does matter. One group includes almost every male alive. The second group includes every woman who derives sexual pleasure from intercourse.

In years past, women weren't supposed to care about the size and shape of a man's penis. That is because they weren't supposed to be interested in sex. But wouldn't you notice the size and shape of something that was about to get stuck into your body? As for how women respond to the actual dimensions of the thing, it clearly varies.

For instance, some women regard the penis as a trophy — the bigger the better; others couldn't care less. Some women prefer the feeling of fullness that a beefier penis has to offer, others prefer giving

blow jobs to a partner who isn't particularly well hung, and some even prefer a smaller penis for intercourse. Most women get the bulk of their pleasure from what a man is able to do with his hands, heart, tongue and intellect. They view the penis as just another body appendage.

For some women, a lover's penis becomes her penis or a part of her body when it's inside of her. Does this mean that she necessarily wants the biggest one in town? Not usually. After all, when women buy dildos, they tend to select medium- to smaller-sized units. (Sorry, but they sometimes upsize later.)

Of course, this isn't to say that women don't have their favorites. Ask a woman to tell you which lover's penis was her favorite, and she will probably be able to give a direct and clear cut answer such as, "It was Randy's" or "There are two or three that stand out, but I'd have to say Todd's takes the prize." However, if you ask about the men behind the penises, and which one she loved the most, Randy or Todd might not be at the top of the list. Maybe the guy she was happiest with didn't have a memorable penis at all, but was able to put it together in other ways.

So while women might prefer one penis over the other, penis size usually isn't a deal-breaker when it comes to choosing a man. It is sometimes disappointing, but usually not the deciding factor.

Psychology note: While some guys grow up worrying if they are hung well enough, women sometimes grow up worrying that guys will be hung too well and might cause them pain or injury. Maybe we humans were simply programmed to worry.

Weenie Enhancement Techniques

Surgery That Makes Your Penis Fat

There is a new surgical technique for penis plumping in which fat cells are harvested from the lower stomach region and injected into the penis. The author of this book called three offices that advertise this procedure and was hit by a wave of sales techniques that he hadn't encountered since joining a health club chain several years earlier.

The heavy sales pitch, which tried to capitalize upon every sexual doubt known to man, made great sense when you consider that these clinics charge $3,000 to $4,000 for a simple outpatient procedure that takes half an hour.

One clinic in Beverly Hills refused to even mail out information about the procedure. They claimed that a brochure had fallen into the hands of a child, resulting in great embarrassment. To prevent such a hideous event from ever occurring again, each caller had to make an office appointment where he could read the brochure and talk to a specialist. "Why an appointment?" "Because we process over 40 men a day." As it turned out, the dreaded brochure contained no pictures or drawings, and was embarrassing only in how it insulted the consumer's intelligence.

This fancy medical clinic insisted that it needed a social security number and health insurance information before discussing the procedure. Each visitor was also required to fill out a separate page about his penis. The wording was designed to make a man feel sexually insecure and blame it all on the size of his weenie.

The Beverly Hills clinic then treated your author to an interview with a clean cut salesman masquerading in a physician's coat, perhaps so people wouldn't confuse him with the kind of salesman who populate used car lots.

None of the three offices offered any studies on the long term safety of the procedure, none agreed on where the fat actually went, and none was willing to say exactly how a penis feels that is encased in a 1/4 inch layer of fat.

It seems that if Mother Nature wanted an extra layer of fat on the penis, she would have put it there herself. Heaven knows, she put it everywhere else. Not even the hot dogs at Dodger stadium have as much fat as a penis that's been cosmetically plumped, and they cost significantly less than $3000 — OK, they cost somewhat less than $3000.

The best we could conclude about this procedure is that a man pays between $3000 and $4000 to give his penis cellulite. Also, some lawyers are starting to specialize in lawsuits from men who were less-than-satisfied with the results of their surgically enhanced penises. And recently, the penis enlargement ads in the sports section of the LA Times have been stating that there is a "new procedure" which is vastly improved over the one used in the past. Perhaps they have forgotten that only a year or two ago their ads for the "old" procedure used to boast about how safe and successful it was.

Would you trust your penis, or any other body parts, to these people?

Weenie Enhancement Techniques

The Vacuum Pump

There is an X-rated video called "How To Enlarge Your Penis" where porn star Scott Taylor pumps himself up with a vacuum device that is supposed to make a guy bigger. Taylor uses the device to plump his penis up fatter than the darned Hindenberg, which he then maneuvers into the apparently spacious vagina of porn starlet Erica Boyer. At no point does Scott's big salami actually get hard; he has to hold his fingers around the base to keep the pressure in. Contrary to what this "self-help" video shows, the vacuum pump is one option that urologists offer male patients who are having trouble getting hard. The "How To Enlarge" info-mercial apparently took several hours to shoot, and even Scott Taylor couldn't stay hard for that long.

The penis pump was first patented in 1917. About sixty years later it became popular in the gay community, both for sexplay and organ enlargement. Some pumpers even started clubs, like Kiwanis or Rotary, where guys get together to pump. Straight men started using the pump in the mid to late 1980s. Pumping provides a sensation that some men find soothing and enjoyable. It also causes the penis to plump up bigger than usual. Most urologists feel that there is no way a guy can make himself permanently bigger with a vacuum pump, and that short term gains occur because the penis is simply swollen. However, the people who manufacture the pumps claim that long term gains are possible. They say that the vacuum pump expands the width of the penis by stretching the walls of the chambers that fill with blood during normal erection. The increase in penis length apparently comes from stretching the ligament that holds almost half of the penis inside the body.

To achieve a "permanent" increase in size, pumpers say that a man has to pump at least a half-hour a day for almost a year. As for the safety of the vacuum pump, it has been approved by the FDA for use with erection problems, but not for use as a weenie enhancement device, not that anyone has applied. (Can you imagine the lab studies that the FDA might require, with hundreds of white rats having their penises pumped for hours on end?) For safety's sake, check with a physician before pumping for long periods of time. That's because there might be a difference between pumping for a few minutes to get hard and pumping for an hour to get bigger. Also ask yourself why you might be focusing so much insecurity onto your penis. No matter what its size, your penis is still a marvelous gift from nature which provides you with tremendous feelings of pleasure.

You would think that the majority of men who pump for size would be those with smaller penises. Not so. A lot of pumpers are fairly well-endowed to begin with. Go figure.

The Bottom Line...

"I once had a lover with an enormous penis. It was a turn-on to look at it, and an ego trip that a man that huge was my partner. But the actual feeling of it inside me didn't give me one-one-hundredth of the pleasure that my more modestly-sized present partner's does. While the size of a man's penis does create different sensations, it is the relationship I have with the man who is attached to the penis that determines what those sensations mean to me." *female age 47*

Before rushing out to get either a pump or cosmetic surgery, please consider the following: If your penis is average- sized or bigger, why do you need to be bigger? What's your problem, anyway? And if your penis is closer to a finger than a phone pole, learn to give great back and foot rubs and become sublime at the art of loving a woman with your lips and tongue. Do this and it is likely that you will be admired by many women, assuming you are a decent human being to begin with. Also try using intercourse positions that might focus more stimulation on the parts of your lover's vagina that give her the most pleasure. The most sensitive areas of a vagina are often located in the first inch or two beyond the vaginal opening. And finally, try to avoid women who are confirmed size-queens. No sense in humiliating yourself needlessly.

A bantam weight penis might feel longer if the female partner bends her knees during intercourse. This results in deeper penetration if that is what she wants. Keeping her legs together will help it feel more snug. A few positions that accommodate bent knees and legs together are rear entry intercourse with both of you on your sides (aka. spoons), or where the woman is on her back and her ankles are resting on the man's shoulders.

As for being embarrassed in front of your locker room buds, sex experts say that it's not fair to compare non-erect penises, because penises that are smaller when flaccid tend to grow a lot when they get hard. But that's of little solace to a guy who's feeling insecure in the showers right after football practice. Hopefully he will learn that there are other ways of earning respect besides having a big penis, assuming that big penises earn respect rather than envy.

Perhaps it might be good to remember that many things in life have a purpose. Whatever it is that you are here on earth to learn, your less-than-memorable member might be one of the keys that helps you find it, especially if it's a bit of humility.

A Note For The Extra-Well Endowed

A small number of men feel angst because they are hung especially well.

For those guys whose girlfriends scream in horror the first time they see the penis erect, relax. Talk about it before you get undressed

("Ah, there's something we need to discuss..."), and flatly rule out the possibility of intercourse for the first couple of weeks. This will allow time for your lover to become comfortable touching and playing with your penis. Ray Stubb's "Erotic Interlude's Part 2" is a very tastefully done videotape which shows a woman massaging the penis of a man who doesn't give up much ground to Trigger. This might be a nice tape to keep around so your girlfriend can see that there are plenty of ways of pleasing you. She can also get you off quite nicely with the oral sex technique which doesn't require her to take your whole penis into her mouth. See the illustration on page 202 for details.

One way of working up to intercourse is if the woman gets on top of the man and experiments with femoral intercourse, which has been described as "intercourse, but not really." With femoral intercourse the penis does not go into the vagina. Instead, the woman holds the well-lubricated penis lengthwise between her labia, like a pencil lying in the binding part of an open book, not that pencil is the most appropriate metaphor here. She can then use the penis to masturbate with, especially by rubbing her clitoris back and forth over the ridge where the head of the penis attaches to the shaft.

After a woman becomes comfortable handling your penis, it's likely that she will eventually want to try vaginal intercourse, for the challenge if nothing else. This will usually work quite nicely as long as the man cools his jets and keeps a low-keyed "stop whenever you want" approach. Use lots of lubrication, and make sure that the woman is the one who puts the thing in and controls the depth and level of thrusting. (Getting popped in the uterus can be just as uncomfortable as getting popped in the testicles.) One position that might be worth trying is where the woman keeps her legs straight but apart. Keep experimenting as certain positions can help a woman's vagina accommodate up to two more inches of penis.

Now, for ways that women mangle their bodies...

---

[1] With apologies to Bruce Springsteen

The Sound Of Leaking Breasts

"I tried out for the cheerleading squad when I was a sophomore in high school. 'This isn't a beauty contest,' the advisor had told us, but we all knew better than that... But you weren't beautiful, Julie Brown, and you knew it. Face facts. You even made a list one time, outlining your numerous faults: breasts too small, buttocks too big, teeth crooked, hair too thin, arms and legs too skinny, feet too long, four inches too tall, nose too bumpy... If you were wealthy, you could make the necessary corrections. If you had enough money, you could have the breast implants you needed, the braces, the nose job, the hairweaving, and with enough money the right cosmetics could be purchased, the ones you saw in the magazines, the ones that would render you flawless..." Julie Brown's "Beauty" pp. 68–70. in the *Michigan Quarterly Review,* edited by Laurence Goldstein, Vol. XXX, No. 1, Winter 1991.

Men aren't the only ones who worry that body parts are too small or not quite right. Women often believe that the world would be a nicer and kinder place if only they had bigger breasts. Some women with petite breasts even feel they would get a better job or promotion if their A cups swelled into majestic E's. Hopes like these have inspired thousands of American women to have their chests packed with funky substances.

Aside from the sheer ridiculousness of getting breast implants, much has been said during the last few years about the safety of them. Silicone molecules seem to leach through the plastic implant pouches. However, it is possible that this isn't any more dangerous to your health than say, living in Detroit or Los Angeles. Saline implants appear to be safer than the silicone, but far less than the original equipment that Mother Nature saw fit to provide.

Silicone Sisters' And The Men Who Love Them

Here in America men with plastic brains are attracted to women with plastic chests. What a perfect combination. What a sad perception of womanhood.

Unfortunately, young girls in America are raised on fashion magazines that highlight gorgeous female models, whatever gorgeous might be. Having grown up under the shadow of super-model breasts, American girls often confuse a combination of anorexia and big breasts for what femininity is all about. As a result, breast implants and bizarre diets have become a way of achieving the fantasy of perfect womanhood.

Perfect womanhood is a costly and precarious myth to pursue. Even if you are able to achieve the right look, it tends to be short-lived and often comes crashing down by the time you reach age thirty-five and can no longer suppress that which in other cultures is considered to be a sign of wisdom. It's too bad America's teenage girls don't get to spend time with America's supermodels. They might get over the super-model fantasy rather quickly.

The Placebo Effect Of Store Bought Boobs

Until recently, some of the biggest proponents of breast implants were the women who got them. Then they had to start spending all that time and energy convincing themselves that the darned things weren't killing them.

One reason why women with plastic chests were so excited about their implants is because life really did get better for many of them. But this guide is willing to bet its left foot that the real reason why life improved is because these women's attitudes got better. It's how they saw themselves that made the difference, not whether their breasts were double A's or triple E's. Feeling more attractive is what made these women more attractive. Granted, there are plenty of men who like the way that big silicone boobs look, but it's quite likely that an increase in confidence without the implants would bring similar results.

Microchip Melons — A New Generation Of Breast Implant?

Unless there is a major shift in the consciousness of American men and women, it is likely that the medical world will find new ways to surgically mangle women's bodies. As long as that is the case, this guide suggests that the next generation of breast implants contain slots for video games. This will help turn the female chest into a full-fledged entertainment center, which is what some men and women apparently expect it to be.

Exercise Video Alert: Truth In Advertising

Exercise videos have been very popular for the past decade. It only seems fair that any actress, model, etc. who does an exercise video ought to list how many cosmetic surgeries she or he has had in order to look the way that she does. (Breast Implants? Ribs removed? Liposuction? Face Lifts? Tummy Tucks? Breast Lifts? Supplemental Hormones?) The videos might then post a warning label such as the following:

WARNING: *With $22,000 Worth Of Plastic Surgery, A Lucky Role Of The Genetic Dice, An Eating Disorder, and The Exercises On This Tape, You Too Can Look More Like Your Video Host.*

Alternatives For Both Men And Women

American advertisers spend millions of dollars to make us think "If only I had this or that, I'd be sexier and happier." It is easy to see why many of us fall for these devious traps. The thought of instantly having bigger or smaller body parts can be terribly seductive.

If cosmetic surgery is what you need, please choose carefully. Do be aware that if you haven't worked through feelings of inferiority, re-aligning body parts may not make you feel any better in the long run. You might simply find new things to feel insecure about.

For alternatives, think about getting your body in good physical shape or dressing better. Breasts that sit on well-developed chest muscles sometimes look bigger, if that is what you are trying to achieve. At the very least, being in good shape makes most people feel and look sexier. And a smaller penis will often look bigger if it isn't being dwarfed by a pot belly, or if the eyes are drawn to nicely developed shoulders and pecs. Also, why not find ways to expand your mind's creativity and intelligence? These are the kind of measures that will make you a better and sexier person.

As for sexual performance, some of the best and most eager lovers are those without ideal dimensions. Since they have less natural endowment to fall back on, they sometimes learn to be extremely attentive and skilled in bed. 🐄 🐄 🐄

End Of Chapter Notes: Some women have breast reduction surgery because it can be severely uncomfortable to lug huge breasts around all of the time. If this is what you are considering, be sure to consult at least two surgeons who specialize in breast reduction surgery. This is not a simple operation, and can leave permanent scaring or disfigurement. 🐄 An interesting dimension of breast implants is their anti-gravitational properties. The things never lie flat, even when a woman is on her back. 🐄 Many women who have implants need additional surgery a few years down the line, and even the salt water boobs make it difficult to screen for cancer.

Chapter 36
When The Tide Turns Red

Once you get into a long term relationship, menstruation is something that happens to both of you. That's why you'll do a whole lot better in life if you try to understand more about it. While we tell you what we can in the pages that follow, the best way for a guy to find out about menstruation is to ask his partner. For instance, does she plod through her periods without much distress, or does she get all swelled-up and bloated? Are there certain things she likes or dislikes when she's having her period? How long does her period usually last? (For most women, it's between three to five or seven days, give or take.) You might eventually ask her to tell you about the first time she menstruated. Almost all women still remember their first period quite vividly.

Learn all she can teach you. You'll be a better person for it, and the two of you might feel more connected as a result. Why not give her the laugh of a lifetime by trying to insert a tampon for her? Some couples will enjoy this; others should never attempt it.

A Brief Historical Note

When people talk about scientific discoveries that have given women more freedom and equality, the birth control pill is often the first thing mentioned. They usually forget that only a couple of generations ago women had to use rags to collect menstrual blood, hence the term "on the rag." The invention of the tampon and sanitary napkin have had more of a positive impact on many women's lives than the birth control pill. And recent modifications to the sanitary napkin have left it far more manageable to use as well as giving birth to the term *panty liner*.

Sex During Periods

Some people fear having intercourse during a woman's menstrual cycle. But the truth is, menstruation causes absolutely no harm to either partner. In fact, the contractions of orgasm push accumulated fluids out of the uterus, which helps decrease menstrual cramping. Can you imagine an American mother telling her fourteen-year-old daughter "Honey, if you're having cramps, why not masturbate?" Instead, they buy Midol.®

Intercourse with a menstruating woman sometimes feels extra nice for the following reasons: 1.) The vagina might be super-lubricated due to menstrual secretions, 2.) The added menstrual swelling might help a woman have a really nice orgasm, and 3.) Some women get extra horny during their periods; this might have to do with a change in hormones, or perhaps they feel more relaxed since it's harder to get pregnant, although pregnancy is still a risk. Other women who don't enjoy having sex with their partner might look forward to their periods as an excuse and respite from sex.

As for the aesthetics of midperiod intercourse, sheets with menstrual lovemaking on them usually wash clean, but so what if they don't? We guys shed that much blood during a hard-fought game of football and consider it a sign of courage.

If you're not into menstrual blood during sex, a great alternative is "Instead," a little disposable cup that fits inside the vagina like a diaphragm, only it is not effective for birth control. You can get it wherever feminine hygiene products are sold. A non-disposable, reusable version is called "The Keeper" (800)680-9739.

Regarding the aesthetics of oral sex during a menstrual cycle, some couples have no problem with it, others do. This is discussed at length in Chapter: 18 — Oral Sex: Vulvas & Honeypots.

Feeling Unlovable

Another thing to be aware of about menstruation is that some women have grown up in households that weren't particularly supportive of their biological processes. As a result, these women may feel unlovable or unattractive when they are having their periods. If this is true for your partner, find a time when she isn't feeling quite so unlovable and discuss it. It's one thing to feel bad when you have done something dumb, but there is nothing dumb about having a menstrual cycle. Besides, if you have ever had to wait out a menstrual period that is seriously late, you will learn to regard the monthly flow as a lover's best friend.

Goofy Facts. Period.

🕊 UC Berkeley scientist Margie Profet believes that menstruation evolved as a way of protecting the female's uterus from harmful bacteria and viruses that might be delivered by male ejaculate. Far from being a waste, she sees menstrual bleeding as the body's way of systematically preventing infection. Other's don't agree.

🕊 In some primitive societies, the native women didn't start suffering from menstrual pain and cramping until they had been "saved" by Western missionaries and their American wives.

🕊 In the 1976 Olympics an American swimmer won gold medals and broke a world record while on her period. (Too bad she didn't get big bucks for endorsing the brand of tampons that allowed her to swim for the gold...)

🕊 There is no evidence whatsoever that a woman's intellectual, academic or job performance is affected by her menstrual cycle. It may not feel great, but it doesn't compromise her ability to think or perform.

The Legacy Of Bleeding

Children are taught from an early age that bleeding is what happens when you have a cut, wound, or other form of trauma. Can you imagine the impact of menstrual bleeding on a young girl who isn't well-prepared? She would probably assume that there is something terribly wrong with her body. "Well-prepared" needs to include more than just the biological facts. It should also incorporate a sense of pride about the body and an awareness that menstrual bleeding is a sign of maturity and health.

Another problem with menstruation is what to do with the blood. Few guys ever have to worry about bleeding through their shorts, but their girlfriends might. One very astute woman reader who is nearly ninety still has dreams that she is menstruating and can't find a sanitary napkin. The feelings of panic remain fresh in her unconscious, although she last menstruated when Harry Truman was president, or was it Dwight Eisenhower. OK — John F. Kennedy.

One feminist writer made an interesting point that if men were the ones who menstruated, they would probably brag about how many ounces they bled each month. At least this would indicate pride rather than shame.

Twinkies And The Onset Of Menstruation

Here in the Western world, the onset of menstruation has slowly but steadily been occurring at a younger age. While this has generally been attributed to better nutrition, it may actually be due to poorer nutrition. A researcher named Rose E. Frisch feels that there is a relationship between the initial onset of menstruation and stores of body fat. Fat tissue is one of the places in the body where estrogen is synthesized.

As a young woman approaches puberty her proportion of body fat increases. In order to start having menstrual cycles she seems to need around 17% body fat, and to ovulate the figure increases to approximately 26%. On the other hand, women who are old enough to menstruate but are seriously overweight tend not to menstruate regularly.

If the level of body fat really does play a role in the menstrual process, then it might be our penchant for junk food and the sedentary life rather than healthy nutrition that is lowering the age of first menstruation. However, there are other theories, too. One suggests that the added stress of the modern world is causing girls to menstruate earlier. Yet if stress were a determining factor, women alive during World Wars I & II would have certainly menstruated at an earlier age.

Women Athletes

It is not uncommon for women athletes to stop menstruating or have irregular periods. One reason is that their body fat is often lower than 17%. If a woman athlete wants to get pregnant but is having difficulty, adding a few pounds might help.

Women athletes might also find that the start of menstruation is delayed due to metabolic reasons. For instance, women athletes and dancers who began their training before the ages of nine or ten often start menstruating a few years later than their nonathletic peers.

It is with great restraint that your author resists telling about the time during his freshman year of college when he lifted weights with the women members of the Soviet National Shot Put Team. He never thought to ask Olga, Svetlana and Georgia if they menstruated regularly.[1]

Note: Children of both sexes who get increased amounts of exercise before puberty have lung capacities that are 10% to 20% greater than their nonexercising peers. The added lung capacity will stay with them for life, which is why it's so important for young children of either sex to exercise and be physically active.

Tampons, Sponges & Toxic Shock Syndrome

Toxic Shock Syndrome (TSS) is a rare but sometimes fatal disease caused by the toxin of certain bacteria that grow in the bodies of both men and women. TSS is now mainly associated with surgery and severe burn cases, but during the early 1980s some women died from TSS following the introduction of a new super absorbent tampon called Rely.

Contrary to what scientists first believed, the killer tampons did not act as a breeding site for the TSS bacteria. Rely contained two synthetic fibers (corboxy methyl cellulose & polyester foam) that are thought to have irritated the vaginal lining in ways that triggered the TSS bacteria to produce a dangerous toxin. Tampons are now made from only cotton and rayon. As a result, the occurrence of TSS among tampon users is rare. Your chances of getting killed in a car wreck are 500 to 1000 times greater than the risk of death by tampon.

---

[1]The former Evil Empire is currently in a bit of disarray. The team of the old Soviet Union (CCCP) no longer exists.

It was originally thought that wearing the same tampon for several hours increased your chances of getting TSS. Not so. However, the risk does go up when you use nothing but tampons throughout your entire period, even if you change them every three hours. If you are a tampon user who wants to greatly reduce her chances of getting TSS, don't wear tampons throughout your entire period. For instance, alternate using tampons and napkins. Also, some people are naturally more susceptible to TSS. If you have ever had TSS or appear susceptible to it, you are better off to not use tampons.

There is a slight increase in TSS among women who use barrier contraceptives e.g. diaphragm, cervical cap, and contraceptive sponge. This risk is very, very, very slight.

One reader comments, "I was put on sea sponges back in the 1980s during the TSS scare. I had used Rely tampons and developed cell abnormalities in my cervix. After ditching all tampons and inserting a clean sea sponge during my period, the abnormal cells disappeared for good. An FDA approved alternative that plenty of women swear by is called "Instead." 🐓🐓🐓

End Of Chapter Notes: Special thanks to Dr. Anne Schuchat from the Center for Disease Control in Atlanta, and Nina Bender at Whitehall Laboratories for their help on TSS.

Chapter 37
Clean Jeans, Tight Jeans, Briefs & Boxers

Clean and Guys: Some guys never recover from the defeat of being toilet trained and get their revenge by avoiding soap and water. It's so easy for a man (and woman) to be clean and smell nice. All it takes is a five minute shower, deodorant, and a toothbrush. If you still have a foreskin, pull the thing back and wash around it.

If you are young or don't have much of a beard, keep your stubble shaved and no one will know the difference. The daily shaving ritual gets old really fast, so count your lucky stars if your beard is wimpy or late in arriving.

Clean and Girls: Regarding sexual hygiene for women, this book defers to the following passage from Betty Dodson's "Sex For One" (Harmony Books) in which Ms. Dodson refers to events that occurred in her various women's groups:

> "During 'Show and Tell' we reviewed our concerns about episiotomy scars from childbirth, inner lips that didn't match, little bumps or moles that looked strange, clitorises that were thought to be too small, and the dreaded vaginal discharge. We talked about genital hygiene and how douching could be available but not as a compulsive routine."

> "Since most women have some clear or white secretion, I always considered that normal. I never used harsh commercial douching preparations... Usually washing the exterior genitalia and reaching just inside the vaginal opening was sufficient cleansing. Before making love, I inserted a finger inside my vagina to smell and taste myself, which made me feel secure."

Regarding Ms. Dodson's reference to tasting herself, it might seem a little strange to some women, but we guys taste you all the time. It's OK, honest. Some of the feminists might say "If we're supposed to taste ourselves, why don't you guys taste yourselves?" Most of us have. Besides, what flavor do you think we get when we kiss you after receiving a blow job?

It's also helpful for women to remember that the hood of the clitoris can sometimes collect the same kind of cheesy stuff as the foreskin of the penis. A Q-Tip dipped in mineral oil will help remove any of these deposits that might be stuck under the hood. Also try to use a low pH soap on your genitals. More about this in the chapter Oral Sex: Honey Pots & Vulvas.

Bidet In A Can?

While we Americans don't allow anything as functional as bidets in our bathrooms, we have invented a totally useless substitute that not only causes irritation but harms the environment as well. It's called feminine hygiene spray.

Feminine deodorants, sprays, powders and commercial douche products with names like "Cherry Orchard Breeze" and "Morning Dew" are key players in Madison Avenue's relentless campaign to create and cash in on every conceivable form of human doubt and fear. The vagina is self-cleaning. Sprays and douches can actually cause odor by disturbing the natural flora and fauna of the vagina. **Note:** Women who douche more than three times a month are said to have a three times greater chance of getting pelvic inflammatory disease than women who don't.

Trimming The Triangle

"I wax and swear by it. Have it done professionally. It's worth the money and then you can start doing it yourself. I use hot wax, not with the strips. Ingrown hairs are sometimes a problem, but it beats having an entire snatch of stubble." *female age 25*

"I shave and just deal with the irritation." *female age 26*

"Shaving is painful and I look about 12-years-old, it grosses me out. Trimming works! Borrow a beard trimmer and go for it! One crew cut coming up!" *female age 29*

"I shave in the summer so that when I wear my bathing suit it doesn't show. Waxing or tweezing is less irritating. When you shave, it itches terribly when it starts to grow back." *female 49*

"My husband really likes to trim my pubic area for me, he gets turned-on by this, and I think it's highly arousing, too." *female 45*

"I'm more aware of myself and my sexuality when I'm shaved. It feels sensual, like the first time you wear silk underwear. It's too much trouble to keep up, though. If there was an easy way, I think I'd do it more often." *female age 36*

All you have to do is walk into your local drug store and see products like "Bikini Bare" and special bikini shavers to realize that a lot of women trim their pubic hair. This is mainly a cultural matter, but here in the U.S. of A. a neatly trimmed triangle can be a nice turn-on. On the other hand, some women view this as an attempt to deface the female body. They equate trimming the triangle with burning down the rain forest.

As for the statistics of muff mowing, some women don't shave anything anywhere; most American women shave their armpits and leg hair, a large number of women trim their pubic hair and some shave all of it off — because they like the way it looks and feels, or because it's summer and they are trying to wear string bikinis without looking like they just stepped off a boat from the Ukraine. Some guys get really turned on by a slick vulva. One advantage is that it's easier to lick; another is the extra visual charge that it seems to offer. Also, a prostitute who previewed this book commented that "Men trim and/or shave too. I see lots of this in my line of work. Yes, big time execs, too." Another female reader says, "I used to have this lovely, neat, wonderfully behaved triangle of pubic hair. And then I turned 30 and the thing started to spread..."

Rainbow Girl Muffs

Some highly adventurous women dye their pubic hair amazing colors such as bright blue, pink, purple or green. Can you imagine? This guide endorses the concept, and would love to hear a woman announce the change by blurting out "Hon, I was abducted by aliens today..." Hopefully, adventurous ladies like these will go out of their way to find non-toxic dyes that won't irritate their tender tissues or stain their boyfriends' teeth.

Tight Jeans & Infections

Of the things in life most irritating to the human organism, bladder infections rate right up there with presidential speeches, unemployment, and earthquake aftershocks. They are not pleasant events. Guys usually don't understand them because they seldom get this type of infection.

Other common female infections involve an overpopulation of yeast cells in the vagina. This can happen when the vaginal environment gets out of balance, as sometimes occurs when taking antibiotics. In fact, the vaginal environment tends to be out of balance when its pH goes above 5.5. This means that a healthy vagina is a bit acidic.

There are some events that might increase the occurrence of both bladder and/or vaginal infections. One is having intercourse when the vagina isn't well-lubricated. Vaginal irritation can also result from using rubbers that aren't adequately lubricated. Putting contraceptive jelly or a water-based lubricant such as KY on the outside of a rubber will help a great deal. Both partners usually enjoy the extra slip'n 'slide feeling.

There may also be a connection between tight jeans and yeast infections. Wearing tight jeans causes a person to sweat between the legs. This allows bacteria from the rectum to hydroplane into the vulva. One solution to the tight jean problem is to trash the tight jeans. But if you are a total slave to fashion, be sure to wear cotton underpants and try cleaning your rear end with a handi-wipe or other moist towelette each time you defecate. This will help cut down on the bacterial version of moon-walking. Also make sure you wipe from the front to the back. Some women find that decreasing the amount of sugar or artificial sweeteners in their diet helps to decrease the number of infections. Lubricants that contain glycerine should also be avoided if you get frequent infections.

Male partners can sometimes carry the infection without having any symptoms themselves. If that's the case, they will need to take the same medication as the woman. Otherwise, the infection will simply ping pong back and forth between partners.

If you get bladder infections often, you might try peeing right after intercourse. It could help flush out whatever little micro-rodents are waiting to make your life miserable. Also, be sure to find out what your doctor, nurse practitioner, or pharmacist has to say about bladder and yeast infections. Some women find that traditional home remedies work best, while others respond better to either prescription or over-the-counter drugs. For instance, some women find that drinking lots of cranberry juice helps with urinary tract infections..

And finally, it might be helpful if both men and women accept the fact that bladder and vaginal infections fall into the category of shared problems rather than just her problem. It might also be nice if the woman felt comfortable enough to tell her lover "I hope that you won't hesitate to let me know if the environment down there gets a little, ah, tropical." The reason we suggest this is because guys who enjoy doing oral sex almost always know a woman's baseline state, and can often tell changes before she might be aware of them. Of course, guys should know that the environment of the vagina changes with the status of a woman's menstrual cycle. For instance, a woman's vagina might become more acidic when she is ready to conceive.

Girlfriends & Testicular Cancer

Cancer of the testicles is the most common cancer for men between the ages of 20-34. While uncommon, it is the leading cause of death for men who are between 15-40. This type of cancer type of cancer is fast growing, but has a very high cure rate as long as it is detected early.

While guys tend to rub their balls several times a day, few make the extra effort to check for early cancer signs. As a result, the first person to discover the cancer is often a man's wife or girlfriend when she notices a pea-sized node on one of his testicles. That's why it's a good idea for women as well men to know how to check for cancer of the testicles.The exam should be done once a month. Instructions for doing a ball check follow.

BALL CHECK!

You need to do a ball check every 30 days or 3,000 strokes, whichever comes first.

The best time to do a ball check is after a warm shower. The worst time is after surfing winter swells.

Use both hands. Grab a ball. Roll it between your fingers. You are looking for any bumps or lumps. They can be smaller than a pea.

BALL NOTES: One ball is usually bigger than the other. Nature made them that way. When you are sexually aroused, your balls tend to swell. It is also normal for balls to go from hard to soft, depending on the weather and level of sexual arousal. If you ever get popped in the balls and the pain lasts for more than ten minutes, it's a really good idea to have them checked by a physician. If not treated quickly, ball trauma can cause your huevos to become sterile.

(3)

Be sure to check all sides, including the top and bottom.

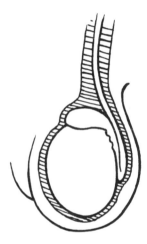

THIS IS YOUR BALL ON DRUGS!

Not really. It's just a cross-section of your ball. There are a couple of spaghetti-like cords that attach to each testicle at the back, towards the top. They form a structure that is shaped like a comma. These might be fuller if you haven't ejaculated in a while. It may feel a little weird, but check out your comma for any little nodes, lumps or changes since the last check.

(4)

(5) Grab your other ball, and have at it.

(6) If either ball has any nodes, bumps or lumps, take it to a physician for a check-up. Chances are, it's only a cyst or infection, but that needs attention, too.

(7) CONGRATULATIONS! You are done. Now go grab your favorite lube and give yourself a congratulatory ball-check orgasm.

BOOB CHECK!

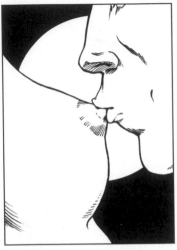

Look, you can do it how the American Cancer Society wants you to—cold, clinical, fear-based and boring. **Or...** You can do it with a real or imaginary lover.

You should be doing a boob check every month for the rest of your life, so why not make it part of a fantasy that not only leaves your breasts tingling, but the rest of your body feeling great? Besides, you're far more likely to do it each month if you spice up the process.

A good time to do a boob check is one week after the start of your menstrual period.

You have nothing on except for one of those skimpy little paper gowns. You hear the door to the examining room open, and suddenly walks in one of the sexiest E.R. hunks you have ever seen. Gulp.

After a few preliminaries, he asks you to stand and open the gown. He says to raise your arms high, "Hold up!" style, then he has you put them on your hips, then you bend forward, and finally you relax your arms at your side. In each position he (Ok, you) look for any changes in the color or texture of the skin and nipple. He also examines each nipple carefully for discharge. You can feel every photon of his caring gaze. You take a deep, deep breath.

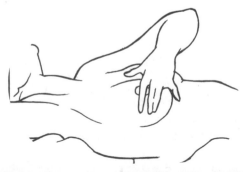

Now he asks you to lay flat on your back with your right arm behind your head.

Your body tenses as the pads of his fingers (your left hand...) begin to examine every inch of your chest. You moan quietly as he moves his fingers in small circles, about the size of a dime. He pauses briefly to put talc or location on your breasts, to help his fingers glide smoothly from one spot to the next, each time making little circles, as if he were hand painting a string of pearls across your breast. He repeats every circle several times before moving his fingers forward, varying the pressure of each circle from light to hard so he can feel all the sensuous layers of tissue.

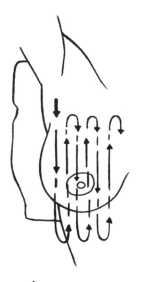

The path he follows is vertical, creating ten to sixteen strands of pearls across your breast.

With your arm relaxed at your side, he reaches under your armpit and explores for any lumps or swollen nodes.

Finally, his fingertips begin to squeeze your nipples to check for discharge that might be more than you usually have.

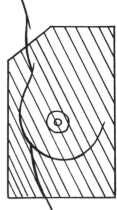 

He pauses; you hear him take a long deep breath. He struggles to maintain his composure as he has you lift your left arm above your head and he begins to feel your other breast...

Return The Favor...

Men should learn how to do routine breast exams on their sweethearts, but never on the first date. Being alert to the early signs of breast cancer can help save the life of a loved one, and breast exams are the way that most problems are discovered and hopefully cured.

Unfortunately, some women won't do routine breast exams because they are afraid they might find something wrong. Perhaps it might help allay some of their fears to know that surgery for breast cancer has come out of the dark ages and is no longer hideously disfiguring. Much of the time, only the lump itself is removed, and even if the whole breast is involved, reconstructive implants can be inserted immediately. Breast reconstruction has become a fine art, with the options ranging from inserting saline implants to grafting fatty tissue from other parts of the body. Most women report being very satisfied with the results.

Women are usually taught how to do breast exams by a gynecologist, family practitioner, or nurse. A woman can then teach her boyfriend how to do the exam, or he can go with her to her next doctor's appointment. That way the doctor or nurse practitioner can teach you both. People sometimes find it strange that a husband or boyfriend would want to join a woman for her pelvic and breast exam. It's just possible that the guy might learn something valuable about his lover's body. Everyone would benefit.

A few things to consider when doing a breast exam are as follows: Breasts tend to be lumpy, and the lower curve of each breast often contains firm tissue. Since the geology of each breast fluctuates with the woman's menstrual status, it is a good idea to do breast exams at the same time each month, preferably after a woman's period. That way you'll establish a baseline reading. With the woman's arms raised above her head, feel each part of her breasts with the pads of your fingers as opposed to using your fingertips. Check all the way to the armpits. Things to look for are lumps that are hard, don't move, feel connected to the breast itself, and/or are still.

NOTE: Contrary to what you might think, women in their twenties can get breast cancer, so start doing those exams now!

Prostate Infections & Irritation

Only men have prostate glands. The prostate gland is located on the floor of the rectum about a finger's length deep. It sits next to the entrance (or is that exit) of the bladder, and wraps around the urethra. When it is not making fluid that contributes to the man's ejaculate, the prostate sometimes swells or gets infected. This is not good, since an irritated or infected prostate can cause severe urinary discomfort or a sudden and powerful need to urinate when the bladder is hardly even half full. For a few unlucky souls, prostate swelling can be so severe that it clamps shut the urethra so the man can't pee at all.

To determine if you have a prostate infection, the doctor needs to stick a finger up your rear and push on your prostate so it drips fluid into your bladder. You then pee into a cup and they culture that. This may sound annoying to those men who have never had prostate problems. However, if your prostate ever becomes seriously irritated, you would probably let King Kong stick his finger up your rear if that could help.

Another potential source of prostate irritation might be cancer. This strikes men over the age of forty and is one of the less dangerous cancers if it is treated early. This is why men over forty should have regular prostate exams.

Is Smoking Sexy?

There are plenty of people who make a phenomenal effort to keep themselves neat, clean and attractive but still fill their lungs with cigarette smoke. Living with this type of contradiction is testimony to how difficult it is to break the nicotine habit, especially when some of the huge tobacco companies have apparently tried to increase the addictive properties of cigarettes.

While there has been a substantial decline in tar sucking among most Americans, young women remain the one group who are still puffing away as much as ever. This fact hasn't escaped the attention of cigarette makers who work hard to attract the interest of young women.

Cigarette ads are populated with shots of sexy women who seem happy, confident and in control, but you almost never see the cigarettes hanging out of their mouths, nor do you see them contorting their lips so they can try to blow the smoke out the side. These ads never have scratch and sniff patches to let you know what your breath will smell like once you begin smoking, nor do they offer free coupons to the cleaners, who you will be visiting more often if you smoke. Young women are also impacted by the fact that most women's magazines make huge revenues from cigarette ads. As a result, women's magazines are hesitant to boycott the ads or run articles about the health hazards of smoking.

Cigarette smoke and birth control pills combine to create a major health risk in women above the age of 33. And all women who take birth control pills and smoke have a greater incidence of bruising. (What about nonsmoking pill takers who are exposed to ambient cigarette smoke? Does the ambient smoke put them at extra risk? One should assume the answer is yes until credible research is done that proves the opposite.) Even dogs who live in homes with cigarette smokers die significantly sooner than those with nonsmoking masters.

Note: Studies show that people who don't begin smoking before the age of 21 aren't likely to ever start. As a result, more and more of the tobacco industry's advertising emphasis will be on getting teenagers to smoke. ◄◄◄

Chapter 38
Abortion? Adoption?

Birth Control Failure: A Sobering Note.

 A large percentage of women who get abortions were using contraceptives at the time of intercourse. That's because even the best contraceptives occasionally fail.

If you are not prepared to make babies, raise babies, or face the issue of abortion or adoption, you shouldn't be having intercourse. Fortunately, there are plenty of fun, erotic, and highly intimate ways of getting each other off besides intercourse. If intercourse is still in the cards, you can greatly minimize your chances of becoming pregnant by using effective birth control methods.

So What If You Just Found Out That You Are Pregnant And Didn't Want To Be?

There are plenty of people who will offer advice. Some of it will be helpful. There are many people who have opted for abortion and many who have had unplanned children. Most will tell you that they did the right thing. Whichever way you decide, keep in mind that millions of people have had to face the exact same thing that you are—although you may feel like the loneliest person on the face of the earth.

In case you are wondering about the emotional aspects of having an abortion, studies show that most women who have abortions don't report an increase in depression (as a group) for any more than a week or two after the abortion, if that. One of these studies was funded by a governmental agency that was hoping to find the opposite result. On the other hand, your own personal beliefs might not allow for abortion, in which case your options will be whether to raise the baby yourself or give it up for adoption. There are plenty of agencies that will help with the latter, but not many that will help the parent of an unplanned child who is trying to raise the child. (It is interesting how some of the strongest anti-abortion proponents are highly supportive while you are still pregnant, but are quite stingy and punitive when it comes to helping the unmarried mom of a toddler or older child.)

Whether you choose to have an abortion or to have the baby, it's important that you make your mind up as soon as possible. People, especially teenagers, who are faced with unwanted pregnancies tend to be indecisive and don't act as soon as they might. If they opt for an abortion it is sometimes later in the pregnancy when the procedure might be more complicated. And if they decide to have the baby, they sometimes don't go for prenatal care until later in the pregnancy. This places them at high risk, endangering themselves and their babies.

A Special Note On Giving Your Baby up For Adoption

There are thousands of loving couples in this country who can't have a baby of their own and desperately want to adopt one. These couples tend to have been married for quite a while. Most have stable homes, good relationships, and solid incomes. They will give your child a lifetime of love and care. Unfortunately, many of these couples must wait as long as seven years before they can adopt a baby, since not many single parents are giving their babies up for adoption these days. Part of the problem is that younger moms are often encouraged by their non-pregnant peers to keep the baby (easy for them to say), and unmarried moms sometimes have the unrealistic fantasy that keeping the baby will make their lives better, or that the baby's father will want to marry them. This usually doesn't happen.

One of the really nice things about giving up a baby for adoption in this day and age is that the pregnant mom gets to interview the couples who want to adopt her baby. She gets to decide which couple she wants to raise the baby. That way she will know her baby is being raised and loved by people she likes.

Chapter 39
Birth Control & Gnarly Sex Germs

Why is it that some young men will care for a car or favorite baseball glove with meticulous love for detail, but forget about birth control when they are having intercourse? Why do so many of America's young women go nearly insane over one little zit or take hours getting dressed for a party, but not insist that a partner wear a rubber when they are sexually active? And why is our nation's rather feeble program to educate its young about sexually transmitted diseases little more than a thinly veiled attempt to discourage them from having sex altogether? It is a program that talks about disease, but rarely mentions pleasure.

It doesn't need to be this way.

This Book's Approach To Birth Control

Most books on sex have birth control chapters that read like the Chilton Manual. Not this one. "War And Peace" maybe, but not the Chilton Manual.

If you are interested in knowing about the various birth control options, go with your partner to a family planning clinic. Perhaps they will have a video you can watch, and a real flesh and blood human being who can answer your questions. Or, if you belong to an HMO, call and ask them to send you a booklet on birth control. Many of these organizations provide excellent birth control services, since it costs them a lot of money when you get pregnant.

Sharing the responsibility for birth control often increases the sexual trust and enjoyment in a relationship. It's the sort of thing that people do when they care about each other, rather than just making it the responsibility of the woman or ignoring the need altogether. Making birth control a mutual project could be the ante for having better sex.

Before saying more about birth control, we need to talk about sex germs. That's because one of the factors in choosing a birth control

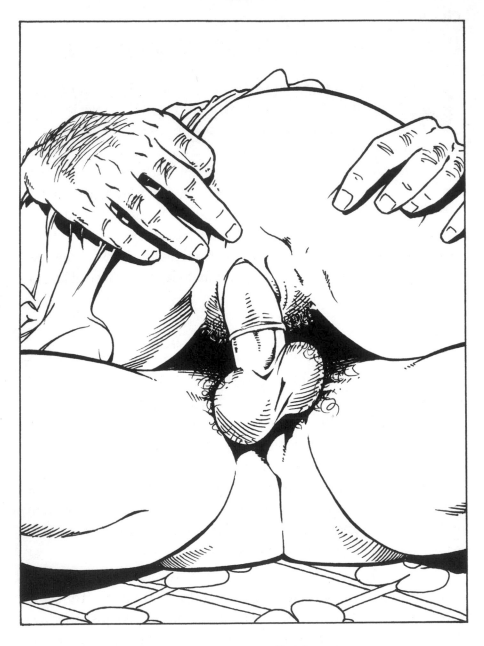

Don't Forget Your Rubbers!

method is whether or not you are at risk for getting a sexually transmitted disease.

GSGs (Gnarly Sex Germs)

Some people believe that AIDS is the most deadly sex disease that
ever was. Actually, the prize goes to syphilis. Even a couple of popes
died from syphilis. That's why this chapter begins with a discussion of
syphilis, and then works its way to AIDS and other diseases that are
associated with sexual contact.

Syphilis — The Great Pox

Before 1492, when Columbus came to America, there had been
no recorded cases of syphilis in Europe. But syphilis did exist in the
part of the New World where Columbus and his crew landed. Shortly
after Columbus' return, a vicious strain of syphilis began to spread
throughout Europe, quickly killing a sizable portion of the general
population. During its first fifty years in Europe, from about 1493 until
1550, syphilis was an even more savage killer than AIDS. Smallpox got
its name because the lesions it caused were small compared to those
of "The Great Pox" syphilis. It's seems that the Spanish army sent
syphilitic prostitutes to infect the enemy Italian army, which is one
of the first recorded instances of biological warfare.

After 1550, syphilis went from being a quick killer to a slow killer,
more like the syphilis we know today. Instead of finishing off its
victims in short order, syphilis began to linger in the body for years
after the initial infection, eventually targeting organs like the heart or
brain. Syphilis remained a potent killer for four hundred more years
(from 1550 to 1940), with almost half of all hospital beds worldwide
filled with its victims. Syphilis is less of a problem today because it
can now be treated in its early phases by antibiotics which weren't
discovered until the 1940s.

Nobel Prize Note: In the 1920s, a medical doctor received the Nobel
Prize for infecting syphilis patients with malaria. The high fever
caused by the Malaria helped to bum out the stubborn syphilis infection. Of course, there was no cure for the new cure. Some scientists

speculate that more people died from the attempts to cure syphilis than from syphilis itself. Until the discovery of antibiotics, popular syphilis therapies included treatment with arsenic and mercury.

Lonely Shepherds, Scared Sheep — Sounds Like AIDS?

Folklore has it that syphilis was originally caused by lonely shepherds who prodded their sheep with something more personal than carved wooden staffs. The reason for the sheep/shepherd rumor is a matter of simple poetry. In 1530 a great physician, poet and scholar named Fracastor wrote a poem about the disease of syphilis which hadn't been named syphilis yet. In the poem, a sixteen year-old shepherd boy named Syphilis made the horrible mistake of building an altar on the wrong plot of land and praying to the wrong gods. This was the 1530s equivalent of wearing the wrong colors in a gang-controlled neighborhood. It seriously angered the god Apollo, who had the youth's genitals struck with a chancre-laden thunderbolt. Ouch! Fracastor's poem tells about the rapid spread of the "new" disease:

> "I sing of that terrible disease, unknown to past centuries, which attacked all Europe in one day and spread itself over part of Africa and Asia..."

Sounds a little like the spread of AIDS. But syphilis behaved and still behaves very much like a sexually transmitted disease. That is not the case with AIDS, unless you are a member of a high risk group.

AIDS

AIDS is a disease or cluster of diseases that involves a shutdown of the immune system. AIDS appears to be transmitted by certain kinds of sexual contact and through certain exchanges of blood. Several factors may be involved in its spread.

AIDS has yet to follow the early predictions about it that were based upon current knowledge of sexually transmitted diseases. For instance, it has not made the highly anticipated cross-over into heterosexual populations. Not nearly enough straight people have been using condoms to prevent the cross-over that would have happened if current viral models were accurate. Many of the AIDS cases that do exist among heterosexuals can be explained by transfusion or IV drug usage. Also, speculation about AIDS running rampant among the general population of Africa may not be holding up to closer scrutiny. More people in Africa appear to be dying from famine and genocide than from sexually transmitted diseases, and medical hygiene is so abysmal that the same syringe is sometimes used to inject hundreds of people with little or no sterilization.

Some straight people will think that this means they don't need to take an informed stance against the spread of sexually transmitted diseases. This would be most unfortunate.

Why Should Straight People Continue To Be Cautious?

Many young straight adults have become wise to the fact that hardly any of their heterosexual peers are coming down with diseases like AIDS. More of their straight peers are dying from drug and alcohol-related causes, not to mention suicide. Of course, this hasn't stopped young people from drinking or doing drugs, so why should they use condoms? It's hard to argue with this kind of logic, except to say that we live in such a fast-paced world that disease contagion will be nearly impossible to stop should an AIDS-like condition begin to prey on the heterosexual population. Those who used condoms might be the ones who survive.

Defining An Acceptable Level Of Risk

Each year 40,000 Americans die in car accidents. Thousands more are seriously injured. Yet most of us consider driving to be an acceptable risk. On the other hand, if people were told about a new sexually transmitted disease that took 40,000 American lives each year and injured thousands more, there would be a great outcry against sex.

Perhaps we believe there is something inherently good about driving, and something inherently bad about sex. Or maybe we get more satisfaction out of driving. Whatever the case, you can greatly decrease your chances of being injured in a car accident by not drinking or doing drugs when you drive, and by driving sensibly. The same is true with having sex.

Staying Well

Rather than focusing only upon AIDS prevention, why not try to keep your entire body healthy? This means staying fit, eating well, and keeping all nonessential drugs out of your body. It also means using rubbers if you are having anal sex whether you are hetero-sexual or homosexual. And if you aren't true blue and monogamous, you should seriously consider using rubbers during vaginal inter-course as well. This will help stop the spread of things likes herpes, syphilis, and perhaps genital warts and chlamydia. It will also help decrease your chances of getting diseases like AIDS.

For many people, an important part of staying healthy also includes having sex. This can be a very good thing. On the other hand, there would probably be a significant drop in the number of sexually transmitted diseases if potential partners dated for a few weeks or months before getting naked together. By then, you would know more about a potential partner than simply how they fill out their blue jeans. Perhaps the sex would be better, too.

As for specifics about staying well, consider the following:

ORAL SEX (mouth-to-crotch): In studies on AIDS and prostitutes, the prostitutes who seem to be coming down with AIDS are those who use intravenous drugs. You would think that if AIDS were trans-mitted by oral sex, women who blow men for a living would be getting it in droves, but they're not unless they also shoot up drugs. While your chances of getting AIDS from oral sex are probably low, you can get other sexually transmitted diseases while doing oral sex that can be harmful to your body. Using a condom while blowing a guy or placing Saran Wrap over a woman's vulva makes sense if you are not in a long term relationship. Also, forget having oral sex without a barrier if there is a cold sore in your mouth. The herpes virus is a switch-hitter that is happy to hop from mouth to genitals or visa versa. If you are a gay or bi-sexual male, it might be an excellent idea to bag whoever you blow, given the current affinity that AIDS has for gay and bisexual males.

ORAL SEX (French Kissing): Besides being a delightful thing to do, French kissing is a way of contracting anything you might get when someone with a cold or flu sneezes in your face. Why not save the making out until you have dated for a couple of weeks, or at least have learned the person's phone number by heart? Then if you think it's a go, go for it.

HAND JOBS: Researcher Bruce Voeller was asked about the chances of catching a sexually transmitted disease from doing your partner by hand. Dr. Voeller compared it to the probability of breaking your neck from falling out of bed, unless you get the fluid into an open cut. Voeller comments: "A good way to know if you have an infectable cut is to rub a piece of lemon over your skin. If a place burns, then you've got a cut that might conceivably get infected."

INTERCOURSE (vaginal): Do you really believe that the great looking fraternity guy who you are about to go to bed with is going to stop and say, "Oh, by the way, I'm totally low risk except for that little butt-fucking incident last month with the captain of the wrestling team." Or what about that sweet-looking former high school cheerleader? Do you honestly believe she will cop to having spiked heroin while going through her rebellious phase last summer? Perhaps it's possible that other people aren't quite as responsible about what goes on with their bodies as you might be with yours.

One should be especially sure to use condoms when sleeping with partners who drink or do drugs, even if it's just brewskis or pot. That's because these substances help to numb the part of the mind which we count on to keep us out of trouble. It's the part that says, "This isn't the kind of person I'd ever sleep with if I weren't stoned," or "I can't even remember this guy's name, but he's got one hand under my shirt and two fingers up my vagina; what's wrong with this picture?" or "I'm sure I will feel much better in the morning if we use a condom tonight."

Note: Pulling out and squirting off to the side doesn't prevent anything, including frustration. Also, it's a good idea to put the rubber on as soon as the penis gets hard enough to wear it. That's because a penis usually starts dripping before it ever goes inside a vagina. And if your partner does speed or cocaine, never have intercourse without using condoms. With such people, you will never know what they have done or with whom. Half of the time, they won't remember themselves. The same is true for heroin addicts and alcoholics, although these substances tend to decrease the ability or desire to have sex.

INTERCOURSE (anal): According to one theory, there might be immune suppressing factors in male ejaculate that help it on its journey up the female reproductive tract. These factors might not contribute to a person's good health when deposited in the rear end.

When compared to the rectum, the vagina has thick walls that keep male sex fluids out of the blood stream. And stomach acids usually kick the daylights out of male ejaculate when it is swallowed. But the jury is still out on what happens to the immune suppressing factors in male ejaculate when it is deposited into the rectum and large colon, which by its very nature, absorbs fluids back into the body. On the other hand, anal sex was popular for several centuries before AIDS was a problem, so it is quite a stretch to assume that anal sex with non-infected partners compromises the immune system. But until more is known about anal sex and the immune system, even totally monogamous husbands and wives are wise to use a condom when having anal sex. This will also help keep the man from getting urinary tract infections, or passing fecal mater into the woman's vagina. (Just washing a penis with soap and water is not enough, as stuff from her rear stays in the peehole.)

URINE: If you are into water sports and not in a long term monogamous relationship, don't shoot urine into any body cavities and keep it off skin that's broken unless the skin is your own.

DRUGS: It is a medically sound idea to eliminate all non-essential drugs from your body, whether prescribed or recreational. This includes anything from poppers and cocaine to antibiotics and anti-fungals. Since many members of the gay community were so amazingly promiscuous during the 1970s and 1980s, sex diseases and parasites were passed around continuously. To combat these, antibiotics and anti-fungals were prescribed in huge amounts, often as a preventative before a guy spent a weekend at the baths or cruised the trails. No one knows what long term effects this might have on the immune system; at the very least it helped create increasingly drug-resistant organisms. Again, avoid taking any drugs that are not essential, whether prescribed or not.

DIET: There is no way the immune system is going to work well if you are malnourished. Most intravenous drug users appear to be malnourished, which might be one of the factors which puts them at high risk for AIDS.

EXERCISE: Exercise is far more important than we like to think. Studies have shown that most people who exercise rigorously often have a delayed onset of serious AIDS symptoms. Also, several of the patients waiting for heart transplants at a major medical center were recently put on a program of exercise. 50% of them no longer needed the transplant by the time it became available. And in most studies on aging, men and women who exercise regularly show a significant decrease in the number of problems typically associated with getting old. They also have sex more often.

AIDS & God

Some people claim that AIDS is a message from God about sexual "immorality." If this is true, then why does God allow millions of right-wing, church going, heterosexual Americans to die each year from cancer and heart attacks — diseases that take far more lives than AIDS? What's the hidden moral message there?

And what about young children who are dying from cancer and various immunological diseases. Is God punishing these two- to six-year-olds for being immoral? How can people say that one disease is caused by the wrath of God, while others aren't? Perhaps the real disease is in the minds of those who are willing to cast the first stone.

This concludes the deadly sex germ part of this chapter. In case you should need it, the phone number of the National AIDS Hotline is (800)342-AIDS.

It's hard to get pregnant in this position.

Not So Deadly Sex Germs & Scruffy Sex Rodents

There are several germs and sex rodents that owe their very lives to people who indiscriminately make love. A highly annoying but generally non-fatal sex rodent is crab lice.

The author of this book first learned about crab lice many years ago while listening to a radical student leader at U.C. Berkeley. The radical leader was speaking to a group of not-so-radical students at a pizza place on the southside of campus. Throughout the entire presentation, the radical leader kept scratching his pubic area with the ferociousness of a junk yard dog. He could barely keep his hands out of his pants long enough to light a Gitanes. Gitanes are French cigarettes that smell really unpleasant. People with bad teeth, radical politics, and itchy balls seem to enjoy them.

At the end of the your author asked a friend if he had noticed something a little, ah, unusual about the radical's social manner. The friend's more experienced face scrunched up like a prune and spit out two very ugly words: *crab lice.* Crab lice are infectious little mites that live in body hair. They can cause serious pubic as well as public itching.

There are other sexually transmitted catastrophes besides crab lice that can be either very mild or very annoying. Some have names that can hardly be pronounced, and more than just radical student leaders get them. Even sorority girls at U.S.C. get herpes, venereal warts, thrush, candida and chlamydia.

If you are sexually active, please keep the following in mind: whenever your genitals, rear end, or mouth sprout warts, grow tiny cauliflowers, lesions, or strange-looking pimples, when there's discomfort as you pee, when your urine is constantly cloudy or has blood in it, when there's a weird discharge or when things don't feel quite right, get yourself to a doctor or a clinic. Most of these problems can be treated without much pain or hassle. But without treatment you could become sterile from an otherwise treatable problem. You can also pass on sex diseases to your partner without experiencing any symptoms yourself. This is not cool.

Anyone who is sexually active should take his or her genitals to a clinic or a private practitioner for a check-up every year or two. Be sure to include a throat culture if you have been doing oral sex, and a rectal culture if you've been taking it up the rear. It's a good idea to get routine check-ups even if you've been using rubbers and don't have symptoms. That's because a subclinical sex disease (without symptoms) can trash your insides and cause you to become sterile.

Note: If symptoms of an STD suddenly go away, DO NOT FOR A MOMENT assume that the disease has gone away!

Herpes, Etc.

The reason this book doesn't include more about sexually transmitted diseases is because it would take about a hundred pages to do a decent job. It would take half that just to cover herpes. More than 20 million people have herpes, and there are entire organizations that do nothing but supply help and information on the subject. Just because millions of people have herpes is no reason to be laissez faire about it. Avoid it by using condoms and sleeping around with fewer rather than more partners.

Herpes is a buff, strong little DNA virus that causes periodic eruptions of small painful blisters on the skin and mucous membranes, usually around the mouth and genitals. Herpes likes to take long siestas, sometimes for years at a time. When it does awaken, it is a little like a creature emerging from the underworld. Stress is sometimes said to trigger the outbreaks, and it helps to have a sense of humor about it. *If you've got it, you've got it. Getting all freaked out about herpes isn't going to help matters one little bit.* Be wise and stay informed. Let yourself become the master of it rather than the other way around. Or, as the Zen folk might say, you and the herpes are sharing the same body. Learn to get along.

If you are having your first outbreak of herpes or any other kind of sexual infection, get to a doctor right away. Proper treatment of the initial herpes outbreak can significantly reduce the severity of future outbreaks. For more information about herpes, check out the various phone numbers and web sites that are in the resources section at the back of this book.

Rubbers & Rubber Wisdom

After much painstaking research, we have come to the conclusion that what you slop on the outside of a rubber is almost as important as what you stuff into it. In addition, the pages that follow describe which cut of rubber seems to feel best, and what to do when your rubber is a lemon.

Rubber Transactions

Nowadays, rubbers can be purchased nearly everywhere except maybe your local post office or Christian Science Reading Room.

But you still need to hand them to a cashier before they are yours to wear, unless you get them from a vending machine.

For some people, the ability to purchase a rubber depends upon who's working the cash register. This is especially true in small towns where there is no such thing as retail anonymity. In some small towns, a person would attract less attention knocking off the local bank than buying a pack of rubbers.

Getting rubbers by mail order helps alleviate this problem, but in some households plain unmarked envelopes garner as much attention as a singing telegram.

Rubber Scoop

Back in his academic days, the author of this book loved the study of viruses and even managed to ace a course on the subject. He was particularly fascinated with slow viruses. As a result, he figured something serious was brewing when reports of a lethal new sex germ started trickling out of San Francisco in the early 1980s. Knowing what happened each night in the bars and baths up there, he assumed it would be an epidemiological nightmare for both gays and straights. Fearing the worst, he began using rubbers before it was fashionable.

When he first started bagging himself his girlfriend scoffed, hissed, puffed and all but threw him out of bed and into the nearby LaBrea Tar Pits. "Those damn things give me bladder infections," she snarled. Sure enough, she got a bladder infection. And that's when he learned that the word pre-lubricated on the outside of the package is someone's idea of a joke. No matter how wet she might be, it's sometimes best to add lubrication when using a condom. Since then he has learned more about rubbers than how to give a woman a bladder infection with them.

Trouble In Rubberland — Not All Rubbers Are Created Equal

Believe it or not, there are no governmental controls over the manufacture of condoms. The FDA leaves quality control up to the makers of condoms. To put it mildly, the foxes are guarding the chicken pen.

To help protect against poorly made rubbers, slop some contraceptive jelly or water-based lubricant on the outside of your rubber before you have intercourse. This will help compensate for a number of rubber ills.

Chronic Rubber Busters

Researcher Bruce Voeller and associates studied a group of young men who were chronic rubber busters. Contrary to what you might think, these chronic rubber busters weren't hung any bigger than average and they hadn't used Vaseline as a lubricant. Petroleum jelly, e.g. Vaseline, is an oil-based lubricant that does to latex rubbers what AIDS does to the body.

Voeller and associates found that almost all of the chronic rubber busters were using ordinary hand creams like Nivea, Johnson's Baby Oil, Vaseline Intensive Care, Corn Huskers, or Jergens to lubricate the outside of their rubbers. These guys assumed that since the hand creams washed off easily they weren't oil-based. WRONG. Almost any type of hand cream will weaken a latex rubber by 90% in less than sixty seconds, especially those that contain mineral oil. The same can be true for body powders. The safest lubricants are contraceptive jellies or water-based products like K-Y Jelly sold at supermarkets or drug stores.

Beware of boutique sex lubricants that are offered at sex specialty stores. Any person or company can make a sex lubricant and sell it over the counter without government regulation. Some boutique lubricants have been found to contain dangerous ingredients, or not contain what's listed on the package. Contraceptive jellies, on the other hand, have to be FDA approved and are likely to be much safer. Since they are made to be used with diaphragms, they will also be safe to use with latex rubbers.

If A Condom Breaks Or Doesn't Come Out When You Do

If you were using a condom for birth control and discover that it broke while in service, consider calling your physician as soon as possible. There is a morning-after pill that is reasonably effective in preventing pregnancy. In the meantime, do not inject birth control foam or jelly into the vagina. The pressure might push the ejaculate up into the cervix. The same is true for douching. Instead, try inserting a contraceptive suppository. Wash your external genitals, pee, and if you have something that contains nonoxynol-9, rub it on your genitals and leave it there for awhile.

Double-Breasted Rubbers?

Some condom companies are now manufacturing rubbers that are extra baggy in the front part right below the head. That's because some men find that baggy rubbers feel better during intercourse. This finding seems to be counterintuitive (not what you'd think). Here's what Dr. Voeller had to say:

"The reason baggy tips feel better is that the head of the penis slides around in that part of the condom. This causes a nice sensation or stimulation. In a tight fitting condom, the penis can't slide around."

At the time of this book's publication, Trojan's Ultra Pleasure condoms are wider around the head. Lifestyles also has a new condom called Xtra Pleasure. It has ore than twice the extra latex around the head, and is also taste and odor-free which makes it better for oral sex. Believe it or not, some guys prefer this type of condom to no condom at all.

The one place where rubbers need to fit snugly is around the base of the penis. Otherwise, they might slip off. The penis usually starts shrinking right after ejaculation, so a guy shouldn't keep thrusting after he comes. He also needs to hold on to the edge of the rubber with his fingers when he's pulling out.

So what about all those situations when a guy who's wearing a rubber comes before his sweetheart? What about her sexual pleasure if he's supposed to suddenly pull out?

If this is a problem, why not help her come before intercourse? That's why Father Nature invented vibrators and oral sex. Or once you begin having intercourse, one of you can reach down with your fingers or the head of a vibrator to help the woman get more stimulation. Another way to increase the stimulation is for the woman to be in a position where she can push against her partner's pubic bone. Also consider doing oral sex after intercourse.

Reservoir Tips?

Some rubber brands make a big deal about having reservoir tips to hold a guy's ejaculate. There are a couple of problems with this concept. The first is that most reservoir tips hold about 2.9 mls. of ejaculate. While half of all guys produce 2.9 mls. or less, there's still another 50% of guys who produce more than 2.9 mls., which means their tips runneth over.

Another problem with reservoir tips is the assumption that they really do hold the fluid. If you think about the physics of intercourse, any fluid ejaculated into the reservoir tip is going to get mashed down the sides with each ensuing thrust. While it's a good idea to leave a half-inch or so of space at the end of the rubber, it doesn't matter if it has a reservoir tip or not.

Rock'n'roll Trivia Note: Did the band 10cc take their name from what they assumed was the volume of the average male ejaculation? If so, they guessed way too high.

Other Rubber Tips & Trivia

A guy who doesn't feel comfortable using rubbers during intercourse might try wearing them while jerking off. This could help him get used to the feel.

Try to find nonlubricated rubbers for blow jobs, since it's the lubrication that tastes bitter. Also, if the initial taste of latex bothers you, try rinsing your mouth out with something like mouthwash, cognac, or toothpaste first.

Most men find that condoms feel better to wear if they put a drop of water-based lubricant inside the tip before unrolling it over the penis. This allows the head of the penis to slosh around inside the condom, which is usually a good thing. It also helps if you will put a little water-based lubricant on the outside of the rubber once it's on the penis.

The average rubber is 7" from stem to stern. This means that the lucky 10% or so of guys who are longer than 7" will feel like geeks in high water pants when using rubbers. The percentage of high-water guys goes up significantly if you remember to leave an extra half-inch of latex at the tip. Fortunately, there are new larger rubbers whose brand names are not difficult to miss.

One recent book on sex cautions against using colored rubbers, since some of the dyes may not be safe or colorfast. They might turn a penis or vagina red, green, blue, yellow, magenta or maybe even hot pink.

Some guys tie off the end of a spent rubber before throwing it in the trash. This is similar to tying the end of a balloon, but for slightly different purposes.

Don't recycle your rubbers. Use a new one for each time you come. Don't carry them around in a wallet or glove compartment of a car. Do experiment with different brands until you find one that you like best, however, don't use the ones with ribs or nubs if you are having anal sex. The next time you want to have extra fun with your friends, sacrifice a couple of latex rubbers by blowing them up really big and letting them fly to the moon.

"Reality"—What Your Parents And Teachers Tried To Force Upon You, Or A New Condom For Women

There is a new female version of a rubber that's inserted into the vagina rather than rolled over a penis. It's called Reality. Here are some of the benefits:

1.) It's made out of polyurethane instead of latex. This means that there won't be as much heat loss between vagina and penis. 2.) Couples won't have to worry about the guy pulling out and leaving it behind, since it stays in place until removed by hand. 3.) It gives women more control in protecting themselves. 4.) Some women report that the ring around the outside of the condom stimulates the clitoris during intercourse.

The women's condom is also being used by both straight and gay couples for anal intercourse, although it's doubtful that the instructions include this small detail.

One possible negative aspect of the new woman's condom is that its birth control properties might be less than optimal. Bummer However, this could be because people aren't using it correctly. Be sure to read the instructions well.

Love You To Death — Not Using Condoms

Researcher Sarah R. Philips reports that young men and women who say they are in love with their partner are far LESS likely to use a condom when having intercourse than those who said they weren't in love. If you have deep feelings for your partner and fear that using one will ruin your spontaneity or somehow dampen the moment, please read the following to him or her:

"I love you way too much to risk putting our relationship through the strain of having to deal with an unwanted pregnancy. I also love you way too much to risk giving you something that I may have gotten from a toilet seat somewhere. (Leave out the part about who you were on the toilet seat with.) So, if we are both serious about being together, let's work on a timetable for ditching the condoms. To do this, we both need to get tested for gnarly sex germs, and we have to start using an effective method of birth control. Then we can dump the condoms, but not before."

Note: In the United States, 50% of pregnancies in women ages 20-34 are neither planned nor intended. The number rises to 75% for women over 40, and more than 80% of pregnant teens had no desire to be that way. Also, 26% of people who use abstinence as their method of birth control become pregnant each year.

The 3-and 5-Year Birth Control Implants: Years Of Protection In The Time It Takes To Fill Up Your Gas Tank

Sexually active people fall into one of two extremes: those who fuck often and those who don't. Believe it or not, the once-every-blue moon group has the lion's share of unwanted pregnancies. There are several reasons for this which could fill an entire book. Please take it on faith that if you don't have intercourse on a regular basis, you are in a higher risk group for getting pregnant. The new birth control implant might be every bit as important for you as for those who hump like bunnies.

The "new" 3- or 5-year implant is a small strip of thin material that's injected under a woman's arm. It could be a very good choice for anyone who enjoys intercourse but doesn't want to get pregnant. The reason this guide scoffs at the term "new" is because the implant has been around since the mid 1970s. It's been widely used in Finland since 1983. America was the 17th country to approve usage for the general public, although American clinics have been testing it for at least fifteen years.

Here's a list of advantages for the birth control implant:

CONVENIENCE: It takes about five minutes to install the implant. You don't even need to get undressed, assuming you've had a recent exam, since the injection goes under your arm. It can be administered by a nurse, and leaves a small black and blue spot for about a week.

SAFETY & HEALTH: Here's a brief comparison of the 3- or 5-year implant to the birth control pill. This comparison is not meant as a criticism of the pill, which works quite well for some women. Birth control pills are given in large enough doses so the chemical is still in a woman's system 24-hours later. To accomplish this, the dosage of each pill is higher than you need during the first 23 hours. It's a little like having to drink enough beer in one sitting to still be buzzed 24-hours later. It is different with the implant. The release rate of the implant is continual, so it never puts out more hormone than you need at any one time. As a result, it releases less than half the amount of chemicals into your body during any twenty-four hour time span, and there are no hormonal ups and downs. Also, the implant doesn't contain estrogen like most birth control pills. It releases only progesterone.

RELIGIOUS CONSIDERATIONS: The birth control implant works by preventing ovulation and by making the cervical mucous more viscous so the male ejaculate has trouble swimming through it. This is an important consideration for couples who believe that life begins with conception. There is no conception, so the question of when life begins does not apply.

SIDE EFFECTS: The side effects of the implant have been lower than with the birth control pill. The only common side effect with the implant is occasional spotting and a tendency towards irregular periods. An unexpected side effect of the implant is that women who use it may actually have a lower incidence of stroke than women who don't. It might be a good idea to use a birth control pill with the same ingredients that are in the implant for three months before actually getting the implant. By then, you will know if it works well for you, although the pill version will be stronger than the implant.

SECOND THOUGHTS: In case you don't like it or want to get pregnant sooner than planned, the implant can be removed at your convenience. Unfortunately, some of the earlier implants were inserted too deeply under the skin to be removed as easily as they might have been. This should not be the case any more.

AS A RUBBER BACK-UP: One problem with rubbers is that they aren't a highly effective method of birth control, so you need to back them up with something else. The implant appears to be a fine choice.

As with any birth control method, check with your physician or family planning center for a full list of side effects. This book's information may be out of date by the time you read it.

Self-Esteem & Birth Control Use

Researcher Meg Gerrard spoke to a random group of college students about sex and birth control. She later gave a series of follow up tests about what she had presented. She found that the students who could remember the most information about the lectures on sex and birth control were the same students who scored highest on measures of sexual-self esteem. Students who felt less comfortable about their own sexuality remembered significantly less about sex and birth control, even if they were A students in other subjects.

These findings were just as true for men as for women. Gerrard found that while being uncomfortable about sex is not enough to keep a person from having intercourse, it is enough to keep him or her from using birth control.

Planning far enough ahead to use birth control makes a clear statement that you want to have sex. One way that people who are ambivalent about sex get around this conflict is by having sex that isn't planned or discussed ahead of time. That way, they can plead temporary insanity if called on the carpet by their own harsh superego, or real life parents if they are still living at home.

Unconscious Reasons For Wanting To Be Pregnant

Here are a few fantasies about getting pregnant and having a baby that might keep a young woman from using birth control: getting pregnant will make her feel grown-up, the baby will love her unconditionally, it's one thing she can do "right," it will help her be respected, it will free her from her parents, the baby's father will want to marry and care for her, she'll be able to care for the child in a way that she wasn't, etc., etc. Unfortunately, most of these fantasies come crashing down once the girl has the baby in her arms and reality rears its uncaring head.

End of Chapter Notes: Women who take triphasic birth control pills report higher libido and sexual pleasure than other birth control pill takers. They even rate higher in these areas than women who take no pills at all. Brand names are Triphasil and Novum 7/7/7. ✦ We are saddened to report the recent death of Dr. Bruce Voeller, a man who couldn't understand why condom makers should be allowed to sell poorly made products. Bruce Voeller was one of the few researchers in this country with the guts and tenacity to take on the condom makers of America. He will be greatly missed.

Late Breaking Note: On the day this edition went to press, a major university reported that the rate of Chlamydia among sexually active teenage girls was 40%. They highly recommend sexually active women get checked for STD's twice a year, rather than the currently recommended once. With this easily cured disease, there are often no symptoms, but internal scarring and sterility can occur just the same.

Chapter 40
Sex During And After Pregnancy

If you hadn't noticed by now, each woman has her own unique way of looking at the world and you can't really predict how she will react to the man who knocked her up. Some pregnant women will want more intimacy than ever before, while others will want space—sometimes huge amounts of space. This can be confusing for a dad-to-be, as he is never quite sure if the love of his life wants to snuggle or pluck his eyes out. Also, don't think that the dad-to-be isn't experiencing his own set of pregnancy-related emotions. These may cause him to hesitate sexually while his child-to-be is turning somersaults half a penis-length away.

Fortunately, the chapter that follows is about sex during pregnancy. It covers all of these issues and more, from orgasm-related uterine contractions and swelling vulvas to fetal brain development and having sex after your baby is born.

WARNING: No matter what you read in this chapter or anywhere else, you absolutely must discuss the matter of having sex while pregnant with a health care provider who is familiar with you and your pregnancy. That's because there are some cases when it might be prudent to altar the way that you and your partner normally enjoy having sex. While this is necessary for relatively few pregnant couples, your personal health care professional is the only one who can help you in making this determination.

Talking To Your Health Care Professional About Sex

Think about this for a moment: you go to a physician, get totally naked, spread your legs wide apart, and your doctor puts her fingers in places where even the IRS doesn't. Yet many of us are nearly paralyzed at asking the simple question "Is it OK for me to have sex while I'm pregnant?"

Some physicians actually encourage couples to have sex during pregnancy. Also, obstetricians like the one you are probably seeing

rely on people having healthy sex lives in order to keep from going bankrupt. So do pediatricians, gynecologists, Lamaze instructors, and everyone else in the health care industry. There is no way your physician wants you getting out of practice with intercourse as long as the possibility exists that you might have more kids further down the line. So don't be afraid to ask.

If your health care provider says it's OK to have sex, go to it… If the answer is "No, it's not OK to be having sex," then it is important to ask more questions. The first is, "Pork Hay?" which is Spanish for "Why not?"

If your health care provider is one of the few remaining dinosaurs who doesn't believe that pregnant women should be having sex, get yourself a second opinion. Most physicians feel that having sex during pregnancy is a completely normal thing to do, unless there are specific reasons not to. Some of these reasons might include a prior history of miscarriages or premature labors, the placenta is attached near the cervix (placenta previa), your water has broken, or when there is bleeding of unknown origin.

If the physician gives a specific reason for why you shouldn't have sex, ask two more questions:

1.) "How long should we not have sex—for the next few weeks, months, or for the entire pregnancy?" All too often, when a physician says "No sex" the couple assumes this means for the entire pregnancy, when the intent was "No sex for the next couple of weeks." If you were to ask the same question in a month, the physician might say "It was just a precaution. Based on how well you are doing now, I see no reason why you shouldn't have sex."

2.) "Does 'no sex' just mean intercourse, or does it include all sexual contact?" For instance, intercourse might pose a potential concern, but it's fine to have orgasms orally or by masturbating. Or, orgasms might be the potential problem, in which case you might ask if you can still have intercourse as long as you don't have an orgasm. For some women, this would be a cruel and unusual compromise, while others might welcome the extra intimacy that the intercourse would allow, orgasm or not.

Urge Surge—The Mood Thing

Mood-wise, some women stay pretty even throughout their pregnancies, while others push the mental envelope. An interesting feature of pregnancy-related moodiness can be the intensity of the mood and the amplitude of its swing. For instance, some pregnant women who are horny feel so intensely horny that they find it hard to think about much else than sex and literally attack the dad-to-be the second he walks through the door. The intensity can be so great that some men feel a little used, while others seize the moment. Other pregnant women don't feel like having sex at all, and some might feel horny one moment and weepy the next.

Survivors of the pregnant mood swing note that a pregnant woman has the potential to feel hurt by comments that few women in their non-pregnant right minds would find offensive.

For the woman whose moods fluctuate, there might be moments when she blames her man for her condition, and other times when she feels elated about being pregnant and is quite happy to know and love the guy who got her that way. Also, it is quite normal for a pregnant woman to feel moments of depression alternating with feelings of elation, and to have dreams of her child being a perfect baby, and fears of her child being handicapped.

Much has been said about the disruptive effects of hormonal changes on a pregnant woman's mood, and this might be quite true. On the other hand, oxytocin levels rise throughout pregnancy, and oxytocin is said to make for better moods. It also causes contractions of the uterus which may help to prepare the woman's body for labor, and it is thought to be involved in a woman's orgasms whether she is pregnant or not.

Beautiful Or Gross?

How you feel about yourself can be an important factor in determining whether you want to have sex. Some pregnant women look in the mirror and feel fat and gross. Others feel they have never been more beautiful. Most women who are pregnant feel somewhere in the middle of these two extremes.

No matter how a woman feels about her pregnant self, it never hurts for her to receive loving reassurance from her partner. While a hard penis and a willing heart might be physical evidence that a man finds the mother of his child to be desirous, loving words, flowers and other romantic gestures speak to a different part of her soul. Do your best to always be available if not always near.

No Fear

One of the nice things about being pregnant is not having to worry about getting pregnant. You can put the diaphragm in the deep freeze, keep the condoms in the bottom drawer, or forget about taking pills each morning. This can make sex during pregnancy particularly relaxed and easy to enjoy. If pregnancy is what you wanted, there's no more "We have to do it now because it's my most fertile three-and-a-half-minutes during the entire next quarter-of-a-century." Even if you didn't plan on getting pregnant, the fact that you can't get pregnant again for nine more months allows some couples to relax and enjoy sex in ways that they might not when consequences are a concern.

Genital Swelling—Slip And Slide

Around the fourth month of pregnancy, most women's genitals begin to swell. And swell. And swell. This swelling can lead to full-time lubrication and can make some pregnant women feel very horny. The increased swelling is due to the growing vascular capacity in the pregnant woman's pelvis. As a result, her vulva often becomes a deeper color and her labia thicken.

Couples find that the added swelling may lead to a delightfully snug feeling during intercourse. Genital swelling during pregnancy also tends to up the intensity of the woman's orgasm. More on this in the pages that follow.

Orgasms During Pregnancy

Plenty of women have no interest in sex or orgasms when they are pregnant. Others not only want orgasms, but report coming in awe-inspiring bursts that are more intense than their most memorable pre-pregnant efforts. For some women, sex during pregnancy presents a slight contradiction: even if she is more easily aroused and her orgasms are more intense, she might take longer to reach orgasm while pregnant than before. The payoff is said to be worth the extra effort.

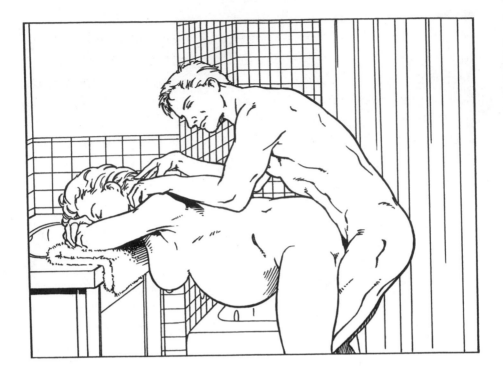

One reason for whopper orgasms during pregnancy might be the increased level of engorgement in the abdomen. With all the extra blood in there, her uterus stays hard for a few minutes after orgasm. As a result, a woman who had single orgasms before pregnancy may experience two or more at a time while pregnant. By the end of the pregnancy, some women find that the swelling in their genitals causes a congested feeling that makes coming feel more frustrating than relieving. Other women continue to have awesome orgasms throughout their entire pregnancies.

Also, it is normal for a pregnant woman to have cramps or Braxton-Hicks contractions either before or after orgasm. These cramps can last for a half-hour or more. The cramping might be due to the extra blood flow in the genitals, it might result from prostaglandins in the man's ejaculate, or it may stem from emotional concerns. Some health care professionals believe that these cramps help improve the muscle tone in a pregnant woman's uterus. If the cramping becomes too uncomfortable, you can eliminate one possible cause by using a condom during intercourse or by having the man pull out before he is about to come. See if this makes any difference over a couple of weeks. Another approach that may help relieve cramping is for the woman's partner to give her a loving foot massage or back rub.

PROSTAGLANDIN NOTE: Prostaglandins are what physicians give to help induce labor (e.g. pitocin). Nature has included very low doses of prostaglandins in male ejaculate. However, these prostaglandins do not influence labor unless the cervix is ripe and ready for labor. This is why some women who are near their due date intentionally have lots of intercourse believing that the prostaglandins work in synergy with a ripe cervix to provide a more gentle labor. A recent study has shown that intercourse during pregnancy does not contribute to premature birth, if anything the opposite might be true. Still, if you are concerned about this or any kind of contractions during pregnancy, be sure to consult with your health care provider.

Another unexpected source of orgasms during pregnancy may be the prolific array of sex dreams that some women report having. "Never had one before, never had one after, but had a large number of sexual dreams during..."

Breasts: Tenderness, Expansion & Leakage

Breast tenderness can happen at any phase during pregnancy, especially during the first trimester. This means that breasts which used to cherish firm handling might suddenly prefer a slight kiss, caress, or no direct stimulation at all. Fortunately, some breasts that are painfully tender during the first trimester morph into major arousal zones during the second trimester. These kinds of changes make it important for pregnant couples to have frequent discussions about "What feels good this week..."

It is normal for the breasts of a non-pregnant woman to swell when she is sexually aroused. However, when a woman becomes pregnant, her breasts may remain swollen all of the time. As a result, she may get swelling on top of swelling when she is sexually excited. This might feel painful, or it may feel wonderfully pleasant, depending on the woman and the stage of her pregnancy. Also, dietary salt content might contribute to the swelling.

For some couples, breast tenderness will make the missionary position a thing of the past long before expansion of the abdomen does. Another potential problem or potential delight, depending on your point of view, might occur if the woman's breasts start to leak during the latter part of pregnancy. Not to worry, this is an ever-so-natural event, and is simply a preview of what's to come.

Intercourse Concerns Part 1—Fetal Concussions

It is not uncommon for couples to worry that the head of daddy's thrusting penis is going to bop junior on the fetal brain and somehow knock him senseless. While it might be nice for dad to think his penis is that powerful, the fetus sits in a sac filled with a fluid that absorbs shocks and provides superb protection. To make it even that far, dad's penis would have to get through mom's cervix and uterine walls.

The most important consideration during intercourse is to find positions and thrusting styles that feel good for mom and her swollen reproductive organs. If it feels good for mom, chances are that the baby will do just fine.

As for questions about squirting junior in the eye with dad's ejaculate, the uterus is sealed off by a mucus plug that is a bit like the cork in a bottle of wine. The amniotic sac provides a secondary barrier that helps keep the ejaculate at bay.

Intercourse Concerns Part 2 —"We Can't, The Baby Will See Us"

Believe it or not, the human fetus is not taking notes on your every action and won't be emotionally scarred by the things you feel or do during pregnancy, even if you listen to—gulp—rock'n'roll instead of classical music. Exceptions, of course, are excessive drinking or doing certain drugs that may compromise the infant's developing brain.

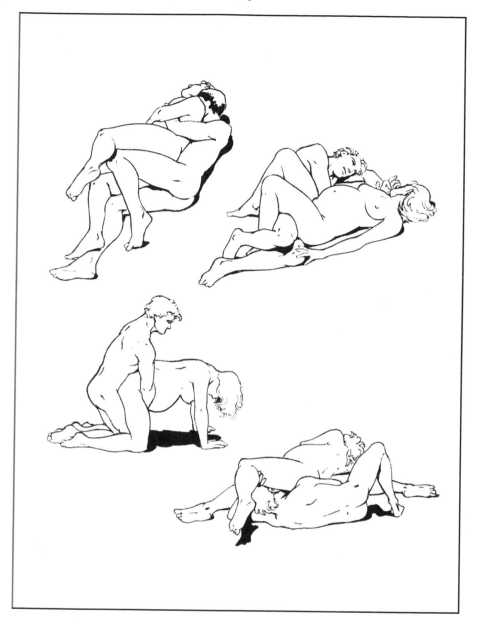

The fetal brain is not like a miniature of the adult brain. Its memory units (called "neurons") are hardly functional at birth. There is simply not enough developed brain structure for the fetus to say "Oh my gosh, mom and dad are having sex and isn't that disgusting" or on a more positive note "Mom and dad are having sex, isn't that wonderful!"

Why Doesn't Victoria's Secret Make Sexy Lingerie For Pregnant Moms?

Sex doesn't stop being an expression of love and intimacy just because a baby is on the way. Yet you can't help but get the feeling that pregnant moms are supposed to be more interested in runny noses and future full diapers than in being lit up sexually or wondering what the new guy at the office looks like naked. You have to search far and wide to get the message that pregnant moms can feel sexy, and that some moms and dads find pregnancy to be sexually exciting.

For a lot of pregnant women, nature turned up the horny knob instead of turning it down. Granted, not all women feel like having sex while pregnant, but enough do that it's difficult to believe that nature would have allowed this urge to go unchecked if it weren't to the benefit of the pregnancy or the species in general.

Intercourse

Some pregnant women cherish the feeling of having both the baby and the baby's father inside of them at the same time. Other women feel like three's a crowd. Dads, too, have their own issues about sex during pregnancy, some of which are discussed later in this chapter. As long as you feel like having intercourse while pregnant, the most important elements are a shared sense of humor and a willingness to explore. Here are some particulars to consider:

Clothes On: Some couples who are trying new positions do so first with their clothes on. This helps them focus their collective energies on the engineering feat at hand, and it allows them to appreciate the humor of the situation without having to worry about feelings of urgency or declining erections. There's always time to get naked and actually go for it once the target positions have been mapped out and a strategy is planned.

Penetration: Some women who are pregnant have the desire for penetration that's deep and assertive while others prefer a more gentle approach than usual. Whatever the case, different phases of pregnancy may require different styles of penetration while the proverbial bun is in the oven. Also keep in mind that the swelling of the cervix and uterus can make certain kinds of intercourse feel uncomfortable, at least the kind where she rides you like a wild bull or clasps her ankles around your neck and shouts "harder, harder, you big stud." Let the woman control the thrusting depth, and if you feel that this somehow cramps your style, be mindful that there are plenty of dads-to-be who aren't getting any at all.

Lubrication: Some women seem to lubricate all of the time when they are pregnant. However, there are plenty of exceptions. If that's the case for you, try adding KY-Jelly. Be sure your lubricant contains no contraceptive goop, as that might cause vaginal stinging.

Dizziness: Some pregnant women experience dizziness or indigestion in certain positions or during certain phases of the pregnancy. This can be particularly true when a woman is on her back. Doing it on her side, on all fours, or while on top might suit her better.

Breast Tenderness: As mentioned earlier in this chapter, breast soreness can be a problem from the earliest part of pregnancy and may require that you abandon the missionary position sooner than you thought.

Romancing The Cervix: The cervix of a pregnant woman often swells due to the extra blood flow into the uterus. It becomes soft, and can sometimes bleed with deep penetration. Try shallower thrusting or use positions where the head of the penis romances the cervix more gently. This may be especially wise during the latter months of pregnancy when the cervix starts to ripen. If you have questions or if there is any bleeding, be sure to consult with your health care professional.

Third Trimester Stretch: By the third trimester, the cartilage in the pelvic region has had several months of pregnancy-related hormones thrown at it. It becomes softer as a result, as part of nature's conspiracy—ah, plan—to ready the pelvic floor for the joys of childbirth. As a result, a woman may find that pressure on her pubic bone feels a little weird. This is another reason why couples need to be creative in their search for comfortable intercourse positions.

Bag It Or Let It Fly? Some physicians believe that a man should wear a condom during the last month or so of the pregnancy, but others feel this is silly. Some experts believe that male ejaculate helps a ripening cervix prepare for an easier labor. Be sure to check with your own health care provider for advice.

Too Much Swelling: For some women, genital swelling may eventually increase to a point where intercourse feels uncomfortable, while for others the desire to have intercourse never wanes. Experimenting with positions where the woman has her legs apart might help.

Backache's & All Fours: With the muscles between her ribs being slowly pried apart and her pelvic floor feeling trampled on, the pregnant female has been known to suffer an occasional backache. Some women find that the rocking motion of intercourse while on all fours can help soothe pregnancy-related backaches. It can also soothe the throbbing between her partner's legs, resulting in a win-win situation for both parties.

The Penile Vice Grip

Some health care professionals feel that it is good for a pregnant woman to tone and exercise the muscles in her pelvic floor (aka doing Kegel exercises). What better way to accomplish this than by having a man insert his penis into your vagina, keeping it stationary while you squeeze it with your pelvic muscles? Most guys would be more than happy to lend a helping penis. And this is an exercise that you might keep doing after the baby is born. (It has been said that some of the finer prostitutes in Asia are able to "massage" a man's penis to ejaculation by squeezing it in this way. Achieving this kind of proficiency might take months or more of practice, but would add a new arsenal to any woman's bedroom technique.)

Intercourse Interruptus—When To Stop

Most physicians in this day and age say it's OK to keep having intercourse until your water breaks. Some couples have intercourse up until the time when labor itself begins, feeling that the prostaglandins in dad's ejaculate help make for a smoother delivery.

There are at least four factors which should influence your decision on when to stop having intercourse: 1.) If it doesn't feel good any longer, 2.) Genital infection of either partner, 3.) Any bleeding or new discharge and, 4.) If your health care provider says to stop.

Oral Sex

The extra lubrication caused by pregnancy can give the vaginal area a stronger taste or smell, which some men notice when giving their pregnant wives oral sex. However, there are no medical reasons to stop giving or receiving oral sex during pregnancy unless the pregnancy is at risk for other reasons.

At the time of this book's printing, one European medical journal was reporting that women who went down on their partners before becoming pregnant had a significantly lower incidence of pre-eclampsia during pregnancy. Pre-eclampsia is a condition where the pregnant woman's blood pressure can rise to potentially dangerous levels. The origin of pre-eclampsia is not known. One medical journal several years ago found that pre-eclamptic conditions decreased significantly in woman whose obstetricians were able to make a solid emotional connection with them, thus pointing to possible psychological factors in pre-eclampsia. It is unlikely, though, that the "solid emotional connection" included giving the obstetrician oral sex. Also, in the more recent study, one would want to know if the decrease in pre-eclampsia was limited to women who swallowed, or if it were also true for women who gave their husbands oral sex but didn't swallow their ejaculate. The latter might suggest that the curative factor is a stronger emotional bond with the husband rather than the ejaculate itself.

Nipple & Perineal Massage

One of the nice things about being pregnant is when the dad-to-be is complaining about all of the things he usually complains about, you have the perfect excuse to say "Shut up and rub my nipples!" That's because as the final months of pregnancy approach, it might be helpful for a woman to have two areas on her body massaged—well, three areas if you count each nipple as having its own private domain. Put a little lotion on each nipple and massage and knead it, assuming it isn't too painful. This will help condition the nipples for nursing, and it may also help release extra oxytocin into the system which seems to be a good thing as the due date approaches. The other area where massage might help is on the perineum, which is the small piece of real estate that's between a woman's vagina and rectum. Some pregnancy afficionados believe that massaging this area may help to make it more pliable and reduce the need for an episiotomy. At the time of this book's publication, you could phone 800-624-4934 to get a booklet titled "Prenatal Perineal Massage" or send $3.20 to ICEA P.O. Box 20048, Minneapolis, MN 55420.

Bleeding

During the first couple of months of pregnancy, bleeding may occur during the time when you would normally have your period. This is usually less reason for concern than bleeding that is random. Be sure to check with your physician when there is any bleeding, just to be on the safe side.

Touch Vs. Sex

Some women may experience a decreased desire for sex during pregnancy, but an increased need for touch and cuddling. This can be difficult for the dad-to-be, because all of the cuddling and touching might make him feel extremely horny. To help the dad-to-be make it through these lean times sexually, his pregnant partner can cuddle beside him and caress his thighs, chest or testicles while he does himself by hand. Or, he can do like a lot of other guys, and jerk off while he's in the shower.

Besides being an important time for holding and touching, pregnancy is a fine time for partners to reassure one another about their feelings of love and attraction—hopefully for each other.

Fears That Bubble Up From The Deep Dark Recesses Of The Human Psyche...

Contrary to how you think you should be feeling, it is not uncommon for perfectly good parents-to-be to have mixed feelings about the baby-to-be. For instance, you may have planned for years to have this baby and wanted it with the deepest of convictions, but then suddenly start feeling "Oh my God, what have we done?" Feelings like these can be fleeting or last for weeks. One reader says that both he and his wife were shocked to discover such feelings, given how their pregnancies were better planned than the average moon walk. Fortunately, they did not experience their bummer moods at the same time. As a result, the one who was feeling good about the pregnancy was able to comfort the one who was feeling tragic.

It is perfectly normal for we humans to be overwhelmed by inner conflicts. These can be especially intense during pregnancy, when so many new demands are about to be placed on you. These are not the sort of feelings that make us want to have sex. It can be very helpful to talk over these conflicts with a friend, partner, or even a counselor if you are feeling particularly jammed by them. One reader adds: "Worries about child care, job security, and having to go back to work after only six weeks can be overwhelming."

Recognizing Dad's Role

During pregnancy, all attention usually focuses on the mom-to-be, which is as it should be. But this is also an important time for the pregnant woman to acknowledge the dad-to-be's role. Potential problems can occur when the woman feels that the baby is her creation alone. This can lead to problems in the relationship between father and child, between the mother and the father, and it is likely that the child will be made to feel guilty when he or she finally attempts to separate from mom.

Dad's Emotional & Sexual Issues During Pregnancy

There are plenty of books devoted to the various feelings that pregnant moms experience. One that we liked a lot is listed at the end of this chapter. Yet dads-to-be experience their own set of pregnancy-related emotions. According to researcher James Herzog, dads-to-be tend to fall into two groups: most attuned, and less and least attuned. The pregnancy spurs the first group of dads into a pathway of personal growth, while the latter group seems to feel threatened by the pregnancy and not particularly fortified by it.

One factor that impacts how a man responds to his wife's pregnancy is the influence of his own father or father substitutes. Herzog noticed that during the second and third trimesters of pregnancy, a number of pregnant dads turned towards their own fathers in an attempt to reconnect with them. They felt that reconnecting with the "good dad" from their early childhood would help them be better dads to their own children. Men in the less attuned group tended to experience a high degree of "father hunger"—growing up without an involved and caring father figure. These men tended to act in unsupportive ways, such as becoming competitive with their wives or being sexually promiscuous; some even had sexual relations with other men. If you find yourself feeling unsupportive or disconnected from your pregnant wife, it might be a great idea to spend extra time with a friend or acquaintance whose fathering skills you admire. Tell him you are feeling on shaky ground; ask him how he manages as a dad when he's feeling uncertain or overwhelmed.

Other things that Herzog found about pregnant dads included the following:

The Right Stuff: Upon learning of the pregnancy, a number of dads-to-be feel quite good about themselves in a masculine and sexual way. The fact of the pregnancy may help allay pre-pregnancy fears that they might not have the right stuff to make a pregnancy happen. With the excitement of being pregnant, a number of couples enjoy sex that is quite intense and intimate, as though sex itself now has a different meaning.

Nourishment As the pregnancy progresses, some men feel as if they are nourishing or symbolically feeding their wives during intercourse, especially when they come inside of them. On some level, the dad-to-be might view his semen as a kind of milk that will help nurture both mother and infant.

Coming Harder: Some men report feeling more depth to their orgasms when their partners are pregnant, with more physical and emotional awareness both before and after ejaculation. At the same time, the dad-to-be might be rethinking who he is; he's a man whose personal identity is expanding. At times this can feel exhilarating, at other times a frightening burden.

Dreams Etc.: There are plenty of ways that dads unconsciously identify with a pregnant spouse or wonder about what's going on inside of her. For instance, by mid-pregnancy, some fathers experience dreams or fantasies about being penetrated as well as being the one who penetrates. Some dream or start to wonder about their own inner body parts. Some put on extra weight, or feel a kind of gastric fullness or upset. Some men have toothaches during this time that land them in the dentist's office. When a man has a toothache of an undetermined origin, some dentists know to inquire if the man's wife is pregnant.

Character Evolution: Being a dad-to-be can help a man to regress in ways that allow him to shed unwanted or outdated parts of his character. The pregnancy becomes both an excuse and a stimulus to mature and become more responsible if he isn't already. Of course, not all men use pregnancy in such a constructive way, nor do all women.

Sex After Giving Birth

Some parents experience the first three to six months after the child's birth as being the most demanding and difficult time of their lives. They might not feel like having sex, or if they do, they might be too exhausted to actually do it. Other couples enjoy sneaking in quickies while the baby sleeps.

There are hugely important considerations that contribute to the frequency of sex among new parents, like whether dad does his fair share of the work around the house and with the baby, and whether mom welcomes his help or is nervous and critical whenever he gets near the baby. (If one parent is an obvious klutz with the baby, there are plenty of other ways that he or she can be helpful than with actual hands-on babycare. In a few months, the baby may have grown enough that you feel more comfortable handling it.)

Even with the best intention and desire, there will be plenty of times when new moms and dads are way too exhausted for sex, especially if there are other children in the family besides the new baby. Keep in mind that plenty of couples struggle when it comes to adapting to their new roles as parents and sexual partners.

Hormones & Libido

Some women don't feel like having sex after pregnancy due to various anti-horny hormones that might be spewing through their veins. On the other hand, women who are nursing are said to produce more anti-horny hormones than women who are bottle feeding, yet statistics show that nursing mothers want sex more often than those who don't nurse. Go figure.

Talking About Sex Before The Baby Is Born

Some of the best advice this book has to offer is that you talk about sex before the baby is actually born. For instance, "I've heard some new parents don't feel like having sex for a few months after giving birth—what are some of the ways we might handle that if it happens to one or both of us?" Or, "What do we do if you've got a raging hard-on and I want to be held and cuddled but don't want to have intercourse?" Or, "What if I want sex but you start seeing me as a mother- type instead of the sexy siren you've hoped I'd always be?"

One of the worst things you can do about sex after pregnancy is to pretend it is not a problem if it actually is. Nothing is to be gained by rolling over and pretending you are asleep to avoid having sex, by getting defensive or by feeling attacked. Like many other aspects of your relationship, this is a time to redefine and put things in a new perspective. Where sex was once taken for granted, it may now need to be planned or scheduled. There will be plenty of times when sexual desire is a casualty to exhaustion. For a while, you might end up masturbating more often.

When Can We Start Having Intercourse?

After the placenta comes out of the womb, it takes time for the place where it was attached to heal. The woman is going to be vulnerable to infections. This is why it might not be such a good idea for things like male ejaculate, store-bought lube and contraceptive jelly to be working their way up there. Also, it might take a couple of weeks for the vagina to heal after it's been stretched from here to China. Some physicians worry that intercourse before the vagina is healed can cause scar tissue to build. This is why most physicians feel it is wise to wait at least a few weeks after birth before you start doing the nasty. Check with your health care provider for specifics. This is particularly true if the woman had an episiotomy, with stitches that need to heal, and don't even think about having intercourse after a C-section until the doctor waves the green flag.

Birth Control

Be sure to stock up on birth control products before the baby is born. Do not leave this important detail for after the birth, as you will have your hands full dealing with other things and are likely to let it slip. It is not fair to you or the new baby to have a repeat pregnancy sooner than you want. Also, don't for a moment believe that moms who are nursing are unable to get pregnant. Nursing moms get pregnant all of the time. Ditto for couples who have unprotected sex during mom's period.

NOTE: Lubricated condoms and condoms with contraceptive chemicals can cause irritation to tender vaginal tissues. If dryness is an issue for you and you are concerned about irritation, check with your obstetrician's office for advice.

Designated Night Out

Once the baby is three-months-old, you would be wise to plan at least one evening a week where you and your spouse go out together, without junior in tow. There are a couple of ways to engineer this, with willing grandparents being top on the list. Every Wednesday night they get the baby and you get each other. If grandparent's aren't an option and a babysitter is either too hard to find or too expensive, call couples from your Lamaze class or find other parents with young babies and arrange to co-op the babysitting. For instance, they take yours every Tuesday, and you take theirs every Thursday.

WARNING: Children know when something important is missing in their parent's relationship. If there is a lack of passion or unity in their parent's relationship, they can suffer almost as much as the parents do. Do not make the mistake of focusing all of your energy into being parents and no energy into being lovers. By the time you notice that something is wrong with your relationship, it may be difficult to repair.

Painful Intercourse?

If you are worried about intercourse being painful, talk to your partner about this ahead of time. Chapter 12 offers plenty of ways you can stimulate tender vaginal tissues with your fingers. Work your way up to intercourse over time. You might also try taking baths together, and sharing a beer or bottle of wine beforehand. Also, it never hurts to have a giant-sized tube of KY Jelly on the nightstand.

Beware The "Husband's Stitch"

Physicians sometimes do a "husband's stitch" when sewing a woman up after delivery if she had tearing or an episiotomy. This is essentially a little tuck and roll that's done at the opening of the vagina. The physician assumes it will make intercourse feel better for the husband. While the philosophy is nice, the "husband's stitch" is better used in upholstery shops than on women's genitals. Tightening the entrance of the vagina just makes the opening smaller and is liable to make intercourse feel painful for the woman. If a woman is concerned about vaginal tone following pregnancy, she would do much better by practicing Kegel exercises, which help to tighten the entire vagina rather than making the opening more difficult to get into. It never hurts to discuss this with your health care provider.

Reader's Comments

"When I was pregnant, I wanted sex more, and felt more free." *female age 44*

"I was extremely horny during my pregnancy and I felt very sexy until the last month or two." *female age 26*

"I had no sexual desire at all." *female age 36*

"I was constantly horny when I wasn't nauseous." *female 35*

"I viewed her expanding body as just more to love, hold and caress." *male age 41*

"Intercourse can hurt towards 39-40 weeks when the baby's head is down lower. Sometimes foreplay was just as satisfying." *female age 25*

"I was more horny than anything. Because of the pregnancy, we needed to start using new positions. Some worked so well that we are still using them today." *female age 25*

"We didn't do anything different during pregnancy, except we didn't have to use rubbers. Yeah!" *female age 38*

"For intercourse while pregnant, I was pretty much always on top." *female age 45*

"Don't worry about the baby. If it is firmly implanted, no orgasm will dislodge it." *female age 35*

"If anything, I admired her more for being able to 'do' a pregnancy. It's a real turn-on to feel an essential part of one." *male age 43*

"When I was pregnant, sex felt extremely good and multiple orgasms happened all the time. They would sneak up on me. Things would be feeling good and if I concentrated hard I could have another and another." *female age 26*

"My wife seemed to be more lubricated, which was great. She seemed more relaxed also." *male age 38*

"Be gentle. Be considerate, encourage her to lead. As for sex after the baby's born, that depends on whether she's in a private room or not." *male age 40* *(Before taking this too seriously, please see "When Can We Start Having Intercourse" on page 493.)*

"Sex after the kids are born? Babysitters, movies for kids, grandmother's house and motel rooms..." *male age 44*

"Lock the door, turn the music up, and put Lion King on the VCR." *male age 39*

"When you've got kids, bedtime is the most convenient time for sex, but it's not always the most exciting time for me. If I wake up early and am horny, I wake my husband up which is something he loves, to have sex when he's just waking up." *female age 45*

"You have to make it clear they can't interrupt. Sometimes I'm just very up front with what we are doing and she knows not to come in." *female age 25*

Chapter 41
Circumcision—The Penile Calamity

 When you compare penises head to head, it is clear that Mother Nature knew exactly what she was doing when she provided the penis with a foreskin. In a recent study published by the British Journal of Urology, 54% of circumcised boys under the age of three had minor problems with their penises (swellings, skin adhesions, etc.), while only 5% of uncircumcised males had problems. In fact, there are not valid statistics that show any reason whatsoever to perform routine circumcisions. Medically speaking, circumcision makes about as much sense as removing a kid's eyelids or cutting out the labia of baby girls.

So why do we still do it in this country? The motives range from medical ignorance to medical greed. But first, a bit of circumcision history.

During the 1880s, a few influential men like John Harvey Kellogg, physician and founder of Kellogg's Corn Flakes, started preaching that the reason boys masturbate is because the foreskin rubs on the head of the penis. Until that time, most American men were not circumcised. As a leading anti-masturbation fanatic, Dr. Kellogg believed that boys who were circumcised at birth would be less likely to play with themselves. His influence helped circumcision to become a routine operation in America. Swell guy that he was, Dr. Kellogg also recommended that girls who masturbate have their clitorses burned out with acid.

Is There A Medical Need For Circumcision?

America's medical establishment has tried to justify its hand in circumcision by saying that it prevents cancer of the penis, cancer of the cervix and numerous other medical calamities. Yet in England, where circumcision used to be performed on 90% of males, physicians have decided that the operation is not such a good idea. As a result, less than 10% of newborn males in England are currently being circumcised.

In Sweden, where few men are circumcised, the rate of cancer of the penis is just as low as in the circumcision-happy United States. It would be interesting to compare the number of penises lost to cancer, which is quite rare, to the number of penises mutilated through botched circumcisions. Also, circumcision does not prevent all cancers of the penis. (One specialist said that the uncircumcised men he has seen with cancer of the penis had two traits in common: they were cigarette smokers and their personal hygiene was terrible.)

Regarding cancer of the cervix, women who live in countries where men aren't circumcised have no higher rate of cervical cancer than women in America. The only penis-related item that increases a woman's chance of getting cancer of the cervix is having numerous male sex partners, circumcised or not. Condom use might help decrease this risk, but circumcision has no impact.

As for other claims, one study did show that circumcised males were less likely to get urinary tract infections during the first year of life. However, in that study the parents of the uncircumcised babies were instructed to pull back their foreskins and wash under them. Most physicians instruct parents to do just the opposite, because nature did not intend for the foreskin to retract before one-year-of-age. It is quite likely that the instructions given to the parents were what caused the higher rate of infections among uncircumcised boys in that particular study. But even if those figures are correct, the number of urinary tract infections is still much greater in girl babies, and no one is recommending preventative surgery for them.

There have also been claims that uncircumcised men are more apt to catch sexually transmitted diseases, including AIDS. However, European men who are mostly uncircumcised don't show any greater incidence of these diseases than American men who are mostly circumcised. Until recently, American men who were uncircumcised tended to be from poor families. Whether circumcised or not, poor people often get diseases of all kinds at a higher rate than those who are rich.

Finally, there exists a myth that large percentages of uncircumcised babies will have foreskins that don't retract ("phimosis"), and that these males will need surgery when they grow older to correct this condition. In reality, fewer than 1 out of every 100 uncircumcised men have this condition, and a foreskin-friendly urologist can almost always help to resolve the problem without having to cut the kid.

So Why Do They Keep Doing It?

A physician makes between $150 and $300 per circumcision. While doing one circumcision per day, five days per week, at a fee of $150 each, minus time out for a six week vacation, a physician makes an extra $34,500 for a procedure that takes less than ten minutes. And that's only one a day at the lower rate. No wonder why pediatricians and obstetricians sometimes fight over who gets to do the circumcision!

Another reason for doing circumcisions is medical bias. Until recently, physicians in this country have had a long-standing bias that hysterectomies are good for women and circumcisions are good for men. Before managed health care, they also had a bias for C-sections over natural births, given how C-sections were much more profitable.

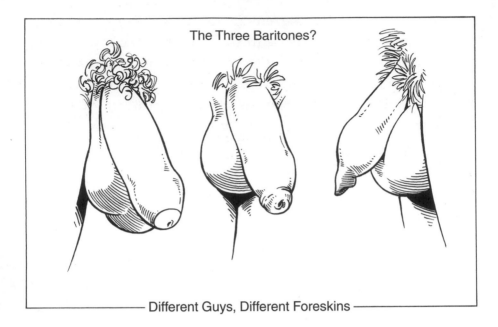

The Three Baritones?

—— Different Guys, Different Foreskins ——

In short, there appears to be no medical reason besides possible income enhancement for doing routine circumcision. There does, however, appear to be a very good reason why nature equipped the penis with a foreskin. Not only is the foreskin rich in pleasure producing nerve endings, but it also keeps the head of the penis moist and the extra skin provides added sliding pleasure during intercourse and masturbation. The foreskin is extremely elastic and is said to be as sensitive to touch as the human lips. Far from being unnecessary, a foreskin is usually a nice thing to have.

"But It Looks Better Circumcised…"

People in countries where female genitals are routinely mutilated believe that female genitals look better when most of them have been cut out. That's what they're used to doing, it's what they're used to seeing. And that's what we're used to seeing in our country— male genitals that have been surgically mutilated.

"Mutilated?"

During male circumcision, they stick a prodding instrument into the foreskin to tear it away from the head of the penis. One-third to one-half of the skin on the penis is then cut off. Traditionally, male circumcisions have not been done with anesthesia, but even when anesthesia is used, there is still pain from the raw scar on the penis.

Religious Considerations

Some people will say "But circumcision is done for important religious and cultural reasons." The same is true for female circumcision, which we in the West refer to as genital mutilation.

Some people might say we are not being respectful of an important ritual in the Jewish faith. This is true. Nor are we respectful of the Catholic Church's ban on birth control and masturbation. If Jewish men want to be circumcised as an expression of their faith, why not let them wait until they are eighteen-years-old and able to call the Moyle themselves? That would be a far greater expression of faith than having the end of your penis chopped off when you're only a few days old and can't tell a Torah from a phone book.

Care Of The Foreskin

Do not try to retract the foreskin of a baby. It is usually best to leave it alone until the child can retract it on his own.

There is actually more care involved for an infant who is circumcised than one who is not. Parents of infants and toddlers are advised to retract any remaining foreskin and wash it carefully, as adhesions can form between it and the head of the penis.

Circumcised or not, if your son's penis is red or irritated for more than three days, be sure to get medical attention. If the physician suggests circumcision, get a second opinion.

Note: While the Goofy Foot Press is able to summarize medical data as well as any other publication, it is not a medical authority nor does it pretend to be. If you have questions about circumcision, be sure to consult with a physician or physicians.

For more information about circumcision, foreskin care, or to find a list of physicians who aren't biased against foreskins, contact NOCIRC, PO Box 2512, San Anselmo, C94979-2512, Tel: (415)488-9883.

Chapter 42
Explaining Sex To Kids

Let's say that little Billy has gone shopping with his dad for the afternoon and you steal half an hour to lie on your bed with stereo headphones bolted to your ears, eyes closed, and fingers massaging a very important place between your legs. You are all alone and the sensations begin to feel wonderful. Next thing you know, the headphones are being yanked off your head by little Billy who is asking "Mommy, what color napkins were we supposed to get for the birthday party?"

Or, perhaps you assume that little Amber is fast asleep and you begin enjoying an all too rare moment of sex when a little hand suddenly taps you on the shoulder and you hear the words: "Daddy, how come Mommy's sucking on your penis?"

The pages that follow don't pretend to have all the answers about children and sex; they are simply a way of getting you to think about the subject long before most parents do, which is sometimes too late for an effective response. Topics range from talking about genitals and masturbation to menstruation, sexplay, and even sex on the internet.

Children's Sexual Development

People often think of sex as something that happens once we become teenagers. Not true. Most of us started having sexual feelings when we were little babies. Each time someone changed our diapers and powdered our private parts we had sexual feelings in the most basic sense — nice physical sensations down where the Pampers go.

As children get a few years older, they often enjoy playing sex games with friends and relatives, same sex or otherwise. Sometimes they just compare and contrast, other times they enjoy doing things that big people do, like sucking on each other's genitals or sticking fingers, penises, and heaven knows what else up each other's front and rear ends. Eventually, you might encounter a third grade child who's sitting there with both hands in his or her pants, happily rubbing away, while claiming how yuckie it would be to ever kiss somebody on the lips...

As children's minds grow and become more complex, so does their ability to have sexual fantasies that include others. With time, the thought of making love doesn't seem so "yuckie" anymore. Eventually, they might even want to read books like the "Guide To Getting It On!" In the meantime, one parent might wonder if it is normal for her four-year-old boy to be playing with his penis, while another might say, "Thank heavens he's got his penis to play with. It's a never ending source of pleasure for him!"

Telling Children About Sexual Enjoyment

Parents usually tell their children all there is to know about things like blowing noses and wiping rear ends, but rarely do they mention that genitals can be the source of good feelings. As a result, children learn that it's OK to seek their parents' wisdom on just about every- thing but sexual feelings. This is most unfortunate, because kids need their parents' guidance on sexual feelings as much as they do on wiping their rear ends or learning to drive a car.

Some parents assume that a three-year-old who is rubbing her genitals has the same intent and fantasies as a twenty-three-year-old. They either try to stop her or simply pretend that nothing is happening. Perhaps it would be helpful for parents to understand that their masturbating three-year-old isn't thinking about how good Johnnie, her daycare buddy, might be in bed! The child is simply touching her genitals because it feels good. It is perfectly normal for little hands to reach between little legs when a child is happy, excited, at naptime or even when you are reading Dr. Seuss to them. All a parent needs to do is say an occasional "It feels good to touch yourself there." This gives mom and dad credibility about such matters and lets the child know it will be safe to talk to his or her parents about things of a sexual nature.

Also, little boys have erections from a very early age, yet parents seldom explain to them that males get erections when they are having fun with their penis, as well as at other times like when waking up in the morning. Parents tell boys that they have nice eyes, ears, or even feet, but they avoid telling a boy about his penis or saying anything nice about it. Nor do they tell a girl positive things about her genitals, or let her know that her vagina will sometimes get wet. Yet girls get wet as often as boys get erections.

Note: Parents who explain such matters to their children may need to distinguish between the sexual kind of wet and the peeing-in-your-pants kind of wet. Also, parents who explain sex in an open and honest way should be prepared for nasty glares from other adults, because their children won't know it is bad to talk about sex; e.g. "Mr. Johnson, my daddy gets erections, do you?" or "Sister Mary Elizabeth, does your vulva tingle when you feel excited?"

Playing With Themselves

Since many parents don't talk about masturbation, their children may regard it as a dirty secret. (See page 301 of this book for a summary of findings on masturbation in children of kindergarten age.)

You can explain masturbation to a younger child by saying that "Masturbation is when you touch yourself between your legs in a way that feels good." If your child asks for details and you feel comfortable about it, you can make a pretend penis with a finger while saying "This is how boys do it" or point two fingers downward and rub the knuckle part to explain how girls do it. Also, it might be reassuring for an older boy to hear his father say "I started masturbating when I was your age" or for a girl to hear her mother say "I masturbate, too."

In doing research for this book, the author met with a class of high school students to talk about sex. Before he had even introduced himself, one of the boys yelled "Do you masturbate?" It's not the sort of question he is used to being asked, let alone by a young punk with baggy pants and a strange haircut. Embarrassing? You bet, yet to have said anything but "Sure" would have created a serious credibility gap, and it would have been dishonest. Beyond that, it would have been inappropriate for him to have discussed details about his private sex life with the young and restless. Hopefully, parents will keep in mind that it is neither necessary nor advisable to discuss the details of their private sex lives with their children. On the other hand, it is fine for

parents to let their children know that sex is a fun and important part of their lives.

Liberal parent alert: For super-permissive parents who feel that putting limits on children destroys their little spirits, keep in mind that children won't feel safe with their sexuality if it is allowed to explode all over the place. If a child is masturbating or exposing him or herself in a public place, there is no harm in saying "I know that feels really good, but the place to do it is in the privacy of your own bedroom." Also, children past the age of four or five who rub their genitals in public areas might be dealing with emotional anxieties that have little to do with sex.

Naming Private Parts

Modern parents usually have no problem telling little boys that they've got a penis and testicles between their legs, although little boys rarely refer to these items by their proper names. For that matter, neither do big boys.

Female sexual anatomy is mislabeled from practically day one. First of all, what you see from the outside is not a vagina, but that has become the generic term for what is nestled between a woman's legs (assuming it's not part of her lover's anatomy!). What you see from the outside is a vulva, which means lips. The vagina doesn't appear until after the vulva is spread open, and even then you only see the outer rim of it. It is also helpful for parents to identify the clitoris. For more on this, please read "Vulvas, Vaginas, Beavers and Bear" on page 86.

Parents might do well to inform boys about girl's genitals and visa versa. This way, girl's genitals won't seem like such a mystery. Also, it is through such talks that parents can teach boys to respect and care about girl's genitals. Otherwise, how are boys expected to learn such things? In a locker room?

The Difference Between Cum And Pee[1]

When you try to explain the concept of ejaculation to a child, the chances are good he or she will assume you are talking about pee. After all, that's what comes out of a penis, right? Kids will likely surmise from early talks about the birds and bees that the man pees into the woman to make her pregnant. One way of avoiding this confusion is to explain that there is a big difference between pee and ejaculate. Pee is thin and mostly clear like water and there is a lot of it, while ejaculate is white, thick, and there is only a teaspoon or two of

---

[1]Bet you'll never see this one in Parent's Magazine!

it at a time. It won't hurt to explain that nature was very smart about all of this, and made it so that a man can pee when his penis is soft, and have an ejaculation when his penis is hard. (This not a hard and fast rule, but no need to go there yet.) Say that when a man has intercourse and his penis is hard, there comes a certain point where his penis feels really good and warm and the ejaculate starts to squirt out. That's the stuff that can get a woman pregnant. You might also explain that this is the exact same stuff that comes out when a man is masturbating. Let them know that boys don't start making this fluid until they go through puberty, which happens sometime between the ages of twelve and sixteen.

Child Abuse Warnings

Now that our society is so revved-up about child abuse, we've got parents and teachers telling young children "Don't let anyone ever touch you down there!" Think about this.

In this day and age, the first time parents mention sex to children is often through warnings about sexual abuse — complete with those deep, measured parental tones that barely hide mom and dad's fear and concern. Consider how dumb it would be if the first thing parents told kids about bike riding is how many scraped knees, broken bones, and fractured skulls they are likely to get. At best, the child would learn to hide his excitement and questions from mom and dad. And if the kid did have a bad encounter on the bike, it is only natural that he or she would try to hide that, too.

Why not establish a good rapport about sex with your child from early on? Then your child can take in your eventual warnings about child abuse with intelligence rather than guilt or trepidation.

As for an actual strategy, try giving young children a sense that their bodies belong to them and no one else. Tell them they don't need to give hugs or kisses if they don't want to. If parent's will respect this in their interactions with the child, then the child will learn from an early age that it's OK to say "NO" to unwanted physical touching. This is a far better approach to preventing child abuse than the stern fear-based warnings that some parents give.

As your child is older and able to speak with you about sexual matters, you can say "no one should touch you in a sexual way unless it's what you want." You can let them know that no adults should ever touch their genitals and bottoms or ask to see them undressed unless it's at the doctor's office and mom and dad are present, or if it is a helping teacher who mom and dad say is OK. Inform them that if anyone ever touches them anywhere on the body and says to keep it a secret, they should tell you anyway. Also encourage them to tell you about any kind of touching that makes them feel strange or uncomfortable.

It is usually not helpful to tell children that some kinds of touch are "good" and some kinds are "bad." It is too easy for children to confuse what is good and what is bad.

Children's Questions About Sex

Some parents have the fantasy that children will ask about sex as the need arises. But when parents volunteer information about all things under the sun except for sexual feelings, children grow up sensing that questions about sex are off limits.

Also, some parents overwhelm young children with biological facts about sex. Folks, a five-year-old can't understand the concept of fallopian tubes! What children need to know are the proper names of the things that they can see or touch, and an acknowledgment that touching or rubbing their genitals can feel quite nice. The latter isn't anything that kids don't know, but it gives them a message that it's OK to talk to mom and dad about things that are sexual.

Some children might need to be told that babies come out of vaginas rather than rear ends. For birds and bees stuff, find a book with fun illustrations that seems neat to you and then read it together with your child.

Once a child asks a question about sex, he has often created an answer or scenario to the question in his own mind. As a result, you may want to pause and ask junior to tell you what he or she thinks the answer might be. That way, you may get more clues about what the child needs. If there is no evidence that he or she is courting a hidden hypothesis, proceed to answer the question the best you can.

When it comes to questions about sex (or anything else for that matter) don't be afraid to tell a child that you don't know the answer. Acknowledge that it's a really good question, and tell junior that you will do your best to find the answer. Then ask a friend, find a book, or call one of the national sex lines. This way your child will feel that you take his or her questions seriously, and will feel free to ask for your opinion in the future.

Keep in mind that you may be asked the same question about sex ten or twenty times. It could be that young children have a profound need for repetition, or maybe they get a secret sense of joy from seeing mom and dad break down into tears after they've been asked the same question for more times than even Job could possibly stand. Also be aware that you will be giving a very different answer to a five-year-old's question about intercourse than you will to the same child when he or she is ten or fifteen. Just because you answered a question when your child was five doesn't mean you won't be answering the same question every couple of years, but each time in a slightly different way.

A Normal Five-Year-Old's Feelings About Sex

"In second grade, a little boy kept squeezing my vulva and it felt so good and tingly and warm and throbbing that I waited quite a while until I told my teacher!" *female age 23*

As part of his training, the author of this guide followed the growth of several normal children from birth on, discussing child development quandaries with their parents as they arose.

One of those children was a five-year-old girl whose lifelong best friend had been a boy of her own age. The girl's mother was shocked one day to find both kids buck naked with the little boy's fingers on her daughter's vulva. The mom's first thought was to break every bone in the little boy's hand, but her daughter was just as happily involved as he. So she went into the kitchen and forced herself to count to twenty. She then decided that the last thing she wanted to do was respond as her own mother would have. Needless to say, your author got a phone call asking for suggestions.

The mom and he discussed how blanket prohibitions about sex often teach children to hide their sexuality from their parents. The child then loses the advantage of having his or her parent's wise counsel about sex. So rather than being guided by her initial response to protect her daughter, the mother asked the little girl how she felt about the way her friend was touching her. Realizing that it was safe to answer truthfully, her daughter replied that it felt so wonderful she simply couldn't find a way to say no!

Since then, this little girl has asked her mother questions about who can touch her genitals and how to say "no" if she doesn't want them to. She asked these questions of her own initiative without being prompted by her parents. Few moms and dads have "perfect" answers for such questions, but just letting your child know that these are good questions and making an effort to discuss them can be amazingly helpful. This kind of discussion helps the child learn how to use reason when dealing with sex.

It is likely that when this little girl becomes a young woman she will have more respect for her own sexuality than the vast majority of her peers. Her sexual decisions may even be the result of good judgment, instead of the all too common adolescent rush to just do it because the opportunity presented itself. **Note:** Please, don't for a moment think that this guide is saying to avoid setting limits on your children's sexual behavior. Parents who set no limits on their children's behavior tend to raise obnoxious brats. Instead, why not think about strategies that might be more effective than simply yelling "NO!" — although there are times when a contemptuous glare or a straightforward "no" are fine parental responses. Hopefully, you will encourage your children to think about their sexuality in ways that are constructive, rather than raising kids who are mindless about sex or have as their criteria "What can I get away with?" or "Screw the consequences—if it feels good, I'm gonna do it!"

When Children See (Or Hear) You Having Sex

If a young child walks in when you are having sex, cover up slowly and try not to look like you were doing something bad, because you weren't. One of you should take the child back to his or her own bed and tuck the kid in. If there are questions about what you were doing, tell the child in a reassuring voice that you were having sex and will be happy to talk about it in the morning. Even if the child doesn't ask any questions, make sure that you raise the issue the next day.

Also, parents who make a fair amount of noise when they are making love should consider telling their young children about it, saying that mom and dad sometimes make noises at night when they are sharing sexual feelings. Explain that these are happy noises which are very different from the noises that mom and dad make when they are fighting. This is an important distinction to make. **Note:** if an older child who should know better is so rude as to barge into your bedroom when you are having sex, GROUND HIM OR HER! Children should be taught from an early age that a closed door requires a knock and a "come in" before they can open it. But don't expect this to work if you always barge in on your own children without knocking.

"Why Can't I Watch You And Mommy Have Sex?"

You've worked hard to be an open, honest parent about sex and your three- to five-year-old suddenly rewards you with the question "I want to watch you and mommy have sex!" Instead of convulsing with panic, regard this as an opportunity to talk about privacy and sex, e.g. "One of the things that makes sex so special for mommy and daddy is that it's private, just between the two of us. Since sex between us is private and personal, I wouldn't feel comfortable having anyone else watching." "Well what about that time I walked into your bedroom and you were kissing mommy"s vulva. Will you kiss mine?" "Your vulva is very sweet and nice. But I wouldn't feel comfortable kissing your vulva like I kiss mommy's because it's a private sexual thing kissing your vulva like I kiss mommy's because it's a private secual thing that I only do with her."

Regular Nudity Vs. Industrial Strength Nudity

"Nudity was a normal part of bathing, dressing, getting up in the morning, or going to bed at night. I think this is ideal. Kids get a lot of reassurance and education from the occasional observation of natural (not contrived) nudity." *female age 35*

Is nudity around the house good or bad? The only research we know of about the subject of nudity in the house was a retrospective study of college students which compared how much nudity they reported when growing up with their current levels of sexual activity. There was no correlation between high levels of nudity at home with sexual promiscuity at college age. Interestingly, kids who reported higher levels of nudity at home seemed to report more feelings of warmth or security when away at college. One reader comments: "My daughter always felt comfortable walking around the house naked, but my teenage son is so modest that nobody can remember seeing him naked since he was five-years-old!"

Parent's Sexual Feelings About Their Children

Our society gives parents little guidance about sexual feelings towards their children, except blanket condemnation. Hopefully, you will find what follows to be a helpful discussion of the matter.

Children of all ages are able to evoke sexual feelings in parents, from a nursing experience that leaves the baby's mother with pleasant genital sensations, to the older teenage son whose developing body might give mom an occasional sexual stirring — perhaps reminding her of the excitement she used to feel when seeing the boy's father when he was the same age. And that's just moms... The problem isn't in having occasional sexual feelings about your children, which plenty of parents feel at times. The problem is in what to do with these feelings.

For instance, let's say that a dad is playfully wrestling with his young daughter and finds that he is getting an erection. A healthy dad will think to himself "Oops!", beg out of the rough-housing, and say to his daughter something like "Why don't you grab the mitts so we can work on your pitching" or "How about a game of Nintendo or Scrabble..." The unhealthy dad, on the other hand, will keep doing the same activity without adjusting to the reality of the situation.

Unfortunately, upon discovering the start of an erection, some very good dads withdraw from any physical and sometimes even emotional contact with the child. In these cases, dad's own harsh superego can ruin a very important parent-child relationship. This can be quite sad for both parent and child. On the other hand, there are some dads who could use a more highly developed superego — or at least develop enough boundaries to recognize that children are not meant to be sexual partners.

As for mother-son feelings, let's say that mom enjoys rubbing her teenage son's back, but finds that she is starting to have a sexual response. Maybe it's time to give junior a quick big hug instead, and realize that it is more appropriate for him to have his back rubbed by girls his own age. Or maybe mom enjoys the way her son's teenage body looks. This is fine, but it starts to cross the line if she ends up in his bedroom whenever he is getting undressed. Particularly troublesome are lonely moms who encourage their sons to share the bed with them, unless such conditions are dictated by abject poverty. The same is true for lonely dads.

Problems sometimes abound in families where the parents' sexual relationship is not a particularly good one. One of the children might decide that it's up to him or her to be a replacement spouse. What's amazing about this kind of mutual seduction is if a therapist suggests that something might be a bit askew, both parent and child may glare at the therapist like he or she is some sort of twisted pervert. Especially destructive are those situations where the parent alternates between being seductive and puritanical.

All things considered, it's not possible to set specific rules and standards for all households. For instance, nudity in one family might be perfectly healthy, while nudity in another family might be part of a syrupy, seductive mess. And while it might be best for parents to put boundaries on one child's sexual expression, another child might do well with the opposite kind of response. For instance, a teenager who is an exhibitionist with his or her naked body can clearly use some limit setting, while a highly inhibited child who is embarrassed about his or her body might find it helpful to hear that it's OK to be naked. Another example is when one young child enjoys masturbating before naps or when tucked into bed as mom or dad are reading a favorite story. This is perfectly normal. However, another young child who masturbates anxiously or throughout the day probably needs emotional help.

It would be nice to say that common sense should prevail, but when it comes to sexual development within the family, there doesn't seem to be an abundance of collective common sense in our culture.

Explaining Puberty

"When I got my first period I was excited, but then my mother wouldn't let me climb trees or play with the guys anymore."

female age 55

"My mom had always been really open with me so I was prepared when my body started changing. I was even glad to get my period ." *female age 19*

"I started growing awfully fast and none of my clothes fit anymore. I'd consume everything in the refrigerator and would still feel hungry. My armpits had never perspired or smelled before. Suddenly, it was like someone had turned on a faucet under each. I dreaded being called on in morning classes, because I'd often have a raging hard-on. My beard was really strange, with isolated man hairs invading my boyhood fuzz, so I appropriated one of my dad's razors and started shaving. I didn't know why I was suddenly having wet dreams, and I used to hide my underwear and wash them myself so my mom wouldn't see the stains. I was sure I was damaging myself by masturbating once a day, but couldn't stop to save my life. Hair started growing from my neck down. And suddenly there were zits. It would have been nice if a parent or some adult had taken a moment to explain some of these things to me."   *male age 44*

It never hurts to let your children know that their bodies will change as they get older. Of course, you will need to address the issue in different ways depending on the child's age. For instance, you can tell your seven-year-old that puberty is what happens when you stop looking like a kid and start looking like an adult—that boys get taller, their voices deepen, they start getting hair under their armpits and around their genitals; that girls' hips start to get wider, they grow breasts, and their armpits and genitals get hair too. Let them know that people can't have or make babies until they go through puberty. *For more about teenage boys and their unwanted erections, see page 63* .

When your child is a few years older, you can explain that puberty is a process that takes a couple of years to complete, and that it usually starts to happen for girls when they turn ten or eleven and for boys when they turn twelve or thirteen. Of course, let them know that puberty is a little like the repair people from the phone company, sometimes they arrive when they're supposed to, sometimes they're awfully late, and occasionally they arrive before you expected. You can also mention that puberty is the time when girls start to menstruate and boys start to ejaculate when they have orgasms, and that the genitals of both girls and boys start to look more like those of adults (bigger and hairier—but best not to mention how easily adult genitals can overwhelm the judgment center of the adult brain).

Keep in mind that kids can be awfully cruel toward other kids who are in the throws of puberty. Let your child know that you'll ring his or her little neck if they make fun of another kid whose body starts to change sooner than theirs, or if they taunt a kid who is really, really late.

Menstrual Bleeding

"Puberty was not a really big deal for me. I read 'Are You There God, It's Me Margaret,' so I knew what my period was when I got it, although my mom never bothered to tell me."   *age 25*

"I was afraid that I would just start bleeding sometime and that it might go through my clothes and I would be embarrassed."

age 49

"My first period was a celebration. I was at my friend's house and I noticed bleeding between my legs. I rushed home to tell my mother, fully aware I was having my period. She was thrilled, and we went out to dinner to celebrate."   *age 18*

The only time when many parents mention sex to their daughters is while explaining menstruation. What an unfortunate association, bleeding and sex. (Now it's even worse, as the first thing young girls often hear about sex from their parents are warnings of sexual abuse.)

As children, we learn that blood is a sign of bodily injury. We are never told that some bleeding is good for us. So when girls start menstruating, the blood that drips from their vulvas is often equated by the unconscious mind as a sign of injury or internal damage. When explaining menstruation, girls should be informed that the bleeding which comes during their menstrual periods is a good thing, and that menstruation is the body's way of keeping the walls of their reproductive organs clean and fresh.

Keep in mind that girls in the year 2000 will be menstruating at ages twelve or thirteen; their grandmothers started menstruating when they were three to four years older. The bodies of these young girls are more developed than their grandmother's were at the same ages, but their emotional development is about the same. This means they will need plenty of encouragement and support from their parents in negotiating the puberty process, especially if they begin menstruating earlier or later than most of their friends.

Growing Girls

Young girls tend to be very self-conscious about physical changes, especially around fathers and brothers, so don't be talking about tampons and training bras when the guys are around. If they mature earlier than their friends, you'll need to be aware that other girls might shun them a bit and boys might tease them. Keep reminding them that things will be fine in a couple of years when everybody else has started to mature. Make sure they are involved in activities like sports, science, 4-H — anything where value is placed on their physical or mental abilities.

If your child is comparing herself in negative ways to actresses on TV, let her know that many of the allegedly "perfect" girls on TV are, for the large part, self-absorbed lunatics who think nothing of barfing up perfectly good food so they won't get "fat." These are people who have more surgery than a BMW in a Tijuana chop shop, and in spite of the stories that their publicists send to People Magazine, few have off-screen lives that are particularly happy. Double ditto for models who are in magazines like Seventeen. (You can take that first hand from a couple of psychoanalysts who work in the heart of Hollywood.)

Get yourself a copy of Mary Pipher's "Reviving Ophelia: Saving The Selves Of Adolescent Girls." Read it yourself, and don't hesitate to share relevant parts of it with your teenage daughter.

Sex On The Internet

Not too long ago one of us went into a search engine on the internet and entered the word "erotic". Thousands of listings appeared. She clicked on one at random, and within a few seconds the computer screen began to show a man's hand that was holding a really large penis that was peeing into the black part of the screen. Then, as more pixels downloaded, the black part of the screen turned into a woman's face. Soon, the screen was filled with a close-up picture of a man peeing into the open mouth of a woman who was looking up at him with an expression of sheepish glee.

Thinking that there must be more to "erotic" than this, she returned to the search engine and clicked on another listing in the erotic category. This time the screen revealed a woman's private parts that were anything but private. She had a penis in every port—one up her rear and one up her vagina.

Having had enough erotic for the day, she entered the word "emate" into the search engine in an attempt to find information about the Apple eMate computer. The screen generated several listings, with the fifth seeming a bit suspicious. As it turned out, this was a site for people who are sexually excited by giving and receiving enemas.

So what does this have to do with explaining sex to kids? Any of these sites are easily within clicking range of the average eight- to ten-year-old child. Worse yet, you don't even have to enter a sex-related word to get sex related sites. (Try entering "toy" or even "beanie babies" which are stuffed animals for kids.) While you can put as many electronic chastity belts on your kid's computer as money can buy, there is simply no way you will keep your child from seeing sites like the ones just described. And while it's admirable to throw roadblocks in junior's way, if your kid can't find sexual sites on his or her own, it's pretty much guaranteed that a friend up the street will.

If you think about it, prohibition has never stopped a single person from doing a single thing that they really wanted to, so it's time to acknowledge that your kids are not only seeing sex on the internet, but that they may be seeing degrees of sexual kink that would boggle the average parent's mind.

Of course, looking for pictures of naked people is nothing new. When we were kids, we'd masturbate for months over a tattered page from Playboy. And while Playboy may not show the most accurate representation of what nature put on the average woman's chest, it is at least an approximation of what you'll get if you're going to have sex. But a certain line gets crossed when a kid sees people peeing into each other's mouths. It's not the sort of thing you should just say "Oh well!" to. You better be ready to help your youngsters digest some of what they are going to be seeing on the internet.

Now you can get all freaked out about this, or you can use it as an opportunity to have some meaningful and helpful conversations with your kids about sex.

One strategy is to let your kids know that it's perfectly normal to be curious about sex, and despite your best efforts, they might see things on the internet that are a little weird and way out of the range of normal. If your kids know that you won't suddenly transform into a total lunatic when the subject comes up, you might ask them about some of the weirdest things they've ever seen on the net. If they have seen sexual sites and are able to tell you about them, your responses might vary from "That sounds really strange; you're not describing any sex acts I'd ever want to do" to "I know it seems weird now, but maybe it's something you'll like to do when you get older" depending, of course, on what they describe.

You might tell your kids that there's sometimes a big difference between looking at pictures of people having sex and what happens when two people actually have a good sexual relationship. Sex with a real-life partner is full of tender and caring moments. You rarely see that kind of tenderness if you are watching sex on the internet or in a video.

Keep in mind that if your children are spending countless hours on the web cruising sex sites or sharing x-rated conversations, it might be due to loneliness and isolation in addition to normal curiosity. Also, as a parent, please understand that if you want your kid to spend less time looking at sex on the internet, it won't happen by treating it like drugs and taking a "just say no" approach. (That never worked with drugs, either.) It's far more effective to get your children involved in extra-curricular activities where their time is structured and they are doing things that make them feel good about themselves .

As a loving parent, you can get your kids through just about anything they see on the internet or anywhere else if you and they are able to talk openly to you about sex, and if they are well-grounded in activities where they learn to feel confident about themselves because they're doing neat things.

Teenagers & Sex

> "I used to pretend my friend Heather was another boy that I liked in school in fifth grade and we would touch each other's vulvas and breasts and have a lot of fun until my Mom found out and sent me to a psychiatrist for being a lesbian!"

> *female age 24*

If you ask a group of sixteen-year-olds if they are emotionally ready to have sex, most will say yes. If you ask their parents whether their sixteen-year-olds are emotionally ready to have sex, most will say no. Chances are, your teenagers do not view sex the way you wish they would. It's also possible that you prefer to see your kids as they once were instead of as the young adults that they are fast becoming.

Parents used to think that the main reason teenage girls have sex is because they are somehow being coerced into it, or are trying to be popular, or are trying to please insistent boyfriends. New studies are showing that a lot of teenage girls are having sex because they think it will feel good. (Guys who need to drug teenage girls into having sex must be total losers!)

Getting Teenagers To Talk About Sex

As a parent, you can't expect a teenager to be verbal about sex just because you have suddenly decided to offer wise counsel. Having an open dialogue about sex is an option that some parents lost when the child was three- to five-years-old. If mom and dad ignored the existence of sexual feelings back then, it might be very uncomfortable for the child who is now a teenager to suddenly start talking about sex. If there is tension between you and the teen, or if the kid is engaged in reckless acting out behavior, you might do better to solicit the help of a favorite aunt, uncle, teacher, or therapist who the teen is more apt to open up to.

When Teenagers Ask On Their Own

Let's say your teenager asks you a question about sex, "How do you know if you're gay?" or "What if you get so nervous before having sex that you feel like throwing up?" or "Would I have to leave home if I got pregnant?" Don't assume that she or he is thinking about being gay, is about to have sex, or is pregnant. It might be something your kid heard on the TV or radio, and is putting him or herself in the other person's place.

Try to respond by saying things that will help expand the question into a discussion, such as "What are your thoughts about that?" or "I'll be able to give you a better answer if you could tell me more about your question." This buys you precious time, which parents can never have enough of when being asked questions about sex, and it helps you squelch any potential screams that are about to explode from the depths of your parental being.

You might take solace from the following words by one of the top sex educators in the country, Debra Haffner: "Like most parents, I have found myself at a loss for words when a question I never expected popped up. Indeed, there have been times when I have responded in ways that I later regretted. For instance, I struggled with how to respond to my daughter when she asked questions about the Bobbit case, and then about Michael Jackson, and now Monica Lewinsky..."

Don't think that you need to come up with perfect answers. The most important thing is to provide an atmosphere where the child can ask questions and know that it's OK to think out loud about sex.

Wouldn't It Be Nice If...

Here are the kinds of questions that you probably never asked yourself before having sex, but hope beyond hope that your teenager will ask him- or herself. Perhaps these questions can act as guides for when you are discussing sex.

⚙ Why does this person want to have sex with me? Is it experimentation, fun, romance, a personal quest?

⚙ Does having sex mean something different to him or her than it does to me?

⚙ What would we do if we had intercourse and became pregnant? Who would we turn to? How would we tell our parents? Would we face it together? Am I ready to be a parent? (No kid should begin dating without seriously discussing this question with his or her parents.)

⚙ Are there ways we could please each other sexually without having intercourse?

⚙ How do I say no to someone who is pestering me for a date, or no to sex without feeling like a coward or geek?

⚙ If we do have sex, how do I get genuine feedback from my partner about what felt good and what didn't? How do I tell him or her what feels good and what doesn't for me?

⚙ Will I feel good about myself the next day?

Even if you don't talk to your kid about sex, make sure that there are things in your teenager's life that give it meaning besides just dating and having relationships.

Towards Higher Expectations

The mere thought of asking an eleven-year-old what qualities she would want in a sexual partner would send most American parents racing to the bathroom for a hit of Tagamet or Imodium. But let's think about it. If you don't introduce the notions of chivalry and respect in sex, where else are your children going to learn them from, MTV?

There is nothing wrong with talking to your child about the difference between a partner who's just trying to get laid as opposed to one who is going to be a caring and loving sexual companion.

For instance, does a partner who is going to be a respectful lover say "I won't go out with you anymore if we can't have intercourse"? Is he or she responsible and caring towards family and friends? Are his or her friends good people? Do they drink or get loaded a lot? And what about introducing the expectation that a truly desirable partner is one who is trustworthy and dependable, and says things like "I'd really like to please you, what can I do?"

It's also a good idea to remind your child that even if he or she falls head-over-heels in love,, it would be wise to wait several months before getting fully sexual. Tell them that teenagers who wait until their relationship is more seasoned before having sex usually end up enjoying the experience far more than those who have sex right away.

Of course, none of this is going to stop your kid from shacking up with one of the local Hell's Angels, but it does kick into motion the idea that an important part of self-respect means choosing your sexual partners carefully. Who knows, with enough intelligent concern and involvement on your part, your kid may even search out a sexual partner who has some of the characteristics and values that you do! Hopefully that's a good thing.

Condom Advice — For Teenage Boys:

Give your teenage boy a couple of condoms and a tube of contraceptive jelly, saying that these are for him to put on when he's alone to see what it feels like. If you have a straightforward relationship with him, you might suggest that he try masturbating with a condom on, which is the condom equivalent of taking a test drive. Tell him to pay attention to how long it takes after he ejaculates before his penis starts to shrink and the condom gets baggy. This is how much time he has to pull out, otherwise the condom might stay in his partner's vagina. Tell him that the shrinking penis factor is why he needs to clasp the condom around the base of his penis as he is pulling out. The contraceptive jelly is to put on the outside of the condom to help it slip and slide better when he is having intercourse, and it will help kill any germs or sperms that accidentally break free.

Condom Advice — For Teenage Girls

Give your daughter a couple of condoms, a tube of contraceptive jelly, and a penis-sized banana. Tell her that one of the condoms is for her to practice putting on the banana, the others are for whatever she wants to do with them. If you have an open relationship with her, try putting the condom on the banana together. This should result in a number of giggles and shared laughs. If it doesn't, you're being way too serious. Explain that she needs to leave a little baggie area at the tip of the penis so it can fill with ejaculate when the guy comes. Also explain that as soon as a guy ejaculates, his penis starts to shrink. This means that she should clasp the condom with her fingers and push it against the base of his penis as he withdraws so he won't leave it inside of her. Let her know that it never hurts to put a little contraceptive jelly on the outside of the condom before having intercourse. This will help give extra protection in case something escapes from the condom that shouldn't. *If you want to include a few more tips on condom usage, see page 465-470 in the chapter on birth control.*

Odds'N'Ends

🙞 If you have a son, make sure he's got a big box of Kleenex next to his bed and when it's all used up in three days don't make smart remarks like "I didn't know you had such a bad cold this week..." Better you have to stock up on extra Kleenex than he be out knocking up some young girl!

🙞 If your child begins to wash his or her own underwear or pajamas, be sure they have proper information about menstruation, masturbation (chapter 22), and wet dreams (chapter 34). You know what happens when boys ejaculate, but some teenage girls get wet spots in their underwear when they become sexually excited.

🙞 Statistics show that sex education does not encourage teens to have intercourse or to be sexually promiscuous. Also, abstinence-only programs do not significantly delay the onset of intercourse. This makes sense when you consider that the entire D.A.R.E. program had no significant impact on drug use. The "just say no" approach works about as well on teenagers as it does on adults! It takes a lot more time, effort and involvement on your part to turn out healthy kids than just saying "no."

🐝 Let your kids know that it's fine to wait until they are older before having sex with a partner, and that masturbation is what you do in the meantime, which is why the Good Lord gave us humans two more fingers than ET.

🐝 Inform them that what they see on TV about sex is usually pretty twisted, exaggerated, and outright incorrect, unless they're watching reruns from "Married With Children"...

A Final Word About Boundaries

If you think your younger teenagers would do better to wait a couple of years before sharing sex with partners, then you might do something other than tempt the fates.

One thing is to talk to your kids about sex and encourage them to talk to you. That way, if they're going to become sexually active, it won't be just to get one up on a mom or dad whose head was stuck in another century. Another thing that helps delay sexual activity is for teenagers to be involved in activities that challenge their minds and bodies—we're talking about things like science fairs and playing soccer or building things. It also helps to keep your kids from going to parties where there's lots of alcohol and pot and unoccupied bedrooms upstairs.

Understand that good kids do not always make good decisions. If you give them enough rope to hang themselves, most will. On the other hand, no kid ever lost a friend because their parents insisted on knowing where they were and with whom. No teenager ever died because his or her parents set a curfew on weekends. No kid ever shriveled up and blew away because one parent called another parent to make sure that an adult would be home when their kid was sleeping over.

Your kids will have plenty of time to do whatever they want once they turn eighteen and are legal adults. Until then, it is your job as parents to get them there safe and sound. 🐸🐸🐸

Chapter 43
Sex When You're Horny & Disabled

A story recently appeared on the internet about a twenty-two-year-old man with cerebral palsy who has virtually no control over his body's movements. The guy started using his wheel chair as a ramming device, running over anything he could. Eventually, this young man wrote on his word board that he was so horny he couldn't stand it any more.

Although his body has the same sexual urges and desires as that of a fully able twenty-two-year-old, he has no ability to walk, talk, or masturbate like the average twenty-two-year-old.

As quickly as they began, this young man's wheel chair tantrums stopped. The reason? A nurse's aid took mercy and began giving him hand jobs. But then she was caught, and fired instantly. The board and care home threatened to file a complaint against her for sexual abuse.

Sexy & Disabled?

If you think you have a good attitude about sex, consider a quadriplegic who wheels by in an electric wheel chair. The person drools a little and steers the chair with a joy stick that's strapped to his forehead. Do you think of this person as being sexual? Do you think he has the same sexual needs and desires as you? Chances are, you'd wonder how good his jump shot is before you'd think of him as having the same sexual needs and desires as yourself.

Many people not only disapprove of sex for the severely disabled, but they might find the concept offensive. They might even feel that we need to protect the disabled from sex.

Dear Dr. Goofy,

I'm a paraplegic from Ohio. From where I sit, I have women's rears and crotches in my face nearly all day long. You have no idea how much restraint it takes to keep my hands to myself. Last week I copped a feel but quickly apologized and blamed it on my "bad driving" and "spastic hand."

Dude,

Just to let you know, there's not an able-bodied guy on the planet who could come face-to-ass with as much anatomy as you do and not want to reach out and touch some. P.S. You must consider a crowded elevator to be a gift from God.

One reason why so many of us blanch at the idea of a disabled person having sex is because the advertising industry spends billions of dollars each year trying to narrow our concept of what sexual attractiveness is. Never do advertisers tell us that sexual appeal might have something to do with integrity and character, given how those can't be paid for with a credit card. As a result, we end up feeling out of the loop if we are bald, short, old, or thirty pounds overweight. Forget even existing sexually if you are missing a few fingers or an entire leg, slur your words when you talk, or are paralyzed from the chest down.

A huge hurdle for many disabled people is being able to accept themselves as being sexual. If you don't accept yourself as being sexual, it is unlikely that others will.

Roll Models

"Prior to my becoming blind, the only person who was blind that I had seen was a beggar. I was horrified to think that this was the only option available to me as a person who was blind."

~From an article on women who are blind by Ellen Rubin in
Sexuality & Disability Vol. 15 #1, 1997.

One of the more discouraging aspects of being disabled is that positive role models are few and far between. For instance, if you ask people to name a famous disabled person, just as many will say The Hunchback of Notre Dame as Franklin Delano Roosevelt. Of the two, FDR was a real life American president who provided people with a real sense of sanctuary, although he was unable to walk unaided. There were reasons why FDR tried to hide his disability. When he was a young man, disabled people were considered a success if they could get a job in the circus.

Different Ways That Disabilities Happen

When people are disabled from crashes and accidents, it is often because the spinal cord was damaged. About 85% of spinal cord injuries happen to men, many in their teens and twenties. That's because men have a penchant for doing things that involve speed or collisions. For instance, if a boy says he needs "pads," you might assume he's talking about something to put under his football jersey. If a girl says she needs 'pads', it's likely that she's referring to sanitary napkins or something to stuff into her bra. In addition to sports injuries and car crashes, disabilities due to injuries might come from shotgun wounds, stabbings, fist fights, or a serious bonk on the head.

Disabilities that result from diseases include arthritis, which can make intercourse painful, or cripple your fingers so much that you can't masturbate. Polio can make it nearly impossible to walk or breathe and it can result in all kinds of problems later in life (post-polio syndrome). Diabetes can keep a guy from having an erection, but it usually doesn't keep him from having an orgasm. Multiple Sclerosis can be mild and manageable, or severe and debilitating. Cancer and the various treatments for it can impact a person's ability and desire to have sex.

There are all sorts of genetic or congenital disorders that can leave a person disabled. Certain chromosome disorders can impact a person's physical growth and/or mental development. Congenital disorders might result in being a midget (top shelf challenged). Medications taken during pregnancy can result in the birth of infants with severe disabilities. Parental exposure to pollutants and chemicals can cause birth defects. Disabilities can also result from things like strokes and heart attacks or cerebral palsy and muscular dystrophy.

Note: If you watch TV talk shows like Jerry Springer, you might think that Siamese twins are born every five minutes, which is not the case, but this is a disability that might impact a person's ability to date. Also, there are people whose genitals are impacted by birth defects, such as hermaphrodites.

Spinal Cord Injury (SCI) Shorthand: When people with spinal cord injuries are talking to other people with spinal cord injuries, they sometimes use a shorthand such as "I'm a C-4 quad" or "I'm a T-3". This code refers to the location on the spine where the injury occurred. For instance, a C-4 injury occurs higher up on the spinal cord (in the neck) than a T-3, so it is likely that a person with a C-4 is paralyzed from the shoulders down (quadriplegic), where a T-3 has use of his or her arms (paraplegic), and an L-4 most likely has more use than a C-4 or T-3 because the injury happened at a point on the spinal cord between the ribs and pelvis. In addition to the location on the cord is whether the injury was complete or incomplete, with the latter supposedly being less severe.

Quad Note: Thanks to Tom Street for this info. Tom is a C-4 quad from an auto accident in 1988. Tom manufactures a computer mouse for quadriplegics called the QuadJoy. This special mouse, combined with extra software that Tom has written, allows the user to run the entire computer including keyboard by mouth. The full range of clicking and dragging happens by virtue of puffing and sucking on the end of the joystick. This can be particularly helpful for a quad who would like to interact with others in chat rooms, or who would like to see internet porn in PRIVATE and without the help of an attendant. Tom can be reached on the internet at: www.quadjoy.com.

Chronic Vs. Acute

There are certain disabilities that happen all at once. They don't keep getting worse. This is true of most spinal cord injuries. There are other disabilities, usually caused by diseases, which have symptoms that get worse over time.

For some people, it is easier to have a disability that stays the same. For instance, once a person with a spinal cord injury is able to learn how to deal with his disability, he can be pretty sure that his condition won't worsen and he won't have to learn a whole new set of skills just to keep even. However, people with chronic illnesses have a more uncertain future and may have to constantly readapt as the illness progresses. The uncertainty of a chronic illness makes it more difficult to get on with your life, as you never know when your disease is going to pull the rug out from under you. Of course, you can say that none of us has any guarantees on the future, but the uncertainty of everyday life is much easier to cope with than the uncertainty of a disease that may be getting worse.

Even the recovery process is different for someone with an acute injury as opposed to a chronic illness. For instance, consider a person who had his leg amputated after being run over in the parking lot at the 7-11 as opposed to having a leg amputated due to complications from diabetes. Outside of not getting to finish his Slurpee, the person who lost his leg at the 7-11 had no pre-existing condition and must only face the problems associated with the amputation itself. The person with progressive diabetes has to cope with numerous problems caused by the diabetes in addition to those that are specific to the amputation.

Also, the treatments for certain disabilities or illnesses can cause sexual problems. For instance, tricyclic antidepressants are often prescribed to help with the neurogenic pain that can occur after spinal cord injury. These drugs can impact the desire to have sex as well as the ability to have an erection and to ejaculate. The same is true for certain cancer treatments that adversely impact the sexuality of both men and women.

Double Your Trouble

If it wasn't bad enough to have your spinal cord injured, accidents that cause the damage are often severe enough to also cause traumatic head injury. Not only does the person have to cope with possible paralysis from the spinal injury, but he may also experience low sexual drive, poor impulse control or unpredictable behavior from the brain injury.

Can Guys In Wheelchairs Get Hard Ons?

It's interesting how people wonder if guys in wheelchairs can get hard ons, but they don't wonder if women in wheelchairs can get wet! Why's that? Contrary to what you might think, a lot of guys who are in   wheelchairs are able to get erections. The stimulation for the erection will often need to come from direct physical contact with he genitals rather than from feeling horny, as the link between the horny center in the brain and the genitals is often damaged. Guys with disabilities can often get good erections with the help of vacuum pumps or injections. Men with higher level spinal cord injuries (usually quads, not paraplegics) tend to get reflex erections. These happen when the penis is being touched and have little connection to feeling horny. They usually go down as soon as the touching stops, but some couples learn how to keep the stimulation going so they can have intercourse.

Able-bodied men often become aware of their own sexual arousal by feeling their penis grow. Men who are paralyzed have to rely on other signals to know when they are aroused, e.g. nipples getting hard, goosebumps, heavier breathing and a heart that beats faster. These aren't any different from what able-bodied men experience, but how many guys notice subtle physical clues when their dicks are screaming "me! me! me!"

Women with spinal cord injuries may find that the sexual wetness in their vagina is decreased or absent. Using a lubricant during intercourse can be very helpful. Many women with spinal cord injuries are able to have orgasms. Bregman and Hadley (1976) interviewed a number of women with spinal cord injuries and found that their descriptions of orgasm were similar to those of women with no spinal cord injury. This suggests that orgasms can be generated by nerves in the body that do not run up the spinal cord. Also, some people with spinal cord injury have orgasms that are referred to as "para-orgasms," which are different from genital orgasms but are quite compelling. Para-orgasms can be so strong that women who are injured above the T-6 level need to be aware of rapid changes in their blood pressure.

Both women and men who no longer have traditional orgasms can learn to experience a type of orgasm that is called an emotional orgasm. This kind of orgasm results in a rush of relaxation and calm in the rest of the body that's like the afterglow of a good hard come.

Whether a person can or can't have an orgasm, the good feelings that most able-bodied people get from being touched and loved are still massively satisfying for someone who is disabled. One person with a spinal cord injury reported in a video that "Before my accident I couldn't get enough stimulation from the waist down; now I can't get enough from the waist up!" When a person is paralyzed in other parts of the body, areas such as the back of the neck and arms can become extremely sensitive in a sexual way. Also, plenty of disabled people report that watching a partner doing something sexual to them can be very satisfying even if they can't feel the actual sensations. The brain is able to fill in the missing pieces.

Vibrator Note: Vibrators can be a very helpful sexual aid for disabled men and women. They can supply the necessary stimulation when a hand is unable. If you tend to be incontinent, consider getting a vibrator that's rechargeable or has batteries. Urine is a far better conductor of electricity than water, making plug-in models a wee bit risky. If your hands are too crippled to use a regular vibrator, see page 613 for someone who might be able to fashion one for you that you can handle.

"Will I Be Able To Have Children"

This seems like a simple, straightforward question. But it is often an indirect way of asking "Will I be able to have sex?" "Will anyone want to have sex with me?" "How in the blazes do I have sex now that I'm like this?" The answer to all of these questions is usually "yes," unless the person stays in a full-time funk and never transitions out of asking "why me." (Try as they might, nobody but God or nature has an answer to the "why me?" question, assuming there is an answer at all.)

Most women who are disabled are able to become pregnant. This is why most disabled women need to use birth control, even if they are paralyzed from the shoulders down. Many men who are paralyzed have problems ejaculating. Physicians are having some success helping these men to ejaculate by sticking electrodes up their rears and shocking the bejesus out of nerves in the prostate region. Some guys with spinal cord injuries above T-12 are able to ejaculate with the help of a vibrator on the penis.

Born With It Vs. Got It Along The Way

Unless they are in a rock 'n 'roll band, people who make it to adulthood without being disabled, have probably achieved certain developmental milestones, aka "maturity." But if a person was disabled at an early age, it is possible that being disabled has gotten in the way of achieving a level of maturity that he or she needs to behave as a responsible and caring adult. For instance, how does a kid who is disabled at age sixteen progress through the usual steps towards independence if he or she needs a parent to get them out of bed and dressed each morning? If he or she is in a rehab center, how do they get the privacy to explore sexually as other kids do? If their hands are crippled, how do they learn to masturbate?

Consider the following questions posed by a therapist who works with the disabled: "How does a young girl in a wheelchair learn how adults are sexual if her parents are afraid to be that way in front of her? How does she explore her parents' drawers when they are out and find books, movies, condoms, sponges, lingerie and so forth—as many youths do—if she cannot get into their bedroom? How can she find her brother's copies of sexually explicit publications if she cannot get under his bed where they are stashed?" (From "Performing A Sexual Evaluation On The Person With Disability or Illness" by Kenneth A. Lefebvre from "Sexual Function in People With Disability and Chronic Illness" by Marca L. Sipski & Craig J. Alexander, An Aspen Publication, 1997).

People who are disabled at a young age will become adults with the same sexual drives and desires as anyone who is not disabled. However, they may be missing a sense of sexual orientation or knowledge of responsible and appropriate ways to satisfy their sexual urges. To help fill in the missing pieces, parents and educators of disabled kids need to be more open about sexual issues rather than less.

Sex & People Who Are Developmentally Disabled

It is not likely that people who are developmentally disabled will be reading this book, although we know of one such woman by the name of Linda who loves looking at the pictures! People with developmental disabilities have the same sexual urges and desires as people without disabilities. They simply go through the stages of sexual development at a slower pace.

The developmentally disabled pose special problems when it comes to sexual training, because they may need a good deal of repetitive explanation about things that many adults feel uncomfortable saying just once. Also, in their drive towards sexual pleasure, developmentally disabled kids may be even less apt to use birth control than their nondisabled partners in crime.

If you are the parent of a disabled child, or you work with people who are disabled, you might be at a loss for finding good references to help you in dealing with your child's sexual growth. One book that might be helpful is by Patricia Patterson, titled "Doubly Silenced, Sexuality, Sexual Abuse, and People With Developmental Disabilities." For ordering information, see the resources section.

Body Image

If a person has been disabled for a long time, particularly from a young age, his body image might also include a wheelchair or braces, scars from various surgeries, hands that are twisted and not particularly dexterous, a voice that slurs words, a head that doesn't sit straight on its shoulders or other features that aren't always like those of models in Vogue or GQ. It may be very difficult for a person who is disabled to feel attractive and effective if they can't see themselves as separate from the devices that help them to survive. As a result, they might need plenty of feedback that you value them as a person in the same way that you do someone who doesn't have a wheelchair, braces or disfigurements.

Dear Dr. Goofy,

We are both have spinal cord injuries and are disabled. Yet we like watching porn that shows able-bodied people having sex. Is this weird?
Dudette,

None of us have eight-inch dicks, last forty-five minutes, come in buckets, or have partners who like taking it in so many different ways, but we like watching pornography too. If most of it weren't so darned boring, we'd watch it more often! Keep in mind that pornography is a fantasy. It helps us go places in our minds that many of us wouldn't go in reality even if we could. Now, here's a question for you: You are not worried about watching able bodied actors in TV or movies, so why is it when it comes to porn you suddenly need to feel so crippledly correct?

Explaining Yourself & Educating Others

"People do have all these kinds of curiosity and you have to find ways of making them feel more comfortable around you at first."

~Steve, a disabled man from the "Sexuality Reborn" video.

Just like people who are able-bodied, people who are disabled need to learn their own sexual strengths and weaknesses, and then teach a partner what they need. They also need to receive plenty of feedback. For instance, for someone who has had a stroke, it might be important to lay on their affected side so they can use their active arm for caressing a partner. Likewise it is important for the partner to give feedback to the stroke victim, as someone with a stroke might have a "visual field cut" which causes them to ignore one side of their partner's body. (This example by way of social worker Sharon Bacharach.)

When it comes to enjoying sex, different disabilities pose different challenges. For instance, if you can't use your hands in a way that allows you to masturbate, then figuring out how to do that will be one of your first challenges. If you need help breathing but want to give a partner oral sex, you might need to alternate sucking on your partner's genitals with sucking breaths of air from your respirator hose. If you can't have intercourse, then you'll need to work out ways

of pleasing both yourself and your partner without it. (This book has plenty of chapters that describe ways of doing that.) Perhaps your disability has left you with little nerve sensation in your genitals, but the opening of your anus is still sensitive and stimulating it might bring you to orgasm. Perhaps your neck, lips, cheeks or nipples are highly sensitized to touch. Maybe it helps if you take a warm bath or shower, or have a beer or glass of wine before having sex. This is just as true for able-bodied people.

Good-Bye To Spontaneity

Some able-bodied couples don't like to use a condom because the thirty seconds it takes to put it on somehow destroys the mood for them. Think of how resilient "the mood" has to be when it takes all sorts of preparations and maneuvers to be ready to have sex! Think of how resilient the mood has to be if one partner cries out in pain and adjustments need to be made in order to continue.

One of the things that people who are disabled loose is the kind of sexual spontaneity that some able-bodied couples take for granted unless they are parents with kids who are still at home. Consider the following advice that recently posted on the internet:

"Patience is truly a virtue in disability-related sex. Disability often destroys something in sex, spontaneity for one thing. Drugs, fatigue, depression, neurological impairment can also be a destructive force. Utilizing the turn-on can sometimes partially make up for what has been taken away. Sometimes erotic books, photos or videos can enhance the performance. The type and degree of disability often demands traveling that extra mile or two." (PeterLove@primenet.com)

Getting Into Relationships

"Why would any man want this body? No woman's going to want this!" Some people who are disabled feel that nobody will find them sexually attractive. As a result, they might push away people who do, or at the other end of the spectrum, offer themselves to the first person who shows interest, even if it is not someone they particularly like or trust. A disabled person without a solid sense of self might be starved for affection or desperately need to prove that he or she is desirable. Of course, one doesn't need to be disabled to have these sorts of hang-ups, but it can be extra difficult when your physical ducks aren't in the same row as everyone else's.

Regarding the subject of dating and the disabled, a woman with cerebral palsy recently commented, "I think women are more accepting of differences than men. I see a lot more disabled men married or in serious relationships. I see a lot more disabled women just giving up." There are plenty of disabled men who say it's equally tough for them. Another disabled woman says one of the reasons why she fell in love with her husband "was the idea that here was a person who looked and acted OK, wanting to have a relationship with me." (Both quotes are from "Dating Issues For Women With Physical Disabilities," in Sexuality And Disability, Vol. 15, No. 4, 1997 by Rintals, Howland, Nosek et. Original source by T. Due, Houston Chronicle, May 24, 1995.)

People who are disabled sometimes shy away from dating other people who are disabled. When you are disabled yourself, there can be a kind of hatred of other people who are disabled—an inner need to say "I'm not like them." There can also be the added problem of social acceptance. Two people in wheelchairs humming down the sidewalk garner far more stares from able-bodied pedestrians than does one.

The Disabled Couple

Perhaps the most difficult aspect of being in a relationship where one or both members is disabled is that ultimately, the couple has to face the same kind of fights, squabbles, disagreements, and difficulties as couples where there is no disability!

As for how disability impacts a couple, keep in mind that some able-bodied couples stay in love with each other only as long as each partner is able to mirror the other's sexual attractiveness. If one member starts to look older than the other, slows down a bit, or becomes disabled, the relationship may quickly dissolve. With other couples, there is a deep love and friendship that transcends physical change.

When there is a new disability, it is not uncommon for both partners to experience frustration, anger, fear, disappointment and helplessness. Roles within the relationship may undergo serious changes. Neither the able-bodied member or the one who is disabled should be afraid to ask for help and advice from social workers and rehab staff.

When it comes to experiencing sexual intimacy, a couple with a new disability may need to learn anew. This might actually be a relief to your partner if you weren't as good in bed as you thought you were! The good news is that couples who had a rewarding sex life before the disability usually find a way to have a good sex life after.

If you are a couple whose primary expression of sexuality was through intercourse, you may have a good deal of adjusting ahead. It will be easier if you are a couple whose sexuality included a full range of sensory experiences, like enjoying the beauty of a sunset, holding hands and caressing each other.

Also, if you can afford it, it would be wise to hire an attendant to perform caretaking functions. Otherwise, a parent/child dynamic can evolve between you and your partner which can intrude on feelings of sexual passion.

With A Deaf Ear & Twinkle In His Eye

A woman who is a friend of the Goofy Foot Press works with deaf people and has also had sex with one or two deaf men. She said that she never realized how much she relies on verbal cues from a partner until she was romanced by a deaf man. For instance, when you are with a deaf person, there is no hearing without seeing. Whether it's being in another room, or looking down when you are having a bowl of soup, the necessary conditions for connection are suddenly missing. She said that the lack of verbal give and take is particularly noticeable during sex, whether it's oral sex or intercourse.

People who are deaf are obviously more comfortable with verbal silence during romance and love-making than are people who can hear. If our friend is sleeping with a man who is deaf, she lets him know that she needs more input than he might be used to giving a partner who is deaf. She also says that it is important to have some of the lights on when you are making love to a deaf person, so they can either see you sign or read your lips. On the other hand, deaf people sometimes sign on the skin of each other or if they are in a spoons position, the person in the back can reach around his partner's body and sign in front of her where she can see it.

Attacking Their Own

It's interesting how people sometimes attack their own. For instance, while many people who are disabled would welcome an increased awareness that they are just as sexual as anyone else, some clearly don't. A year ago, when a mainstream, glossy magazine for disabled people ran a story on sex and the disabled, some readers were so upset that they canceled their subscriptions. When hearing about this, you might think that the story was Hustler-like and included photos of the naked disabled doing things that would have pleased Caligula. In reality, the article was so tame that it could have been published in Parade Magazine or even House & Garden.

Perhaps the subject of sex brings up huge amounts of frustration and sadness for some disabled people, to the point of where they simply get angry at sex itself.

So You Won't Have To Read The "Sex During Pregnancy" Chapter Of This Book Unless You Want To

Women can get pregnant in a wheelchair just as easily as they can get pregnant in any other chair. Don't think for a moment that just because you are disabled or paralyzed from the shoulders or waist down you somehow can't get pregnant. Be sure that you speak to each other and to your physician about birth control. **Note:** Until recently, it was believed that birth control pills, shots, and implants might be unsafe for some women who are in wheelchairs. It's not the wheelchair that's the problem, but proneness to circulatory problems and blood clots that can be increased by the birth control pill. However, the newer low dose pills and shots are thought to be quite safe. If your gynecologist isn't used to working with women who have disabilities, check with the National Spinal Cord Foundation for a referral.

Attendants And Caregivers—The Good And Bad Of It

Powerful feelings can develop between people who are patients and those who are hired to care for them—both loving and hateful. It is beyond the scope of this book to explore the various possibilities, except to say that it does little good to turn a blind eye to the dynamics that can arise between caretaker and caregiver.

If you are able-bodied, consider for a moment the issue of privacy. The kind of privacy that able-bodied people take for granted might not exist for someone who is disabled. This can range from bathing and completing bowel movements to preparing for masturbation and sex. It may be necessary for a disabled person to share private aspects of themselves with an attendant that some able-bodied people don't feel comfortable sharing with a partner of many years.

Considering the level of dependency that some disabled people have, the opportunity for abuse by attendants is rife. This is a huge issue and is unfortunately quite common. It is important that disabled people speak up against assistants who are abusive. If this is a concern for you, please contact your local center for independent living.

Helping The Helpers

In order to have fulfilling sex lives, people with disabilities often need the help of several different medical subspecialities. These might include neurology, psychology, urology, oncology, endocrinology, physical and rehabilitative medicine and sex therapy. Unfortunately, getting medical specialists to work together in a collaborative effort requires that professional egos be set aside. This can be as difficult as getting Catholics, Mormons, Jews and Southern Baptists to join forces. The problem multiplies when the issue is sex, since many of the professionals who need to work together might be ever so uncomfortable with the subject at hand.

If you are a disabled person who is struggling to get assistance with your sexual needs, maybe it will help if you gave your health care provider a copy of this book opened to this chapter. Perhaps it will help them feel more at ease in aiding you with sexual matters. After all, it's quite likely that they, too, enjoy sex and would be more than happy to help you if they were just able to feel more comfortable.

Rehab Note: When rehab therapists get around to mentioning sex, it is usually in combination with discussions about bowel and bladder functioning. This is quite unfortunate. People who are newly disabled need access to positive information about sexuality early in their rehabilitation. Even if they reject the information, it is something positive that will remain in their consciousness, to be accessed at another time.

Stroke Studies—Interesting For A Number Of Reasons

Stroke survivors, as a group, experience a decrease in sexual activity. Until recently, this was thought to have physical, rather than emotional causes. However, a study of stroke survivors by Buzzellie, di Francesco, Giaquinto, and Nolte concluded that "psychological issues, rather than medical ones, account for disruption of sexual functioning in stroke survivors." ("Sexuality Following Stroke" in Sexuality & Disability, Vol. 15, Number 4, Winter 1997.)

It is especially significant that the researchers found no differences in the sexual functioning of people with right-brained lesions as opposed to left-brain lesions or contralateral lesions. This seems to contradict our modern tendency to view almost all behaviors as coming from one side of the brain or the other. This study indicates that sexuality is neither "right-brained" nor "left-brained."

Resources On Sex For People Who Are Disabled

Please check out the resources section at the end of this book for a huge listing of resources for people who are disabled. Fortunately, we include a doctor who customizes sex toys to fit your particular disability. For instance, if your fingers are too crippled to hold a vibrator, you might be able to negotiate one that is embedded in a Nerf ball.

General—Video

SEXUALITY REBORN. Highly recommended. An excellent tape where four likeable and articulate couples tell about their personal experience with sex and disability. At least one person in each couple is wheelchair bound. Very helpful for both disabled and able-bodied viewers. College instructors who use the Guide To Getting It On! in their classes are highly encouraged to show this tape to their students. A great deal of humanness is conveyed without a moment of pity or self-absorption. There is something about the honesty and genuineness of the couples who speak in this video that gives able-bodied people a more realistic and grounded perception of people who are disabled. There are parts of the tape where the couples are naked and having sex, but it isn't in a pornographic way that's going to ruffle the feathers of your dean or regents. The only criticism that reviewers had was that the occasional comments by the talking head medical specialists seemed unnecessary and perhaps detracted rather than added to the tape's effectiveness.

UNTOLD DESIRES. Highly recommended. A series of interviews about sex with people who have all kinds of disabilities. This award-winning documentary contains no nudity and makes an excellent companion tape for "Sexually Reborn". We seriously hope that anyone going through a rehab program would get to see both tapes. Included in this tape is a wonderful interview with a woman who has severe cerebral palsy. She is amazingly astute, funny, and energetic. The tape provides subtitles when she speaks because her speech is so CP-involved. The interviews with several other disabled people are equally valuable. As an additional bonus, there is footage of one chair-bound guy skiing down a steep mountain that is pretty spectacular, as well as a chair bound dude racing down stairs and streets. Redefines the term "No Fear." Highly recommended for people who are disabled as well as those who aren't. ✎✎✎

Chapter 44
Dyslexia Of The Penis — Learning To Improve Your Sexual Hang Time

Coming too soon is an unfortunate joke that a man's body plays on itself. His penis suddenly feels like its had twenty minutes worth of intercourse before he has finished his first couple of strokes. Rather than being able to enjoy the warmth and excitement of having his penis inside a lover's body, he is left fending off an unwanted orgasm and the feelings of disappointment that tend to follow.

Equally as frustrating is the numbing effect that premature ejaculation has on the woman's level of excitement. That's because she often holds back in an attempt to help the man last longer. In cases where she might want to wrap her legs around her lover's body and have him thrust away at a hefty clip, she learns to lay still; and if she wants long deep strokes, she learns to not even ask.

Since coming too soon effects both partners, this chapter takes a partner's approach to solving it. For instance, it talks about the need for a couple to increase rather than decrease the level of sexual excitement in their relationship. It offers exercises that can help the man learn to tolerate a depth of sexual feeling in his penis that he probably doesn't even know exists. It also suggests that a couple's entire relationship can be strengthened when the woman helps the man to improve upon a problem that he has been helpless to fix on his own. Few women realize the depth of gratitude that most men feel when a partner helps them with a problem like premature ejaculation.

Note: You are encouraged to read about premature ejaculation in other books on sex, or to consult with a trained sex therapist. You may find other programs more to your liking.

Increasing The Woman's Sexual Excitement And Self-Sufficiency

Retraining a dyslexic penis can take several months, and it is important to consider the female partner's sexual pleasure as well. For instance, the couple might explore various ways that the woman can experience high levels of sexual satisfaction. This is important for a number of reasons:

⌣ She won't feel resentful or frustrated (assuming she doesn't already).

⌣ He won't feel guilty (assuming he doesn't already).

⌣ It's likely to be fun. (Hopefully, much fun!)

⌣ Both partners will get to experience what it is like when the woman is able to open up sexually, no longer needing to mute her excitement to help her man last longer.

Fortunately, a lot of men learn to compensate for premature ejaculation by becoming really good at pleasing a woman with oral sex and different kinds of massage. If not, this would be a fine time to learn. Also, there is no reason why the woman can't masturbate while her partner holds her. Besides being nice for her, this allows the man to feel her body in his arms as she experiences intense levels of sexual pleasure.

Why Does It Happen?

There are different theories about why men come too soon. One theory blames the masturbation habits of teenage boys, saying that they teach themselves to come quickly by jerking off as fast as they sometimes drive. Another theory says that the body cannot distinguish anxiety from sexual excitement, and that high amounts of anxiety fool the body into thinking that it has been having intercourse for much longer than it really has. A third theory proposes that a man who comes too soon holds tension in his genitals and rear end, and is unable to relax that part of his body during intercourse. The constant muscle contraction makes for a quick come. A pair of Korean researchers claim that some men's penises are naturally more sensitive than others, and this causes them to come sooner. They are working on a special motion lotion to help increase your intercourse mileage. And finally, there is a zoological perspective, which recognizes that most male animals ejaculate after only a few thrusts. This helps them to live longer, since a steamy two-hour lovemaking session in a jacaranda tree greatly increases the chances that a pair of mating primates will fall off a limb or be eaten by predators, and we're not talking oral sex here.

Whatever the cause, it is generally agreed that men who come too soon go from erection to ejaculation without much adroitness at the steps in-between. Often times they try to prevent ejaculation by thinking about something other than sex, which is about as productive as an Indy race driver thinking about golf as he's entering a high speed turn. Although all of us are occasionally distracted when having sex, this is not a good way to last longer. Quite to the contrary, the exercises that follow encourage a man to be more present sexually rather than absent.

The Other 97%

Whether you come too soon or not, it never hurts a couple to take the time to gently caress and massage each other's bodies. It is especially important for the man with a dyslexic penis to get away from his thoughts and into his body — and not just the part that sticks out from between his legs. Not enough can be said about allowing a partner to touch you from head to toe while you empty your mind and let your body completely relax.

Calibrating The Penis — Teaching An Old Dog New Tricks

The goal of this exercise is to help the man expand his range of sexual feeling. Of course, men who come too soon sometimes believe that they feel too much rather than too little, when the opposite is actually true. If a man can learn to tolerate a fuller range of sexual feeling, then greater amounts of pleasure won't automatically trigger an ejaculation.

The mechanics of calibrating the penis are fairly simple. It begins with the woman rubbing or massaging the penis in any way that both she and her partner enjoy. This can be done with the penis dry (traditional hand job strokes), with the penis lubricated, with oral sex, or even with a vagina, although the latter is usually not recommended until the man has mastered the basic field maneuvers. How you stimulate the penis will also depend on how quickly the man comes. For instance, some guys who come quickly with intercourse can last nearly forever when being given a traditional hand job. The woman's arm could literally fall off from stroking the penis before such a guy comes. She might find it more fun to calibrate her partner's penis orally or by lubricating it and massaging it.

The scale of calibration is usually from 0-to-10, with zero representing absolutely no arousal whatsoever, e.g. "Your grandmother just slipped you the tongue..." A ten represents orgasm and ejaculation. As the woman is stimulating the man's penis, he tells her where he senses himself to be, e.g. "1," "3," "5," "6", "8". At first, the man will just be guessing, but after a while he will know exactly where he is on his own personal scale. Guys who come too soon often go from 3 to 9 rather suddenly, while other men can stay at a 6 or 7 for five, ten or more minutes.

As the man lands on a specific number, his partner should try to keep him there for a few minutes, and then back off before going higher. She shouldn't hesitate to call it a day and let him ejaculate after fifteen to thirty minutes of doing the exercises. With time, he will be able to tolerate hovering at a constant 6, 7, or 8 for prolonged periods, but don't expect that to happen right away. That's because his body might resist staying at a 7 or 8, when these levels are currently experienced as mere bleeps on the way to a speedy ejaculation.

The Point Of No Return

To successfully calibrate the penis, it is important to recognize when the man is approaching the POINT OF NO RETURN. The point of no return is when nothing short of stepping on a land mine will keep a man from ejaculating. The point of no return is usually an 8.5 or 9 on the scale of 10. As mentioned in an earlier chapter, signs that a man is approaching the point of no return are as follows:

The veins in his penis may start to bulge or his penis might give a sudden throb, the color of the head may darken, his testicles might suck up into his groin, his muscles will tighten, his hips may thrust, and he might suddenly start to groan like a dying bull or invoke the names of various saints. Appreciate how well you are doing when you can keep him close to the point of no return for several minutes without letting him go over the edge.

When first calibrating a penis, a woman should probably stop all stroking as a man approaches the point of no return. She then waits around ten seconds before resuming stimulation. A goal to eventually shoot for (so to speak) is for the woman to be able to switch stroking techniques rather than stopping the stimulation altogether. For instance, if she is rubbing the shaft and finds that the thing is about to blow, she might switch and begin to rub only the head, with the change in focus being the cue that helps the man power through the urge to come. But please don't try this until you have spent a couple of months feeling really comfortable with the prior routine. Remember, guys who come too soon need to learn sexual patience; rushing through the process simply contradicts everything you are trying to achieve.

As for erections, don't worry about them. What you are working toward is the capacity to tolerate more sensation. Don't be confused by the presence or absence of hardness. Some men will start to get hard at only a 3, while others won't stiffen until a 7 or higher. When receiving genital massage or oral sex, a man can experience incredibly high levels of sexual feeling while sporting only half of an erection. It's quite possible to come without an erection at all.

Penis Pull Ups

There is much hype these days about genital squeezing exercises called Kegels. Unfortunately, some people in the sex business claim that doing Kegel exercises will literally make the dead walk and the blind see. No research has ever shown that Kegel exercises can cure premature ejaculation or make an impotent penis hard, nor will they allow a man to dial a rotary phone with his penis. However, Kegel exercises can be valuable in helping a man become more aware of feelings in his penis and pelvic region before and during orgasm.

Kegel exercises are pretty simple and straightforward. They involve squeezing or contracting the muscles that stop the flow of urine — the ones you squeeze when the phone begins ringing after you just started taking a long leak and think it might be a seriously important call. Here are four ways to help build up these muscles:

1. Squeeze as you would when you are peeing and want to cut off the flow of urine. Do this nine or ten times in succession. For the first couple of weeks hold the squeeze for only a few seconds. After a month or two, try holding the squeeze for up to ten seconds. (The peeing reference is so you will understand which muscles to squeeze; it's best not to do these exercises when actually taking a leak, lest your urinary tract begin to revolt.)

2. Try the above exercises without pause, squeezing and relaxing the muscles in rapid sequence, like when shooting at ducks in an arcade game.

3. Squeeze for a couple of seconds, and then push all the way out like you are trying to have a bowel movement. Repeat this several times. The first two exercises can be done just about anywhere: at work, at school, at church, inside a crowded elevator, or when commuting. However, consider doing this exercise in privacy, as the push out part might cause you to pass gas.

4. Optional exercise for guys who have way too much time on their hands: When your penis is erect, sit or stand with your legs apart and try wagging the thing up and down or sideways by squeezing the muscles in your groin. (Some wives and girlfriends find this amusing to watch.) Eventually toss a wash cloth or small towel over the penis to add resistance, but be careful that you don't strain. If you are a jock and work really hard at it, Nike only knows what you might be able to hang on the end of your penis some day! Of course, check with your physician or personal trainer first, and never attempt anything that causes pain or strain.

Possible Benefits Of Doing Penis Pull Ups

At first, most men won't be able to isolate the muscles that anchor the penis. Instead, they will tense the whole pelvic region, including the rectum. With time, they can teach themselves to better isolate the various muscle groups in the pelvic floor, even the ones that stop the flow of urine from the ones that wag the end of the penis. This can help a man become aware when he might be tensing these muscles unintentionally. For instance, doing exercise #3 above should help a man become aware when he is unconsciously contracting the muscles in his rear end. Speculation has it that tension in the anal sphincters not only contributes to premature ejaculation, but to hemorrhoid formation as well — two conditions that are greeted with similar amounts of glee. Some sex therapists say that one of the keys to lasting longer is being able to relax the muscles in the pelvic floor and rear end when having intercourse. Also, some men claim to get extra mileage by pushing out, which is the exact opposite of squeezing. Another purported benefit of doing penis pull ups is that they may help to expand the feelings of orgasm itself.

Including Intercourse

It can take a couple of months to fully calibrate the dyslexic penis. By then it's time to start having intercourse, after you can keep the penis between 6-and-7 for a good five or ten minutes without needing to ejaculate.

Having intercourse again can be tricky. That's because the woman will be tempted to fall into old habits of muting her sexual excitement in order to help the man last longer. At the same time, the man can't be expected to make his new calibration skills work during intercourse without gradually easing into it. Keeping both needs in mind, it might not be a bad idea for the woman to plan on having independent orgasms before or after the couple has intercourse. Then maybe you can view intercourse as a further way of calibrating the penis, with the woman using her vagina to calibrate the penis instead of her hands or mouth. For specifics about intercourse, consider the following:

⌣ The man should avoid using the muscles in his rear end for thrusting. This causes his butt to tense up and may contribute to premature ejaculation. Perhaps this is one reason why a lot of men seem to last longer when the woman is on top; not having to thrust allows the man to relax his pelvic muscles more. The same has been said for when he is standing. When the man is thrusting, he should experiment with using his back muscles instead of his rear end to propel the in-out part of intercourse.

⌣ You might consider starting with femoral intercourse for a few weeks before doing full penetration. This is where the shaft of the penis glides through the lips of the vagina, like a hot dog in a bun. The penis doesn't actually go into the vagina, and does need to be lubricated ahead of time. Femoral intercourse can be done with the woman on top. Even if the penis doesn't go into the vagina, it's a good idea to use contraception when doing this.

⌣ Some men can last much longer in one position rather than another. Also, certain intercourse positions might cause anxiety which can contribute to premature ejaculation. Yes, intercourse positions carry their own unconscious baggage.

The Realm Of Sensation

You would be amazed at how many people, both male and female, teach their bodies to ignore gentle sensations. For instance, a man might have learned to ignore his body's more subtle sensations when he was a boy. Perhaps this happened the first time he had to throw a block on a nasty looking linebacker.[1] Also, some men (and women) find it scary to become passive or to allow themselves to receive subtle pleasure.

---

[1]This isn't to say that a boy or girl shouldn't compete in contact sports, but that they need a parent's help in learning that there is a time and place for butting heads and an equally important but different time and place for experiencing sensual feelings.

It can't be emphasized enough that the purpose of the exercises in this chapter is to allow the man to tolerate (and enjoy) a fuller depth of physical pleasure. This, rather than trying to stop coming, needs to be your goal.

One of the first things mentioned in this chapter was how nice it can be to share touch and massage. This can help to allow more sensation. Some couples enjoy using a variety of materials and fabrics to massage the body from head to toe.

For instance, good results can be had with a feather or furry mitt, as well as a silk scarf or piece of rayon. Some couples might also be into leather, latex or rubber. Others find the feel of a partner's fingertips to be exquisite.

A Note On The Squeeze Technique

Sex therapists since the time of the Ming Dynasty have recommended doing one form or another of the squeeze technique to help relieve premature ejaculation. To do the squeeze technique, the woman brings the man close to the point of no return and then squeezes his penis to stop the impending orgasm. While the squeeze technique has worked for many couples, it may be preferable to go the extra distance and actually calibrate the penis.

The latter is a process that helps build more familiarity and trust between the man and woman than simply squeezing a dyslexic penis into submission.

The Most Important Ingredients...

In helping a man to last longer, attributes such as patience, love, and a tolerance for frustration are essential for a woman to have. That's because her man is probably fighting a private battle with his own penis that doesn't include much kindness. And for heaven's sake, don't forget to have a sense of humor. Humor is the sexual lubricant for the soul.

Visualization Exercises

Visualization is not a traditional exercise for premature ejaculation — unless the man is trying to visualize something that's totally nonsexual in an attempt to last longer. Hopefully, you can now appreciate how unproductive this kind of visualization can be. Here are a few visualization exercises designed to help a man stay in the saddle by becoming more, rather than less, aware of his body's processes. If they make sense to you, then you might give them a try.

1.) Close your eyes and feel yourself having intercourse. After you are able to feel yourself thrusting in and out, concentrate on relaxing the muscles in your butt cheeks, rectum, and genitals. Each time you feel these muscles contract or tense up, concentrate on relaxing them.

2.) Repeat the prior exercise, only this time concentrate on your breathing. Try to relax by taking slow, deep Zen-like breaths. These are done by expanding and contracting your abdomen instead of your chest.

3.) Close your eyes and feel yourself having intercourse. Keep thrusting until your mind starts to wander or until you visualize yourself ejaculating. At the point that your mind wanders or you see yourself ejaculating, start to visualize something pleasant and non-demanding, such as lying in the warm sun on a private beach. Relax in this way for a few minutes, and then let your senses have another go at intercourse. Keep returning to the pleasant, non-demanding place whenever you feel conflicts arising from intercourse. (The point of this visualization is not to decrease sexual sensation, but to help relax any anxiety that might be causing you to come too soon.)

Relationship Fears & Resistances

Since most of these exercises involve both partners, it is reasonable to expect that a man might have a certain amount of apprehension about seeking his partner's involvement. It is also possible that his partner may have certain resistances or fears about what might happen if her man is able to last longer.

Sex therapist Helen Singer Kaplan, whose book on premature ejaculation is recommended at the end of this chapter, mentions that many of the men who were unable to successfully complete her come-too-soon program had wives or girlfriends who did not necessarily want them to last longer.

The following examples are about three different couples where the man came sooner than he would have liked:

Zeus suspected that his wife didn't want him to improve his sexual function and that she would resist helping him do something about it. As it turned out, he was right. His wife didn't particularly enjoy sex, and the faster he came the better. In addition, she didn't want him having sex with anyone else. She assumed that he would be less likely to have extra-marital affairs if his problems remained in tact.

Lancelot was afraid that his girlfriend wouldn't want to invest the time and effort in helping him to last longer. He was mortified to even ask. As it turned out, he was wrong as could be. She was happy (and relieved) that he wanted her help in solving the problem. They took on the problem together, with historic results.

Heathcliff had a secret and didn't know if Catherine would want to help or not. While caring greatly for each other, their sex life had never been a central part of their relationship. After several years, he finally asked for her help with his premature ejaculation, and received an unexpected reply. She told him that she often masturbated after he went to sleep, keeping her sexual needs to herself because she didn't think he was interested. They began masturbating together and started feeling sexually intimate for the first time in their lives. Eventually they worked to solve his problems with premature ejaculation. By this time, Heathcliff he had become such a changed man that not even his neighbors could recognize him anymore.

Rather than bulldozing ahead with the kind exercises that are mentioned in this chapter, why not start by having a couple of long talks about it first? The two of you might do well to talk about your entire sexual relationship and any fears or concerns that you are having.

Also, some of the most annoying aspects of premature ejaculation that women report are the constant apologies and self-deprecation that men express after coming too soon. They say that this whining and bellyaching puts them off. If you decide to work on these exercises together, the man needs to promise that he will no longer apologize or berate himself for coming too soon!

Drugs For Coming Too Soon?

We live in an age when everything from normal fatigue to bad moods are being medicated with anti-depressants and various mood altering drugs. When used prudently, these drugs can be quite helpful and even life saving. However, this guide cautions you against using drugs to "cure" sexual problems when effective alternatives exist. For instance, a lot of men who come too soon can find relief from exercises like those mentioned in this chapter. More importantly, the process itself will help most couples to heighten their mutual trust and intimacy.

On the other hand, researchers are trying to isolate the specific component in a particular anti-depressant which has the side-effect of causing men to last longer. In a couple of years, it may become the Viagra of premature ejaculation. While many men will flock to such a drug, it is questionable if these will ultimately help them become better lovers.

Note: A sex worker who has read this chapter mentions that cocaine is used by some men to keep the penis hard and numb. While this may help them to last longer, she emphasizes that it certainly doesn't make them better lovers. Too often, we forget how satisfying the outcome can be when a man and woman make the effort to work through a sexual problem together rather than going for the magical cure.

If You Went For Years Without Coming Too Soon, And Then...

Some men go for years, or is that come for years, without experiencing premature ejaculation. Then they find themselves coming too soon. If that has happened to you, it is a good idea to get a prostate exam. A prostate gland that is only slightly irritated can make the body think that it is getting more sexual stimulation than is really the case. While less likely, the sudden occurrence of premature ejaculation may also be caused by neurological problems. ⌣⌣⌣

Resources: Helen Singer Kaplan's short little book titled "PE-How to Overcome Premature Ejaculation" is a good resource. If you come too soon, it is a good idea for both you and your partner to read this book. Dr. Kaplan recommends that men do the calibrating exercises by themselves with a lubricated hand until they learn to maintain a level of 5 to 7 for at least five minutes. After a few weeks or months, the woman takes over. During the self-calibration period, the woman can lay besides her man and masturbate, do her nails, read the newspaper, sleep, you name it! As for Dr. Kaplan's book, Brunner/Mazel, its publisher, has given it one of the more stupid covers we have ever seen, with the letters PE in huge block print, as though the average reader knows what PE is. Everyone here said "physical education" and preceded to swap stories about weird PE teachers from high school... Still, this is an improvement over the older cover. Another helpful book is Barbara Keesling's "Sexual Pleasure."

Chapter 45
When Your System Crashes

While this is a chapter on sexual problems, please keep in mind that it's only a brief overview. Hopefully you will find it to be an intelligent and thought provoking overview. At the same time, you are encouraged to read other books on sex that offer a more traditional perspective, and even check with a sex therapist or physician (preferably a urologist) if that seems indicated.

Sex Problems Typically Ascribed To Men

The Bummer In Your Pants

It is amusing to look at the impotence ads in the sports section of various major newspapers. They are usually located next to the ads for hair implants and toupees, above the ads for nude female mud wrestling and sometimes on the same page as the penis enlargement ads. Most of the men in the impotence ads are really old. Does this mean that erection problems are a part of old age, or are these men simply bored limp with the type of sex that they've been having for most of their lives?

Contrary to what the erection ads show, hard-on problems (hard-offs?) happen to men of all ages, from teenagers on up. For instance, it's not unusual for erection problems to occur at the start of a sexual relationship. Call it performance anxiety, call it fear, it's not unusual for a guy to need a couple of weeks or months to find a comfortable groove. Giving him any less time to get it up is silly and short-sighted, as long as your relationship is solid and there is a strong sense of mutual attraction. The real danger is not with the lack of erection, but with what each of you makes of it, e.g. short term problems can become long term problems if the man sees himself as a failure or the woman needs his erection to validate she's desirable.

Several different kinds of erection failure are discussed on the pages that follow — from those caused by physical impairment to those resulting from emotional concerns. Whatever the cause,

hopefully you will be able to utilize these otherwise bothersome moments as a great time for the man to please his partner with his hands and mouth, and as a fine time for her to please him in more ways than by simply letting him stick his penis inside her. For instance, genital massage does not require a man to have an erection, and oral sex can feel just as good on a penis that's soft as hard. On the other hand, some people feel that it's best to focus attention on other body parts whenever a penis stalls out. Perhaps it depends upon the situation and how comfortable you are talking to each other about sex. If you decide to keep stimulating a pokey pecker, make sure it's understood that you are doing so only to give it pleasure rather than trying to squeeze an erection out of it. Otherwise, the guy will feel like a total dud and probably have performance anxiety next time. Also, it's usually helpful if the woman will tell the man that she wants him to get her off in some other way, e.g. by necking for a long time, by hand, with oral sex, with a vibrator or her favorite dildo, or maybe she enjoys masturbating while he watches or holds her. That way, he'll at least feel useful and she'll get her share of sexual satisfaction. And more importantly, a potentially disappointing situation might be turned into something sweet.

Often times, the biggest problem with impotence isn't the lack of erection. Rather, it's a lack of playfulness and resourcefulness on the part of the man and woman when they are confronted with a hard-on that's a no-show.

When Your Posse Won't Ride

Popular books on sex often use terms such as "self-hatred," "self-loathing," and "devastating" to tell us how a man feels when he is — gulp — impotent; you know, the horror that a man goes through when he can't get it up.

Perhaps this guide is way out of step or maybe it's just plain insensitive, but devastating is what happens when your wife or child dies or when you've just been told that you only have six months to live. Self-hatred is what you feel if your business flops or if you've just blown your life's savings. Self-loathing is what you experience when you've just had a major stroke or accident and can't feed or bathe yourself anymore.

Call us callous, call us rude, but we can think of about a thousand things worse than if a man's hard-on takes a hiatus, even if it is forever. Sure, it's frustrating and even humiliating at times, but so are a lot of other things in life. The fact is, you still have your fingers and mouth for giving pleasure, and you still have what's in your heart to love your partner with. And if you can't count at least five things in your life to be thankful for, even if your dick never gets hard again, then your priorities are seriously in bad shape.

Contrary to what you'll read elsewhere, this guide believes that erection problems, regardless of the cause, are an opportunity to have better sex rather than worse. Fortunately, there are plenty of ways that modern medicine can help a recalcitrant penis to get hard, but it seems a shame to employ a quick cure without allowing yourself and your relationship to grow in the process.

A woman who is overcoming orgasm problems has to welcome an entirely new way of embracing her body and her sexuality. It's a journey, a process. And men and women who survive heart attacks and cancer often learn to approach life differently as a result of the disease. Impotent men, on the other hand, just want their dicks to get hard-no learning, no journey.

The Sufis have a saying that you have to let yourself die before you are truly born. Sometimes a guy has to give up his penis as a symbol of masculinity before he can get on with his life.[1] Sometimes he has to realize that there's more to being a man than getting a hard-on, and that there's more to sex than just intercourse. Then he has to convince his wife...

---

[1] Some men who have problems sustaining erections need to do just the opposite — to stop fearing what it means to be masculine and to enjoy a healthy display of their own aggression and masculinity. Such men may have been given the mis-message early in life that to be strong in a sexual way is a bad thing. They may hide their sexual excitement or sexual competence when a partner would delight in a show of strength. They would do well to sport a hard-on with pride!

This is not to say that a man shouldn't inquire about the various remedies that modern medicine has for erection problems. He should also have a full physical to make sure that the erection problem is not a symptom of something else. If there are medical problems, they need to be treated. At the same time, it's worth noting that some medical problems are the body's way of making a statement. Perhaps the man has important lessons to learn about himself and the world around him. If he is able to accomplish the kind of changes and growth that are necessary, and if his partner can grow and evolve in her own way, then maybe he'll start getting hard again. But by then it won't matter as much, because he and his partner will have discovered new ways to give each other sexual pleasure and emotional support.

Note: No kidding about getting a physical exam. Men past the age of 40 who begin to experience a gradual increase in impotence might be seeing the first signs of an impending stroke or heart attack. In fact, studies are now showing that impotence in some men may be an even greater predictor of impending stroke or heart attack than the highly regarded physical stress test. It seems that the arteries in the penis start to gum up before those in the rest of the body. Pursuing it at such an early point may allow the medical profession to give a man the help he needs before something really bad happens.

A More Traditional Approach To The Great Groin Grinch

If you are having hard-on problems, it is likely that you are muttering under your breath that we can take our Sufi logic and stuff it where the sun don't shine. You want a more traditional Western approach. You want a magic bullet that does not require introspection or lifestyle changes. Good enough. The advice that follows is a spoof on a typical sex book approach to fixing erection problems. While it conveys a certain amount of wisdom, it still focuses on fixing the penis instead of helping the man behind it and the woman in front of it. It is an approach that attempts to turn the clock back to a time when the penis worked just fine. It's a regressive fix rather than a step forward, one that is oblivious to lessons that might be learned or frontiers of trust that are waiting to be crossed.

Dear Dr. Goofy:

My bowling partner recently started having erection problems and is too embarrassed to seek help. Can you offer some advice?

Akron, Ohio.

Dear Akron:

If your bowling partner has stopped throwing strikes for more than a couple of weeks, it's a good idea for him to take his poky pecker to a physician for a checkup. It's smart to rule out underlying medical conditions of which his floppy dog could be a symptom. It is estimated that almost 50% of erection problems have physical causes from Diabetes to who-knows what.

One of the things the physician will ask is if your friend is able to get erections at all, like in the morning upon waking, or when he jerks off. He may even be sent home with a device he attaches to his penis when he sleeps at night. While this device won't help get him off (darn) it will measure whether or not he has erections in his sleep and for how long. Doctors figure that if a man can get a sustained erection in his sleep, then the origin of the problem resides in his psyche. However, researchers are now finding that certain types of depression can keep you from getting an erection even in your sleep.

Another thing the physician should carefully check is if your friend is taking any medications that might be cold-cocking his rooster. Medications can range from alcohol and heroin to numerous prescriptions or even over-the-counter drugs. Even Tagamet can do it, honest. Also, a lifetime of cigarette smoking can do the same thing to a man's penis that it does to his lungs and heart. It may also contribute to getting cancer of the penis.

The doctor might also give your friend's penis a shot of something that causes most men to get an erection. Don't worry, it's an itty-bitty wisp of a shot. No one is going to pull out a massive syringe with a hollow nail for a needle and suddenly say "Drop your drawers." If the penis gets hard and is able to stay that way, then the plumbing is probably intact and the problem might be caused by some sort of emotional pain or struggle. It is unlikely but also possible that there is a neurological problem which is somehow disabling the body's ability to begin the hard-on process. If your friend were a car, this might be similar to having a defective start-up motor or when the key is turned but no current is sent.

If the shot does not make the penis hard, or it gets hard but doesn't stay that way for long, then it's likely there is a circulation problem. This can be anything from hardening of the artery (strange term for when it happens in the penis) to leaky valves. More tests would need to be done to peg the exact cause. In the event that surgery is recommended, get a second and even a third opinion.

If it turns out the problem is emotional rather than physical, your friend might consider doing a little private detective work, or detective work on his privates. For instance, what was going on in his life around the time when his soldier stopped marching? Did his ability to get an erection decline gradually, like the fall of Rome, or did it shut down all at once like the Bank of Boston? Was there a change in his job status? Did his insurance company cancel him without cause? Did his team not go the Superbowl because of a lousy call in the closing seconds of the final playoff game? Or did his team used to be the L.A. Rams? Was there a change in his relationship with his sweetheart? Did his wife leave him for another man? Did she leave him for another woman? Was he pulled from an important project, or lose a promotion he had his heart set on? Did he receive an unkind inquiry from the IRS?

Also, it is important to inquire about the quality of his relationship with his spouse. If he is asked about this and instantly says "Naw, it's fine," ask him to describe some of the things that are fine about it. See if he conveys a sense of love and fondness, or if it seems like he is reading the instructions on a bottle of Kaopectate. If the relationship has fallen on — dare we say — hard times, then he and his wife need to focus on fixing that rather than upon fixing his penis which is merely the messenger.

As for curing this kind of penile narcolepsy, your friend and his partner might try to forget all that they know about each other and start over again as if they'd just met. This can be difficult, especially if they have had some really lousy times together. They might try taking a month or two doing things like hugging, touching, and talking, with no attempt at intercourse. They also might try sharing romantic dinners, movies, and the type of things they enjoyed doing when they first met. How about racking their bowling balls and taking a trip around the country in the Winnebago? They might discover that there really is life after bowling. On the other hand, some couples do better when they spend less time with each other. This can be especially true when they are newly retired and suddenly find themselves in each other's face for 24-hours a day. Other couples do really well with the extra time together.

There is also the possibility that your friend had erection problems before he and his wife met. Then he might find it helpful to get some psychological help on his own.

And if none of that seems to help there's this Sufi saying...

The Tour de France In Your Pants

Extensive research is just beginning on the relationship between bike riding and impotence or numbness of the penis. It seems that several thousand men who are serious bike riders may be damaging their penises in the process. Especially unkind are incidences where the foot slips off the pedal and the crotch goes crunch on the bicycle frame. While most bicycle related numbness appears to be temporary, a special surgery has been devised to help those men whose penises have suffered permanent injury. There are now special gel-filled seats that help absorb road shock. This might be a wise choice for the serious rider. One we know of is the Triflex Dual Density seat by Trico.

Viagra

You've heard about Niagra® right? It's the spray that starches your shirts. Well, they've managed to put something very similar into a pill, and instead of calling it Super Niagra, they called it Viagra. Instead of starching your shirts, it starches your schlong. Nuff said?

Our favorite quote about Viagra is from Boston Globe columnist Ellen Goodman:

> "I can't help wondering why we got a pill to help men with performance instead of communication. Moreover, how is it possible that we came up with a male impotence pill before we got a male birth control pill? The Vatican, you will note, has approved Viagra while still condemning condoms."

Viagra had only been released for a month or two before this book's publication. The headlines are full of every little detail, and will be a better source of information than the current edition of the Guide.

A urologist in Colorado suggests they combine Viagra with Prozac and make one little pill that cures everything. Even women are taking Viagra, perhaps to help with their erections too.

Chemicals That Make You Hard

There are a couple of compounds which cause a diehard erection when injected into the penis, assuming enough of the penile plumbing is intact to be able to hold an erection once the penis gets hard. A compound called Papervine was formerly used for this purpose, but that's been replaced by a type of prostaglandin that has fewer side effects. Also, there is a new kind of prostaglandin which the man simply places in his urethra (peehole) a few minutes before he needs an erection. No injection is needed, and the drug seems to work well for erection failures that are more psychological in origin. It is apparently like one of those little fertilizer sticks that you shove in the soil next to your droopy houseplants, only you shove it in your urethra instead. It is possible that other drugs will be available in the near future. Please consult a urologist for more information.

There are other orally prescribed drugs that help some men to get hard. One drug that is sometimes prescribed by urologists is called Yohimbine. Yohimbine is a native tropical of Africa. It can often be found in health food stores. Since the cost of yohimbine isn't much more in prescription form, why not get it from a urologist? That way you will be monitored for side-effects and you will be sure that you are getting the Yohimbine in consistent doses, which is not true for the Yohimbine sold in health food stores. The urologist can also rule out other possible causes of the erection problem. Other drugs for impotence are currently being tested, including some that are administered in cream form, but none have been released at the time of this guide's printing.

Mechanical Devices For Getting Hard

Some men find that the vacuum pump is a useful erection aid. It is a little bulky and cumbersome, but worth a try if you are in search of your lost erection. It might also be wise to try the vacuum pump first before subjecting your genitals to various types of surgery, including implants. What do you have to lose? Urologists are happy to tell you about their surgical successes, but don't expect them to tell you about their failures or show you pictures of penises that have been surgically mangled. While surgery can be very helpful, it's still surgery and it still has risks. See the resources section of this book for Vacuum pump suppliers. Be sure they include special gaskets which keep your scrotum from getting sucked up into the tube.

Surgical Implants

There are different kinds of surgical implants, from semi-rigid shanks to implants with little pumps that you activate when you want an erection. Please research this subject carefully and consult with at least two urologists before making a decision.

Lousy Hang Time — Premature Ejaculation

The term "premature ejaculation" didn't exist in our society before the 1960s. That's when sex researchers realized that a woman might want more than a couple of thrusts during intercourse. Golly.

This book has an entire chapter on the subject of premature ejaculation. It's titled "Dyslexia Of The Penis—Improving Your Sexual Hang Time" It is extremely thorough. You might also read what other books on sex have to say about premature ejaculation. Most have chapters on it.[1]

Problems Of Either Sex

'Gasm Spasm

One of the nice things about being naked together and having sex is getting to experience an occasional orgasm or two. Of course, most couples realize that there are times when orgasms either don't happen or you need to supply your own afterwards. This is so normal that it would be silly to call it a sex problem. On the other hand, there are some men and women who don't orgasm at all, or it only happens when they are alone and not in the presence of a lover. That's what the next couple of sections are about.

Not Being Able To Come With A Partner

Retarded Ejaculation: Some guys ("retarded ejaculators," honest) are able to get hard and have intercourse for hours, but can't reach orgasm. These men might be able to come while masturbating, but

---

[1]Believe it or not, Helen Singer Kaplan wrote an excellent book on this very subject that has the words "Premature Ejaculation" plastered across the cover. In doing research for this guide, your author has borrowed or bought every title imaginable — from "The Classic Clitoris" to "The Kama Sutra." The only book he wouldn't take up to the retail counter to purchase is Kaplan's book with the words PREMATURE EJACULATION written boldly across the front. Come on, Helen, have your publisher rent a brain. **2nd ed. note:** Helen is no longer with us. Hopefully, she's in a better place. And her publisher has gone from the idiotic to the just plain stupid by replacing the words "premature ejaculation" on the cover of Helen's book with huge block letters that say "PE".

not while having intercourse. Men with this sort of problem often try to thrust faster and harder, thinking this will help them come. Unfortunately, this is one of the worst things to do, because after you are at it for a while, thrusting that is hard'n'fast tends to desensitize the penis.

The causes for delayed ejaculation can be many, from concerns about losing control or becoming too vulnerable to an unconscious fear of getting a partner pregnant or somehow causing her damage. Or the problem may be strictly physical and have no psychological underpinnings.

Whatever the reason for not coming, the man is probably not experiencing a full range of erotic sensation. To help change the situation, he needs to focus on experiencing more physical and sexual excitement instead of trying so hard to come. To help accomplish this, his partner might spend time tickling his inner thighs and groin with a feather, silky fabric, her fingers, or lips. The man might also do well to try masturbating with a different grip and lighter touch. A few moments before coming, he should roll over into a position that he usually doesn't come in and finish masturbating to orgasm. Also, if he is able to come when masturbating, he might try alternating hand strokes with intercourse.

In designing a treatment strategy, it is best for a couple to consult books whose focus is on treating sexual problems. Both of you should read the books, so you can talk it over and decide which suggestions are worth trying as opposed to those which would never work. Sex therapy might also be helpful. Some couples have found Barbara Keesling's "Sexual Pleasure" from Hunter House Press to be helpful. Also, if delayed orgasm is a new problem and nothing has changed in the relationship, a man would be wise to consult with a urologist to rule out any possible physical causes.

When A Woman Can Come On Her Own But Not With A Man

Many women don't come during intercourse because there isn't enough stimulation or not the kind they need for an orgasm. Hopefully the man is able to fill the gap with manual stimulation, oral sex, or a big old vibrator. However, sometimes a woman is able to give herself orgasms when she is alone, but can't generate one in the presence of a man even if he's able to stimulate her to near perfection. The reasons for this might be similar to those mentioned for men who can't come with women. Also, some women are so frightened by men or just plain angry at them that they would sooner give birth to triplets than come in a man's presence. Other women aren't hostile but feel there is something about their sexuality that needs to be hidden, or they might feel frustrated or absent in the presence of a man. Therapy can often be helpful if that's what you want to do. There are several good books and a few video tapes on the subject. See "Women's Orgasm Problems" which follows in two more pages.

Problems With Excitement

Some people can't tolerate much excitement. Somewhere along the line they got the feeling that sexual excitement might be dangerous or disorganizing. As a result, they experience all sorts of conflicts when they become sexually excited. One solution they might adopt is to perpetually numb themselves between the navel and knees. Another solution is to destroy desire itself, e.g. to become unaware of sexual excitement in the way that an anorexic is unaware of her body's need for food. That way they don't have to face the antic-ipated dread or catastrophe that sexual excitement holds in their imagination. The good news is, they don't have to go through all the effort and nonsense that horny people do when they feel the need to get laid.

People who want to work through excitement problems should allow pleasurable feelings to evolve slowly and without goals such as having an orgasm. Pressure to feel sexual takes them out of the moment and makes them feel numb. With time and effort, sexual excitement can be tolerated in the here and now, assuming that's what the person wants. Other people might have trouble managing sexual excitement when they are alone, e.g. they can't masturbate or even feel very sexual on their own, but do just fine when they are with a partner. Perhaps they need to experience a partner's excitement about them before they can feel their own excitement.

A Question of Desire

Just because a person doesn't like sex is no reason to view them as being abnormal. Perhaps it's a choice that works well for them. On the other hand, if they are in a relationship with a partner who does like sex, it is worth exploring various forms of compromise. For instance, it might be tacitly understood that the other partner gets his or her sexual needs met elsewhere. Or maybe it's worth considering the situation in therapy.

Sometimes the lack of desire results from problems in the relationship, even if things appear to be wonderful on the surface. Other times a person doesn't want to have sex regardless of who he or she is involved with. Whatever the case, lack of desire is one of the hot new areas among sex therapists. That's because desire is the ante for having sex.

David Schnarch's book "The Sexual Crucible" deals nicely with this and other sexual issues. It's worth struggling through Schnarch's own struggle with the English language to see what he has to say. Fortunately, the lucid parts of the book are the case material, which is very enlightening to read.

Orgasm Fears & Tears

Although orgasms are usually welcome events, this is not always the case. For instance, young girls or boys who are having their first adult-like orgasms might feel that they have done something wrong or broken something inside.

Adults occasionally have mixed feelings about their own orgasms, especially when feelings of sadness or loneliness are triggered by the orgasm. The sadness can sometimes be for a former real-life partner, or maybe the orgasm taps into a deep emotional pain that suddenly gets released. Some people cry after a good come just because it feels right.

There are also people who treat their own orgasms with a kind of cold detachment, especially when they feel a need to masturbate. Perhaps the need for orgasm brings up feelings of weakness or self-loathing. Whatever the case, they are not particularly gentle or tender when handling their own genitals. And finally, there are people who dislike orgasms because they experience them as a form of losing control.

It's a fine testament to the power of orgasm that more people in our society don't have problems with them, given how we tend to be a bit sexually repressed.

Painful Intercourse

This can happen to both men and women, but is more often experienced by women. The causes can be physical or emotional. Also, the problem may have originally been physical, but has since evolved into an emotional struggle.

If you are having pain during intercourse, be sure to check with a physician. Also, try to determine whether the pain is experienced at the opening of the vagina or if it is caused by deep thrusting. Deep thrusting pain can sometimes be caused by constipation or pelvic inflammatory disease. Shallow thrusting pain has a larger range of possible causes, from adhesions under the clitoral hood and episiotomy scars to yeast infections, herpes sores, or vaginal changes associated with menopause.

Painful intercourse might also occur when there is a poor match in sexual anatomy between male and female, but it is more likely that the couple is clumsy or sexually unsophisticated. At this point, most sex books would suggest that the male might be a clumsy lover, but a passive female who accepts a male's clumsiness is just as sexually inept — oops! sexually challenged — as he. Or maybe both partners are trying the best they can, but need a little extra help. Whatever the case, it is the couple, rather than just the man, who needs the help.

Other questions to explore about painful intercourse include whether it happens all the time, how long has it been happening, if it happens with all partners or just one, and if added lubrication helps. Then it might be wise to consult with someone whose expertise is human sexuality. At the very least, read up on the subject in a couple of books on sex problems and see what they have to say. *See the resources section for the "Vulvar Pain Foundation."*

Problems Typically Ascribed To Women:

Women's Orgasm Problems

We caution you about the notion that a woman who can't have an orgasm during intercourse has a sexual problem. Plenty of women don't have orgasms with thrusting during intercourse. This doesn't mean that they have sexual problems. All it means is that both partners need to explore what gets the woman off and include it as part of their lovemaking, unless it happens to be the man's best friend. Then again, some couples enjoy that, too.

Also, some therapists in this day and age automatically assume that sexual problems are the result of prior sexual abuse, especially if the patient is a woman. Yet plenty of men and women who never had a shred of physical abuse still have sexual problems. For instance, being raised in some religious households can cause sexual problems that appear very similar to those of sexual abuse, including the person's feeling vacant, depersonalized or numb when having sex. Such a person might find it extremely difficult to have an orgasm.

For women who haven't had an orgasm yet, the classic reference book remains "For Yourself: The Fulfillment Of Female sexuality" by Lonnie Barbach. Also see page 609 for a list of other books that might be helpful.

Vaginismus — Shutdown

Vaginismus is when the muscles surrounding the vagina close so tightly that they won't allowing anything to go inside. The reaction is sometimes so severe that a woman can't even insert a tampon.

Vaginismus might result from the body holding onto scary memories. it could be from a bad experience that was simply too overwhelming to be fully processed by the mind and is still being held within the body. Such a problem can result from something as acute as rape or as chronic as a messed-up family situation. It might or might not include physical abuse. Also, vaginismus may have a physical origin, such as those listed in a prior part of this chapter under the subheading of "Painful Intercourse."

If you have this kind of problem, try reading up on the subject. There are simple behavioral techniques that can be used to help the vagina to eventually relax. You would also do well to seek out a psychotherapy consultation. Problems of this nature tend to be a powerful statement that the body is holding onto something that needs to be worked through. 🐜 🐜 🐜

End Of Chapter Notes: There are a number of common drugs that can adversely impact your sex life. For instance, Tagamet can be a libido downer. Not to worry about giving it to your teenager when he or she has an acid stomach, but for yourself, consider using Pepcid or Zantac instead. For men or women who are looking for a book to help with Sexual problems, Barbara Keesling's "Sexual Pleasure" can be very helpful and a good place to start. You may not agree with all that she says, but there is much in the book that is worthwhile. On the other hand, her later book, "How To Make Love All Night" sucks the big weenie. Also, Bernie Zilbergeld's "The New Male Sexuality" provides a lengthy but very competent look at guy stuff.

Chapter 46
Sex Laws

Each state has it's own unique set of sex laws. Fortunately, they are seldom enforced—mainly when people are having sex in public places, or when adults are having sex with minors. It's a good idea to be aware that in many states, the government has jurisdiction over what you do when your pants are down.

Sodomy

Most people think that sodomy laws have to do with anal intercourse among homosexuals, or with farmers who have sex with Bossy. Actually, if you are a sexually active man or woman who has never had anal sex, never done a homosexual act, and never transgressed upon the dignity of a sheep, cow or chicken, the chances are still excellent that you have broken a number of state sodomy laws. That's because each state has it's own definition of what sodomy is.

In Maryland if you have oral sex anywhere in the state, including your own bedroom, you have just broken the sodomy law. The same is true for Pennsylvania, unless you are married. In Louisiana, if you and your spouse get caught having oral sex (unnatural carnal copulation), you have committed a felony and could do time in state prison. In Virginia, if a wife doesn't want to give her husband a blow job, all she needs to do is wave her finger in her husband's face and say "Suckin' on that thang is a crime!" She'd be right.

In Washington D.C., it is a felony for anyone to have oral sex. So let's say you live at 1600 Pennsylvania Avenue and you were to engage in oral sex, would you be guilty of a crime?

Fornication

Fornication is generally defined as unlawful sexual intercourse when at least one partner is unmarried. It can also refer to living together without being married. In Florida, it is illegal for an unmarried man and woman to "lewdly and lasciviously associate and

Against The Law
In Florida

Because this
couple isn't
married.

Against The Law
In Maryland

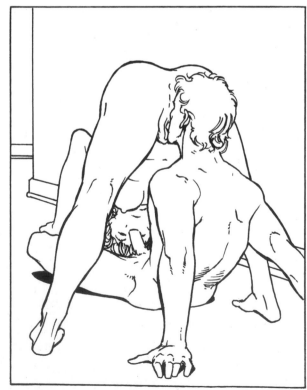

Against The Law   In
Arkansas

Against The Law
In California

But what about
Wyoming?

cohabit together." Interestingly, many of the people who violate this law in Florida are senior citizens who live together but don't officially marry because it would drastically reduce their social security payments. In Minnesota and Georgia, you don't even have to live together to be fornicators.

Oklahoma! Oklahoma!

A man meets a virgin female, they fall in love, he asks her to marry him, she says yes and they make passionate love to celebrate. A few months later, he breaks up with her. This sequence of events is a crime in Oklahoma.

In California, there is a law governing the matter of who gets to keep the ring if you break off an engagement. If he paid for it and she broke it off, he gets the ring back. If he breaks it off, she gets to keep the ring. Just being unmarried and engaging in sexual activities is enough.

Adultery

If you are married and have an extra-marital affair, you have committed adultery.

In Washington D.C., if a married woman sleeps with an unmarried man, they are both presumed guilty. However, if a married man sleeps with an unmarried woman, only the man is guilty. In Idaho, if a married woman has sex with a single man, she has just committed a felony. In Maryland, adultery is illegal, but it is only a ten dollar fine. It is not illegal in Vermont, but it is grounds for divorce.

"Jake, You Beast, Take Me!"

In most states, it is illegal to engage in sexual conduct with an animal. This includes poultry, fish and game. The name of the crime is "bestiality" or "buggery."

Wyoming has no statute that specifically outlaws bestiality. Perhaps it has something to do with those long, cold winters, or maybe they handle it on a local level.

Prostitution

Prostitution is defined as "performing, offering or agreeing to perform any act of sexual intercourse, fellatio, cunnilingus, masturbation or anal intercourse in exchange for anything of value" (Colorado), for compensation (Montana), for pecuniary benefit (Maine), for money or anything of value (Illinois). It's a good thing the law isn't written that way here in Southern California. Much of the entertainment industry would be behind bars.

Polygamy

Polygamy is being married to multiple partners at the same time. This is illegal in all states. However, if you come from a country where plural marriages are accepted and you want to travel with your wives to visit in the U.S., you won't be charged with polygamy. (May we suggest giving each of your wives her very own copy of the Guide To Getting It On?)

Age of Consent

In most states, you need to be eighteen years of age to marry without parental consent. As for having sex, it varies from state to state. In some states, the punishment increases greatly if one partner is three or more years older than the other, while in other states, it is illegal for minors to engage in intercourse at all. If you are under eighteen, or are having sex with someone under eighteen, know your states laws about the age of consent and realize that you can be put in jail for violating them.

Chapter 47

Dr. Dog & The Stolen Toast

Dr. Dog is a collie, and if he has just had a bath and you are standing a half-mile away you might think that he looks like Lassie. Of course, Lassie never spent hours licking his private parts, attacked fleas with a ferociousness that left his own skin bleeding, or took a dump on the sidewalk in front of the Sheriff's station. Another thing Lassie never did is steal toast.

If you offer Dr. Dog a piece of toast fresh from the toaster he couldn't care less. But the minute you are off to answer the phone or are hypnotized by the newspaper's account of how badly your team got beat last night, Dr. Dog grabs the toast from your plate. Legal toast has no appeal to his canine senses, but forbidden toast might as well be sirloin steak.

When it comes to sex, we humans are a bit like Dr. Dog. Sex that has an air of danger or forbidden urgency sometimes gets us excited. In fact, sex that's just a bit dirty or nasty can be downright wonderful for no other reason than the element of erotic suspense.

For sex to be as good as stolen toast, some experts claim that it needs to reveal things about you that were previously hidden — little mysteries of the heart and soul. This is easy the first couple of times, since you know so little about each other. But over the long term it takes love and effort to keep sex sexy. It requires that you keep exploring hidden dimensions within yourself and within your partner.

Carrot Humps Cornelius

Carrot is a 13-year-old Irish Setter who is mostly deaf, arthritic, and until recently sat around all day like a canine couch potato. Then Carrot's owner got a new roommate who started taking Carrot to the local doggie park where dogs of all kinds get to run free and play.

On his first day at the doggie park, Carrot hobbled for a couple of yards and that was it. But after visiting the doggie park every day for a week, Carrot was no longer as invested in the sedentary lifestyle. While not exactly Rin Tin Tin, Carrot began staying on his feet for the better part of an hour. He could even be found following other dogs around, sniffing their rear ends just like the younger pups do. And when Carrot did sit down, it was often in a big patch of mud where some of the bird dogs and Nordic breeds with blue tongues and thick coats liked to lay.

After a few more weeks at the doggie park, Carrot could sometimes be found trying to hump Cornelius, a sweet but lame and stone-deaf Great Dane or "demi-Dane" since some of his Great Dane chromosomes appear to be counterfeit.

For better or worse, Carrot's plight is not dissimilar from what happens to us humans. As many of us get older we tend to sit around without much physical or mental stimulation. (Sorry, but watching TV does not count as mental stimulation.) Then we slowly rot away, just like Carrot had been, and we assume that this is a normal part of aging.

Although a steady diet of physical and mental stimulation won't be enough to keep the Reaper at bay forever, it can help a person to stay vital and productive. Perhaps this is why middle-aged people who work out three times a week often have sex as frequently as couples who are twenty years younger, and physically fit people in their sixties have sex as often as couples in their forties. As for the notion that people automatically have less sex as they get older, a pair of seventy-year-olds who recently contacted the Goofy Foot Press have been swinging sexually with other couples for thirty years. This couple has more sex at their weekend mate-swapping parties than most young newlyweds have all week long. Between Carrot and the Gray Panther Swingers, one needn't fear old age if it's approached with the proper attitude.

An Important Note

In our questionnaires, we asked people to describe their sexual pleasure now versus when they were younger. Whether they were in their thirties, forties or fifties, nearly each and every person said that sex is better now for them than it was in their early twenties. This was just as true for males as females.

Chapter 48
Sex On The Interstate
(One For The Road)

The spirit of America: For some people, there's nothing like cruising down a deserted interstate with one hand on the wheel and the other on their lover's sweet spot. It doesn't matter if you are rich or poor, mongrel or blueblood, this is one time when our motor driven culture nips you in the rear and makes you feel good all over.

For instance, it might be particularly nice when your brain's in a narcoleptic funk from the hilly monotone of Nebraska backroad and your sweetheart slyly grabs your free hand and slips it into the warm wet space between her legs. Or what about when you're driving across the plains of Texas or through the Bonneville Salt Flats and the wind's not the only thing that's doing the blowing?

If you and your partner have a long term relationship the memory just keeps getting better. About ten years after the fact, one of you will occasionally find yourself saying "Honey, remember that time going 'cross Kansas..." and you'll both stop whatever you are doing, smile, and shut out the rest of the world for a precious moment or two. But first, please consider the following...

Winnebegos On The Continental Divide

While it's important to do things that inspire fond memories, it's also nice to stay alive so you can enjoy them. Keeping your bearings on the road while experiencing certain types of physical pleasure is a talent that not all people have or should ever attempt. For instance, it's not something to try if your eyelids clamp shut during moments of sexual bliss or you aren't an excellent driver to begin with. And no matter how much driving experience you have, it's really stupid to be messing around when road conditions require your extra attention, like on a busy freeway or when you're taking a Winnebego over the Continental Divide. On the other hand, just about anything that wakes you up when you're on a rural road might be safer than trying to drive when you feel sleepy. Thousands of people die each year from falling asleep at the wheel. (The best solution? If you find yourself feeling sleepy, get yourself some coffee or pull far off the road and take a nap.)

Perhaps the best use of a car for sex, besides for driving to your sweetheart's house to get some, is when parking at a romantic spot and seeing how quickly you can steam the windows up. People who live in the inner-city often don't have cars, so they sometimes find a favorite rooftop or "tar beach" with a romantic view where they can make love. Just be sure it's not a spot where junkies like to shoot up; you don't want to roll over on someone's hidden apparatus.

Note: We are in no way encouraging you to share sexual pleasures while driving, as it is often illegal and sometimes dangerous. There are safer ways to have sex in your car, although most of these are illegal, too. (Public indecency, lewd acts, etc.)

Sex On The Rail Of The Hoover Dam

Some people like to have sex in public places where other people will see. While this might be a fine form of release for all parties involved, it is not what this section is about. What's being described is that rare moment in life when you and your partner get to make love in a natural setting which is so magnificent that nature's sweet vibration nearly explodes inside of you. What transpires can be so expansive that it's difficult to think of it as just sex — or maybe it's what sex was meant to be before we started living in abominations of nature such as high rises and condominiums.

There are plenty of natural settings where you don't have to be too cautious about getting it on, like in a meadow filled with wildflowers, on a deserted beach, or under a god-sized rainbow in the Montana Big Sky. But there are other equally compelling locations, like dams, bridges, trains, planes, and various national monuments, where a well-honed sense of cunning and mischief are absolutely essential. The following are but a few suggestions that you might find helpful:

⚡ Bug repellent. Don't forget the bug repellent if you are baring your all next to some humid bog or anyplace where the average mosquito would take one look at your naked butt cheeks and think it had died and gone to heaven.

⚡ For sex in public places, it can be more than helpful if the woman wears one of those really full 1950s type of dress or sundress. It's the equivalent of wearing her own private dressing room— she won't need to take a single thing off except for her underwear, unless she's not wearing any.

⚡ If you are doing it at the beach or on a sandy river bed, be sure to take two large blankets. There's something about being on top of two blankets instead of one that helps keep sand from getting inside your crotch. Also, extra lube might help take the abrasive edge off any sand that makes its way inside.

⚡ Sex in water provides its own set of challenges, given how water washes away natural lubrication. Try coating your genitals with a silicone-based lube ahead of time.

Caution: One reader comments, "A close friend of mine went to jail for having sex in public, it was her first arrest and very traumatic." So please be aware that while it's perfectly legal for a couple to have a really loud and nasty fight in public, having sex in public (or maybe even in your back yard) is likely to break all sorts of local, state and federal statutes and might get you arrested. Of course, some people say that the risk is half the fun. ⚡ ⚡ ⚡

Chapter 49
A Goofy Good-Bye

 This is the final chapter of the Guide To Getting It On! It talks about things like hippies, cash flow, meaning, integrity, and then says good-bye.

What Puff The Magic Dragon's Tears Were Really All About.

Back in the 1960s, a small group of hippies suddenly appeared in this country. These hippies didn't think like the rest of us and probably arrived from another planet. The nation became infatuated with them.

After the arrival of the real hippies, there suddenly appeared millions of hippie wannabes. These were often college students who didn't have to work because they were getting money from home. They spoke a great deal about love and peace, but you had the feeling they didn't know much about either. They were also going to save the world from anything that was even remotely like their own mom and dad.

By the time the mid-1970s rolled around, the hippie wannabes started getting degrees in fields like law, business and medicine. Guys started cutting their hair and women stuffed their breasts back into bras, all in preparation for an important American ritual called "the job interview." Words like *marketing* and *standing to sue* took the place of bitchin' and groovy, and designer labels became more important than flowers and beads. Things changed.

Few people had time anymore to hold hands, take walks, or talk about a problem before it became a major crisis. Instead, there was the constant specter of work, often sixty hours a week, with a person's whole life mapped out according to which rung of the law firm or corporate ladder he or she planned on hanging from.

It may seem strange that a book on sex would mention things like jobs and money, but in the course of our lifetimes most of us will fret more over money than love. The people at Mastercharge will probably know more about us than our sex partners do. Yet, no matter

how much money or social status we acquire, we can never leave who we are or what we've become on the floor at the edge of the bed. Sex may be a wonderful thing, but it can't make up for an existence that has little integrity, value or meaning.

A Better Place

There are still a few of us from way back when who didn't abandon our hopes and dreams for a better society. We weren't radical or reactionary, we simply hoped to leave the world a better place than how we found it. This book is an attempt in that direction.

This guide may not have the head rush of good drugs and it doesn't pretend to have many answers. But it is a more advanced view of sex than most of us had when we first started getting it on. Thank you for being patient with its efforts to be more than just another how-to manual on sex.

This book has almost 700 pages, and it still can't define sex. Hopefully you will be able to define it on your own, or at least have a beautiful time trying.

Vaya Con Dios!

Thanks! Thanks! Thanks!

(Jon Westover)^2, Toni Johnson, Morgan & Burce Yarrosh, Suzanne LaPlacette Mike Fischler, Wanda Moore, Veronica Monet, Monte Farrin, Rebecca Wood, Catherine & Peter Gilson, Dixie Marquis, Mike Conway, Karen Saliba, Carol Tavris, Michael Kogutek, Katherine Almy, Richard Curtis, BJ Robbins, Ken Sherman, Bob & Kim Otto, Linda Szymialis, Kristi Walsh, Duncan & Lilly Rouleau, Tom Reynolds, Bill Applebaum, Nancy Reaven, Bruce Voeller, Andre Deuschanes, Meridith Tanzer, Roan, Evan Rapostathis, Janet Snow, Kenny Wagner, Ross Rubin, Barry Richmond Carolyn Andre, Paula Samuels, Daphnicious Delicious Rosewoman-Kingma, Cathryn Michon, Diane Driscoll, Billy Rumpanos, Paula & David Wayne, John Van Dixhorn & Members of The Newport Psychoanalytic Institute, Diana Heiselu, Judy Seifer, Randi Lockwood, Brent Ryder, Breta Hedges, Emily LeBeff, Ken Stubbs, Loren & Steve Kapelo, Laurel Shaffer, Brent Myers, Ron Goosen, Pat Lincoln, Alison Rosenzweig, Michael, Bill, Marty, Joan, Don, Julie, Tricia, Ray, John, Mike Gail, Fred, Lisa, Betty, Eleanor & Cheech (R.I.P.)

Heather Cameron, Paul Rooney, Leslie Davisson, Elise Cannon, Kim Wylie, Sabrina Young, Marcia Loeffler and Ron & all the Reps & everyone else at Publishers Group West, Gary Todoroff-best wishes wherever & whatever, Marty & Dianne Gilliland, Val Littou, Krista Foley, Lee Horn, Gunter, Becky & the gang at Gilliland Printing, Mat Honig at Wells Fargo Bank, Mike Mansel & Eric Ruiter at Argo, Sheryl Palese, Janice Hamilton, Chip Rowe, Rodney Fingelson & Steve Frankiel, Kathy Herdman, Janet at Greenery Press, Jack McHugh, Joe Marzucco, Michael Meller, Todd Seigel & Jessica, Alex Foti, Adam Moore, Avedis Panajian, Pat Patterson, Dana Smart, Peter Stoller, Genanne Walsh, Laura Corn, Harry Gilmartin, Elizabeth Olsen, K.C. "errata not erotica" Rourke, Pam Winter, Bill Brent, Dan Poynter, Mike Conway at Atlas Design, Theresa Benedick, Brandon Klock, Joe Sparling, Carol Queen, Robert,Westwood Kinkos, Lily, Bill & Louie at Sir Speedy, Monte at Input/Output, the staff at Book Soup, How at Kinkos Westwood, Nathan & Bob at Kinkos Ventura, the librarians at UCLA (Biomed, URL & the former Ed/Psych) & LA County Library, staff at A Different Light bookstore (West Hollywood) Brentanos (Century City & Beverly Hills), & Borders (particularly Fawn in

Honolulu) Marty & Craig at First Interstate Bank (R.I.P.), everyone at Holiday Printing, Joe Marsh, the managers and staff at the wonderful Waterstone's Book Store Chain including Matt Comito, Christine, Maura, Jill, Sandy, Dave, Peter, Jay, Doug, Terry, Travis, Ann, Betty, Jane, & Eric Horndog Deville, Jan Nathan at PMA, Victoria Hamilton, Mike Moskowitz, Juliann Popp & Jason Aronson At Jason Aronson, Bill & Berryl Johnson, Lew & staff at Font Shop in San Francisco, Karen Seemueller & friends at Blue Sky in Portland, Pam White, Larry Hedges, Avedis Panajian & Bill Young.

Mr. Verne Graham & Christianna Billman, who provided wise counsel and worked insane hours to get the 2nd edition to press. Bravo!

A very special thanks to Drs. William Erwin & Donald Marcus.

Resources

Centers for Sexual and Health Related Information

Picnic Supplies?

STD Information

American Association for Health Education
Provides information on STD's and other sexual health issues.
1900 Association Drive
Reston, VA 22191
(703) 476-3437

American Social Health Association
An independent organization devoted to the prevention and control of all sexually transmitted diseases.
PO Box 13827
Research Triangle Park, NC 27709
(800) 342-2437(AIDS), (800) 344-7432 Spanish, (800) 243-7889 Hearing Impaired
www.asha.std.org

Center For Disease Control National Prevention Network & AIDS Clearinghouse
Offers prevention information, free written information and local referrals including
financial services and testing.
P.O. Box 6003
Rockville MD 20849
(800) 458-5231
www.cdcnac.org   sunsite.unc.edu/ASHA/

Hepatitis Hotline
American Liver foundation. Provides information, free literature, referrals to support groups and to local liver specialists.
(800) GO-LIVER
www.liver-foundation.org   info@liverfoundation.org

National Herpes Hotline
American Social Health Association. Offers information, counseling and support group referrals.
(919) 361-8488
sunsite.unc.edu/ASHA/

National STD Hotline
Offers prevention information, free written information and local referrals for over 20 diseases, including herpes.
(800) 227-8922
sunsite.unc.edu/ASHA/

Condoms

Condom Resource Center
Nonprofit organization which coordinates and provides condom education and National Condom Week: 2/14-2/21
Men's Support Center
P.O. Box 30564
Oakland, CA 94604
(510) 533-3412

Condomania
The Sears of condom supplies and other fun items to light up your night life.
7306 Melrose Avenue
Los Angeles, CA 90046
(213) 933-7865

351 Bleecker Street
New York, NY 10014
(212) 691-9442

Reality—The Female Condom
Listen carefully for options, ask for a free condom.
(800) 274-6601 ext. 241

Naked & Nude Stuff

American Association for Nude Recreation
Publishes a reference guide to nude beaches and recreation areas, public and private, in Northern America.
1703 N Main Street, Ste. E
Kissimmee, FL 34744-3396
(800) 879-6833 (TRY NUDE)
email try-nude@aanr.com

Educator Resources

ETR Associates
Publishes pamphlets, books, videos and curriculum on sexual health, rape, birth control, STD's, abstinence, HIV and relationships. Call for a catalog.
P. O. Box 1830
Santa Cruz, CA 95061-1830
(408) 438-4060
www.ETR.org

Focus International
Free mail-order catalog of pamphlets and videos. A good resource for teachers. Lots of good information.
1160 E. Jericho
Huntington, NY 11743
(516) 549-5320, (800) 843-0305 Orders, (516) 549-2066 Fax
www.focusint.com   ms@focusint.com

Multi Focus
Large selection of videos, films and slides on all aspects of human sexuality from disease transmission to bisexuality.
1525 Franklin Street
San Francisco, CA 94109-4592
(415) 673-5100, (800) 821-0514

Veronica Monet
Extremely articulate sex worker available to speak on sexuality at colleges and universities. Also makes adult videos and writes intelligently on being involved in the sex industry.
1850 Union Street #1014
San Francisco, CA 94123
(415) 631-7696 Fax
www.een.com/welcome   email: tapdiver@aol.com

Sex Education

Girls Incorporated National Resource Center

Programs and sexual education for girls 6-18. Check website for most up-to-date info or write for a list of available pamphlets.

441 West Michigan Street

Indianapolis, IN 46202

(317) 634-7546

www.girlsinc.org

IASHS (Institute for the Advanced Study of Human Sexuality)

School with a postgraduate degree program in human sexuality studies. IASHS also produces educational pamphlets, books, videos and safer sex supply kits.

1523 Franklin Street

San Francisco, CA 94109

Network: (900) CAN-HEAR ($2/min.)

SIECUS (Sexuality Information and Education Council of the U.S.)

A national, nonprofit advocacy organization that develops, collects and disseminates information, promotes comprehensive education about sexuality and advocates the rights of individuals to make responsible sexual choices.

Contact SIECUS for a list of sexual health clinics and training programs in your area.

130 W, 42nd Street, Suite 350

New York, NY 10036-7802

(212) 819-9770

www.siecus.org

siecus@siecus.org

Circumcision

An anti-circumcision organization, provides helpful info on foreskin health and problems.

NOCIRC

P. O. Box 2512

San Anselmo, CA 94960

Penis Pumping

Osbon ErecAid Classic

FDA approved, $350.00, 24-hour helpline and is available in drugstores or by calling (800) 438-8592.

Rejoyn Vacuum Therapy System

FDA approved, $150.00 and available through drugstores or by calling (888)209-8609

Vacu-tech
www.vacutech.com
Penis pumping, ball pumping and foreskin restoration.
www.newart.com/pump

Phallic Replication

Hard Art
From a simple-to-use, do-it-yourself molding kit, this company will make a statue of your penis in any form or function you desire.
4213 Cromwell Ave.
Los Angeles, CA 90027-1355
(323) 667-1501
www.hardart-phallic.com   info@hardart-phallic.com
Jerry@delosnet.com

General Information

Center for Sex Research, California State University, Northridge
Has an extensive resource center on campus with information on the history of human sexuality from sex laws to cross dressing.
College of Social and Behavioral Sciences
18111 Nordhoff St.
Northridge, CA 91330-8318
(818) 677-3844
www.csun.edu/~sr2022/index.htm

Human Awareness Institute
An organization that produces workshops on love, intimacy, and sexuality.
1730 S. Amphlett Blvd., Suite 225
San Mateo, CA 94402-2712
(650) 571-5524
www.hai.org   office@hai.org

The Kinsey Institute for Research in Sex, Gender and Reproduction
Supports the interdisciplinary study of human sexuality. Pregnant with information including the latest MA & Ph. D. research on subjects related to sex.
Indiana University
Bloomington, IN 47405
www.indiana.edu/~kinsey/

Sinclair Institute
Adult sex education videos. Call for free catalog.
P. O. Box 8865
Chapel Hill, NC 27515
(800) 955-0888

Society For Human Sexuality
Great web site with lots of info and links to almost everything having to do with sexuality: magazines, books, videos, information lines, organizations, conferences, mail-order resources, plus local resources in Seattle, WA and Portland, OR.
University of Washington
SAO 141
Box 352238
Seattle, WA 98195
weber.u.washington.edu/~sfpse

SSSS (The Society for the Scientific Study of Sexuality)
An international organization dedicated to the advancement of knowledge about sexuality
P.O. Box 208
Mount Vernon, IA 52314
(319) 895-8407

Sex Info Lines

San Francisco Sex Information
A free information and referral service that provides anonymous, accurate, nonjudgmental information about sex including reproduction, birth control, safer sex, HIV, gender identity and more.
P.O. Box 881254
San Francisco, CA 94188-1254
(415) 989-SFSI (7374)
www.sfsi.org

Seattle Sex Information
An answer line for any earnest, sex-related question.
(206) 328-7711

Web Site Resources

General Information

American Public Health Association
Deals with sex related issues.
www.apha.org

(CPS) Coalition for Positive Sexuality
A quick and easy online tour through the most important topics for teens who are sexually active or thinking about having sex.
www.positive.org
Healthy Sexuality
As part of HealthGate's Healthy Living series, the on-line publisher has added "Healthy Sexuality," a short, on-line magazine covering subjects such as infertility, erectile difficulty and safe sex.
www.healthgate.com/healthy/sexuality/fs.index.html

InteliHealth
Deals with general health information including information re: sexuality issues.
www.intellihealth.com

Male Health Center
Tons of male-specific health information, including articles on sex, fitness and aging.
malehealthcenter.com

Massage Therapy
This Southhampton University Massage Club is the site for a step-by-step guide to home massage as well as links to massage professionals around the world.
www.soton.ac.uk/~ktakeda

Masturbation Resource Guide
This one-page site lists links to solo-sex sites, guides, forums and products everywhere on, and off, the Internet.
www.viaverde.com/sex/mast.htm

Men's Health Online
Information on all sorts of male health, sex, fitness and lifestyle issues.
www.menshealth.com
Museum of Menstruation
Amazing site on every aspect of menstruation that a woman or man would possibly want to know, including medical updates on the subject.
www.mum/org

National Men's Resource Center
Lists a comprehensive directory of men's services and books.
www.menstuff.org

Nerve Magazine
Up-front, artful photographs, erotic fiction, book & film reviews and essays.
www.nerve.com
Sexuality Database
Extensive collection of articles pertaining to sex.
www.sexualitydata.com

Prostate Information

Chronic Prostatitis
Sponsored by urologist Ivo Tarfusser, M.D.. Treatment information as well as many simple tips to help alleviate discomfort are included.
www.parsec.it/summit/po.htm

Prostate Cancer Information
Features journal abstracts, a support section and database on treatment and side-effects.
www.prostate.com

Prostate Cancer Support
Daily updates on research, full-text medical journal articles, pamphlets and even book chapters from this helpful site. There's also an opportunity to "chat" with other men who have had prostate cancer.
www.shn.net/?c=prc

Circumcision

Circumcision Facts
A helpful site, maintained by Glenn Epps, which includes general information and information about foreskin problems in its "Intact Handbook."
www.gepps.com/circ.htm

Condoms

Condom Country
You can browse through an extensive catalog, complete with photos, or search the index for your favorite brand. Includes advice on use and safety.
www.condom.com/

Condomania
Excellent site for condoms, lube, books, games, etc.
www.condomania.com

Advice Sites

Femme Productions
Run by Candida Royalle, Femme produces erotic videos from a woman's perspective, along with this informative Web site. Online catalog, interactive forums, and the "Ask Candida" advice column.
www.royalle.com

Go Ask Alice
A great website for sex advice and most highly recommended. One of the oldest and most respected sources of sexual information on the Internet. Run by Columbia University Health Service, this site allows you to submit your own question or browse hundreds of previous questions and replies.
goaskalice.columbia.edu

Sex Clinic
This site, run by a therapist, offers advice on having better sex. The confessions section provides a candid glimpse into the difficulties and pleasures experienced by other couples.
www.sexclinic.com

Sexuality Bytes
Illustrated encyclopedia of sex and sexual health. If you need something they don't have, you can E-mail one of the experts for a free confidential consultation.
www.sexualitybytes.com.au

General Books On Sex

101 Nights of Great Sex, by Laura Corn, Park Avenue Publishers, New York, NY 1995 (800) 547-2665.

The Go Ask Alice Book of Answers; For all ages, written by a very, very competent group of health care providers at Columbia University, Henry Holt Publishing, New York, NY 1998, (888) 330-8477.

Good Sex: Real Stroies fromReal People, by Julia Hutton, Cleis Press, San Francisco, CA 1992 (800) 780-2279.

Joy of Sex; by Alex Comfort, Simon & Schuster, NY. NOT RECOMMENDED, Although a perennial best seller, the Joy of Sex is poorly written, heavy handed and contains enough stereotypes to gag a Haitian military dictator. The revised edition has been 90s-ized, which means it has a prozac-like, delibidinized edge that makes it way too uncreative and really, really boring. Thank heavens for the great illustrations!

Mismeasure of A Woman: Why Women Are Not the Better Sex, the Inferior Sex, or the Opposite Sex, terrific book by Carol Tavris, Simon & Schuster, NY 1992.

Romantic Interludes: A Sensuous Lover's Guide, by Kenneth Ray Stubbs, Secret Garden Press, 1986.

Sex Tips for Girls, by Cynthia Heimel, Simon & Schuster, NY.

The Sexuality Library; A wonderful catalog that has all kinds of sex books and erotic literature, (800) BUY-VIBE

Tricks: More Than 125 Ways to Make Good Sex better, Vol. 1 & 2; by Jay Wiseman. If you only find five usable sex tips in each book, that's nine more than you will likely find in the entire "Joy of Sex" (yawn!) A number of interesting, fun suggestions that can help perk up anyone's sex life. Greenery Press, 3739 Balboa Ave., #195, San Francisco, CA 94121, (888) 944-4434, www.bigrock.com/~greenery

The Ultimate Kiss; Although a bit dated, somewhat sexist and too wordy in parts, this is a really helpful book on oral sex, by Jacqueline and Steven Franklin, order from the Sexuality Library, (800) 289-8423.

Say No To Circumcision! 40 Compelling Reasons, by Thomas J. Ritter, M.D. & George C. Denniston, M.D., Hourglass Book Publishing, Aptos, CA 1996, (408) 688-7535.

Books To Help With Sexual Problems

Becoming Orgasmic, by Julie Heiman & Joseph LoPiccolo, Fireside Books, New York, 1988. (They also have a video that's nicely done)

Night Thoughts: Reflections of a sex therapist, revised edition, by Avodah K. Offit, Jason Aronson Publishing, New Jersey, 1995.

Treating Sexual Disorders, Randolph S. Charlton, Ed. and Irvin D. Yalom, Gen. Ed., Jossey-Bass Publishers, San Francisco, 1997.

Magazines & Newsletters

Libido: A quarterly journal of erotic poetry, photography and short stories; To subscribe: (800) 495-1988.

Sex and Health Newsletter

Highly recommended newsletter stuffed full of helpful information. It's also a great conversation starter for men and women about sex.

Sex and Health Newsletter

P.O. Box 7312

Red Oak, IA 51591-2312

(800) 666-2106

Sex Over Forty Newsletter

S/40

P.O. Box 1600

Chapel Hill, NC 27515

SexLife

A magazine geared towards couples in their 20s and 30s. To Subscribe Call:

(650) 968-7851

Family Issues

Child Custody Made Simple: Understanding the Laws of Child Custody & Child Support; by Webster Watnik, Single Parent Press, Claremont, CA 1997, (909) 624-6058.

Real Boys; A most helpful perspective if you are raising boys; by William Pollack, Random House, NY 1998, (212) 751-2600.

Stepfamilies; If you're aboout to blend or have blended, read it. It will help, by James Bray Ph. D., Broadway Books, NY 1998, .

Highly recommended: any books on parenting by T. Barry Brazelton, M.D.

Sex and Disability Resources

Abledata

A huge database of technology, assistive devices, and information.

(800) 227-0216

(AASECT) American Association of Sex, Educators, Counselors and Therapists
Send a self-addressed, stamped envelope for a list of AASECT-certified counselors.
435 North Michigan Ave., Ste# 1717
Chicago, IL 60611
(312) 644-0828 (Voice)

American Board of Sexology
Refers patients to licensed therapists..
1929 18th St. NW, Ste.# 1166
Washington, DC 20009
(202) 462-2122

American Heart Association
Order these pamphlets: *Sex & Heart Disease* and *Sex After a Stroke*
(800) 242-8721

American Cancer Society
Publishes a male and female version of a free pamphlet called *Sexuality & Cancer.*
National Office
1599 Clifton Rd. NE
Atlanta, GA
(800) ACS-2345

Arkansas Spinal Cord Commission
Publishes information sheets on spinal cord injury and sexuality including:
Male Spinal Cord Injury and Fertility, by Shirley McCluer, M.D.
Vibrator Technique for Ejaculation, by Shirley McCluer, M.D., 1992
1501 N. University, Ste. 400
Little Rock, AR 72207
(501) 296-1788

Arthritis Foundation
Publishes a brochure, *Living and Loving,* on arthritis and sexuality.
(800) 283-7800
Brain Injury Association
Ask for articles on brain trauma and sexuality.
105 N. Alfred St.
Alexandria, VA 22314
(800) 444-NHIF

Covenant Rehabilitation Center
Dr. Verdyun is a well-recognized, certified sex therapist dealing with sexuality and disabilities. Published papers address spinal cord injuries and pregnancy.
Walter Verduyn, M. D.
2055 Kimball Avenue, Ste.#120
Waterloo, IA 50702
(319) 234-0109

The Disability Rag
This publication regularly covers sexuality issues.
P.O. Box 145
Louisville, KY 40201
(502) 894-9492

Handicap Introductions (H. I. National Computer Matching)
35 Wisconsin Circle, Ste.# 205
Chevy Chase, MD 20815
(301) 656-8723 (Voice)

ILRU (Independent Living Research Utilization) Program
This information clearinghouse provides a complete list of independent living centers and programs in the U.S. and Canada in their quarterly. Extensive resources on independent living.
23233 South Shepherd, Ste.#1000
Houston, TX 77019
(713) 520-0232, TTY 713 520 5136

Interdisciplinary Special Interest Group on Sexuality and Disability
Basically a networking source for physicians and therapists.
American Congress of Rehabilitation Medicine
4700 W. Lake Ave.
Glenview, IL 60025
(847) 375-4725

It's Okay!
Quarterly newlsetter which explores the world of sexuality and disability.
It's Okay! c/o Phoenix Counsel, Inc.,
1 Springbank Dr., St. Catharines,
Ontario, Canada L2S 2K1.
(905) 687-3630

Lawrence Research Group (Xandria Collection)
Publishes a "special edition" catalog ($4.00) which seems to be their regular products with a few pages tacked on about disability stuff.
165 Valley Drive
Brisbane, CA 94005
(415) 468-3812, (800) 242-2823

National Multiple Sclerosis Society
Ask for a reprint of the *Inside MS* article, *"Sexual Problems Your Doctor Didn't Tell You About."*
205 E. Forty-second St.
New York, NY 10017
(800) 344-4867, (212) 986-3240

National Rehabilitation Information Center and Able Data
Offers the largest library of research, support services and consumer products.
8455 Colesville Rd., Ste.# 935
Silver Spring, MD 20910-3319
(301) 588-9284, (800) 346-2742

National Spinal Cord Injury Association
Publishes some fact sheets on Sexuality & Disability including:
Sexuality After Spinal Cord Injury, Fact Sheet No.3
Male Reproductive Function After Spinal Cord Injury, Fact Sheet No.10
8300 Colesville Rd., Ste. 551
Silver Spring, MD 20910
(800) 962-9629

One Step Ahead: A Newsletter for People With Disabilities, Their Families and Their Friends.
Often contains sex and relationship-related articles.
EKA Publications
P. O. Box 65766
Washington, DC 20035

PeopleNet DisAbility DateNet Home Page
The site serves as a meeting place for people with disabilities and a source of information and sharing.
P.O. Box 897 Levittown, NY 11756-0897
www.idt.net/~mauro   Mauro@idt.net

ProjectLINK

A free service to provide individuals and caregivers with consumer information on finding specific products they require (eg. customized wheel chairs, personal aids, etc.).
Center for Assistive Technology
515 Kimball Tower
Buffalo, NY 14214
(800) 628-2281

Sexuality and Disability Training Center
Publishes the *Journal of Sexuality and Disability.*
Boston University Medical Center
720 Harrison, Ave., Ste.# 906
Boston, MA 02118
(617) 638-7358

Spinal Cord Injury Information Network
Publishes *New Mobility* Magazine and a catalog called *Spinal Network: The Total Wheelchair Book.*
23815 Stuart Ranch Rd.
Malibu, CA 90265-8987
(800) 338-5412
www.sci.rehabm.uab.edu

TASH (The Association For The Severely Handicapped)
29 West Susquehanna Ave. Ste. 210
Baltimore, MD 21204-5201
(410) 828-8274

United Cerebral Palsy Association
A mother organization for local service centers for people dealing with CP.
1522 K Street NW, Ste.# 1112
Washington, DC 20005
(800) 872-5827, (202) 842-1266

Vulvar Pain Foundation
Publishes a newsletter and connects people to support groups.
P. O. Drawer 177
Graham, NC 27253
(336) 226-0704, (336) 226-8518 Fax

Western New York Association for Sexuality and Disability
Information and help for people who are physically disabled; also provides helpful sex information for the developmentally disabled.
c/o Susan Caruso
17 Bellwood Lane
Depew, NY 14043
(716) 878-7015

Wings Convenient Clothing
Catalog ($2.00) of "easy wear-easy care" clothes with front and back Velcro closures. For men and women.
WCC Catalog
Vocational Guidance Services
2239 East Fifty-fifth Street
Cleveland, OH 44103
(216) 431-7800

Sexual Aids For Disabled People

Loveswing
Attaches to the ceiling and elevates one partner above the bed or ground. This allows the other partner to have intercourse with them while standing, or oral sex while sitting up either in a regular chair or a wheelchair. It's actually kind of fun, and is worth a check out for the sexually adventurous able-bodied people as well as the disabled. Swings can also be extremely helpful if you have a sore back or neck and prefer to give oral sex while sitting comfortably. The best and most reasonably priced, swing we have seen is made by a guy in Southern California whose name is Richard. You can check out his website or phone him at: loveswing.com   (888) love-088

Steven E. Kanor, Ph.D.
Finally! A doctor who can retrofit any sexual aid (vibrators, dildos, etc.) to suit the physical ability and disability of the user. Can be controlled by mouth-piece, hand control, etc. without the embarrassment of asking a caretaker for help.
385 Warburton Ave.
Hastings-On-Hudson, NY 10706
(914) 478-0960

Web Site Resources

Doug's Gimp Page
A humorous and helpful site with links and information for the disabled. Also available in large print.
www.primenet.com/~lathrop/gimp.html

Empowerment Zone
Lots of links including a few on sex and disabilities.
www.empowermentzone.com

Polio Survivors' Page
"Page dedicated to those who fought dragons in their youth and now — when the world has grown cold — must fight again."
www.eskimo.com/~dempt/polio.html

Books On Sexuality and Disabilities

Doubly Silenced: Sexuality, Sexual Abuse and People with Developmental Disabilities, by Patricia Miles Patterson, MSSW, Wisconsin Council on Developmental Disabilities, Madison, WI 1991, (608) 267-3906.

Enabling Romance: A Guide To Love, Sex And Relationships For The Disabled; A helpful and encouraging book that covers a wide range of disabilities, by Ken Kroll & Erica Levy Klein, Woodbine House, Bethseda, MD 1995, (800) 843-7323.

No Less A Woman: Femininity, Sexuality & Breast Cancer; Excellent! by Deborah Hobler Kahane, MSW, Hunter House Inc., Alameda, CA 1995, (800) 266-5592.

Reproductive Issues for Persons with Physical Disabilities, ed. Florence Haseltine, Sandra Cole & David Gray, Brookes Publishing, Baltimore, MD 1993, (800) 638-3775.

Sexual Function in People with Disabilities and Chronic Illness: A Health Professional's Guide, Ed. Marca Sipski & Craig J. Alexander, Aspen Publishers, Gaithersburg, MD 1997, (800) 638-8437.

Sexuality After Spinal Cord Injury; by Stanley Ducharme & Kathleen M Gill, Brookes Publishing, Baltimore, MD 1997, (800) 638-3775 .

Women With Physical Disabilities: Achieving & Maintaining Health & Well-Being, Danuta M. Krotoski, Margaret A. Nosek & Margaret A. Turk, Brookes Publishing, Baltimore, MD 1996, (800) 638-3775.

Videos On Sex & The Disabled

Sexuality Reborn
See review in Chapter 43. Available from the Kessler Institute, West Orange New Jersey. Call to order (973) 731-3600.

Untold Desires
See review at end of Chapter 43. This excellent but pricey video is meant to be ordered for group presentations, rental fee $75, purchase price $350.
Filmaker's Library
124 East 40th Street
New York, NY 10016
(212) 808-4980, (212) 808-4983 fax
www.filmakers.com   info@filmakers.com

Pregnancy Information & Resources

Emergency Contraception Hotline

Information on emergency contraception. Gives you names of doctors and hospitals in your area that prescribe emergency contraception. English and Spanish. 24hours/day, 7days/week.

(888) NOT-2-LATE

opr.princeton.edu/ec/hotline.html

National Abortion Federation Hotline

Provides a resource, referral and information source.

(800) 772-9100

www.prochoice.org

Planned Parenthood Federation of American

Offers resources for sexual and reproductive health, birth control, family planning, pregnancy, STIs, HIV, sex education and abortion. English and Spanish. 24hours/day, 7days/week.

(800) 230-PLAN

www.ppfa.org   www.igc.apc.org/ppfa/

Vista Del Mar

A well-respected adoption agency that has been around for years. Mothers admitted have health and living costs covered as well as a say in selecting the adoptive parents. They deal with mothers all over the country and provide free counseling.

3200 Motor Ave

LA, CA 90034

(310) 836-1223

Web Site Resources

Alan Guttmacher Institute

A well laid-out site with contraception and family planning as its main focus. Has contraception information by state.

www.agi-usa.org

Association of Reproductive Health Professionals

Provides newsletter links and information on family planning, HIV, STD's, urogenital disease, menopause, cancer prevention/detection and infertility.

www.arhp.org

AVSC International
Organization that works with over 50 countries around the world to ensure that women and men receive quality reproductive care.
www.avsc.org

National Family Planning and Reproductive Health Association
Provides family planning facts.
www.nfprha.org

Planned Parenthood Resources: Birth Control & Family Planning
www.igc.apc.org/ppfa/lev2bc.html

Presbyterians Affirming Reproductive Options
Presbyterian stance on abortion and homosexuality. More informational than preachy.
www.pcusa.org/info/issues.htm

Religious Coalition for Reproductive Choice
42 national religious organizations are listed in this basically political site which supports the "right to choose."
www.rcrc.org
Resources for Teenage Pregnancy
Provides public health information, statistics, educational resources, photo documentary of two teen mothers and links to other teen help sites.
pegasus.cc.ucf.edu/~feecwg/teen.html

Suggested Literature

ICEA Bookcenter
Clearinghouse for pregnancy resources including books, pamphlets, etc. like *Prenatal Perinatal Massage*
P.O. Box 20048
Minneapolis, MN 55420
(612) 854-8772 , (800) 624-4934

Bonding: Building the Foundations of Attachment and Independence; great book for pregnant moms and dads to read; thoughtful, provocative and informative, by Marshall H. Klaus, M.D., Phyllis H. Klaus, C.S.W., M.F.C.C. and John H. Kennell, M. D., Addison-Wesley Publishing, 1995.

The Girlfriends' Guide to Pregnancy; There are dozens of competent books on pregnancy but this is the only one we know of that has a sense of humor, by Vicki Iovine, Simon & Schuster.

Highly recommended: any books on parenting by T. Barry Brazelton, M.D.

Centers for Crisis Victims

Child Help U. S. A. Hotline
Provides support for children suffering from abuse, neglect, incest and molestation, for adults in crisis and for adults who were abused as children.
(800) 422-4453

National Domestic Violence Hotline
Handles issues relating to domestic violence. Women in domestic situations can call to find out about emergency shelters in their area. Spanish and many other languages.
(800) 799-SAFE, (800) 787-3224 hearing impaired

RAINN (Rape, Abuse, Incest National Network)
(800) 656-HOPE
Victim's Assistance Hotline For Gays & Lesbians
A new non-profit hotline to assist all victims of anti-gay incidents and provide them with a centralized source of information and documentation.
(800) 259-1536

Gay, Lesbian, Bisexual and Transgender Information

Affirmation: United Methodists for Lesbian/Gay/Bisexual Concerns
P. O. Box 1021
Evanston, IL 60204
(708) 733-9590

Anything That Moves
Magazine and Web site
c/o BABN
2404 California Street #24
San Francisco, CA 94115

Bisexual Resource Center
Information and referrals pamphlet: $1.00 with SASE. Publishes *Bisexual Resource Guide.*
P.O. Box 639
Cambridge. MA 02140
(617) 424-9595
norn.org/pub/other-orgs/brc/index.html   BRC@norn.org

BiNet USA, Southwest Region
8601 Zuni #105
Denver, CO 80221-7411

Boston Bisexual Women's Network
Publishes the Bi-Women, bi-monthly newsletter.
P.O. Box 639
Cambridge, MA 02140
(617) 424-9595

EIDOS
Grassroots, free-thinking newspaper for consenting adults.
P.O. Box 96
Boston, MA 02137-0096
(617) 262-0096, (800) 4UEIDOS
eidos4sex@pipeline.com

FTM
Information and peer support for female-to-male transsexuals and cross-dressers. Publishes quarterly newsletter and resource guide.
5337 College Ave #142
Oakland, CA 94618
(510) 287-2646
FTM News@aol.com   www.ftm-intl.org/

Gay and Lesbian National Hotline
Provides information and referrals to over 14,000 gay resources, such as social groups, doctors, businesses, therapists, etc. Also provides peer counseling by trained volunteers.
(888) THE-GLNH
www.glnh.org/

GLPCI (Gay and Lesbian Parents Coalition International)
Provides support, referrals and information to LesBiGay parents and their children regarding custody, insemination, adoption, surrogacy and legal rights.
GLPCIN@ix.netcom.com

Gayellow Pages
Free listings for LesBiGay groups and services of all kinds. Call for a free book or listing.
5200 Montrose Blvd Ste 480
Houston, TX 77006
(212) 691-8960

Homosexuality: Common Questions & Statements Addressed
www.geocities.com/WestHollywood/1348/

International Foundation for Gender Education
Answers questions dealing with transgender issues. Provides information and referrals to local support groups and local therapists specializing in gender issues.
P.O. Box 229
Walcham, MA 02254
(781) 894-8340
ifge@world.standard.com   office@ifge.org

IYG (Peer support for gay, lesbian and bisexual youth)
(800) 347-TEEN

Open Hands
Published by the lesgay group of United Methodists.
P. O. Box 23636
Washington, DC 20026
(202) 863-1586, (202) 488-1423 FAX

PFLAG (Parents, Friend & Families of Lesbians & Gays)
Provides support and referrals for friends and families of gays and lesbians, education for the public and advocacy and support for those dealing with prejudice.
(202) 638-4200, (202) 638-0243 FAX
www.pflag.org/
info@pflag.org

Queer Resources Directory
QRD has over 20,000 files and links about everything queer.
www.qrd.org

Seattle Bisexual Woman's Network
Publishes the North BI NorthWest Newsletter.
P. O. Box 30645
Greenwood Station
Seattle, WA 98103-0645

UUBN (Unitarian Universalist Bisexual Network)
Provides a newsletter, an International Directory of Bisexual Groups and more with $10.00 membership.
P. O. Box 10818
Portland, MN 04104

LesBiGay And Transgender Web Site Resources

Alternate Sources

The only global CD-ROM, directory and Web site search engine for all the alternate sexuality communities. They also publish a directory.

www.alternate.com

Alt Sex

A Web site dedicated to BDSM, homosexuality, bisexuality, polyamory, sexual health and transgender issues.

www.altsex.org

Androgeny RAQ (Rarely Asked Questions)

wavefront.com/~raphael/raq/raq.html

ASTRAEA National Lesbian Action Foundation

Political, social events and volunteer information.

www.astraea.org

Bi Married Men of America

www-personal.umich.edu/~dastony/bmma.html

Sexual Health InfoCenter

A public service of Renaissance Discovery, this Web site has a guide to safer sex, STDs, lesbian/gay/bisexual issues and sexual problems.

www.sexhealth.org/infocenter/infomain.htm

Gay, Lesbian & Bisexual Books

A Different Light Bookstore

Over 17,000 titles for and about lesbian and gay people

· (800) 343-4002

The Black Book; An annual web/phone/media/consumer directory for kink & fetish with all sorts of USA resources listed; ed. Bill Brent, P. O. Box 31155 -GF, San Francisco, CA 94131-0155, (415) 431-0171.

Good Vibrations Guide to Sex, by Anne Semans and Cathy Winks, Cleis Press, San Francisco 1998.

The Other Side Of The Closet: The Coming-Out Crisis for Straight Spouses and Families, by Amity Pierce Buxton, Ph.D., John Wiley & Sons, New York, NY 1994, (212) 850-6000.

The Sexuality Library; Call for a catalog of books on sex & erotic literature,(800) BUY-VIBE

When Husbands Come Out Of The Closet, by Jean Schaar Gochros, Ph.D., Harrington Park Press, Binghampton, NY 1989, (607) 722-5857.

Kink, SM/BD & Alternative Lifestyle Resources

APEX (Arizona Power Exchange)
A non-profit organization that explores consensual BDSM relationships with
respect, caring and dignity.
www.xroads.com/apex/

The Black Book; An annual web/phone/media/consumer directory for kink & fetish with all sorts of USA resources listed; ed. Bill Brent, P. O. Box 31155 -GF, San Francisco, CA 94131-0155, (415) 431-0171.

E-SIG
Special-interest group for enema erotica.
c/o AMTI
P.O. Box 64307
Virginia Beach, VA 23467-4307
(757) 495-2546 Fax
//204.141.230.178/esig-www/pages/info.htm#Index
Wateruv@etzine.com

Lifestyles Organization
Promotes alternative lifestyles and sexuality;
sponsors annual Lifestyles convention.
P.O. Box 6978
Buena Park, CA 90622
(714) 821-9953
Lifestyles@Playcouples.com
www.playcouples.com

North American Swing Club Association
An umbrella organization for many smaller groups, NASCA offers, among many other services, a directory of these swinger's clubs in North America.
(714) 229-4870

QSM

If you're into S&M or enjoy fantasizing about it, get the free QSM catalog.

P.O. Box 880154

San Francisco, CA 94188

(415) 550-7776

info@qualitysm.com

www.qualitysm.com

Sandmutopian Guardian; A high-quality, practical SMBD magazine & website.

The Utopian Network

P. O. Box 1146

New York, NY 10156

(516) 842-1711, (516) 842-7518 (FAX)

www.catalog.com/utopian

Slippery When *Wet*

A 'zine growing in popularity which promotes sex and radical sexuality.

More! Productions

P. O. Box 3101

Berkeley, CA 94703

slippery@net.com

Alternative Books & Presses

A Hand In The Bush: The Fine Art of Vaginal Fisting, by Deborah Addington, Greenery Press, San Francisco, CA (888) 944-4434.

Consensual Sado Masochism: How To Talk About It and Do It Safely; Highly recommended for people into SM, by William A. Henkin, Ph.D. & Sybil Holiday, CCSSE, Daedalus Publishing, San Francisco, CA 1996, (415) 626-1867.

Daedalus Press; call for catalog. Specializes in books on S/M

584 Castro St. # 518

San Francisco, CA 94114

Greenery Press; publishes a number of books on S/M, kink and sexual practices such as vaginal fisting.

3739 Balboa Ave #195

San Francisco, CA 94121

(415) 831-2220, (888) 944-4434, (415) 752-4138 Fax

www.bigrock.com/~greenery

Trust: The Handbook; The classic book on anal fisting, by Bert Herrman, Alamo Square Press, P. O. Box 14543, San Francisco, CA 94114

The Ultimate Guide to Anal Sex for Women, by Tristan Taormino, Cleis Press, San Francisco, CA , 1998, Call for catalog (800) 780-2279.

Some of the top books on S/M: Screw the Roses, Send Me the Thorns, by Philip Miller & Molly Devon, Mystic Rose Books, Fairfield CT; S/M/ 101, by Jay Wiseman , Greenery Press, San Francisco; *Leather Sex: A Guide for the Curious Outsider and the Serious Player*, by Joseph Bean, Daedalus Press, San Francisco; *Miss Abernathy's Concise Slave Training Manual*, by Christine Abernathy, Greenery Press; *The Sexually Dominant Woman: A Workbook for Nervous Beginners*, by Lady Green, Greenery Press; *Kinky Crafts: 101 Do-It-Yourself S/M Toys*, by Lady Green with Jaymes Easton, Greenery Press; *The Bottoming Book: How to Get Terrible Things Done To You By Wonderful People*, by Dossie Easton & Catherine A. Liszt, Greenery Press.

Shopping Guide

Mail-Order Catalogs

Adam and Eve

Mail-order catalog of toys, videos and lingerie.

P.O. Box 800

Carrboro, NC 27510

(919) 644-1212, (800) 274-0333

www.aeonline.com

Behind Closed Doors

Mail-order catalog of toys, books and videos for women.

P.O. Box 93

Woonsocket, RI 02895-0779

(800) 350-3314

ccondon@tiac.net

Blowfish

Mail-order catalog of toys, books and videos. Fun!

2261 Market Street #284

San Francisco, CA 94114-1600

(415) 252-4340, (800) 325-2569

www.blowfish.com info@blowfish.com

Good Vibrations
Run by women -- highly recommend that you get their catalog.
938 Howard Street #101
San Francisco, CA 94103
(415) 974-8990, (800) 289-8423
www.goodvibes.com   goodvibe@well.com

Xandria
A good catalog!
165 Valley Drive
Brisbane, CA 94005
(415) 468-3812, (800) 242-2823

Retail Stores

Ambiance, The Store For Lovers
Retail stores in Ohio of all places, offering toys, books, lingerie and other nasty stuff.
Mentor: (440) 942-4669
Cleveland: (216) 676-0669
North Olmstead: (216) 779-4100
Parma Heights: (216) 885-2001
Shaker Heights: (216) 751-2003
N. West Kanton: (330) 497-4488

A Woman's Touch
Toys, books and safer sex supplies.
600 Williamson Street
Madison, WI 53703
(608) 250-1928
wmstouch@aol.com

Betty Dodson, Ph.D.
Self-loving books and videos, private sex coaching, group training for professionals.
P.O. Box 1933 Murray Hill
New York, NY 10156
(212) 679-4240
bettydodson.com   site@bettydodson.com

Come Again Erotic Emporium
Store and mail-order catalog ($4.00) of toys, books and lingerie.
353 E. 53rd Street
New York, NY 10022
(212) 308-9394

Come As You Are
Toys, books, videos, lingerie.
701 Queen Street West
Toronto, Ontario
Canada M6J 1E6
(416) 504-7934

Condomania
The Sears of condom supplies and other fun items to light up your night life.
7306 Melrose Avenue
Los Angeles, CA 90046
(213) 933-7865

351 Bleecker Street
New York, NY 10014
(212) 691-9442
www.condomania.com

Crimson Phoenix
Retail store of books, toys and novelties.
1876 SW 5th Avenue
Portland, OR 97201
(503) 228-0129

Erotic Cabaret
Lingerie, books, video, massagers, clothes.
1222 Westheimer
Houston, TX 77006
(713) 528-4565

Fantasy Gifts
Lingerie, books, videos, toys, massages oils, gifts, etc.
Minnesota Stores
Bloomington (612) 884 6535
Burnsville (612) 882 0313
Coon Rapids (612) 755-7629
Crystal (612) 504-0428
Fridley (612) 572-1075
St. Paul (651) 665-0622
St. Louis Parks (612) 922-0838
Minneapolis (612) 824-2459
New Jersey Stores
Marlton (609) 596-0676
Turnersville (609) 228-7002
www.fantasygifts.com

Fantasy Lane
Toys, books, magazines, etc.
8016 Atlantic Blvd
Jacksonville, FL 32211
(904) 724-9009

Fantasy Unlimited
Retail store of toys, books, magazines and fetish wear.
2027 Westlake Ave
Seattle, WA 98121
(206) 682-0167

Focus International
Free mail-order catalog of pamphlets and videos. A good resource for teachers. Lots of good information.
1160 E. Jericho
Huntington, NY 11743
(516) 549-5320, (800) 843-0305 Orders, (516) 549-2066 Fax
www.focusint.com   ms@focusint.com

Good Vibrations
Highly Recommended. Books, toys, videos, vibrators, you name it!
Stores:
1210 Valencia Street
San Francisco, CA 94110
(415) 974-8980
2504 San Pablo Avenue
Berkeley, CA 94702
(510) 841-8987

Grand Opening
Retail stores and free mail-order catalog of books, toys and videos.
318 Harvard Street #32
Arcade Building, Coolidge Corner
Brookline, MA 02146
(617) 731-2626
www.grandopening.com   grando@tiac.net

It's My Pleasure
Feminist retail store of toys, books and videos.
3106 NorthEast 64th Blvd.
Portland, OR 97123
(503) 280-8080

Kiss & Make Up
Lingerie, toys, oils, books.
5432 Patterson Ave
Richmond, VA 23226
(804) 285-0326

Lovecraft
Retail stores and on-line catalog of toys, books, videos and lingerie.
63 Yorkville Ave.
Toronto, Ontario
Canada M5R 1B7
(416) 923-7331

2200 Dundas Street East
Mississauga, Ontario
Canada L4X 2V3
(905) 276-5772
www.regesex.com/lovecraft

Lover's Package Retail lingerie, books, magazines, etc.
3959 Martin Way East, Ste. D
Olympia, WA 98506
(360) 456-0997

Loveseason / Secret Pleasures
Retail stores and mail-order catalog ($4.00-good towards first order) of toys, videos, books
and lingerie.
4001 198th Street SW #7
Lynnwood, WA 98036
(425) 775-4502 (800) 500-8843

12001 NE 12th Street
Bellvue, WA 98005
(425) 455-0533

Passion Flower
Retail store of toys, books, videos and lingerie.
4 Yosemite Ave.
Oakland, CA 94611
(510) 601-7750

The Pleasure Chest
Retail store and catalog of toys and clothing.
7733 Santa Monica Blvd
West Hollywood, CA 90046
(213) 650-1022 store, (800) 75-DILDO mail-order
www.the pleasure.chest.com

Romantasy
Retail store and catalog of toys, books and lingerie.
2191 Market Street
San Francisco, CA 94114
(415) 487-9909
info@romantasy.com   www.romantasy.com

Sensuous Things
Lingerie, videos, books, etc.
239 W. Hibiscus Blvd.
Melbourne, FL 32901
(407) 725-3862

Spice Of Life
Lingerie, swimsuits, leather, fetish, etc.
2940 SW 30 Ave Suite #2
Pembroke Park, FL 33009
(954) 458-5200
www.spiceoflife.com

Tasty's Gift Factory
Potpourri, candles, adult novelties, books, etc.
4014 West 96 Street
Indianapolis, IN 46268
(317) 471-8606
Tender Moments

Lingerie magazines, books
4635-3 Coronado Parkway STE.3
Cape Coral, FL 33904
(941) 945-1448

Toys in Babeland
Retail store and catalog of toys, books and videos.
707 Pike Street Check
Seattle, WA 98122
(206) 328-2914, (800) 658-9119
Babeland@aol.com   letters@babeland.com   www.babeland.com

Tres Chic Lingerie
Lingerie, books, gifts, etc.
11902 Jones Road
Houston, TX 77070
(281) 894-8814

Use Your Imagination
Lingerie, toys, books, oils, novelties.
15250 S. Tamiami Trail Unit E1
Fort Myers, FL 33908
(941) 433-0606

The Goofy Glossary

Definitions of Words Pertaining To Sex, Local Culture & Sport

Hmmm... Would this be a CIRCLE JERK or a CALVIN KLEIN UNDERWEAR AD?

AC•DC—1. someone who is bisexual 2.well known metal rock'n'roll band whose members are now really old

ACORN—slang term for the glans or head of the penis

AFTERNOON DELIGHT—1. a nooner 2. sex in the afternoon

AIRHEAD—1.perfect date for a guy who is easily overwhelmed by intelligent women 2. in a discussion on the effects of nuclear winter, an airhead would want to know how the global dust cloud would affect her tan lines 3. song by Thomas Dolby; see "bimbo"

ANAL—refers to anal sex

ANAL BEADS—string of beads that goes up a partner's rear end and is pulled out at the point of orgasm

ANALINGUS—"kissing ass" minus the metaphorical intent; aka "rimming"

ANAL PLUGS—see "butt plugs"

ANDROGYNOUS—1. not clearly masculine or feminine 2. can you name three androgynous rock'n'roll musicians?

APHRODISIAC—1. food, drug or other substance that is given (or taken) to increase sexual desire 2. be wary of anything that is called an aphrodisiac because it is usually people and not chemical concoctions that turn other people on; see "Spanish fly" and "Yohimbine"

ARSE—British for the slang term ass, e.g. "piece of arse" "up your arse"

ASHRAM—1. house or mansion where gurus live 2. important to know in case your sweetheart forsakes volleyball and string bikinis for incense and meditation.

ATROPHY—1. scientific term for "use it or lose it" 2. fear that many guys have concerning their penis, especially when they haven't had sex for an epoch or two. atrophy happens to muscles; the penis, for better or for worse, does not seem to be one. one's penis sometimes gets a better workout from jerking off than intercourse, so if you are worried about atrophy...

BACK DOOR MAN—interesting song by the doors. what's it referring to, anyway?

BAD LESBIAN—1. among politically stiff lesbians, a "bad lesbian" is a gay woman who has sex with a man or fantasizes about it (heaven forbid!) 2. writer Carol Queen attributes this kind of rigid thinking to "the lezzie thought police"

BAG IT—to wear a rubber

BALL—to have intercourse with (past tense is "balled")

BALLS TO THE WALL—1. a state of mind where one powers through a situation with tenacity and guts 2. a semi-equivalent term is "pedal to the metal" 3. origin~the air force.

BANGER—British term for sausage or penis, plural may refer to testicles

BARNEY—person with anemic surfing skills; see "grommet"

B/D—bondage/discipline

BEARD—date or marriage arranged for a homosexual person to make them appear straight. Gay men or women who aren't out of the closet will sometimes have a friend of the opposite sex act as a beard when mom and dad are in town

BEARD BURN—1. inner thigh hazard that women face who receive oral sex from men with five o'clock shadow 2. can be prevented by draping thighs with towels, plastic wrap, or a quick shave on Thor's part

BEAT OFF—slang term for when a male masturbates

BEAT YOUR MEAT—slang term for when a male masturbates

BEAUTY PAGEANT—event where beautiful women get to meet other beautiful women

BEAVER—1. term for someone who attends Oregon State University 2. refers to the female sex oregons 3. great bumper sticker: Eat A Beaver, Save A Tree

BEEFCAKE—1. photos of nude males 2. a nude mall

BEN WA BALLS—1. a pair of metallic balls that are inserted into the vagina for sexual pleasure while rocking back and forth or squeezing the thighs together. more hype than reality since they don't work for most people 2. the ultimate ben wa story comes from the people at Good Vibrations in San Francisco: a woman who had inserted a pair of ben wa balls just before a flight was apprehended by airport security personnel as she tried to pass through the metal detector 3. aka Burmese Bell, which is probably the cadillac of ben wa balls

BESTIALITY—when your sexual partner has four legs and a tail

BELLY—beach talk for "babe"

BIDET—1. an oval-shaped porcelain bowl that is plumbed with a fountain of water over which a woman squats to clean and sometimes stimulate her genitals 2. found in traditional European bathrooms 3. found in few American bathrooms.

BIMBO—1. woman who looks great but falls one or two IQ points short of Albert Einstein; See "airhead"

BIOLOGICAL CLOCK—procreational urge that overwhelms some people between the ages of 34 and 42

BISEXUAL—person who feels varying degrees of arousal for both sexes. aka "switch hitter or ac-dc"

BLADDER INFECTION—1. when a totally obnoxious bacteria with a pain-wrenching kick establishes residency in the human bladder 2. a person so affected would be willing to pawn her great grandmother's wedding ring for a hit of antibiotics 3. is more common in women because the passageway from the bladder to the outside of the body is much shorter, allowing bacteria easier access 4. women susceptible to vaginal and bladder infections should avoid soaps with fragrances, wear underpants with cotton crotches, wipe from front to back, and wash their hands before playing with their genitals. aka "cystitis"

BLIND DATE—aptly named social event; see "loch ness monster"

BLOW—cocaine

BLOW JOB—oral sex that's done on a guy

BLUE BALLS—1. refers to a condition where a male has been sexually stimulated but not to orgasm 2. sometimes actually hurts, and is rumored to cause a blue tint to the scrotum 3. can easily be cured by jerking off 4. at one time was thought to have caused physical damage, but recent evidence does not support this fear 5. get used to it, dude

BODY SHOTS—when doing tequila shooters, you have to suck the salt from whatever part of your lover's body that he or she puts it on, and then suck the lime from his or her mouth. somewhere in between, you down the tequila

BODY MODIFICATION—piercing or tattooing. see "piercing"

BOFF—to have intercourse

BOINK—to have intercourse

BONE —less than gentle term used by less than gentle men in referring to intercourse; e.g. "To bone a babe"

BOOTY—rear end, or can be used in referring to sex

BOTTOM—sexually submissive, s/in term. see "top & bottom"

BOXERS OR BRIEFS?—1. a question every guy ponders at one time or another 2. for a brief treatise on men's underwear and testicular cancer, see chapter 34

BRA HOOK—1. maidenform waterloo 2. no single device known to humankind has caused more guys (and some women) more angst than the hook of the bra 3. apparently, Obewan Kinobe originally taught Luke Skywalker about "the force" in order to help him unhook Princess Leia's bra. Given that they eventually turned out to be brother and sister, it's fortunate for Messrs. Spielberg and Lucas that Leia's bra hook proved even tougher than the force

BREEDER—a gay term for a straight person

BROWN SUGAR—refers to a sexy black lady or to having sex with a black lady

BUFF—1. having well-developed muscles 2. having a chest and arms (guns) that are pumped up but still cut 3. refers to someone who is in great physical shape

BUGGERY—an academic tradition; sodomy that's commonly done to boys and young men who attend boarding schools as well as in other places where men are warehoused

BUM— british for "rear end"

BUSH—slang term for female pubic hair

BUTCH—1. a lesbian who has adopted the male role and run with it 2. an exaggerated form of maleness, a few notches beyond macho

BUTT PLUG—1. diamond shaped object that goes in the rear end to give a feeling of fullness 2. usually made of plastic or silicone with a special flanged end so it won't get lost where the sun don't shine 3. plugs come in different sizes and shapes, some even vibrate, and one is made that is called a triple ripple, honest

CABOOSE—last guy when a woman is pulling a train

CANDY—1. when used as sexual slang, refers to sex or a person who is sexually arousing; e.g. "I want candy" 2. can refer to certain drugs that are snorted; e.g. nose candy

CASTING COUCH—Hollywood term referring to a process where certain directors and producers receive sexual favors in exchange for casting an actor/actress in a movie or TV

CELLULAR PHONE—male equivalent of breast implants, important to display where ever you go

CERVICAL CAP—1. birth control device 2. little rubber beanie that sits on top of the cervix to discourage male ejaculate from entering 3. differs from a diaphragm in several ways: it's smaller, stays in longer, is usually not filled with birth control jelly, and may not be as effective for some people

CERVIX—1. hat rack for a diaphragm 2. the cervix is the bottom part of the uterus. it can be found in the back part of the vagina, the cervix can be as small as a cherry in a woman who has not delivered a baby through her vagina. otherwise, it can be much bigger 3. the cervix might have a different feeling during different times of the month, and usually feels softer when the woman is ovulating, during that time, mucus passes through the cervix opening and bathes the vagina 4. male ejaculate passes through a small passageway in the center of the cervix on its way to do that conception thing

CHAKRAS—1. an eastern concept (Nepal, not New Jersey)—focal points where body energy gets supercharged and passed upward, or so they say

CHERRY—1. virginal or like new 2. hymen 3. maidenhead (in case you read Shakespeare)

CHICKEN & CHICKEN FOX—chicken refers to a boyish looking young man who wants to be picked up and cared for (or purchased) by an older man who is known as a chicken fox.

CHICKS WITH DICKS—person who appears to be a woman in all ways except for the genital region; can be a transvestite, partially fixed transsexual, or hermaphrodite (possessing both a penis and a vagina); in the latter case, the clitoris may have been enlarged prenatally due to a late dose of male-type hormones bathing a female fetus. aka she-he or he-she

CHIGGER—blood sucking little mite

CHLAMYDIA—1. called "the silent sexually transmitted disease" because women often don't know they have it, although men usually have symptoms 2. there are about 3-to 5 million cases each year 3. although often without symptoms, chlamydia can cause sterility and also increases the chances of having an ectopic pregnancy. sexually active people, especially adolescents, should get a test for it every year 4. sexually active women can easily have the test done during pelvic exams. the test is inexpensive and doesn't hurt a bit 5. treatment involves giving antibiotics to both sexual partners, not just the one with the symptoms. otherwise, it won't work 6. you can carry it for years before displaying actual symptoms of the infection

CHOCOLATE—1. one of the few adequate substitutes for really good sex; traditionally used in the wooing process 2. may impact the female body on a physiological level as an anti-depressant, honest to goodness

CIRCLE JERK—when guys masturbate together

CIRCLE JERKS—semi-notorious punk band of the 1980's

CIRCUMCISION (GOYIM)—a routinely performed medical procedure of debatable value, originally done in this country to prevent masturbation.

CIRCUMCISION (JEWISH)—1. "the way a Jewish mother lets her son know who's in charge"—jmw 2. you decide: a profound statement of faith-or-when a father won't stand up to his own father to protect his son 3. what's the harm in allowing Jewish boys to wait until they turn eighteen and are able to phone the moyle themselves? why not let them decide if being circumcised is a way that they want to express their faith?

CLAMPS—see "nipple clips"

CLAP—gonorrhea, one of the old timers in the field of sexually transmitted diseases. can cause burning sensation when peeing or unusual discharge. easily treated, but can do severe damage if not attended to

CLITORIS—Latin for "darned thing was here just a second ago" 1. the only organ in either the male or female body whose sole purpose is pleasure—which from a biological perspective might indicate that the female genitals are more highly evolved than the male's 2. sometimes regarded as the Emerald City of women's orgasmic response 3. not to be approached in haste 4. sometimes wants to be caressed with vigor, other times can hardly tolerate being breathed upon 5. while the clitoris is a fine organ to lavish huge amounts of attention upon, qualities such as tenderness, playfulness and respect also contribute largely to orgasmic response

CLUSTER FUCK—1. army term for when you are in a really bad situation 2. three-way sex

COCK~AND~BALL TOYS— little harness-like assemblies that snap around the base of the male genitals to pull the testicles up and apart, or to pull down on the scrotum. some men hang weights on these things

COCK RING—1. a ring made of rubber or sometimes leather that fits tightly over the base of a hard penis. some also fit over the penis and testicles a bit like a halter 2. the purpose is to help maintain an erection when the mind and body are otherwise unwilling. may also make the male genitals appear larger 3. supposedly holds shut the veins near the surface so none of the penile blood pressure can escape 4. of dubious value 5. don't wear one for more that 20 to 30 minutes without taking it off for a few minutes. otherwise you may risk permanent damage

COITUS—scientific term for sexual intercourse, taken from the root word "coit" which is a carpet and drapery cleaning business in Northern California

COKE WHORE— person who is so strongly addicted to cocaine that he or she will do anything (or anyone) to feed the habit

COLORED CONDOMS—1. just so you'll know, some of the color pigments used in colored condoms might be carcinogenic, and others may leave permanent stains on your skin 2. if you want to change the color of your penis, why not take it to Earl Sheib and get it dipped in acrylic?

COME—to have an orgasm

COME CUP—1. device that attaches to the head of a vibrator and fits over the glans of the penis 2. use lots of lube, dude

COMING TOO SOON—when a male sexual partner has lousy hang time; aka premature ejaculation

COMPUTER BULLETIN BOARD (BBS)—all kinds of interchanges via computer modem—e.g. specific bbs to download porn, have conferences, get dates

CONDOM—1. fancy name for a rubber 2. a rubber by any other name is still a rubber 3. only jerks brag about having to wear extra-large condoms

CORNHOLE —1. to have anal sex 2. the slang origin probably arose because dried corn cobs are sometimes used in the place of toilet paper; not to be confused with the term "cornhusker" (can you name the cornhusker state?)

COTTONTAIL—term that nude sunbathers sometimes use for people who wear bathing suits; see "textile"

COWPER'S GLANDS—tiny structures near the urethra inside the base of the penis. produce the clear silky drops of fluid known as "precum." see "precum"

CRABS—1. what people often see on Card 10 of the Rorschach (ink blot) test 2. funky little lice-like creatures that hang out on body hair (pubic or otherwise). can sometimes make you itch to the point of near insanity 3. reason for turning bright crimson when your pharmacist yells all the way across the store "Harvey, can you show this young person where the shampoo for crab lice is located?" 4. washing your pubic hair and external genitals with alcohol (70%) will likely zap the crab lice, although it may sting somewhat

CRAMPS—1. rock'n'roll band whose cult hits include "What's Inside A Girl", "Bikini Girls With Machine Guns", "Can Your Pussy Do The Dog", and "Don't Eat Stuff Off The Sidewalk" 2. what women sometimes get during their periods, the intensity of which can sometimes be diminished by orgasms

CRANK—1. speed (methamphetamine) 2.nasal decongestant propylhexedrine, often used to get a quick rush

CROSS-DRESSING—when a person of one sex makes a serious attempt to dress like a member of the other sex—and we're not talking about a woman simply wearing her boyfriend's shirt or boxer shorts

CRUMPET—1. British term for sexual activity. 2. piece of arse? 3. bakery product

CUJONES-Spanish for "balls"

CUM (COME)—male ejaculate, white sticky stuff that usually squirts out of a penis during male orgasm, much of which is produced by the prostate gland 2. most males average about a teaspoonful of cum per ejaculation 3. varies in consistency and sometimes taste among different guys

CUNNILINGUS—1. "cunnus" is Latin for vulva (the part of a woman's genitals that are on the outside) and "lingere" means to lick—put'em together and figure it out for yourself 2. has any living human being ever used the term "cunnilingus" outside of an academic setting, except of course, for telling the renowned "Connie Lingus" jokes?

CUNT—1. from the Latin "cunnus" (meaning vulva), a somewhat harsh term for women's genitals, but is currently being used in feminist literature in a positive way 2. a derogatory way of referring to a woman

CUP—1. plastic device that manly guys wear to protect their genitals from potential calamities like dick-high line drives, bad hops, or catching for pitchers who throw screwballs and split finger fastballs 2. there are now two styles of hard cup, and a cup made of softer material for sports with less severe contact. the old style of hard cup is somewhat pear shaped, while the new style is banana shaped—reflecting changes in the shape of male genitals since the women's movement of the 1960s. both types of hard cup are held in place by a special type of supporter 3. wearing a cup over shorts (briefs, boxers etc.) may help it feel less strange; for instance, a friend of this guide who has been a baseball catcher for more than twenty-five years wears an old style cup in a supporter over his briefs, and then puts on a pair of lycra sliding pants (a little like bicycle shorts) to hold it in place better

CUPID'S HOTEL—vagina

CURVED DICK—1. there are some penises that curve as they get hard, most likely due to a tight ligament, this is perfectly normal unless it causes physical pain, in which case it should be taken to a physician for consultation 2. since some guys with curves feel self-conscious, consider the following pearl of information: one highly experienced woman told this guide that the best sex she ever had was with an Italian guy who had a curved penis 3. if you've got a curve, experiment with different intercourse positions that might provide an advantage over guys who don't have a curve. especially effective might be a position that allows the head of your penis to massage the roof of the vagina

CUT—1. a guy who has been circumcised 2. weightlifting term for muscles that have great definition

CYSTITIS—see "bladder infection"

DANCING WITH MYSELF—1. see "masturbating" 2. great song by Billy Idol

DATE—without this event, men might never cut their toenails

DEADHEAD—1. a grateful dead groupie. 2. what you do to flowering plants to keep them blooming

DIESEL DYKE—1. manly lesbian, "bulldyke" 2. opposing term is "lipstick lesbian"

DEPILATORY—cream for removing body hair

DIAPHRAGM—1. cross between a condom and a frisbee, maintaining the flexibility of the condom and aerodynamics of the frisbee 2. contraceptive barrier device that holds contraceptive jelly against the opening of the cervix

DIAL~A~PORN—1. phone sex at the rate of $2.00+ a minute 2. masturbation enhancement device for those who like their stimulation over the phone 3. male equivalent of an eating disorder; aka "dial-a-fuck"

DICK—1. male equivalent of the clitoris, urethra, vagina and inner labia. 2. person who is being a jerk

DICK- HEAVY COMPANIES —businesses where the bosses are men and the secretaries (oops! assistants) are women

DIEN BIEN PHU'D—("phu'd" sounds like food) 1. getting your butt kicked; e.g., "our football team got Dien Bien Phu'd last night by the Twin Peaks Beaver

2. town in North Vietnam where the French were soundly defeated in 1954. the 72-day siege on Khe Sanh during 1968 nearly became America's Dien Bien Phu **DILDO**—1. penis-shaped object which a woman puts into her vagina for sexual satisfaction 2. not to be confused with a vibrator, which is a mechanical humming device usually placed on the outside of a woman's genitals rather than being inserted 3. can be worn in a harness and be used as one would an erect penis 4. term for a person who is being a jerk or moron

DILDO HARNESS—1. jock-strap like device that a dildo attaches to 2. gives a dildo penis-like properties of suspension and thrustability

DOCKING—1. when an uncircumcised male pulls his foreskin over the head of another man's penis 2. no reason why it can't be pulled over a woman's nipples, assuming she's into that sort of thing

DOGGIE STYLE—1. intercourse from behind, not to be confused with intercourse in the behind 2. more popular than the missionary position in some parts of the world 3. often results in better stimulation of the vaginal roof, which some women prefer

DOOBIE—a joint

DO THE WILD THING—to make love

DOUBLE BAGGED—to wear two condoms at once

DOUBLE DILDO—dildo that seats two

DOUBLE PENETRATION—1. penises in the vagina and rear end at the same time 2. two penises in the same vagina at the same time

DOUCHE BAG—1. gravity driven device for feminine hygiene 2. uncomplimentary term for a woman or gay man 3. women who douche three times a month are three times more likely to develop pelvic inflammatory disease than women who don't douche at all

DRAG—when a man wears women's clothing

DRAG QUEEN—1. man who dresses and behaves as if her were a woman 2. can sometimes be differentiated from transvestites because a drag queen is usually attracted to men, whereas a transvestite tends to be more heterosexually oriented 3. drag queens tend to be a bit more boisterous than either transsexuals or transvestites. when you are in a room with a drag queen you often know she's there

DRESSED TO THE RIGHT OR LEFT—guys who wear boxer shorts have to make a very basic decision in life: on which side of the fly to rest their genitals. this is no big deal (sorry) unless you get your Wranglers tailor made, in which case the tailor will inquire "sir, do you dress to the right or to the left." he will then leave extra denim on whichever side you indicate

DRY HUMP—1. traditional sport of young couples, especially at Italian wedding receptions, where pubic regions are feverishly rubbed together while both participants are fully clothed 2. can result in severe chafing, irritation, orgasm, or all three, aka frottage

D/S-domination/submission

DYKES ON BIKES—a type of all-girls motorcycle club

DYSFUNCTIONAL—is this the most overused word in the English language? does it have any meaning anymore? would the world be any worse off if no one used the term "dysfunctional family" for the next ten years?

EAT OUT— neat oral thing that a man (or woman) does to a woman; see "muff diver," "go down on" and "cunnilingus."

ECTOPIC PREGNANCY—1. pregnancy where embryo implants into the wall of the fallopian tube instead of the uterus 2. a very dangerous condition which can result in maternal death

EIGHTY-SIX'D (86'd)—1. put out of commission 2. left behind 3. dropped 4. term used in restaurants to signify that they are out of a particular menu item, or when the item has been pulled from the menu because it has caused at least three customers to throw-up before reaching the parking lot 5. can also refer to someone who is being thrown out of a bar or restaurant

EJACULATION—1. the big squirt 2. usually accompanies orgasm in the male and sometimes follows orgasm in the female

ELBOW GREASE—brand of lubricant often used for anal sex, well known in the gay community

ENURESIS—1. peeing in your sleep 2. happens to almost as many girls as guys and can last until adulthood 3. a really lousy thing to have, sometimes very difficult to shake

EPISIOTOMY—1. an incision made in the bottom of a woman's vagina to increase its size so she can deliver a baby without tearing herself 2. the delivery room equivalent of "we've got to destroy this village in order to save it" 3. in America, up to 90% of first time mothers are given episiotomies; in the Netherlands, only 20%-30% of first time mothers are given episiotomies. there is speculation that American doctors don't understand the second stage of labor and sometimes mismanage deliveries. On the other hand, if it's a 9 lb. baby.

EROTICISM—state of tension fueled by sexual desire, resolved through sexual contact that quenches at least some of this desire

EUNUCH—guy without balls, literally

FAG HAG — woman who hangs out with gay men, claims to be heterosexual, but seems to fear sexual intimacy with straight men

FAYGELEH—yiddish term for gay male

FANNY—in Britain, a vulva or vagina, in America, a rear end

FEEL UP—to touch or stimulate a partner's genitals with your hand

FELCHING—licking male ejaculate out of whichever orifice it's been shot into, usually done by the male who put it there

FELLATIO—1. from the Latin "fellare" which means to suck 2. oral sex as performed on a male; blow job

FEMALE EJACULATION—with extra stimulation, some women squirt fluid from the urethra as part of having an orgasm

FEMORAL INTERCOURSE—1. when a lubricated penis slides back and forth between the labia like a hot dog in a bun, but is not stuck inside the vagina. 2. also refers to intercourse with the thighs being used as the vagina

FEMME—feminine looking lesbian as opposed to a diesel dyke. "lipstick lesbian"

FETISH—1. when a person relies on a particular prop (leather, rubber, underwear, shoes, etc.), body part (feet, hair, breasts, etc.), or scenario to get themselves off sexually 2. the prop can be fantasized or exist in actuality 3. one philosopher has described "fetish" as a hungry person sitting down at a dinner table and feeling full from simply fondling the napkin

FIST FUCK (FISTING OR HANDBALLING)—placing a fist into the rectum or vagina, honest

FLAGGING—practice in the gay community where one signals the kind of sexual acts he likes with a specific color of handkerchief that he tucks in his back pocket

FLAPPER—term used to describe a sexually liberated woman during the 1920's who flaunted her nonconventional approach to life

FLOG THE LOG—masturbate

FORESKIN—1. male equivalent of the clitoral hood 2. flap of skin that extends from the shaft of the penis over the glans (head) to keep the latter moist and safe 3. gets chopped off during circumcision

FORNICATE—intercourse between people who are not married

FRAZIER—1. manliest lion to ever live in captivity, once had intercourse more than 160 times in less than 3 days 2. died shortly thereafter

FRENCH—term for oral-genital contact, not to be confused with "French kiss," (however, one often leads to the other)

FRENCH KISS—1. kissing with mouths open as opposed to closed 2. usually involves transfer of tongues (in the nonbiblical sense)

FRENCH TICKLER—any form of condom that has little bumps, projections on it, ridges, marketed to increase a woman's sexual pleasure. maybe it works for French women, but not for anyone we know. instead of buying French ticklers, spend the extra money on flowers and you'll both be happier

FRENULUM—extra-sensitive part of the penis just below the head on the side of the shaft that faces away from the abdomen

FRIENDS IN LOW PLACES—1. wonderfully expressive (ok, totally kick ass) song written by Dewayne Blackwell and Earl Bud Lee and performed by Garth Brooks 2. musical balm for the lovelorn; if the live version doesn't help to get you out of a funk, seriously consider anti-depressants 3. by the way, the wildly successful Mr. Brooks worked at a Nashville shoe store while every record label passed on his demo tapes. ("reality is no friend of the dreamer" says he.) what tricksters the fates can be

FRIG—British for jerk off

FROTTAGE—see "dry hump"

FUCK BUDDY—friend or acquaintance who you occasionally (or often) have sex with. while the sex might be serious, the relationship isn't

GANG BANG—when a woman has intercourse with several men in rapid succession, at her invitation as opposed to gang rape which is sexual assault, aka "pulling a train" 2. it's interesting how a man who has sex with five women in the same room might be considered a stud, lucky, or at the worst wild and reckless, while a woman who has sex with five men in the same room is considered trash and risks being given a psychiatric diagnosis or at the very least is called a nymphomaniac

GANG BANGER—member of a street gang

GANG OF FOUR—1. the name of a very solid post-punk rock'n'roll band 2. Jiang Qing, Wang Hongwen, Yao Wenyuan, and Zhang Chunqiao. if you don't know who they are, look up the "gang of four" in an encyclopedia, it won't do you any harm

GANG RAPE—when several men rape a woman, demonstrating incredible cowardice and supporting the notion that we humans reside on a limb far from the top of the evolutionary tree

GENDER-BENDER—someone of one sex who is in the process of becoming the other or alternates between the two

GETTING OFF—coming or having an orgasm; aka getting your rocks off

GIVE HEAD—to perform oral sex, can be on a woman, but the term is often synonymous with blow job

GLANS—head of the penis

GLORY HOLE— hole in the wall into which a man sticks his penis to have it indiscriminately sucked, or through which one person spies on the other; primarily gay

GO DOWN ON—to perform oral sex on a woman

GO-GO DANCER—ask your grandparents

GOLDEN SHOWERS—1. when peeing becomes a sexual turn-on, aka water sports 2. a tree of the legume family, native to India, whose Latin name is cassia fistula.

GONAD—1. sex gland 2. dweeb

GOOFY-SPOT—see "g-spot"

GREEK—anal

GROMMET—1. a rookie surfer who often substitutes gumption for intelligence, and hyperactivity for poise; aka groin, surf rat, or weed 2. surfing mag reports that sex is a matter of great concern and mystery for the young groin: "what does one do?" "for how long?" "is it all right if I don't get completely naked?"

GROUP SEX—see "swinging"

G-SPOT—1. controversial place on the roof of the vagina named after the lucky man (grafenberg) who claims to have discovered it

G-STRING—oh, about a quarter of a bikini bottom

GUSHER—term for when a man has an orgasm at the same time that his prostate is being massaged. some men say it feels spectacular

JOHN THOMAS—British term for penis. "to frig your John Thomas" is a redundant phrase, "playing with your john thomas" is cricket

HANDBALLING—see "fist fuck"

HAND JOB—to bring either yourself or a partner to orgasm with your hand

HAND WARMERS—Australian term for breasts, perhaps explaining something about the way Australian men regard Australian women

HARDBODY—person who is in great physical shape

HEART—1. that which contains all love, caring, passion, tenderness, happiness, courage, loyalty, gentleness, awe, hope, beauty, feeling, play, laughter, trust, charity and joy 2. an important thing to have

HERMAPHRODITE—1. a rare condition when nature allows a baby to be born with both male and female sex organs 2. sometimes caused by an unintended bath of androgen (male-type hormone) during pregnancy. can result in a vagina whose clitoris has grown into a fully developed penis (pseudohermaphrodite) 3. in modern times the parents are offered the choice of which sex they want to raise the child. the medical community then backs up the decision with surgical and/or pharmacological interventions 4. in spite of what your friends say, you're probably not, but think of the possibilities if you were.

HERPES—virus that affects the mouth and/or the genitals with a rash, lesions, or chancre sores. it is usually harmless when hibernating, which is most of the time, but occasionally surfaces with a vengeance, it hibernates deep in the nerves that surround the mouth and/or genitals. avoid sex without a latex barrier when there are active herpes lesions, because that's when it is usually transferred back and forth from the mouth to the genitals, mouth to mouth, or genitals to genitals. however, it is possible to get it when there is no apparent lesion. if you have herpes, spend time reading up on it and learn as much as you can; that way you become the master of it rather than it becoming the master of you. (there's a national organization; call your local planned parenthood or sex- related clinic for information)

HERSHEY HIGHWAY—refers to anal sex

HICKEY—1. love bite 2. for some, a cause of embarrassment and reason to wear a turtleneck no matter what the weather, for others, a sign of desirability.

HIT A HOME RUN—to have intercourse

HOLMES—1. homeboy 2. gang talk for "dude"

HONKY—a white person

HOOCH—1. illegal liquor 2. a hut or shack, often where a prostitute lives

HORNDOG—a male whose reputation for sleaziness precedes him

HORNY—1. the sexual urge 2. refers to a situation where "she's got to have it" (hi tracy!) or he's got to have it

HUMP—the way a poodle or dachshund often greets the arm or leg of an unsuspecting human. see "dry hump" and "frottage"

HUNG—a male with large sex organs

IMPOTENCE—when a guy can't get it up on a regular basis

INCEST—sex among immediate family members who are blood relatives

IRIE—1. rasta or reggae term meaning cool, relaxing, calm and collected 2. how you hopefully feel after making love

JACKING OFF—rubbing your genitals in a way that causes pleasant or wonderful sensations, generally resulting in orgasm

JACK'N'JILL PARTIES—1. gatherings of sexually uninhibited men and women who attend in their underwear and masturbate in front of each other 2. by-product of concern about aids.

JADE STOCK—Buddhist term for penis

JANEY—lesbian slang for vagina

JELLY ROLL—jazz term for female genitals

JERKING OFF—see "jacking off"

JOANI 'S BUTTERFLY—a small vibrator that can be strapped in place for use during intercourse or when out on the town

JOCK STRAP—jog bra with only one cup

JOHN—someone who pays a prostitute for sex, aka "trick"

JOHNSON—Old fashioned slang term for penis

JUNKIE—1. a heroin addict 2. anyone who's infatuated with someone or something, not necessarily a negative term

KEGEL EXERCISES—1. genital aerobics—when you squeeze or contract the muscles surrounding your genitals in a way that would stop the flow if you were taking a leak. 2. some people claim that these exercises will fix everything from a floppy penis to an uninspired vagina, research results do not support these claims, however the exercises can be useful in becoming more aware of genital sensations, and some people say they result in stronger orgasms

KILLER PUSSY—1. rock'n'roll group who sang the cult classic hit "Teenage Enema Nurses In Bondage" as well as "Pepperoni Ice Cream," "Pocket Pool" and "Bikini Wax " 2. how guys occasionally refer to a vagina that feels extra wonderful 3. how guys occasionally refer to steamy looking women

KINDNESS—perhaps the greatest sex aid of all

KINK—doing what others only think about

KINSEY AVERAGE—1. oh, about two and a half minutes 2. the amount of time sex researcher Alfred Kinsey estimated that it takes the average American male to come during intercourse, because of increased public awareness, the Kinsey average has probably increased in the last 30 years, perhaps even doubled

KNICKERS—1. undergarments worn by your great, great grandmother 2. what your great great grandfather dreamed of getting into

KNOCKED UP—pregnant

K-Y JELLY—1. a brand name of a water soluble lubricant that a lot of people use to help increase the all important slip—slide coefficient during intercourse, especially when using a rubber 2. the first generation of water soluble lube, you might like some of the newer ones better 3. if it starts to dry out during use, add a few drops of water or saliva, not more KY

LEFT HAND—what a right-handed person sometimes uses to masturbate with to help it feel like someone else is doing it

LESBIAN—woman who prefers sex with women

LESBO—straight term for lesbian, can be derogatory, equivalent to saying fag

LIBIDO—what Freud said is the fuel for our desire to make an emotional connection with others

LIFESTYLES ORGANIZATION—1. large organization for couples who like to have sex with other couples (thousands of couples belong), based in Anaheim, California, pride of Orange County (you know, home of God, Country, Chapter 13, and Swinging!) 2. if you went to one of the weekly dinners or dances sponsored by this organization, you would think you were among a group of police (husbands and wives) or teachers 3. interestingly, a large number of police and teachers really do belong

LINGAM—sanskrit term for penis

LIZARD—someone who tries to move in on your sweetheart when you're not there

LOCHNESS MONSTER—1. a rather frightening mythical creature of Scottish origin aka: nessi 2. sightings of the lochness monster are sometimes reported by men and women who have just returned from a blind date

LONG FLANNEL NIGHTGOWN—1. very effective birth control device worn by American women 2. the cadillac of flannel nightgowns used to be made by lanz®

LOPPY TUNA—surfer term for women's genitals, first coined between Redondo and Hermosa beaches

LOVE-a special and precious way that we have of relating to one another

LUCKY PIERRE—a gay or bisexual term, referring to 3-way sex; lucky Pierre is the man in the middle. so what about lucky Giselle?

MAGIC WAND®—Hitachi's laptop for women, has two speeds, a big round head, and vibrates like a federation freighter at warp 9

Why the 1960s phrase "MAKE LOVE — NOT WAR"
never had a chance?

MAINLINE—1. to shoot up a drug (injection into the vein) 2. great way to get fatal diseases

MAINTAIN—a level of behavior one attempts to achieve when dealing with parents, teachers and officers of the law

MAN'S SHIRT—1. object of male clothing which girlfriends often lay claim to and love wearing, especially to bed 2. the very feel and smell of it gives the lovelorn woman comfort 3.any man who had a similar attachment to a piece of woman's clothing would be called weird or kinky

MASHER—1. rather insensitive perpetually horny male who gets physically closer than the situation calls for2. a term used in playing marbles.

MASOCHIST—a person who invites pain and passively controls others in the process; a bottom or submissive

MASTURBATION—a date with your own genitals

MATANUSKA THUNDER FUCK–Term used in Alaska, Matanuska being a region in Alaska known for its herb production.

MENAGE A TROIS—(sounds like "men-aj-ah-twa") 1. when three French people are sharing sexual intimacy 2. includes either two men and a lucky woman or two women and a lucky man

MERCY FUCK—intercourse done from a sense of duty or pity rather than burning desire

MILE HIGH CLUB—to have had sex in a plane

MISSIONARY POSITION—1. intercourse position where the man and woman are horizontal and face to face, usually with the man on top 2. term coined by savages who associated this position with conquering missionaries 3. too much of this position may lead to a boring sex life

MONILIA—type of vaginal yeast infection that can be very uncomfortable for the woman. can cause thicker discharge than is normal, extreme itching, and painful intercourse

MONS PUBIS—fleshy mound at the top of the vulva from which pubic hair grows

MONTGOMERY NODES—1. little bumps that often form on the nipples after puberty, especially prominent when you feel a chill or are sexually aroused.

MORNING AFTER PILL—1. pill which can be taken the next day following unprotected intercourse which greatly reduces the chances of becoming pregnant. call your physician 2. an alternative if you discover that the rubber broke

MOTHER FIST AND HER FIVE DAUGHTERS—British masturbation term referring to the hand. The equivalent American term is Rosie palm and her five sisters

MUFF DIVER—someone who enjoys oral/genital contact with a woman

NEWMAN, ALFRED E.—1. goofy guy emeritus, joining Bullwinkle the Moose and Larry, Moe & Curly as major childhood influences for many a male and some hip females 2. hopefully Mr. Newman appreciates his location in the goofy glossary between "muff diver" and "nipple clips"

NIPPLE CLIPS—1. variation of a roach clip that is placed on each nipple as part of sex play 2. used by people who like to have their titties tweaked 3. applies varying degrees of pressure, depending on the type of clip used 4. there are clip styles, clamp styles, and even electrified nipple clips, as well as those that vibrate 5. some people like them on their labia or scrotum 6. B. Cohen, formerly of the LA Weekly, claims to use then as sweaterguards. aka "nipple clamps"

NOCTURNAL EMISSION—wet dream

NONOXYNOL-9—1. active ingredient in most contraceptive foams and jellies that renders the male ejaculate infertile by changing its ph (acid—base balance) 2. if used with rubbers may help control the spread of aids and herpes 3. not recommended for teeth brushing, but if you happen to swallow some during oral sex you're not going to die or anything.

NORDIC COMBINE—refers to members of the other sex who are fair—haired, blue—eyed, and physically gifted; term coined by author Dan Jenkins

NSU—non-specific urethritis common infection of the urinary tube

NUCLEAR—1. intense 2. massive release of energy 3. orgasmic

OCT (OPTIMAL COME TIME)—1. when a guy lasts long enough during intercourse to please both himself and his partner 2. a guy with good hang time

ONANISM—refers to masturbation, named after the bible's onan who spilled his seed (pulled out and came)

ON THE RAG—to be menstruating; before tampons and sanitary napkins were invented, rags were used to catch menstrual flow

OUTING—a vicious process where gays publicly expose gays who aren't out of the closet, supposedly to show the straight world that some of its biggest heroes and stars are really gay

PACKING—1. codpiece for genderbenders 2. when a woman who is cross-dressing as a man wears a penis shaped object in her pants to make it look like she is well hung 3. worn by some male rock'n'roll singers 3. more realistic when made of a soft material rather than silicone. (a good packing device does not make a good dildo)

PANDERING—pimping

PANTY LINER—extra large tampon that's been flattened out like the insole of a shoe, has stick'um instead of string, and is worn on the outside of the body rather than inside

PAPAVERINE— drug injected into the penis which causes it to get hard

PEDERAST—older male who has sex with boys or young men; aka "chicken fox"

PEEING WHILE STANDING—1. a wonderful ability that nature (combined with cultural habit) bestowed upon men and denied women 2. particularly useful while in theatres, stadiums and other places with crowded or filthy restrooms

PEEING WITH A HARD-ON—1. a misery inflicted on the human male nearly every morning, though much worse when he's young 2. a very difficult act to achieve, since the passageway to the bladder is closed off when a male gets an erection (see the definition of "waking with a hard-on" for why) 3. phenomena that originally caused Buddhists to invent meditation, with the earliest mantra being "lord, let this hard-on subside before my bladder bursts"

PELVIC INFLAMMATORY DISEASE (PID)—inflamation of the female reproductive organs, often the fallopian tubes, usually caused by a bacterial infection.

PERINEUM—1. demilitarized zone of the human crotch 2. the area between the asshole and genitals in men and women 3. Zen types get all weak in the knees when talking about the perineum, which they consider to be quite sensitive

PHILISTINE— smug, jock-like jerk with a bad attitude

PIERCING—1. term that refers to placing a pierced earring, safety pin, or facsimile through a person's nose, lip, nipples, navel, genitals or anywhere else that skin grows   2. piercing enthusiasts might enjoy reading the "piercing fans international quarterly." ask at your local library 3. people into piercing are often into tattoos as well. see page 234

PINK PEARL—pink, bullet-shaped vibrator made to be inserted into the vagina

PIT JOB—intercourse using the arm pit as vagina

POCKET POOL—rubbing of the testicles brought about by the invention of pants with pockets

POLYMORPHOUS PERVERSE—kinky

POONTANG—word of dubious origin that refers to a woman's genitals or what one hopes to get from them

POPPERS—1. sold over the counter as a liquid air deodorizer, poppers were originally made of amyl nitrate (which is for heart patients). then the formula was switched to butyl nitrate because the amyl formulation could no longer be legally sold over the counter. when butyl nitrate was outlawed, popper makers switched the formula to a type of isopropyl alcohol which is fairly dangerous, but legal nonetheless 2. poppers are very popular in the gay community 3. popper vapors are inhaled immediately before orgasm with the resulting sensation described by some as amazing and totally indescribable 4. one problem with poppers is that the current formulation can kill you if you have hidden heart problems. some people feel that popper usage might weaken the immune system, but there's no research on the matter

PRECUM—slick, silky, clear drops of fluid that drip out of the urethra of the penis when it is very hard and very excited. most people assume that this is nature's own form of k-y jelly, however, nature seems to have had something else in mind. urine, which frequently travels through your urethra, is acidic. this is not good for the more alkaline parts of your ejaculate that cause conception. precum helps to deacidify the urethra and make it more slick so your ejaculation will be even more likely to get your girlfriend pregnant. see "cowper's glands"

PREPUCE—foreskin

PRIAPISM—1. a hard-on that won't quit. not a good thing. so you will know, having an erection for 3 to 4 hours straight without it going down can result in permanent damage. while this is not a common occurrence, emergency room visits should be planned accordingly 2.named after Priapus, son of Dionysus and Aphrodite, god of male reproductive power

PRODUCER—1. person who controls movie and TV projects in the entertainment industry 2. older men who often sleep with actors/actresses who are half their age 3. has much power in an industry where just about anyone will sleep with anyone to realize their celluloid dreams 4. producers who are principled, kind and actually creative are to be truly appreciated

PRINCE ALBERT—a type of body modification (piercing) where a ring is put through the urethral opening of the penis and comes out the underside of the shaft. (dare we say "ouch?")

PROSTATE—1. weird walnut-shaped gland located on the floor of a man's rectum nearly a finger's length up his bum 2. it's what generates about 30% of the fluid that comes out when a man ejaculates 3. contracts seconds before orgasm, resulting in an exquisite feeling 4. gets bigger with age 5. sometimes becomes inflamed and can even crimp the urethra making it difficult to pee. (prostatitis) 5. some men (straight, gay—it doesn't matter) enjoy the feeling that results from having the prostate massaged. others would sooner be caned than let someone stick a finger up their rear, see "gusher"

PSA—1. what southwest airlines used to be called. 2. abbreviation for "prostate specific antigen" which tends to be elevated in men who have prostate cancer. they can check your psa when doing a blood test.

PUDENDA—anatomical term for women's genitals (vulva); from the Latin word "pudere" which means to be ashamed

PULLING A TRAIN— see "gang bang"

PUNANNY—rasta or reggae term for sex; "I wan' punanny!"

PUSSY POSSE—vice squad

PUSSY WHIPPED (PW'D)—a mental illness whereby the male hovers, grovels and begs in excess of what is normally required to have sex

PUSSY WHIPPER—a sexual partner who is very controlling and rarely satisfied. she often wishes aloud that her man would be more aggressive, yet would annihilate him the second he dared

QUANTUM—major

QUIM—British for vulva or vagina

RANDY—Australian term for horny

RAPE—1. sexual bodily assault 2. because the developmental arrest is so profound and the capacity for empathy is so diminished, rapists rarely seek out psychotherapy or respond to it. there are men who are capable of committing rape and an hour later going home to have what appears to be normal sex with their suburban wives, most rapists don't view their acts as being criminal or brutal, and are apt to justify themselves by saying that the woman wanted it, needed it, or deserved it

RAPE FANTASIES—1. when a person is aroused to images of being raped, but would never want it to happen in real life 2. the "rapist" in rape fantasies is often a person who the "victim" would very much like to have sex with anyway.

RASTA—1. short for rastafarianism, a religion originally from Jamaica, with the belief that Africa is the promised land and that former Ethiopian emperor Haile Selasie was the messiah 2. having to do with reggae and reggae music.

REAM JOB—to have your anus licked. aka "rim" "rimming~~ "ream" 2. what a conscientious plumber does to the inner lip of any pipe that he or she has just cut.

RETARDED EJACULATION—When a guy's sexual hang time is so long that nobody cares.

RETROGRADE EMISSION—1. when an ejaculating penis backfires. caused by either prostate problems or when a guy who's jerking off clamps the end of his penis shut **note:** an important reason why Kleenex and toilet paper were invented was so guys could have something to shoot their wad into when masturbating. 2.restricting the flow from a penis when ejaculating can cause severe plumbing problems and should only be done in the most dire of circumstances, unless you want to end up at the doctor's office doubled over with pain having to answer some really embarrassing questions

ROAD ERECTION—unwanted wood having nothing to do with sexual thoughts. can happen any time a guy is sitting in a vehicle that vibrates (bus, car, tractor, etc). it is caused by a combination of the vibration which sends extra blood into the penis, and sitting which tends to shut the veins that carry blood out of the penis

ROID RAGE—unpleasant mood states that occur in some people who take steroids

RIMMING (RIM JOB)—kissing ass, literally

RUBBERS—common name for condoms. origin: before the invention of latex, condoms in this country were made of vulcanized rubber

SANGER, MARGARET—(1883-1966) famous birth control advocate at a time when dispensing information about birth control was illegal in this country

SAPPHO—poetess on the island of Lesbos noted for her use of nonphallic imagery

SAFE WORD—in bondage, a special prearranged word or expression that the submissive partner (bottom) can say to the dominant partner (top) which means to stop.

SCHLONG—jewish term for penis

SCUM BAG—1. condom 2. term for someone you don't like

SEVEN-OF-NINE—human thinking may be illogical, human reasoning may be flawed, but human crotches collectively swell when this piece of borg perfection becomes one with the screen. assimilate/ejaculate/resistance is futile. (so who's resisting?)

SEX BEFORE THE GAME—1. refers to masturbating or having sex less than twenty-four hours before a major sporting event 2. Mirkin & Hoffman in their "the sports medicine book" have looked into the topic and found there's no correlation between sex before the game and decreased athletic performance. they report that in a recent olympics one athlete had sex approximately one hour before the event and won a gold medal, another Olympian had sex right before his event and ran a sub four-minute mile. Mirkin & Hoffman quote Casey Stengal on the matter: "It isn't sex that wrecks these guys, it's staying up all night looking for it." 4. masturbating or having sex before a game might help you feel more relaxed or energized—it's strictly a personal matter.

SEX DREAMS—nature's way of making sleep more interesting

SEX ON THE BEACH SHOOTERS—1. on the west coast, a drink consisting of vodka, peach schnapps, o.j., and cranberry juice 2. on the east coast, a drink consisting of melon liqueur, raspberry liqueur and pineapple juice. how did this happen?

SEXUALITY—an altered state of mind that's often quite enjoyable. usually includes varying degrees of erotic or sensual feeling

S.F. JACKS—1. somewhat notorious men's jerk off club in San Francisco 2. a by-product of extreme horniness, a desire to socialize, and concern about aids 3. sympathies to the janitor

SHAKE'N'BAKE—to make love; do the wild thing

SHAVED—see "slick"

SHE-HE (OR HE-SHE)—see "hermaphrodite"

SHORT ARM INSPECTION—1. military term for examining an enlisted man's penis 2. supposedly for the detection of VD.

SHORT HAIRS—refers to pubic hair

SHOT MY WAD—ejaculate

SHRED-surf & skateboarding term, means to excel

SHRED BETTY—a woman who excels at what she does, particularly in volley-ball, surfing and frisbee tossing

SIXTY-NINE (69)—1. when a man and woman perform oral sex on each other at the same time. 2. when French people do 69 they call it "soixante-neuf."

SIZE QUEEN—1. a woman who likes guys who are hung like elephants 2. a guy who likes guys who are hung like elephants

SKANK—person who is short on physical and social graces

SKIN FLICK—porno film

SLAM—a really bad wipeout

SLICK—1. refers to genitals that have been shaven, often to accommodate various forms of bikini design 2. some people enjoy the look and feel of being slick as a sexual turn-on

SLIT—British for vulva

SLOPPY SECONDS—intercourse when you are not first in line

SLOW DANCING—1. event that sometimes causes guys to get erections, especially during the teenage years 2. when girls congregate in the women's restroom during dances, do they tell each other things like "it felt like Billy got hard while we were slow dancing" or do they limit themselves to mundane stuff like "this new bra is killing me"?

SMEGMA—cheesy stuff that forms beneath the foreskin and under the hood of the clitoris

SNAP ON TOOL—1. brand name of various types of wrenches, sprockets, and power tools 2. slang term for a dildo that some women wear in a harness and use as if it were an erect penis

SNATCH—see "beaver"

SODOMY—anal sex; see "buggery"

SPANDEX—that which gives bikinis their zing

SPANISH FLY—1. alleged aphrodisiac made from powdered blister beetles, causes severe irritation of the bladder and urethra (peehole), and can be very toxic. women have died from it. the effect is not dissimilar from drinking draino 2. giving her roses and a foot rub will get you much further and won't endanger anyone's health

SPECTATORING—a term used by sex therapists to describe what happens when a person is worried or obsessing about his or her sexual performance instead of just being able to enjoy it; sometimes experienced by women who can't reach orgasm or by guys who can't get it up

SPLASH CONCEPTION—Geting pregnant from doing anal sex without a rubber, when the male ejaculate oozes out of the woman's rear end and drips into her vaginal. Are people conceived in this way doomed to have anal personalities?

SPUNK—British term for male ejaculate

SPRUNT—1. feminine hygiene deodorant spray. a useless and sometimes harmful product foisted on the American public by corporate marketing types who exploit social fears. 2. what women use who are either misinformed about feminine hygiene or feel that their genitals are dirty

STUD—someone who is manly without effort, sometimes a derogatory term

STUD MUFFIN—1. a woman, sometimes of amazonian proportion, who takes absolutely no guff from anyone 2. some misguided souls confuse the term and use it in refering to a "hot" male

STYLIN'—lookin' good

SURFING—to have sex with waves

SWEET DEATH—literary term for intercourse

SWINGER—husband or wife swapper

SWINGING—often refers to group sex or private parties where couples go and have sex with different partners

SWITCHES—people into s/m who enjoy alternating between top & bottom roles

SWITCH HITTER—bisexual, ac-dc

TAMPONS—cotton plugs that are placed in a vagina to collect menstrual flow

TAR BEACH—1. mainly an east coast term, refers to a rooftop where people do things like sunbathe, grow plants, make out or shoot up drugs

TEDDY—woman's lingerie that is a combination of tank-top and panties, sometimes snaps at the crotch, usually made of silk, lace acetate, or leather

TEXAS TWO-STRAP—highly regarded brand of dildo harness

TEXTILE—term that nude sunbathers sometimes use for people who wear bathing suits. see "cottontail"

3RD DEGREE CLEAVAGE—1. refers to breasts that are quite large 2. some guys salivate over 3rd degree cleavage, some couldn't care less, and some are more aroused by women with petite breasts 3. a good personality and solid heart are usually sexier than big boobs, unless you are trying to get a job mud wrestling at the Tropicana. unfortunately, a lot of flat-chested women don't understand this and develop complexes or get surgical implants

THREESOME—sex with two women and a man or two men and a woman. see "manage a trois"

THRUSH—vaginal infection caused by candida or monilia fungus. men can also get it, but not in the vagina

TIENANMEN SQUARE—1. a place in China where democracy recently took it on the chin 2. a powerful reminder that governments can and do turn upon their own people, pointing to the need for a vigorously enforced system of checks and balances, and a well-protected bill of rights, do you know what those rights are here in America? how many state governments have the right to jail people for sexual acts that we perform in our own homes as mutually consenting adults? is your state one? is oral sex between married heterosexual couples legal in all states? check again

TIPPED UTERUS—1. a woman's uterus is usually parallel to her spine, a uterus that is tipped points somewhat towards the back 2. depending on the severity of the tipping, the ability to conceive can be affected; the ability to wear a diaphragm can also be affected 3. has little or no effect on sexual enjoyment

TIT—FUCKING—when a well-lubricated penis is thrust back and forth between a woman's breasts

TOP & BOTTOM—1. a top is someone who prefers doing and a bottom is someone who prefers having it done to them 2. in domination or bondage, the top is the master, mistress or dominator, the bottom is the servant, submissive, or slave 3. in anal sex, the bottom is the one who prefers being the receiver (split end)

TOUCH UP-British term for doing another person by hand

TOXIC SHOCK SYNDROME—rare and sometimes lethal infection sometimes associated with tampon use

TRAINING BRA—training wheels for the chest

TRIBADISM—when two women rub their vulvas together, resulting in exquisite sexual pleasure, or so they say

TRICK—1. customer of a prostitute; aka "john". 2. sexual act as done by a prostitute, e.g. "turn a trick"

TROPHY WIFE—physically stunning woman who appears to be the ultimate entertainment industry or corporate wife. the relationship between a trophy wife and her husband is best described as consensual parasitism. trophy wives are often involved in charities for dying children, when they are not messing up the minds of their own. it would be a mistake to throw all trophy wives into a neat, predictable group of status & security seeking barracuda. some trophy wives are complex people, capable of displaying levels of feeling besides just abusing maids, caterers, florists,and gardeners. trophy wives can be downright hospitable, especially if you are able to help their husband's career. sexually speaking, it's possible that some trophy wives do feel sensation between their legs, but this is frowned upon because allowing true sexual feelings might result in making sloppy decisions when selecting a mate. trophy wives view wealth, power and security as the ultimate orgasm, as do the men who bed and wed them

TUBAL LIGATION—female sterilization where the fallopian tubes are surgically sealed off

TWINK– young gay guy

UNCONTROLLABLE URGE—a powerful phenomenon that overwhelms the senses, cannot be ignored, and will only pass with the help of a loving partner, vibrator, or caring hand

UNCUT—not circumcised

URGE TO MERGE—horniness, sometimes with a romantic edge

VAGINAL MOISTURIZER—as the former lover generation hot flashes its way into the next century, we will be seeing more and more special potions that get squirted into dry vaginas to help make them slippery. aka slip'n'slide

VAL—1. San Fernando Valley (southern California) version of a bimbo or airhead, unique in that this particular species of bimbo has evolved its own tribal dialect perhaps caused by the added weight of lip gloss and braces, or it is possible that tanning booth rays and string bikinis combine to adversely effect the speech center of the human brain 2. begs the question of whether children should be allowed to hang out in places called The Galleria 3. immortalized in song by Moon Unit Zappa and icon dad Frank

VANILLA SEX—what people into S/M call sex that doesn't include S/M

VASECTOMY—snip, snip

VASELINE— that which melts rubbers (latex condoms) 2. should never be used as a sexual lubricant either with or without a rubber, as it interferes with the vagina's ability to self-clean. 3. the reason Vaseline melts latex rubbers is because both are made of petroleum by-products. the Vaseline acts as a solvent and dissolves the latex rubber

VERTICAL REENTRY—1. difficult but important surfing trick which involves coming out of the wave and doing a skateboard-like maneuver to get back into it 2. similar maneuver is called for during intercourse when a guy pulls out too far

VIBRATOR—electrical device which makes some women very, very happy

VIBRATING SLEEVE—1. soft, tube-like device with a vibrator in the end which men stick a lubricated penis into 2. masturbation device

VOYEUR—someone who enjoys watching other people undressing or having sex

VULVA—1. the external female genitals 2. people often say vagina when they are referring to the vulva 3. what you're looking at when you cop a beaver shot

WAD—male ejaculate

WAKING WITH A HARD-ON—here are three reasons for why guys often wake up with hard-ons, take your pick, mix and match, or invent your own: 1. during r.e.m. (dream) sleep males usually get hard-ons and females' genitals swell and lubricate, since we humans have a much greater proportion of dream sleep towards the morning, men frequently awaken in the morning with r.e.m. related hard-ons 2. when a male has an erection the prostate gland swells. this blocks off the entrance to the bladder and forces a man's ejaculation to squirt towards the outside of his body instead o1 backfiring into his bladder. nature may give an erection to a sleeping man with a full bladder to keep him from wetting his bed. it's also why a guy has to lose some of his erection before he can start peeing once he's awake 3. many males awaken with elevated levels of male sex hormone in their blood, while this doesn't necessarily make them any hornier, it's possible that it contributes to the tendency to get hard-ons in the morning

WANK—British term that means to masturbate

WANKER—name that the Queen of England calls Andy and Charlie when they are being lazy or bad

WANK MAGS-British term for pornographic magazines

WANNA BE—1. pretender 2. person who tries to act like someone or something that he or she isn't 3. people with a good sense of self don't need to be something that they're not

WATER SPORTS—see "golden showers"

WEENIE—a dweeb

WEST HOLLYWOOD—the darnedest little place, where totally buff construction workers wear earrings under their hard hats and actually mean "cat" when they say "pussy"

WET DREAM—slang term for sex dream; isn't totally accurate because people have sleep orgasms without ejaculating

WET SPOT—1. a mixture of male and female sexual fluids, which results in a wet patch on the mattress. 2. couples sometimes go through very complex and often totally irrational negotiations to determine who sleeps on the wet spot

WHACKING OFF— see"jacking off"

WHITE MAN'S DISEASE—when a person has absolutely no sense of rhythm

YANG—male essence, according to eastern religions

YEAST INFECTION—1. group of party-hearty fungi (yeasties) that live in warm, wet places like in vaginas and between toes. 2. when environmental conditions get out of balance,the yeasties go nuts, causing major discomfort

YIN—female essence, according to eastern religions

YOHIMBINE (OR YOHIMBE)—tropical plant from Africa used to help men get erections

YONI—sanskrit for female genitals

ZIPLESS FUCK—quick meaningless intercourse, term coined by Erica jong in her book "Fear Of Flying"

Examples of Slang In Other English Speaking Countries

United Kingdom:
England, Scotland, Ireland
ARSE—rear end
ARSE OVER TIT—head over heels
ARSEHOLE—asshole
BENDER—gay male
BOLLOCKS—testicles
BUM—rear end
BUN IN THE OVEN—pregnant
FANNY—female genitals
FRIG—female masturbation
GAGGING FOR IT—horny
GIGGLE BANDS—garters
HAVING IT OFF—intercourse
JOHN THOMAS—penis
JONNIE, JOHNY, JIFFIE—condom
JUGS—breasts
KNICKERS—panties
KNOCKERS—breasts
LEMONS—lesbians
PASS WIND—fart
PISS & WIND—meaningless words
PINS, PEGS—legs
PRICK PARADE—army talk for STD check

ROGER—penis

SHARKING—prowling for sex

SLAPPER, SLAG—rude female

SMALLS—underwear

SNOGGING—french kiss

SPUNK—male ejaculate

STIFFY—erection

STROKE DOLLY 'TIL SHE CRIES—masturbation

SUCKING OFF—blow job

SWAGGERS—breasts

TART, PROSSIE—prostitute

THE BOBBY'S HELMET—penis

THRAP THE BISHOP—masturbation (also BASH THE BISHOP)

TO GET OFF—kiss

TO HAVE A WANK—male masturbation

TOTTY—female who is sexy & available

JONNIE, JOHNY, JIFFIE—condom

UP THE BUM—anal intercourse

WANKED HIM OFF—hand job

WANKER—asshole

WILLY—penis

Down Under:

Australia, New Zealand

ARSE, BUM—rear end

CHUBBY, TO CHUB UP—erection

COCK TAX—alimony

COW—obnoxious female

CRACKING A FAT—erection

CRACK A WIDE—female lubrication

CRUMPET—woman

EXERCISE THE ARMADILLO—to have sex

FA'AFAFINE—transvestite (soinoa)

FANNY—female genitals

FENCE JUMPER—bisexual

FLIP YOURSELF OFF—masturbate

FRENCH LETTER—condom

FROTTING—petting

FUCKWIT, FUCKNUCKLE—jerk

GET A STIFFY—erection, horny

GREAT HAIRY LASSO OF LIFE—vagina

GRUDS—panties

HAND WARMERS—breasts

HAVE DOGGIES—doggy style

HIDE THE SAUSAGE—intercourse

LOVE BOX, HONEY TREE—vagina

MAIDENHEAD—woman's virginity

MAN IN THE BOAT—clitoris

MAP OF TAZY (TASMANIA)—vulva

MRS. PALMER AND HER 5 HELPERS—masturbation

NORK—woman's breast

PASH, PASHING—french kiss

PILLOW BITER—anal sex

PORK SWORD—penis

PUD PULLING—male masturbation

PUPPIES, HEADLIGHTS—breasts

RANDY—horny

RIDING THE PORK BUS TO TUNA CITY—intercourse

SHEILA—woman

SNORKER—penis

SPOOF—male ejaculate

SPOOFING—to ejaculate

SPRAY PAINT THE OVARIES WHITE—intercourse

SUCKING OFF—blow job

TACKLE (FISHING TACKLE)—male genitals

TAN TRACKER—gay man

THE WAR DEPARTMENT—wife

THREE PIECE SUIT—male genitals

TIT ROOTING—intercourse between breasts

TRAMPOLINE—diaphragm

UP THE DUFF—pregnant

WET PATCH—wet spot

WOMEN IN COMFORTABLE SHOES—lesbian

A helpful book on sexual slang is "Talking Dirty: Slang, Expletives, and Curses From Around The World" by Jeremy R. Ellis, Citadel Press/Carol Publishing Group, Secaucus, NJ 1996.

Index

About the Author

Paul Joannides is a research psychoanalyst. This means he went to college for way too long. In addition to teaching and doing research, Paul writes a syndicated column for college newspapers. He is also the publisher of the Goofy Foot Press.

About the Illustrator

Daerick Gross is an internationally recognized illustrator of fantasy and comic book art. His list of publications could fill the next five pages.

About the Goofy Foot Press

How it began. It was 1994, and all of the major American publishing houses had passed on the "Guide To Getting It On!" for the second time in two years. According to them, books on sex are supposed to look like the "Joy Of Sex" or at least pay homage to it. "Would you be willing to soften the tone?" "Our people in marketing have no idea how they can sell it. Is it sex—is it humor?" Publishers at the bigger houses apparently don't mix the two.

And so, Paul started the Goofy Foot Press. After the 1st edition of the Guide had won an award and was being assigned as required reading on college campuses, the big publishing houses started to call. "Why didn't you submit this to us in the first place?" They were suddenly offering big bucks and promising to distribute the book far better than the tiny Goofy Foot Press. This sounded inviting, but it would mean that the same marketing people who didn't get it in the first place would become its new owner. People who don't believe that sex and humor go together would be making final decisions on the book's content. Could this be?

Three of us and a dog manage the offices here at the Goofy Foot Press. That's about as corporate as we ever hope to be. As you can see from the pages of this book, there's nothing about being small that means you can't be just as good, if not better, than the big publishing houses.

Order Form
$$$$$$$$$$$$$$$$$$$$$$$$$$$$$$$$$$

To order by phone, call toll free
(800) 310-PLAY

or fax this to:
(310) 652-2995

or it mail to:
The Goofy Foot Press
P.O. Box 69365
West Hollywood, CA 90069-0365

The cost for "The Guide To Getting It On!" is $19.95
Plus State sales tax if you live in California.
Shipping and handling only 5¢.
See other side of this page for details.

Please include the following:

Name: _____

Street Address: _____

P.O. Box (if no street address):_____

City:_____State: ____ Zip :_____

Telephone (_____) _____

❑Visa ❑ MasterCard ❑Amex

Card number: _____

Name on card: _____ Exp. date:___ / ___

❑Personal check (Sorry, but we must allow 3 - 7 working days for personal checks to clear at the bank before shipping.)

You may return any books for a full refund as long as they are in new condition and you have purchased them within the past 30 days.

Never fear, we will not give your name to any other business or organization. The only junk mail you might occasionally receive will be from The Goofy Foot Press, and it will be tasteful, intelligent, and funny.

> This book contains sexually explicit material.
> You must be at least 18-years-old to order.

═══(over)═══

Goofy Foot Press
Order Form

1 copy of "The Guide To Getting It On!"... $19.95

___ additional copies @ $16.00 each .... _____
Must be part of the same order & sent to the same address.

Shipping & handling (CHEAP!!!) .... .05

Sales tax (if you live in California)[1]... _____

TOTAL................... _____

Make checks payable to *The Goofy Foot Press*. Please do not send cash, since there is no paper trail to protect you in case it is lost or stolen.

[1]California Residents:
If you are a California resident, you need to pay sales tax. Bummer.
California residents must pay 8.25%, or $1.65 for the first book, and $1.32 for each additional book ordered.

Books are sent in a plain package except for The Goofy Foot Press logo and address.

=(over)=

Order Form

$$$$$$$$$$$$$$$$$$$$$$$$$$$$$$$$$$

To order by phone, call toll free
(800) 310-PLAY

or fax this to:
(310) 652-2995

or it mail to:
The Goofy Foot Press
P.O. Box 69365
West Hollywood, CA 90069-0365

The cost for "The Guide To Getting It On!" is $19.95
Plus State sales tax if you live in California.
Shipping and handling only 5¢.

See other side of this page for details.

Please include the following:

Name: _____

Street Address: _____

P.O. Box (if no street address):_____

City:_____State: _____ Zip :_____

Telephone (_____) _____

❑ Visa ❑ MasterCard ❑ Amex

Card number: _____

Name on card: _____ Exp. date:___ / ___

❑ Personal check (Sorry, but we must allow 3 - 7 working days for personal checks to clear at the bank before shipping.)

You may return any books for a full refund as long as they are in new condition and you have purchased them within the past 30 days.

Never fear, we will not give your name to any other business or organization. The only junk mail you might occasionally receive will be from The Goofy Foot Press, and it will be tasteful, intelligent, and funny.

> This book contains sexually explicit material.
> You must be at least 18-years-old to order.

═══(over)═══

Goofy Foot Press
Order Form

1 copy of "The Guide To Getting It On!"... $19.95

___ additional copies @ $16.00 each .... _____
Must be part of the same order & sent to the same address.

Shipping & handling (CHEAP!!!) .... .05

Sales tax (if you live in California)[1]... _____

TOTAL................... _____

Make checks payable to *The Goofy Foot Press*. Please do not send cash, since there is no paper trail to protect you in case it is lost or stolen.

[1]California Residents:
If you are a California resident, you need to pay sales tax. Bummer.
California residents must pay 8.25%, or $1.65 for the first book, and $1.32 for each additional book ordered.

Books are sent in a plain package except for The Goofy Foot Press logo and address.

Dear Readers,

Your input is needed to help improve future editions of the "Guide To Getting It On!" Please take a moment to send us your comments and suggestions. Also, if you liked this book, please tell a friend.

Goofy Foot Press
P.O. Box 69365
West Hollywood, CA 90069-0365

Fax: (310) 652-2995

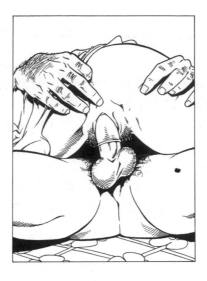

The End